Public & Private Families

AN INTRODUCTION

ANDREW J. CHERLIN
Johns Hopkins University

9e

PUBLIC AND PRIVATE FAMILIES: AN INTRODUCTION, NINTH EDITION

Some ancillaries, including electronic and print components, may not be available to customers outside the United States.

This book is printed on acid-free paper.

1 2 3 4 5 6 7 8 9 LWI 23 22 21 20

ISBN 978-1-260-81327-2 (bound edition)
MHID 1-260-81327-4 (bound edition)
ISBN 978-1-260-24082-5 (loose-leaf edition)
MHID 1-260-24082-7 (loose-leaf edition)

Product Developer: *Alexander Preiss*
Marketing Manager: *Amy Reed*
Content Project Managers: *Danielle Clement/Katie Reuter*
Buyer: *Laura Fuller*
Designer: *David Hash*
Content Licensing Specialist: *Brianna Kirschbaum*
Cover Image: *CARACOLLA/Shutterstock*
Compositor: *SPi Global*

Library of Congress Cataloging-in-Publication Data

Names: Cherlin, Andrew J., 1948- author.
Title: Public & private families : an introduction / Andrew J. Cherlin, Johns Hopkins University.
Other titles: Public and private families
Description: Ninth edition. | New York, NY : McGraw-Hill, [2021] | Previous edition published in 2017.
Identifiers: LCCN 2019041911 | ISBN 9781260813272 (hardcover)
Subjects: LCSH: Families–United States. | Families. | Family policy.
Classification: LCC HQ536 .C442 2021 | DDC 306.850973–dc23
LC record available at https://lccn.loc.gov/2019041911

mheducation.com/highered

For Claire and Reid

About the Author

Courtesy of Will Kirk, Johns Hopkins University

Andrew J. Cherlin is Benjamin H. Griswold III Professor of Public Policy and Sociology at Johns Hopkins University. He received a B.S. from Yale University in 1970 and a Ph.D. in sociology from the University of California at Los Angeles in 1976. His books include *Labor's Love Lost: The Rise and Fall of the Working-Class Family in America* (2014), *The Marriage-Go-Round: The State of Marriage and the Family in America Today* (2009), *Marriage, Divorce, Remarriage* (revised and enlarged edition, 1992), *Divided Families: What Happens to Children When Parents Part* (with Frank F. Furstenberg, Jr., 1991), *The Changing American Family and Public Policy* (1988), and *The New American Grandparent: A Place in the Family, A Life Apart* (with Frank F. Furstenberg, Jr., 1986). In 1989–1990 he was chair of the Family Section of the American Sociological Association. In 1999 he was president of the Population Association of America, the scholarly organization for demographic research. He is a member of the American Academy of Arts and Sciences, the American Academy of Political and Social Science, and the National Academy of Sciences.

In 2005 Professor Cherlin was awarded a John Simon Guggenheim Memorial Foundation Fellowship. He received the Distinguished Career Award in 2003 from the Family Section of the American Sociological Association. In 2001 he received the Olivia S. Nordberg Award for Excellence in Writing in the Population Sciences. In 2009 he received the Irene B. Taeuber Award from the Population Association of America, in Recognition of Outstanding Accomplishments in Demographic Research. He has also received a Merit Award from the National Institute of Child Health and Human Development for his research on the effects of family structure on children. His recent articles include "Nonmarital First Births, Marriage, and Income Inequality," in the *American Sociological Review;* "Family Complexity, the Family Safety Net, and Public Policy," in the *Annals of the American Academy of Political and Social Science;* "Goode's *World Revolution and Family Patterns:* A Reconsideration at Fifty Years," in *Population and Development Review;* and "The Deinstitutionalization of American Marriage," in the *Journal of Marriage and Family.* He also has written many articles for *The New York Times, The Washington Post, The Nation, Newsweek,* and other periodicals. He has been interviewed on the *Today Show, CBS This Morning,* network evening news programs, National Public Radio's *All Things Considered,* and other news programs and documentaries.

Contents in Brief

Contents

Part Three Sexuality, Partnership, and Marriage, 151

Chapter 6 Sexualities, 153

Chapter 7 Cohabitation and Marriage, 179

Part Five Conflict, Disruption, and Reconstitution, 291

Chapter 11 Domestic Violence, 293

List of Boxes

Families and Public Policy

How Do Sociologists Know What They Know?

Preface

The sociology of the family is deceptively hard to study. Unlike, say, physics, the topic is familiar (a word whose very root is Latin for "family") because virtually everyone grows up in families. Therefore, it can seem "easy" to study the family because students can bring to bear their personal knowledge of the subject. Some textbooks play to this familiarity by mainly providing students with an opportunity to better understand their private lives. The authors never stray too far from the individual experiences of the readers, focusing on personal choices such as whether to marry and whether to have children. To be sure, giving students insight into the social forces that shape their personal decisions about family life is a worthwhile objective. Nevertheless, the challenge of writing about the sociology of the family is also to help students understand that the significance of families extends beyond personal experience. Today, as in the past, the family is the site of not only private decisions but also activities that matter to our society as a whole.

These activities center on taking care of people who are unable to fully care for themselves, most notably children and the elderly. Anyone who follows social issues knows of the often-expressed concern about whether, given developments such as the increases in divorce and childbearing outside of marriage, we are raising the next generation adequately. Anyone anxious about the well-being of the rapidly expanding older population (as well as the escalating cost of providing financial and medical assistance to them) knows the concern about whether family members will continue to provide adequate assistance to them. Indeed, rarely does a month pass without these issues appearing on the covers of magazines and the front pages of newspapers.

In this textbook, consequently, I have written about the family in two senses: the *private family,* in which we live most of our personal lives, and the *public family,* in which adults perform tasks that are important to society. My goal is to give students a thorough grounding in both aspects. It is true that the two are related–taking care of children adequately, for instance, requires the love and affection that family members express privately toward each other. But the public side of the family deserves equal time with the private side.

Organization

This book is divided into 6 parts and 14 chapters. Part One ("Introduction") introduces the concepts of public and private families and examines how sociologists and other social scientists study them. It also provides an overview of the history of the family. Part Two ("Gender, Class, and Race-Ethnicity") deals with the three key dimensions of social stratification in family life: gender, social class, and race-ethnicity. In Part Three ("Sexuality, Partnership, and Marriage"), the focus shifts to the private family. The section examines the emergence of the modern concept of sexuality, the formation of partnerships, and the degree of persistence and change in the institution of marriage. Finally, it covers the complex connections between work and family.

Part Four ("Links across the Generations") explores how well the public family is meeting its responsibilities for children and the elderly. Part Five ("Conflict, Disruption, and Reconstitution") deals with the consequences of conflict and disruption in family life. It first studies intimate partner violence. Then the formation and dissolution of marriages and cohabiting unions are discussed. Finally, in Part Six ("Family, Society, and World") family change around the world and social and political issues involving the family and the state are discussed.

Special Features

Public and Private Families is distinguishable from other textbooks in several important ways.

First and foremost, it explores both the public and the private family. The public/private distinction that underlies the book's structure is intended to provide a more balanced portrait of contemporary life. Furthermore, the focus on the public family leads to a much greater emphasis on government policy toward the family than in most other textbooks. In fact, most chapters include a short, boxed essay under the general title, "Families and Public Policy," to stimulate student interest and make the book relevant to current political debates.

In addition to this unique emphasis on both the *Public and Private Families,* the text:

- **Addresses the global nature of family change.** Although the emphasis in the book is on the contemporary United States, no text should ignore the important cross-national connections among families in our globalized economy. The text includes a chapter on "International Family Change" that provides a comprehensive treatment of the major types of change that are occurring in family life around the world (Chapter 13).
- **Includes distinctive chapters.** The attention to the public family led me to write several chapters that are not included in some sociology of the family textbooks. These include, in addition to the new chapter on international family change, Chapter 14, "The Family, the State, and Social Policy," and Chapter 10, "Older People and Their Families." These chapters examine issues of great current interest, such as income assistance to poor families, the costs of the Social Security and Medicare programs, and the extension of marriage to same-sex couples. Throughout these and other chapters, variations by race, ethnicity, and gender are explored.
- **Gives special attention to the research methods used by family sociologists.** To give students an understanding of how sociologists study the family, I include a section in Chapter 1 titled, "How Do Family Sociologists Know What They Know?" This material explains the ways that family sociologists go about their research. Then in other chapters, I include boxed essays under a similar title on subjects ranging from national surveys to feminist research methods.

Pedagogy

Each chapter begins in a way that engages the reader: the controversy over whether the Scarborough 11 in Hartford, Connecticut, constitute a family (Chapter 1); the transgender moment (Chapter 3); the courtship of Maud Rittenhouse in the 1880s (Chapter 7); and so forth. And each of the six parts of the book is preceded by a brief introduction that sets the stage.

Several *Quick Review* boxes in each chapter include bulleted, one-sentence summaries of the key points of the preceding sections. Each chapter also contains the following types of questions:

- *Looking Forward*—Questions that preview the chapter themes and topics.
- *Ask Yourself*—Two questions that appear at the end of each of the boxed features.

- *Looking Back*—Looking Forward questions reiterated at the end of each chapter, around which the chapter summaries are organized.
- *Thinking about Families*—Two questions that appear at the end of each chapter and are designed to encourage critical thinking about the "public" and the "private" family.

What's New in Each Chapter?

As with every edition, all statistics in the text have been updated whenever possible. The structure of the chapters in the book remains the same as in the 8th edition. Changes include the following:

CHAPTER 1. PUBLIC AND PRIVATE FAMILIES.

- I have slightly altered the definition of the private family to accommodate alternative families such as the Scarborough 11 and the voluntary-kinship based families formed by some LGBTQ individuals. I explicitly say that family members do not all need to be related by blood or marriage.
- I now use *voluntary kinship* as the term for what I previously called *created kinship,* since the *voluntary* term is more common in the literature.
- I have deleted reference to a 1999 New York Times survey in which people were much more pessimistic about other families than about theirs. It is too dated, and I cannot find a more recent administration of the survey questions.
- I have added a fifth theoretical perspective: queer theory. In previous editions, I had discussed it briefly in other chapters, and I still do in this edition. But due to its popularity among scholars, I have now given it equal status with other important theoretical perspectives. I introduce several new key terms in this chapter: cisgender people, transgender people, heteronormativity, monogamy, polyamory, and queer theory.
- I have moved the discussion of intersectionality from Chapter 3 (gender) to this chapter. The intersectional perspective has become more prominent among social theorists.

CHAPTER 2. THE HISTORY OF THE FAMILY

- I have moved the section on the historical emergence of sexual identities from Chapter 6 in the previous edition to Chapter 2 of this edition. This move reflects my view that the material on sexuality and the family has become more central to sociological research and should be introduced earlier.
- I have deleted the section on the origins of family and kinship, which described hunter-gatherer society and lineages; however, I have added back in material on lineages in the section on American Indians later in the chapter.
- I have deleted a discussion of African roots of African American cultural patterns, which reflects my sense that historians are no longer pursuing this topic.
- I have added to the section on emerging adulthood a subsection on gay and lesbian emerging adults in the period from 1945 to 2000.

CHAPTER 3. GENDER AND FAMILIES

- I include an update on attention to transgender issues, including an estimate of how many transgender people there are in the United States.
- In this edition, I have introduced the concept of intersectionality in Chapter 1, rather than in this chapter. Here I write briefly about the origin of the concept in gender studies and give an example of its usefulness.

Chapter 4. Social class and Family Inequality

- I present new estimates of the lifetime prevalence of homelessness among the baby boom generation.
- I have deleted an out-of-date discussion about how couples decide what class they are in.
- There is a new section on the rise in "deaths of despair" due to alcohol poisoning and drug overdoses among whites without college degrees, but not among African Americans and Hispanics without college degrees. It draws upon a book and articles that I have written on the working-class family over the past several years.

Chapter 5. Race, Ethnicity, and Families

- I include an update on racial and ethnic categories to be used in the 2020 Census, (See boxed feature, "How Should Multiracial Families Be Counted?")
- In the section on Hispanic families, I present more information on migration from Central America. I note that Salvadorans are now a larger group in the United States than are Cubans. I have added a subsection, "Salvadorans."

Chapter 6. Sexualities

- Historical material on the emergence of sexual identities has been moved to Chapter 2.
- A new section on LGBTQ family life has been added, focusing on defining and forming families, becoming parents, and dividing the household labor.
- I present evidence that men's heterosexuality may be more precarious than women's.
- I discuss up-to-date twin studies and GWAS gene-sequencing studies on biological influences on sexuality.
- Evidence is presented that a greater increase in same-sex sexual activity has occurred among women than among men.

Chapter 7. Cohabitation and Marriage

- A new section on online matchmaking and commitment is included.
- I present a new estimate of the number of Americans who are in living-apart relationships.
- I also report that a majority of all same-sex couples in the United States who are living together are now married.

Chapter 8. Work and Families

- A new chapter opener contrasts the amount and kind of child care that male physicians and male emergency medical technicians tend to do (from Clawson & Gerstel, 2014).
- A new subsection presents research showing that single and cohabiting mothers tend to do less housework, have more leisure time, and sleep more than married mothers.
- I discuss the results of studies of the division of labor in same-sex couples.
- I have rewritten the section on work hours, formerly titled "Overworked and Underworked Americans." Among other updates, the new section emphasizes the "normal unpredictability" (new key term) of work hours among less-educated workers.

Chapter 9. Children and Parents

- I consider controversial research suggesting that the amount of time that mothers spend with their children is not associated with how well the children are faring. (See the section, "What's Important?")

- I include a new subsection on the difficulties that unauthorized-immigrant parents face in raising their U.S.-born children.

CHAPTER 10. OLDER PEOPLE AND THEIR FAMILIES

- I have written a new subsection on grandfamilies (called in previous editions, skipped-generation households): families in which grandparents are raising grandchildren without the parents being present. It draws upon a recent book by Rachel Dunifon (2018).
- I have deleted the subsection on the effects of divorce and remarriage. I include more on post-dissolution relationships in Chapter 12.

CHAPTER 11. DOMESTIC VIOLENCE

- I discuss new research showing that during the Great Recession men acted in a more coercively controlling way toward their partners in areas where the unemployment rate was increasing rapidly, even after taking into account whether the men themselves were unemployed (Schneider, Harknett, & McLanahan, 2016).
- I draw attention to the sharp rise in the number of children in foster care due, in large part, to the opioid addiction and death crisis. See the boxed feature, Families and Public Policy: The Swinging Pendulum of Foster Care Policy.

CHAPTER 12. UNION DISSOLUTION AND REPARTNERING

- I have greatly revised this chapter: It was too focused on divorce. It now notes that the rise of cohabiting unions has been the major factor driving dissolution and repartnering among young adults over the past few decades.
- A new chart (Figure 12.1) showing that while the overall percentage of children experiencing parental union disruption hasn't changed much, the source has: Children born to cohabiting parents constitute a larger share of all children experiencing dissolution than in the past.
- I present evidence from the Panel Study of Income Dynamics that families with older stepparents or adult stepchildren exchange less assistance up and down the generations than do families with only biological parents and children, which suggests a problem for future generations in societies (such as the U.S.) that rely on family members to provide assistance and care (Wiemers, Seltzer, Schoeni, Hotz, & Bianchi, 2019).

CHAPTER 13, INTERNATIONAL FAMILY CHANGE

- The great rise of cohabitation in many regions of the world necessitates an expanded, separate section on the "cohabitation boom."

CHAPTER 14, THE FAMILY, THE STATE, AND SOCIAL POLICY

- I discuss recent bipartisan activity on the issue of paid parental leave that raises the possibility that national legislation will be enacted in the near future.

The 9th edition of *Public & Private Families* is now available online with Connect, McGraw-Hill Education's integrated assignment and assessment platform. Connect also offers SmartBook 2.0 © for the new edition, which is the first adaptive reading experience proven to improve grades and help students study more effectively. All of the title's website and ancillary content is also available through Connect, including

- A full Test Bank of multiple-choice questions that test students on central concepts and ideas in each chapter.
- An Instructor's Manual for each chapter with full chapter outlines, sample test questions, and discussion topics.
- Lecture Slides for instructor use in class.

FOR INSTRUCTORS

You're in the driver's seat.

Want to build your own course? No problem. Prefer to use our turnkey, prebuilt course? Easy. Want to make changes throughout the semester? Sure. And you'll save time with Connect's auto-grading too.

65%
Less Time Grading

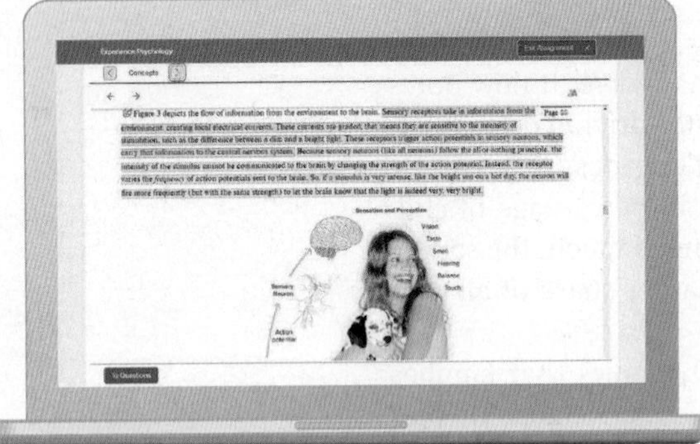

Laptop: McGraw-Hill; Woman/dog: George Doyle/Getty Images

They'll thank you for it.

Adaptive study resources like SmartBook® 2.0 help your students be better prepared in less time. You can transform your class time from dull definitions to dynamic debates. Find out more about the powerful personalized learning experience available in SmartBook 2.0 at **www.mheducation.com/highered/connect/smartbook**

Make it simple, make it affordable.

Connect makes it easy with seamless integration using any of the major Learning Management Systems—Blackboard®, Canvas, and D2L, among others—to let you organize your course in one convenient location. Give your students access to digital materials at a discount with our inclusive access program. Ask your McGraw-Hill representative for more information.

Padlock: Jobalou/Getty Images

Solutions for your challenges.

A product isn't a solution. Real solutions are affordable, reliable, and come with training and ongoing support when you need it and how you want it. Our Customer Experience Group can also help you troubleshoot tech problems—although Connect's 99% uptime means you might not need to call them. See for yourself at **status.mheducation.com**

Checkmark: Jobalou/Getty Images

FOR STUDENTS

Effective, efficient studying.

Connect helps you be more productive with your study time and get better grades using tools like SmartBook 2.0, which highlights key concepts and creates a personalized study plan. Connect sets you up for success, so you walk into class with confidence and walk out with better grades.

Study anytime, anywhere.

Download the free ReadAnywhere app and access your online eBook or SmartBook 2.0 assignments when it's convenient, even if you're offline. And since the app automatically syncs with your eBook and SmartBook 2.0 assignments in Connect, all of your work is available every time you open it. Find out more at **www.mheducation.com/readanywhere**

"I really liked this app—it made it easy to study when you don't have your text-book in front of you."

– Jordan Cunningham,
Eastern Washington University

Calendar: owattaphotos/Getty Images

No surprises.

The Connect Calendar and Reports tools keep you on track with the work you need to get done and your assignment scores. Life gets busy; Connect tools help you keep learning through it all.

Learning for everyone.

McGraw-Hill works directly with Accessibility Services Departments and faculty to meet the learning needs of all students. Please contact your Accessibility Services office and ask them to email accessibility@mheducation.com, or visit **www.mheducation.com/about/accessibility** for more information.

Top: Jenner Images/Getty Images, Left: Hero Images/Getty Images, Right: Hero Images/Getty Images

Acknowledgments

To write a book, this comprehensive requires the help of many people. At McGraw-Hill, Product Developer Alexander Preiss and freelance Development Editor Anna Howland provided valuable editorial guidance. Brianna Kirschbaum, Senior Content Licensing Specialist, managed rights and permissions, and Danielle Clement, Content Project Manager, smoothly managed the production process.

Part One

Introduction

The family has two aspects. It is, first, the place where we experience much of our private lives. It is where we give and receive love, share our hopes and fears, work through our troubles, and relax and enjoy ourselves. Second, it is a setting in which adults perform tasks that are of importance to society, particularly raising children and assisting elderly parents. To be sure, people undertake these tasks not to perform a public service but rather to express love, affection, and gratitude. Nevertheless, family caretaking benefits us all by raising the next generation and by reducing our collective responsibility for the elderly. Indeed, people today frequently express concern over whether changes in the family have reduced parents' abilities to raise their children well. This book is about both the private and public aspects of families. It examines the contributions of family life not only to personal satisfaction but also to public welfare. The first two chapters provide an introduction to this perspective. Chapter 1 explores the most useful ways to think about families, and it examines the approaches that sociologists and other social scientists use to study families. Chapter 2 provides an overview of the history of the family. Over the past half-century family historians have produced many studies that provide useful insights. A knowledge of family life in the past can help us to understand families today.

Chapter One

Public and Private Families

Looking Forward

1. What do families do that is important for society? What do families do that is important for the individuals in them?
2. How do sociologists go about studying families?
3. What are the leading theoretical approaches to studying families?
4. How does individualism influence American family life?
5. How is globalization changing family life?

In August 2014, a group of friends consisting of two couples with children, a couple without children, and two other individuals bought a house together on Scarborough St. in Hartford, Connecticut. To drive down Scarborough is to pass mansion after mansion on what may be Hartford's most elegant street. But the eight-bedroom home that they purchased had fallen into disrepair and had been on the market for four years. The Scarborough 11, as they came to be called, deemed it perfect. "We didn't see the need to live in these isolated nuclear family units," said one of the residents. "It's sustainable for the earth, it makes economic sense, and it's a better way to raise our children. We didn't need a multifamily house with separate kitchens and separate living areas."[1] The group includes two school teachers, a college professor, employees of a clinic and of a cultural center, and a stay-at-home dad. They share the renovation costs, the monthly bills, and the household chores. Each pair of adults cooks dinner for everyone one night a week.

The problem is that Hartford's zoning law prohibits three or more unrelated individuals from living together in a single-family home. The law defines a family as two or more people who are related by blood, marriage, civil union, or adoption—which is pretty much the definition that the U.S. Census Bureau still uses. Defenders of the zoning law argue that it is necessary to protect residential neighborhoods from the establishment of rooming houses or (worse yet!) fraternities. By this standard, the Scarborough 11 comprised *too many* families: a Census-taker in the hallway might see one family consisting of parents and children to her left, a second family of parents and children to her right, a third family formed by the childless couple in the next room, and two other unrelated people making dinner in the kitchen. By her rules, which Hartford follows, none of the three families is related to each other, nor to the two singles. So there are more than two "unrelated" people in household, which violates the zoning law. Yet the Scarborough 11's radical claim is that they are *one* family and should therefore be allowed to live in a single-family home. "We have systems in place to ensure that we are functioning not just as a house but as a collective relationship," a resident told a reporter.

Shortly after the Scarborough 11 moved in, some neighbors complained to the Hartford Zoning Board that the group did not meet the zoning law and therefore

[1] My account is drawn from stories in the *Hartford Courant,* including "Zoning Squabble: Family Is What Family Does," November 21, 2014; "Scarborough 11's Family Dynamic One to Be Envious of," February 26, 2015; "Hartford Upholds Action against Scarborough Street Family," February 17, 2015; and "City of Hartford Withdraws Suit in 'Scarborough 11' Case," October 27, 2016; and in addition, "When 8 Adults and 3 Children Are a Family," *The Daily Beast,* May 10, 2015.

did not have the right to occupy the home. The attorney for the Scarborough 11 disagreed: "They may not look like your or my family but they are a family nevertheless and have a right to live there." But the zoning board sided with the complainants and ordered the Scarborough 11 to vacate the property. The Scarborough 11 appealed the ruling and lost. When they did not give up their home, the City of Hartford sued them. In response, the Scarborough 11 sued the city in federal court, challenging its definition of a family. A year later, bowing to public pressure, Hartford withdrew its suit and allowed the Scarborough 11 to remain in their home without penalties.

At the heart of the controversy over the Scarborough 11 is the question of what constitutes a family. It was a question that seemed to have a clear answer in the 20-year period after World War II, 1945 to 1965, when nearly all adults got married, divorce rates were modest, living together outside of marriage was frowned upon, and having a child out-of-wedlock was downright shameful. Back then, families centered on the marriage-based unit of husband, wife, and children. Starting in the 1970s, however, family life began a period of intense change that continues today. Divorce rates rose, cohabitation prior to marriage became the majority experience, young adults postponed marriage or forwent it entirely, childbearing outside of marriage became common, the family roles of women and men changed, and same-sex marriage became legal. Alternative family forms that extend beyond relationships based on blood or marriage, such as the Scarborough 11, have appeared. The uniformity of the post–World War II era gave way not to a dominant new family form but rather to a diversity of forms. It is therefore difficult today to impose a single definition of the family.

Yet the idea of family remains central to most people's sense of themselves and their intimate connections in life, even as it has become harder to define exactly what a family is. In this regard it is similar to some other sociological concepts such as *social class* and *race* that are difficult to define precisely but too valuable to do without. Moreover, the definition of the family is important economically: It determines who is eligible for billions of dollars in government and corporate benefits that depend on rules about who is a family member. For example, if a low-income parent applies for food stamp benefits, now called the Supplemental Nutrition Assistance Program (SNAP), how much she receives depends on how large her officially defined family is. We must place some boundaries around the concept of family, some limitations on its shape, or else it will lose its usefulness. But how do we determine what the key aspects of family life are today and how can we best specify what we mean by the term *family?*

What Is a Family?

At one extreme, some observers claim that families are so diverse that the concept may not even be useful anymore. At the other extreme are those who press politicians to use the singular form "family" (instead of the plural "families") to signify that there is only one proper kind of family—the married couple living with their biological children.

For example, I am eligible for health insurance coverage through my employer for my "family," which is defined as a spouse and children under 18. If I were unmarried but living with a woman who was the mother of my children, I could insure the children but not their mother. If I had been living for years with a man whom I considered my lifelong partner, I could not insure him in some states.

Moreover, how one defines a family plays an important role in the debate over whether the family has declined.

I would argue that there is no single definition of a family that is adequate for all purposes. Rather, how you define a family depends on what questions you want to answer. Two key questions are

1. How well are family members taking care of children, the chronically ill, and the frail elderly?
2. How well are families providing the emotional satisfaction people value so highly—intimacy, love, personal fulfillment?

These questions address, respectively, the public responsibilities and the private pleasures the family is called upon to meet. For each of these questions, I submit, one of two definitions of the family will be helpful; I will call them the public family and the private family. These definitions provide two useful ways of looking at the same reality—and often the very same group of adults and children. Some observers may impose their own theological definitions of what constitutes a family from religious works such as the Bible or the Koran. But social science cannot determine the moral essence of the family, nor need it do so.

THE PUBLIC FAMILY

In examining the concept of the public family, it's useful to borrow a few terms from the field of economics. Economists who specialize in public welfare have introduced the notion of **externalities,** of which there are two types. First, **negative externalities** occur when an individual or a business produces something that is beneficial to itself but imposes costs on other individuals or businesses. For example, factories that release sulfur dioxide through smokestacks impose a cost on everyone else by polluting the air. The factory gains by producing goods without having to install expensive smokestack scrubbers, but everyone else loses. Second, **positive externalities** occur when an individual or business produces something that benefits others but for which the producers are not fully compensated. For example, a corporation may start an expensive job-training program in order to obtain qualified workers; but some of the workers may take jobs with rival firms after completing the training. The other firms obtain skilled workers without paying the cost of their training.

externalities benefits or costs that accrue to others when an individual or business produces something

negative externalities the costs imposed on other individuals or businesses when an individual or business produces something of value to itself

positive externalities benefits received by others when an individual or business produces something, but for which the producer is not fully compensated

public goods things that may be enjoyed by people who do not themselves produce them

Some positive externalities involve the production of what are called **public goods.** These goods have a peculiar property: It is almost impossible to stop people who don't produce them from enjoying them. As a result, public goods are often produced in smaller quantities than is socially desirable. Suppose a town raises taxes to build a water filtration plant that cleans a polluted river. It cannot stop residents of other towns downstream from enjoying the cleaner water, yet these fortunate residents have paid nothing for the cleanup. In a situation like this, it is clearly in each town's interest to have some other town farther up the river produce the public good—the treatment plant. Yet if no town builds the plant, no one will enjoy cleaner water. One solution to this dilemma is for the county or state government to raise taxes in all the towns and then build the plant. Another is for the towns to reach an agreement whereby one will build the plant but all will contribute to the costs. Either solution compensates the producer of the public good for the benefits that others obtain.

Although it may seem like a long leap from factories to families, the concepts of externalities and public goods still apply. Families do produce valuable public goods—most notably, children (England & Folbre, 1999). For example, when

Americans retire, they hope to receive a Social Security check from the government each month. The funds for those checks come from payroll taxes paid by workers. During the next decade or so, the many men and women born during the post–World War II baby boom will reach retirement age. Currently, there are about five persons of working age for each retired person; but by 2030 there may be only three persons of working age for every retired person.[2] This means that the burden of supporting the elderly will increase greatly. It's in society's interest, then, for families to have and rear children today who will pay taxes when they grow up. Children, in this sense, are public goods.

More generally, it's in society's interest that today's children become good citizens with traits such as obeying the law, showing concern about others, and being informed voters. It's also in society's interest that they be productive workers who are willing and able to fill the needs of the economy. To be sure, critics charge that families often raise children in ways that reproduce existing inequalities between women and men (see Chapter 3) or between the working class and middle class (see Chapter 4). Nevertheless, what they do is of great public value. They are greenhouses growing the workers and citizens of tomorrow.

But children are costly to raise, and a retiree will receive the same Social Security check whether or not the workers were raised by her. Therefore, it's in each retiree's economic interest to remain childless and to have every other family raise children. Yet if everyone followed this strategy there would be no next generation. This dilemma is sometimes known as the **free-rider problem:** the tendency for people to obtain public goods by letting others do the work of producing them—metaphorically, the temptation to ride free on the backs of others. Luckily, people have children for reasons other than economic self-interest. At the moment, however, they are barely having enough to replace the current generation of parents. Everyone benefits from the child rearing that parents do.

free-rider problem the tendency for people to obtain public goods by letting others do the work of producing them—metaphorically, the temptation to ride free on the backs of others

In addition, families provide other services that have the character of public goods. As will be noted in Chapter 10, adult children still provide the bulk of the care for the frail elderly. If I am old and ill, I will benefit if I have adult children who will care for me. But others will also benefit from the care that my family provides, because without them, I would need more assistance from the government-funded medical insurance programs for the elderly (Medicare) and for the poor (Medicaid). Consequently, the care my family provides will keep government spending, and hence taxes, lower for everyone. The same logic applies to care that family members provide for the chronically ill.

The first definition, then, concerns the view of the family you take when you are concerned about the family's contribution to the public welfare—the useful services family members provide by taking care of one another. It is a definition of what I will call the **public family:** *one or more adults who are jointly caring for dependents, and the dependents themselves.* Dependents are defined as children, the frail elderly, and the chronically ill. By "jointly" I mean working as a cooperative unit. The family members usually reside in the same household, but that is not essential. For example, an elderly woman may live in her own apartment but still receive daily assistance from her daughter or son. Nor is it essential that the family members be married or of different sexes. Caregivers who are not related to the dependents by blood or marriage may nevertheless be considered as family members (Voorpostel, 2013).

public family one or more adults who are jointly caring for dependents, and the dependents themselves

[2] Considering 20 to 64 as working age and 65 or older as retirement age. See U.S. Bureau of the Census 2018.

The important fact is that they are taking care of dependents and, in doing so, producing public goods. This definition would include, of course, a married couple and their children or their elderly parents. But it would also include a divorced (or never-married) mother and her children, a cohabiting couple with children, a same-sex couple who are raising children, or a close friend who is the main caregiver for a frail older person. It would also include the Scarborough 11, who are jointly raising children. ("I love living here," one of the children told a reporter, "If you need company there's always someone there for you.") Note also who would be excluded by this definition: a childless married couple with no dependent or elderly relatives, or different-sex or same-sex cohabitors without children, the elderly, or ill dependents.

The production of public goods invites public scrutiny, and public families are easily identifiable to outsiders by the presence of dependents. Because society has an interest in how well families manage the care of dependents, the law allows for some regulation of these families–despite strong sentiment in the United States against intervening in family matters. For example, we require families to send their children to school until age 16. And state social welfare agencies have the power to remove children from homes judged to be harmful. More recently, several states have required medical personnel to report suspected cases of physical abuse of children. The public family, then, is about caretaking and dependency. It points us toward the kinds of kinship ties that are important for nurturing the young and caring for the elderly and the ill. It is a useful perspective for answering questions such as: How adequately will our society raise the next generation? How will we care for the growing number of elderly persons?

THE PRIVATE FAMILY

At the same time, the family is much more than a public service institution. It also provides individuals with intimacy, emotional support, and love. Indeed, most people today think of the family and experience it in these private terms. Although some of the intimacy is expressed sexually, the family is also where we get and give support to others. An appropriate definition of the private family must, therefore, encompass intimate relationships whether or not they include dependents. Yet if we are to maintain our focus on families, the definition still must encompass some rules for defining what kinds of intimate relationships constitute a family and what kinds do not. Where exactly is the boundary between family life and less intensive forms of intimacy? How do we develop a definition of the private family that applies to the married partnerships that still dominate durable, intimate relationships in American society and yet is broad enough to encompass alternative families such as the Scarborough 11?

First, we could observe that both the smaller marriage-based versions and the larger Scarborough-like versions of families involve emotional connections and commitments to each other. Second, we could see that both also involve almost daily interaction, sharing, and cooperation. One of the Scarborough family members told a reporter, "We have systems in place to ensure that we are functioning not just as a house but as a collective relationship" (Ryan, 2015). They take turns cooking; they pool money for home repairs; and they make life decisions based on each other. Third, we could note an important difference: The smaller version is tied to relationships formed by blood (intergenerational descent) and marriage, whereas the larger version includes some family members who have no biological or marital ties to others. The same Scarborough person said that the City of Hartford's suit was "a threat to anyone who's had people in their home who are not blood but who they care for and love no matter what" (Ryan, 2015). If we are to accommodate alternative families, we must expand our definition to include emotional bonds among people who are not related through blood or marriage.

Let me offer, then, this definition of the **private family:** *two or more individuals who maintain a close, emotional relationship and a commitment to each other, and who usually live in the same household and pool their incomes and household labor.* The phrase "two or more" allows for larger groups. I do not require that all members of the group be related by blood or marriage or that they be of different sexes. By a "close, emotional relationship," I mean a relationship that is intimate but not necessarily sexual. By "commitment," I mean that the individuals expect the family to endure indefinitely. This definition also includes the notion that the family is typically household-based and is economic as well as intimate—shared residence, common budgets. Nevertheless, I have added the qualifier "*usually* live in the same household" to allow for family members who live apart but in other ways meet the criteria.

private family two or more individuals who maintain a close, emotional relationship and a commitment to each other, and who usually live in the same household and pool their incomes and household labor

In fact, families are becoming so diverse and complex that it is hard to determine their boundaries from either the public or the private perspectives. Suppose that after a divorce a father makes regular child support payments to his ex-wife and sees his children often. You might argue that he is still sharing parenthood and therefore part of the family. If he doesn't make regular payments, on the other hand, and sees his children sporadically, you might not consider him to be part of the family any longer. When families are very complex, even the people who are involved may disagree about who's in them. Take the example of a large national survey that asked the mothers of teenage children who else was living in their household. Several hundred mothers said that they were living with a man who was not the father of the teenager. In other words, according to the mothers' reports, these were what might be called "cohabiting stepfamilies" that were similar to stepfamilies except that the stepfather and mother were not married. The survey also asked the teenage children in these households who besides their mothers was living with them. Strikingly, nearly half of them did not mention the man at all, as if their mothers were single parents (Brown & Manning, 2009). Perhaps in some of those households the men were present only half the week and the children considered them to be visitors; or perhaps the children rejected them as father figures. The correct answer, then, to the question of who is in the family is sometimes unclear. This is an example of **boundary ambiguity,** a state in which family members are uncertain about who is in or out of the family (Carroll, Olson, & Buckmiller, 2007). It is more common now than it was a half-century ago, when rates of divorce, remarriage, and childbearing outside of marriage were substantially lower and when alternative families such as the Scarborough 11 were less common.

boundary ambiguity a state in which family members are uncertain about who is in or out of the family

To be sure, individuals also receive emotional support and material assistance from kin with whom they are not in a close emotional relationship. The word "family" is sometimes used in the larger sense of relationships with sisters, uncles, cousins, close friends, and so forth. These broader kinship ties are still an important part of the setting in which people embed their intimate relations to spouses, partners, and children. The usual definition of "kin" is the people who are related to you by descent (through your mother's or father's line) or marriage. Yet the concept of kinship is also becoming broader and harder to define. In settings as varied as sharing networks among low-income African Americans, family networks among lesbian, gay, bisexual, transgender, or queer (LGBTQ) individuals, and middle-class networks of adults who are related only through the ties of broken marriages and remarriages, people are expanding the definition of kinship, creating kin, as it were, out of relationships that don't fit the old mold. In fact, throughout the book I will distinguish between what I will call **voluntary kinship**—kinship ties that people construct with others who are not related to them by blood or marriage (Braithwaite et al., 2010)—and **assigned kinship**—kinship ties that people more or less automatically acquire when they are born or when they marry.

voluntary kinship kinship ties that people construct with others who are not related to them by blood or marriage

assigned kinship kinship ties that people more or less automatically acquire when they are born or when they marry

Voluntary kinship is particularly valuable to people who can't find adequate support among blood-based or first-marriage-based kin. LGBTQ individuals, for example, often construct families that mix biological relatives with friends and partners (Hull & Ortyl, 2018; Soler, Caldwell, Córdova, Harper, & Bauermeister, 2018). Poor African American mothers who cannot find suitable spouses exchange help not only with their mothers and grandmothers but also with close friends, creating kinship-like relationships. A divorced mother whose ex-husband provides little support can receive assistance from a live-in partner or second husband. Yet even people who could find adequate support in conventional arrangements may intentionally create new forms that fit their preferences and needs (Nelson, 2013). You will recall that one of the Scarborough members said, "We didn't see the need to live in these isolated nuclear family units."

Some observers look at all of these new forms of intimate relationships and conclude that the concept of family is outmoded. Some of the criticism has come from scholars in Europe, where rates of marriage are lower than in the United States and where, in many countries, long-term cohabiting relationships are more common (Roseneil & Budgeon, 2004). Family is a "zombie category," wrote two social theorists (Beck & Beck-Gernsheim, 2002), a dead body walking around that we mistakenly think is still alive. The critics note the boundary ambiguities of many families and the ways in which people are constructing new forms of kinship. They point to phenomena such as couples in intimate, committed relationships who are living in separate households because they value their independence, don't think they are ready to live together, or have practical constraints such as jobs in different cities (Liefbroer, Poortman, & Seltzer, 2015). Some conclude that we should give up on the term "family" and use a broader, more inclusive descriptor, such as "personal community" (Pahl & Spencer, 2004, 2010). But I think that in an American context, we are not at the point where we should give up on the concept of family. Its boundaries are fuzzy, it takes diverse forms, it is stressed and strained by social change, but for the current day it is, I suggest, still worth retaining.

TWO VIEWS, SAME FAMILY

Table 1.1 reviews the basic distinction between these two perspectives. The first row shows examples of families as seen through the public and private family perspectives. The second row shows the main functions of the family in the public and private domains. In raising the next generation of children—the workers, citizens, and parents of the future—parents and other caregivers are best viewed as carrying out the functions of the public family. The same can be said for caregivers of the frail elderly or for disabled individuals. In contrast, when providing love, intimacy, and emotional support, family members are carrying out the functions of the private family. The third row shows the key challenges families face in these two guises. It's in people's narrow self-interests to let others do the hard work of raising children

Table 1.1 Two Ways of Looking at the American Family

	THE PUBLIC FAMILY	THE PRIVATE FAMILY
Examples	Married couple, cohabiting couple, or single parent with children Single person caring for ailing parent Cohabiting person caring for seriously ill partner	Married or cohabiting couples without children Network of committed LGBTQ adults providing love and support to each other.
Main Functions	Raising the next generation Caring for the elderly Caring for the ill and disabled	Providing love and intimacy Providing emotional support
Key Challenge	Free-rider problem	Boundary problem

Source: The table is the author's, but it is based on Giddens (1991, 1992), Beck & Beck-Gernsheim (1995, 2002), and Beck, Giddens, & Lash (1994).

or caring for the elderly—activities that benefit society as a whole. (And much of this care is provided by women outside of the paid workforce. See Chapter 8.) But if too many people try to ride free, our society may not invest enough time and effort in producing the next generation or in caring for the elderly. In fact, some social critics believe American society has already reached this point. As for the private family, its key challenge is maintaining its place as the setting where people experience emotional gratification. Today there are many kinds of relationships that provide intimacy, love, and sex. Will the private family continue to cohere as a social institution, or will its boundaries collapse into a sea of diverse personal relationships?

In sum, to examine the contributions of families to the public welfare is to look at relationships through the lens of the public family. To examine the family's provisions of intimacy, love, and fulfillment is to look through the lens of the private family. Sometimes, both lenses apply to the same situation. Think of a married couple with children. Through the lens of the private family, we may see the partners providing each other with love and emotional support. Through the lens of the public family, we may see them raising children. Both perspectives are embedded in each of the chapters that follow. Which is better? Neither. They are two takes on the same reality. Many textbooks emphasize the private family by focusing primarily on interpersonal relationships, cohabitation, and marriage. In doing so, they pay less attention to the socially valuable work that families do. Although this book, too, will have much to say about the private family, it will also emphasize the public family. Most chapters will include a short essay on families and public policy; and the concluding chapter, "The Family, the State, and Social Policy," is directed primarily toward public issues.

Quick Review

- Families are more diverse in their forms than was the case in the mid-twentieth century.
- No single definition of the family is adequate for all purposes.
- This book takes two perspectives and proposes two definitions:
  - The "public family," which focuses on the care that family members provide for dependents.
  - The "private family," which focuses on the love and emotional satisfaction family members provide for each other.
- Both definitions can be applied to the same family unit because most families have both a public and a private dimension.

How Do Family Sociologists Know What They Know?

objectivity the ability to draw conclusions about a social situation that are unaffected by one's own beliefs

scientific method a systematic, organized series of steps that ensures maximum objectivity and consistency in researching a problem

hypothesis a speculative statement about the relationship between two or more variables

Sociologists collect and analyze data consisting of observations of real families and the people in them. For the most part, they strive to analyze their data using objective, scientific methods. **Objectivity** means the ability to draw conclusions about a social situation that are unaffected by one's own beliefs. But it is much more difficult for a sociologist to be objective than it is for a natural or physical scientist. Sociologists not only study families, they also live in them. They often have strong moral and political views of their own (indeed, strong views about social issues are what lead many people to become sociologists), and it is difficult to prevent those views from influencing one's research. In fact, there are some sociologists who argue that objectivity is so difficult to achieve that sociologists shouldn't try. Rather, they argue, sociologists should acknowledge their values and predispositions so that others can better interpret their work (see *How Do Sociologists Know What They Know?:* Feminist Research Methods, in Chapter 3).

But most sociologists, although aware that their views can influence the way they interpret their data, model their research on the scientific method. For a detailed examination of the scientific method in sociology, consult any good introductory sociology textbook. For example, Schaefer (2007, p. 29) defines the **scientific method** as "a systematic, organized series of steps that ensures maximum objectivity and consistency in researching a problem." The essence of the scientific method is to formulate a hypothesis that can be tested by collecting and analyzing data. (A **hypothesis,** Schaefer writes, is "a speculative statement about the relationship between two or more variables" [p. 45].) It's easy to come up with a hypothesis (God is a woman), but the trick is to find one that can be shown to be true or false by examining data. Sociologists therefore tend to formulate very specific hypotheses about family life that can be confirmed or disconfirmed by observation. For example, sociologists have hypothesized that having a first child as a teenager lowers, on average, the amount of education a woman attains; and statistical data are consistent with this claim.

Even so, there are inherent limitations in how well social scientists can use the scientific method. The best way to confirm or disconfirm a relationship between two factors is to conduct an experiment in which all other factors are held constant. Scientists do this by randomly assigning subjects to one of two groups: a treatment group and a control group. For example, to study whether a new drug speeds recovery from an illness, doctors will assemble a group of volunteers, all of whom have the illness, and then randomly give half of them (the treatment group) the new drug. By randomizing, the doctors hope that all other confounding factors (such as past medical history) will be equalized between the two groups. Then they compare the average recovery times of the treatment group and the control group (those who did not receive the drug).

But it is rarely possible for sociologists to conduct randomized experiments on families. Without randomization, there is always the possibility that another, unobserved factor, lurking just beneath the surface, is causing the relationship we see. Consider again teenage childbearing. Women who have a first child as a teenager tend to come from families that have less education and less money, on average, than do other women. So the reason that teenage mothers attain less education may reflect their disadvantaged family backgrounds rather than having a child; in other words, they might have had less education even if they hadn't had children as teenagers. To truly settle this issue, a truth-seeking but cold-blooded sociologist would want to obtain a list of all families with teenage girls in the United States and then to assign *at random* some of the girls to have children and others to remain childless until their twenties. Because of the random assignment, teenage childbearing would be about as likely to occur in middle-class families as in poor families. In this way, the social scientist could eliminate family background as a cause of any differences that emerge between teenage mothers and nonmothers.

For very good ethical and legal reasons, of course, sociologists simply cannot conduct this type of study. Without random assignment, we can't be sure that having a child as a teenager *causes* a woman to have less education. Still, the lack of randomized experiments does not mean that sociologists should abandon the scientific method. Astronomers, after all, can't do experiments either. But this limitation makes the task of deciding whether a sociological study confirms or disconfirms a hypothesis more difficult.

If not from experiments, where does the data that family sociologists use come from? Generally, from one of two research methods. The first is the **survey,** a study in which individuals or households are randomly selected from a larger population and asked a fixed set of questions. Sociologists prepare a questionnaire and give it to a professional survey research organization. The organization then selects a sample of households randomly from an area (a city, a state, or the entire nation) and sends interviewers to ask the questions of one or more family members in the households. The responses are coded numerically (e.g., a "yes" answer is coded 1 and a "no" is coded 0), and the coded responses for all individuals are made available to the sociologists as a computer file.

survey a study in which individuals from a geographic area are selected, usually at random, and asked a fixed set of questions

The random selection of households is done to ensure that the people who are asked the questions are representative of the population in the area. This kind of random selection of households shouldn't be confused with conducting a randomized experiment. A random-sample survey is not an experiment because the households that are selected are *not* divided into a treatment group and a control group. Nevertheless, data from surveys provides sociologists with the opportunity to examine associations among characteristics of a large number of individuals and families. (See *How Do Sociologists Know What They Know?:* The National Surveys, in this chapter.)

The advantage of the survey method (assuming that the households are randomly selected) is that its results are representative not only of the sample that was interviewed but also of the larger population in the area. The main disadvantage is the limited amount of information that can be gathered on each person or family. Most people won't participate in an interview that takes more than an hour or two. Moreover, the same set of questions is asked of everyone, with little opportunity to tailor the interview to each participant. Another disadvantage is that it's difficult to determine whether the people in the sample are responding honestly, especially if the questions touch upon sensitive issues. (See *How Do Sociologists Know What They Know?:* Asking about Sensitive Behavior, in Chapter 6.)

The second widely used research method is the **observational study,** also known as *field research,* in which the researcher spends time directly observing each participant in the study—often much more time than an interviewer from a survey organization spends. The researcher may even join the group she or he is studying for a period of time. The individuals and families to be studied are not usually selected randomly; rather, the researcher tries to find families that have a particular set of characteristics he or she is interested in. For example, in a classic observational study of a low-income area of Boston, Herbert Gans (1962) moved into an Italian

observational study (also known as **field research)** a study in which the researcher spends time directly observing each participant

neighborhood for eight months and got to know many families well. He was able to argue that the stereotype of slum families as "disorganized" was not true. The strength of the observational method is that it can provide a much more detailed and nuanced picture of the individuals and families being studied than can the survey method. Sociologist-observers can view the full complexity of family behavior and can learn more about it.

The disadvantage of observational studies is that it is hard to know how representative the families being studied are of similar families. Because it takes a great deal of time to study a family in depth, observational studies typically are carried out with far fewer families than are surveys. Moreover, sociologists who do observational studies usually can't choose their families randomly by knocking on doors or calling on the telephone because they must win a family's cooperation and trust before the family will agree to be studied in such detail. So although observational studies may yield a great deal of information about a small number of families, we may be unsure that we can generalize this knowledge to other similar families that weren't in the observational study.

Surveys and observational studies, then, have complementary strengths and limitations. If the knowledge from sociological studies could be stored in a lake, a survey-based lake would be wide (because of the large number of people reached) but shallow (because of the limited time spent with each family), whereas an observationally based lake would be narrow but deep. Ideally, it would be best to employ both methods to study a problem, and some research projects attempt to do so. But to choose a large number of families randomly and then to send in sociologists to observe each family intensively over weeks and months is too expensive to be feasible. Moreover, the set of skills necessary to do survey research versus observational research is so distinct that sociologists tend to specialize in one or the other.

Social scientists sometimes use other research methods as well. For some topics, it is useful to examine historical sources. Chapter 7 describes a study in which magazine articles from 1900 to 1979 were used to study changing conceptions of marriage (Cancian, 1987). Occasionally, it is even possible to do an experiment. In the 1990s, the Department of Housing and Urban Development conducted an experiment in which some low-income families living in public housing in five cities were randomly selected to receive a voucher that they could use to subsidize their rent if they moved to lower poverty neighborhoods. These "treatment-group" families were compared to "control-group" families that received less assistance. Four to seven years later, families that had received the vouchers were living in safer neighborhoods and were less poor; in addition, the daughters in these families had better mental health than daughters in the control-group families. Ten to fifteen years later, young adults who had moved with their parents to better neighborhoods before age 13 had higher incomes (Chetty, Hendren, & Katz, 2015).

These are the major methods that sociologists use to study families. In several of the chapters of this book, we will examine the methodology of key studies so that you may better understand how family sociologists develop their research findings.

Quick Review

- Survey research and observational research are the two methods most commonly used by sociologists.
- The two methods have complementary strengths and limitations.
- Table 1.2 summarizes the differences between the two methods.

Table 1.2 Comparing Survey Studies and Observational Studies

WHO IS STUDIED	HOW THEY ARE STUDIED	STRENGTHS	LIMITATIONS
SURVEY STUDY			
Large, random sample of individuals or families	An interviewer asks questions from a predesigned questionnaire and records the answers	Results can be generalized to the population of interest	Only limited knowledge can be obtained; hard to judge honesty of responses
OBSERVATIONAL STUDY			
Small, purposefully chosen sample of individuals or families	A researcher observes them in depth over a long period of time, sometimes participating in their daily activities	Detailed knowledge is obtained	Findings may not be representative of other, similar individuals or families

Sociological Theory and Families

The methods sociologists use and the questions they ask are influenced by sociological theory. Let me present a brief introduction to five perspectives that I think are most actively used by family researchers today: exchange, symbolic interaction, feminist, postmodern, and queer. I will draw on these perspectives often in this book.

THE EXCHANGE PERSPECTIVE

The sociological approach known as **exchange theory** is similar to the model of human behavior that economists use. People are viewed as rational beings who decide whether to exchange goods or services by considering the benefits they will receive, the costs they will incur, and the benefits they might receive if they chose an alternative course of action. In the rational choice-based theory of the family that won Gary Becker the 1992 Nobel Prize in economics, women often choose rationally to exchange the performance of household and child care services in return for receiving the benefits of a man's income. If men are more "efficient" at market production—meaning they can earn higher wages—and women are more "efficient" at home production—meaning they are better at raising small children—then both partners gain from this exchange, argues Becker (1991). Thus, Becker's model was used to explain the prevalence in the mid-twentieth century of the **breadwinner–homemaker family**—a married couple with children in which the father worked for pay and the mother did not. His theory implied that the division of labor in this type of family is best for both husband and wife. Becker did not anticipate same-sex marriage. In Chapter 8 we will examine whether this model applies to same-sex spouses.

exchange theory a sociological theory that views people as rational beings who decide whether to exchange goods or services by considering the benefits they will receive, the costs they will incur, and the benefits they might receive if they were to choose an alternative course of action

breadwinner–homemaker family a married couple with children in which the father worked for pay and the mother did not

In the hands of others, exchange theory can lead to very different conclusions. Many sociologists maintain that exchanges take on a different character if the two actors come to the exchange with unequal resources. Richard Emerson and his colleagues developed a version of exchange theory that is useful in studying families (Cook, O'Brien, & Kollock, 1990; Emerson, 1972). According to Emerson, if person A values goods or services person B has to offer, and if person A has few alternative

How Do Sociologists Know What They Know?

The National Surveys

Sociologists who study the family in the United States draw many of their findings from a series of national surveys that have been conducted over the past few decades. These surveys interview randomly selected samples of the U.S. population. They are similar to the opinion-poll surveys you see in news sites online (e.g., what percent of the public thinks the president is doing a good job?), but they differ in several important ways:

- *They are larger* The surveys reported online typically interview 500 to 1,500 individuals. The social scientific surveys typically interview 5,000 to 10,000 individuals or more. Because of this larger size, the social scientific surveys can provide reliable information on subgroups of the population, such as couples who are living together outside of marriage, currently divorced individuals, and never-married adults.
- *They are mainly carried out using in-person interviews* In contrast, most of the online polls are conducted by randomly dialing telephone numbers and speaking to people over the telephone. In-person interviews can be longer and more detailed (because people tire of telephone conversations more quickly than in-person conversations) and can be more flexible (e.g., the interviewer can give the subject a self-administered questionnaire for her husband or partner to fill out). But in-person interviews are also much more expensive to carry out.
- *They are longitudinal* Whereas the typical online poll is a one-time activity, social scientists prefer a **longitudinal survey,** meaning a survey in which interviews are conducted several times at regular intervals. This design allows social scientists to study social change. The surveys typically select families or individuals at random and then reinterview them annually or biennially about how their lives are changing.
- *They are intended to be public resources* Most online polls are meant for **primary analysis,** meaning they are analyzed by the people who collected the information. The data from these polls are then forgotten. The social scientific studies are designed for **secondary analysis,** meaning analysis of the data by people other than the group that collected it. The questionnaires are intentionally broad so that the interviewers can collect a wide range of information that will be of interest to many researchers. The results are coded numerically into electronic files and made available to anyone who wants to analyze them.
- *They are conducted by academic research centers rather than by commercial polling firms* The academic centers, such as the NORC at the University of Chicago and the Survey Research Center at the University of Michigan, typically take extra steps in designing and carrying out a survey so that the

longitudinal survey a survey in which interviews are conducted several times at regular intervals

primary analysis analysis of survey data by the people who collected the information

secondary analysis analysis of survey data by people other than those who collected it

sources of obtaining these goods or services, then person A is said to be dependent on person B. The degree of dependency is greater the more highly A values these goods or services and the fewer alternative sources A has. For example, if a husband (person B in this case), by virtue of his greater earning power, can offer to purchase many goods and services, and if his wife (person A) values these goods and services but can't purchase them on her own because she can't earn as much, then she is said to be dependent on her husband. Her dependency is greater if she has fewer alternative sources of income, perhaps because she took time away from paid work to have children and now finds it hard to find a good job. Moreover, according to Emerson, the more A is dependent on B, the greater is B's power over A. When one person is more powerful than another, he or she may be able to shape the exchange so that he or she receives greater benefits and incurs fewer costs than does the other person. Husbands, many writers have suggested, are in a stronger bargaining position when they are the sole earners in their families because their wives have fewer alternative sources of income. According to exchange theory, when wives earn money on their own, their dependence decreases and therefore their husbands' power over them decreases. They can drive a better bargain for who does the housework.

results are of better quality (e.g., the data conforms better to the statistical theory underlying random sample surveys; a greater percentage of the selected subjects are reached and interviewed).

Because of the large sample size, longitudinal design, use of in-person rather than telephone interviews, and extra care in the fieldwork, the social scientific surveys are very expensive. Most are sponsored by U.S. government agencies such as the National Institutes of Health, the National Science Foundation, or the Bureau of Labor Statistics. The agencies support those large surveys to provide information on many research questions so that hundreds of researchers can analyze the data.

One such project is the Fragile Families and Child Wellbeing Study, which was designed to learn more about unmarried parents and their children. Interviews were conducted between 1998 and 2000 in urban hospitals around the country with nearly 5,000 mothers, about three-fourths of them unmarried, just after their child's birth. The researchers also interviewed the fathers of the children when possible, and they are still following these so-called fragile families almost 20 years later. They found that half of the unmarried mothers were living with the fathers of their children at the time of birth (McLanahan et al., 2003).

Another study is the Panel Study of Income Dynamics. In 1968, researchers at the University of Michigan interviewed 5,000 American households selected at random. They have reinterviewed the members of these households every year or two since then. When children grew up and left home, or adults divorced and moved out, the study followed them and interviewed them in their new households. The Panel Study of Income Dynamics greatly increased our knowledge of the economic fortunes of families over time. For example, the results indicate that few families are poor every year, but over the course of a decade many families, perhaps one-fourth, experience at least a year in which they are poor (Duncan, 1984).

Throughout the book, findings from these and other national surveys will be presented. Although not without limitations (see Chapter 6, *How Do Sociologists Know What They Know?*: Asking about Sensitive Behavior), they constitute a valuable resource to everyone interested in families, households, parents, and children.

Ask Yourself

1. Besides researchers, who else might be interested in the results of social scientific surveys? Can you think of any practical use for this information?
2. Why do you think researchers would want to see survey results for particular racial and ethnic groups or specific types of families?

THE SYMBOLIC INTERACTION PERSPECTIVE

Exchange theorists tend to see the social world as a concrete reality with easily perceived costs and benefits and they view individuals as rational, calculating beings, as if we each had a computer in our head, taking in data, calculating costs and benefits, and deciding how to act. The adherents of **symbolic interaction theory,** however, see the social world as a much more fragile and unstable place, in which individuals are continually creating and sustaining meanings, often without much conscious thought to costs and benefits (Stryker & Vryan, 2003). The major figure in symbolic interaction theory was philosopher George Herbert Mead, who taught at the University of Chicago early in the twentieth century. His foremost interpreter in sociology was Herbert Blumer (1962). According to these theorists, people do not react to the world like computers respond to mouse clicks, but rather they *interpret* what others do based on shared understandings they may take for granted. We interpret symbols—gestures, words, appearances—whose meanings we have come to understand. This interpretation occurs in situations in which we interact with someone. It is this process of the interpretation of symbols during social interaction that the symbolic interactionists study.

symbolic interaction theory a sociological theory that focuses on people's interpretations of symbolic behavior

For instance, when women and men interact with each other, they vary the way they dress, the gestures they use, and the tone of voice they employ according to whether the situation is a friendly conversation or a potentially romantic encounter. Each person in the interaction picks up on the symbols used by the other in order to understand which type of situation is being experienced. Most of the time the symbols are so clear and so routine that we don't even think about what's happening. In fact, we rely on not having to think about what kind of social situation we are in—we don't have the mental energy to continually scrutinize the basic facts of our social encounters. Instead, we rely on taken-for-granted symbols and meanings.

But these symbols and meanings can reinforce inequalities between women and men in subtle ways. When a man holds a door open for a woman, both people may see this as merely a display of courtesy. Yet a woman is much less likely to hold a door open for a man. Does this mean that women are less courteous than men? Of course not. Rather, the symbol of a man holding a door open has an additional meaning: It reinforces the cultural message that men are physically stronger than women and should take care of them, like gallant medieval knights ushering their ladies through the castle gates. In this way, the simple gesture of holding the door becomes a symbol of the cultural differences between men and women. And done again and again on a daily basis, it reinforces gender differences. There are many such interactions. For example, husbands who don't want to change their babies' diapers may make a display of fumbling at the changing table when called upon by their wives, thus exhibiting their male "inferiority" at the task.

The interactionist perspective is also useful in analyzing situations in which family relations seem less institutionalized, less set in concrete—such as in newly formed stepfamilies. How a stepfather acts toward his stepchildren when they misbehave, for instance, is a symbol of his emerging role: Does he speak loudly and angrily and admonish them, or does he leave that kind of language to the children's mother and avoid the role of disciplinarian? In general, the interactionist perspective helps sensitize us to the ways in which people create shared understandings of how family members should act toward one another. These shared understandings become the bases of the social roles people play in families—spouse, parent, breadwinner, homemaker, child, and so forth.

THE FEMINIST PERSPECTIVE

feminist theory a sociological theory that focuses on the domination of women by men

gender the social and cultural characteristics that distinguish women and men in a society

Feminist theory is a perspective developed to better understand, and to transform, inequalities between women and men. It draws upon both the exchange and the symbolic interaction perspectives. The central concept in feminist theory is **gender,** which is usually defined as the social and cultural characteristics that distinguish women and men in a society (see Chapter 3). Feminist theorists argue that nearly all the gender differences we see in the roles of women and men are of cultural origin and have been socially constructed. By socially constructed, they mean arising not from biological differences but rather from culturally accepted rules, from relationships of power and authority, and from differences in economic opportunities. For example, the culture might include a rule that women should not work outside the home (as was the case among the American middle class from the mid-nineteenth to the mid-twentieth centuries). Or, the opportunities for women might be limited to jobs that tend to pay less than comparable jobs in which most workers are men.

Moreover, feminist theorists assert that these cultural differences are constructed in ways that maintain the power of men over women (Thorne, 1992). For instance, feminist theorists criticize the notion that the breadwinner–homemaker family provided an exchange that was equally beneficial to women and men. Rather, like Emersonian exchange theorists, they note that women's direct access to money through paid employment was restricted in this type of family, which maintained women's dependence on men. They also note that men's relationships with their children were often limited. The cultural belief that "women's place is in the home" and the lower wages paid to women employed outside the home compelled married women to give up the idea of paid employment. Under these constraints, their best strategy may indeed have been to trade household services for a male income; but it was a forced choice set up by a social system that favored men.

In addition, feminist theorists argue that the kinds of work that women tend to do are valued less highly in our culture than the kinds that men do. In particular, they say, the work of caring for other people is undervalued because we value individualism and autonomy from others more than we value connections with others (Tronto, 1993). Women have historically done much of the work of maintaining connections with kin and caring for young children and the frail elderly. They have done much of it for free as part of their family responsibilities; in fact, we may not even consider a mother who is raising children full time to be "working." But today women also constitute most of the employees at hospitals, nursing homes, day care centers, and other settings where people are cared for. Their pay tends to be low: As we will see in Chapter 8, aides at child care centers make less, on average, than parking lot attendants. Their low wages reflect, at least in part, the devaluing of caring work, sociologists say (England, 2005). Until we value care more highly, they say, we will continue to have less caring labor than is optimal. For instance, the low pay of child care workers will continue to cause high job turnover and less stable caregiving to young children.

Feminist theory makes us aware that the experience of living in a family is different for women than it is for men. Arrangements that make men happiest don't necessarily make women happiest. A husband might prefer that his wife stay home to care for their children and do household work full time. His wife might prefer to combine a paying job with housework and child care, and she might wish that he would share more of the household tasks. In other words, women's interests in the family are not necessarily the same as men's interests. The breadwinner–homemaker bargain may have been great for men (except for those who wanted an active role in raising their children), and it may have been great for women who wished to raise children and do housework full time, but it frustrated other women by restricting the possibility of developing a satisfying career outside the home. Feminist theory urges us to view families through a prism that separates the experiences of men and women rather than just considering what's best for the family as a whole.

THE POSTMODERN PERSPECTIVE

A number of theorists of modernity claim that personal life has changed fundamentally over the last several decades. They argue that the modern era—the long period that began with the spread of industrialization in the mid-to-late nineteenth century—effectively ended in the last half of the twentieth century. It has been replaced, they state, by what they call the **late modern era** (Giddens, 1991) or sometimes the **postmodern era.** Looking back at the modern era, they emphasize that individuals moved through a series of roles (student, spouse, parent, housewife, breadwinner) in a way that seemed more or less natural. Choices were constrained.

late modern or **postmodern era** the last few decades of the twentieth century and the present day

In mill towns, two or three generations of kin might work at the same factory. Getting married was the only acceptable way to have children, except perhaps among the poor. Young people often chose their spouses from among a pool of acquaintances from their neighborhood, church, or school. Life's stages flowed in a way that one accepted and didn't have to question.

But in the late modern era, the theorists maintain, individuals must make choices about nearly all aspects of their lives (Beck & Beck-Gernsheim, 2002). You can't get a job in the factory where your father and grandfather worked because overseas competition has forced it to close, so you must choose another career. Rather than allowing your relatives to help you find a partner, you sign on to an Internet dating service and review hundreds of personal profiles. As other lifestyles become more acceptable, you must choose whether to get married and whether to have children. In ways such as these, your identity in the late modern age is transformed from a "given" to a "task" you must undertake (Bauman, 1992, 2002).

self-identity a person's sense of who he or she is and of where he or she fits in the social structure

reflexivity the process through which individuals take in knowledge, reflect on it, and alter their behavior as a result

As these choices are made, it is said, questions of self-identity become more important. By **self-identity,** I mean a person's sense of who he or she is and of where he or she fits in the social structure. In societies such as ours, individuals must construct their self-identities; they cannot rely on tradition or custom to order their daily lives. "We are not what we are," wrote social theorist Anthony Giddens (1991), "but what we make of ourselves." Developing one's self-identity becomes an important project that individuals must work on. People do the work of developing their identities through **reflexivity,** the process through which individuals take in knowledge, reflect on it, and alter their behavior as a result (Beck, Giddens, & Lash, 1994). In other words, people pay attention to their experiences and regularly ask themselves: How am I feeling? Do I find my life fulfilling? How do I want to live the rest of it? Depending on the answers to questions such as these, people may change the way they are living their lives. The postmodern theorists believe that the rise of reflexive change is a key characteristic of what they call the late modern era: the last few decades of the twentieth century and the beginning of the twenty-first. Table 1.3 compares the current era with the modern era that began with industrialization and ended in the mid-twentieth century (although, in a broader sense, modernization can be traced back to the Enlightenment in eighteenth-century Europe). In reality, the periods are not quite as distinct, and the differences not as sharp, as the table suggests.

Behavior, according to the theorists, was *rule-directed* in the earlier era, meaning that (1) rules such as social norms, laws, and customs strongly influenced personal life and (2) the actions of individuals did not change those rules. Marriage was the only acceptable context for having children. Divorce was frowned upon and harder to obtain. Despite occasional movements to liberalize divorce laws, the norms and customs did not change much. In the current era, behavior is *rule-altering* to a much greater extent because the lifestyle choices individuals make can alter the laws and customs pertaining to families. For instance, as more gay and lesbian couples began to live openly together, many municipalities, in reaction, enacted domestic-partnership laws that gave same-sex couples privileges similar to those of married couples (such as requiring that employers who offer health insurance benefits that cover the spouses of their employees also cover their same-sex partners). These new laws altered the rules about what constituted a legally valid partnership. And as same-sex partnerships became more acceptable, activists urged the legalization of marriage for same-sex partners. A 2015 Supreme Court decision (Obergefell v. Hodges, 2015) legalized it nationwide.

Table 1.3 Aspects of Personal Life in the Late Modern Era

	MODERN ERA	LATE MODERN ERA
Time period	Industrialization to mid-twentieth century	Since mid-twentieth century
Behavior	Rule-directed	Rule-altering
Lifestyle choices	Restricted	Mandatory
Kinship ties	Assigned	Voluntary

Note: The table is the author's, but it is based on Giddens (1991, 1992), Beck & Beck-Gernsheim (1995, 2002), and Beck, Giddens, & Lash (1994).

Lifestyle choices, as Table 1.3 suggests, were *restricted* in the earlier era. For example, people were much less likely to choose a spouse of a different religion or racial-ethnic group. In the current era, choices are not only greater but also *mandatory:* You must make choices in nearly all aspects of personal life. Having to make so many decisions has its good and bad points. It opens the possibility of developing a self-identity that is deeply fulfilling; and it allows people to seize the opportunities that may be before them. On the other hand, choices can bring insecurity and doubt. The risk of making the wrong ones can weigh on you, creating a burden as well as a boon.

Finally, kinship ties tend to shift from being assigned to being *voluntary.* In the past, you acquired your relatives at birth; then, when you married, you acquired a spouse and in-laws. There was little choice in the matter. Today, people in a variety of settings are more likely to draw upon others, such as close friends, with whom they voluntarily—that is, by free choice—construct a kinship network.

People who choose not to rely on lifelong marriage must construe kinship differently. They must do the hard work of constructing a group of kin, a broader family, that they can rely on. These ties require continual attention to maintain. In contrast, relations of blood and first marriage are supported by strong social norms and the law. Lacking this support, people must actively keep up voluntary kinship ties. If they are allowed to lapse, there is no guarantee that they can be revived.

Postmodern theory is consistent with a view of families as diverse, changing, and developing in unpredictable directions. It can help us make sense of family life at a time when individuals must continually make choices in uncertain circumstances, for which there are no clear rules. For instance, same-sex marriage is new enough that no general agreement exists on how spouses should divide up the tasks of work at home and in the labor market. Divorce and remarriage are new enough on a large scale that stepparents and stepchildren have little guidance on who is part of their family and how they should act toward them. (We will examine stepfamilies in Chapter 12.) These new circumstances bring both opportunities for fashioning mutually beneficial arrangements and the costs of the anxiety and conflict that working out new rules can cause.

THE QUEER THEORY PERSPECTIVE

The perspective known as **queer theory** questions common assumptions about sexual and gender identities, monogamy, and the definition of the family. Queer theorists reject the idea of fixed, stable sexual and gender identities (Oswald, Blume, & Marks, 2005). For instance, they reject the idea that the paired categories of gay

queer theory the view that sexuality and gender are artificially organized into categories that reflect the power of heterosexual norms

Table 1.4 Theoretical Perspectives on the Family

THEORETICAL PERSPECTIVE	MAIN THEME	APPLICATION TO FAMILIES
Exchange	Individuals with greater resources and more alternatives can drive better bargains.	Husbands' power over wives is greater when wives do not earn money on their own.
Symbolic interaction	Individuals interpret the actions of others and act in ways consistent with their interpretations.	Individuals give, and look for, symbolic cues about how to conduct the activities of everyday family life.
Feminist	Society is organized in ways that privilege men over women.	A system of male dominance gives husbands more power than their wives.
Postmodern	Individuals reflexively influence their social environments.	Individuals choose how they will act in new family forms such as stepfamilies.
Queer	Sexuality and gender are fluid categories	Individuals create families from a mixture of biological kin and friends

versus straight or homosexual versus heterosexual are adequate to describe the sexual desire and behavior of everyone in society. Rather, they argue, sexuality is a continuum along which individuals may position themselves. Consistent with the postmodernists' assertion that people construct their self-identities and may choose to change the way they are living their lives, queer theorists argue that individuals may choose to change their sexual identities by moving along the continuum; or they even choose to reject the notion that they have a firm sexuality. Thus, the term *queer,* which prior to its adoption by theorists in the 1990s was pejorative (Blasius, 2001), refers to individuals who see themselves as operating in a more complex and changing sexual space than we typically assume, and who may see themselves as neither straight nor gay.

Queer theorists make a similar argument about gender: the male-female dichotomy is inadequate, they claim, to fully understand the meaning of gender. They distinguish, for instance between cisgender individuals and transgender individuals. **Cisgender people** are those whose sense of their own gender is consistent with the gender that they were assigned at birth on the basis of physical characteristics. **Transgender people** are those who sense of their own gender is inconsistent with the gender they were assigned at birth—a feeling that may emerge years or decades after they were born. Transgender people may wish to transition from one gender to the other. Yet even the cisgender/transgender distinction preserves the two gender model: transgender people are thought of as either transwomen and or transmen. Queer theorists would go further to question the basic idea that a person must have a fixed, stable gender identity as a woman or a man. Rather, they assert, some individuals may see themselves as moving fluidly and repeatedly along the continuum between women and men.

cisgender people people who identify with the identity they were assigned at birth

transgender people people who identify with a gender other than the one they were assigned at birth

Moreover, queer theorists question the definition of a family. According to the conventional definition, such as the one that the Bureau of the Census uses, a family consists of two or more people who are related by birth, marriage, or legal adoption and who reside together. Queer theorists argue that we should be willing to include family ties among people who establish close bonds but are not related by any of the Census rules and who don't necessarily live together (Oswald, Blume, & Marks, 2005). For instance, as part of their families, people may include friends to whom they have close, emotional bonds and from whom they receive love and support. Going further, some queer theorists question the norm of **monogamy**—the belief that a person should have only one long-term partner at a time, usually through marriage—whether that partner is of the same sex or of a different sex. They write of "de-centering" marriage, that is, moving it out of its central position in our conception of what a family is (Willey, 2016). They point to alternatives such as **polyamory**, the practice of having more than one open romantic relationship at a time (Schippers, 2016). Indeed, to queer theorists the supremacy of the conventional birth-marriage-or-adoption definition of the family is a prime example of **heteronormativity**, the idea that heterosexual relationships are the only normal and natural relationships, and that, by contrast, intimate relationships outside of the conventional heterosexual model are abnormal. Queer theorists argue that the dominance of heteronormativity limits the definition of a family and restricts individuals whose intimate relationships do not coincide with it.

monogamy The belief that a person should have only one long-term partner at a time, usually through marriage

polyamory The practice of having more than one open romantic relationship at a time

heteronormativity The idea that heterosexual relationships are the only normal and natural relationships

Most queer theorists also reject the view that there are important biological influences on how society organizes sexuality and gender. Rather, they argue that we unconsciously re-create the illusion of heterosexual "masculinity" and "femininity" in everyday interactions (Butler, 1990). In this way, queer theory has some similarities with the symbolic interactionist approach that views people as continually creating and sustaining meanings in daily life. Both contest the notion that people have stable, "natural" identities that exist separately from the social world they live in. But there is a difference (Green, 2007): Symbolic interactionists try to explain how we construct gender and sexual identities that seem durable and lasting to us and to those around us. But queer theorists tend to argue against the whole idea of durable gender and sexual identities; rather, they see fixed identities as deeply problematic. Queer theory, then, is deconstructive; it attempts to take apart the idea of a stable self-identity.

This perspective leads observers to question the validity not only of traditional conceptions of family life but also of some recent ones. Consider same-sex marriage. Between the early 2000s and 2015, same-sex marriage went from being illegal everywhere to being the law of the land. In large part, this transformation was due to the work of gay and lesbian social activists. While most queer theorists would consider the legalization of same-sex marriage to be an advance, they have an ambivalent stance toward it. The very term *same-sex* assumes that there are fixed gender categories and that we can easily tell whether the partners are the same or different. And the fight for the right to marry reinforces the idea that marriage is the central form of family life, a position that most queer theorists reject. Thus, some queer theorists considered the push for same-sex marriage to be misguided and argued against pursuing it (Lehr, 1999). In this way, queer theorists refute conventional categories, be they favorites among the political left or the right.

Queer theory constitutes a challenge to standard approaches to the sociology of the family (Acosta, 2018; Allen & Mendez, 2018). It rejects the idea that society should prefer fixed sexual and gender identities over fluid and changing ones. It rejects the rule that family members must be related by blood or marriage. It rejects the norm that marriage should hold a privileged place among intimate relationships. It sees the domination of these forms as privileging heterosexual monogamous relationships (and lately same-sex monogamous relationships) over other forms of family life. How might it influence a textbook such as this one? First, it would suggest that the definition of the family should be expanded beyond the conventional blood-or-marriage-related-and-living-together definition, as I have done in the definition of the private family in this chapter. Second, it would suggest that the author should be alert throughout the book to the complexities that queer theory exposes in standard treatments of gender, sexuality, marriage, and kinship. This I will also do throughout the book. It may also suggest de-emphasizing marriage and other long-term, two-person intimate unions–be they of the same sex or different sex. Here I will respectfully part ways with queer theory. Although I will write about other family forms, such as single-parent families or alternative families like the Scarborough 11, I will focus to a large extent on marriage-like relationships (including unmarried cohabitation) because they remain by far the most common form of intimate partnerships in American society today.

Quick Review

- Five widely used theoretical perspectives are exchange, symbolic interaction, feminist, postmodern, and queer.
- Table 1.4 summarizes the main theme of each perspective and its application to studying families.

INTERSECTIONALITY

intersectionality the principle that inequalities related to one social identity often overlap with inequalities in other identities

One further theoretical point: After a look at the history of the family in Chapter 2, I will present four chapters on major sources of identity and inequality as they relate to families: Chapter 3 on gender, Chapter 4 on social class, Chapter 5 on race and ethnicity, and Chapter 6 on sexuality. Although these chapters will be separate, the topics overlap. Sociological theorists maintain that in order to fully understand inequalities in one domain, we often must consider the others. Think of a person standing at the intersection of four circles: one that represents inequalities tied to class, one for inequalities tied to race, one for inequalities tied to gender, and one for inequalities tied to sexual identity. In order to comprehend the situation of, say, a working-class African American woman who identifies as queer, a sociologist must examine the joint effects of all four of her sources of inequality: her class, race, gender, and sexuality. And there may be other overlapping circles that sometimes need to be drawn, such as age or physical challenges. The theoretical principle that inequalities that are related to one social identity often overlap with inequalities that are related to other identities is called *intersectionality* (Crenshaw, 1991). The analyst using this perspective focuses on the struggles and conflicts in the overlapping domains (Allen, Walker, & McCann, 2013; Ferree, 2010).

The idea of intersectionality arose in the 1980s and 1990s, when scholars who studied minority groups criticized feminist theorists for not linking gender with race (and its close cousin ethnicity) and class–essentially, for focusing heavily on the lives of white, middle-class women (Collins, 2000; Glenn, 2000). The critics agreed that gender is as much a part of social stratification as race and class, but they noted that members of minority groups experience gender and race together, and often in combination with class. More recently, queer theorists have argued that sexual identity constitutes another overlapping circle of inequality that should be added to gender, race, and class (Allen and Mendez, 2018; Acosta, 2018).

The idea of intersectionality raises a caution for both the reader and the author of textbooks such as this one. It is true that one often needs to study a situation from all overlapping lenses at the same time in order to fully comprehend it. That is to say, when individuals experience inequality, they tend to experience it in multiple ways at once. Yet in a textbook, the author must impose some separation on these inequalities so that students can begin to comprehend them. If every section of the chapter on gender, for instance, referred to all other sources of inequality, the reader's basic understanding of gender would likely suffer. Therefore, when you read Chapters 3 through 6, you should keep in mind that although I am focusing on one domain per chapter, they exist in relation to each other. I will attempt to help the reader by noting ways in which an intersectional viewpoint is helpful.

Quick Review

- Individuals often experience interlocking inequalities that simultaneously involve domains such as gender, class, racial/ethnic position, and sexuality.

Globalization and Families

These days, many sociologists are applying their theories to the study of a major social trend that has occurred over the past few decades: **globalization,** the increasing flow of goods and services, money, migrants, and information across the nations of the world.

globalization the increasing flow of goods and services, money, migrants, and information across the nations of the world

Globalization is evident in the movement of factory work overseas so that, for instance, virtually every piece of clothing you own was probably made outside of the United States. You face it when you call the technical service line for help with a laptop problem and are connected to someone in India. You have seen it if you know one of the many middle-class families who have hired women from countries such as Mexico or the Philippines to help care for their children while the parents work. You have experienced it on news sites that collect Twitter feeds and cellphone videos keep you apprised of uprisings in distant lands. Globalization is tying together the lives of people around the world in a way that was not possible before late-twentieth-century advances in computing, communications, and transportation. It has been aided by the ascendency of a political viewpoint known as neoliberalism that supports free movement of investment funds and free trade of goods across nations, open borders, and individual initiative.

No national government controls this trend. Rather, globalization operates at world level above the nation state, as money, people, and information transit the globe. It is affecting family life in nearly every region of the world, although its effects differ from region to region (Trask, 2010). In developing countries, the new factories have created millions of low-wage jobs that have drawn mothers into the paid work force. As in the United States, the employment of mothers with young children can create child care problems, which are often worsened by the lack of any government child care assistance and by workers' inability to pay for care. But the jobs, modest in pay though they are, have also provided women with a greater degree of independence in their family lives, increasing their bargaining power with their husbands and allowing some to escape abusive marriages. Therefore, globalization is changing the relations between women and men in areas where manufacturing work has grown. In addition, the style of romantic love and companionship to be found in the United States and other wealthy countries seems to be spreading across much of the developing world.

Western nations the countries of Western Europe and the non-European, English-speaking countries of the United States, Canada, Australia, and New Zealand

The effects of globalization on family life can also be seen in the **Western nations,** the countries of Western Europe and the non-European, English-speaking countries of the United States, Canada, Australia, and New Zealand. This book's main focus will be on the family in the United States, but there are strong similarities between the American family and the family in other Western nations.

In the United States, the movement of manufacturing jobs overseas has made it more difficult for high school educated young adults to find decent jobs. As a result they frequently are hesitant to marry, and they form short-term cohabiting relationships instead. Meanwhile, college-educated young adults, who have an easier time finding the kinds of well-paying professional and technical jobs that still remain in the United States, finish their education, marry, and enjoy a higher standard of living. In this way, globalization is creating a gap between the family lives of the college graduates and those with less education.

Moreover, international migration is creating family forms that span the developed and developing countries in ways that have never been seen before. Whereas in the past most people who migrated from their home country to another country were men, today almost half of all international migrants are women (United Nations, 2017). Many of them are mothers who leave their children at home. For instance, the women who migrate to the United States to care for the children of working parents often leave their own children in the care of others in their home countries. They typically send back most of their salary to pay for the children's school fees, better clothes, or a nicer house. A grandmother may be minding the children during the years that the mother is gone, or the family may be paying someone else to do the caring. In this way, the immigrant nannies create transnational families in which mothers and children can be thousands of miles apart and yet keep in touch through phone calls, text messages, and Skype sessions.

Globalization, then, can influence family life both positively and negatively. In less developed countries it can induce parents to work long hours for wages that are low by Western standards and it can create child care crises. But the increase in household income does represent a step up in the families' economic fortunes, and it elevates the position of women. In the home countries of the women who migrate to the Western countries to do caring work, children are separated from their mothers by hundreds or thousands of miles; yet their opportunities are increased by the money their mothers send home. In the West, globalization has improved the economic prospects of highly educated young adults, most of whom are still forming marriage-based families, while eroding the ability of young adults with less education to form stable, long-term family bonds.

The world is too interconnected to consider what is happening to families in the United States without also considering what is happening elsewhere. Consequently, Chapter 13 will be devoted to international family change.

Quick Review

- During the past few decades, the international flows of goods and services, money, migrants, and information have increased greatly, in a process known as globalization.
- Globalization has affected family life throughout the world, although its effects are different in Western countries than in other regions.

Family Life and Individualism

A family life centered on marriage remains the preference of most Americans. When young adults are asked their plans for the future, the overwhelming majority respond that they plan to marry and to have children. But it is a different kind of marriage than it used to be. In most societies at most times in the past, marriage was the only acceptable setting for sexual activity and childbearing. As recently as the mid-twentieth century, marriage, childbearing, and sexual activity overlapped to a great extent, possibly even greater than in prior times. Sexual intercourse, for the majority of women at least, was restricted to marriage (or to the men they were engaged to); consequently, few children were born outside marriage. Cohabitation was rare except among the poor. Marriage was more nearly universal than at any other time in the twentieth century. The probability that a marriage would end in divorce, although substantially higher than in the nineteenth century, was much less than it is today. To be respectable, it was necessary to be married before living with a partner or having a child; to stay respectable, it was necessary to avoid divorce if at all possible.

By the 1990s, the power of marriage to regulate people's personal lives was much weaker than in the past. Cohabitation before marriage had become common and acceptable to most people. Although childbearing outside marriage was still frowned upon by many, it was tolerated by most. Divorce was considered to be unfortunate but acceptable if a partner wished to end a marriage. Lifelong singlehood, although still uncommon, was also acceptable. In general, there was a greater acceptance of nonmarried adults.

There are several reasons for the lesser role of marriage and the greater tolerance of those who are not married. Marriage is less economically necessary than when most people needed to pool their labor and earnings with a spouse in order to subsist. Moreover, the movement of married women into the paid workforce—a major trend of the past half-century—has lessened women's economic dependence on men. Even though women's wages remain, on average, lower than men's, it is less difficult now for a woman to support herself and her children. Also, the job prospects for young men without college educations have worsened as jobs are transferred overseas or lost to automation, discouraging young adults from marrying.

But in addition, the decline of marriage and greater tolerance for alternative lifestyles reflects the rise of a more individualized view of family and personal life. By **individualism,** I mean a style of life in which individuals pursue their own interests and place great importance on developing a personally rewarding life. Individualism in American life is of two types (Bellah, Madsen, Sullivan, Swidler, & Tipton, 1985). The older, more-established type is **utilitarian individualism:** a style of life that emphasizes self-reliance and personal achievement, especially in one's work life. Benjamin Franklin was the quintessential utilitarian individualist. In his *Poor Richard's Almanack,* he advised that "early to bed and early to rise, makes a man healthy, wealthy, and wise" and that "God helps them that help themselves." Today, this is the style of the person determined to succeed on his or her own or to get to the top of the corporate ladder. It is also the style of a single mother who works two jobs to pay for her children's college tuition. The second type, newer on a large scale, is **expressive individualism:** a style of life that emphasizes developing one's feelings and emotional satisfaction. This is the style of the person who wants to connect emotionally with a romantic partner, express his or her innermost thoughts to a trusted friend, and develop a good body at the health club. It is

individualism a style of life in which individuals pursue their own interests and place great importance on developing a personally rewarding life

utilitarian individualism a style of life that emphasizes self-reliance and personal achievement, especially in one's work life

expressive individualism a style of life that emphasizes developing one's feelings and emotional satisfaction consistent with the focus on self-identity that, according to the postmodern theorists, characterizes our day.

The Supreme Court decision that legalized same sex marriage nationwide, *Obergefell v. Hodges* (2015), exemplifies these individualistic views. Writing for the majority, Justice Anthony Kennedy stated:

> *A first premise of the Court's relevant precedents is that the right to personal choice regarding marriage is inherent in the concept of individual autonomy.*

Individual autonomy: Kennedy implies that autonomy is a basic right under the constitution. *Personal choice:* autonomous individuals must be able to choose whether or not to marry, regardless of sexual orientation. As he writes elsewhere in the decision, "the decision whether and whom to marry is among life's momentous acts of self definition." Getting married is here conceived of not as a social norm that people should follow (and that might restrict marriage to different sex couples) but rather as a constitutionally protected choice that individuals must be free to make on their own.

In an individualistically oriented society, adults are expected to construct their family lives in ways that are consistent with their self-development. Today, most Americans still want to marry, but they have less of a need to do so than in the past. Marriage must compete with alternatives such as staying in school longer to obtain a higher degree, taking more time to develop a career, living with a partner without marrying, or having children outside of marriage. Some people may be ambivalent about marriage, at once drawn by its promise of intimacy and wary of its commitments and constraints. Family life therefore becomes much more diverse than it was a half-century ago. Even though most Americans choose to marry and a majority choose to have children within a marriage, they tend to respect the choices that other, freely acting individuals may make.

Compared to a half-century ago, what's most notable is that people have so many choices. They don't have to be married in the sense that adults at midcentury did. Predictably, people spend less of their lives married and fewer children are raised by two married parents. Moreover, people tend to marry at a later point in their lives than they did a half-century ago. Individuals used to get married prior to living together, having children, and establishing careers. Today, before marrying you may live with your future spouse or with someone else, you may spend several years establishing yourself in the labor market, and you may even have children. It is not a status to enter into lightly; rather, you wait until you're sure it's going to work. Marriage is a status you work toward, a personal achievement, a mark of distinction. In some ways, then, marriage's symbolic value has increased even as its practical significance has decreased (Cherlin, 2004). For instance, although you and your partner can have children without marrying and still be respectable, you may choose to marry to show everyone that you have achieved a successful personal life. For some people, then, marriage has become the ultimate family merit badge.

As the postmodernists argue, a key way in which family and personal life differ today from the way they were in the past is that you not only *can* make choices, but also you *must* make choices. You have to choose whether to live with someone, whether and when to have children, whether to marry, and sometimes whether to end a marriage. You must make these decisions yourself because your options are less constrained by parents and social norms. One's family life, according to two social theorists, becomes a permanent do-it-yourself project (Beck & Beck-Gernsheim, 2002). And so you get out your hammer and nails and construct a cohabiting relationship with someone, try it out, see how you like it, renovate or clean house, or maybe remodel with someone else. You construct it and reconstruct it; every person is his or her own architect. This is a very individualistic approach to marriage and family life because it centers on your personal evaluation of how much satisfaction you are getting, on your sense of whether you are growing and developing as a person, and on whether your partnership is meeting your emotional needs. It has led to the growth of what I will call later in this book the "individualistic marriage": a union based on individual rewards rather than on the approval of family, friends, and community. These are different criteria for judging whether your family life is a success from the criteria your grandparents' generation used. What this transformation means for the personal life of adults today, as well as for the lives of the children and elderly they care for, is one of the fundamental questions that underlies this book. It is a vital concern because so much depends on it: the well-being of the next generation, the health and comfort of the growing older population, and the emotional rewards we so highly value.

Quick Review

- Americans tend to take individualistic perspectives on adult life.
- Utilitarian individualism emphasizes self-reliance and personal achievement.
- Expressive individualism emphasizes one's feelings and emotional satisfaction.
- People must choose the kind of family life they will have.

A Sociological Viewpoint on Families

As noted earlier, some sociologists would argue that no one can conduct completely objective research. Therefore, they say, one must examine, reflexively, how one approaches the subject. Only by frankly examining and stating one's viewpoint can one provide a framework others can use to properly evaluate one's own research. In that spirit, let me briefly discuss the viewpoint I bring to the writing of this textbook. In reading this book, you should keep these convictions in mind. I believe that families perform services of value to society and therefore should be publicly supported when necessary. Despite their increasing diversity, families, in my opinion, still constitute a coherent social category worth studying. I believe that, other things being equal, stable, long-term partnerships—different-sex or same-sex—provide the best environment for raising children. These partnerships need not be marriages, but getting married seems to enhance the chances of long-term stability and to increase the investments parents make, at least in the United States. I also believe that alternative family forms, with adequate support, can provide good environments for children.

In addition, I think it is likely that our evolutionary history has produced some inherent differences between the ways that women and men go about finding partners and building family lives. But I don't believe these differences are significant enough to prevent equality for women and men, which is a goal that I think we should strive for in the early twenty-first century. Biologically based differences, if any, would stem from the different roles that men and women played in the hunter-gatherer bands in which most humans and their evolutionary predecessors lived until about 8,000 B.C. Women, on average, may be predisposed to value sex in the context of relationships and commitment more than men, whereas men may be predisposed to value sex outside of relationships and to behave aggressively more than women. But even if we do have biological predispositions toward some behaviors and away from others, whether we exhibit these behaviors depends on the social circumstances of our lives: the upbringing we received from our parents; the cultural influences we absorbed from peers, neighbors, ministers, and the media; and the economic constraints or racial prejudices we may have faced. These social factors may exaggerate whatever biological differences there may be between women and men, so that the differences we see are greater than biology alone would create. Biological predispositions, then, would not determine a person's behavior. Rather, they would create tendencies and leanings. On average, a group of people who share a predisposition (toward, say, aggressive behavior) would be likely to show more of it than would a group who does not share it; but it is difficult to predict how any single member of the group would behave.

social institution a set of roles and rules that define a social unit of importance to society

In this book, I will use the singular form "the family" rather than the plural form "families" when discussing the family as a **social institution.** This term refers to a set of roles and rules that define a social unit of importance to society. The roles give us positions such as parent, child, spouse, ex-spouse, stepfather, partner, and so forth. The rules offer us guidance about how to act in these roles. But the use of the singular is not meant to imply that there is only one kind of family. On the contrary, there are many forms. Similarly, one might write about "the corporation" in a textbook on social organizations without implying that there is no difference between ExxonMobil and a chain of grocery stores. Or, an author might discuss "the hospital" in a text on medical sociology while recognizing the difference between a giant teaching hospital in a central city and a community hospital out in the suburbs. In addition, referring to "the family" is not meant to imply that the interests of wives, husbands, and children are always identical—any more than that the interests of workers and managers in corporations are identical.

In all of these cases, the use of the singular would signal the study of a social institution rather than just a set of relationships. An institution can grow stronger or weaker over time; it can take on somewhat different forms at different times and places; and it can be difficult to define at its margins. But it is a visible structure that people can recognize and understand. It also does something important for society. I think the "family" still fits this description. Its important functions include rearing children, caring for the elderly, and providing comfort and emotional support to its members. Nevertheless, people's actions are greatly changing the family and eroding its institutional basis. Stability and change in the family are the subject matter of this book.

Currently, most Americans seem to view their own families primarily in emotional, personal terms—the terms of the private family—and to pay less attention to the commitments and obligations of the public family. This emphasis on sentiment and self-fulfillment might lead one to assume that the private family is the older, more established perspective. But that isn't so. The emergence of the private family is a relatively new development in history. Its origins lie in the upper-class and merchant families of Western Europe in the 1600s and 1700s. It did not spread to the masses until the late 1800s and 1900s. Most people have used the public perspective in thinking about families throughout most of history. The historical development of the family is the subject of the next chapter.

Looking Back

1. **What do families do that is important for society? What do families do that is important for the individuals in them?** Families contribute to society by raising the next generation and caring for the ill and the elderly. On an individual level, families are settings in which people give and receive love, intimacy, and social support. This book proposes two definitions of the family—one for each of these questions. The public family perspective defines the family in terms of the presence of caregivers and dependents. The private family perspective defines the family in terms of an emotionally close relationship between two or more individuals who are committed to each other and who usually live in the same household and share the fruits of their labor. These two perspectives constitute different views of the same reality; a given family unit might fit both of them.

2. **How do sociologists go about studying families?** Sociologists observe real families and the people in them, and for the most part, they try to analyze their data objectively using the scientific method. Sociologists formulate hypotheses that can be tested, although there are limits to their use of the scientific method. The two most common research methods sociologists use are (1) the survey, a study in which a randomly selected group of individuals or families are asked a fixed set of questions and (2) the observational study, in which the researcher spends time directly observing each participant in the study.

3. **What are the leading theoretical approaches to studying families?** Five widely used perspectives are exchange theory, which examines how family members bargain based on their resources and their alternatives; symbolic interaction, which focuses on how individuals interpret the social world; feminist theory, which analyzes the sources of gender inequality in families; postmodernism, which emphasizes the choices individuals must make in constructing family lives; and queer theory, which emphasizes the fluidity of sexuality and gender.

4. **How does individualism influence American family life?** In general, Americans take an individualistic perspective toward family life. An older form, utilitarian individualism, emphasizes self-reliance and achievement. A new form, expressive individualism, emphasizes personal feelings and emotional satisfaction. Individuals must choose the kind of family life they want, rather than relying on their parents or customs to define their lives for them.

5. **How is globalization changing family life?** In developing nations, it has created factory jobs that have drawn mothers into the paid workforce, creating childcare problems for those women, but also giving mothers more bargaining power within marriage. In the developed, Western nations, it has opened a gap between the marriage-based family lives of the college-educated and the family lives of the less-educated.

Study Questions

1. Do you think that the Scarborough 11 are one family?
2. What are the two components of American individualism?
3. Why might children be considered a "public good"?
4. What kinds of daily activities are better analyzed by thinking of the family as a public rather than a private institution?
5. Conversely, what daily activities are better analyzed by thinking of the family as a private institution?
6. Are there daily activities that could be viewed as having both a public and a private component?
7. Why can't sociological research be as objective as research in physics or chemistry?
8. How do people develop their self-identities today?
9. Are "straight" and "gay" fixed sexual categories?

Key Terms

assigned kinship 10
boundary ambiguity 9
breadwinner–homemaker family 15
cisgender people 22
exchange theory 15
expressive individualism 27
externalities 6
feminist theory 18
free-rider problem 7
gender 18
globalization 25
heteronormativity 23
hypothesis 12
individualism 27
intersectionality 24
late modern or postmodern era 19
longitudinal survey 16
monogamy 23
negative externalities 6
objectivity 12
observational study 13
polyamory 23
positive externalities 6
primary analysis 16
private family 9
public family 7
public goods 6
reflexivity 20
scientific method 12
secondary analysis 16
self-identity 20
social institution 30
survey 13
symbolic interaction theory 17
transgender people 22
utilitarian individualism 27
voluntary kinship 10
Western nations 26
queer theory 21

Thinking about Families

The Public Family	The Private Family
What are some of the ways that your family has carried out its "public" functions?	**How has your family carried out its "private" functions?**

References

Obergefell v. Hodges, 576 (U.S. 2015).

Acosta, K. L. (2018). Queering family scholarship: Theorizing from the borderlands. *Journal of Family Theory & Review, 10*(June), 406–418.

Allen, K. R., Walker, A. J., & McCann, B. R. (2013). Feminism and families. In G. W. Peterson & K. R. Bush (Eds.), *Handbook of marriage and the family* (pp. 139–158). New York: Springer.

Allen, S. H., & Mendez, S. M. (2018). Hegemonic heteronormativity: Toward a new era of queer family theory. *Journal of Family Theory & Review, 10*(March), 70–86.

Bauman, Z. (1992). *Intimations of postmodernity.* London: Taylor and Francis Books.

Bauman, Z. (2002). Individually, together. In U. Beck & E. Beck (Eds.), *Individualization* (pp. xiv–xix). London: Sage Publication.

Beck, U., & Beck-Gernsheim, E. (2002). *Individualization: Institutionalized individualism and its social and political consequences.* London: Sage Publications.

Beck, U., Giddens, A., & Lash, S. (1994). *Reflexive modernization: Politics, tradition and aesthetics in the modern social order.* Cambridge: Polity Press.

Becker, G. S. (1991). *A treatise on the family (enlarged edition).* Cambridge, MA: Harvard University Press.

Bellah, R., Madsen, R., Sullivan, W. M., Swidler, A., & Tipton, S. M. (1985). *Habits of the heart: Individualism and commitment in America.* Berkeley: University of California Press.

Blumer, H. (1962). Society as symbolic interaction. In A. M. Rose (Ed.), *Human behavior and social processes* (pp. 179–192). Boston, MA.: Houghton Mifflin.

Brown, S. L., & Manning, W. D. (2009). Family boundary ambiguity and the measurement of family structure: The significance of cohabitation. *Demography, 46,* 85–101.

Butler, J. (1990). *Gender trouble: Feminism and the subversion of identity.* New York: Routledge.

Cancian, F. M. (1987). *Love in America: Gender and selfdevelopment.* Cambridge, England: Cambridge University Press.

Carroll, J. S., Olson, C. D., & Buckmiller, N. (2007). Family boundary ambiguity: A 30-year review of theory, research, and measurement. *Family Relations, 56,* 210–230.

Chetty, R., Hendren, N., & Katz, L. F. (2015). *The effects of exposure to better neighborhoods on children: New evidence from the moving to opportunity experiment.* Working Paper No. 21156. Cambridge, MA, National Bureau of Economic Research.

Cherlin, A. J. (2004). The deinstitutionalization of American marriage. *Journal of Marriage and Family, 66*(4), 848–861.

Collins, P. H. (2000). *Black feminist thought* (Vol. Routledge): New York.

Cook, K., O'Brien, J., & Kollock, P. (1990). Exchange theory: A blueprint for structure and process. In G. Ritzer (Ed.), *Frontiers of social theory: The new syntheses*

Crenshaw, K. (1991). Mapping the margins: Intersectionality, identity politics, and violence against women of color. *Stanford Law Review, 43*(6), 1241–1299.

Duncan, G. J. (1984). *Years of poverty, years of plenty.* Ann Arbor: Institute for Social Research, University of Michigan.

Emerson, R. M. (1972). Exchange theory, part 2: Exchange relations and network structures. In J. Berger, M. J. Zelditch, & B. Anderson (Eds.), *Sociological theories in progress* (Vol. 2, pp. 53–87). New York: Houghton Mifflin.

England, P. (2005). Emerging theories of care work. *Annual Review of Sociology, 31,* 381–399.

England, P., & Folbre, N. (1999). The cost of caring. *The Annals of the American Academy of Political and Social Science, 561,* 39–51.

Ferree, M. M. (2010). Filling the glass: Gender perspectives on families. *Journal of Marriage and Family, 72*(June), 420439.

Giddens, A. (1991). *Modernity and self-identity.* Stanford, CA: Stanford University Press.

Glenn, E. N. (2000). The social construction and institutionalization of gender and race. In M. M. Ferre, J. Lorber, & B. B. Hess (Eds.), *Revisioning gender* (pp. 3–43). Walnut Creek, CA: AltaMira Press.

Green, A. I. (2007). Queer theory and sociology: Locating the subject and the self in sexuality studies. *Sociological Theory, 25*(1), 26–45.

Lehr, V. (1999). *Queer family values: Debunking the myth of the nuclear family.* Philadelphia: Temple University Press.

McLanahan, S., Garfinkel, I., Reichman, N., Teitler, J., Carlson, M., & Audiger, C. N. (2003). The fragile families and child well-being study baseline national report, revised March 2003. Retrieved October 23, 2015, from www.fragilefamilies.princeton.edu/documents/nationalreport.pdf

Oswald, R. F., Blume, L. B., & Marks, S. R. (2005). Decentering heteronormativity: A model for family studies. In V. L. Bengtson, A. C. Acock, K. R. Allen, P. Dilworth-Anderson, & D. M. Klein (Eds.), *Sourcebook of family theory and research* (pp. 143–154). Thousand Oaks, CA: Sage Publications. Nelson, T. J., & Edin, K. (2013). *Doing the best I can: Fathering in the inner city.* Berkeley: University of California Press.

Roseneil, S., & Budgeon, S. (2004). Cultures of intimacy and care beyond "the family": Personal life and social change in the early 21st century. *Current Sociology, 52,* 135–159.

Schaefer, R. T. (2007). *Sociology* (10th ed.). New York, NY: McGraw-Hill.

Stryker, S., & Vryan, K. D. (2003). The symbolic interactionist frame. In J. Delamater (Ed.), *Handbook of social psychology* (pp. 3–28). New York: Kluwer Academics/Plenum Publishers.

Thorne, B. (1992). Feminist rethinking of the family: An overview. In B. Thorne & M. Yalom (Eds.), *Rethinking the family: Some feminist questions (revised edition)* (pp. 3–30). Boston, MA: Northeastern University Press.

Trask, B. S. (2010). *Globalization and families: Accelerated systemic social change.* New York: Springer.

U.S. Bureau of the Census. (2018). Detailed age and sex composition of the population. *2017 National Population Projections Tables.* Retrieved November 20, 2018, from https://www2.census.gov/programs-surveys/popproj/tables/2017/2017-summary-tables/np2017-t3.xlsx

United Nations. (2017). *International migration report 2017 Department of Economic and Social Affairs, Population Division* Retrieved from http://www.un.org/en/development/desa/population/migration/publications/migrationreport/docs/Migration Report2017_Highlights.pdf

Willey, A. (2016). *Undoing monogamy.* Durham NC: Duke University Press.

Chapter Two

The History of the Family

Looking Forward

1. What functions have families traditionally performed?
2. How did American families change after the United States was founded?
3. How have the family histories of major ethnic and racial groups differed?
4. How did the emotional character of the American family change during the early twentieth century?
5. When did the idea of a sexual identity develop?
6. What important changes occurred in marriage and childbearing in the United States in the last half of the twentieth century?
7. How does the life course perspective help us to understand social change?

The serious study of the history of the family began in 1960, when the manager of a tropical fruit importing firm in France, a self-described "Sunday historian," published a book about the history of childhood (Ariès, 1960). Philippe Ariès, curious about family life in the Middle Ages, had examined works of art dating back 1,000 years. Any artist will tell you that children's heads are larger in proportion to the rest of their bodies than adults' heads. Yet many early medieval artists used adult proportions when painting children's heads and bodies, as if their subjects were, in fact, small adults. Moreover, the artists dressed children in the same clothes as adults. From such evidence, Ariès concluded that the concept of childhood was a modern invention.

Of course, there always had been children, but until the 1700s, wrote Ariès, the long stage of life we call childhood wasn't recognized by most people. American historian John Demos put forth a similar argument about the Puritans in Plymouth Colony in the 1600s: "Childhood as such was barely recognized in the period spanned by Plymouth Colony. There was little sense that children might somehow be a special group, with their own needs and interests and capacities" (Demos, 1970). According to historians such as Ariès and Demos, parents withheld love and affection from infants and toddlers because so many of them died. The great French essayist Montaigne wrote in the late 1500s, "I have lost two or three children in their infancy, not without regret, but without great sorrow."[1] *Two or three*—Montaigne couldn't even remember how many. If children survived, wrote Ariès and Demos, they were treated as little adults. By age seven, boys and girls performed useful work—helping fathers in the fields or mothers at the hearth—and played the same games and attended the same festivals as adults.

Ariès argued that it was only with the spread of schooling and the decline in child deaths—neither of which occurred on a large scale until the 1800s outside the noble and middle classes—that the notion of a protected, extended stage of childhood emerged.

Ariès's influential book launched a new generation of historians who studied ordinary families rather than royal families. His contribution is still respected even though many historians now believe that he underestimated parents' appreciation of childhood as a stage of life. For every Montaigne, the revisionist historians have

[1] From vol. 2, no. 8, of Montaigne's *Essais*. Quoted on p. 39 of Ariès (1960).

found a Martin Luther, who wrote in the 1500s after the death of his infant daughter, "I so lamented her death that I was exquisitely sick, my heart rendered soft and weak; never had I thought that a father's heart could be so broken for his children's sake."[2] When historian Linda Pollock located and read 68 diaries written by American and British parents in the 1600s and 1700s, she found that most of them were aware that children were different from adults and that they needed parental guidance and support. The diarists frequently referred to their children as "comforts" and showed pride in their accomplishments. "I doe not think one child of 100 of his age durst doe so much," wrote one proud father (Pollock, 1983). (See also Nicholas [1991], Ozment [2001].) Nevertheless, parents of this period did seem less saddened by the death of an infant than that of an older child.

The family history industry that Ariès spawned has produced thousands of books and articles. Related fields such as the history of women, gender, and sexuality have grown just as fast. Together, these fields provide an anchor for the study of the contemporary family. They describe the context in which the contemporary family has developed. Among other things, they tell us that the public family is as old as human civilization but that the private family blossomed only during the past few hundred years. For the sociologist studying the contemporary family, the historical literature is a wonderful source of insights. This chapter will provide a brief guided tour of that literature. Of necessity, it will be a highly selective tour, focused on the United States.

First, we will look at what the colonial and American Indian families were like prior to 1776. Afterward, we will follow the changes in the American family that took place between 1776 and the start of the twentieth century. We will then study the diversity of racial and ethnic American families in the twentieth century, the emergence of sexual identities, and the rise of what I call "the private family." Then we will consider the changing "life course" and new life stage, emerging adulthood.

The American Family before 1776

There were several kinds of American families prior to the Revolution. There were, first of all, the families of the indigenous people who would become known as American Indians. There were the families of the European colonists. And there were the families of the African slaves, who were transported involuntarily to the Americas beginning in the 1500s. I will discuss the history of African American families later in this chapter. For now, let us examine the American Indian family and the European colonists' family before 1776.

AMERICAN INDIAN FAMILIES: THE PRIMACY OF THE TRIBE

The term **American Indian** is often used for a subset of the original, indigenous people who had settled in North America thousands of years before Columbus, namely, those who had settled in the territory that later became the 48 contiguous United States (Snipp, 2007). Indeed, it was because Columbus mistakenly believed that he had reached India that he gave this aboriginal population the misnomer "Indian." Although there is little direct evidence about American Indian societies

American Indian the name used for a subset of all Native Americans, namely, those who were living in the territory that later became the 48 contiguous United States

[2] Quoted in Ozment (1983).

lineage a form of kinship group in which descent is traced through either the father's or the mother's line

patrilineal describing a lineage in which descent is traced through the father's line

matrilineal describing a lineage in which descent is traced the mother's line

before the 1800s, scholars think that most American Indians lived in tribal societies based on **lineages:** kinship groups in which people trace their descent either through the father's or through the mother's line but not both. If descent is traced through the father's line, the lineage is described as **patrilineal;** and if descent is traced through the mother's line, the lineage is described as **matrilineal.** These groups may seem odd, at first, to contemporary Western readers, who trace descent through both the father's and mother's line, but the structure served a purpose in territories where no strong government other than the tribe existed. Among other virtues, lineages limited the number of people who were related to a person and with whom that person must share land, water, animals, and other resources. If I am in a lineage that traces descent through the father's line, my sons will marry women from outside the lineage; then the couples will live near me (sometimes with me) and remain in my lineage. My grandsons will do the same. But my daughters and granddaughters will marry men from other lineages, move to their land, and leave my lineage. Consequently, I need to share my resources with, and to defend, only those persons related to me through my father, my brothers, and my sons. If a maternal uncle needs assistance, that's his lineage's problem; I am not my mother's brother's keeper.

The American Indian population was devastated by diseases brought by Europeans, such as smallpox–diseases to which the native population had developed no immunities. Moreover, we know that large numbers of American Indians were killed in wars and massacres (Snipp, 2007). How these catastrophic events modified family and kinship is unclear. In the absence of direct evidence, scholars have assumed that the numerous accounts of American Indian societies in the 1800s and early 1900s can be generalized back in time. Although the assumption that present arrangements accurately reflect the past ignores the historical changes that occurred to American Indian societies after the arrival of the Europeans, the outlines of American Indian family and kinship seem clear.

Both patrilineal and matrilineal tribes existed. Related lineages were often organized into larger clans that provided the basis for social organization and governing. In matrilineal tribes such as the Hopi, for example, a person traced his or her relatives through his or her mother's line.[3] If you were a child, your father was a guest in your mother's home. Although strong bonds existed between wives and husbands, a woman's ties to her maternal kin–her mother, her mother's brothers, her maternal cousins–were generally stronger. Consequently, your maternal uncles played an important role in your upbringing. They, not your father, had to approve your choice of spouse. Still, if you were a boy, you did learn many of the skills of an adult male–growing crops, herding animals–from your father. It was as if you had two kinds of fathers: a biological father who taught you skills and an uncle-father who held greater authority over you. If you were a girl, you spent less time with your father.

When Hopi boys reached puberty, they moved out of the household, sleeping in the men's ceremonial house and eventually marrying into another clan. Girls, on the other hand, remained in or near their mothers' homes throughout their lives, bringing husbands from other clans into their dwellings. In general, American Indian children were more independent than European American children: They were given more freedom and experienced less physical punishment (Mintz, 2004). In all tribal societies, the common requirement that individuals marry someone

[3] This account of Hopi kinship draws from Queen, Habenstein, and Quadagno (1985).

outside their clan forged alliances across clans. If clan A and clan B frequently exchanged young adults as marriage partners, the two clans would likely consider themselves as allies in any disputes with other clans in the tribe. Thus, the lineage and clan organization of American Indian societies served to strengthen the social order and to protect individuals against unfriendly outsiders.

Kinship was also matrilineal among the Apache of Arizona. Soon after a girl's first menstruation (which probably occurred several years later in her life than is the case today), her lineage held a four-day Sun Rise ceremony, after which she was eligible to marry (Joe, Sparks, & Tiger, 1999). Marriages were typically arranged by elders from the prospective bride's and groom's lineages. (Marrying someone from the same lineage was forbidden.) A series of gifts was exchanged by the bride's and groom's families, which culminated in the groom's family bringing him to the home of the bride. The bride's family then constructed a separate home for the couple. The gifts between families symbolized the importance of establishing an alliance with a family in another lineage. It's not that love between the young couple was necessarily lacking, but their marriage also served the larger purpose of tying together members of two lineages who could provide assistance in times of trouble or need.

EUROPEAN COLONISTS: THE PRIMACY OF THE PUBLIC FAMILY

Among the European colonists, there were no lineages. There were only the smaller kinship groups known as the **conjugal family** of husband, wife, and children, and the **extended family,** comprising the conjugal family plus any other relatives present in the household, such as a grandparent or uncle. These families provided services that were of great value to the community. Consider education. In Plymouth Colony, children received their basic education from their parents or, if they were working as servants, in another family's home. Parents and masters were required by law to teach reading to their children and young servants, so they could at least "be able to duely read the scriptures" (Demos, 1970). Why weren't these children learning to read in school? Because there was no school—or rather, because the family *was* school. In addition to providing schooling, all Plymouth Colony families were expected to provide vocational training. Through apprenticeship and service, working next to an adult, children and youths learned the skills they needed to farm, trade, garden, cook, and make clothes. All families were also expected to supplement church services by engaging in "family worship," praying and meditating daily.

conjugal family a kinship group comprising husband, wife, and children

extended family a kinship group comprising the conjugal family plus any other relatives present in the household, such as a grandparent or uncle.

Selected Plymouth Colony families also functioned as

- *Hospitals* Some adults who supposedly had specialized knowledge took sick persons into their homes for treatment.
- *Houses of correction* Judges ordered some idle or criminal persons to live in the homes of upstanding families to learn how to change their ways.
- *Orphanages* Children whose parents had died—and death rates were very high (Navin, 2012)—were taken in by a relative or family friend.
- *Nursing homes* Frail elderly parents were cared for in their homes by their children.
- *Poorhouses* Families sometimes took in poor relatives who needed food and shelter. (Demos, 1970)

Today, all these activities, with the exception of caring for the elderly, are carried out primarily outside the home, mostly by publicly supported institutions. In Plymouth Colony, then, the family's public role was much broader than it is now.

In contrast, the family's private role was much smaller. The kind of privacy that Westerners today take for granted hardly existed a few hundred years ago, as is apparent to anyone who visits the Puritan houses that still stand in Massachusetts. The downstairs area of a typical house contained one or two rooms. The larger of them was an all-purpose room called the "hall," in which the members of the household spent most of their indoor waking hours. It was dominated by a huge fireplace used for heating and cooking. In smaller houses, the second downstairs room would contain little except bedding. Most houses also had one or two second-story lofts with beds. Often, only the hall contained furniture for any activity other than sleeping. In this one room, fathers, mothers, children (Plymouth families had an average of seven or eight children), servants or apprentices, and perhaps a grandparent ate, cooked, talked, prayed, sewed clothing, relaxed, and received visitors. Individuals simply could not find a place to get away from other household members.

Not only did individuals have difficulty maintaining privacy but the conjugal family also had difficulty maintaining privacy from other households. The colonists did not regard the conjugal family as separate from society, but rather as an integral part of it. To a great extent, a family's affairs were considered public business. For example, Puritan laws required that married couples maintain harmonious relations and raise their children properly—and imposed fines on those who didn't. Friends and neighbors commonly called at one another's houses without advance notice. Given all the ways in which privacy was prevented, the idea of a private, conjugal family with its own separate space—and of individual privacy within the family—may not have been in the mind-set of most people. At best, privacy was probably dismissed as unattainable.

FAMILY DIVERSITY

But not all colonial families fit the ideal of two married, biological parents and their children. Particularly outside of New England, families were diverse. For one thing, death rates were so high that children commonly lost a parent and lived in a stepfamily after their remaining parent remarried (Navin, 2012; Uhlenberg, 1980). In addition, people sometimes proclaimed themselves married in front of family or friends, without the participation of clergy, and were accepted as married by their communities. Europeans, it turns out, had a long tradition of informal marriage. Until the Council of Trent in 1563, the Catholic Church accepted as a marriage any public statement by a couple that they considered themselves married to each other, as long as neither partner coerced the other and their marriage did not violate church laws about who could marry whom. Until 1753 the Church of England, which had broken with the Catholic Church during the reign of Henry VIII, recognized informal marriage (Therborn, 2004). Even as late as 1850, informal marriage was common in England among the poorer classes (Gillis, 1985). People used the phrase "living tally" to describe couples living as married but who had never wed in the church.

Informal marriage was particularly common in the Middle Colonies (New York, New Jersey, Pennsylvania, Delaware, and Maryland) and the Southern Colonies (Virginia, North Carolina, South Carolina, and Georgia), where the Anglican Church (the American wing of the Church of England) did not provide enough clergy, and in frontier areas where social control was looser. An Anglican minister in eighteenth-century Maryland said, "if . . . no marriage should be deemed valid that had not been registered in the parish book, it would I am persuaded bastardize nine-tenths of the People in the Country."[4] In other words, most couples who considered themselves married never had a church ceremony to make it official. As in England, informal marriage persisted into the nineteenth century. In 1833, the Chief Justice of the State of Pennsylvania wrote that if the state truly enforced its marriage laws, the "vast majority" of the state's children would be considered illegitimate. A form of bigamy also sometimes occurred: A man who left his wife and migrated to a faraway state or territory was unlikely to be followed, so he could marry anew without much fear of prosecution (Hartog, 2000). In the nineteenth and early twentieth centuries, in contrast, families probably became *less* diverse over time, as churches established control of marriage and as fewer parents died while their children were young.

Quick Review

- Lineages and clans constituted the main social organization of American Indian tribal societies.
- In American colonial society, families had many public functions but a smaller private role than today.
- Parental death and informal marriage produced diverse types of families.

The Emergence of the "Modern" American Family: 1776–1900

Pinpointing the beginnings of social change is always difficult; rarely can we discern a great divide between an older way of life and an emerging one. Nevertheless, the decades surrounding the American Revolution seem to have been a watershed in the history of the American family. Between 1776 and 1830, the outlines emerged of a kind of family that would remain prominent well into the twentieth century. Clearest among the white middle class, it had four new characteristics:

- Marriage was increasingly based on affection and mutual respect rather than on male authority and custom. As a consequence, women experienced increasing autonomy in the family. (But, I would add, they were increasingly restricted to the home.)
- The primary role of the wife became the care of children and the maintenance of the home. Women came to be seen as morally superior to men, and the home came to be seen as "women's sphere."
- The attention and energy of the husband and wife were increasingly centered on their children. Children came to be seen as needing not only discipline and economic support, but also attention, affection, and loving care.
- The number of children per family declined, in part as a consequence of the greater investment of emotion and time that they were seen to need.

The role of romantic love probably increased within marriage during this period, at least among the middle and upper classes who left diaries and letters that historians can read today (Bloch, 2003). But romantic love needed to be tempered by a careful judgment of whether a potential spouse was a reliable and dependable

[4] Quoted in Cott (2000). The Anglican minister is quoted on p. 32; the Chief Justice, on p. 39.

person—someone with whom one could build a family. These practical considerations were particularly important for women, who became legally and socially bound to their husband's authority upon marrying. During courtship, women needed to assure themselves that feelings of love were leading to a safe choice of husband (Blauvelt, 2007). To be sure, young adults today still care about a partner's character, but the stakes are not as high as in the past because it is possible for women to lead independent adult lives and because ending an unhappy marriage through divorce is much more acceptable. In the early 1800s, then, both emotion and practicality played important roles in choosing a spouse.

Despite these changes, marriage retained a moral basis in custom and law through the nineteenth century. According to historian Nancy Cott (2000), political philosophers argued that lifetime marriage with the husband as the head was similar to American governance: It involved democratic rule by a leader (the husband) with the voluntary consent of the governed (the wife). Preserving marriage was seen as essential to maintaining a democratic moral order. Consequently, government support for marriage—such as laws that made obtaining a divorce difficult—was viewed as necessary and proper. Cott's thesis suggests that the family's contribution to public welfare was conceived more broadly than today. I defined the "public family" in terms of its valuable care for dependents. Prior to the twentieth century, many Americans also thought that marriage served as the foundation of national morality. This view of marriage as the moral and political backbone of society would erode during the twentieth century.

FROM COOPERATION TO SEPARATION: WOMEN'S AND MEN'S SPHERES

Another spur to family change was the transition from subsistence farming to wage labor. Instead of growing crops and tending animals, more husbands took paying jobs. It began sometime in the 1700s and early 1800s, with the growth of commercial capitalism—an economic system that emphasizes the buying, selling, and distribution of goods such as grain, tobacco, or cotton. Commercial capitalism created jobs for merchants, clerks, shippers, dockworkers, wagon builders, and others like them, who were paid money for their labor. The opportunity to earn money outside the home undermined the authority of fathers. Because sons had alternatives to farming, fathers no longer had a near monopoly on the resources needed to make a living. This greater economic independence facilitated the growth of individualism. The transition accelerated in the mid-1800s with the spread of industrial capitalism, which created factory work for the great masses of immigrants and their descendants.

The heart of this change was the movement of men's work out of the home. Instead of working together in a common household enterprise, husbands and wives now worked on separate enterprises—he exchanging his labor for wages, she maintaining the home and raising the children. Instead of working in close proximity, the two were physically separated during the workday. Moreover, wage work held no intrinsic value for most men, and in nineteenth-century factories it was frequently exhausting and dangerous.

The sharp split between a rewarding home life and an often alienating work life led to the emergence of the idea of "separate spheres": men's sphere being the world of work and, more generally, the world outside the home; and women's sphere being the home, relatives, and children. Whereas men's sphere was seen as being governed by the rough ethic of the business world, women's sphere came to be seen as morally pure, a place where wives could renew their husbands' spirituality and character. And whereas men's sphere was seen as providing no reward other than a paycheck, women's sphere was the center of affection and nurturing, the emotional core for husbands and children.

Thus, developed a nineteenth-century ideology, a set of beliefs, which historian Barbara Welter (1966) named "the cult of True Womanhood." The True Woman was, first of all, a pious upholder of spiritual values. She was also pure: She was to have no sexual contact before marriage—although men might try to tempt her—and none afterward except with her husband. Moreover, the True Woman was submissive to men, particularly her husband. And finally, she was domestic: Her proper place was in the home, comforting her husband, lovingly raising her children.

Woman's sphere in the 1800s at once limited women's opportunities and glorified their domestic role. It was a more restricted economic role than wives in the colonial and revolutionary eras had experienced (O'Connor, 2009). To be sure, the colonial wife was also home most of the day, but she was collaborating with her husband in the family economy; and often buying and selling goods; without her contribution, her husband might not have been able to feed and clothe their children. Then the movement to wage labor separated women from paid work. Men went out every morning into the wider social world, but their wives could not follow. In a culture that had begun to celebrate individualism, women were supposed to give up much of their individualism to care for their husbands and children. Seen from this vantage point, one might argue that women's lives were worse in the 1800s than they had been before the Revolution—more restricted, less productive, more dependent and more isolated. Indeed, many historians have argued as much.

But other historians, while acknowledging the restrictions and dependency inherent in the domestic sphere, argue that it nevertheless offered some benefits. Appointing women the guardians of moral values and giving them the major role in rearing children provided them with substantial influence. However circumscribed, it may have allowed wives to counter the authority of their husbands, which had been so pervasive in the colonial period. Moreover, the ideology of women's sphere may have created a self-consciousness of, and an identification with, women as a group. Women established and maintained deep friendships with other women, reinforced by the segregation of their lives and by female rituals surrounding childbirth, weddings, illnesses, and funerals (Smith-Rosenberg, 1975). Some joined together in public associations to promote values consistent with domesticity, such as greater devotion to religion, assistance for the poor, or enlightened child-rearing. These friendships and associations may have been a prerequisite for the development of feminist organizations in the nineteenth and twentieth centuries. Historian Nancy Cott captured the dual nature of women's sphere in the title of her book, *The Bonds of Womanhood* (1977), for the bonds that tied women to the domestic sphere also bound them together in a subculture of sisterhood that prefigured their social and political movements decades later.

Quick Review

- In the late 1700s and early 1800s, American marriage seemed to change.
  - Greater importance was given to affection and mutual respect rather than male authority.
  - Increasing attention was paid to the loving care of (a declining number of) children.
- Under the emerging doctrine of "separate spheres," men's sphere was the world outside the home, women's, the home, relatives, and children.
- Women's sphere restricted their opportunities but also fostered friendships and participation in public organizations.

African American, Mexican American, and Asian Immigrant Families

Europeans, of course, were not the only immigrants to the United States in the 1700s and 1800s. Three other groups were present early in the nation's history. Africans had been forced to immigrate–captured or bought in West Africa, transported across the ocean under horrible conditions that killed many, and sold as slaves upon arrival. Mexicans, in search of grazing land, had pushed north into the area that is now the Southwest. Asian immigrants first arrived in large numbers in the mid-nineteenth century, when they were used as laborers by the railroads and other enterprises. The family lives of all three groups differed from those of the Europeans. Like white working-class women, those from racial and ethnic minority groups had to contribute economically outside, as well as inside, the home (Cherlin, 2014).

AFRICAN AMERICAN FAMILIES

Until the appearance of new scholarship in the 1970s, most historians thought that the oppression and harsh conditions of slavery had destroyed most of the culture African slaves brought with them, leaving little in its place. The writings of both white and black scholars emphasized the losses imposed by slavery: the uprooting from Africa, the disruption of families through sales of family members to new owners, the inability of fathers to protect their families from the abuses imposed by masters. In an influential 1939 book, E. Franklin Frazier, a sociologist and an African American, argued that white masters had destroyed all social organization among the slaves. As a result, he wrote, slave family life was disorganized; the only stable bond was between mothers and their children:

> *Consequently, under all conditions of slavery, the Negro mother remained the most dependable and important figure in the family. (Frazier, 1939)*

From Frazier and others, then, came the idea that both during and after slavery, most African American families were headed by women and that African American men were relatively powerless in and outside the home. But in 1976, historian Herbert Gutman published a comprehensive study of plantation, local government, and census records that suggested a much different picture (Gutman, 1976). Gutman found substantial evidence that whenever possible, slaves had married and lived together for life and that they knew and kept track of uncles, aunts, cousins, and other kin. He cited letters such as one the field hand Cash sent to relatives on a Georgia plantation after he, his wife, Phoebe, and some of their children were sold away:

> *Clairissa your affectionate Mother and Father sends a heap of love to you and your Husband and my Grand Children. Mag. & Cloe. John. Judy. My aunt sinena . . . Give our Love to Cashes brother Porter and his Wife Patience. Victoria sends her Love to her Cousin Beck and Miley. (Gutman, 1976)*

Moreover, Gutman argued, before and after slavery, in both the North and the South, most African American families included two parents. These family ties were forged despite the frequent sale of husbands, wives, and children to other masters, despite the sexual abuse of slave women by owners, and despite high rates of disease and death.

Still, there were some differences, both before and after the Civil War, between black and white families. For example, young slave women often had a first child before marrying; if so, they were usually married within a few years, although not necessarily to the father (Jones, 2010). This pattern may have occurred in part because slave owners valued women who had many children, increasing the owner's wealth. Enslaved women living on farms with a small number of slaves were more likely to be living apart from the fathers of their children than on farms with many slaves—perhaps because there were more marriages that crossed the boundaries of the smaller farms (Miller, 2018). Moreover, slave marriages had no legal standing and could be broken apart by owners at any time. Overall, slave families took a variety of forms, including marriage-based, single-parent, and multigenerational. The most lasting form, however, was the mother and child unit, which would remain after a father was sold away (Hunter, 2017).

After the Civil War, the U.S. Freedmen's Bureau, which was formed to assist former slaves, enforced marriage by arresting cohabiting individuals who had not married. In this way, government policy moved from not recognizing marriage legally before the war to punishing cohabiting couples who were not married in the years after the war (Hunter, 2017).

Another difference between black and white families after the Civil War was that wives in rural black families worked seasonally in the fields, whereas rural white women didn't. According to 1870 census figures for the Cotton Belt states, about 4 in 10 African American wives had jobs, almost all as field workers. In contrast, 98 percent of white wives said they were "keeping house" and had no other job (Jones, 2010). The differences reflect a mixture of economic pressure and culture. The plots of land African American sharecroppers farmed in the late nineteenth century provided such a marginal standard of living that men and women (and often children) were needed in the fields, at least at harvesttime. Historian Jacqueline Jones (2010) has also noted that "the outlines of African work patterns endured among enslaved laborers," in that African women often bore the major responsibility for cultivating food.

Moreover, although most black families still had two parents, black mothers were more likely to be living without a male partner than white mothers. This racial difference stemmed partly from the high mortality rates of black men; by one estimate, 42 percent of black wives were widowed by ages 45 to 50 around 1900 (Preston, Lim, & Morgan, 1992). But a difference still remains after mortality is taken into account (Morgan, McDaniel, Miller, & Preston, 1993). A much larger racial difference in household structure would emerge after about 1960 (see Chapter 5).

When black families migrated to Northern cities in the twentieth century, black women continued to work outside the home in larger numbers than white women. Thirty-one percent of married black women worked outside the home in the 1920s and 1930s, compared with 8 percent of married white women (Bouston & Collins, 2014). Because of discrimination, black men were offered only low-paying, physically challenging jobs that couldn't support a family. Staying home simply was not an option for most black wives, who also faced discrimination and found work mainly as domestic servants. As intersectionality theorists have argued (Collins, 2000), black women faced inequalities due to both gender and race. Not until the 1960s did black women break out of domestic service into occupations previously reserved for white women. Today, women of both races still lag behind men in earnings, and black men's employment situation, though improved, remains difficult (Katz, Stern, & Fader, 2005).

MEXICAN AMERICAN FAMILIES

Like African Americans, Mexican Americans established a presence early in the history of what is now the United States. In the early nineteenth century, well before migrants from the eastern United States arrived, Mexicans settled the frontier of what was then northern Mexico (Martínez, 2001). These pioneers crossed deserts and fought with American Indians to reach as far west as California and as far north as Colorado. Their early settlements generally included an elite landowning family and poorer farmer-laborer settlers. The landowning elite tended to be (or claimed to be) of nearly pure Spanish descent. Some owned vast tracts of land on which they grazed cattle or sheep. They arranged their children's marriages with care and celebrated elaborate weddings and feasts, so as to preserve or merge their holdings with other wealthy families or with wealthy Anglo (non-Mexican) immigrants (Griswold del Castillo, 1979).

mestizo a person whose ancestors include both Spanish settlers and Native Americans

More numerous were the laborers who worked the great estates or farmed or grazed animals on their own smaller holdings. They tended to be **mestizos,** people whose ancestors included both Spanish settlers and Native Americans from Mexico (Caldera, Velez-Gomez, & Lindsey, 2015). There is some evidence that informal marriages were more common among this group (Griswold del Castillo, 1979). Informal marriages allowed couples to evade the control of their parents and other kin; and with fewer resources to protect than among the elite, the *mestizo* classes had less reason to control who married whom. These small landholders and laborers attempted to enlist the sponsorship and support of the well-to-do through the tradition of **compadrazgo,** a godparent relationship in which a wealthy or influential person outside the kinship group became the *compadre,* or godparent, of a newborn child, particularly at its baptism. The godfather and godchild were expected to retain a special relationship, and the godparent was supposed to assist his godchild, for example, by providing or finding a job for him (Mintz & Wolf, 1950).

compadrazgo in Mexico, a godparent relationship in which a wealthy or influential person outside the kinship group is asked to become the *compadre*, or godparent, of a newborn child, particularly at its baptism

This social structure was disrupted by a series of wars, revolts, and land grabs by U.S. troops and immigrants during the 1830s and 1840s. When it was over, the United States had acquired, by conquest, the current Southwest. Soon thereafter, most of the Spanish elite lost their land to taxes, drought, and Anglo squatters. Instead of ranchers and farmers, Mexicans became more of a working-class community, employed by the growing numbers of Anglos (Caldera, Velez-Gomez, & Lindsey, 2015). And as the number of Anglo immigrants rose, Mexican Americans were forced into **barrios,** segregated neighborhoods in the city. Residents of the *barrios* faced high unemployment or low income if they provided low-wage labor to Anglo employers.

barrio a segregated Mexican-American neighborhood in a U.S. city

A slow migration from Mexico continued until the start of World War II, consisting mostly of immigrants who stayed in the United States for a short period of time to earn money and then returned to Mexico (Rosenblum & Brick, 2011). In 1942, the U.S. and Mexican governments established the Bracero Program, under which Mexicans could enter the United States as guest workers. But it was not until the mid-1960s that legal and unauthorized Mexican immigration began to occur on a large scale due to economic difficulties in Mexico; the demand for low-wage labor by American employers in fields such as construction, farming, and maintenance; and changes to immigration law. The Mexican-origin population grew rapidly, and a new flow of immigrants began from Central American countries such as El Salvador, Guatemala, and Honduras. In 2015, 63 percent of all Americans who identified as Hispanic said that they were of Mexican descent (Pew Research Center, 2017).

ASIAN IMMIGRANT FAMILIES

The Asian Heritage Before the middle of the twentieth century, most Asian American families in the United States consisted of immigrants from China and Japan and their descendants. Family systems in East Asia (where China and Japan are located) were sharply different from those in the United States and other Western countries, although these differences are currently diminishing (Cherlin, 2012; Goode, 1963). In the traditional East Asian family, parents had more authority over family members than is true in the West. For example, parents usually controlled who their children would marry and when. In addition, kinship was patrilineal, or traced through the father's line. In China, the ideal was that a man's sons (and eventually his grandsons) would bring their wives into his growing household. Daughters would be sent at marriage to live in their in-laws' households. When parents grew old, sons and their wives were expected to live with them and care for them. In Japan, the oldest son carried the main responsibility for the care of elderly parents. Thus, East Asian cultures placed a greater emphasis on children's loyalty to their parents than Western culture. For a son or daughter, happiness in marriage was less important than fulfilling obligations to parents and other kin.

Asian Immigrants Chinese immigrants first began to arrive during the California gold rush in the 1850s. After the Civil War, they were hired to build the railroads of the Southwest. Because the vast majority of these immigrant laborers were men, relatively few new families were formed. In fact, some left wives behind (Takaki, 1998). In California and most other western states, laws prohibited Chinese (and later Japanese) immigrants from marrying white Americans or becoming citizens. In fact, American sentiment against Chinese immigrants was so strong that in 1882 Congress passed the Chinese Exclusion Act, which restricted Chinese immigration until after World War II. As late as 1930, 80 percent of the Chinese population was male (Takaki, 1998).

In the 1880s, significant numbers of Japanese immigrants began to arrive in Hawaii (which the United States would soon annex) and the mainland United States. The ratio of women to men was more balanced among the Japanese than among Chinese immigrants, so more families were formed. Both Chinese and Japanese families were patrilineal. The father's authority was strong, and ties to extended family members such as brothers or grandparents were important. Traditionally, parents or other relatives arranged their children's marriages (Wong, 1988). Since immigrants usually left their extended families behind, they developed other ways of building family-like ties in the United States. For example, people from the same region of China or Japan formed mutual aid societies (Bergquist, 2005).

Like the Chinese, Japanese immigrants faced discrimination. After the war with Japan began in 1941, some Americans warned that Japanese immigrants might be disloyal, even though many had lived in the United States for decades. Bowing to these fears, the government rounded up Japanese immigrants, most of whom lived in California, and sent them to internment camps. Aside from the imprisonment, humiliation, and economic losses the Japanese suffered there, the camps eroded the traditional authority of Japanese parents (Kitano & Daniels, 1988). They had little to offer children, who were exposed to American activities such as dancing to the music of the latest bands. Young Japanese American men could even volunteer to join a much-decorated U.S. Army unit that fought in Europe. After the war, the autonomy children had experienced in the camps contributed to sharp changes in Japanese American marriage patterns. Whereas the older generation's marriages had been arranged by relatives who stressed obligations to kin and emotional restraint, the younger generation much more often chose their own spouses based on romantic love and companionship (Yanagisako, 1985).

1965 Immigration Act act passed by the U.S. Congress which ended restrictions that had blocked most Asian immigration and substituted an annual quota

Overall, Asian immigration was modest until Congress passed the **1965 Immigration Act,** which ended restrictions that had blocked most Asian immigration and substituted an annual quota. Since then, the Asian population of the United States has expanded rapidly. Moreover, Asian immigrants have become more likely to arrive as families than in the past (Takaki, 1998). According to the American Community Survey, there were 18.3 million people of Asian origin in the United States in 2016, a 54 percent increase from 2000 (U.S. Bureau of the Census, 2012). The three largest groups were Chinese, (Asian) Indians, and Filipinos.

bilateral kinship a system in which descent is reckoned through both the mother's and father's lines

Filipino immigration began as a small stream of mostly students after the United States captured the Philippines in the Spanish-American War of 1898. After 1965, many Filipino immigrants were professionals, most notably nurses. Unlike Chinese and Japanese families, Filipino families trace descent through both the father's and mother's line, a system called **bilateral kinship** (the system followed in the United States). Such a system usually provides women more independence than patrilineal kinship, so Filipino American women have been more likely to work outside the home than women in Chinese or Japanese families (Kitano & Daniels, 1988). Immigration from India was modest until after 1965, and even in 2010, 88 percent of Indian-American adults were foreign born. Indian-Americans are the most highly educated immigrant group; 70 percent of adults age 25 and over in 2010 had a college degree (DeSilver, 2014).

Quick Review

- The family lives of groups that emigrated from Africa (through slavery), Mexico, and Asia differed from the family lives of European immigrants.
- The women in all immigrant families were more likely to contribute economically than were middle-class women.
- African American families have maintained stronger ties to extended kin and borne a higher percentage of children outside of marriage than have European American families.
- Most African American families had two parents, even during slavery.
- Early Mexican settlers included a landed elite and a larger population of *mestizos.*
- Mexican families use the tradition of *compadrazgo* to obtain assistance for children.
- Chinese immigration was heavily male at first, and immigrants sent home remittances to family.
- Japanese families were sent to internment camps during World War II.
- Both Chinese and Japanese families were traditionally patrilineal, with arranged marriages.

The Emergence of Sexual Identities

In April 1779, Alexander Hamilton wrote to John Laurens, with whom he had served in the American Revolution:

> *Cold in my professions, warm in [my] friendships, I wish, my Dear Laurens, it m[ight] be in my power, by action rather than words, [to] convince you that I love you. I shall only tell you that 'till you bade us Adieu, I hardly knew the value you had taught my heart to set upon you.*

In September, after almost giving up hope of receiving a letter from Laurens, Hamilton wrote of his joy at finally receiving one:

> *But like a jealous lover, when I thought you slighted my caresses, my affection was alarmed and my vanity piqued. I had almost resolved to lavish no more of them upon you and to reject you as an inconstant and an ungrateful–. But you have now disarmed my resentment and by a single mark of attention made up the quarrel.* (Katz, 1976)

Upon discovering this correspondence, it is the instinct of the contemporary reader to wonder whether Alexander Hamilton was gay. Yet historians argue that such a question represents the myopia of a person steeped in contemporary culture peering back at another time. The categories of gay and straight did not yet exist, and therefore eighteenth- and early-nineteenth century people did not need to fit into them. Whether or not Hamilton's intimate friendship ever involved a sexual act was not its defining feature. As historian Jonathan Katz notes, even if many of the phrases in letters that men wrote to each other were merely rhetorical flourishes, it is striking how easy it was for men to use language that today would be seen as indicating a sexual relationship. In fact, what seems so different about relationships such as Hamilton and Laurens's is the seeming ease with which two same-sex individuals could engage in intimacies, such as declaring their love for each other, without these acts marking the relationship sexual. A broad range of public affection and intimacy was open to same-sex friendships in a way that, for most men at least, it is not today (Adam, 2004).

Alexander Hamilton was one of many eighteenth- and nineteenth-century Americans who wrote intimate letters to other men.

Source: Library of Congress Prints and Photographs Division [LC-DIG-ppmsca-17523]

The best-known study of same-sex intimacy in the late eighteenth and nineteenth centuries is Carroll Smith-Rosenberg's "The Female World of Love and Ritual" (Smith-Rosenberg, 1975). Smith-Rosenberg explored the separate sphere of middle-class women and found that they often formed strong emotional bonds with other women. Some of their correspondence seems, by today's standards at least, to have a romantic and even erotic tone. Smith-Rosenberg writes of Sarah Butler Wister and Jeannie Field Musgrove, who first met as teenagers during a summer vacation, attended boarding school together for two years, and formed a lifelong intimate friendship. At age 29, Sarah, married and a mother, wrote to Jeannie, "I shall be entirely alone [this coming week]. I can give you no idea how desperately I shall want you." Jeannie ended one letter "Goodbye my dearest, dearest lover" and another "I will go to bed . . . [though] I could write all night—A thousand kisses—I love you with my whole soul."

The point of studying exchanges such as these, as Smith-Rosenberg herself argued, "is not whether these women had genital contact and can therefore be defined as heterosexual or homosexual." Rather, the point is that these women lived in a social context that allowed them the freedom to form a friendship that was quite intimate without the friendship's being labeled as anything more than that. Middle-class women's bonds could be loving and sensual without necessarily being sexual; it is likely that even if they were, the sexual acts would not be seen as the defining characteristic of the relationship. The social context allowed women more flexibility in creating intense emotional ties than is the case today, when we tend to think that close, sensual same-sex relationships must be "gay" or "lesbian."

But in the late-nineteenth and twentieth centuries, this more fluid conception of sexuality congealed into two master categories that people saw as central to their senses of themselves—two sexual identities, then known as heterosexual and homosexual. Of course, there is nothing new about sex, or about people having sexual preferences and attractions. What's new—or at least no more than 150 years old—is the way that sexual acts and preferences are organized into sexual identities. By a **sexual identity,** I mean the formation in people's minds of an identity such as heterosexual, gay, lesbian, or bisexual based on romantic and sexual attraction. Our sexual identity, in turn, becomes an important part of our sense of who we are. Furthermore, we see this as "natural"—everyone, we assume, has a sexual identity.

sexual identity the formation in people's minds of an identity such as heterosexual, gay, lesbian, or bisexual based on romantic and sexual attraction

SEXUAL ACTS VERSUS SEXUAL IDENTITIES

Until the nineteenth century, not only the terms "homosexual" and "heterosexual" but also the idea of "being" homosexual or heterosexual had not yet been invented. There were only two categories of sexual activities: the socially approved (sexual intercourse within marriage, in moderation, and undertaken mainly to have children) and the socially disapproved (all other activities, including acts between persons of the same sex, masturbation, oral sex regardless of the genders of the partners, and so forth). To perform any of the latter was sinful, but such behavior did not define a person as having a particular sexual identity. Then, during the nineteenth century the concept of an orientation toward the same sex began to emerge. Men and women were recognized and sometimes punished and persecuted for their same-sex attraction, and some participated in clandestine social clubs and searched for persons of similar orientations. Yet the nature of one's sexual orientation was not as central in defining one's sense of self as it would become in the late-nineteenth and twentieth centuries (Robb, 2003). The concept of a sexual identity requires a self-consciousness and self-examination that was not prominent until the late nineteenth century.

THE EMERGENCE OF "HETEROSEXUALITY" AND "HOMOSEXUALITY"

Americans defined these categories in part by mounting a public campaign against homosexuality beginning in the late nineteenth century. At that time, an influential body of medical literature began to describe not merely homosexual acts but homosexual persons—distinctive individuals who were seen as suffering from a psychological illness that altered their sexual preferences. Their supposedly unnatural condition was labeled "homosexuality," and it was said to pervade their personalities. They were no longer just men or women who engaged in sexual acts with a same-sex partner; they were homosexuals—seriously ill people (Foucault, 1980). In contrast to them, the same writers defined a "normal" sexual preference for the opposite sex as "heterosexuality." Heterosexuals were seen as mentally healthy as opposed to sick. This was the way sexuality entered our everyday language and our consciousness: as a means of organizing people into two contrasting sexual identities, one viewed as normal and one disparaged as diseased.

The medical model remained dominant until 1973, when the American Psychiatric Association removed homosexuality from its list of mental disorders (Silverstein, 1991). The medical model stigmatized gay people and served as a basis for prejudice and discrimination. But the very force of the critique also created a group identity for individuals who had previously had none. Much as the ideology of separate spheres created conditions that allowed for social and political action by women's groups, so the discourse on homosexuality as an illness created conditions that ultimately provoked social and political actions by gays and lesbians. "Homosexuality began to speak in its own behalf," wrote Michel Foucault, "to demand that its legitimacy or 'naturality' be acknowledged, often in the same vocabulary, using the same categories by which it was medically disqualified" (Foucault, 1980).

There are intellectuals and researchers today who claim that these identities are becoming more fluid again and some who argue against even using the concept of a sexual identity anymore. There are sociologists who state that people who do not follow the dominant heterosexual model are creating new modes of living that challenge the usefulness of the concept of "the family" or even of diverse "families" to describe personal life in the twenty-first century. In Chapter 6, we will examine the rise, and perhaps the beginning of the fall, of sexual identities and the implications for studying family life.

Quick Review

- The idea that people have a sexual identity did not arise until the late nineteenth century.
- Homosexuality was initially defined as a psychological illness, whereas heterosexuality was seen as normal.

The Rise of the Private Family: 1900–Present

THE EARLY DECADES

An increase in premarital sex. A drop in the birthrate. A new youth culture rebelling against propriety, dressing outrageously, and indulging in indecent dance steps. And a rapidly rising divorce rate. These were the concerns of American moralists, politicians, and social scientists during the first few decades of the twentieth century. The flourishing new youth culture was exemplified in the 1920s by the "flapper" girls. Independent, often employed outside the home, and brazen enough to bob their hair and wear lipstick and eyeliner in public, the flappers patronized dance halls and movie theaters with their male companions. Historian Stephanie Coontz (2005) notes that interest in and openness about sexuality grew during this period. A good marriage, people increasingly thought, required a good sex life, although the husband's satisfaction still seemed to matter more than the wife's. By the 1920s, birth control pioneers such as Margaret Sanger had opened clinics, and public discussion about ways to prevent births was widespread.

Perhaps the greatest source of concern, the divorce rate had risen to the point where a marriage begun in 1910 had about a 1-in-7 chance of ending in divorce. This may seem like a small risk today, but it represented a substantial increase over the 1-in-12 chance in 1880 or the 1-in-20 chance at the end of the Civil War (Cherlin, 1992). Yet the period from the 1890s through the 1920s was generally one of increasing prosperity—which raises the question of why an increase in divorce would occur. In part, it was made possible by the growing economic independence of women, who were now better educated, had fewer children, had likely worked outside the home before marrying, and therefore had greater potential to find work outside the home if their marriages ended (O'Neill, 1967). But that is not the whole story, for the marriage rate kept rising right along with the divorce rate. What had occurred, in addition, is that both women and men came to expect a greater amount of emotional satisfaction from marriage (May, 1980). More than ever before, they sought happiness, companionship, and romantic love in marriage. If they found their marriages fell short of their expectations, they were more likely to ask for a divorce. As Coontz (2005) writes, the trend had begun in the latter part of the 1800s:

> *The people who took idealization of love and intimacy to new heights during the nineteenth century did not intend to shake up marriage or unleash a new preoccupation with sexual gratification. . . . In the long run, however, they weakened it. The focus on romantic love eventually undercut the doctrine of separate spheres for men and women and the ideal of female purity, putting new strains on the institution of marriage.*

The emphasis on love and companionship, and the accompanying strain on marital bonds, spread in the early 1900s.

And so women and men came to see marriage and family as central to their quest for an emotionally satisfying private life. Before the twentieth century, emotional satisfaction had been less important to both husbands and wives, but not because they were ignorant of the concept—no Ariès-like claim is made here that people of the twentieth century discovered happiness. Rather, before the twentieth century the standard of living had been so low that most people needed to concentrate on keeping themselves clothed, housed, and fed. Before 1900, pursuing personal pleasure was a luxury few could indulge in. Most were too busy just trying to get by.

Still, Americans (and the citizens of other Western nations) were gradually enlarging the scope of the *private family*. They were defining marital success in emotional terms, not material terms, and were beginning to derive their greatest satisfaction not from the roles they played (breadwinner, homemaker, father, mother) but from the quality of the relationships they had with their spouses and children. This process had certainly begun long ago among the more prosperous classes, and it continued throughout the twentieth century. But in some eras its ascendancy was more noticeable than in others, and the first few decades of the twentieth century were such an era.

As these developments were occurring, the family was becoming less of a dominant force in people's lives. The many public goods the colonial family had provided gradually diminished: Compulsory schooling replaced education at home; hospitals replaced sickbeds; department stores replaced home crafts; and so forth. As marriage became less necessary economically and materially, it was redefined as a means of gaining emotional satisfaction. A well-known text on the family described this transformation as a shift "from institution to companionship" (Burgess & Locke, 1945). (See Chapter 7.) In this process, marriage became more fragile, for the bonds of sentiment were weaker than the ties forged by working a family farm or the unchallenged authority of the patriarch. Soon, an institution that had been designed to enhance survival and security began to creak under the weight of expectations that it provide so much emotional satisfaction. One result was a more or less continuous increase in the divorce rate, which reached a high plateau about 1980.

Privacy also increased after 1900. Two demographic trends contributed to this increase. First, the birthrate declined, which meant, among other things, fewer persons per room. Second, adult life expectancy increased due to advances in medicine and a rising standard of living. As a result of these trends, parents were younger when they finished the child-rearing stage of life, and they lived longer after their last child left home. Consequently, a new stage of family life, the "empty nest" phase of married life after all children have left home, became common. Between 1900 and 2000 the proportion of 45- to 64-year olds who were empty nesters tripled from 11 to 34 percent (Fischer & Hout, 2006).

Greater prosperity also meant that more apartments were built, and more people could afford to live on their own. And the rise in individualism probably made more unmarried people *wish* to live on their own. Consequently, boarding and lodging–in which a single person paid to rent a room and have meals cooked in a family's home–went from commonplace to rarity during the first half of the century (Laslett, 1973). In 1950, 9 percent of all households contained one person; by 1970 the figure was 17 percent; and by 2017 it was 28 percent (Kobrin, 1976; U.S. Bureau of the Census, 2017). Even so, during the first few decades of the century, about two-thirds of young women and perhaps 40 percent of young men did not leave home until they married. If they did, it was often because their parents lived in rural areas, where young adults couldn't find jobs. Later, in the 1940s and 1950s, the age at which young adults left home fell sharply, both because of earlier marriage and because many young men left home to join the military during World War II and the Korean War (Goldscheider & Goldscheider, 1994).

The first few decades of the twentieth century, then, were an important time of change in the American family. The basis for marriage moved away from an economic partnership and toward emotional satisfaction and companionship. Men and women became more economically independent of each other. As a result of these developments, the bonds of marriage became weaker, and divorce became more common. In addition, prosperity, lower birthrates, and longer life expectancy accelerated the trend toward privacy, as exemplified by child-free older couples and people living alone.

THE DEPRESSION GENERATION

The prosperity of the early decades of the century was interrupted by the Great Depression, which began in 1929 and continued until the late 1930s. In addition to its severe effects on family finances, the Depression also undermined the authority and prestige of the father. If he lost his job, his family might view him as having failed in his role as breadwinner. If his wife or his children were forced to find jobs, as many were, their labor was a constant reminder of his inability to fulfill their expectations.

The economic hardships forced many young adults to postpone marriage and childbearing. The Depression was so long and so severe that some couples never had the opportunity to have children. As a result, lifetime childlessness was more common among women who reached their peak childbearing years in the 1930s than in any other generation of women in the twentieth century: About one in five never had a child (Rindfuss, Morgan, & Swicegood, 1988). In contrast, only about one in ten of the women who reached their peak reproductive years during the 1950s baby boom never had a child.

As fathers and mothers struggled to make a living, their children helped out. Teenage boys took whatever jobs they could find; teenage girls took over more of the household work for mothers who were forced to work outside the home. The result was what Glen Elder, Jr., called "the downward extension of adultlike experience": Girls took on the role of homemaker; boys took on the role of breadwinner. Elder (1999) examined the records of a group of children who were first observed in 1932, at age 11, and then followed through adulthood. He found that when they reached adulthood, the men and women in the group who came from economically deprived families valued marriage and family life more highly than those whose families hadn't experienced hardship. Women from deprived families married at younger ages than other women. Perhaps the difficulties their families had faced when they were adolescents made the deprived group eager for a secure marriage, or perhaps they viewed families as an important resource in hard times. In any event, when they reached adulthood, these young men and women turned inward to build their own family lives.

Quick Review

- In the twentieth century, people increasingly viewed family life through the perspective I have called the *private family.*
  - People began to derive their greatest pleasure from the quality of their personal relationships.
  - People increasingly viewed marriage primarily as a means of obtaining emotional satisfaction.
  - Divorce became more common.
  - Privacy itself increased as standards of living rose, birthrates dropped, and life expectancy rose.
- The hardship of the Great Depression forced a generation to alter their family lives by, for example, delaying or forgoing marriage and childbearing.

THE 1950s

In fact, when the young adults of the Depression generation began to marry and have children after World War II, they created the most unusual and distinctive family patterns of the century. They married younger and had more children than any other twentieth-century generation. Nearly half of women delayed having sex until after they were married, which was an easier task than it is now because of the young ages at marriage (Wu, Martin, & England, 2017). Figure 2.1, which displays the percentage of 20- to 24-year-old men and women who had never been married, from 1890 to 2017, shows how unusual the 1950s were. Note that the percentage

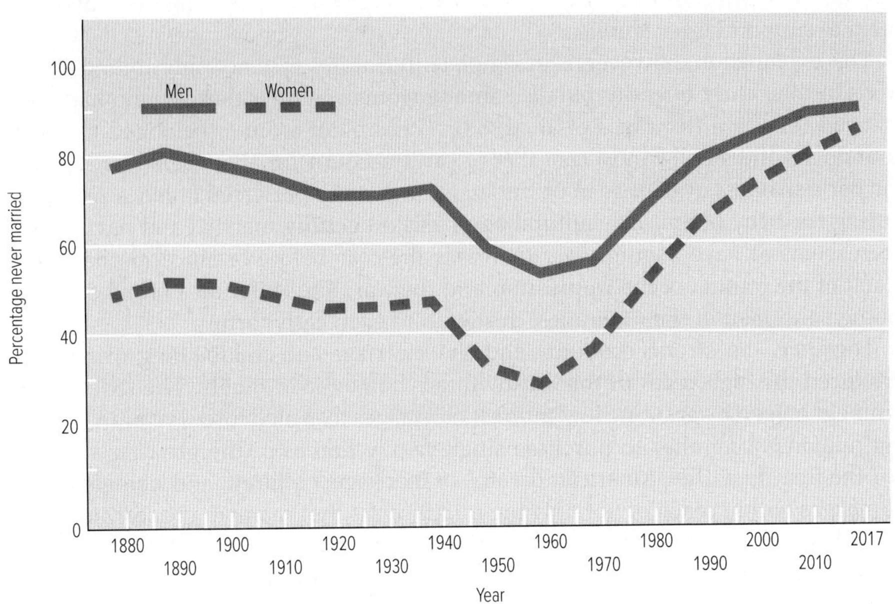

FIGURE 2.1
Percentage never married among men and women aged 20 to 24, 1890 to 2017. (*Sources:* for 1890–1990, Carter et al. (2006); for 2000–2017, U.S. Bureau of the Census (2018).)

is highest at the beginning and end of this chart, indicating that young men and women were most likely to be single (and therefore to marry at an older age) in the late 1800s and the current era. The percentage who had never been married declined slowly during the first half of the twentieth century and then plunged to its lowest point during the 1950s. After 1960, it rose so much that by the 2010s, young adults were marrying later than at any time since at least 1890.

The years after World War II were also the time of the great **baby boom.** Couples not only married at younger ages but also had children faster–and had more of them–than their parents' generation or, as statistics would later show, than even their children's generation. Indeed, the late 1940s through the 1950s was the only period in the past 150 years during which the American birthrate rose substantially. It spiked dramatically just after the war, as couples had babies they had postponed having during the war. After a few years it dropped, but then began to climb again, peaking in 1957. Women who married during the 1950s had an average of slightly more than three children, the highest fertility rate of the century (Evans, 1986; Carter et al., 2006).

baby boom the large number of people born during the late 1940s and 1950s

Although the causes of the baby boom are not fully clear, a strong post–World War II economy and a renewed cultural emphasis on marriage and children were certainly contributing factors. One explanation focuses on the unique circumstances of the young adults who married during the 1950s. Since most of them were born during the Depression, when birthrates were low, they constituted a relatively small **birth cohort,** as demographers call all the people born during a given year or period of years. After the bad luck of growing up during the Depression and the war, they had the good fortune to reach adulthood just as the economy was growing rapidly. The Allied victory in World War II had left the United States with the strongest economy in the world. Employers needed more workers, but the small size of the cohort meant there were fewer workers to hire (especially given the widespread preference during the 1950s that married women forgo work

birth cohort all people born during a given year or period of years

outside the home). In this tight labor market wages rose for young men, allowing them to support larger families.[5]

This explanation, however, is incomplete. Birthrates rose not only among newlyweds in their early twenties but also among women in their thirties who had been married for years (Rindfuss et al., 1988). These older women belonged to larger cohorts, so the small-cohort-size theory can't account for their behavior. Rather, the pervasiveness of the rise in births suggests that the preferred family size shifted during the baby boom. The cultural emphasis on getting married and having children seems to have been greater than was the case before or since—perhaps as a result of the trauma of the Depression and the war. The shift had a broad effect on women and men in their twenties, thirties, and even early forties.

Together, the strong economy and the marriage-and-childbearing orientation produced the high point of the breadwinner–homemaker family. The federal government helped by granting low-interest mortgages to armed forces veterans, allowing millions of families to purchase single-family homes in the growing suburbs. For the first time, the "American dream" of marriage, children, and a single-family home was within reach of not only the middle class, but many in the working class as well. Yet some homemakers missed the world of paid work and school they had left behind and felt constrained by their economic dependence on their husbands (Weiss, 2000).

Moreover, overlooked during the 1950s because of all the attention given to the baby boom was a countercurrent that would loom large later in the century. Increasingly, homemakers went back to work outside the home after their children were of school age. They took jobs that had been typed as women's work—jobs that were relatively low paying but still required some education, such as secretary, nurse, or salesclerk. And some urged their daughters to postpone marriage in order to pursue higher education and professional careers (Weiss, 2000). In fact, women received contradictory messages in the 1950s: Motherhood was valuable, but so was having an independent self (Plant, 2010).

THE 1960s THROUGH THE 1990s

Just as social commentators confidently announced a return to large families, the roller-coaster car reached the top of its track and hurtled downward. The birthrate plunged from the heights of the baby boom to an all-time low in the 1970. Women who were in their peak childbearing years in the 1970s had an average of 1.8 children (Carter et al., 2006). The baby boom had begotten the baby bust. The drop was aided by the introduction in 1960 of the birth control pill, the first highly effective medical method of contraception. By 1964, it was the most popular contraceptive in the nation (May, 2010). In addition, young women and men were marrying at later and later ages; between the mid-1950s and 2000, the age at which half of all first marriages occur increased by about five years for men and women (U.S. Bureau of the Census, 2018). So the percentage of young adults who had never married, as Figure 2.1 shows, surpassed the levels of the early twentieth century.

What were they doing during these five additional years before marriage? In part, they were living on their own. In the first half of the twentieth century, it was rare for an unmarried person in his or her twenties to be living alone. Either you remained with your parents or you rented a room in another family's house. Young

[5] The relative-cohort-size theory was expounded by Easterlin (1980).

people couldn't afford to live on their own; there was a shortage of adequate housing; and anyway it was morally questionable, especially for an unmarried woman, to live alone. But by 2000, the proportion of unmarried twenty-somethings heading their own households had risen to 36 percent for women and 28 percent for men (Rosenfeld, 2007). Not all of these young household heads, however, were *truly* alone. After about 1970, **cohabitation**—the sharing of a household by unmarried persons in a sexual relationship—accounted for some of the postponement of marriage (Smock, 2000). In other words, some young adults substituted cohabiting relationships for early marriages. Moreover, they were increasingly having children prior to marrying. In 1950 only 4 percent of births occurred outside of marriage; but by 2000, 33 percent did (U.S. National Center for Health Statistics, 2005). Most of these births occurred among less-educated women. In 2000, 70 percent of unmarried high school dropouts aged 25 to 44 had already given birth, as had 53 percent of comparable high school graduates. But only 9 percent of unmarried college-educated women in the same age range had given birth (Fischer & Hout, 2006). Although the conventional path of marrying before having children is still prevalent among the college-educated, many of the less-educated are having children prior to marrying.

cohabitation the sharing of a household by unmarried persons who have a sexual relationship

Change occurred not only in how and when people entered marriage but also in how and when they ended marriage. The divorce rate, which had been stable during the 1950s, doubled during the 1960s and 1970s. Since then, divorce rates have diverged by educational level: the rate has declined for the college-educated, remained stable for people with high school degrees or a few years of college, and increased for people without high school degrees (Härkönen & Dronkers, 2006; Martin, 2006). At the rates prevalent near the end of the century, about one-third of the marriages of college graduates would end in separation or divorce, whereas over half of the marriages of people without college degrees would end in separation or divorce (Raley & Bumpass, 2003). Here again, a person's level of education has become an important marker of the kind of family life she or he leads.

What all of these developments have meant for the living arrangements of children during the twentieth century is shown in Figure 2.2. It is based on the answers of people of differing ages to the question "Were you living with both your own mother and father around the time you were 16?" in a series of national surveys. If they said no, they were asked whether they weren't living with both parents due to a parent dying or for other reasons—most often, divorce or separation but also, as the century progressed, being born outside of marriage. In the 1910s, according to the answers to these questions, about 25 percent of children (adding up 17 percent from the purple bar and 8 percent from the blue bar) around age 16 were not living with both parents. Note that by far the most common reason for not living with both parents was that a parent had died. A fair number of children experienced family disruption a century ago but mostly because of parental death. The percentage not living with both parents stayed relatively stable for the first two-thirds of the century (the purple and blue bars total about 25 percent at each time point through the 1960s), although the reasons changed: By mid-century parental death rates had declined but disruptions for other reasons had increased. Yet beginning in the 1970s, the percentage not living with both parents began to rise, and by the 1990s (when the purple and blue bars total 44 percent) it greatly exceeded the level of the 1910s, even though it was quite uncommon to have a parent die. Over the century,

FIGURE 2.2
Percent of children not living with their own mother and father at age 16 because a parent died or for other reasons, 1910s to 1990s.
Source: Ellwood & Jencks, 2004, Figure 1.1.

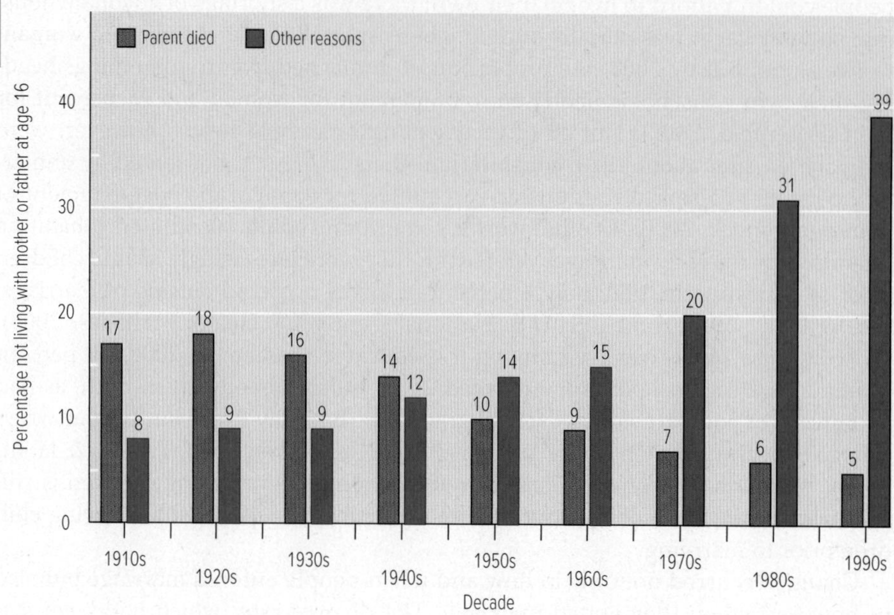

then, two changes occurred: First, the reasons why adolescents weren't living with both parents changed dramatically from the death of a parent to divorce or separation or being born to an unmarried parent. Second, beginning in the 1970s, the total number of adolescents not living with both parents rose.

After the 1950s, married women continued to work outside the home in ever larger numbers. Even women with pre-school-aged children joined the workforce in large numbers. By 2000, 77 percent of all married women with school-aged children and 63 percent of married women with pre-school-aged children were working outside the home (U.S. Bureau of the Census, 2011). Whereas in the 1950s, married women tended to drop out of the paid workforce when they were raising small children, today married women are much more likely to remain at their jobs throughout the child-rearing years. This change in women's work lives has had a powerful effect on the family.

Quick Review

- The 1950s produced the most distinctive family patterns of the twentieth century, notably early marriage and larger numbers of children.
- Rising wages and a cultural shift toward home and family may have caused the 1950s baby boom.
- Family trends reversed in the 1960s: Young adults married later; birthrates fell; divorce rates rose.
- In addition, married women with young children began to enter the workforce in large numbers in the 1960s.
- The percentage of children not living with both parents rose toward the end of the century because of increases in marital separation and divorce and births to unmarried parents.

The Changing Life Course

We have seen that family and personal life changed greatly during the twentieth century. One way to understand these changes is to compare the experiences of groups of individuals who were born in different time periods. This approach is known as the **life-course perspective:** the study of changes in individuals' lives over time and how those changes are related to historical events.

life-course perspective the study of changes in individuals' lives over time, and how those changes are related to historical events

SOCIAL CHANGE IN THE TWENTIETH CENTURY

Consider Figure 2.3. In the middle of the figure is a time line for the twentieth century, divided into 10-year intervals. The top half shows the time lines for three different birth cohorts born 30 years apart. The first group was born in 1920; I have labeled them the "depression cohort" because they were nine years old when the Great Depression began in 1929. The second group, the "baby boom cohort," was born in 1950, just after the start of the baby boom. The third group, born between 1980 and 2000, is often referred to as the "millennials" because they began to reach adulthood after 2000, which was the turn of the new millennium. The bottom half of Figure 2.3 shows time lines for the occurrence of major historical events and trends that have changed family and personal life. For example, the Great Depression lasted from 1929 until about 1940, and the baby boom occurred from the late 1940s to the early 1960s.

One can think of the top and bottom halves of Figure 2.3 as showing two kinds of time. The top half displays what we might call "individual time": the passing of time in people's lives as they age. This is the usual way we think of time. The bottom half displays what might be called "historical time": the beginning and ending of key events and social trends that have influenced family life during the century. The figure's usefulness is that it allows a comparison of individual time and historical time; or put another way, it places the course of an individual's life in historical context.

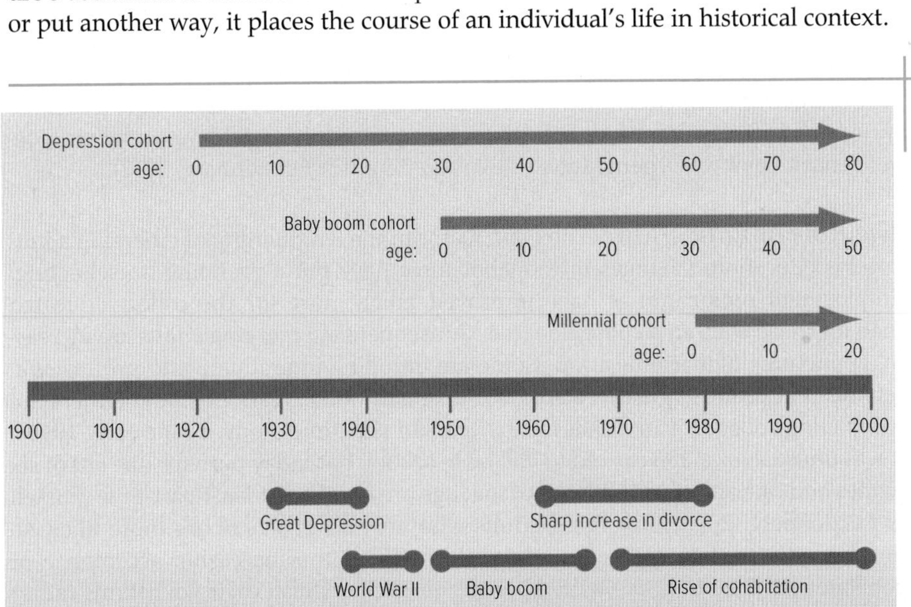

FIGURE 2.3
A life-course perspective on social change in the twentieth century.

For example, the figure shows that in 1950, as the baby boom started, members of the depression cohort were still in their childbearing years; therefore, they became the parents of the baby boomers. The figure also shows that by the time the baby boom cohort reached age 30 in 1980, a sharp rise in divorce had occurred. As a result, the baby boomers have had a much higher rate of divorce than the depression cohort. In addition, the figure shows that the millennial cohort is the first to have lived their early childhood years after the sharp rise in divorce. That is why far more millennial cohort members experienced the breakup of their parents' marriages than previous cohorts.

This way of looking at changes in family and personal life is an example of the life-course perspective. Rather than study families as an undifferentiated group, sociologists and historians who use this perspective tend to study the lives of individuals within families. They examine how historical developments affect the course of these individuals' personal and family lives. Elder's work on the depression cohort (defined in his case as people born in 1921) is probably the most influential study of this genre (Elder, 1999). The life-course perspective is particularly attractive to scholars who wish to study social change over time. And as this chapter has made clear, the twentieth century was a time of great change in the kinds of family lives individuals led.

THE NEW LIFE STAGE OF EMERGING ADULTHOOD

emerging adulthood period between mid-teens and about age 30 when individuals finish their education, enter the labor force, and begin their own families

labor force all people who are working for pay or who are looking for paid work

Recently, social scientists have used the life-course perspective to suggest the appearance of a new stage of life: **emerging adulthood** (Arnett, 2000; Settersten, Furstenberg, & Rumbaut, 2005). I will define it as the period between the mid-teens and about age 30 when individuals finish their education, enter the labor force, and begin their own families. (The **labor force** is defined as all people who are working for pay or who are looking for paid work.) It is the stage of life when one makes the transition from adolescence (itself only a century old, as we will see in Chapter 7) to adulthood. As I noted earlier in this chapter, most young people made the transition to adulthood quickly in the mid-twentieth century, marrying at historically young ages and having children soon afterwards. Today, this transition has become longer and more varied and complex. It is more difficult for emerging adults to achieve economic independence than it was a generation or two ago (Sironi & Furstenberg, 2012).

The Role of Education The main factor in the lengthening of emerging adulthood is education. Changes in the labor force have put a premium on schooling: Employment opportunities have improved much more for the college-educated than for those without a college degree. Consequently, emerging adults are increasingly pursuing higher education. Some are enrolling in graduate and professional schools that promise great rewards but take additional years of study. Others are completing college, even if that means years of part-time study. In the early 1990s, it was unusual for a 25-year-old to still be in school; but today perhaps one out of six whites and one out of eight blacks of that age are enrolled at least part-time (Fussell & Furstenberg, 2005). Emerging adults who are still in school are more likely to defer decisions about careers and families. Given the increasing acceptance of cohabitation, they may live with a partner until they finish their educations rather than marry. Or they may marry but postpone having children. Although they may be working for pay to help defray the costs of their education, they delay starting on a career ladder until after they have the appropriate degree in hand.

Constrained Opportunities Emerging adults with more limited education take other, usually shorter, paths to reach the traditional markers of adulthood. Most of those who don't graduate from high school, or who graduate but don't go on to college, enter the job market well before their college-bound peers. Some take college courses but don't achieve a bachelor's degree. Their opportunities are more constrained than were the opportunities of similarly educated individuals a half-century ago (Hill & Yeung, 1999). As I will explain in Chapter 4, the movement of manufacturing jobs overseas and the growth of automation have reduced the demand for non-college-educated workers. The kinds of decent-paying blue-collar factory jobs that sustained a generation of workers and their families a half-century ago are in short supply. Sociologists argue that non-college-educated entrants into the labor force often must take "stopgap jobs"—short-term, often part-time jobs such as working at a fast-food restaurant—that give them a modest income for a short time but don't help to develop a career (Oppenheimer, Kalmijn, & Lim, 1997).

Consequently, some non-college-educated adults are postponing marriage not because they are still studying but rather because they (or their prospective marriage partners) don't think their economic prospects are good enough to support a marriage. But forgoing marriage no longer means one must forgo having children because childbearing outside of marriage has become more acceptable. Some emerging adults father, or give birth to, children without marrying. In 2000, 5 percent of white 25-year-olds and 28 percent of black 25-year-olds were unmarried parents. They have made more progress toward traditional markers of adulthood than their childless contemporaries still in school because they have had children and are often working. But their work lives are erratic and usually consist of a series of low- and moderate-paying jobs rather than a career. And they may not marry for a long time, if ever.

Many emerging adults are living independently of their parents, a situation we will examine more closely in Chapter 7. But the probability that an independent emerging adult will move back in with his or her parents—if, for example, he or she loses a job or breaks up with a partner—has increased since the mid-twentieth century (Goldscheider, 1997). This trend toward returning to the nest is another reason why emerging adults often achieve lasting independence—and full adulthood—in fits and starts over a longer period of time. Nevertheless, by age 30 the differences between the college-educated and the less-educated in marriage, parenthood, and employment are smaller. What education does is make a difference in how they got there—how they experience emerging adulthood.

LGBTQ Emerging Adults and Their Families We know less about emerging adulthood among LGBTQ individuals, but a study of white, middle-class gay and lesbian emerging adults during the last half of the twentieth century suggests that they often had ambivalent relations with their parents and other biological kin (Murray, 2010). During the late 1950s, when homosexuality was classified by psychiatrists as a "sociopathic personality disturbance" (Bayer, 1981), gay and lesbian emerging adults were frequently hesitant to tell their parents about their sexual orientation. Fearing rejection and anger, they discreetly kept their sexual lives to themselves when talking with relatives. At a time when gay men could be arrested and imprisoned even for consensual sex (lesbians were less likely to be subject to these laws), some of them married opposite-sex partners in order to publicly lead conventional family lives. Then in the 1960s and 1970s, coming out—publicly declaring one's homosexuality—became possible as liberation movements (gay, feminist, civil rights) swept the country. But coming out to one's parents remained fraught with potential difficulties for gay and lesbian emerging adults. In some families, parents rejected children who came out to them. In others, parents tacitly acknowledged their child's sexuality but chose not to talk about it.

Yet by the late 1970s and 1980s, a significant number of parents were accepting their children's sexuality. A new organization, Parents, Families, and Friends of Lesbians and Gays, grew into a national movement in the 1980s to provide support to gay and lesbian emerging adults. Also in the 1980s, the deadly epidemic of AIDS arose and began to cause the deaths of thousands of gay men per year. Some parents reacted with shock and shame to the news that their child had AIDS, whereas others were sympathetic and comforting (Murray, 2010). As gay men cared for each other and lesbians cared for them (and each other) too, gays and lesbians began to include friends and caregivers as members of their family (Weston, 1991). Throughout the last half of the century, in the words of the historian who studied the topic, the biological family "might be simultaneously alienating and accepting" and it "might combine many elements of oppression and love" (Murray, 2010).

EMERGING ADULTHOOD AND THE LIFE-COURSE PERSPECTIVE

The growing literature on emerging adulthood is a good example of the life-course perspective for several reasons. It focuses on a key transition in the lives of individuals–in this case the lengthening period from adolescence to adulthood. It demonstrates the substantial social changes that have occurred in this stage of life. And importantly, it places that transition in historical perspective by showing the influences of the decline in manufacturing jobs, the growing employment opportunities for the well-educated, and the greater acceptance of cohabitation and childbearing outside of marriage. As they make the transition today, emerging adults steer a course in a different sea than was sailed in the past. Many reach their destinations later, and by different routes, than their parents and grandparents.

Quick Review

- The life-course perspective seeks to study the course of individual lives in historical context.
- Emerging adulthood is the term for an emerging life stage between adolescence and adulthood.
- The pursuit of higher education is the main factor lengthening emerging adulthood.
- Emerging adults without college degrees start the transition to full adulthood sooner.
- LGBTQ emerging adults often had ambivalent relations with their parents and other biological kin.

WHAT HISTORY TELLS US

The history of the family tells us that Americans come from regions of the world that have different family traditions. To some extent, the American mixing bowl blends those traditions together and reduces the differences. The result is that the family lives of today's ethnic and racial groups have more in common than not. Still, the historical record can help us understand some of the variation we see today.

Americans of European ancestry hail from a system that has emphasized the conjugal unit of the married couple and children more than have family systems in other regions of the world. In the nineteenth and early twentieth centuries, European American conjugal families developed a sharp division of labor between the husband, who worked outside the home, and the wife, who by and large worked inside the home. That sharp division, however, broke down in the last half of the twentieth century as more married women entered the workforce. And during the twentieth century, Americans placed increasing weight on personal satisfaction as the standard people should use in judging the quality of their relationships. European American family traditions are important because they have been the basis for American law and custom. For example, American law gives parents nearly exclusive rights over children and gives far less authority to grandparents or other kin.

The family systems of American Indians and of Americans from other regions (such as Latin America, Asia, and Africa) have traditionally placed more emphasis on kin beyond the conjugal family. Sometimes these family systems consisted of tightly organized lineages. Think of the matrilineal tribes of the Hopi. At other times and places, they consisted of extended families in which grandparents, uncles, aunts, and others from both sides of a person's family might contribute to her or his well-being and even share a home. And as the Mexican tradition of *compadrazgo* showed, sometimes individuals without any ties of blood or marriage were recruited into a person's kin network.

Marriage was still central to most of these systems. But married couples were embedded in larger family structures that could provide assistance and support. This tradition of support is important because marriage declined among all American racial and ethnic groups during the last half of the twentieth century, although less among those with college degrees. The weakening of marriage left European American families in a particularly vulnerable position because they had less of a tradition of extended family support to fall back on. The story of recent changes in marriage and family life, and their impact on Americans with different heritages, will be told in subsequent chapters.

Looking Back

1. **What functions have families traditionally performed?** Family and kinship emerged as ways of ensuring the survival of human groups, which were organized as bands of hunter-gatherers until about 10,000 years ago. Until the past 250 years or so, most families performed three basic activities: production, reproduction, and consumption. Most American Indian tribes were organized into lineages and clans that provided the basis for social organization and governing. Colonial American families performed functions such as education that are now performed by schools and other institutions. These kinds of families can be said to follow the familial mode of production. The colonial American family performed many activities that are now done mainly outside the family: educating children, providing vocational training, treating the seriously ill, and so forth.

2. **How did American families change after the United States was founded?** Between 1776 and about 1830, a new kind of family emerged among the white middle class in the United States, one in which marriage was based on affection rather than authority and custom. Over time, the primary role of women in these families became the care of children and the maintenance of the home. Children came to be seen as needing continual affection and guidance, which mothers were thought to be better at providing than

fathers. As families became more centered on children, the number of children they raised declined. At the same time, a movement toward greater individualism weakened parents' influence over their children's marriage decisions and family lives. Working-class families, because of difficult economic circumstances, did not change as much.

3. **How have the family histories of major ethnic and racial groups differed?** Before the Civil War, African slaves married and lived together for life, wherever possible, and knew and kept track of other kin. After the Civil War, discrimination shaped their family lives. For example, out of economic necessity, rural black wives worked in the fields, and urban black wives worked for wages outside the home, more than white wives did. As for Mexican Americans, after U.S. troops and immigrants seized their land, they became more of a working-class community, increasingly confined to *barrios.* Over time, more and more women headed households, in part because their husbands often worked as migratory farm workers. Chinese and Japanese families also faced discrimination. Traditionally patrilineal, their authority over their children has declined over the generations. Filipinos, the second largest Asian immigrant group in the United States today, are descended mostly from people who immigrated in the twentieth century. Filipinos have a bilateral kinship structure more similar to the kinship system of Europeans.

4. **How did the emotional character of the American family change during the early twentieth century?** During the early decades of the twentieth century, rising standards of living allowed for greater attention to an emotionally satisfying private life. As the search for emotional satisfaction through family life became an important goal, the private family emerged. Eventually, the success of marriage came to be defined more in emotional terms than in material terms. People experienced more privacy in their personal lives through the increasingly common empty nest phase of marriage and the rise in the number of individuals living alone.

5. **When did the idea of a sexual identity develop?** The idea that individuals have a coherent sexual identity involving a preference for either opposite-sex or same-sex partners did not exist until the nineteenth century. Before then, though religious doctrine and civil law forbade numerous sexual practices, a person who broke those laws was not thought to have a different personality from people who displayed conventional sexual behavior.

6. **What important changes occurred in marriage and childbearing in the second half of the twentieth century?** In the 1950s, young adults married at earlier ages and the birthrate rose to a twentieth-century high. The baby boom was caused in part by the small cohort size and good economic fortune of the cohort that reached adulthood in the 1950s. In addition, a greater cultural emphasis on marriage and childbearing seems to have been present. The 1950s was the high point of the breadwinner–homemaker family, which was dominant only during the first half of the twentieth century. Since then the trends in marriages, divorces, and births all reversed: Age at marriage increased sharply, the divorce rate doubled, and the birthrate reached its lowest level. Cohabitation became common. Moreover, married women were increasingly likely to work outside the home even when their children were young.

7. **How does the life-course perspective help us to understand social change?** Sociologists examine how the course of individuals' lives is affected by historical events such as the Great Depression of the 1930s or the large rise in divorce rates in the 1960s and 1970s. Because young adults today have better job opportunities if they obtain a college degree, many are postponing marriage and childbearing until they finish their studies. Life-course scholars now use the term "emerging adulthood" for this life stage.

Study Questions

1. How did belonging to a lineage help a family in a tribal, agricultural society?
2. What did the colonial family do that modern families do not? What do modern families do that the colonial family did not?
3. How did marriage change during the late 1700s and early 1800s?
4. What were the costs and benefits to women of their restriction to the "women's sphere"?

5. In what ways did the scope of the "private family" increase after 1900?
6. In what ways was family life in the 1950s distinctive compared to earlier or later in the century?
7. Why didn't the decline of parental death lead to an increase in children living with both parents?
8. What does it mean to take a "life-course perspective" on the study of social change?
9. Why is the concept of "emerging adulthood" appearing now rather than 50 or 100 years ago?

Key Terms

1965 Immigration Act 48
American Indian 37
baby boom 55
barrio 46
bilateral kinship 48
birth cohort 55
cohabitation 57
compadrazgo 46
conjugal family 39
emerging adulthood 60
extended family 39
labor force 60
life-course perspective 59
lineage 38
matrilineal 38
mestizo 46
patrilineal 38
sexual identity 50

Thinking about Families

The Public Family	The Private Family
Why were the American family's public responsibilities much broader in the colonial period than is the case today?	**Why are emotional satisfaction, intimacy, and romantic love more important in American family life today than they were 100 years ago?**

References

Aries, P. (1960). *L'enfant et la vie familiale sous l'ancien regine.* Paris: Librairie Plon.

Arnett, J. J. (2000). Emerging adulthood: A theory of development from the late teens through the twenties. *American Psychologist, 55,* 469.

Bayer, R. (1981). *Homosexuality and American psychiatry: The politics of diagnosis.* New York: Basic Books.

Bergquist, K. J. S. (2005). Asian Americans and social welfare (United States). In J. M. Herrick & P. H. Stuart (Eds.), *Encyclopedia of social welfare history in North America* (pp. 31–35). Thousand Oaks, CA: Sage.

Blauvelt, M. T. (2007). *The work of the heart: Young women and emotion 1780–1830.* Charlottesville: University of Virginia Press.

Bloch, R. H. (2003). Changing conceptions of sexuality and romance in eighteenth-century America. *William and Mary Quarterly, 60,* 13–42.

Boustan, L. P., & Collins, W. J. (2014). The origin and persistence of black-white differences. In L. P. Boustan, C. Frydman, & R. A. Margo (Eds.), *Human capital in history: The American record* (pp. 205–240): University of Chicago Press.

Burgess, E. W., & Locke, H. J. (1945). *The family: From institution to companionship.* New York: American Book Company.

Caldera, Y. M., Velez-Gomez, P., & Lindsey, E. W. (2015). Who are Mexican Americans? An overview of history, immigration, and cultural values. In Y. M. Caldera & E. W. Lindsey (Eds.), *Mexican American children and families: Multidisciplinary perspectives.*

Carter, S. B., Gartner, S. S., Haines, M. R., Olmstead, A. L., Sutch, R., & Wright, G. (2006). *Historical statistics of the United States: Millennial edition online.* Cambridge: Cambridge University Press.

Cherlin, A. J. (1992). *Marriage, divorce, remarriage: Revised and enlarged edition.* Cambridge, MA: Harvard University Press.

Cherlin, A. J. (2012). Goode's "*World Revolution and Family Patterns:*" A reconsideration at fifty years. *Population and Development Review, 38,* 577–607.

Cherlin, A. J. (2014). *Labor's love lost: The rise and fall of the working-class family in America.* New York: Russell Sage Foundation.

Collins, P. H. (2000). *Black feminist thought* (Vol. Routledge): New York.

Coontz, S. (2005). *Marriage, a history: From obedience to intimacy, or how love conquered marriage.* New York: Viking.

Cott, N. F. (1977). *The bonds of womanhood: "Women's sphere" in New England, 1780–1835.* New Haven: Yale University Press.

Cott, N. F. (2000). *Public vows: A history of marriage and the nation.* Cambridge, MA: Harvard University Press.

Demos, J. (1970). *A little commonwealth: Family life in Plymouth colony.* Oxford: Oxford University Press.

DeSilver, D. (2014). 5 facts about Indian Americans. *Pew Research Center.* Retrieved April 27u, 2019, from http://www.pewresearch.org/fact-tank/2014/09/30/5-facts-about-indian-americans/

Elder, G. H., Jr. (1999). *Children of the Great Depression: Social change in life experience* (25th Anniversary Edition ed.). Chicago: University of Chicago Press.

Ellwood, D. T., & Jencks, C. (2004). The spread of single parent families in the United States since 1960. In D. P. Moynihan, T. Smeeding, & L. Rainwater (Eds.), *The future of the family* (pp. 26–65). New York: Russell Sage Foundation.

Evans, M. D. R. (1986). American fertility patterns: A comparison of white and nonwhite cohorts born 1903–1956. *Population and Development Review, 12,* 267–293.

Fischer, C. S., & Hout, M. (2006). *Century of difference: How America changed in the last one hundred years.* New York: Russell Sage Foundation

Foucault, M. (1980). *The history of sexuality.* New York: Vintage Books.

Frazier, E. F. (1939). *The Negro family in the United States (revised and abridged edition).* Chicago, IL: University of Chicago Press.

Fussell, E., & Furstenburg, F. F., Jr. (2005). The transition to adulthood during the twentieth century. In R. A. Settersten, Jr., F. F. Furstenburg, Jr., & R. Rumbaut (Eds.), *On the frontier of adulthood: Theory, research, and public policy* (pp. 29–75). Chicago: University of Chicago Press.

Goldscheider, F. K. (1997). Recent changes in the U.S. Young adult living arrangements in comparative perspective. *Journal of Family Issues, 18,* 708–724.

Goldscheider, F. K., & Goldscheider, C. (1994). Leaving and returning home in the 20th century America. *Population Bulletin, 48*(4).

Goode, W. J. (1963). *World revolution and family patterns.* New York: The Free Press.

Griswold del Castillo, R. (1979). *The Los Angeles barrio, 1850–1890: A social history.* Los Angeles: University of California Press.

Gutman, H. G. (1976). *The black family in slavery and freedom, 1750–1925.* New York: Pantheon Books.

Härkönen, J., & Dronkers, J. (2006). Stability and change in the educational gradient of divorce. A comparison of seventeen countries. *European Sociological Review, 22*(5), 501–517.

Hartog, H. (2000). *Man and wife in America: A history.* Cambridge, MA: Harvard University Press.

Hill, M. S., & Yeung, W. J. (1999). How has the changing structure of opportunities affected transitions to adulthood? In A. Booth, A. C. Crouter, & M. J. Shanahan (Eds.), *Transitions to adulthood in a changing economy* (pp. 3–39). Westport, CT: Praeger.

Hunter, T. W. (2017). *Bound in wedlock: Slave and free black marriage in the nineteenth century:* Harvard University Press.

Joe, J. R., Sparks, S., & Tiger, L. (1999). Changing American Indian marriage patterns: Some examples from contemporary Western apaches. In S. L. Browning & R. R. Miller (Eds.), *Till death do us part: A multicultural anthology on marriage* (pp. 5–21). Greenwich, CT: JAI Press.

Jones, J. (2010). *Labor of love, labor of sorrow: Black women and the family from slavery to the present* (Revised ed.). New York: Basic Books.

Katz, M. B., Stern, M. J., & Fader, J. J. (2005). The new African American inequality. *The Journal of American History, 92*(1), 75–108.

Kitano, H. H. L., & Daniels, R. (1988). *Asian Americans: Emerging minorities.* Englewood Cliffs, NJ: Prentice-Hall.

Kobrin, F. E. (1976). The fall of household size and the rise of the primary individual in the United States. *Demography, 13,* 127–138.

Laslett, B. (1973). The family as a public and private institution: An historical perspective. *Journal of Marriage and the Family, 35,* 480–492.

Martin, S. P. (2006). Trends in marital dissolution by women's education in the United States. *Demographic Research, 15,* 537–560.

Martínez, O. J. (2001). *Mexican-origin people in the United States: A topical history.* Tucson: University of Arizona Press.

May, E. T. (1980). *Great expectations: Marriage and divorce in post-Victorian America.* Chicago: University of Chicago Press.

May, E. T. (2010). *America and the pill.* New York: Basic Books.

Miller, M. C. (2018). Destroyed by slavery? Slavery and African American family formation following emancipation. *Demography, 55*(5), 1587–1609.

Mintz, S. (2004). *Huck's raft: A history of American childhood.* Cambridge, MA: The Belknap Press of Harvard University Press.

Mintz, S. W., & Wolf, E. R. (1950). An analysis of ritual co-parenthood (compadrazgo). *Southwestern Journal of Anthropology, 6*(4), 341–368.

Murray, H. (2010). *Not in this family: Gays and the meaning of kinship in postwar North America.* Philadelphia: University of Pennsylvania Press.

Navin, J. J. (2012). 'The time of most distress: Plymouth Plantation's demographic crisis. *Journal of Family History, 17*(4), 387–396.

Nicholas, D. (1991). Childhood in medieval Europe. In J. H. Hawes & N. Hiner (Eds.), *Children in historical and comparative perspective* (pp. 31–52). New York: Greenwood Press

O'Connor, E. H. (2009). *The ties that buy: Women and commerce in revolutionary America.* Philadelphia: University of Pennsylvania Press.

O'Neill, W. L. (1967). *Divorce in the progressive era.* New York: New Viewpoints.

Oppenheimer, V. K., Kalmijn Oppenheimer, V. K., Kalmijn, M., & Lim, N. (1997). Men's career development and marriage timing during a period of rising inequality. *Demography, 34*(3), 311–330.

Ozment, S. (1983). *When fathers ruled: Family life in reformation Europe.* Cambridge, MA: Harvard University Press.

Ozment, S. (2001). *Ancestors: The loving family in old Europe.* Cambridge, MA: Harvard University Press.

Pew Research Center. (2017). How the U.S. Hispanic population is changing. *Fact Tank.* Retrieved April 27, 2019, from http://www.pewresearch.org/fact-tank/2017/09/18/how-the-u-s-hispanic-population-is-changing/

Plant, R. J. (2010). *Mom: The transformation of motherhood in modern America.* Chicago: University of Chicago Press.

Pollock, L. A. (1983). *Forgotten children: Parent-child relations from 1500–1900.* Cambridge, England: Cambridge University Press.

Preston, S. H., Lim, S., & Morgan, P. S. (1992). African American marriage in 1910: Beneath the surface of census data. *Demography, 29,* 1–15.

Queen, S. A., Habenstein, R. W., & Quadagno, J. S. (1985). *The family in various cultures* (5th ed.). New York: Harper & Row.

Raley, R. K., & Bumpass, L. L. (2003). The topography of the divorce plateau: Levels and trends in union stability in the United States after 1980. *Demographic Research, 8,* 245–259.

Rindfuss, R. R., Morgan, S. P., & Swicegood, G. (1988). *First births in America: Changes in the timing of parenthood.* Berkeley, CA: University of California Press.

Robb, G. (2003). *Strangers: Homosexual love in the nineteenth century.* New York: W. W. Norton.

Rosenblum, M. R., & Brick, K. (2011). U.S. Immigration policy and Mexican/central American migration flows: Then and now. *Migration Policy Institute.* Retrieved May 14, 2016, from http://www.migrationpolicy.org/research/RMSG-us-immigration policy-mexican-central-american-migration-flows

Rosenfeld, M. J. (2007). *The age of independence: Interracial unions, same-sex unions, and the changing American family.* Cambridge, MA: Harvard University Press.

Settersten, R. A., Jr., Furstenberg, F. F., Jr., & Rumbaut, R. G. (Eds.). (2005). *On the frontier of adulthood: Theory, research, and public policy.* Chicago: University of Chicago Press.

Silverstein, C. (1991). Psychological and medical treatments of homosexuality. In Gonsiorek & Weinrich (Eds.), *Homosexuality* (pp. 101–114). Newbury Park CA: Sage.

Sironi, M., & Furstenberg, F. F. (2012). Trends in the economic independence of young adults in the United States: 1973–2007. *Population and Development Review, 38*(4), 609–630.

Smith-Rosenberg, C. (1975). The female world of love and ritual: Relations between women in nineteenth-century America. *Signs, 1*(1), 1–29.

Smock, P. J. (2000). Cohabitation in the United States: An appraisal of research themes, findings, and implications. *Annual Review of Sociology, 26,* 1–20.

Snipp, C. M. (2007). An overview of American Indian populations. In G. H. Capture, D. Champagne, & C. C. Jackson (Eds.), *American Indian nations: Yesterday, today, and tomorrow* (pp. 38–48). Lanham: Altamira Press.

Takaki, R. (1998). *Strangers from a different shore: A history of Asian Americans* (Update and Revised ed.). Boston: Little Brown.

Therborn, G. (2004). *Between sex and power: Family in the world, 1900–2000.* London: Routledge.

Uhlenberg, P. (1980). Death and the family. *Journal of Family History, 5,* 313–320.

U.S. Bureau of the Census. (2011). The 2012 statistical abstract. Retrieved July 17, 2018, from https://www2.census.gov/library/publications/2011/compendia/statab/131ed/2012-statab.pdf

U.S. Bureau of the Census. (2012). The Asian population: 2010. Census 2010 brief 11. Retrieved November 23, 2015, from https://www.census.gov/prod/cen2010/briefs/c2010br-11.pdf

U.S. Bureau of the Census. (2017). Table H1. Households by type and tenure of householder for selected characteristics: 2017. Retrieved July 16, 2018, from https://www2.census.gov/programs-surveys/demo/tables/families/2017/cps-2017/tabh1-all.xls

U.S. Bureau of the Census. (2018). Table MS-2. Estimated median age at first marriage, by sex: 1890 to the present. *Historical Marital Status Tables.* Retrieved November 16, 2018, from https://www2.census.gov/programs-surveys/demo/tables/families/time-series/marital/ms2.xls

U.S. National Center for Health Statistics. (2005). Number and percent of births to unmarried women, by race and Hispanic origin: United States, 1940–2000. Retrieved October 30, 2015, from http://www.cdc.gov/nchs/data/statab/t001x17.pdf

Weiss, J. (2000). *To have and to hold: Marriage, the baby boom, and social change.* Chicago: University of Chicago Press.

Welter, B. (1966). The cult of true womanhood. *American Quarterly* (Summer), 151–174.

Weston, K. (1991). *Families we choose: Lesbians, gays, kinship.* New York: Columbia University Press.

Wong, M. G. (1988). The Chinese American family. In C. H. Mindel, R. W. Habenstein, & J. W. Roosevelt (Eds.), *Ethnic families in America: Patterns and variations* (pp. 230–257). New York: Elsevier Science Publishing.

Wu, L. L., Martin, S. P., & England, P. (2017). The decoupling of sex and marriage in the United States: Cohort trends in who did and did not delay sex until marriage. *Sociological Science, 4,* 151–175.

Yanagisako, S. (1985). *Transforming the past: Tradition and kinship among Japanese Americans.* Stanford, CA: Stanford University Press.

Part Two

Gender, Class, and Race-Ethnicity

Families are affected by the larger social structures in which they are embedded. Three main axes of social stratification are gender, class, and race-ethnicity. How gender is structured greatly affects the ways that men and women relate to each other in families. Social class differences influence the ways that family life is organized. Racial and ethnic groups also differ in their family lives. Moreover, gender, class, and race-ethnicity are linked because all three are structures in which a more powerful group (men, the wealthier classes, whites) dominate the less powerful; and all three can affect a family simultaneously. Consequently, the content of the next three chapters should be seen as overlapping and interlocking, even though for educational purposes it is useful to have one chapter focus on each of these core constructs of sociology. Chapter 3 examines the construction and maintenance of gender differences, a core source of differentiation in family life. It presents several different approaches to understanding gender. Chapter 4 explores differences in family life among social classes. It includes an examination of how trends in the economy have affected families. Chapter 5 considers the consequences for families of the divisions in society along racial-ethnic lines. The family patterns of African Americans are discussed. The chapter also examines commonly used categories such as "Hispanic" and "Asian," which include groups that vary greatly in their family patterns.

Chapter Three

Gender and Families

Looking Forward

1. How do sociologists distinguish between the concepts of "sex" and "gender"?
2. How might fetal development affect the behavior of women and men?
3. How do children learn how women and men are supposed to behave?
4. How does everyday life reinforce gender differences?
5. Are gender differences built into the structure of society?
6. Overall, how should we think about gender differences?
7. Is there more than one kind of masculinity?

The Transgender Moment

The 2010s will be remembered as the time when the term *transgender* entered into common usage in the United States. News stories on the topic were published or posted online about 30 times more often in 2017 than in 2010, according to citations in Google News. And as the term became widespread, Americans' familiarity with transgender issues grew. Sociological research began to appear in the 1990s and increased greatly after 2000 (Schilt & Lagos, 2017).

To be sure, the phenomenon is not new. A study of changes of name and sex that people requested in their Social Security records found evidence of small numbers of seemingly transgender individuals going back to the mid-1930s (Cerf, 2015). The topic became widely known in 1952 when an army veteran, George Jorgensen, underwent sex-reassignment surgery and hormone treatments in Europe and returned in 1953 as Christine Jorgensen. She became a media star, ridiculed by many and understood by few. Serious attention to the phenomenon increased during the next half-century. But the key public moment may have occurred in 2015: The news media breathlessly covered the story of Caitlyn Jenner, who before her transition from a man to a woman was Bruce Jenner, an Olympic gold medalist who had married into a family of reality television stars, the Kardashians. In addition, transgender woman Laverne Cox, who portrayed an incarcerated transgender woman in the video series, *Orange Is the New Black,* caught the attention of the general public, as did *Transparent,* a video series about a father who is transitioning to a woman and his relationships with his family.

Consequently, transgender people, whom we defined in Chapter 1 as people who identify with a gender other than the one that they were assigned at birth, have become part of the public discourse. The best estimates suggest that about one-half of one percent of the population in the United States identifies as transgender (Flores, Herman, Gates, & Brown, 2016; Meerwij & Sevelius, 2017). That may seem to be a small number, but it amounts to more than one million people. Gender, their actions show, is a characteristic that can change over the course of a person's life–an enormous shift from the way gender was understood in the past. The place of transgender people in society is still controversial and contested: States and localities have debated laws that would prohibit discrimination on the basis of gender identity, with some passing these laws and some rejecting them.

Transgender people make a transition from male to female, or from female to male. In either case, they more or less follow the idea that there are only two genders. Another revolutionary idea was spreading at about the same time: gender is a continuum rather than a two-valued (male and female) status. According to this view, one might think of the gender spectrum as consisting of two poles with a pathway between them. Although most people reside at one of the poles, others may be somewhere on the pathway, and they may move back and forth along the pathway as they so choose. Thus, new terms such as *gender nonconforming* arose to describe the sexual identities of people who do not see themselves as having an unchanging male/female identity. Consider one such term, *genderqueer,* which is used to describe individuals who reject the idea that one must take on a fixed gender identity. The term appeared about 40 times more often in news articles in 2017 than in 2010, according to Google News citations.

Some societies have long had gender categories that were neither male nor female. Until the twentieth century, many Native American cultures had a place for **two-spirit people,** men or women who dressed like, performed the duties of, and behaved like members of the opposite sex (Jacobs, Thomas, & Land, 1997; Leland, 2008). As neither ordinary men nor ordinary women, two-spirits could undertake special tasks that women and men could not perform as easily, such as negotiating a marriage between a woman's family and a man's family or settling a dispute between a man and a woman. But what's new about gender-nonconforming individuals today is that they reserve the right to move along the pathway between the poles as often as they wish, and some further reject the idea that one needs a gender identity at all.

two-spirit people in Native American societies, men or women who dressed like, performed the duties of, and behaved like a member of the opposite sex

Why has there been such an increase in fluid conceptions of gender in American society? The postmodern theorists tell us that questions of self-identity have become more important in contemporary life. Individuals must work on their sense of who they really are. They are expected to make choices about the kind of personal life they want to live. In contrast, during the high modern era of the mid-twentieth century, people were taught to play the social roles that society expected of them: to marry heterosexually, to abide by strict rules about how men were supposed to behave (good providers, good fathers, stereotypically masculine) and how women were supposed to behave (good housewives, good mothers, stereotypically feminine), and to not ask many questions of themselves. Today, they are supposed to ask questions.

Thus, a man in the 1950s who felt uncomfortable about his gender identity might nevertheless get married, have children, and act like society expected a man to act. He might not be fully aware of the stirrings within him; or even if he were aware, he might repress them. He didn't have a name with which to label them. And he knew he would be rejected by everyone around him if he stepped outside of the conventional male role. In contrast, a similar man today may be influenced by expressive individualism, a set of values discussed in Chapter 1 that emphasize developing one's own feelings and emotional satisfaction. He is expected to pay attention to these feelings and to construct a genuine, true self. One of Jenner's daughters from a previous marriage told a reporter that he was a better parent when he began to transition and "was moving toward his authentic self" (Bissinger, 2015).

Today, if a person wants to transition to another gender, he or she will see role models in the media and perhaps in his or her own daily life. "We are in a place now," Cox told a reporter, "where more and more trans people want to come forward and say, 'This is who I am'" (Steinmetz, 2014). Moreover, a person in discomfort about his or her gender identity can find information more easily than in the past due to the rise of the Internet. Someone who questions the idea of a fixed gender identity can quickly find a supportive online community. A transgender woman who began her transition in middle age said to a reporter, "If the Internet had existed, in any meaningful sense, when I was 21, I would have figured it out" (Steinmetz, 2014).

sex the biological characteristics through which one can classify a person as female or male

Most sociological writings distinguish between sex and gender. We can define **sex** as the biological characteristics through which one can classify a person as female or male: sex chromosomes, sex-specific hormones, reproductive organs, and physical characteristics. Gender, which we defined in Chapter 1, refers to the social and cultural characteristics that distinguish women from men. In our society, such characteristics include the different clothing that men and women wear or the expectation that boys shouldn't cry when they are hurt. Gender is said to be a social creation; sex is said to be a biological creation. Nevertheless, drawing a line between the two concepts is sometimes more difficult than these definitions suggest. The example of transgender people shows that some individuals born with biological characteristics that lead them to be classified as one sex may have an intense identification with the other sex that seems to be inherent in their personalities rather than socially imposed.

Gender, then, is clearly a complex phenomenon, basic to most people's sense of themselves and yet less stable than is commonly thought. It is also fundamental to family life in many ways, from the biology of having children to strong social norms about how partners and parents are supposed to act. It has been a site in which men have exercised power over women. In fact, some scholars would restrict the definition of gender to characteristics that reflect male power over women or would argue more broadly that nearly all gender differences reflect gender politics (Ferree, 2010; Scott, 2000).

To understand families, we must understand gender. And to understand gender, we must begin before birth, for the paths of women and men begin to diverge in the womb. The origins and consequences of gender differences in childhood, and their maintenance in adulthood through social interaction and social structure constitute the subject of this chapter. (A more general examination of how parents raise their children will be the subject of Chapter 9.)

The Gestational Construction of Gender

gestation the nine-month development of the fetus inside the mother's uterus

For the first several weeks of **gestation** (the term for the nine-month development of the fetus inside the mother's uterus), the external sex organs of soon-to-be girls and boys are identical. These primitive genitals can develop into either a clitoris, vagina, and ovaries or a penis, scrotum, and testes. But soon male embryos begin to develop testes. In the second trimester (the middle three months) of gestation, the testes in soon-to-be boys produce male sex hormones called androgens. These hormones cause the genitals to develop into the male form. In the absence of high levels of androgens, the genitals develop into the female form. After only a few months, then, the developing child's genital sex is determined by the level of male sex hormones.

Some scientists believe that the androgens that circulate in male fetuses do more than cause the genitals to take on the male form. They claim that parts of the fetus's brain develop differently depending on the level of androgen that is present. In other words, the brains of males and females may be organized somewhat differently because of the presence or absence of high levels of male sex hormones during the second trimester of gestation (Leaper & Farkas, 2015). If so, then some of the gender differences we recognize in women and men could be influenced by differences in prenatal (before birth) hormone levels. Nevertheless, brain studies suggest that there is much variability and inconsistency in the gendered nature of women's and men's brains (Joel et al., 2015).

Those who believe that both biological and social factors have important influences on human development (Harris & McDade, 2018) may take a **biosocial approach** to gender differences. The biosocial perspective does not suggest that hormones and chromosomes are destiny nor that biology always wins out over social influences. In fact, those who believe biological influences do affect gendered behavior would add at least three qualifications. First, biologically based differences in gendered behavior exist only "on average"; individuals can show a wide range of behavior and a substantial overlap (Hyde, 2005). If we were to select a large group of women and another large group of men at random and measure the incidence of some biologically influenced behavior, we would find the behavior occurred more frequently among one group than the other. For example, if the behavior were physical aggression, we might find that, on average, aggression levels were moderately higher among the men than among the women. But not all men, nor all women either, would show the same level of aggression. A modest number of women would be very aggressive, and a modest number of men not at all aggressive. To take another example, even if, on average, women are more predisposed than men to engage in nurturing behavior, as some observers suggest, in any randomly selected group, some women will not be very nurturing and some men quite nurturing.

biosocial approach (to gender differences) the theory that both biological and social factors influence gender differences

Second, whether biological predispositions lead to actual behaviors depends on the environment in which a person is raised. For example, a child who is predisposed to be physically aggressive may not behave aggressively if his or her parents provide supportive but firm guidance and control. But a comparably predisposed child might behave very aggressively if his or her parents are neglectful. Biology and environment—nature and nurture—work together to produce behavior. It makes little sense, therefore, to attempt to determine how much of children's observed behavior is "genetic" or "environmental" because the interaction of nature and nurture is what produces the behaviors we see (Handel, Cahill, & Elkin, 2007).

Third, social influences can counteract biological predispositions. For instance, even if, on average, men are predisposed to be more physically aggressive than women, our society can control overly aggressive behavior through moral education, public pressure, and, for extreme aggression, law enforcement. Why, then, should biological predispositions matter at all? Because counteracting the influence of genes or hormones on human behavior is a bit like rolling a stone uphill: It can be done, but it takes continuing effort. If society were to decide that all biologically based gender differences in behavior should be eliminated, strong, deliberate steps would need to be taken to achieve that goal. And the stronger the biological predisposition, the stronger those steps would need to be. Understanding the biological bases of behavior, then, can help us to understand persistent differences between women and men and to estimate the ease or difficulty of bringing about social change.

Quick Review

- Some researchers think that the brains of male and female fetuses may be organized somewhat differently, but there is much overlap and inconsistency.
- Sociologists taking the biosocial approach to human behavior believe that both biologically based predispositions and social experiences influence gendered behavior.
- Biologically based differences, if any, exist only "on average."
- Social influences can counteract biologically based predispositions.

The Childhood Construction of Gender

Once born, children face multiple influences on their behavior. The most obvious influence comes from their parents, who typically treat girls and boys differently. In addition, children receive messages about gender from television and other media. And when they play together at a day care center or in their neighborhood or at school, they again are taught lessons about how girls and boys are supposed to behave.

PARENTAL SOCIALIZATION

socialization the processes by which we learn the ways of a given society or social group so as to adequately participate in it

socialization approach (to gender differences) the theory that gender identification and behavior are based on children's learning that they will be rewarded for the set of behaviors considered appropriate to their sex but not for those appropriate to the other sex

Researchers have argued that people first learn how women and men act through socialization during childhood. **Socialization,** according to the definition in one widely cited book, encompasses "the processes by which we learn and adapt to the ways of a given society or social group so as to adequately participate in it" (Handel, Cahill, & Elkin, 2007). It is how individuals learn to take on the attitudes and behaviors considered culturally appropriate for them. The emphasis in the **socialization approach** to gender differences is on conscious, social learning: Children are rewarded for behavior adults think is appropriate for their gender and admonished or punished for behavior that is not considered appropriate. By watching parents, teachers, television actors, and others, children learn the behavior of both genders, but they soon learn that they will be rewarded for one set of behaviors and not for the other. For example, although at first little boys cry as much as little girls, they are admonished not to, so that as men they cry less often than women. More generally, men are encouraged to be competitive and independent, whereas women are encouraged to be more nurturing to children and adults and better at enabling and maintaining personal relationships.

In the standard model of socialization, children passively learn lessons from their parents. Many researchers now think this model is too simplistic and that, in reality, both children and parents influence each other's behavior as socialization proceeds (Maccoby, 2007; McHale & Crouter, 2003). A brother and sister may respond differently to their parents' attempts at discipline because they have different predispositions for disruptive behavior or merely because the younger child is acting differently from the older one in order to compete for the parents' attention. The parents may then respond differently to the two children, perhaps becoming stricter with one than the other. This response, in turn, may encourage the two children to become even more different in their actions. Or parents may buy a toy building set as a birthday present for a son in response to his interest in playing with blocks; and this present may make him even more interested in stereotypically male toys than his sister. In other words, a feedback loop is created in which differences in siblings' predispositions, whether biologically based or based on earlier treatment, may make parents respond differently to each of them, which in turn will make their behaviors even more distinctive from each other.

THE MEDIA

Nor is gender socialization confined to parents; children learn lessons from books and television, among other sources. As recently as the 1960s, schools made little effort to balance the gender content in the books children were assigned to use. Publishers produced stories and histories that focused mainly on boys and men. Then, spurred by the feminist movement, school systems began to demand more balanced literature. As a result in most children's books, girls and boys receive much more equal treatment. Gooden and Gooden (2001) examined 83 picture books for young readers that had been designated as "notable" by the American Library Association between 1995 and 1999. They found that female main characters (human or animal) were just as common as male main characters, a sharp difference from the better than two-to-one edge that male main characters had in a similar study 25 years earlier. Still, male characters were rarely seen doing housework or child care.

Over the past few decades, books have lost ground to electronic media as a source of information for children. In 2016, the average 12- to 17-year old in the United States spent 14 hours per week watching television and an additional 7 hours per week on a game console, internet-connected desktop or laptop, or multimedia device; the average 2- to 11-year old spent almost 20 hours per week watching television, along with four hours per week on desktops, laptops, game consoles, and multimedia devices (Statistica, 2018). Video games have been shown to reinforce gender stereotypes: Men are portrayed as muscular heroes who often shoot weapons, whereas women (who appear less often than men) are portrayed as sexy and innocent and who often wear revealing clothing (Miller & Summers, 2007).

PEER GROUPS

Researchers also suspect that much of the development of gender-specific behavior occurs from an early age in children's **peer groups**—similar-age children who play or perform other activities together. Between the ages of two and three, children begin to sort themselves into same gender peer groups. Psychologist Eleanor Maccoby argued that these same gender peer groups strongly influence the distinctive behavior patterns of boys and girls (Maccoby, 1998). In observing pairs of children who were on average 33 months old, Maccoby and her colleagues found that these youngsters were far more likely to show social behavior—offering or grabbing a toy, hugging or pushing, vocally greeting or protesting, and so forth—to children of the same gender than to children of the opposite gender. Maccoby suggests that boys' peer groups tend to reinforce a competitive, dominance-oriented interaction style that carries over into such adult male communication tactics as interrupting, boasting, contradicting, and threatening, which restrict conversation. Girls' groups, she suggests, reinforce a different style that carries over into adult communication. Through expressing agreement or support, asking questions rather than making statements, and acknowledging other persons' comments, girls continue interactions rather than restricting them. These styles, Maccoby asserts, may influence adult, mixed gender interactions in school, at the office, and in families.

peer group a group of people who have roughly the same age and status as one another

How Do Sociologists Know What They Know?

Feminist Research Methods

Sociologist Barrie Thorne (1993) begins her influential book about children's play groups, *Gender Play: Girls and Boys in School*, by writing not about her subject but about herself. She recalls that the segregation of girls and boys on the playgrounds of the elementary school she attended was considered "natural." She tells the reader that her views on gender were transformed by the women's movement of the 1970s and 1980s, which argued that the differences between the genders are not natural but rather a social construction. She describes her commitment to raise her own children in a nonsexist way.

Thorne then discusses how, in her own research, she took pains to learn the terminology that the subjects themselves used: "kids" rather than "children." She explained, "I found that when I shifted to 'kids' in my writing, my stance toward the people in question felt more side-by-side than top-down" (p. 9). Using "kids" helped her to adopt the viewpoint of her subjects, as opposed to the viewpoint of an adult feminist scholar.

In fact, Thorne's entire first chapter consists of preliminary material about herself and her relationship with her subjects. The chapter illustrates an orientation that is called *feminist research methods*. It emerged from the feminist movement of the 1970s and 1980s and is linked to feminist theory and to the postmodern perspective. Researchers are encouraged to *reflexively* examine the nature of the research process that they are undertaking (Broom, Hand, & Tovey, 2009). Two feminist methodologists write approvingly of "the tendency for feminists to reflect on, examine critically, and explore analytically the nature of the research process" (Fonow & Cook, 2005, p. 2218).

Researchers are also encouraged to learn the point of view of the subjects they are studying. Moreover, they are also encouraged to minimize power differences between researchers and the groups they study (Harding & Norberg, 2005). That is why Thorne sought to use language and methods that made her more of a "side-by-side" observer than a "top-down" observer.

Researchers are also encouraged to conduct socially engaged research that may create social change, particularly by reducing the oppression of women—and also by ending the gender constraints placed on men (Ferree, 2010). Feminist researchers explicitly acknowledge this political agenda. "The goal of feminist thinking, research, and practice," according to one overview, "is social change—in the academy, in the community, and in the hearts and minds of individuals" (Allen, Walker, & McCann, 2013, p. 142).

More important, they argue that *all* social scientific research reflects the social and political beliefs of the researchers but that most social scientists hide their beliefs—sometimes even from themselves. In contrast, most sociologists try to follow the *scientific method*. A key assumption of the scientific method as it is often practiced is that researchers are neutral figures who stand outside the phenomena they study. The researcher's point of view, it is said, should not influence the methods she or he uses or the conclusions that she or he makes. In this way, social scientists strive for objectivity—a way of viewing the social world that is independent of personal beliefs.

But feminist researchers argue that objectivity is nearly impossible to achieve (Ruddick, 1996). They argue that much supposedly "objective" social scientific research actually reflects male bias. The very categories that social scientists use often reflect prevailing political agendas (Harding & Norberg, 2005). For example, they note that not long ago, the U.S. Bureau

Symbolic interactionists say that children develop a sense of self through activities such as peer group play—a "gendered" sense of self, in this instance. As a girl (or a boy) formulates what she will say or do in the group, she imagines how the others are likely to respond. This process of imagining how others will respond is what George Herbert Mead called "taking the role of the other" (Blumer, 1962). It is, interactionists say, how children develop an internalized sense of appropriate behavior.

But not all girls and boys follow these stereotypical scripts. When Barrie Thorne (1993) observed children in elementary schools, she found that most play groups comprised either all girls or all boys. But a modest number of girls and boys played in groups with the other gender, and there was much crossing of the gender border—for example, when boys and girls chased one another or invaded the other gender's space. The degree of separation between girls' and boys' worlds, Thorne concluded, was overstated. Thorne's approach to her study reflects many of the principles of feminist research methods (see *How Do Sociologists Know What They Know?:* Feminist Research Methods).

of the Census, in its surveys, defined the husband as the "head of household" in a married-couple family, no matter what the family's situation was. Similarly, violence against women by husbands and partners was greatly underreported in crime statistics until feminists focused attention on the problem.

Proponents of feminist research methods frequently try to show that there is substantial variation from person to person in the ways in which women and men act. They do so because they oppose generalizations about women that might be used to restrict their independence and equality (e.g., the belief, prevalent at mid-century, that the husband should earn the money and the wife should stay home and care for the children). They sometimes carry out research with the intent of demonstrating that generalizations about women are wrong. Thorne warns, for instance: "One should be wary of what has been called 'the tyranny of averages,' a misleading practice of referring to average differences as if they are absolute" (pp. 57–58).

So Thorne ventured out to the elementary school playground to disprove the idea that boys and girls are inherently different in their play styles—boys more aggressive, more concerned with dominance in groups; girls more concerned with relationships with a small number of friends. On the playground, girls and boys did separate, for the most part, in the ways the generalizations about them predict. They were not, however, completely separate. Thorne provided an insightful analysis of contact between girls and boys during the "border work" that maintained their separation, such as invading the other gender's spaces and chasing one another. She also found that a few children defied the stereotype, such as a boy who played jump rope and an athletic girl who played sports with the boys. And she documented occasional mixed games of dodgeball and the like.

From evidence such as this, Thorne concluded that gender "has a fluid quality" (p. 159) and that the claim that boys and girls have separate cultures "has outlived its usefulness" (p. 108). However, as one reviewer noted, the number of times that boys and girls cross the gender boundaries "are a tiny minority of her observations" (England, 1994, p. 283). Consequently, claiming that the average differences between boys and girls aren't important because some individuals cross the boundaries may be an overstatement.

But where "scientific" researchers may see averages, feminist researchers often see variability, diversity, and the possibility of social change. Scientific researchers attempt to describe the world as it seems to them. They ask "what is" questions: What is the nature of a situation currently, what is cause and what is effect? Feminist researchers place more emphasis on "what could be" questions: What could be an alternative social arrangement that would be more just? What could be changed about the positions of women and men in the system they are studying? In doing so, they attempt to fuse sociological research with their commitment to ending the social inequalities that disadvantage women.

Ask Yourself

1. Does your gender affect the way you react to Barrie Thorne's research? Explain.
2. What are the advantages and disadvantages of feminist research methods and of the scientific method? Why?

In sum, studies of young children's preferences and activities suggest numerous influences on the different behaviors of girls and boys. Society's expectations about how to behave are transmitted to children through channels such as parents, electronic media, books, and peer groups. In these ways, cultural differences between women and men are reproduced in the next generation. Yet the evidence also suggests that children may have innate predispositions that affect gender differences in their behavior. These predispositions appear to be stronger for boys than for girls. Boys seem to prefer rough play more than girls, on average, regardless of their parents' opinions about how they should play. Thus, the influence of same gender peer groups may reflect both socialization and biological predispositions.

Quick Review

- Sociologists who take the socialization approach to gender differences believe that children learn they will be rewarded for some types of behavior but not others.
- Parents both act and respond to their children by rewarding them for behavior they think
- appropriate and withholding rewards for behavior they think inappropriate.
- The media—television, video games, books—often portray boys and girls, and men and women, behaving in gender-stereotypical ways.
- Children's same-gender peer groups often reinforce gender-stereotypical behavior.
- Feminists have developed research methods that challenge key assumptions of the standard social scientific model. (See *How Do Sociologists Know What They Know?*: Feminist Research Methods.)

The Continual Construction of Gender

Over the past few decades, sociological research on the construction of gender differences has moved away from studying socialization or predispositions formed in childhood. In this recent way of thinking, gender is more fluid, more fragile, and more in need of constant reinforcement. Scholars argue instead for an approach that focuses on the continual construction and maintenance of gender differences throughout adulthood.

DOING AND UNDOING GENDER

interactionist approach (to gender differences) the theory that gender identification and behavior are based on the day-to-day behavior that reinforces gender distinctions

Candace West and Don H. Zimmerman (1987) developed this approach in an influential article, "Doing Gender." At the time, their perspective was so new and different that it took them 10 years of rejections and revisions to find an academic journal that was willing to publish it (West and Zimmerman, 2009). To develop their framework, which is commonly known as the **interactionist approach,** the authors hearkened back to symbolic interaction theory (Blumer, 1962).[1] "We argue," West and Zimmerman (1987, p. 129) wrote, "that gender is not a set of traits, nor a role, but the product of social doings of some sort." These social doings occur through "situated conduct"—interactions between men and women in particular settings (such as a kitchen or a job interview). Gender is an achieved property that is created through countless social interactions that reinforce gender differences.

For example, how do a wife and husband come to understand that she should do most of the housework? Socialization theory suggests that doing the housework is part of the behavior women learn beginning with the dolls and teacups they are given in childhood and the praise they get for helping their mothers wash the dishes. But the symbolic interactionists, while not denying that socialization occurs, emphasize that questions such as who does the housework are settled again and again in daily life. For example, in a study conducted by Sarah Fenstermaker (2002), a woman who was asked "What household work does your husband do?" replied:

> *He tries to be helpful. He tries. He's a brilliant and successful lawyer. It's incredible how he smiles after he sponges off the table and there are still crumbs all over. (p. 113)*

[1] They actually adhere to a variant of the interactionist approach called ethnomethodology (Wickes & Emmison, 2007).

Here the husband's smile—the symbol—indicates to his wife that he is incapable of sponging all the crumbs off the table, despite having enough brains to be a brilliant and successful lawyer. It is a way for the husband to express a feigned helplessness, which he and his wife both interpret as meaning that she's the only one who can do a good job of cleaning up after dinner. Daily scenes such as this, Berk and others argue, not only produce clean tables but also produce—and reproduce—gender distinctions. The interactionists focus on people's actions in concrete situations such as this one in order to determine how social meanings—in this case the shared understanding of who should do the housework—are produced.

According to this line of reasoning, people must continually "do" gender—do the work of creating a shared sense of what the relations between men and women should be (West & Zimmerman, 1987). Gender becomes a verb, usually in the passive voice: Housework is gendered, work for wages is gendered, childcare is gendered, over and over in hundreds of situations. The household, in Fenstermaker's phrase, becomes a gender factory that produces the shared reality of gender relations along with crumb-free tables (Fenstermaker, 2002).

In a sense, the interactionist approach turns the logic of the socialization approach on its head. The socialization view is that men offer to carry packages for women because men and women are taught to believe that women aren't strong enough to manage on their own; the interactionist view is that men and women believe that women can't manage on their own because men keep offering to carry their packages. The setting is a woman walking to her car in a supermarket parking lot carrying a manageable load of groceries; the interaction is that a male friend of hers approaches and offers to carry the bags for her; she smiles politely and accepts his offer with thanks, even though she could have made it to the car herself. The achievement is reinforcing and, in effect, re-creating gender differences—in other words, doing gender. You can think of many other daily situations that have similar properties; add them up and multiply by the thousands of days in the average life, say the interactionists, and you get a powerful mechanism for reproducing a society with gender differences so strong that people think they are natural.

Today, the idea of doing gender and the interactionist perspective that underlies it are still relevant. Yet not all interactions between women and men should be thought of as doing gender. The intention of West and Zimmerman was to examine interactions that reinforce inequality between women and men (Risman, 2009). But some interactions may narrow inequality between women and men. For instance, women who enter traditionally male occupations may have interactions with their male coworkers that will help them to accept women on the job. A couple who try to establish shared parenting may use their interactions to establish a more equal relationship to each other. One author suggests that we reserve the term "doing gender" for interactions that reproduce gender differences, and use a new term, "undoing gender," for interactions that reduce gender differences (Deutsch, 2007). After several decades of change in family and work lives, an increasing share of the daily interactions between women and men may be undoing gender.

Quick Review

- Sociologists who take the interactionist approach believe that gender is not a fixed role or trait but rather a social construction that must be actively maintained throughout adulthood.
- Through situated conduct—interaction in concrete settings—in everyday life, women and men unthinkingly reproduce and sustain gender differences.

Gender as Social Structure

social structure the fundamental set of positions that organize society as a whole

Another body of writing about the construction and maintenance of gender differences focuses not only on social interaction or socialization, but also on the very structure of society: its hierarchies of dominance and power and its economic and political systems. According to this line of reasoning, gender differences are social creations deeply imbedded in society (Risman, 2004). Think of **social structure** as the fundamental set of positions that organize society as a whole. Social structure consists, in part, of the distribution of material resources such as wealth and education among individuals and groups. Those with more material resources tend to have power over those with fewer resources, the way the wealthy exercise power over the poor or whites exercise power over blacks. Resources and power are the bricks and mortar out of which social structure is built. Like class (see Chapter 4) and race (see Chapter 5), gender is said to be a basic part of social structure, a central way in which a society is stratified into more and less powerful groups.

For instance, a study of 22 countries suggests that how a couple divides the housework is not just a matter of their personal beliefs. Rather, the degree of gender equality that exists at the national level also influences them. Consider two couples, A and B, who both believe that ideally housework should be divided equally. Suppose couple A lives in a country such as Russia or Japan, where few women are in parliament, few have powerful or prestigious occupations, and few earn high salaries. Suppose couple B, in contrast, lives in a country such as Sweden or Canada, where women have much more political and economic power at the national level. Then couple B will tend to divide the housework more equally than will couple A, even though their personal beliefs are the same. How they live their home lives, the study suggests, is influenced by the power and influence that women have in their national political and economic systems (Fuwa, 2004).

Or consider the way the economy runs. In Western nations, people must purchase the goods they need with money (as opposed to making their own clothes and building their own houses). Western societies are organized so that men have access to more money than women: Men are more likely to work for pay, and when they do, most earn higher wages and salaries than women. To be sure, men tend to have more work experience than women, in part because many women withdraw from the paid workforce to bear and rear children. Gender theorists argue, however, that the wage gap is far wider than differences in education and work experience would predict—and recent economic studies suggest that their argument is correct. (See *Families and Public Policy:* Do Employers Discriminate Against Women?) In a number of ways—such as when parents encourage sons more than daughters to have careers, when employers discriminate against women in hiring or pay, and when long-established rules provide men with higher pay than women for comparable work—society creates and reinforces men's economic domination.

Social structure also has a cultural component that contains the rules about how to act when relating to other people. In order to simplify the task of determining what's an appropriate way to act in everyday situations, individuals rely on simple mental models of behavior. Gender is one of the basic mental models, or cultural frames as Ridgeway (2011) calls them, that people use for this purpose. Others are age and race. When you meet someone, you almost instantaneously categorize them according to gender without even thinking about it; and that categorization affects how you act toward the other person. What's more, the cultural frame of gender contains inequalities: Men are expected to be more dominant and aggressive than women, and women are expected to be nicer and more nurturing. These mental models not only influence how we behave toward men and women but also reinforce and recreate stereotypical gender differences. An employer hiring for a management position may be predisposed to view male applicants more positively than women applicants, whereas an employer hiring for a child care center may be predisposed toward women. Thus, the sociological argument that gender is a basic part of social structure has two parts: First, men typically have material advantages (e.g., higher earning potential) that can lead to greater power over women (e.g., doing less housework and child care). Second, the cultural frame of gender subtly influences men and women to interact in ways that reinforce male privilege. Even when men's material advantages erode, the cultural frame of gender may change more slowly, thus slowing the movement toward gender equality.

Quick Review

- Many theorists view gender as a basic part of the social structure, like class and race.
- Men tend to have material resources (money, education) that place them in positions of power over women.
- Mental models, or cultural frames, of the characteristic of women and men are also part of the social structure.

Thinking about Gender Differences Today

The outpouring of scholarship on the sociology of gender has transformed the way we view gender differences in family life and the workplace. Let's assess where knowledge, discussion, and debate are today.

CAUSES AT MULTIPLE LEVELS

The growing consensus among scholars is that gender differences are produced and reproduced at all the levels we have examined in this chapter: biosocial, childhood socialization, interactional, and social structural (England, 2009; Ridgeway, 2011). As for the biosocial level, there may be some biologically based differences in personality or preferences between women and men that are relevant to gender differences, although there would also be a big overlap that included many women who are aggressive at work and many men who are nurturing at home. But even if biology plays a role, the social world greatly expands and amplifies these differences. It does so at the level of socialization by providing thousands of little lessons for children and adolescents to learn from sources as diverse as friends, teachers, and video games. It does so at the level of the continual, daily interactions of men and women. In these interactions, women and men often do gender: They respond to each other using the cultural frame of stereotypical gender differences and in the process reinforce those differences. And it does so at the level of social structure, where the greater material resources of men often give them an advantage in hiring decisions or negotiations about housework. Because gender differences are created and strengthened at so many levels, they are deeply embedded in our view of the social world—so much so that we sometimes tend to see all gender differences as "natural." Yet gender relations that seemed natural in the 1950s don't seem natural today; and what we view as natural today probably won't seem so natural a generation or two from now.

Families and Public Policy

Do Employers Discriminate Against Women?

In the late 1970s, the weekly earnings of the average woman who worked full-time were only about 63 percent of the weekly earnings of the average man who worked full-time. Progress has been made toward gender equality in earnings since then. In 2015, the average woman working full time earned 81 percent of what the average man earned. But an earnings gap continues to exist (U.S. Bureau of Labor Statistics, 2017). Why in most occupations do women still earn less than men? And why are women workers still overrepresented in lower-paying jobs? Do employers discriminate against women? Are they less likely to hire a woman than a man, and do they pay women less? Or are other factors responsible for the differences between women and men in the labor market?

Some social scientists have argued that the earnings gap primarily represents the different social roles that women choose. That is, they assume that women prefer to devote a larger share of their lives to raising children than do men. Consequently, according to this line of reasoning, women tend to choose jobs that they can leave for a period of time and then reenter, and they leave voluntarily when they have young children. These jobs tend to be in the lower-paying occupations and industries. In addition, they have less work experience and invest less in their careers (e.g., by taking fewer job-training courses). Since employers pay lower wages to people with less work experience, they pay women less than men.

The evidence, however, suggests that this is not the whole story of the earnings gap. When two economists looked at the wage gap and took into account differences between women and men in education, work experience, and occupation and industry, they still could not explain a substantial part of the gap (Blau & Kahn, 2007). It's possible, as they suggest, that some or all of the remaining gap in earnings is due to discrimination in how much employers pay women compared to men.

A change in the world of classical music provided an unexpected window on the question of whether employers discriminate against women. Until the 1970s the conductors of the major symphony orchestras in the United States, all of whom were male, made decisions about hiring new players to fill vacancies based on recommendations from musicians they knew and on seeing and hearing the top candidates audition for the jobs. Nearly all of the new hires were men. Then in the 1970s most of the major orchestras switched to so-called blind auditions. Orchestras first advertised for vacancies; and then, in the preliminary round of auditions, a committee of orchestra members listened to the musicians

THE SLOWING OF GENDER CHANGE

After rapid changes in the 1960s through the 1980s, the pace of gender change has slowed. The amount full-time female workers earn per every dollar full-time male workers earn—81 cents in 2015—has not increased since 2005 (U.S. Bureau of Labor Statistics, 2017). Men increased the time they spent in housework between the 1970s and the 1990s, but there has been no increase since then (Sayer, 2015). Why might change have slowed? One possibility is that women with dependent children remain at a disadvantage in a labor market that still seems to assume that workers have a spouse at home to take most of the responsibility for child care. It remains difficult for the primary caregivers of children to work full time, especially in lower-wage service and clerical jobs where a mother cannot take a personal phone call and can be fired for missing a day. The U.S. government provides less assistance to working parents than does any other wealthy country, as we will discuss in Chapter 8. Another possibility is that the cultural frame of gender has changed less than one might expect given the increases in mothers working outside the home—an instance of what sociologists have called **cultural lag** (Ogburn, 1964).

cultural lag the tendency for attitudes and values to change more slowly than the material circumstances that underlie them

from behind a screen. Since the committee members could not see the players, they could not determine their genders. Some symphonies went so far as to run a carpet from where the applicants entered the room to the screen so that the committee could not guess the gender of the musicians by the sound of their footsteps. The audition committee selected candidates for the final round of auditioning without knowing their names or genders—they relied purely on the sound of their playing. Conductors still made the final decision in most cases, but only among the candidates who made it through the preliminary round.

Did the introduction of the blind audition result in more hiring of women players? Yes, concluded Claudia Goldin and Cecilia Rouse, who obtained detailed information about auditions and rosters of players from 11 major American orchestras (Goldin & Rouse, 2000). They estimate that the screen increased the likelihood that a woman would advance beyond the preliminary rounds of auditions by 50 percent and sharply increased the likelihood that a woman would be hired to fill a vacancy. Since the 1970s, the percentage of women players in the major symphonies has increased greatly (about one-third of the players in the New York Philharmonic are women), and the authors estimate that 25 percent of that increase is the result of blind auditions.

It seems clear that discrimination in hiring was one of the factors that kept the percentage of women players low until the 1970s. Is there still discrimination in hiring today in other occupations? Quite likely: A study of 2000 Census Bureau data showed that 20 percent of the earnings gap between women and men could not be accounted for by differences in education, occupation, and work experience (Weinberg, 2007).

Nevertheless, progress is being made. Among young adults ages 25 to 34, the median hourly wages of women were 89 percent of the wages of men in 2017—in part because young women are now more likely to graduate from college than are young men (Pew Research Center, 2018).

Ask Yourself

1. Have you ever compared notes with your coworkers and discovered that the women in your group are being paid less than men? If so, how did you and the other employees interpret the earnings gap?
2. Can you think of reasons other than work experience and discrimination that would help explain the earnings gap?

People tend to interpret new situations in ways that are consistent with their existing cultural expectations; they discount evidence of change and pay more attention to evidence of continuity until the evidence for change is overwhelming. The result is that gender stereotypes change more slowly than do material circumstances such as women's changing roles at work and at home (Ridgeway, 2011). Even the expansion of higher educational opportunities may have slowed the pace of gender change. As one's choice of a major comes to be seen as a way to express one's personal preferences, men's and women's senses of what are stereotypically "male" and "female" occupations may lead them to choose gender-typical majors. In the most economically advanced nations, such as the United States and Western European countries, women tend to cluster more highly in the social sciences and the humanities and men in the natural sciences than is the case in less wealthy countries (Charles & Bradley, 2009).

THE ASYMMETRY OF GENDER CHANGE

When preteens at a middle school in a southeastern city were asked how a hypothetical girl who tried to start a girls' football team would be treated, a few expressed concerns that she would be teased, but most thought she would be accepted. When asked, however, about a hypothetical boy who tried to become a cheerleader, nearly all the students said that he would be the target of ridicule. Many said he would be called "gay," which was the worst insult a boy in the school could receive, according to the authors of the study (Risman & Seale, 2010). Yet the label of "gay" seemed to have less to do with sexual orientation than with acting outside of boundaries of expected behavior. Boys (and some girls) strictly policed the boundaries of masculinity by taunting boundary crossers. High school boys, other studies show, do the same (Pascoe, 2007). Yet girls at the middle school could easily cross the boundaries of femininity to be good athletes and to compete with boys for academic success in ways that their mothers and grandmothers could not. In other words, the changes in gender expectations in middle school seem to have made it OK for girls to act like boys but not for boys to act like girls.

asymmetry (of gender change) the greater change in women's lives than in men's lives

This is an example of the **asymmetry of gender change** over the past few decades. If change were symmetric, it would be the same on both sides: as much movement toward crossing the boundaries of traditional masculinity and femininity among men as among women. In contrast, there has been more change in women's behavior than in men's. To take another example, far more women than men have moved into occupations that were traditionally held by the opposite sex. Between 1975 and 2017, the percentage of physicians who were women increased from 13 percent to 40 percent; and yet the percentage of registered nurses who were men rose from 3 percent to only 10 percent. Over the same period, the percentage of college teachers who were women rose from 31 to 47 percent, while the percentage of men who were elementary and middle school teachers increased from 15 percent to only 21 percent (U.S. Bureau of Labor Statistics 2018; Wootton, 1997). England (2016) argues that men's resistance to entering occupations staffed largely by women reflects the persistent devaluation in our culture of roles and activities that are seen as feminine. This devaluation may reflect deep-seated patterns of socialization as well as the "doings" of gender display. Gender differences may be reinforced by the taunting a boy knows he will receive if he steps outside the bounds of acceptable school-age male behavior. While today's school girls may be learning lessons that lead some of them to become doctors, today's school boys are still learning lessons that lead most of them to avoid becoming nurses.

INTERSECTIONALITY

Many of the older sociological studies of gender that are cited in this chapter are based on samples of individuals and family members who are largely white and middle class. The contemporary feminist movement is said to have begun with the publication of Betty Friedan's book, *The Feminist Mystique,* in 1963. Friedan identified a "problem that has no name" that was affecting married women in the 1950s and early 1960s: A dissatisfaction with their restriction to full-time child care and housework (Friedan, 1963). Friedan's book was almost entirely based on her observations of white middle-class women. This focus was typical of feminist writing until the 1980s and 1990s, when women from minority groups began to criticize the movement for ignoring race and class. They argued that poor women and women from minority racial and ethnic groups experience the social inequalities differently from middle-class white women and that researchers must incorporate these multiple perspectives (Collins, 2000; Glenn,

2000). This viewpoint became known as *intersectionality,* which was defined in Chapter 1 as the principle that inequalities related to one social identity often overlap with inequalities in other identities. Two gender theorists write that "there is no single category (race, class, ethnicity, gender, nation, or sexuality) that can explain human experience without reference to other categories" (Dill & Kohlman 2012, p. 170).

For example, the number of workers who provide support and caring to middle-class families has increased in the past decade or two. (And, in fact, a new subfield of *care work studies* has developed around these workers, as we will discuss in Chapter 8.) They include nannies, house cleaners, home health care aides, day care center staff, and others. These jobs tend to be typed as women's work (when's the last time you saw a male nanny?), so issues of gender are clearly important in understanding their growth. But it is also true that a substantial number are African American, Hispanic, or Asian and that most are lower class or working class. A recent immigrant woman from Mexico or Jamaica who lacks proper documents may be channeled into the nanny business, where she will accept low pay and quite possibly send home part of her earnings to pay someone to care for her own children (Parreñas, 2002). To understand her story, you will need to see how her gender, ethnicity, and class position intersect to place her in a suburban American home.

Quick Review

- Gender differences are produced and reproduced at multiple levels, including the biosocial level, the socialization level, the level of interaction, and the social structural level.
- The pace of gender change has slowed in recent decades. Possible reasons include work-family conflict and the persistence of a cultural frame that supports gender stereotypes.
- Gender change has been asymmetric: There has been more change in women and girls' behavior than in men and boys' behavior.
- Studies of gender differences should recognize variations according to domains such as race and class.

Men and Masculinities

Sociological writings on gender have commonly focused on the conditions under which women and girls live their lives. This orientation reflects the roots of gender studies in the feminist movement that began in the 1960s. Although men have not been absent from gender studies, they tended to be included mainly because of the ways in which they influence or control women. Beginning in the 1980s, however, both a scholarly and a popular literature emerged that was focused on men. This body of literature grew greatly in the 1990s and 2000s, as social movements aimed at men gained strength. The main topic of these writings was **masculinity**—the set of personal characteristics that society defines as being typical of men.

masculinity the set of personal characteristics that society defines as being typical of men

These writers reject the idea that masculinity has a singular essence (Coltrane, 1994). Instead, they argue that what we often think of as the "essence" of masculinity—aggressiveness, attempts to dominate, emotional detachment, aversion to homosexuality, and so forth—is merely a social construction. These authors write not of masculinity but of *masculinities,* the title of an influential book by R. W. Connell (1995) that implies that there is more than one way to be masculine. Connell and others argue that the social influences that prop up the Western version of masculinity are so pervasive they become invisible to us. Consequently, we assume incorrectly that the current version of masculinity is the way men naturally are (Kimmel, 2012).

Can men swim against the tide of the current construction of masculinity and be nurturing and caring? This is an important question because most mothers now work outside the home rather than caring for children full-time. Is it possible for fathers to become the principal caregivers in the home and do the kind of caring that mothers routinely do? Studies suggest that at least some fathers can do caregiving well (Coltrane & Adams, 2008). For instance, Andrea Doucet set out to interview fathers who were primary caregivers in and around Ottawa, Canada (Doucet, 2006). Through advertisements and word of mouth, she identified over 100 fathers. She found that these men cared for and nurtured their children in ways that resembled the kind of care mothers provided, but with a noticeable difference: Fathers emphasized playfulness, physical activity, risk taking, and autonomy more than mothers typically did. These kinds of activities have long been seen as part of fathers' repertoires (Parke, 1996). This doesn't mean that fathers aren't nurturing, Doucet argues, but rather that they tend to nurture in a somewhat different way than mothers typically do. If more fathers were to become primary caregivers in the coming years, we might see more of this style of nurturing.

Quick Review

- Sociologists argue that the characteristics that comprise "masculinity" as we know it are socially constructed rather than natural.
- Fathers are capable of nurturing children but may do so somewhat differently than mothers do.

The Contributions of Gender Studies

We have reviewed several approaches to the study of gender differences (Table 3.1, p. 91). Despite their different perspectives—or perhaps because of them—sociologists who have studied gender (along with their colleagues in anthropology, history, and psychology) have made important contributions to our understanding of the family. First, they have demonstrated that the roles men and women play in families are in large part socially and culturally constructed. Indeed, many sociologists would argue that such differences are almost entirely constructed by conscious social forces. But all would agree that biology cannot explain why the great 1950s liberal Adlai Stevenson told the 1955 graduating class of Smith College (a private liberal arts college for women) that

Table 3.1 Approaches to the Study of Gender Differences

APPROACH	HOW GENDER IS CONSTRUCTED	EXAMPLES
Biosocial	Through biologically based (e.g., genetic, hormonal) differences that have evolved over the history of the human existence.	Boys will sometimes insist on playing with trucks and tools even if they are given dolls and stuffed animals.
Socialization	Through learning from adults, the media, peers, and teachers what kinds of behavior are expected of women and men.	Boys are given trucks and tools for birthday presents; girls are given dolls and stuffed animals. Boys are admonished not to cry; girls are allowed to cry.
Interactionist	Through continual reinforcement of gender differences because of the everyday behaviors of women and men.	Husbands who are very competent outside the home will claim they're not good at washing dishes or changing diapers, and their wives will agree with them and do these tasks.
Structural	Through the distribution of resources and power that favors men over women.	Women are paid less than men for working at the same job. Women who work outside the home are still expected to be the primary caregivers to children, even if they are married.

their place in politics was to "influence man and boy" through the "humble role of housewife" (Chafe, 1972). Moreover, biology can't explain the social changes in family life that have occurred over the past few decades, or even the past few centuries, because evolutionary change is slow. Consequently, the biological approach may not be very useful to a sociologist who is trying to explain social change—although it might be helpful in determining the difficulty of bringing about social change. In this book the social and cultural construction of gender will be relevant to discussions of changing conceptions of sexuality (Chapter 6), patterns of courtship, dating, and spouse choice, and the relationships between married or cohabiting couples (Chapter 7).

Second, sociologists of gender have taught us that gender distinctions sometimes (some would say *always*) reflect differences in power between men and women. Adlai Stevenson's speech was meant to convey to the Smith graduates how important their restricted political role was. But women whose only political influence is through their husbands are not equal in political power to men. After the rise of the feminist movement in the 1960s and 1970s and the increases in the number of women elected to political office, no male politician would make Stevenson's statement. Feminist scholars argue, moreover, that power differences do not stop at the family's front door; rather, the roles women play within marriages often reflect their husbands' greater power—in particular, his greater economic power. Said differently, the lesson is that families are not islands isolated from the rest of society; rather, the relations of power and inequality that hold outside the home can also extend within it. Differences in power and the allocation of work within the household will be examined in Chapter 8. Other chapters will include discussions of the effects of male domination on domestic violence against women (Chapter 11), the economic circumstances of divorced women (Chapter 12), and family law and policy (Chapter 14).

Looking Back

1. **How do sociologists distinguish between the concepts of "sex" and "gender"?** Sociologists use the term *sex* to refer to biological characteristics through which one can classify a person as female or male and *gender* to refer to differences between women and men that are social and cultural, and therefore constructed by society. Gender differences often reflect male domination over women. Nevertheless, in some instances social and biological influences on gender differences are difficult to disentangle.

2. **How might fetal development affect the behavior of women and men?** There is some evidence that biological differences in the development of male and female fetuses could account for some of the gender differences in children's and adults' behavior. Biologically based differences only exist "on average"; individuals can show a wide range of behavior. And social influences such as parental upbringing and education can counteract biological predispositions.

3. **How do children learn how women and men are supposed to behave?** According to the socialization approach, young children learn stereotypical behavior from parents, peers, teachers, and the media. The emphasis in this approach is on conscious, social learning. In general, children are taught to think that boys and men are aggressive, competitive, and independent, whereas girls and women are less aggressive, more nurturing, and better at enabling and maintaining personal relationships. From these lessons, children mentally construct the concept of gender.

4. **How does everyday life reinforce gender differences?** Sociologists who take the interactionist approach believe that gender differences need continual reinforcement throughout life. In their view, gender differences are reproduced in daily interactions between women and men in settings such as the home and the workplace. Without being conscious of it, individuals do the work of maintaining gender differences.

5. **Are gender differences built into the structure of society?** Many gender theorists argue that gender differences are built into the social structure in a fundamental way like social class or race. Men tend to have material advantages that place them in positions in the social structure where they have power over women. People also use pervasive mental models, or cultural frames, of the characteristics of women and men that are built into the social structure. They use these cultural frames to guide their interactions. The cultural frames reinforce inequalities, such as the idea that men are more dominant and aggressive than women. Even if the material advantages of men decline, the cultural frames can remain strong enough to reinforce gender differences.

6. **Overall, how should we think about gender differences today?** Gender differences are created and maintained on many levels, which is why gender is such a strong factor in people's identities and in how societies are organized. Biosocial factors predispose people to act in gendered ways and childhood experiences socialize them to do so. Gender differences are reinforced in everyday interactions between women and men. And differences in power and influence are built into the social structure. After several decades of rapid change in gender differences, the pace of change has slowed; moreover, the amount of change in women's lives has been greater than in men's lives. The influences of gender often depend on the social class and racial context of a situation. Minority group women often experience gender, class, and racial or ethnic inequality simultaneously.

7. **Is there more than one kind of masculinity?** Sociologists suggest that the dominant kind of masculinity, with its aggressiveness, emotional detachment, and so forth, is socially constructed and is not the only kind of masculinity. They argue that many men can be nurturing caregivers to children, even though they may do the work of caring in a way that emphasizes physical activity, play, and autonomy more than mothers typically do.

Study Questions

1. What do news stories about transgender people teach us about gender?
2. Let us suppose for the moment that prenatal male hormone levels influence aggressive behavior. Would we then expect all boys to be aggressive and all girls to be unaggressive?
3. Do frequently visited websites and video games impart messages about women's and men's proper behavior?
4. Is "doing gender" in daily life—the daily reinforcement of gendered behavior through social interaction—strong enough to maintain the gender differences we see in society?
5. Do you agree, as many feminist researchers do, that it is impossible to be completely objective when studying gender?
6. Why might the pace of gender change have slowed?
7. Why has gender changed more for women than for men?
8. Are fathers capable of nurturing children?

Key Terms

asymmetry (of gender change) 86
biosocial approach (to gender differences) 75
cultural lag 84
gestation 74
interactionist approach (to gender differences) 80
masculinity 87
peer group 77
sex 74
social structure 82
socialization 76
socialization approach (to gender differences) 76
two-spirit people 73

Thinking about Families

The Public Family	The Private Family
Do parents, peers, and teachers prepare boys for success in the work world more than they prepare girls?	**Does everyday life reinforce gender differences in families in ways we usually don't notice?**

References

Allen, K. R., Walker, A. J., & McCann, B. R. (2013). Feminism and families. In G. W. Peterson & K. R. Bush (Eds.), *Handbook of marriage and the family* (pp. 139–158). New York: Springer.

Bissinger, B. (2015, June). Caitlyn Jenner: The full story. *Vanity Fair, 57.*

Blau, F. D., & Kahn, L. M. (2007). The gender pay gap. *Economists' Voice, June,* 1–5.

Blumer, H. (1962). Society as symbolic interaction. In A. M. Rose (Ed.), *Human behavior and social processes* (pp. 179–192). Boston, MA.: Houghton Mifflin.

Broom, A., Hand, K., & Tovey, P. (2009). The role of gender, environment and individual biography in shaping qualitative interview data. *International Journal of Social Research Methodology, 12*(1), 51–65.

Chafe, W. H. (1972). *The American woman: Her changing social, economic, and political roles, 1920–1970.* New York: Oxford University Press.

Charles, M., & Bradley, K. (2009). Indulging our gendered selves: Sex segregation by field of study in 44 countries. *American Journal of Sociology, 114,* 924–976.

Collins, P. H. (2000). *Black feminist thought* (Vol. Routledge): New York.

Coltrane, S. (1994). Theorizing masculinities in contemporary social problems. In H. Brod & M. Kaufman (Eds.), *Theorizing masculinities* (pp. 39–60). Thousand Oaks, CA.: Sage Publications.

Coltrane, S., & Adams, M. (2008). *Gender and families.* Lanham, MD: Rowman & Littlefied.

Connell, R. W. (1995). *Masculinities.* Cambridge, UK: Polity Press.

Deutsch, F. M. (2007). Undoing gender. *Gender & Society, 21,* 106–127.

Dill, B. T., & Kohlman, M. H. (2012). Intersectionality: A transformative paradigm in feminist theory and social justice. In S. N. Hesse-Biber (Ed.), *Handbook of feminist research: Theory and praxis* (pp. 154–175). Thousand Oaks CA: Sage.

Doucet, A. (2006). *Do men mother? Fathering, care, and domestic responsibility.* Toronto: University of Toronto Press.

England, P. (2009). A gender lens on marriage. In H. E. Peters & C. M. K. Dush (Eds.), *Marriage and family: Perspectives and complexity* (pp. 57–74). New York: Columbia University Press.

England, P. (2016). Sometimes the social becomes personal: Gender, class. And sexualities. *American Sociological Review, 81,* 4–28.

Fenstermaker, S. (2002). Work and gender. In S. Fenstermaker & C. West (Eds.), *Doing gender, doing difference: Inequality, power, and institutional change* (pp. 105–118). New York: Routledge.

Ferree, M. M. (2010). Filling the glass: Gender perspectives on families. *Journal of Marriage and Family, 72* (June), 420–439.

Flores, A. R., Herman, J. L., Gates, G. J., & Brown, T. N. T. (2016). How many adults identify as transgender in the United States? *The Williams Institute.* Retrieved April 27, 2019, from https://williamsinstitute.law.ucla.edu/wpcontent/uploads/How-Many-Adults-Identify-as-Transgender-in-the-United-States.pdf

Fonow, M. M., & Cook, J. A. (2005). Feminist methodology: New applications in the academy and public policy. *Signs: Journal of Women in Culture and Society, 30,* 2211–2236.

Fuwa, M. (2004). Macro-level gender inequality and the division of household labor in 22 countries. *American Sociological Review, 69,* 751–767.

Friedan, B. (1963). *The feminine mystique.* New York: W. W. Norton.

Glenn, E. N. (2000). The social construction and institutionalization of gender and race. In M. M. Ferree, J. Lorber, & B. B. Hess (Eds.), *Revisioning gender* (pp. 3–43). Walnut Creek, CA: AltaMira Press.

Goldin, C., & Rouse, C. (2000). Orchestrating impartiality: The impact of "blind" auditions on female musicians. *American Economic Review, 90,* 715–741.

Gooden, A., & Gooden, M. (2001). Gender representation in notable children's picture books: 1995–1999. *Sex Roles, 45,* 89–101.

Handel, G., Cahill, S., & Elkin, F. (2007). *Children and society: The sociology of children and childhood socialization:* Oxford University Press. Handler, J. (1995). *The poverty of welfare reform.* New Haven: Yale University Press.

Harding, S., & Norberg, K. (2005). New feminist approaches to social science methodologies: An introduction. *Signs: Journal of Women in Culture and Society, 30,* 2009–2015.

Harris, B. C. (2015). Likely transgender individuals in U.S. Federal administrative records and the 2010 Census. *Center for Administrative Records Research and Applications, U.S. Census Bureau, Working Paper 2015-03.* https://www.census.gov/content/dam/Census/library/working-papers/2015/adrm/carra-wp-2015-03.pdf

Harris, K. M., & McDade, T. W. (2018). The biosocial approach to human development, behavior, and health across the life course. *RSF: The Russell Sage Foundation Journal of the Social Sciences, 4*(4), 2–26.

Hyde, J. S. (2005). The gender similarities hypothesis. *American Psychologist, 60*(6), 581–592.

Jacobs, S., Thomas, W., & Lang, S. (Eds.). (1997). *Two-spirit people: Native American gender identity, sexuality, and spirituality.* Champaign-Urbana: University of Illinois Press.

Joel, D., Berman, Z., Tavor, I., Wexler, N., Gaber, O., Stein, Y., Shefi, N., Pool, J., Urchs, S., Margulies, D. S. (2015). Sex beyond the genitalia: The human brain mosaic. *Proceedings of the National Academy of Sciences, 112*(50), 15468–15473.

Kimmel, M. (2012). *Manhood in America: A cultural history* (Third ed.). New York: Oxford University Press.

Leaper, C., & Farkas, T. (2015). The socialization of gender during childhood and adolescence. In J. E. Grusec & P. D. Hasting (Eds.), *Handbook of socialization: Theory and research* (Second ed., pp. 541–565).

Leland, J. (2008, October 8). A spirit of belonging, inside and out. *The New York Times,* pp. D1, D6.

Maccoby, E. E. (1998). *The two sexes: Growing up apart, coming together.* Cambridge, MA: Harvard University Press.

Maccoby, E. E. (2007). Historical overview of socialization research and theory. In J. E. Grusec & P. D. Hasting (Eds.), *Handbook of socialization: Theory and research* (pp. 13–41). New York: Guilford Press.

McHale, S. M., & Crouter, A. C. (2003). How do children exert an impact on family life? In A. C. Crouter & A.

Booth (Eds.), *Children's influence on family dynamics: The neglected side of family relationships* (pp. 207–220). Mahwah, NJ: Lawrence Erlbaum Associates.

Miller, M. K., & Summers, A. (2007). Gender differences in video game characters' roles, appearances, and attire as portrayed in video game magazines. *Sex Roles, 57,* 733–742.

Ogburn, W. F. (1964). Cultural lag as theory. In O. D. Duncan (Ed.), *William F. Ogburn on culture and social change: Selected papers* (pp. 86–95). Chicago: University of Chicago Press.

Parke, R. D. (1996). *Fatherhood.* Cambridge, MA: Harvard University Press.

Parreñas, R. S. (2002). The care crisis in the Philippines: Children and transnational families in the new global economy. In B. Ehrenreich & A. R. Hochschild (Eds.), *Global woman: Nannies, maids, and sex workers in the new economy* (pp. 39–54). New York: Henry Holt.

Pascoe, C. J. (2007). *Dude, you're a fag.* Berkeley: University of California Press.

Pew Research Center. (2018). The narrowing, but persistent, gender gap in pay. Retrieved July 23, 2018, from http://www.pewresearch.org/fact-tank/2018/04/09/gender-pay-gap-facts/

Ridgeway, C. L. (2011). *Framed by gender: How gender inequality persists in the modern world.* Oxford: Oxford University Press.

Risman, B. J. (2004). Gender as social structure: Theory wrestling with activism. *Gender & Society, 18,* 429–450.

Risman, B. J. (2009). From doing to undoing: Gender as we know it. *Gender & Society, 23*(81–84).

Risman, B. J., & Seale, E. (2010). Betwixt and between: Gender contradictions among middle schoolers. In B. J. Risman (Ed.), *Families as they really are* (pp. 340–361). New York: W. W. Norton.

Ruddick, S. (1996). Reason's "femininity". In Ruddick, S. (1996). Reason's "femininity". In N. R. Goldberger, J. M. Tarule, B. M. Clinchy, & M. F. Belenky (Eds.), *Knowledge, difference, and power: Essays inspired by women's ways of knowing* (pp. 248–270). New York: Basic Books.

Sayer, L. C. (2015). Trends in women's and men's time use, 1965–2012: Back to the future? In S. M. McHale, V. King, J. Van Hook, & A. Booth (Eds.), *Gender and couple relationships* (pp. 43–78). Dordrecht: Springer.

Scott, J. W. (2000). Some reflections on gender and politics. In M. M. Ferree, J. Lorber, & B. B. Hess (Eds.), *Revisioning gender* (pp. 70–96). Walnut Creek, CA: AltaMira Press.

Statistica. (2018). Children and the media in the U.S. https://www.statista.com/topics/3980/children-and-media-in-the-us/

Steinmetz, K. (2014, June 9). America's transition. Time, 183, 38–46.

Thorne, B. (1993). *Gender play: Girls and boys in school.* Thorne, B. (1993). *Gender play: Girls and boys in school.* New Brunswick, NJ: Rutgers University Press. New Brunswick, NJ: Rutgers University Press.

Weinberg, D. (2007). Earnings by gender: Evidence from census 2000. *Monthly Labor Review* (July/August), 26–34.

West, C., & Zimmerman, D. H. (1987). Doing gender. *Gender and Society, 2,* 125–151.

West, C., & Zimmerman, D. H. (2009). Accounting for doing gender. *Gender & Society, 23,* 112–122.

U.S. Bureau of Labor Statistics. (2017). Women in the labor force: A databook. *Report 1071.* Retrieved October 13, 2018, from https://www.bls.gov/opub/reports/womens-databook/2017/home.htm

U.S. Bureau of Labor Statistics. (2018). Labor force statistics from the current population survey: 11. Employed persons by detailed occupation, sex, race, and Hispanic or Latino ethnicity. *Household Data Annual Averages* Retrieved October 13, 2018, from https://www.bls.gov/cps/cpsaat11.htm

Wootton, B. H. (1997). Gender differences in occupational employment. *Monthly Labor Review* (April), 15–24.

Chapter Four

Social Class and Family Inequality

Looking Forward

1. How have changes in the American economy since the 1970s affected families?
2. How have the family lives of people with college degrees diverged from the family lives of those with less education?
3. What factors determine the social class position of families?
4. Are there social class differences in kinship?
5. Are there social class differences in how parents raise children?

In the fall of 2018, the Census Bureau released its annual report on income and poverty (U.S. Bureau of the Census, 2018). Among other statistics, it showed that the median male full-time worker earned less in 2017 than did his counterpart in 1972. (The median is the midpoint: half of men had higher incomes and half had lower incomes.) Forty-five years had gone by in which the size of the American economy grew and the productivity of the work force improved, and yet the median worker had made no progress.

Who is that median worker? It is typically someone with a high school degree but no college degree. A generation ago, we called these workers "blue collar," after the iconic chambray shirt that workers wore to their factory jobs. Today, many of those factory jobs are gone. Every old city has seen the closing of factories that had formerly provided full-time jobs at good wages to workers without college educations. The Singer Sewing Machine Company dominated Elizabeth, New Jersey, from its founding in 1873 until it closed in 1982–its market reduced by ready-to-wear clothes and its competitive edge lost to plants in developing countries that paid workers far lower wages. One longtime worker told anthropologist Katherine Newman

> *I worked there forty-seven years and one month. I was one of many people in my family. My niece worked there. My two brothers, my father. You see, Singer's in the old days, it was a company that went from one generation to the other. (Newman, 1988)*

Advances in communications and transportation allowed managers to close plants such as Singer and import their goods from factories in developing nations in Latin America, South Asia (e.g., India), Southeast Asia (e.g., Indonesia or the Philippines), or East Asia (e.g., China) where wages were much lower. American factory workers lost their jobs, while opportunities grew for the well-educated managers who imported and marketed goods. In other industries, computers allowed employers to replace less-skilled workers with machines, including workers who used to answer the telephone. When I call Amtrak to make a train reservation, a perky voice answers by saying, "Hi, I'm Julie, Amtrak's automated agent," and continues to give me options until I yell "operator" several times and am finally connected to a human being. Julie could not function without a voice recognition system that depends upon fast, powerful computers and complex software that did not exist until about two decades ago. Before then, sales agents, most of whom did not have college degrees, answered the phones. Jobs like theirs are also disappearing. At the same time, jobs for the well-educated people who design systems like Amtrak's are increasing.

The result has been a **polarization** of the labor market since the 1970s: Job opportunities have increased for the most-educated workers and for the least-educated workers, while declining for workers with moderate levels of education and skill (Autor, 2010, 2014; Kalleberg, 2011). Managers (such as business executives) and professionals (such as lawyers) are still needed, as are the low-skilled service workers (such as restaurant staff) who cook their meals and the sales workers (such as cashiers) who sell them their clothes. Managers and professionals tend to have high salaries, while service and sales workers typically have low wages. Meanwhile the percentage of workers who have jobs in manufacturing has declined as plants like Singer closed. And the percentage who work in moderately skilled white-collar jobs like the people who used to answer Amtrak's phones has declined, too. The American occupational structure looks more and more like an hourglass, bulging at the top and the bottom but narrow in the middle (Massey & Hurst, 1998).

polarization (of the labor market) a growth of job opportunities at the top and bottom of the job market but a lessening of opportunities in the middle

Employment has also become more precarious, with less security and shorter periods of employment. For example, employers increasingly contract out work to temporary agencies instead of hiring their own workers. They downsize quickly when demand for their products or services drops. Ride-hailing services such as Uber consider their drivers to be independent contractors rather than employees and therefore do not provide the drivers with health insurance, vacations, or guaranteed hours. As a result of these developments, workers feel less loyalty to their employers and are more likely to change jobs when an opportunity arises. What some call the psychological contract between employers and employees—employers promise job security and advancement while employees promise loyalty and hard work—strengthened in the mid-twentieth century as American manufacturing prospered; but it has since broken down (Kalleberg, 2011). As a result of the greater polarization and precariousness of employment today, people feel anxious and insecure about jobs. Young people entering the labor market, especially those without college degrees, have less confidence that they can find a good job today. And that feeling of insecurity can lead them to postpone starting a family.

Families and the Economy

In fact, since 1980 only men with college degrees and women with at least some college courses have experienced substantial wage growth (Autor, 2014). The result is a great increase in what I will call **family inequality,** the extent to which some families obtain more income and wealth than do others. Moreover, we will see that families that are doing well are increasingly headed by married, well-educated couples, whereas the ones that are not doing as well are increasingly headed by cohabiting couples or single parents, most of them without a college education.

family inequality the extent to which some families obtain more income and wealth than do others

THE GROWING IMPORTANCE OF EDUCATION

Over time, the amount of education that people obtain has become a stronger predictor of the types of families that they live in and how well-off they are. In contrast, education was a much less important factor in determining family income in the

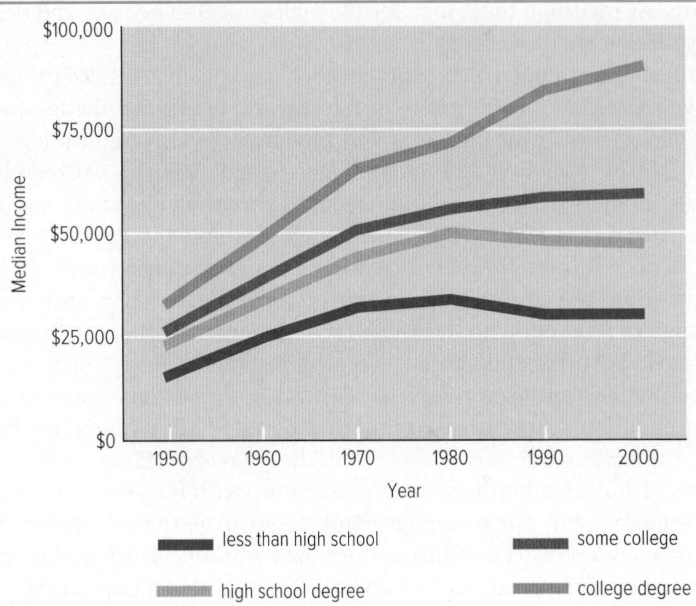

FIGURE 4.1 Adjusted family-of-four income medians, by education, 1950 to 2000. (*Source:* Fischer & Hout, 2006) Note: Income expressed in 1999 dollars and adjusted for family size (see Fischer & Hout, 2006).

middle of the twentieth century. Figure 4.1 shows the median income for a typical family of four, by education of the family head, for the period 1950 to 2000. You can see that the lines start closer together, and then in the 1970s they begin to move farther apart. As the lines diverge, the income advantage of families with college-educated family heads increases over families whose heads had less education; and the income disadvantage of families whose heads did not graduate from high school grows. In 1950 a family whose head had a college degree earned about twice as much as a family whose head had not completed high school. In 2000 that family earned about three times as much.

There is another important reason why the families of the college educated were pulling away from other families: they were more likely to have two parents in the household. Over the past several decades, single-parent families have increased in the United States due to rising rates of divorce and to more childbearing outside of marriage. But the increase has been faster among the less educated. Of all families with children whose heads had a college degree in 2016, 14 percent were headed by an unmarried mother. In contrast, 31 percent of families with children whose heads did not have a college degree were headed by an unmarried mother (U.S. Bureau of the Census, 2017b). Single-parent families must rely on the money that one parent brings in; moreover, women's earnings (most single-parent families are headed by women) are usually lower than men's. Two-parent families, in contrast, can pool the incomes of both adults. Since the 1980s, the median income of married-couple families in which both spouses work has increased much more rapidly than has the median income of other types of families (U.S. Bureau of the Census, 2017c). Because the families of the college educated could rely on two earners more than families with less education could, the gap between the incomes of the college educated and the less educated widened (Western, Bloome, & Percheski, 2008).

Quick Review

- Family inequality has increased over the past several decades.
- The kinds of jobs that used to allow high school educated adults to support a family have become scarce because of automation and the globalization of production.
- Widespread higher education is a recent phenomenon; high school degrees were uncommon and college degrees rare in 1900. College attendance rose rapidly in the second half of the 1900s.
- The incomes of families, where the head of the family is college educated, have risen more rapidly than the incomes of families when the head of the family is less educated.
- A person's education is a more important predictor of the kind of family life he or she leads than it was in the past.

DIVERGING DEMOGRAPHICS

Since about 1980, the family patterns of people with college degrees have moved in different directions from those of people with less education. Today, college-educated Americans are more likely to marry (although they take longer to do it), more likely to wait until after marriage to have a first child, and less likely to divorce than are less-educated Americans.

Age at Marriage People with four-year college degrees are displaying a pattern we might call catch-up marriage: Until age 25, relatively few of them marry, which is consistent with the societywide trend toward later marriage. But by age 30 they are slightly *more* likely to have married than are the less educated (Pew Research Center 2010). In other words, if you just followed a group of young adults until their mid-twenties, you would conclude that college graduates have lower marriage rates, and you might even predict that fewer of them will ever marry. You would be missing, however, the action that occurs later on, after men and women have completed their higher education and begun to establish careers, which more than compensates. By mid-life, four-year college graduates are more likely to have married than are the less educated (Martin, Astone, & Peters, 2014).

Childbearing Outside of Marriage Most college-educated women also wait to have children until after they are married—childbearing outside of marriage remains almost as uncommon among them as it was a half-century ago (Wu, 2017). Among women without college degrees, however, and especially among women who have never attended college, far fewer wait until marriage to have children than was the case a half-century ago. Figure 4.2 shows how the percentage of women who are married when they give birth varies by education. You can see how sharply the percentage rises as education increases. It is as if marriage and childbearing—so closely linked in Western culture—remain so only for those with bachelor's degrees. Among the moderately educated—those with a high school degree but not a bachelor's degree—being married at the time of birth seems optional, and for the least-educated—those without high school degrees—it is downright uncommon.

A study of young women in low-income Philadelphia-area neighborhoods found that many of them think it unlikely that they could find suitable marriage partners (Edin & Kefalas, 2005). They see few men who are earning steady, decent incomes—still a requirement for a husband in the United States—and who are free of the problems such as substance abuse and illegal activity that often come with limited

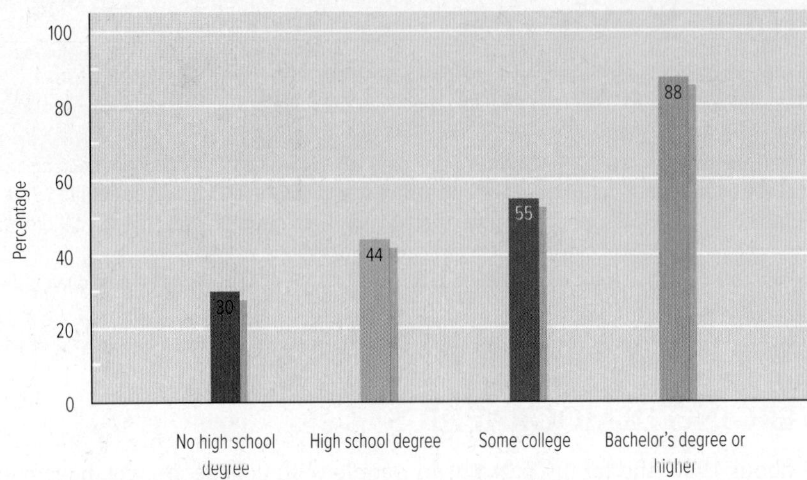

FIGURE 4.2
Percentage of women who were married when they gave birth, by education, 2010–2014. (*Source:* Wu, 2017)

earning potential. Consequently, they think that to postpone having a child until one is married carries a high risk of never having children—a risk they are unwilling to take. And they do not think that having a child outside of marriage will hurt them subsequently in the marriage market. Moreover, they do not expect to attend college. So they often follow the strategy of having children at a relatively early age without marrying and then thinking seriously about marriage many years later. The authors, Kathryn Edin and Maria Kefalas (2005), write

> *Unlike their wealthier sisters, who have the chance to go to college and embark on careers—attractive possibilities that provide strong motivation to put off having children—poor young women grab eagerly at the surest source of accomplishment within their reach: becoming a mother.*

Young women who are confident that they will graduate from college, on the other hand, can reasonably expect to find a suitable husband afterwards and to have children after they marry. Most of them can make the conventional strategy—finish your education, marry, and then have children—work successfully. Thus, the most- and least-educated groups tend to follow different strategies for ensuring that they will have children. The groups in the middle of the educational distribution ranges are somewhat more likely than the college educated to have children outside of marriage, and they increasingly do so in cohabiting unions rather than marriage. I will discuss the role of cohabitation in more detail in Chapter 7.

The Marriage Market Education has become a more important factor in who marries whom over the past half-century or so. Sociologists call the tendency of people to marry others similar to themselves **assortative marriage.** In the 1930s, religion was a more important determinant of who marries whom than was education: A college-educated Protestant was more likely to marry a Protestant high school graduate than to marry a college-educated Catholic. But since the middle of the twentieth century, college graduates have become much more likely to marry each other than to marry people with the same religion but less education. Religion remains a factor, but the college educated have largely

assortative marriage the tendency of people to marry others similar to themselves

removed themselves from the rest of the marriage market (Kalmijn, 1991). And since the 1970s, people who did not complete high school have become less likely to marry people with more education; rather, they have become more isolated in the marriage market (Schwartz & Mare, 2005). In the middle of the educational distribution, on the other hand, more marriage across educational groups exists (e.g., a marriage between a high school graduate who did not attend college and someone who attended college but did not get a bachelor's degree). In sum, the marriage market today seems to be stratified by education into three submarkets of people who choose partners primarily like themselves: people with bachelor's degrees; people who graduated from high school and may have attended college but did not get a bachelor's degree; and people who did not graduate from high school. To be sure, some marriages still cross these boundaries, but on the whole these divisions exist.

Divorce The trends in divorce also show a divergence. In the 1960s and 1970s the risk of divorce was rising for all groups, but starting about 1980 the risk began to decrease. The drop was greatest for college graduates. By the 2000s, college graduates had a substantially lower lifetime risk of divorce than the less educated (Schwartz & Han, 2014). So, as is the case with marriage, the risk of divorce also seems to be stratified, with a college-educated group at the low end. We will consider divorce in more detail in Chapter 12.

Putting the Differences Together To sum up this picture of diverging demographics, several trends in marriage, childbearing, and divorce suggest that the family patterns of individuals have moved in different directions in the past few decades:

- College graduates delay marriage but ultimately have a higher lifetime probability of marrying than do people without college degrees.
- People increasingly choose a spouse with a similar level of education.
- College graduates are much less likely to have a child without marrying.
- The chances of divorce have been declining more for college graduates than for the less educated.

It is likely that the restructuring of the American economy, which improved the life chances of those with the most education and reduced them for those with the least education, influenced this divergence. But it did not act alone; rather, a broad cultural shift probably played a role: Alternatives to marriage (having a child as a single parent or cohabiting) have become more acceptable, and the meaning of marriage has changed. I will return to the theme of cultural change in marriages and partnerships in Chapter 7.

In any event, people with different levels of education increasingly experience the life stage of emerging adulthood in different ways. The college educated continue their schooling into their twenties, postpone both marriage and childbearing, but eventually marry and have a lower risk of divorce. Individuals who did not graduate from high school are increasingly isolated in the marriage market, and are much more likely to have a child prior to marrying. In addition, when and if they marry, their risk of divorce is high. Finally, individuals with a high school degree and perhaps some college credits are in the middle range with regard to marriage and childbearing.

Defining Social Class

social class an ordering of all persons in a society according to their degrees of economic resources, prestige, and privilege

life chances the resources and opportunities that people have to provide themselves with material goods and favorable living conditions

status group a group of people who share a common style of life and often identify with each other

It's clear from the previous sections that people who differ in the level of education they have attained also tend to experience the job market and family life differently. When sociologists think about differences in economic resources, they often use the concept of **social class,** an ordering of all persons in a society according to their degrees of economic resources, prestige, and privilege. All agree that income and wealth are core elements of this ordering. But the German sociologist Max Weber added other standards (Gerth & Mills, 1946). One is the broader idea of **life chances,** the resources and opportunities that people have to provide themselves with material goods and favorable living conditions. People's life chances may be augmented by the higher education they obtain or their family's contacts in the labor market. Their life chances may be limited by discrimination or racial segregation. So education can be considered an economic resource, too. A second concept is a more subjective category: the **status group,** a group of people who share a common style of life and often identify with each other. They are sometimes distinguished by prestige—the honor and status a person receives—such as the prestige of medical doctors or university professors. They often differ in their level of privilege—that is, their access to special advantages such as attendance at elite universities. Are the concepts of social class and status groups useful in helping us understand the variations in family life today?

SOCIAL CLASSES AND STATUS GROUPS

ideal type a hypothetical model that consists of the most significant characteristics, in extreme form, of a social phenomenon

Let us examine the four social class categories commonly used in public discussions and sociological research: upper class, middle class, working class, and lower class. But think of them as ideal types rather than concrete realities. Introduced by Weber, the **ideal type** refers to a hypothetical model that consists of the most significant characteristics, in extreme form, of a social phenomenon. It is useful for understanding social life, even though any real example of the phenomenon may not have all the characteristics of the ideal type.

The Four-Class Model Americans understand the four-category scheme, but they overwhelmingly say they are either middle class or working class. For instance, in the 2016 General Social Survey (GSS), a biennial national survey of adults, 3 percent of the respondents said they were upper class, 40 percent said middle class, 47 percent said working class, and 10 percent said lower class (Smith, Davern, Freese, & Hout 2017). Both extremes apparently sound unpleasant to people, probably because of the stigma of being "lower class" and the embarrassment of admitting to being "upper class." By most reasonable criteria, however, the lower class is larger than 9 percent. For instance, 12.3 percent of Americans had incomes below the official poverty level in 2017 (U.S. Bureau of the Census, 2018).

upper-class families families that have amassed wealth and privilege and that often have substantial prestige as well

There is little consensus on the size of the upper class or on just how to define it. In general, **upper-class families** are those that have amassed wealth and privilege and that often have substantial prestige as well. They tend to own large, spacious homes, to possess expensive clothes and furnishings, to have substantial investment holdings, and to be recognized as part of the social and cultural elite of their communities. Upper-class husbands tend to be owners or senior managers of large corporations, banks, or law firms. Their wives are less likely to work for pay outside the home than women in other social classes, and they may be instrumental in maintaining ties to wealthy kin.

Middle-class families are those whose connection to the economy provides them with a secure, comfortable income and allows them to live well above a subsistence level. Middle-class families can usually afford privileges such as a nice house, a new car, a college education for the children, fashionable clothes, a vacation at the seashore, and so forth. The jobs that middle-class men and women hold usually require some college education and are performed mainly in offices and businesses. Middle-class men tend to hold higher-paying jobs such as a lawyer, pharmacist, engineer, sales representative, or midlevel manager at a corporation. Jobs such as these usually have some prestige and include fringe benefits such as health insurance, paid vacations, paid sick leave, and retirement pensions. Women in general are underrepresented in the higher-paying professional and managerial occupations, although their numbers are growing in fields such as law and medicine. Women professionals still tend to be found in occupations that require a college education, such as nursing and teaching, but that don't pay as much as male-dominated professions.

middle-class families families whose connection to the economy provides them with a secure, comfortable income and allows them to live well above a subsistence level

Working-class families are those whose incomes can provide reliably for the minimum needs of what people see as a decent life: a modest house or an apartment, one or two cars, enough money to enroll children at a state or community college, and so forth. Working-class men tend to hold manual jobs in factories, automobile repair shops, construction sites, and so forth, that involve little or no authority over others. Layoffs are more common in manual occupations than in the office and business jobs middle-class men tend to have, so working-class men are more vulnerable to periods of unemployment. Moreover, working-class men and women are less likely to work a full week and have fringe benefits. As women's educational attainment has overtaken men's, women in working-class families may work at professional jobs such as nurse or teacher and earn more than their husbands.

working-class families families whose income can reliably provide only for the minimum needs of what other people see as a decent life

Lower-class families are those whose connection to the economy is so tenuous that they cannot provide reliably for a decent life, either because they work steadily at low-paying jobs (the so-called working poor) or because they are frequently unemployed. They may live in deteriorated housing in neighborhoods with high crime rates. They may not be able to afford adequate clothing for winter, and they may need government-issued food stamps to purchase enough food. They are susceptible to homelessness (see the boxed feature *Families and Public Policy:* Homelessness, by the Numbers). Lower-class men, who have little education and few occupational skills, can find jobs that pay only at or slightly above the minimum wage and that have few, if any, fringe benefits and little security.

lower-class families families whose connection to the economy is so tenuous that they cannot reliably provide for a decent life

Three Status Groups Although these four categories seem ingrained in both social scientific research and popular thought, the definitions are so broad that it is very difficult to draw a clear distinction between middle-class and working-class families or between working-class families and lower-class families. Moreover, given the increasing importance of education, it may be more useful to group people by the amount of education they have. These groupings are more like Weber's status groups. The first group comprises people with a college degree. I will draw this boundary based on two arguments: First, the restructuring of the American economy has increased the life chances of those with college degrees to a much greater extent than those without college degrees; and second, the college educated form a

Families and Public Policy

Homelessness, by the Numbers

Homelessness is the kind of issue that tugs at people's heartstrings. Whether they believe that poverty is the fault of the individual (the poor don't work hard enough) or of society (too little opportunity, too much discrimination), most people think that everyone ought to have a place to sleep. They are troubled by homelessness and at once appalled and fascinated by reports of individuals and families who live in the streets or in shelters. But although the problem has been long on empathy, it has been short on numbers. Ever since the issue gained currency a few decades ago, good information on the homeless population has been scarce. It is, after all, difficult to count people who sleep in alleyways and move in and out of shelters.

Only in the past 10 or 15 years can we finally get good estimates of the homeless. That's because in 2007 the Department of Housing and Urban Development set up a system of reports from community institutions across the country. On a single night in January 2017, according to the most recent report, there were 553,742 homeless people sleeping in shelters or on the streets (U.S. Department of Housing and Urban Development, 2017). One-third of them were families with children. Homelessness is an urban phenomenon. For instance, nearly one out of four homeless people lived in New York or Los Angeles. Nearly half of all people experiencing homelessness identified as white; 45 percent identified as African American.

That is the one-night snapshot. We can also look over a year's worth of time. In 2016, 1.42 million individuals used shelters for the homeless or transitional housing at some point during the previous year. Of this total, about one-third were families with children; the rest arrived without children (U.S. Department of Housing and Urban Development, 2017). Shelter families overwhelmingly consist of single mothers and their children. Single parents are more vulnerable to homelessness because they do not have a second adult earner to help pay the rent.

What about lifetime levels of homelessness? A 2012 national survey of older Americans found that 6.2 percent of the baby boom generation (born between 1946 and 1964) had experienced a period of homelessness during their lives. Blacks were much more likely to have experienced homelessness (16.8 percent reported a spell) than were Hispanics (8.1 percent) or non-Hispanic whites (4.8 percent) (Fusaro, Levy, & Shaefer, 2018).

The number of homeless people counted in the single-night estimates has decreased by 14 percent since the first assessment in 2007. The decline may reflect more effective government programs, which now emphasize putting individuals into supportive housing first and dealing with the personal or family problems after that (Lee, Tyler, and Wright, 2010).

Either of the two estimates of the size of the homeless population, the number homeless on a night in January or the number who rely on a shelter during the course of the year, is a small percentage of the total population with incomes below the federal poverty line. This doesn't mean that homelessness isn't a serious problem or that we should ignore it. On the contrary, we should strengthen our efforts to combat it. But the numbers do suggest that for every poor homeless person there are many poor people who are precariously housed—behind on the rent or trying the patience of a friend whose living room couch they are sleeping on. Helping this larger number of people stay housed is an important part of the solution, for if the precariously housed lose their places to live, their numbers could overwhelm the already-stressed shelter system. The homeless problem and the larger poverty problem are not as separate as they may seem.

Ask Yourself

1. Has anyone in your family ever been forced to move into a friend's or relative's home, or perhaps into a homeless shelter? If so, what caused the crisis?
2. What can the government do to prevent families from becoming homeless? What can families themselves do?

status group, in the Weberian sense of sharing a common style of life, because their patterns of marriage, divorce, and childbearing appear to be diverging from the patterns of people without college degrees. About one-third of all adults between the ages of 25 and 54 have a four-year college degree. In addition, some individuals who have a two-year college degree are able to attain this style of life.

The second group comprises people who graduated from high school and most of those who have attended college but did not obtain a four-year degree; they are the most difficult to categorize in terms of social class because they sometimes share the characteristics of the groups above and below them. The third group comprises people who did not graduate from high school, whose family patterns in some respects are diverging from both groups above them. These three status groups are roughly equivalent to what people think of as the "middle class," "working class," and "lower class," respectively; but these labels are so imprecise that I will avoid them for the most part.

Quick Review

- Social scientists use the concept of social class to order all individuals in a society.
- Max Weber maintained that one needs to consider status groups as well as classes to understand how a society is stratified.
- Wives and husbands both consider each other's income, education, and occupation in identifying their social class, but wives do so more than husbands.
- Sociologists typically assume that four broad social classes exist: the upper class, middle class, working class, and lower class.
- Differences in life chances and styles of living suggest that three status groups , people with a college degree, people who have graduated from high school and may have attended college, and people who have not graduated from high school, may be as useful as the four broad social classes.

Social Class Differences in Family Life

Earlier in the chapter, Figure 4.1 showed that the median incomes of families with different levels of education have diverged since the 1970s: The incomes of families whose heads are college educated have risen compared to other families, and the incomes of families whose heads have not completed high school have fallen compared to other families. Subsequent sections showed that parallel patterns of marriage, divorce, and childbearing have diverged. There are other long-standing social class differences that are important but have not necessarily diverged. One is the kind of assistance family members received from relatives living in their household or elsewhere. A second is the way parents approach child rearing. They are not completely different, of course; similarities run across status groups that would be apparent to someone visiting from a non-Western culture where, for instance, parents are heavily involved in helping their children choose spouses, newly married couples move in with the husband's family, and adult children care for their aged parents in their homes.

ASSISTANCE FROM KIN

As differences in whether people have children before marrying show, there is variation around the norm of the two-parent-and-children conjugal family. Families differ not only in terms of marriage but also in terms of their ties to other kin, both the kin that a person is born to or acquires at marriage and the kin that some people construct from distant relatives, friends, partners, partners' families, and so forth. These kinship patterns differ by social class, although some of the class differences appear to be fading or overstated.

Kinship among the Poor and Near Poor A large literature dating back to the Great Depression shows that a husband's place in the family is heavily dependent on whether he has a job. In the cultures of all industrialized nations, men have been viewed as the main earners; providing a steady income has been seen as their responsibility. Rightly or wrongly, women's economic contribution has been viewed as secondary, although this perception may be changing as women increasingly work outside the home and in some cases out-earn their husbands. When wives choose not to work for pay, or when they lose their jobs, they are not looked down upon. But when husbands lose their jobs, as happens frequently to husbands in poor and near-poor families, their authority in their homes decreases, their self-respect declines, and other family members treat them with less respect as well. Chapter 9 examines in more detail how a husband's unemployment affects a married couple and their children.

Chronic Poverty and Kin Networks When a man's unemployment problems are chronic–when he is unable or unwilling to find steady employment over many years–he may be viewed, and may view himself, as having failed to fulfill a central role in his life. In a community with many chronically unemployed men, young mothers rely less on marriage and more on other kinship ties for support. Commonly, in poverty areas, young mothers, many of them unmarried, receive help from their own mothers in raising their children. They may also get money or assistance from sisters and brothers, friends, and, sometimes, the fathers of their children. The result is **women-centered kinship,** a kinship structure in which the strongest bonds of support and caregiving occur among a network of women, most of them relatives, who may live in more than one household. Mothers, grandmothers, sisters, and other female kin hold most of the authority over children and provide most of the supervision.

women-centered kinship a kinship structure in which the strongest bonds of support and caregiving occur among a network of women, most of them relatives, who may live in more than one household

The extended kinship ties of the women-centered network help its members survive the hardships of poverty. If the members of a household have little to eat or are evicted from their homes, relatives and friends in their network will provide whatever assistance they can. Sisters or aunts who are themselves poor will nevertheless give food or money because they know that in the future they may need emergency help. In this way, the kinship networks of the poor spread the burdens of poverty, cushioning its impact on any one household and allowing its members to get by from day to day. In a widely cited study of The Flats, a low-income African American neighborhood in the Midwest, anthropologist Carol Stack found that individuals could draw upon a complex network of relatives and friends that extended over many households (Stack, 1974).

The Limits of Kin Networks Yet membership in such a kinship network is not without cost. Because an individual's meager income must be shared with many others, it is difficult for her or him to rise out of poverty. Stack described what happened when an older couple unexpectedly inherited $1,500. At first, they wished to use the money for a down payment on a house. Then other members of their network, upon learning of the windfall, asked for help. Several relatives needed train fare to attend a funeral in another state; another needed $25 so her telephone wouldn't be turned off; a sister was about to be evicted because of overdue rent. Moreover, the public assistance office cut their children off welfare temporarily. Within six weeks, the inheritance was gone. The couple acquiesced to these requests because they knew they might need assistance in the future. Even someone who finds a good job may not withdraw from a network unless she is confident that the job will last a long time.

Moreover, it's not clear how widespread these networks are today. Studies show that very disadvantaged parents tend to receive less support from kin, either because the people in their networks have fewer resources to provide or because they are not in a network (Harknett & Hartnett, 2011). In general, low-income parents are more likely to receive practical support from their kin, such as child care assistance, than to receive financial support, whereas middle-class parents are more likely to receive financial support (Swartz, 2009). Assistance from kin takes different forms among the poor and nonpoor but seems to be important for both.

Kinship among the Nonpoor The core of kinship among the nonpoor in the United States has been the conjugal family of wife, husband, and children, at least ideally (Schneider & Smith, 1973). The married couple is expected to spend their income on their children and themselves rather than to provide financial assistance to siblings or other relatives. Any assets or savings are passed from parents to children, rather than being spread throughout a kin network. Income sharing is not as necessary, to be sure, because the standards of living of kin tend to be higher than among the poor. Yet standards of living are higher in part *because* it is expected that the conjugal family will spend its savings on a down payment for a house rather than doling it out to relatives who need train fare to attend funerals or to pay bills and *because* it is expected that the family will move away from kin, if necessary, to pursue better job opportunities.

Adults in nonpoor families feel most obligated to assist their parents and their children. These vertical kinship ties—up and down the generations from parents to children to grandchildren—engender stronger feelings of obligations than do aunts, uncles, nieces, nephews, and cousins (Rossi & Rossi, 1990). The image of middle-class kinship suggested by these findings is of a tall, solid tree trunk with skinny branches: The vertical axis is strong as one moves from parents to children to grandchildren, but the horizontal links are weaker as one moves from parents to uncles, or from children to nieces (Bengtson, 2001). Resources are passed from a person's parents to his or her spouse and children, and then to the grandchildren. Assistance to elderly parents is likely to be much more substantial and more common than assistance to elderly aunts and uncles.

SOCIAL CLASS AND CHILD REARING

Families also differ by social class in how they raise their children. In general, college-educated parents often act in ways that encourage autonomy and independence, whereas less-educated parents more often encourage conformity and obedience to (and distrust of) authority. Not all parents fit this pattern, of course; there is substantial variation within social classes. Moreover, as the twentieth century progressed, parents in all social classes moved toward emphasizing independence (Alwin, 1988). On average, though, intriguing class differences remain.

Social Class and Parental Values Beginning in the 1960s, Melvin Kohn pioneered a line of research showing the connections between the conditions a person experiences on the job and his or her child-rearing values (Kohn, 1969). He noted that working-class employees (by which he meant blue-collar industrial workers), for the most part, are closely supervised, work with physical objects (as would carpenters), and perform simple tasks repetitively (as on an automobile assembly line). It is important for workers in these jobs to obey their supervisors and to accept the discipline of doing repetitive tasks. In contrast, middle-class workers (by which he meant white-collar professional and technical workers), are less closely supervised, usually work with data (as would computer programmers) or people (as would personnel managers), and perform a variety of tasks (as would physicians). Middle-class jobs, Kohn argued, encourage more independence than working-class jobs and often reward creativity and individual initiative.

When working-class and middle-class parents are asked to select the most important characteristics that children should have, their preferences reflect their occupational positions. Working-class parents are more likely to select obedience to authority, conformity, and good manners, whereas middle-class parents are more likely to select independence, self-direction, curiosity, and responsibility (Alwin, 1990). Working-class parents emphasize the kinds of characteristics their children would need if they were to enter blue-collar jobs. To work on an assembly line for 40 years requires obedience and conformity; someone who is creative and independent might have a harder time tolerating the job. In contrast, to be a successful manager requires independence and initiative. Thus, each class socializes its children to fill the same positions their parents have filled. Because of his or her conformist upbringing, a child from a working-class family may be less successful as a manager than a self-directed child from the middle class. In this way, socialization by parents both is influenced by and helps to perpetuate the social class divisions in the United States.

Concerted Cultivation versus Natural Growth More recently, sociologist Annette Lareau intensively studied 12 families with third-graders and found class differences in the way parents view the task of raising children (Lareau, 2011). These differences, which are consistent with Kohn's research, applied to both African American and European American children in her sample; at least for these families, class, more than race, determined parents' approaches to child rearing. Lareau defined a group of families in which the parents had jobs requiring college or more advanced degrees as "middle class" and a group with jobs requiring less education as "working class" or "poor." Middle-class families tended to actively enhance children's talents, opinions, and skills, a cultural style she calls "concerted cultivation"—as if parents were cultivating a garden so its plants would grow as well as possible. Working-class (and poor) parents, on the other hand, did not focus on developing their children's special talents; rather, they emphasized providing a safe environment and love and letting children grow on their own. Lareau calls this cultural pattern the "accomplishment of natural growth." In everyday life, these different styles affected children's time use, language use, and family ties. Middle-class parents filled their children's weeks with a whirlwind of formal activities such as lessons, sports, tutoring, and play dates, whereas working-class parents were often content to let their children hang out at home or in the neighborhood. Middle-class parents talked with their children more, reasoning with them rather than telling them what to do. Children from working-class and poor families had closer ties to uncles, aunts, and children than did middle-class children.

Moreover, other studies show that highly educated parents spend more time with their children and focus more on developmentally enriching activities (Thomsen, 2015; Sayer, Gauthier, & Furstenberg, 2004). They also spend more money on their children's development; and the difference is increasing: The gap between what parents in the top 20 percent of the income distribution spent on their children and what parents in the bottom 20 percent spent tripled between the early

1970s and the mid-2000s (Kornrich & Furstenberg 2013). And the sensibilities that children learn may stay with them through their own marriages, according to a study of cross-class marriages in which one spouse came from a blue-collar background and one from a white-collar background (Streib, 2015). Their parenting styles often reflected the social class that they were raised in, despite years of marriage to someone with a different style.

Because of greater parental investments of time and money, middle-class children have advantages in school and, later, in the job market: They are more assertive with authority figures such as teachers and coaches, they are more verbal, and they have a more independent sense of self. Working-class and poor children (and their parents) are less likely to speak up for themselves and challenge authority; they are more deferential and less trusting of authority. Middle-class children gain a sense that they are entitled to a stimulating, rewarding daily life, whereas working-class and poor children get a sense that their opportunities are constrained. So as they grow up, middle-class children are in a better position to achieve a middle-class lifestyle themselves. The main point, for Lareau as for Kohn, is that the social class of the family you grow up in affects the way you think about school, authority figures, and work.

CLASS, RACE, AND DEATHS OF DESPAIR

As the intersectionality theorists would remind us, the ways in which class affects people's lives may vary among racial or ethnic groups. One counterintuitive example is trends in death rates. For decades, rates of death in the United States from all causes fell as health care improved and standards of living rose. But since the late 1990s, death rates for whites without college degrees have stagnated or increased from causes related to alcohol abuse, such as cirrhosis of the liver, drug abuse, such as fatal overdoses, and suicide (Case & Deaton 2015, 2017). In contrast, death rates for African Americans declined until 2014 and since then have leveled off, while death rates for and Hispanics have continued to decline (Shiels et al., 2017; U.S. National Center for Health Statistics, 2019). A study that compared two national surveys, one conducted from 1995 to 1996 and the other from 2011 to 2014, found a deterioration in psychological health that was strongest for whites of low socioeconomic status (Goldman, Glei, & Weinstein, 2018).

Why might less-educated whites, but not less-educated African Americans or Hispanics, be more prone to abuse alcohol and drugs to the point of death in recent years? it's a puzzling question because we know that whites still have higher incomes, on average, than African Americans or Hispanics. One possible explanation comes from **reference group theory,** the idea that in order to understand how people think and behave, one must know to whom, or to what, they are comparing themselves (Merton, 1968). And in thinking about how their lives are going, people often compare their standard of living with the standard of living that their parents had (Cherlin, 2016b).

reference group theory the idea that to understand how people behave, one needs to know to whom, or to what, they are comparing themselves

When less-educated whites make these mental comparisons, they can often remember fathers who benefitted from the strong industrial economy of the mid-to-late twentieth century. Although high school educated white women haven't experienced the same reversals in the job market, they may look at their husbands—or, if they are single, to the men they choose not to marry—and reason that their married parents' standard of living was better when they were growing up. In contrast, African Americans, received a smaller share of the blue-collar prosperity of the era. They may look back to a time when discrimination deprived their parents of equal opportunities. Many Hispanics may look back to the lower standard of living their parents experienced in their countries of origin. In sum, whites are likely to compare themselves to a reference group that leads them to feel worse off. Blacks and Hispanics compare themselves to reference groups that may make them feel better off. Consistent with this idea, the national study of psychological health mentioned earlier also found that whites were more likely to say that they were doing worse than their parents than were economically comparable African Americans and Hispanics (Glie, Goldman, & Weinstein, 2018).

Sociologist Timothy Nelson and I saw this pattern of thinking in interviews we did with non-college-educated men (Cherlin, 2014). White men were more likely to make unfavorable comparisons with the past. A 35-year-old white man who did construction jobs said, "It's much harder for me as a grown man than it was for my father." He remembered his father saying that back when he was 35, "'I had a house and I had five kids or four kids.' You know, 'Look where I was at.' And I'm like, 'Well, Dad, things have changed.'" Blacks were more optimistic, even though they may be earning less than their white counterparts today. One man told us, "I think there are better opportunities now because first of all, the economy's changing. The color barrier is not as harsh as it was back then." It is possible, then, that the rise in self-destructive substance abuse among less-educated whites reflects a profound disappointment that the adult lives that they expected to live when they were growing up are now out of reach—a casualty of the outsourcing and computerization of the blue-collar jobs that sustained their parents' generation.

Quick Review

- Poor families often depend on women-centered kinship networks, in large part because men cannot consistently earn enough to support a family.
- Nonpoor families typically center on a wife, husband, and children who have obligations to their parents and their grandchildren but are otherwise independent of kin.
- Middle-class parents tend to emphasize independence and self-direction in raising children.
- Working-class parents tend to emphasize conformity and obedience to authority in raising children.
- Middle-class parents are increasing the amount of money they invest in their children's development.
- Deaths from substance abuse have risen among less-educated whites, possibly due to the difficulty of attaining the standard of living of their parents.

Social Class and the Family

In the middle of the twentieth century, most families with children, rich or poor, had two parents and one earner. As recently as 1973, 51 percent of all poor families consisted of married couples; by 2016, 38 percent were married-couple families (U.S. Bureau of the Census, 2017a). Meanwhile, a majority of well-off families have two parents and two earners. Thus, the association between the type of family you live in and your social class position is stronger today than in the past. This great sorting out of families by social class has occurred for both economic and cultural reasons. On the economic side, two developments stand out: the movement of married women into the workforce and the declining employment prospects of men without college educations. On the cultural side are the rise in expressive individualism and people's higher aspirations for material goods.

In the 1960s and 1970s, social commentators debated whether it was "necessary" for married women to work. After all, standards of living had been far lower in the first half of the twentieth century, and yet few married women had worked outside the home. However, the economic slide that gained momentum in the 1980s more or less ended that debate. Among those without college educations, objections to married women working outside the home faded as decent-paying entry-level blue-collar jobs—the kind of jobs young husbands used to take—dwindled. Whereas in the 1970s wives' employment was seen by many as a sign of a husband's failure to provide adequately for his family, now it is seen as a necessary and acceptable contribution.

Among couples with college educations, the employment situation has been better; still, only two-earner couples have been beating inflation consistently. Moreover, the price of housing has risen far faster than wages, placing the American dream of homeownership out of reach of more and more single-earner couples. In the 1950s and 1960s, payments on a median-priced home required just 15 to 18 percent of the average 30-year-old man's income. That figure rose to 20 percent in 1973 and then doubled to 40 percent in 1987 (Levy & Michel, 1991). Housing affordability deteriorated further through the 2000s (U.S. Bureau of the Census, 2013). Consequently, for college-educated couples, too, wives' employment was seen as necessary and acceptable. (In the mid-2000s the availability of so-called subprime mortgage loans to families with modest incomes may have created the illusion that homes were more affordable, but many of the families who took out these loans defaulted on the payments, triggering the Great Recession of the late 2000s.)

Concurrently, adults in a more individualistic culture were freer to choose not to marry or to end marriages. Having children outside of marriage became more acceptable. People's expectations about what constitutes a good life also changed. Young middle-class couples could, in theory, aspire only to the standard of living of the late 1940s and early 1950s—which for many consisted of an apartment or a small, one-story home, one car, a clothesline in the backyard for drying the laundry, one telephone, no stereo system, few restaurant meals, no airplane travel, and, of course, no DVD players or computers—and still keep one parent home all day. This is not an appealing prospect in a country where people have gotten used to a higher standard of living that is promoted by advertising and reinforced by the media.

With regard to what women and men do in families, however, class differences may have lessened over the past few decades. To be sure, the women-centered kinship networks of low-income families remain distinctive. Yet not all low-income families have functioning networks, and the number of single-mother families has increased among the nonpoor as well. The distinctive working-class gender segregation and resistance to wives' employment, presented in several widely read mid-twentieth-century studies (Bott, 1957; Gans, 1962; Rubin, 1976), seems to have faded. Child-rearing patterns do still seem different, with college-educated parents instilling in their children a sense of independence and of entitlement to a rewarding life, while less-educated parents tend to stress obedience, safety, and natural growth. These class differences in child rearing could affect the quality of education that children obtain and the type of occupations they will eventually get.

Until the 1980s, families at all educational levels seemed to move in parallel as rates of marriage, divorce, and childbearing rose and fell in waves. Since then, however, we see evidence that families at the top and bottom of the social ordering are moving in different directions. The college educated appear to be consolidating their gains in the restructured economy: Young adults postpone marriage while obtaining advanced educations, then they marry spouses who also have college degrees, and only then do they have children. Their marriages have become more stable in recent years, quite possibly reflecting their improved economic position. In contrast, individuals without high school degrees seem increasingly marginalized. They are isolated in the marriage market, as if shunned by those with better economic prospects. They often have children years before marrying, if they marry at all. And their marriages still have a high risk of divorce. These are not encouraging trends in a nation that thinks of itself as a land of equal opportunity.

Social class is not the only way that American society classifies families. Racial and ethnic distinctions are also frequently made, and it is to these differences in family patterns that we now turn.

Looking Back

1. **How have changes in the American economy since the 1970s affected families?** The restructuring of the U.S. economy since the 1970s has caused a shortage of well-paid semiskilled and skilled jobs that do not require a college education—the kind of jobs less-educated young men used to rely on to support their wives and children—and has increased the importance of education. Since the 1970s, incomes have increased the most among families headed by college graduates and the least among families headed by persons who did not graduate from high school.

2. **How have the family lives of people at the top and bottom of the social order diverged recently?** People with college educations are more likely to marry than are people with less education, although they marry at later ages. Their marriages are less likely to end in divorce, and they are less likely to have a child outside of marriage. In general, people are more likely than in the past to marry someone with a similar level of education. The typical life course of people who obtain college degrees involves completing one's education, then marrying someone else who is a college graduate, and then having children. For a person who does not graduate from high school, the life course may involve having children well before marrying, having a restricted choice of marriage partners, and having a high risk of divorce if one does marry at all.

3. **What factors determine the social class position of families?** Sociologists agree that income and wealth are important. In addition, they examine whether the worker belongs to a status group with shared levels of prestige, privilege, and lifestyle. Since many families have more than one earner, the social class position of families can be ambiguous. Therefore, the four social classes that are usually defined—upper, middle, working, and lower—should be considered as hypothetical models (ideal types). Recent trends suggest that it may be useful to use people's educational levels to define a set of three status groups.

4. **Are there social class differences in kinship?** Poor and near-poor families are distinctive because many of them consist of single-parent units embedded in kin networks although these networks may be less prevalent than in the past. These networks share resources in order to ease the burdens of poverty. Nonpoor families consist mainly of two-parent households that are relatively independent of kin except for vertical ties to grandparents and grandchildren.

5. **Are there differences across classes in how parents raise children?** Poor and working-class parents tend to emphasize obedience and conformity in raising children, whereas middle-class parents are more likely to emphasize independence. As a result, sociologists suggest, poor and working-class children are not as assertive with authority figures such as teachers. They also show less self-direction and independent initiative. Middle-class children develop a sense that they are entitled to a rewarding life. These child-rearing differences tend to steer poor and working-class children toward blue-collar and service work and to steer middle-class children toward professional and managerial work.

Study Questions

1. How has the movement of factory production to other countries affected American family life?
2. How has the growth of single-parent families affected the incomes of families with different levels of education?
3. What are the strengths and limitations of the four-class (upper, middle, working, lower) model of social status in the United States?
4. What is a "status group" and how does it relate to the concept of social class?
5. How has the role of education in the marriage market changed over the past several decades?
6. Why might a young woman with little education choose to have a child without marrying?
7. What are the costs and benefits of the sharing networks commonly used by low-income families?
8. Why might working-class whites be more despairing about economic opportunities than working-class African Americans or Hispanics?

Key Terms

assortative marriage 100
family inequality 97
ideal type 102
life chances 102
lower-class families 103
middle-class families 103
polarization (of the labor market) 97
reference group theory 109
social class 102
status group 102
upper-class families 102
women-centered kinship 106
working-class families 103

Thinking about Families

The Public Family	The Private Family
What obligations do you think extended kin like grandparents, uncles, and aunts have to aid parents and children?	**How are the relationships between men and women different from social class to social class?**

References

Alwin, D. F. (1988). From obedience to autonomy: Changes in traits desired in children, 1924–1978. *Public Opinion Quarterly, 52*(1), 33–52.

Alwin, D. F. (1990). Historical changes in parental orientations to children. In N. Mandell (Ed.), *Sociological studies of child development* (pp. 65–86). Greenwich, CT: JAI Press.

Autor, D. H. (2010). The polarization of job opportunities in the U.S. Labor market: Implications for employment and earnings. *Brookings Institution: The Hamilton Project.* Retrieved May 23, 2014, from http://www.brookings.edu/~/media/Files/rc/papers/2010/04_jobs_autor/04_jobs_autor.pdf

Autor, D. H. (2014). Skills, education, and the rise of earnings inequality among the "other 99 percent." *Science, 344*(6186), 843–851.

Bengtson, V. L. (2001). Beyond the nuclear family: The increasing importance of multigenerational bonds. *Journal of Marriage and Family, 63,* 1–16.

Bott, E. (1957). *Family and social network.* London: Tavistock.

Case, A., & Deaton, A. (2015). Rising morbidity and mortality in midlife among white non-Hispanic Americans in the 21st century. *Proceedings of the National Academy of Sciences, 112*(49), 15078–15083.

Case, A., & Deaton, A. (2017). Mortality and morbidity in the 21st century. *Brookings papers on economic activity, 2017,* 397.

Cherlin, A. J. (2014). *Labor's love lost: The rise and fall of the working-class family in America.* New York: Russell Sage Foundation.

Cherlin, A. J. (2016, February 22). Why are white death rates rising? *The New York Times,* P. A19.

Edin, K., & Kefalas, M. J. (2005). *Promises I can keep: Why poor women put motherhood before marriage.* Berkeley: University of California Press.

Fischer, C. S., & Hout, M. (2006). *Century of difference: How America changed in the last one hundred years.* New York: Russell Sage Foundation

Fusaro, V., Levy, H., & Shaefer, H. L. 2018. Racial and ethnic disparities in the lifetime prevalence of homelessness in the United States. *Demography, 55*(6), 2119–21218.

Gans, H. J. (1962). *The urban villagers: Group and class in the lives of Italian-Americans.* New York: The Free Press.

Gerth, H. H., & Mills, C. W. (1946). *From Max Weber: Essays in sociology.* New York: Oxford University Press.

Glie, D. A., Goldman, N., & Weinstein, M. (2018). Perception has its own reality: Subjective versus objective measures of economic distress. *Population and Development Review, 44(4),* 695–722.

Goldman, N., Glei, D., & Weinstein, M. (2018). Declining mental health among disadvantaged Americans. *Proceedings of the National Academy of Sciences of the United States of America, 115*(7290–7295).

Harknett, K. S., & Hartnett, C. S. (2011). Who lacks support and why? An examination of mothers' personal safety nets. *Journal of Marriage and Family, 73*(4), 861–875.

Kalleberg, A. L. (2011). *Good jobs, bad jobs: The rise of polarized and precarious employment systems in the United States, 1970s to 2000s.* New York: Russell Sage Foundation.

Kalmijn, M. (1991). Shifting boundaries: Trends in religious and educational homogamy. *American Sociological Review, 56*(6), 786–800.

Kornrich, S., & Furstenberg, F. (2013). Investing in children: Changes in parental spending on children, 1972–2007. *Demography, 50*(1), 1–23.

Lareau, A. (2011). *Unequal childhoods: Class, race, and family life, second edition.* Berkeley: University of California Press.

Lee, B. A., Tyler, K. A., & Wright, J. D. (2010). The new homelessness revisited. *Annual Review of Sociology, 36,* 501–521.

Levy, F., & Michel, R. C. (1991). *The economic future of American families: Income and wealth trends.* Washington, DC: Urban Institute Press.

Martin, S. P., Astone, N. M., & Peters, H. E. (2014). Fewer marriages, more divergence: Marriage projections for millennials to age 40. Retrieved January 12, 2015, from http://www.urban.org/UploadedPDF/413110-Fewer-Marriages-More-Divergence.pdf?RSSFeed=Urban.xml

Massey, D. S., & Hirst, D. S. (1998). From escalator to hourglass: Changes in the U.S. Occupational wage structure 1949–1989. *Social Science Research, 27*(1), 51–71.

Merton, R. K. (1968). *Social theory and social structure, enlarged edition.* New York: The Free Press.

Newman, K. S. (1988). *Falling from grace: The experience of downward mobility in the American middle class.* New York: The Free Press.

Pew Research Center. (2010). The reversal of the college marriage gap. Retrieved November 21, 2015, from http://www.pewsocialtrends.org/2010/10/07/the-reversal-of-the-college-marriage-gap/

Rossi, A. S., & Rossi, P. H. (1990). *Of human bonding: Parent-child relations across the life course.* New York: Aldine de Gruyter.

Rubin, L. B. (1976). *Worlds of pain: Life in the working-class family.* New York: Basic Books.

Sayer, L. C., Gauthier, A. H., & Furstenberg, F. F., Jr. (2004). Educational differences in parents' time with children: Cross-national variations. *Journal of Marriage and Family, 66*(6), 1152–1169.

Schneider, D. M., & Smith, R. T. (1973). *Class differences and sex roles in American kinship and family structure.* Englewood Cliffs, NJ: Prentice-Hall.

Schwartz, C. R., & Han, H. (2014). The reversal of the gender gap in education and trends in marital dissolution. *American Sociological Review, 79*(4), 605–629.

Schwartz, C. R., & Mare, R. D. (2005). Trends in educational assortative marriage from 1940 to 2003. *Demography, 42*(4), 621–646.

Shiels, M. S., Chernyavskiy, P., Anderson, W. F., Best, A. F., Haozous, E. A., Hartge, P., et al. (2017). Trends in premature mortality in the USA by sex, race, and ethnicity from 1999 to 2014: An analysis of death certificate data. *The Lancet, 389*(10073), 1043–1054.

Smith, T. W., Davern, M., Freese, J., & Hout, M. (2017). General social surveys, 1972–2016. Machine readable data file. Chicago: National Opinion Research Center.

Stack, C. B. (1974). *All our kin: Strategies for survival in a black community.* New York: Harper and Row.

Streib, J. (2015). *The power of the past: Understanding cross-class marriages.* New York: Oxford University Press.

Swartz, T. T. (2009). Intergenerational family relations in adulthood: Patterns, variations, and implications in the contemporary United States.

Thomsen, M. K. (2015). Parental time investments in children: Evidence from Denmark. *Acta Sociologica, 58*(3), 249–263.

U.S. Bureau of the Census. (2013). Who could afford to buy a home in 2009? Retrieved November 21, 2015, from https://www.census.gov/prod/2013pubs/h121-13-02.pdf

U.S. Bureau of the Census. (2017a). Historical poverty tables: People and Families, Table 4. Retrieved July 24, 2018, from https://www.census.gov/data/tables/time-series/demo/income-poverty/historical-poverty-people.html

U.S. Bureau of the Census. (2017b). Table F-2. Family households, by type, age of own children, and educational attainment of householder: 2016. Retrieved July 23, 2018, from https://www.census.gov/data/tables/2016/demo/families/cps-2016.html

U.S. Bureau of the Census. (2017c). Table F-7. Type of family (all races) by median and mean income: 1947 to 2016. Retrieved July 23, 2018, from https://www.census.gov/hhes/www/income/data/historical/families/

U.S. Bureau of the Census. (2018). Income and poverty in the United States: 2017. *Current Population Reports, Series P60-263.* Retrieved November 20, 2018, from https://www.census.gov/content/dam/Census/library/publications/2018/demo/p60-263.pdf

U.S. National Center for Health Statistics. (2019). Mortality trends by race and ethnicity aamong adults aged 25 and over: United States, 2000–2017. *NCHS Data Brief No. 342.* Retrieved September 6, 2019, from https://www.cdc.gov/nchs/products/databriefs/db342.htm

U.S. Department of Housing and Urban Development. (2017). The 2017annual homeless assessment report (AHAR) to Congress, part 1: Point-in-time estimates of homelessness. Retrieved July 23, 2018, from https://www.hudexchange.info/resources/documents/2017-AHAR-Part-1.pdf

Western, B., Bloome, D., & Percheski, C. (2008). Inequality among American families with children, 1975 to 2005. *American Sociological Review, 73,* 903–920.

Wu, H. (2017). Trends in births to single and cohabiting mothers, 1980–2014. *Family Profiles, FP-17-04, National Center for Family and Marriage Research.* Retrieved July 23, 2018, from https://www.bgsu.edu/ncfmr/resources/data/family-profiles/wu-trends-births-single-cohabiting-mothers-fp-17-04.html

Chapter Five

Race, Ethnicity, and Families

Looking Forward

1. How are racial and ethnic groups constituted?
2. How has African American family life changed over the past several decades?
3. What are the family patterns of the major Hispanic ethnic groups?
4. What are the distinctive characteristics of the family patterns of Asian Americans?
5. How does the concept of "social capital" apply to immigrant families?
6. How is intermarriage affecting racial and ethnic groups?

On January 20, 2009, over a million people crowded the mall in Washington to witness the inauguration of Barack Obama as the 44th president of the United States. Many were African Americans, there to celebrate the election of the nation's first African American president. On that day it was hard to imagine that just two years earlier a debate had raged in the African American community about whether Obama was really an authentic African American. Everyone knew, of course, that President Obama had a white mother from Kansas and a black father from Kenya. Yet the basis of the charge that he was, in the phrase sometimes used, not black enough (Coates, 2007) was not that he had a white mother. Most African Americans have some white ancestry in their backgrounds, due to sexual relationships between slaves and their masters (think of the descendants of Thomas Jefferson's likely liaison with Sally Hemings) and to interracial relationships and sexual violence after emancipation. Moreover, an American with even a trace of African ancestry has traditionally been classified as black according to the so-called one-drop rule of American culture: People are said to be black if they have any "black blood" in their veins. No, Obama's mixed parentage wasn't the heart of the matter.

Rather, the main objection was that he was not descended from African slaves. Critic Stanley Crouch wrote in a column in the *New York Daily News*, "Obama did not–does not–share a heritage with the majority of black Americans, who are descendants of plantation slaves" (Crouch, 2006). In this reading, race depends not just on physical characteristics but also on historical experiences. Obama understood this position but argued subtly that he was an African American because he was treated by whites as if he were one. When asked at a Democratic Presidential Primary debate to respond to charges that he was not authentically black enough, he replied, "You know, when I'm catching a cab in Manhattan ..."–an allusion to taxi drivers who will not stop to pick up a black man for fear that his destination will be a dangerous neighborhood (*The New York Times*, 2007). Cab drivers, Obama implied, never tell him he's not black enough.

In fact, what turned around black public opinion on the matter of Obama's race was how white America began to treat him and his family–especially when that treatment seemed disparaging. After Obama won the South Carolina primary, Bill Clinton dismissively compared the win to Jesse Jackson's ultimately fruitless victory in South Carolina 20 years earlier. To some ears, Clinton's comment suggested that Obama was just another inconsequential black aspirant whose candidacy would soon fade away. When Michelle Obama said that for the first time in her adult life she was proud of her country, she was accused of being unpatriotic because she had not been proud all along. When clips of the fiery sermons of the Obamas' black minister, Jeremiah Wright, were shown endlessly on television, the Obamas were forced to resign from their church. As these events cumulated, African Americans rallied around Obama and defined him as one of them. By the time of his inauguration, he was universally and triumphantly hailed as the first black president. And he had won 95 percent of the African American vote.

Racial-Ethnic Groups

Obama's swift transition from not being an authentic African American to being a symbol of African American pride suggests that the definition of what constitutes a "race" is fluid. We tend to think of races as if they are natural categories clearly defined by physical characteristics–skin color, hair texture–and unchanging over time. But if that were true, then Obama couldn't have been transformed from a racially ambiguous, mixed-parentage person to an unambiguous African American in two years. Rather, his transformation shows that the racial categories we use are socially constructed. That doesn't make them any less important, just more subject to change and redefinition than is commonly thought (as when Obama's identity changed in the minds of many blacks), more reflective of the beliefs of the dominant group (as when whites began to define Obama as black), and more dependent on a particular time and place. At other times, in other places, race can be defined quite differently than it is in the United States today. In New World countries such as Brazil, there is no sharp division between black and white but rather a continuum of skin color distinctions. As recently as 1910, the U.S. Census included a mixed black and white ancestry category labeled "mulatto." Yet during the twentieth century, the image of two distinct groups, black and white, became fixed in American culture, despite the mixed racial ancestry of many Americans, such as Barack Obama.

Other racial categories remain more flexible, in part because none carries the long history of slavery and racial discrimination faced by African Americans. Consider the individuals in the United States who are descended from the original, indigenous peoples of North America. These peoples include American Indians, the name still often used for Native Americans in the contiguous 48 states, and Alaska natives, such as the Eskimo and Aleut. The 2010 Census questionnaire presented "American Indian or Alaska native" as one of 15 "race" categories. Of the 5.2 million people who chose it, 44 percent chose a second category, most often "white" (U.S. Bureau of the Census, 2011a). Since the 1970 Census, the American Indian population has increased at a far higher rate than counts of births and deaths during the 1970s would suggest (Snipp, 2002). The increases in reporting were greater in California and the East than in traditional American Indian population centers. This pattern suggests that individuals residing in metropolitan areas far from tribal lands and having some Native American ancestry have become more likely to think of themselves as American Indians. Nagel (1995, 1996) wrote of an "ethnic renewal" in which people of mixed heritage have increasingly identified themselves as American Indians due to factors such as American ethnic policies and American Indian political activism.

CONSTRUCTING RACIAL-ETHNIC GROUPS

Defining an ethnic group is even more difficult than defining a racial group. Most generally, an ethnic group consists of people who think of themselves as distinct from others by virtue of common ancestry and shared culture–but not necessarily physical characteristics. For example, the skin color and physical features of Mexican Americans range from distinctly European to distinctly Native American, with most people displaying a mixture of the two. Given the ambiguities and overlap between race and ethnicity, let me combine them and define a **racial-ethnic group** as people who share a common identity and whose members think of themselves as distinct from others by virtue of ancestry, culture, and sometimes physical characteristics. Often racial-ethnic group members' shared identity is reinforced by the way they are treated by outsiders. For instance, racial prejudice and, until the 1960s, racially discriminatory legislation have contributed to the sharp distinction between African Americans and whites.

racial-ethnic group people who share a common identity and whose members think of themselves as distinct from others by virtue of ancestry, culture, and sometimes physical characteristics

Thus, racial-ethnic groups are social creations, reflecting cultural norms, social inequality, and political power. Consequently, people can redefine these groups or create new ones as circumstances dictate. The clearest recent example of the redefinition of a racial-ethnic group in the United States is the rise of Hispanic ethnicity. In this chapter, the term **Hispanic** refers to persons in the United States who trace their ancestry to Latin America.[1] An alternative term, Latino, is sometimes used instead. In the mid-twentieth century, the terms Hispanic and Latino were hardly used; rather, one referred to specific groups such as Puerto Ricans, Mexican Americans, or Cuban Americans. There was no Hispanic category, for example, in the full 1970 Census. During the 1970s, however, political leaders of Latin American ancestry formed alliances based on their shared interest in improving the lives of their disadvantaged constituents. A Hispanic caucus was formed in Congress, the category "Hispanic" was added to the census, and Hispanics came to be seen as a coherent racial-ethnic group. In the 1980 Census, after the individual responding for the household checked boxes indicating which of the so-called races each person in the household belonged to, she or he was asked "Is this person of Spanish/Hispanic origin or descent?" The categories were: (1) No; (2) Yes, Mexican, Mexican American, or Chicano; (3) Yes, Puerto Rican; (4) Yes, Cuban; and (5) Yes, Other Spanish/Hispanic.

Hispanic a person living in the United States who traces his or her ancestry to Latin America

A similar scheme was used in the 2010 Census in which 16.3 percent of the U.S. population chose one of the Hispanic categories. This question was asked separately from the racial question because Hispanics can be of any race. In 2010, 37 percent of people who listed themselves and their household members as Hispanic checked none of the specific racial categories but rather the catchall racial category "Some other race" (U.S. Bureau of the Census, 2011a). That 37 percent of Hispanics considered themselves to be neither white nor black may reflect both the Latin American tradition of intermediate racial categories and also the sentiment that Hispanics are a separate group from European whites and African blacks.

Similarly, the category **Asian American** has become an umbrella for an extremely diverse group of people who hail from nations as far apart as Japan and Pakistan– people who differ in language, religion, alphabet, and physical features. For instance, South Asians, such as Indians, Pakistanis, and Bengalis, are

Asian American a person living in the United States who comes from or is descended from people who came from an Asian country

[1] Strictly speaking, "Hispanic" also includes people who trace their ancestry directly to Spain.

mostly Hindus or Muslims; and they speak languages belonging to the same Indo-European family from which English evolved. Unlike the category "Hispanic," there was no overall "Asian" category in the 2010 Census but rather a list of many Asian nationalities (e.g., "Chinese," "Asian Indian") in the "race" question. Census tabulations of Asian Americans sometimes include U.S. residents who are Pacific Islanders—people indigenous to Hawaii and to the Pacific islands that are territories of the United States.

Marriage patterns are one sign that the umbrella categories of "Asian" and "Hispanic" are beginning to take on a life of their own. In the marriage markets of many metropolitan areas in the United States, the number of marriages in which the bride and groom are both "Asian," meaning any Asian racial category at all, or are both "Hispanic," meaning any of the Hispanic groups, is substantially larger than we would expect by chance (Rosenfeld, 2001). In other words, it's not just that Japanese Americans are more likely to marry each other but also that Japanese Americans are more likely to marry anyone from the many groups that make up the Asian category—and the same holds for Mexican Americans and the Hispanic category. The author of the study suggests that we are seeing the emergence of "pannational" identities in which people identify as "Asian" or "Hispanic."

Nevertheless, for studying family life, the category "Hispanic" or "Latino" is not very useful, and "Asian American" is not much better. As will be discussed, there is nearly as much variation in family patterns among the various subgroups of the Hispanic population as there is between Hispanic families and non-Hispanic families. Indeed, there is substantial variation in family patterns within each of the major racial-ethnic groups. Still, the political discourse on racial-ethnic groups in the United States is increasingly structured around five racial-ethnic groups: African Americans, Hispanics, Asian and Pacific Islanders, Native Americans, and a category we can call **non-Hispanic whites,** meaning people who identify their race as white but do not think of themselves as Hispanic. These categories are still a subject of debate and controversy. (See *Families and Public Policy:* How Should Multiracial Families Be Counted?)

non-Hispanic white people who identify their race as white but do not think of themselves as Hispanic

"WHITENESS" AS ETHNICITY

Do non-Hispanic whites—the majority group—have an ethnicity? In the past, most scholars wrote as if the concept of ethnicity applied only to minority groups. But of late, many academics have begun to study the social construction of "whiteness" as an ethnicity that ordinarily provides power and privilege (Rasmussen, Klinenberg, Nexica, & Wray, 2001; Twine & Gallagher, 2007). Whiteness is not an inherent characteristic of people; rather, those considered white can differ over time and from place to place (McDermott & Samson, 2005). For example, when European immigrants from Ireland and Italy first began arriving in the United States in the 1800s, they weren't considered white. Only as they moved out of poverty and into the middle class did they acquire "whiteness" and the privileges that go with it.

Since nearly all whites are descended from European immigrants, their family and kinship patterns derive from the European historical experience. In fact, some scholars now prefer the label "European American" to "white," in order to emphasize the origins of white culture. As noted in Chapter 2, the conjugal family of husband, wife, and children dominated the European family.

Families and Public Policy

How Should Multiracial Families Be Counted?

How can a child whose parents have different races have only one? Logically impossible, you might think; but until 1997, federal government statistical policy required that individuals check just one race for themselves or their children on official forms such as the Census of Population. People such as Barack Obama had to choose one race prior to 1997 even if they thought of themselves as belonging to more than one. And before 1997, the government recognized four races: (1) white, (2) black, (3) Asian and Pacific Islander, and (4) American Indian and Alaska Native. It also required its agencies, in a separate question, to ask about membership in one ethnic group: Spanish or Hispanic origin.

In 1993, Representative Thomas Sawyer of Ohio, who was then the chair of the subcommittee of the House of Representatives that oversees the census and statistical policy, listened to the testimony of Susan Graham, an advocate for multiracial children and a mother of two of them. She told Representative Sawyer:

> *When I received my 1990 census form, I realized there was no race category for my children. I called the Census Bureau. After checking with supervisors, the Bureau finally gave me their answer, the children should take the race of the mother. When I objected and asked why my children should be classified as their mother's race only, the Census Bureau representative said to me, in a very hushed voice, "Because in cases like these, we always know who the mother is and not the father." (U.S. House of Representatives, Committee on Post Office and Civil Service, Hearings, 1994)*

Ms. Graham said her son had been classified as white by the census but black by the school he attended. Her solution: Add a new category, "Multiracial," to the official government list and to the 2000 Census. Yet this seemingly logical step was opposed by many of the political leaders of the minority groups that would be most affected. They opposed a multiracial category because the statistics that agencies collect are used not just to describe the population but also to determine whether federal laws have been carried out. Congress and the courts use the information on race and ethnicity from the census to determine whether congressional districts are providing fair representation to blacks and Hispanics. Agencies that oversee banks use the information to determine whether banks are willing to loan money to members of racial-ethnic groups. Other agencies use the information from employers to determine whether employers are discriminating on the basis of race or ethnicity. Consequently, the political leaders opposed a multiracial category because they feared it would lower

Moreover, European families did not appear to rely on kin for support as much as families in other regions of the world (Goode, 1963). This heritage can still be recognized today. Figure 5.1 shows the differences in children's living arrangements among five racial-ethnic groups. It comprises all children under 18 who were living in households at the time of the 2009 Survey of Income and Program Participation conducted by the Bureau of the Census (a small number were in juvenile institutions, group homes, or the military). As the purple columns show, 86 percent of Asian children and 77 percent of non-Hispanic white children were living with two parents. Hispanic, American Indian and Alaska Native, and African American children were less likely to be living with two parents. As the burnt orange columns show, Asian and non-Hispanic white children were least likely to be living with neither parent—an arrangement that is much more common among American Indian and African American children. Many of these children were living with grandparents or other relatives. Figure 5.1 suggests, then, that the roles of marriage and of the extended family vary considerably across racial-ethnic groups—an insight we will pursue in the following sections.

the number of blacks, Hispanics, or Asians counted in the census and would therefore dilute the political power that comes with greater numbers (Wright, 1994).

Faced with this dilemma, the government considered what, if anything, to do about Susan Graham's children and the many others like them when it fielded the 2000 Census of Population. In 1997, a government statistical committee decided that the 2000 Census (and all other government surveys) would allow individuals to choose more than one race; but it rejected a separate "multiracial" category. It also decided to place the question about Hispanic ethnicity before the question on race (rather than after it, which was the old policy), a change that probably increased the number of people who said they were "Hispanic."

When Americans filled out the 2010 Census, they were asked whether they were "Hispanic, Latino, or Spanish origin," and then they were asked their race. There were 15 choices, and as in 2000, Americans were allowed to check all the categories that applied to them. Overall, only 2.9 percent of the population checked two or more race categories. But 7.4 percent of those who checked "Black, African American, or Negro" also checked another category, as did 15.3 percent of those who checked one of the Asian categories, 43.8 percent who checked "American Indian or Alaska Native," and 55.9 percent who checked "Native Hawaiian" or "Other Pacific Islander" (U.S. Bureau of the Census, 2011a). Clearly, many members of minority groups think of themselves as having more than one race.

Still dissatisfied with Americans' responses to the term "race," the Census Bureau considered dropping the word altogether in the 2020 Census. It tested a set of questions that would simply ask "which category best describes" a person, followed by a long list of racial and ethnic groups, including white, black or African American, Hispanic or Latin, Asian, and so forth. People would be told that they could select more than one group. It also tested a new racial category, "Middle Eastern or North African," which was requested by Americans of Arab descent, who do not feel comfortable identifying as white, Asian, or black. But the Bureau ultimately decided not to add this new category and to maintain the distinction between race and ethnicity in the 2020 Census (U.S. Bureau of the Census 2018b).

Ask Yourself

1. Have you ever been frustrated by questionnaires that require you to select just one racial or ethnic group to describe yourself or a family member?
2. Relate the controversy over the wording of the census questions to the concepts of the public and the private family. What was the private family's interest in this matter? The public family's interest?

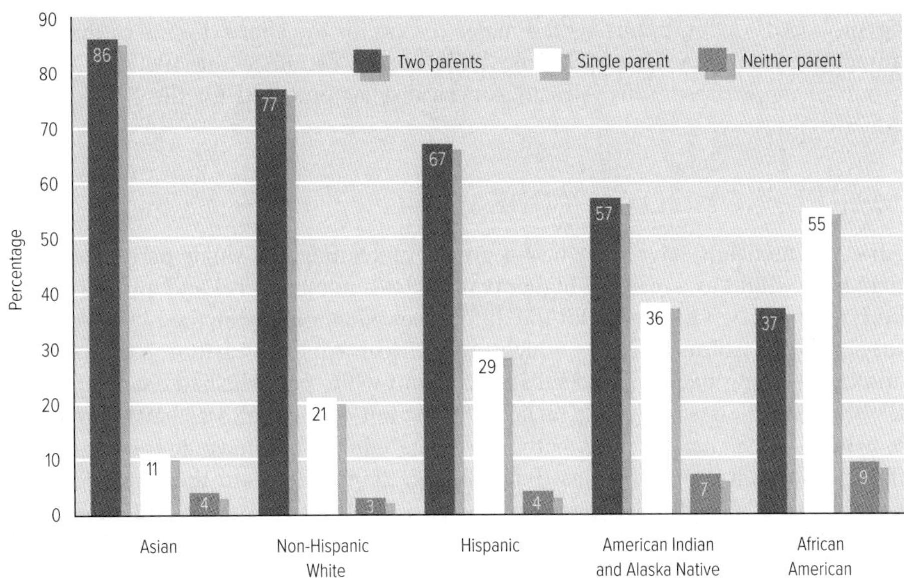

FIGURE 5.1
Percentage of children under 18 living with two parents, a single parent, or neither parent, for all children living in households in 2009, by race and ethnicity. Note: Percentages for American Indians and Alaska Natives are for 2001. (*Source:* U.S. Bureau of the Census, 2011b)

Quick Review

- Racial-ethnic groups are socially created and vary from society to society and from time to time.
- Two broad racial-ethnic groups that have emerged recently are "Hispanics" (sometimes called "Latinos") and "Asians."
- Some scholars are now studying the social creation of "whiteness" as an ethnicity that provides power and privilege.
- The roles of marriage and the extended family vary considerably across racial-ethnic groups.

African American Families

The economic ups and downs of the second half of the twentieth century and the first two decades of the twenty-first century had a profound effect on African Americans. In the 1960s, as the economy boomed and the civil rights movement lowered barriers, African Americans made unprecedented gains in employment and income. But the post-1973 economic slowdown hit African Americans hard, especially the men (Levy, 1998), many of whom had moved into industrial jobs in the 1950s and 1960s. In the 1970s, as growth in manufacturing jobs slowed, African American men who did not have a college education watched their economic prospects plummet. African American women had established a position in the growing service sector, so the changing economy did not affect them as much.

These great economic changes, in turn, had a significant impact on less-educated blacks. Without a stable economic base, some African American men were reluctant to marry, for fear they could not provide for their families. And some African American women were reluctant to marry them. In fact, William Julius Wilson argued in two influential books that the drop in semiskilled and skilled blue-collar jobs–their flight to low-wage nations such as China, their disappearance into the circuit boards of computers–is the major reason for the sharp decline in marriage among African Americans (Wilson, 1987, 1996). Yet since the 1960s, a sizable group of more prosperous African Americans has emerged for the first time in American history.

MARRIAGE AND CHILDBEARING

African Americans have long had a greater percentage of single-parent families than have whites as a result of higher death rates among parents and more children born to unmarried mothers. But the differences widened during the twentieth century, peaking around 1970, by which time African American patterns of marriage and childbearing had changed substantially but white patterns had changed much less. Since then, in some ways, racial differences in family patterns have narrowed, as whites–particularly whites without college educations–have altered the ways they go about forming families (Furstenberg, 2009). Here are three measures of family life that provide a window on how African Americans and whites compare. The numbers are summarized in Table 5.1.

Marriage In the 1950s, nearly nine in ten African Americans married at some point during their adult lives, usually in their late-teenage or early adult years. The 1950s were the high point of marriage for all groups; and 95 percent of whites married. But since then, the likelihood of ever marrying has dropped much more for African Americans than for whites. As Table 5.1 shows, only about half of young adult African American women will ever marry at current rates, far fewer than in the 1950s. The decline has been less steep for non-Hispanic whites, for whom the likelihood of marrying has declined to 84 percent for young adult women. So over the past half-century, a substantial gap in the marriage rates of whites and blacks has appeared. Marriage may play a lesser role in black family life today than it does among whites.

Childbearing Outside of Marriage Although African American women are postponing or forgoing marriage, they are not forgoing having children. Fewer and fewer of them are willing to wait until marriage to have their first child. A large majority of all African American children–70 percent, as Table 5.1 shows–are born to unmarried women. In other words, for every 100 African American women giving birth, 70 are unmarried at the time. Young African American women, especially those who are not on track to attend college, look around and see few successful models of the wait-until-marriage style of childbearing. Moreover, they live in a time when the stigma of having a child outside of marriage has declined greatly from the levels of the mid-twentieth century. But in this regard they are similar to other non-college-educated women, all of whom, regardless of race, have become more likely to have a child without marrying. That includes non-college-educated whites, who are much more likely to give birth without marrying than was the case a few decades ago (Furstenberg, 2009). Consequently, the racial gap in nonmarital childbearing, unlike the marriage gap, has actually been narrowing. As Table 5.1 shows, the percentage of births to unmarried women has more than quadrupled among non-Hispanic whites since 1970 while not quite doubling among blacks.

Single-Parent Families The high rates of childbearing outside of marriage among African Americans, combined with high levels of divorce and separation (see Chapter 12), combine to create a high level of single-parent families. Currently, as Table 5.1 shows, more than half of all African American family households are headed by a single parent. For non-Hispanic whites, the comparable figure is 27 percent. But note that the white figure has more than doubled since 1970–a faster rate of change than among African Americans. Overall, the numbers in Table 5.1 suggest these conclusions: (1) African Americans have high levels of childbearing outside of marriage and single-parent families and low levels of marriage; (2) but whites are changing, too; (3) in particular, childbearing outside of marriage has grown at a faster rate among whites in recent decades, leading to a narrowing of this racial difference.

EXPLAINING THE TRENDS

How can we explain the decline in marriage among African Americans and the increase in the proportion to children born to unmarried African American

Table 5.1 Indicators of the Decline of Marriage among African Americans and Whites

INDICATORS OF THE DECLINE OF MARRIAGE	AFRICAN AMERICANS	WHITES
The percentage of young women who will ever marry has fallen more for African Americans than for whites[a]	88% in 1950s → 51% in 2010s	95% in 1950s → 84% in 2010s
The percentage of children born to unmarried mothers has risen for both African Americans and whites[b]	38% in 1970 → 70% in 2016	6% in 1970 → 29% in 2016
The percentage of family households with children headed by one parent has risen for both African Americans and whites[c]	36% in 1970 → 59% in 2017	10% in 1970 → 27% in 2017

[a]Rodgers & Thornton, 1985; Martin, Astone, & Peters (2014).

[b]U.S. National Center for Health Statistics, 1995, 2018a.

[c]U.S. Bureau of the Census, 2018a.

mothers? Studies suggest that both the availability of suitable partners—not incarcerated, steadily employed—and cultural differences play a role.

Availability As noted earlier, changes in the labor market in the 1970s and 1980s affected all young men without college educations, and they hit African Americans particularly hard. Studies in the 1990s suggested that for every three black unmarried women in their twenties, there was roughly one unmarried black man with earnings above the poverty line (Lichter, McLaughlin, Kephart, & Landry, 1992). The situation is unlikely to be any better today.

In addition to job losses—or perhaps as a result of them—there are other reasons why young black women may face a difficult time finding a suitable spouse. Consider the terrible toll that violence and drugs are taking on young black men. Homicide rates for young African Americans have risen to appalling levels over the past two decades. If the rates in 2016 were to continue, about 1 of every 43 black 15-year-old boys would die violently before reaching age 45.[2] The rates of imprisonment and institutionalization of young black males are also strikingly high. The number of Americans incarcerated—in prison or jail—has soared since the 1980s to levels far above any other country, and black men are eight times more likely to be incarcerated than are white men. Imprisonment is concentrated among the least educated: According to one estimate, 69 percent of black men without high school degrees are likely to be incarcerated by the time they are in their early thirties. This "mass incarceration" of black males, as it has become known, removes men from the pool of eligibles while they are in prison and makes it difficult for them to find jobs after they are released (Western & Wildeman, 2009).

What if we could place African Americans in an environment where there is less unemployment and discrimination—would their marriage rates go up? To answer that question, researchers examined the marriage histories of young African Americans in the military, arguing that military life provides a natural experiment of sorts: There is no unemployment, little racial segregation, and less racial discrimination. They found no difference between the marriage rates of black and white soldiers, which suggests that greater unemployment and discrimination in the

[2] Author's calculation from homicide rates for black males 15–44 in U.S. National Center for Health Statistics (2018b).

civilian world may be depressing black marriage rates (Lundquist, 2004; Lundquist & Smith, 2005). Another study found that black men who had served on active duty had higher rates of marriage than black reservists or non-veterans (Teachman, 2007). These findings are an intriguing suggestion that economic conditions and racial discrimination do make a difference in African Americans' propensity to marry.

Is the decline in marriage, then, due to the shortage of men who are available and "marriageable," as Wilson calls them? Overall, the research suggests two conclusions: (1) The employment problems of black men and the high rates of incarceration and homicide are indeed important factors in the decline in marriage. For instance, a study that has followed thousands of Americans for about 45 years suggests that the worsening employment situation of African American men has played a role in declining rates of marriage and that African American women are less likely to marry in areas where incarceration rates are higher (Schneider, Harknett, & Stimpson, 2018) (2) Nevertheless, a racial difference in marriage patterns remains even after these problems are taken into account.

A similar pattern can be seen in a comparison of census data on the percentage of black and white families that are headed by a married couple (as opposed to an unmarried woman or man). Figure 5.2 shows this comparison for families at different income levels. As the reader can see, for both African Americans and non-Hispanic whites, the higher the family's income, the greater is the percentage that are headed by a married couple. Clearly, among both African Americans and non-Hispanic whites, married couples are less commonly found in low-income households. Note also, however, that at each income level, non-Hispanic white families are more likely to be headed by a married couple than black families. Even when there are no income differences between the families being compared, a racial gap still exists, and the gap is particularly pronounced among the poor and near poor. Economics, it seems, is part of the story of racial differences in family structure; but it is not the whole story.

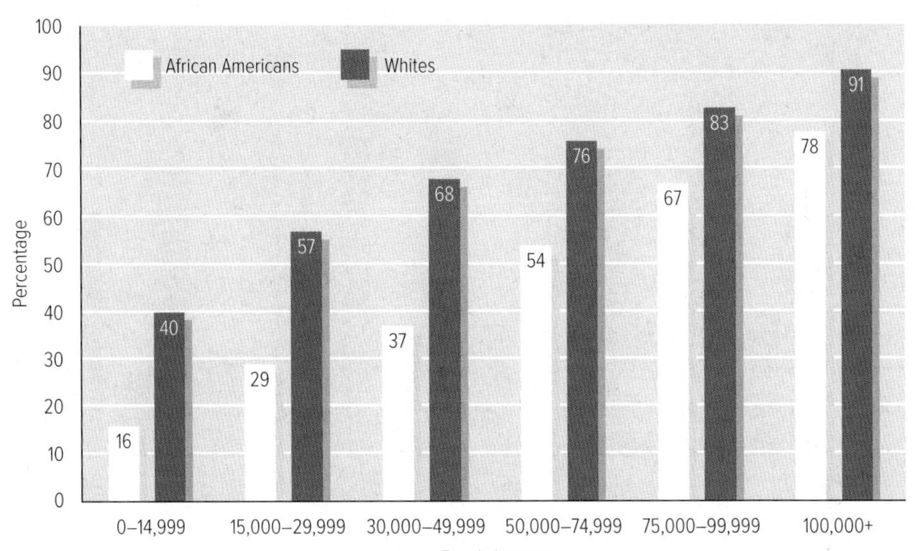

FIGURE 5.2
Percentage of families that were headed by a married couple, by family income, for African Americans and whites, 2016. (*Source:* U.S. Bureau of the Census, 2017)

Culture To more fully understand the differences in the family patterns of African Americans and whites, we must turn from economics to culture. There has been a resistance among liberal social scientists and activists to acknowledge the role of culture in shaping African American family patterns. In part, this concern arises from the entirely negative way in which black families are often portrayed: problem-ridden, weak, overwhelmed. The strengths of black families are often overlooked. Figure 5.3 helps to show where these strengths may lie. Graphed across income levels from low to high are the percentage of family households that are "extended"—that is, the percentage that contain relatives other than parents (or stepparents) and their children. Often the additional relatives are grandparents. Note that at all income levels—even among those earning more than $200,000—black family households are much more likely than white households to include a grandparent or other relative.

Indeed, grandparents play a stronger role in African American families, on average, than they do among white families (Bertera & Crewe, 2013). In 1982, just before Frank Furstenberg and I carried out a national survey of grandparents, we visited a group of black grandmothers at a senior citizens' center in Baltimore. The grandmothers told us how involved they were with their grandchildren's upbringing. Most of them had lived at least temporarily with their grandchildren. One woman, for example, said about her grandchildren:

> *I was always named "sergeant"—"Here comes the sergeant." I loved them. I did for them, and gave to them, so that they had an education, so that they had a trade. I went to school regularly to check on them; they didn't know I was coming. (Cherlin & Furstenberg, 1992)*

Very few white grandparents had this kind of hands-on involvement and authority. Our national survey confirmed that black grandparents, on average, were more involved in parentlike activities with their grandchildren than were white grandparents. Moreover, this racial difference still remained when we compared black

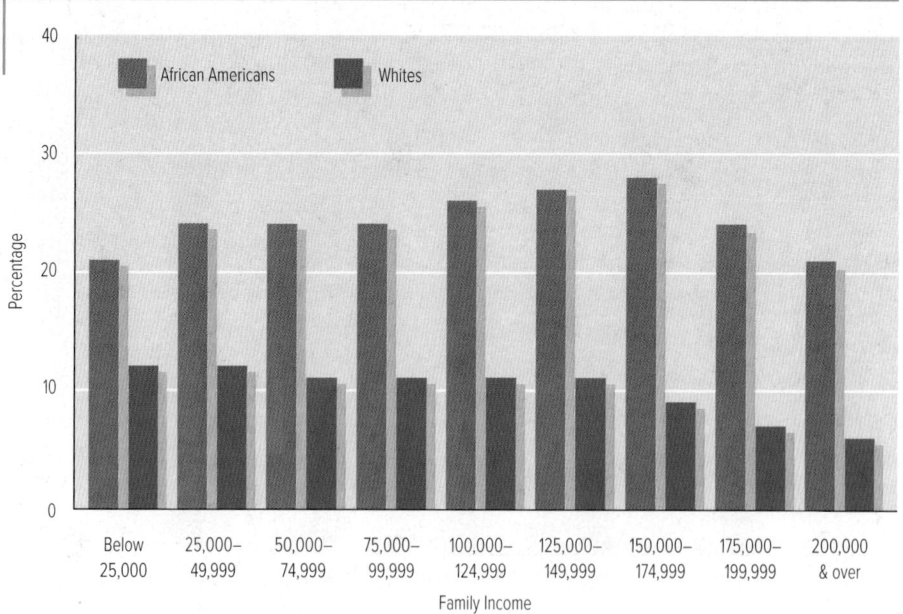

FIGURE 5.3 Percentages of family households that are extended (contain relatives other than parents and their children), by family income, for African Americans and whites, 2004. (*Source:* Tabulations by Reynolds Farley from 2004 U.S. Bureau of the Census American Community Survey data)

and white grandparents of similar incomes. Even among more prosperous families, black grandparents seem to play a stronger role than white grandparents.

More generally, in African American families, ties to a network of kin are more important, compared with marital ties, than is the case in white families. When Alice and Peter Rossi measured the strength of people's feelings of obligations toward kin, they found that African Americans felt much stronger obligations to aunts, uncles, nieces, nephews, and cousins than did whites (Rossi & Rossi, 1990). It follows, then, that when African Americans face adversity, they are probably more likely to seek help from kin than are whites. Moreover, African cultural patterns may still be influential: In West Africa marriage is more of a process than an event, with childbearing sometimes occurring before the process is completed.

The chapter on class also discussed the strengths and weaknesses of relying on kin for support. Briefly, membership in a network of kin helps people subsist because it allows them to spread the burdens of poverty by borrowing when they are in need and lending when they are able. It also, however, makes escaping from poverty more difficult because it is difficult and risky for poor people to withdraw from the network. Ever since Stack's (1974) influential account of African American kinship networks in "the Flats," many writers have assumed that black families receive more assistance from their networks than do white families. Several statistical studies, however, have cast doubt on that conclusion (Hofferth, 1984; Roschelle, 1997). It may be that the poor have fewer resources to share now than in the 1970s. We know that the share of income going to families whose heads did not graduate from high school has been declining. Some kin networks, therefore, may be overwhelmed by their members' needs. Or it may be that blacks and whites differ in the kind of support they provide rather than in the quantity of support. According to one study, white women were more likely to give financial support to kin and to receive it (in large part because they had more money to give) than were black women; but black women were more likely to give and receive help with child care, transportation, and housework (Sarkisian & Gerstel, 2004).

Reconciling the Explanations Some observers think the changes in families are entirely due to changes in the economy; others believe that culture may have played a role. I think that both were likely involved. As one sociologist has argued, culture is a sort of "tool kit" (Swidler, 2001). It provides people with a particular set of tools they know how to operate. When faced with difficulties, people tend to reach into their tool kits to fix the problem. For African Americans over the past several decades, the problem has been a very unfavorable economic environment. Not only did they battle discrimination, but as globalization and automation proceeded, they also faced a growing shortage of the kinds of jobs that can sustain families in which the parents do not have college educations. The job situation was worse for black men than for black women because the latter group had attained a foothold in the kinds of service-sector jobs (secretaries, waitresses, health care workers) that grew while blue-collar factory jobs disappeared.

Faced with this problem, African Americans increasingly reached into their tool kits and seized the kind of family support system that their history and culture provided: extended kinship networks rather than married-couple families. These networks usually relied heavily on women—mothers, sisters, grandmothers—who were able to find jobs or were able to qualify for government assistance to single-parent families. Women-centered kinship was part of the cultural repertoire of African American families. Had it not been, African Americans might not have retreated as much from the marriage-centered kinship patterns of European Americans.

Relying on extended kin has risks, but it can allow low-income families to obtain the support they need to make it from day to day.

GENDER AND BLACK FAMILIES

Both black men and black women face discrimination and economic disadvantages. But black feminist writers argue that black women face an additional source of disadvantage because of their gender. For example, unlike black men they may face the earnings gap between jobs primarily held by men and jobs primarily held by women. As women, they are more likely to be victims of domestic violence (see Chapter 11). But their situation also is unlike that of white women; they have always had to work outside the home, so the role of homemaker was rarely available to them. Social scientists with this perspective stress the intersectionality of black women's situation: the extent to which their lives are affected by overlapping systems of class, racial, and gender-based disadvantage (Hill, 2005). It is as if black women stand at the intersection of overlapping circles of race, class, and gender. This perspective challenges the idea that there is a universal black experience shared by all African Americans. Instead, it emphasizes the diversity of the black experience, the extent to which it differs for women and men and also for middle-class families and low-income families.

THE RISE OF MIDDLE-CLASS FAMILIES

In fact, a small group of prosperous African Americans has long existed, often through the efforts of two-earner married couples. Landry (2000) presents evidence that in the late nineteenth and early twentieth centuries, more prosperous black women pioneered the ideology that women should combine marriage, careers, and community service. Because black women had been excluded from the "cult of True Womanhood" that enveloped white women in the late 1800s, they were freer to pursue careers. At all times during the twentieth century, the percentage of black women who worked for pay was higher than that of white women. Moreover, the wealthiest black women had the highest rates of paid work, suggesting that better-off black women were working for satisfaction as well as income.

Since the 1960s, the number of relatively prosperous blacks, whom observers tend to call the "black middle class," has expanded substantially. It has been growing long enough that a second generation has moved into higher education. Among black freshmen entering 28 selective colleges in 1999, 60 percent had a father who graduated from college, 25 percent came from families earning over $100,000 per year, and 72 percent said that their parents owned their home (Massey, Charles, Lundy, & Fischer, 2003). Still, middle-class black families tend to have less money in assets (savings, investments, homes, cars) than comparable white middle-class people. In a study of the assets of respondents to the Census Bureau's Survey of Income and Program Participation in 1987 through 1989, Oliver and Shapiro (1995) found much larger differences, on average, in wealth (assets) between blacks and whites than in income. Comparing college-educated blacks with college-educated whites, for instance, they found that whereas the blacks earned 76 cents for each dollar earned by the whites, blacks had assets of just 23 cents for every dollar of white assets. And if homes and cars were excluded from assets (leaving savings accounts, stocks, small businesses), black college graduates had *one cent* of assets for every dollar of white assets. Oliver and Shapiro ascribe the difference to three factors: (1) whites are more likely to inherit some wealth or borrow money for a down payment on a home or car from their parents; (2) whites can more easily obtain home mortgage loans from banks; and (3) homes in predominantly black neighborhoods don't appreciate in value as much as homes in white neighborhoods.

The lower amount of wealth among blacks also affects whether they marry. Wealth ownership is a marker of income security that young adults use to judge whether they and their partners can make a successful marriage. Young men and, to a lesser extent, young women who own a car or have a bank account are more likely to marry, independently of how much money they earn. Since blacks tend to have fewer assets, the wealth differences between whites and blacks account for a portion of the black-white differences in the likelihood of marrying (Schneider, 2011).

Because of residential segregation, middle-class black neighborhoods tend to be closer to poor black neighborhoods, and their neighborhoods usually contain some poor families. Pattillo (2005) writes of the "inbetweenness" of the black middle-class experience. Middle-class blacks tend to live in neighborhoods that have less crime and poverty than the neighborhoods of low-income blacks, but much more crime and poverty than the neighborhoods of middle-class whites. As a result, middle-class African American parents may struggle to shield their children from the lure of street life, with its criminal behavior and drug usage. And middle-class African Americans must coexist with neighbors and relatives in the underground economy in ways most whites need not (Pattillo-McCoy, 1999). Still, the growth of the African American middle class is a success story that is too often lost in the understandable focus on the African American poor.

Black churches have been a great source of social support to African Americans who have newly gained middle-class status. Throughout African American history the church and the family have been the enduring institutions through which black families could gain the strength to resist the oppression of slavery, reconstruction, segregation, and discrimination (Berry & Blassingame, 1982). The church has served as a **mediating structure,** a midlevel social institution (other examples are civic groups, neighborhoods, and families themselves) through which individuals can negotiate with government and resist governmental abuses of power (Berger & Berger, 1983). It has been the greatest source of continuity, outside of the family, in the African American experience. Today the church also serves as a link between the black middle class, many of whom have moved out of inner-city neighborhoods, and the black poor. Often by virtue of sanctuaries that are still in poor neighborhoods, churches provide a direct way for middle-class congregants to provide assistance to the poor (Gilkes, 1995). In some of the poorest black neighborhoods, which have lost both population and organizations over the past few decades (Wilson, 1996), churches are among the few nongovernmental institutions left (McRoberts, 2003).

mediating structures midlevel social institutions and groupings, such as the church, the neighborhood, the civil organization, and the family

Quick Review

- Marriage has declined among African Americans even more than among whites; childbearing outside of marriage has increased for both groups.
- The impact of economic restructuring—and the employment problems it has caused for African American men—is an important factor in the decline of marriage.
- But cultural differences between African Americans and whites are probably important too.
- In general, African American families rely on ties to extended kin more than white families do.
- African American women's family lives are affected not only by their race and class but also by their gender.
- Over the past several decades, a substantial African American middle class has emerged for the first time.

Hispanic Families

The label "Hispanic" covers groups that are so diverse with respect to family patterns that it makes little sense to combine them, yet that is the direction public discussions have taken. It lumps together recent immigrants with citizens whose families have been in the United States for generations, and lighter-skinned, well-educated political émigrés with darker-skinned, poorly educated laborers looking for work. Americans of Mexican origin are by far the largest group, constituting 63 percent of all Hispanics in 2015 (Pew Research Center, 2017a). Since 2007, however, more Mexicans have left the United States than have entered it (Pew Research Center, 2015b). The reversal of the Mexican migration stream is due to factors such as stricter border enforcement, the declining Mexican birth rate, and improvements in the Mexican economy (Pew Hispanic Center, 2012). In contrast, immigration from Central America has surged. The number of immigrants from the northern triangle formed by El Salvador, Guatemala, and Honduras rose by 25 percent from 2007 to 2015 (Pew Research Center, 2017d). Salvadorans have recently become the third largest Hispanic group in the United States, exceeded only by Puerto Ricans (all of whom are American citizens) and Mexicans. Cubans are the fourth largest, and people hailing from the Dominican Republic are the fifth largest (Pew Research Center, 2017a). Figure 5.4 shows an example of the diversity in Hispanic family patterns. It presents the percentage of households headed by a woman with no husband or cohabiting partner present for four Hispanic groups and, for comparison, non-Hispanic whites and non-Hispanic blacks. At one extreme, Dominicans have levels of households headed by women that are nearly identical to the high levels among non-Hispanic blacks. At the other extreme, Cubans have levels that are not much higher than the low levels among non-Hispanic whites. Consequently, any statement about overall Hispanic levels of households headed by women would mask this great diversity. Any statistic you read about Hispanics as a whole tends to reflect the experience of Mexicans, since they are by far the largest group; but such statistics lump together groups that sharply differ from one another.

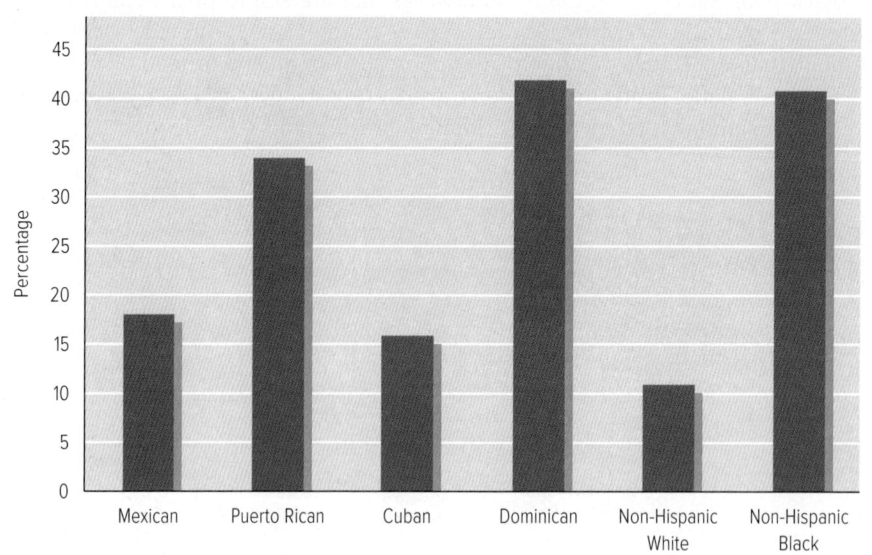

FIGURE 5.4
Percentage of households headed by a woman without a husband or partner present, for Hispanic groups, non-Hispanic whites, and non-Hispanic blacks, 1998–2002. (*Source:* Landale, Oropesa, & Bradatan, 2006)

MEXICAN AMERICANS

The United States and Mexico share a long history and a long border—the longest border between a developed and a developing country in the world. Some of the estimated 35.8 million people of Mexican origin in the United States in 2015 (Pew Research Center, 2017a) are the descendants of the early settlers of the Southwest. Others are second- or third-generation Americans, while still others are recent immigrants. Americans of Mexican origin have some distinctive family patterns:

- *Marriage.* Mexican Americans marry at a younger age than other Hispanics, non-Hispanic whites, or African Americans. In 2000, for instance, 46 percent of 20- to 24-year-old Mexican American women had already married, compared to 32 percent of comparable white non-Hispanics (Landale & Oropesa, 2007). Even though Mexican Americans are more economically disadvantaged, which should lower their likelihood of marrying, they still marry younger. Moreover, two-parent, single-earner families are more common among Mexican American families than among other Hispanic families (Lichter & Qian, 2004).
- *Number of children.* The Mexican-origin population has a high birthrate by American standards. The **total fertility rate** (TFR) is the average number of births that a woman would have over her lifetime if current age-specific birthrates were to remain the same. Mexican American women had a TFR of 2.0 in 2014, the highest of any major racial-ethnic group. Other Hispanics have fewer children. Puerto Ricans had a TFR of 1.7, while Cubans had a TFR of 1.6; both figures are lower than the TFR for non-Hispanic whites (1.7) and non-Hispanic blacks (1.9) (U.S. National Center for Health Statistics, 2017). Births show, once again, the diversity of the Hispanic population.

total fertility rate (TFR) the average number of children a woman will bear over her lifetime if current age-specific birthrates remain the same

What make the ages at marriage low and the birthrates high among the Mexican-origin population, it turns out, are the family patterns of recent immigrants, rather than of Mexican Americans who were born in the United States. In Mexico the average age at marriage is younger than in the United States (Raley, Durden, & Wildsmith, 2004), so immigrants come from a culture where early marriage is more common. Moreover, many Mexican immigrants are already married when they get here. Because most legal immigrants receive visas under a program to reunite them with relatives already living in the United States, many spouses immigrate; in fact, a majority of Mexican women who migrated after age 15 did so after marrying. Moreover, immigrants who arrive in the United States before marrying have an incentive to marry because it will usually allow them to apply for permanent residence. In contrast, Mexican-origin individuals who were born in the United States—who are more distant from Mexican culture and who may have less incentive to marry—marry at similar ages to non-Hispanic whites (Raley et al., 2004). In addition, Mexico had a higher birthrate than the United States until recently. Mexicans who immigrate have grown up in a society that values higher fertility, and they have more children than do non-Hispanic whites. But the children of Mexican immigrants are more influenced by American values and their level of childbearing is not much different from that of non-Hispanic whites. In fact, the TFR for the Mexican-origin population fell sharply in the early 2010s as net immigration dropped (Cherlin, Cumberworth, Morgan, & Wimer, 2013).

Yet even with the lower birthrates among those born in America, the massive scale of Mexican immigration prior to its leveling off in 2007 greatly affected the size of the American population. Between 2000 and 2004, for instance, births to new Hispanic immigrants (a large share of them from Mexico) and births to Hispanics already in the United States accounted for half of the nation's population growth (Haub, 2006). One demographic study predicts that by 2040, Mexican immigrants since the 1980s and their descendants will have produced 36 million additional births (Johnson & Rendall, 2004).

Hispanic households, including Mexican-origin households, also are more likely than non-Hispanic white households to live in extended families rather than conjugal families (Landale, Oropesa, & Bradatan, 2006). A family's household is said to be extended horizontally when a relative in the same generation as the household head–a brother, sister, or cousin–lives there. It is said to be extended vertically when a relative in the generation above the household head–a parent, an uncle, or an aunt–lives there. Mexican-origin households are more likely to be both horizontally and vertically extended than are non-Hispanic white households, in large part due to the migration of relatives (Glick, Bean, & Van Hook, 1997). An extended family can assist newly arrived kin, or older parents can provide child care assistance to their children and grandchildren. Other immigrant groups, particularly Asians, are also more likely to live in extended family households.

PUERTO RICANS

All Puerto Ricans are U.S. citizens because the island of Puerto Rico is a U.S. territory. Consequently, Puerto Ricans, unlike all other major Hispanic groups, are free to move to the mainland if they wish, and many have done so. By 2012, more than half of all people who identified themselves as Puerto Ricans were residing on the mainland (Pew Research Center, 2015a), and the migration from the island to the mainland has continued since then (Pew Research Center, 2015c). Puerto Ricans have a high percentage of children born to unmarried mothers. Yet some of the formally unmarried Puerto Rican mothers are living in a partnership that they consider to be a marriage. In Puerto Rico and other Caribbean islands, a long tradition of **consensual unions** exists. These are cohabiting relationships in which couples consider themselves to be married but have never had religious or civil marriage ceremonies. From the viewpoint of the state and the Church, people in consensual unions are unmarried; but from the viewpoint of the couples and their peers, they are in a marriagelike relationship. Still, Puerto Rican couples who are formally married do exhibit some differences; for instance, married men are more likely to pool their incomes with their partners' incomes (rather than, say, to give their partners an allowance) than are men who are not formally married (Oropesa, Landale, & Kenkre, 2003). Whether consensual unions are still as common as they were in the past is unknown; little research has been conducted recently.

consensual union a cohabiting relationship in which a couple consider themselves to be married but have never had a religious or civil marriage ceremony

SALVADORANS

Large-scale immigration from El Salvador, as well as from neighboring Guatemala and Honduras, began in the 1980s, as Salvadorans and Guatemalans fled long civil wars and economic hardship (Lesser & Batalova, 2017). In 1998 a devastating hurricane hit Central America, which led to further migration. The United States government granted Central American refugees from the hurricane and other natural disasters Temporary Protected Status (TPS), which allowed them to remain in the United States for a limited time but did not provide them with permanent residency or citizenship. The government has extended the amount of time immigrants can remain in the Unites States under TPS several times. By the mid-2010s, about 200,000 Salvadorans were benefitting from TPS protection (Messick & Bergeron, 2014). In 2018, however, the United States government announced an end to TPS protection for Salvadorans and directed all of them to leave the country by September 2019 (Jordan, 2018). It is possible that this decision will be overruled and TPS protection will be extended yet again, but if not, the beneficiaries will be faced with the decision to either return to El Salvador or remain illegally in the United States (Jordan, 2018). A second migration stream, which has not been granted TPS protection, strengthened in the 2010s as Salvadorans fled gang violence and high homicide rates (Chishti & Hipsman, 2016).

Immigrants who have been in the United States under TPS protection are in legal limbo: They are not illegally in the country, but they also are not permanent residents or citizens (Menjívar, 2006). Their ambiguous status affects their family lives. For instance, they are not allowed to travel outside of the country except with special permission that is difficult to obtain. As a result, they cannot visit spouses or children that they may have left behind without incurring the risk that they would not be let back in the country. They sometimes owe thousands of dollars in debt to smuggling operations that managed their passages from Central America to the United States; and until they pay off the debt, they are limited in how much money then can send back home to help family members (Menjívar, 2012). Even if they come from areas where consensual unions are common, they may need to marry their partners in order to present the strongest application for permanent residence (Menjívar, 2016). Women may have less difficulty finding full-time work, leading them to out-earn their partners and therefore to upend the patriarchal authority of men in Central American families (Menjívar, 1999). In these ways, immigration policies and the labor market influence the family lives of both the immigrants and the family members who depend on them in the United States and in their home countries.

CUBAN AMERICANS

The first wave of Cuban Americans came to the United States not to look for higher paying jobs nor to escape natural disasters or violence but rather to flee the Communist government of Fidel Castro, who had led a successful revolution in 1959. The U.S. government allowed Cuban citizens to enter the country as political refugees. Indeed, the early migrants were drawn from the Cuban upper and middle classes, the elite that Castro's Communist party overthrew. These immigrants arrived with substantial amounts of education, skills, and capital. In addition, they were largely white in racial appearance. The U.S. government, sympathetic to their plight and wishing to isolate and embarrass Castro, welcomed them enthusiastically and provided assistance in retraining (Suarez, 1993).

Despite government efforts at resettlement, most Cuban immigrants chose to settle in the Miami metropolitan area. Classic sociological theories of immigration held that immigrants would adjust better and prosper more if they assimilated into the mainstream. (**Assimilation** means the process by which immigrant groups merge their culture and behavior with that of the dominant group in the host country.) In the U.S. context, assimilation implies learning English, sending children to public schools, and dispersing geographically. Many Cuban immigrants chose, instead, to remain clustered in the Cuban neighborhoods of one metropolitan area, to listen to Spanish-language radio stations, to buy their food at markets owned by Cuban Americans, to eat at Cuban restaurants, and to send their children to private Cuban schools. They limited much of their lives to a large, dense, single-ethnic-group, almost self-sufficient community of the type that has been called an **immigrant enclave** (Wilson & Portes, 1980).

assimilation the process by which immigrant groups merge their culture and their behavior with that of the dominant group in the host country

immigrant enclave a large, dense, single-ethnic-group, almost self-sufficient community

According to classic immigration theory, then, Cuban immigrants should have suffered. Instead, they prospered. By 1970, the median income of Cuban American families was higher than that of any other Hispanic group or of African Americans, at 80 percent of the median income of non-Hispanic white families; and by 1980 it had reached 88 percent of the median income for non-Hispanic white families (Bean & Tienda, 1987). Some observers claim that Cuban immigrants successfully used the ethnically based connections of the enclave to obtain loans to start businesses when no Anglo bank would lend to them; they also used their connections to find jobs at Cuban enterprises. (See the section, later in this chapter, Social Capital and Immigrant Families.) Portes argues that the enclave strategy is a viable way for an immigrant group to achieve economic success.

Yet it must be remembered that these immigrants started out with a friendly reception from their hosts, arrived with substantial education and skills, received government assistance, and had white skin. These advantages were not shared by those who were part of a later wave of Cuban immigration that began in 1980, when Castro allowed a flotilla of small boats to depart from the port of Mariel. Unlike the first wave of Cuban immigrants, who arrived during an economic boom, the Mariel Cubans arrived at a time of stagnant wages and high unemployment. They were not welcomed enthusiastically or assisted, and they experienced discrimination from the earlier wave of immigrants. By 2001, the median income of Cuban-origin families had declined, reflecting the influx of Mariel refugees. Nevertheless, Cuban Americans had the second highest median household income of the five largest Hispanic groups, trailing only Salvadorans (Pew Hispanic Center, 2012).

The prosperity of Cuban Americans is derived in large part from business ownership. Cuban immigrants have become entrepreneurs, opening new businesses in far greater numbers than other Hispanic immigrants. Many of the businesses were organized on a family basis. As Figure 5.4 showed, Cubans are more likely to form two-parent families than are other Hispanics. Married Cuban men were more likely to be self-employed, even after taking into account differences between married and unmarried men in education, work experience, citizenship, and English proficiency. If the men had children, they were even more likely to be self-employed (Portes & Jensen, 1989). Cuban immigrants appear to have used conjugal families as a means of pooling the labor and accumulating the capital necessary to start a business. Too many adults represented a drain on capital that could be used for the business; too few children or the absence of a spouse, on the other hand, resulted in insufficient labor or outside income (as from a wife's job) for starting a firm.

Quick Review

- Mexican Americans have high birthrates and marry at younger ages, in large part because of the extensive migration from Mexico.
- Mexican immigrants and their descendants are contributing greatly to the American population growth.
- Puerto Ricans are the most economically disadvantaged of the major Hispanic groups.
- Puerto Ricans have a tradition of consensual unions, in which couples consider themselves married although their unions have never been formalized.
- Cubans, many of whom settled in immigrant enclaves, established family businesses more than other Hispanic groups.
- Many Salvadorans have entered the Unites States through a Temporary Protected Status program that left them in legal limbo.

Asian American Families

Less has been written about Asian American families than about African American and Hispanic families because of their modest numbers prior to the 1965 immigration act. For example, the Korean population increased from an estimated 69,000 in 1970 to 350,000 in 1980 and to 1.8 million in 2015 (Lee, 1998, Pew Research Center, 2017c). In the 2015 American Community Survey, 20.4 million people identified as belonging to one of the Asian racial categories, a 72 percent increase over the 2000 Asian population (Pew Research Center, 2017b). The family patterns in the many sending nations are diverse, but, in general, Asian cultures emphasize interdependence among kin more, and individualism less, than Western culture (Goode, 1963). Asian families place a greater emphasis on children's loyalty and service to their parents than do Western families. In fact, Asian immigrant parents are more likely to live in households in which their adult children provide most of the income (Glick & Van Hook, 2002).

These Asian ways can conflict with American ways. Two researchers, for instance, read a series of vignettes to a sample of Chinese American immigrants from Taiwan and their parents in Chicago and Los Angeles. Here is one:

> *Wang Hong has to transfer three times on public transportation to get from where he lives to his office. Because of the time and inconvenience of taking public transportation, Wang Hong has tried very hard to save money to buy a car before winter. However, Wang Hong's parents have a need for money and ask Wang Hong to give them the money Wang Hong has saved.*

Both the parents and their adult children were asked to react to this vignette. The authors noted that when a similar vignette had been read to a general U.S. sample of the elderly and their caregivers, about three-fourths of both groups had thought that the child should buy the car. Yet a majority of the Chinese adult children and parents said that Wang Hong should give the money to his parents—placing obligation to one's parents over convenience of transportation (Lin & Liu, 1993).

Immigrants' families frequently pool economic resources to start businesses or to buy homes. Several Asian-origin groups have very high rates of business ownership, often accomplished by borrowing funds from kin and close friends. As for homeownership, shared residence and income pooling often help, as one Vietnamese immigrant told an interviewer:

> *To Vietnamese culture, family is everything. There are aspects which help us readjust to this society. It is easy for us because of [the] tradition of helping in the family.*
>
> *We solve problems because [the] family institution is a bank. If I need money and my brothers and my two sisters are working, I tell them I need to buy a house. I need priority in this case. They say OK, and they give money to me. After only two years, I bought a house.*
>
> *Some Americans ask me, "How come you came here with empty hands and now you have a house?" I told them, it is easy for us because my brother and sister help with the down payment. Now I help them. They live with me and have no rent. (Gold, 1993)*

This is not to say that all Asian immigrants adjust well and prosper. The first wave of Vietnamese immigration occurred in the immediate aftermath of the Vietnam War in 1975. Like the initial Cuban influx, it was a political migration of middle-class business and military personnel who were assisted on arrival. They have been successful as a group. Yet like the Mariel immigration, a later, less-educated stream of Vietnamese immigrants escaped in overcrowded boats to refugee camps in Southeast Asia. Those who have emigrated to the United States have fewer skills, have received less assistance, and have encountered a sluggish economy. A 1984 study of some of the later immigrants found that 61 percent had household incomes of less than $9,000 (Gold, 1993). Nevertheless, Asian Americans are a prosperous group overall. In 2015, the median household income for Asians was $73,000, which was 36 percent higher than the median for all families, an impressive achievement for a population that includes so many recent immigrants (Pew Research Center, 2017b).

The extent to which Asian-style patterns will survive through the second and third generations of Asian Americans remains to be seen. Among Asian Americans whose families have been in the United States for a few generations, the traditional Asian patterns are less apparent. For instance, the relations between women and men are more egalitarian in third-generation Japanese American families than in the older, immigrant generation (Ishii-Kuntz, 2000). And rates of interracial intermarriages are high among Asians, a topic to which I will turn in a few pages.

Social Capital and Immigrant Families

social capital the resources that a person can access through his or her relationships with other people

The recent literature on immigrants refers often to a concept developed by the French sociologist Pierre Bourdieu (1980) and expanded on by the American sociologist James S. Coleman (1988). **Social capital** is the resources that a person can access through his or her relationships with other people. To understand this concept, think about the social connections that might allow you to get a ticket to a sold-out concert (because your friend's cousin works in the box office), to be admitted to a competitive college (because your mother is an alumna), or to get your first job after college (because your roommate's father runs the company). In all these cases, the resources you would draw on would not be monetary (which social scientists refer to as "financial capital") or educational (which social scientists call "human capital"), but rather your social links to a network of people who can help you reach a goal you might otherwise fail to achieve.

That is the essence of the concept of social capital. In the literature on immigrants it is sometimes used more broadly to refer to a person's links to an entire immigrant community. The idea is that the community provides members with resources that help them to achieve goals they could not achieve alone, or even as families working together. For example, to explain why the children of Vietnamese immigrants in Versailles Village do better in school than their low social class would predict, Zhou and Bankston (1998) point to the social capital created by the close-knit Vietnamese community. They describe a Vietnamese Catholic church that offers after-school courses, and the Vietnamese Education Association, a community group that holds an annual awards ceremony to honor high-achieving students. Through these institutions, the authors argue, the Vietnamese community in Versailles Village provides social capital that boosts school achievement among Vietnamese students.

As I mentioned earlier, the literature on Cuban immigrants provides another example of the use of social capital. One reason for the growth in the number of Cuban American–owned firms from the late-1960s to the 1980s was that immigrants could use their social standing in the Cuban community in Miami to obtain the initial loans needed to start a business. In the mid-1960s, a few small banks owned by South Americans hired Cuban immigrant ex-bankers. The Cubans began to make loans to their fellow immigrants that other financial institutions would have thought risky. As one Cuban banker said:

> *At the start, most Cuban enterprises were gas stations; then came grocery shops and restaurants. No American bank would lend to them. By the mid-sixties we started a policy at our bank of making small loans to Cubans who wanted to start their own business, but did not have the capital. These loans of $10,000 or $15,000 were made because the person was known to us by his reputation and integrity. All of them paid back; there were zero losses. With some exceptions they have continued being clients of the bank. People who used to borrow $15,000 on a one-time basis now take $50,000 in a week. In 1973, the policy was discontinued. The reason was that the new refugees coming at that time were unknown to us. (Portes & Sensenbrenner, 1993)*

Whereas American banks would have required more proof that an applicant would be able to pay back a loan, the Cuban bankers relied solely on the applicant's "reputation and integrity." That reputation was established through a network of ties within the Cuban enclave in Miami. The banker might have known someone who had married the sister of the applicant and could vouch for the applicant's character. To enforce the terms of the loan, the banker relied on the humiliation and, perhaps, ostracism that would befall a person who defaulted. In this way, Cuban immigrants were able to use their ties to a network of relatives and friends to obtain the money they needed to buy a grocery store or restaurant.

American Indian Families

Before the twentieth century, kinship ties provided the basis for governing most American Indian tribes. A person's household was linked to a larger group of relatives who might be a branch of a matrilineal or patrilineal clan that shared power with other clans. Thus, kinship organization was also political organization. Under these circumstances, extended kinship ties reflected power and status to a much greater extent than among other racial-ethnic groups in the United States. American Indian kinship systems allowed individuals to have more relatives, particularly distant relatives, than did Western European kinship systems (Shoemaker, 1991). Even in recent times, extended family ties retained a significance for American Indians that went beyond the sharing of resources that has been noted among other groups (Harjo, 1993). Kinship networks constitute tribal organization; kinship ties confer an identity.

Only 22 percent of American Indians or Alaska Natives lived in tribal areas or other trust lands in 2010 (U.S. Office of Minority Health, 2018). As noted earlier, a substantial share of the growth of the American Indian population in urban areas in the East and on the West Coast reflects a rise in the number of people who considered themselves to be American Indians. In addition, migration from reservations to urban areas may have accounted for some of the drop in the percentage living near tribal lands.

American Indians remain an economically disadvantaged population. Their median household income is about the same as that of African Americans according to the American Community Survey. Consistent with their high levels of poverty, the percentage of American Indian families headed by an unmarried woman is substantial: As Figure 5.1 showed, 36 percent of American Indian families with children in 2009 were headed by a single parent. Consistent with these figures,

68 percent of American Indian and Alaska Native mothers who gave birth in 2016 were unmarried–a percentage that is comparable to African Americans (U.S. National Center for Health Statistics, 2018a). The percentage of adults who are divorced is also higher among American Indians than among the U.S. population as a whole (Sandefur & Liebler, 1997).

It's likely that many of the unmarried mothers were enmeshed in kinship networks that provided assistance. Little research, however, has been done on contemporary American Indian family patterns–especially among American Indians outside tribal lands. Beyond these lands, intermarriage and shifting conceptions of American Indian ethnicity make the study of families more complex. It is increasingly difficult to talk of the "American Indian family": There always has been diversity in family patterns among Indian tribes and among persons residing on reservations versus persons not on reservations, and now an American Indian family is often a multiracial family, as the next section discusses.

Quick Review

- Asian family patterns traditionally have placed a greater emphasis on children's loyalty and service to parents than have Western family patterns.
- Ties to family and community can provide social capital to immigrants.
- Kinship networks traditionally provided organization and identity to American Indians.
- The high intermarriage rate and shifting conceptions of identity make American Indian family patterns diverse.

Racial and Ethnic Intermarriage

When Barack Obama was born in Hawaii to an interracial married couple in 1961, at least 15 states had laws forbidding marriages between whites and nonwhites. Then, in 1967 the Supreme Court, ruling on a case brought against the state of Virginia by a white man, Richard Loving, and his black wife, Mildred Jeter, declared such laws unconstitutional (*Loving* v. *Virginia*, 1967). In 1972, when the General Social Survey started its annual survey of American adults, 37 percent of whites still favored laws against racial intermarriage (Smith, Davern, Freese, & Hout, 2017), and interracial married couples comprised only about 1 percent of all American married couples (Lee & Edmonston, 2005). By 2002, just 11 percent of whites favored these laws, and the General Social Survey stopped asking the question. Meanwhile interracial and interethnic marriage have surged to an all-time high.

VARIATION IN INTERMARRIAGE

Although intermarriage is much more common among all racial-ethnic groups than in the past, some groups marry out more than others, as Figure 5.5 shows. There are so many whites in the United States that even though millions of them marry a nonwhite, the percentage of white people who intermarry is lower than for other groups. Still, in 17 percent of all new marriages between 2008 and 2010 that involved at least one white spouse, the other spouse was African American, Hispanic, Asian, American Indian, or Alaska Native. The racial-ethnic group with

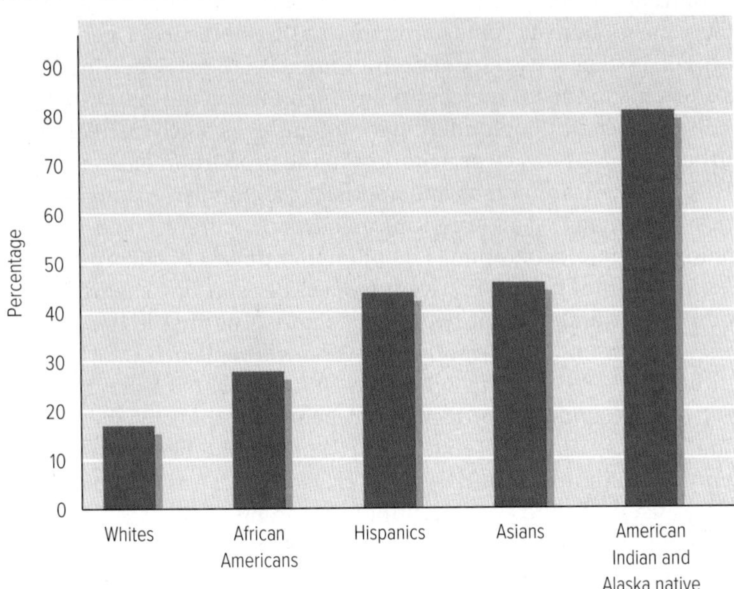

FIGURE 5.5
Percentage of Intermariages among Major Racial-Ethnic Groups, 2008 to 2010 (*Source:* Frey, 2015).

the next higher percentage of intermarriage is Africans Americans: Among new marriages in 2008 to 2010 that involved at least one African American spouse, 28 percent had a non-African-American second spouse—a much higher proportion than in the past. The historic racial barrier that was formally overturned in the aptly named *Loving* decision may finally be breaking down. Toward the high end of the intermarriage continuum are Hispanics at 44 percent and Asians at 46 percent, meaning that nearly half of all new marriages that involved at least one spouse from these groups were out-marriages. And among American Indians and Alaska Natives, 81 percent were out-marriages, reflecting the large share of the American Indian population that do not reside on reservations and that consider themselves to be multiracial.

There are gender differences in intermarriage, too. African American men are more likely to marry out than are African American women. Twenty-four percent of African American men who married in 2010 married someone other than an African American, compared to 9 percent of African American women who married in 2010 (Taylor, 2014). The lower out-marriage rate for African American women may reflect both their preference for finding a partner within their racial-ethnic group and the low rate at which white men approach them in dating markets (Banks, 2011; Lin & Lundquist, 2013).[3] Among Asian Americans, on the other hand, women are more likely to marry out than are men: 36 percent of Asian American women who married in 2010 married someone other than an Asian American, compared to 17 percent of Asian American men (Taylor, 2014). Some observers have suggested that white men seek Asian-origin women because they are seen as submissive, sexual, and stereotypically feminine (Nemoto, 2006); but Internet dating site contacts suggest that Asian American women actively send and respond to messages from white men (Lin & Lundquist, 2013). The racial-ethnic gender differences remain not well understood.

[3] An old literature claimed that African American men with substantial incomes can trade their socioeconomic status for low-income white wives who possess the culturally dominant standard of beauty (Davis, 1941; Merton 1941); but demographic evidence does not support this theory (Rosenfeld, 2005).

If these rates continue into the future, far more people could identify as "multiracial" when the Census Bureau comes around to ask about race a generation or two from now. For instance, as the children of interracial marriages involving American Indians reach adulthood, the continuing high rates could result in a further decline in the number of people identifying themselves solely as American Indians and a further increase—to a clear majority—in the proportion of people who identify themselves as American Indians and another race. Similarly, a majority of U.S.-born Americans with an Asian American or Hispanic parent could identify themselves as multiracial in a generation. The ultimate number of such people in the United States in the mid–twenty-first century will depend on whether intermarriage increases further and also on two other factors. The first is the level of immigration: Immigrants from Latin America and Asia will replenish the Hispanic and Asian American single-race groups while the U.S. members of these groups continue to marry out. Second, the propensity of people to think of themselves as multiracial could rise. Consider the golfer Tiger Woods, who became a symbol of twenty-first-century multiracial identity. He described his race as "Cablinasian": His father was black, Chinese, and American Indian, and his mother is Thai, Chinese, and white. If having a multiracial identity becomes more acceptable, it could provide a further boost to the multiracial numbers that the census will count.

INTERSECTIONALITY AND INTERMARRIAGE

The intersectionality perspective has been used to understand the role of marriage in the lives of college-educated black women (Banks, 2011; Clarke, 2011). Between 1970 and 2008, the proportion of young black women (age 25 to 34) with four-year college degrees increased sharply from 6 percent to 22 percent (Autor, 2010). They are more likely to marry than are black women without college degrees; this suggests that their class position, as measured by education, gives them an advantage in the marriage market. However, black women with college degrees are still far less likely to be married than are white women with college degrees (Isen & Stevenson, 2011). So their race puts them at a relative disadvantage compared to white women with the same level of education. In addition, black women are much less likely to marry someone of a different race than are black men. Since more black men are marrying out, the pool of potential spouses for black women is reduced. So the marriage rates of college-educated black women reflect their class position (they marry more often than less-educated black women), their race (they marry less often than white women), and their gender (they outmarry less often than black men). To understand their situation fully, one must consider their class position, race, and gender all at once. This unique intersection of class, race, and gender reduces the marriage rates of college-educated black women below that of comparably educated white women.

Quick Review

- Racial and ethnic intermarriage has increased greatly over the past few decades.
- Rates vary greatly, with intermarriages of Asians and American Indians at the high end and those of African Americans and non-Hispanic whites (due to their large population size) at the low end.
- Intermarriage has the potential to reshape individual and group identities over the next half-century.

Race, Ethnicity, and Kinship

Family ties have been central to the successes and the struggles of racial-ethnic groups in the United States. All the minority groups that have been discussed in this chapter have relied on their relatives for support—whether that support be food for dinner or money to buy a restaurant. Their reliance on extended kinship contrasts with the nuclear family ideal among non-Hispanic whites. To be sure, there are substantial differences among racial-ethnic groups in the kinds of family lives they tend to lead. Some of these differences reflect economic forces. Put another way, sometimes what we think of as ethnic or racial differences may, in large part, be class differences. For example, to compare Puerto Ricans on the mainland with Cubans on the mainland is to compare an economically disadvantaged group with a more economically privileged one.

Still, in Chapter 4 and this chapter, we have seen similarities across racial-ethnic groups in the ways low-income families organize family and kinship. Among these disadvantaged groups, the strongest family tie is often between a mother and her adult daughter. In what I have called women-centered kin networks, low-income women organize exchanges of support that extend across households, linking networks of people who share their meager resources.

Nevertheless, the precise form of kinship varies from group to group, reflecting, in my opinion, long-standing cultural differences. For example, the distinctive characteristic of Puerto Rican households is the consensual union, although there are also many households headed by women without live-in partners. Single-parent households, or grandmother-daughter-grandchild households, are common among low-income African Americans, with young mothers often residing with their own mothers for several years. For all these groups, assistance from family members other than one's spouse or partner is crucial for subsisting from day to day.

Among many immigrant groups, family ties provide critical assistance to individuals who wish to start small businesses. Most banks will not lend money to new immigrants because they are not sure they will be repaid. Immigrants tend not to have homes or other assets that they can use as collateral to secure a bank loan. Sometimes, however, they can obtain start-up loans from members of their kinship and community networks. Those who loan the money rely upon kinship and community ties as a form of moral collateral: A borrower puts his reputation and standing among his peers on the line when he or she obtains a loan. If the borrower were to default, he or she would be dishonored before family and friends. Thus, kinship ties provide a form of social capital that immigrants can use to obtain the financial capital—money, equipment, storefronts—needed to start an enterprise. These same ties also become recruiting networks through which members of the group can find jobs.

The immigrant entrepreneurs utilize what we might call marriage-centered kin networks. These exchanges tend to connect households that are headed by husbands and wives. It is the married couple that starts and maintains the business, although other relatives may work in it. Ties to a wider network of kin provide financial assistance that the married couple is allowed to manage largely for its own benefit. In contrast, women-centered kin networks require that any surplus be shared. In this way, the kin networks of the poor allow the maximum number of people to get the resources they need to avoid becoming destitute. Thus, the two kinds of kinship networks have different functions: Marriage-centered networks allow for the accumulation of resources by the husband-wife household, whereas women-centered networks allow for the maximum sharing of resources across predominantly single-parent households.

I would suggest that these two forms of kin networks have different strengths and limitations. The women-centered networks are superior for easing the hardships of persistent poverty. They have allowed many poor individuals to subsist from day to day. Yet they make it difficult for network members to accumulate the resources necessary to rise above poverty. The marriage-based networks, on the other hand, are superior for allowing people to be upwardly mobile by accumulating enough resources to start a business or move to a better neighborhood. Yet they make it difficult for network members to provide assistance to all kin who need it. The differences between the two networks suggest, therefore, a tension that many people with low incomes may face: helping all of one's kin who need assistance versus accumulating enough money to better the position of one's own household. Different racial-ethnic groups resolve this tension in different ways.

This is not to suggest that whether a household escapes from poverty is solely, or even primarily, a matter of kinship networks. For instance, education also matters. Asian Americans have a higher percentage of college graduates than non-Hispanic whites (Pew Research Center, 2017b). In addition, a case could be made that, although there has been discrimination against Asian Americans, it has not been as institutionalized and as pervasive as has discrimination against African Americans. Moreover, the restructuring of the economy has had a major effect on the family lives of African Americans because of the loss of manufacturing jobs that black men used to take. Still, within these constraints, family and kinship patterns appear to make a difference in the life chances of the members of racial-ethnic groups, allowing many to survive and some to prosper.

Looking Back

1. **How are racial and ethnic groups constructed?** Racial and ethnic groups are socially constructed rather than reflecting natural, timeless divisions among people. Beliefs about what constitutes race in the United States have changed over time. Two examples of the changing definitions of race and ethnicity are the categories of "Hispanic" and "Asian." Each was created in the United States and each includes very diverse subgroups from many nations. Even whiteness can be considered as a socially constructed ethnicity.

2. **How has African American family life changed over the past several decades?** African Americans have been adversely affected by economic changes that have reduced the number of semiskilled and skilled blue-collar jobs available to American workers. In part as a result of this economic transformation, the importance of marriage in African American families has declined substantially relative to ties to extended kin such as grandmothers. The link between childbearing and marriage has also weakened; about two-thirds of black children are now born to unmarried mothers. African Americans have responded to these changes by drawing on the network of kin for mutual support. During the same period, however, a substantial African American middle class has emerged.

3. **What are the family patterns of major Hispanic ethnic groups?** The largest Hispanic group, Mexican Americans, is characterized by early marriage and relatively high birthrates. These reflect the distinctive behavior of recent immigrants; Mexican-origin Americans who were born in the United States, on the other hand, are not as different from other Americans in marriage and

childbearing. Among Puerto Ricans, the poorest of the major Hispanic groups, a relatively high number of children are born to unmarried mothers. But some of these mothers live with partners in consensual unions that they consider to be like marriages. Cuban Americans are the most prosperous Hispanic group, although recent immigrants have reduced the group's economic standing. Most Cuban Americans settled in an immigrant enclave in the Miami area and many started family-based businesses.

4. **What are the distinctive characteristics of the family patterns of Asian Americans?** More than in any other group, including non-Hispanic whites, Asian American families are headed by married couples. These families also have comparatively few children born outside of marriage and low divorce rates—characteristics that probably reflect a greater emphasis on the interdependence and mutual obligations of kin. Although some Asian subgroups are poor, Asian American families as a whole have a higher median income than non-Hispanic white families. A majority of young adult Asian Americans now marry non-Asians.

5. **How does the concept of "social capital" apply to immigrant families?** Some Hispanic immigrant groups, most notably the Cubans and many Asian immigrant groups, use ties to others in their ethnic community to achieve certain goals, such as starting a business. This use of social connections to advance oneself is an example of what sociologists call social capital.

6. **How is intermarriage affecting racial and ethnic groups?** Rates of intermarriage have increased greatly in recent decades. For some groups, such as Asians and Hispanics, rates are so high that a majority of each group may soon identify as multiracial. Rates of intermarriage are lower among African Americans, although they also have increased substantially.

Study Questions

1. What are the pros and cons of the use of "umbrella" racial-ethnic group designations such as "Hispanic" and "Asian"?
2. Does it make sense to consider "whites" as a racial-ethnic group?
3. What does research suggest about economic and cultural influences on the decline of marriage among African Americans?
4. Why might middle-class African American families have more difficulty maintaining their status than middle-class white families?
5. Why might Mexican American and Puerto Rican family patterns be different?
6. What are the likely implications of the high rates at which Asian Americans and American Indians marry outside of their racial-ethnic groups?
7. How does the concept of intersectionality help us to understand the marriage rates of college-educated black women?
8. Why might marriage-centered kin networks be advantageous to immigrant entrepreneurs?

Key Terms

Asian American 120
assimilation 135
consensual union 134
Hispanic 120
immigrant enclave 135
mediating structures 131
non-Hispanic white 121
racial-ethnic group 120
social capital 138
total fertility rate (TFR) 133

Thinking about Families

The Public Family	The Private Family
Should more native-born Americans care for their aging parents the way many immigrant groups do?	**Interracial and interethnic marriages are widespread among Asian Americans and American Indians, common among Hispanics, and uncommon but increasing among African Americans. How might intergroup marriage change American families in the early decades of the twenty-first century?**

References

Autor, D. (2010). The polarization of job opportunities in the U.S. Labor market: Implications for employment and earnings. *Brookings Institution: The Hamilton Project.* Retrieved May 23, 2014, from http://www.brookings.edu/~/media/Files/rc/papers/2010/04_jobs_autorA34_jobs_autor.pdf

Banks, R. R. (2011). *Is marriage for white people? How the African American marriage decline affects everyone.* New York: Dutton.

Bean, F. D., & Tienda, M. (1987). *The Hispanic population of the United States.* New York: Russell Sage Foundation.

Berger, B., & Berger, P. L. (1983). *The war over the family: Capturing the middle ground.* Garden City, New York.

Berry, M. F., & Blassingame, J. W. (1982). *Long memory: The black experience in America.* New York: Oxford University Press.

Bertera, E., & Crewe, S. E. (2013). Parenthood in the twenty-first century: African American grandparents as surrogate parents. *Journal of Human Behavior in the Social Environment, 23,* 178–192.

Bourdieu, P. (1980). Le capital social: Notes provisaire. *Actes de la recherche en sciences sociales, 3,* 2–3.

Cherlin, A. J., Cumberworth, E., Morgan, S. P., & Wimer, C. (2013). The effects of the Great Recession on family structure and fertility. *Annals of the American Academy of Political and Social Science, 650*(November), 214–231.

Cherlin, A. J., & Furstenberg, F. F., Jr. (1992). *The new American grandparent: A place in the family, a life apart.* Cambridge, MA.: Harvard University Press.

Chishti, M., & Hipsman, F. (2016). Increased Central American migration to the United States may prove an enduring phenomenon. *Migration Policy Institute.* Retrieved April 27, 2019, from https://www.migrationpolicy.org/article/increased-central-american-migration-united-states-may-proveenduring-phenomenon

Clarke, A. Y. (2011). *Inequalities of love: College-educated black women and the barriers to romance and family.* Durham: Duke University Press.

Coates, T.-N. P. (2007, February 1). Is Obama black enough? *Time.*

Coleman, J. S. (1988). Social capital in the creation of human capital. *American Journal of Sociology, 94 Supplement,* S95–S120.

Crouch, S. (2006, November 2). What Obama isn't: Black like me on race. *New York Daily News.*

Davis, K. (1941). Intermarriage in caste societies. *American Anthropologist, 43,* 376–395.

Furstenberg, F. F. (2009). If Moynihan had only known: Race, class, and family change in the late twentieth century. *Annals of the American Academy of Political and Social Science, 621,* 94–110.

Gilkes, C. T. (1995). The storm and the light: Church, family, work, and social crisis in the African-American experience. In N. Ammerman & W. C. Roof (Eds.), *Work, family, and religion in contemporary society* (pp. 177–198). New York: Routledge.

Glick, J. E., Bean, F. D., & Van Hook, J. V. W. (1997). Immigration and changing patterns of extended family household structure in the United States: 1970–1990. *Journal of Marriage and Family, 59,* 177–191.

Glick, J. E., & Van Hook, J. (2002). Parents' coresidence with adult children: Can immigration explain racial and ethnic variation? *Journal of Marriage and Family, 64,* 240–253.

Gold, S. J. (1993). Migration and family adjustment: Continuity and change among Vietnamese in the United States. In H. McAdoo (Ed.), *Family ethnicity* (pp. 300–314).

Goode, W. J. (1963). *World revolution and family patterns.* New York: The Free Press.

Harjo, S. S. (1993). The American Indian experience. In H. McAdoo (Ed.), *Family ethnicity* (pp. 199–207).

Haub, C. (2006). Hispanics account for almost one-half of U.S. Population growth. Retrieved February 22, 2006, from http://www.prb.org

Hill, S. A. (2005). *Black intimacies: A gender perspective on families and relationships.* Walnut Creek, CA: AltaMira Press.

Hofferth, S. (1984). Kin networks, race, and family structure. *Journal of Marriage and the Family, 46,* 791–806.

Isen, A., & Stevenson, B. (2011). Women's education and family behavior: Trends in marriage, divorce, and fertility. In J. B. Shoven (Ed.), *Demography and the economy* (pp. 107–142). Chicago: University of Chicago Press.

Ishii-Kuntz, M. (2000). Diversity within Asian-American families. In D. H. Demo, K. R. Allen, & M. A. Fine (Eds.), *The handbook of family diversity* (pp. 247–292). New York: Oxford University Press.

Johnson, S. H., & Rendall, M. S. (2004). The fertility contribution of Mexican immigration to the United States. *Demography, 41,* 129–150.

Jordan, M. (2018). Trump administration says that nearly 200,000 Salvadorans must leave. *The New York Times.* Retrieved, April 27, 2019, from https://www.nytimes.com/2018/01/08/us/salvadorans-tps-end.html

Landale, N. S., & Oropesa, R. S. (2007). Hispanic families: Stability and change. *Annual Review of Sociology, 33,* 381–405.

Landale, N. S., Oropesa, R. S., & Bradatan, C. (2006). Hispanic families in the United States: Family structure and process in an era of family change. In M. Tienda & F. Mitchell (Eds.), *Hispanics and the future of America* (pp. 138–178).

Landry, B. (2000). *Black working wives: Pioneers of the new family revolution.* Berkeley: University of California Press.

Lee, S. M. (1998). Asian Americans: Diverse and growing *Population bulletin* (Vol. 53). Washington, DC: Population Reference Bureau.

Lee, S. M., & Edmonston, B. (2005). New marriages, new families: U.S. Racial and Hispanic intermarriage. *Population Bulletin, 60*(2), 1–36.

Lesser, G., & Batalova, J. (2017). Central American immigrants in the United States. *Migration Policy Institute.* Retrieved April 28, 2019 from https://www.migrationpolicy.org/article/central-american-immigrants-unitedstates#Immigration_pathways

Levy, F. (1998). *The new dollars and dreams: American incomes and economic change.* New York: Russell Sage Foundation.

Lichter, D. T., McLaughlin, D. K., Kephart, G., & Landry, D. J. (1992). Race and the retreat from marriage: A shortage of marriageable men? *American Sociological Review, 57,* 781–799.

Lichter, D. T., & Qian, Z. (2004). Marriage and family in a multiracial society. *The American People: Census 2000.* New York and Washington: Russell Sage Foundation and Population Reference Bureau.

Lin, C., & Liu, W. T. (1993). Intergenerational relationships among Chinese immigrants from Taiwan. In H. McAdoo (Ed.), *Family ethnicity* (pp. 271–286).

Lin, K.-H., & Lundquist, J. (2013). Mate selection in cyberspace: The intersection of race, gender, and education. *American Journal of Sociology, 119*(1).

Loving v Virginia, 347 1 (U.S. 1967).

Lundquist, J. H. (2004). When race makes no difference: Marriage and the military. *Social Forces, 83,* 731–757.

Lundquist, J. H., & Smith, H. L. (2005). Family formation among women in the U.S. Military: Evidence from the NLSY. *Journal of Marriage and Family, 67,* 1–13.

Martin, S., Astone, N. M., & Peters, H. E. (2014). Fewer marriages, more divergence: Marriage projections for millennials to age 40. Retrieved January 12, 2015, from http://www.urban.org/UploadedPDF/413110-Fewer-Marriages-More-Divergence.pdf?RSSFeed=Urban.xml

Massey, D. S., Charles, C. Z., Lunday, G. F., & Fischer, M. J. (2003). *The source of the river: The social origins of freshmen at America's selective colleges and universities.* Princeton: Princeton University Press.

McDermott, M., & Samson, F. L. (2005). White racial and ethnic identity in the United States. *Annual Review of Sociology, 31,* 245–261.

McRoberts, O. M. (2003). *Streets of glory: Church and community in a black urban neighborhood.* Chicago: University of Chicago Press.

Menjífvar, C. (1999). The intersection of work and gender: Central American immigrant women and employment in California. *American Behavioral Scientist, 42*(4), 601–627.

Menjífvar, C. (2006). Liminal legality: Salvadoran and Guatemalan immigrants' lives in the United States. *American Journal of Sociology, 111*(4), 999–1037.

Menjífvar, C., & Abrego, L. (2012). Legal violence: Immigration law and the lives of Central American immigrants. *American Journal of Sociology, 117*(5), 1380–1421.

Menjívar, C., & Lakhani, S. M. (2016). Transformative effects of immigration law: Immigrants' personal and social metamorphoses through regularization. *American Journal of Sociology, 121*(6), 1818–1855.

Merton, R. K. (1941). Intermarriage and the social structure: Fact and theory. *Psychiatry, 4,* 361–374.

Messick, M., & Bergeron, C. (2014). Temporary protected status in the United States: A grant of humanitarian relief that is less than permanent. *Migration Policy Institute.* Retrieved April 27, 2019, from https://www.migrationpolicy.org/article/temporary-protected-status-united-states-grant-humanitarianrelief-less-permanent

Nagel, J. (1995). American Indian ethnic renewal: Politics and the resurgence of identity. *American Sociological Review, 60,* 947–965.

Nagel, J. (1996). *American Indian ethnic renewal: Red power and the resurgence of identity and culture.* New York: Oxford University Press.

Nemoto, K. (2006). Intimacy, desire, and the construction of self in relationships between Asian American women and white American men *Journal of Asian American Studies, 9*(1), 27–54.

Oliver, M., & Shapiro, T. M. (1995). *Black wealth/white wealth: A new perspective on racial inequality.* New York: Routledge.

Oropesa, R. S., Landale, N. S., & Kenkre, T. (2003). Income allocation in marital and cohabiting unions: The case of mainland Puerto Ricans. *Journal of Marriage and Family, 65,* 910–926.

Pattillo, M. (2005). Black middle-class neighborhoods. *Annual Review of Sociology, 31,* 305–329.

Pattillo-McCoy, M. (1999). *Black picket fences: Privilege and peril among the black middle class.* Chicago: University of Chicago Press.

Pew Hispanic Center. (2012). Net migration from Mexico falls to zero—and perhaps less. *Pew Hispanic Center.* Retrieved January 2, 2019, from http://assets.pewresearch.org/wp-content/uploads/sites/7/2012/04/PHC-Net-Migration-from-Mexico-Falls-to-Zero.pdf

Pew Research Center. (2012). The 10 largest Hispanic origin groups: Characteristics, rankings, top counties. *Hispanic Trends.* Retrieved January 3, 2019, from http://www.pewhispanic.org/2012/06/27/the-10-largest-hispanic-origin-groups-characteristics-rankings-top-counties/

Pew Research Center. (2015a). Hispanics of Puerto Rican origin in the United States, 2013. *Hispanic Trends.* Retrieved January 3, 2019, from http://www.pewhispanic.org/2015/09/15/hispanics-of-puerto-rican-origin-in-the-united-states-2013/

Pew Research Center. (2015b). More Mexicans leaving than coming to the U.S. *Pew Research Center.* Retrieved January 2, 2019, from http://www.pewhispanic.org/2015/11/19/more-mexicans-leaving-than-coming-to-the-u-s/

Pew Research Center. (2015c). Puerto Ricans leave in record numbers for mainland U.S. *Fact Tank.* Retrieved January 3, 2019, from http://www.pewresearch.org/fact-tank/2015/10/14/puerto-ricans-leave-in-record-numbers-for-mainland-u-s/

Pew Research Center. (2017a). How the U.S. Hispanic population is changing. *Fact Tank.* Retrieved April 27, 2019, from http://www.pewresearch.org/fact-tank/2017/09/18/how-the-u-s-hispanic-population-is-changing/

Pew Research Center. (2017b). Key facts about Asian Americans, a diverse and growing population. *Fact Tank.* Retrieved January 2, 2019, from http://www.pewresearch.org/fact-tank/2017/09/08/key-facts-about-asian-americans/

Pew Research Center. (2017c). Korean population in the U.S., 2000-2015. *Social and Demographic Trends.* Retrieved January 3, 2019, from http://www.pewsocialtrends.org/chart/korean-population-in-the-u-s/

Pew Research Center. (2017d). Rise in U.S. Immigrants from El Salvador, Guatemala and Honduras outpaces growth from elsewhere. *Hispanic Trends.* Retrieved January 3, 2019, from http://www.pewhispanic.org/2017/12/07/rise-in-u-s-immigrants-from-el-salvador-guatemala-and-honduras-outpaces-growth-from-elsewhere/

Portes, A., & Jensen, L. (1989). The enclave and the entrants: Patterns of ethnic enterprise in Miami before and after Mariel. *American Sociological Review, 54*(6), 929–949.

Portes, A., & Sensenbrenner, J. (1993). Embeddedness and immigration: Notes on the social determinants of economic action. *American Journal of Sociology, 98,* 1320–1350.

Raley, R. K., Durden, T. E., & Wildsmith, E. (2004). Understanding Mexican-American marriage patterns using a life-course approach. *Social science quarterly, 85,* 872–890.

Rasmussen, B. B., Klinenberg, E., Nexica, I. J., & Wray, M. (Eds.). (2001). *The making and unmaking of whiteness.* Durham, NC: Duke University Press.

Rodgers, W. C., & Thornton, A. (1985). Changing patterns of first marriage in the United States. *Demography, 22,* 265–279.

Roschelle, A. R. (1997). *No more kin: Exploring race, class, and gender in family networks.* Thousand Oaks, CA: Sage.

Rosenfeld, M. J. (2001). The salience of pan-national Hispanic and Asian identities in the U.S. Marriage markets. *Demography, 38,* 161–175.

Rosenfeld, M. J. (2005). A critique of exchange theory in mate selection. *American Journal of Sociology, 110* (March), 1284–1325.

Rossi, A. S., & Rossi, P. H. (1990). *Of human bonding: Parent-child relations across the life course.* New York: Aldine de Gruyter.

Sandefur, G. D., & Liebler, C. A. (1997). The demography of American Indian families. *Population Research and Policy Review, 16,* 95–114.

Sarkisian, N., & Gerstel, N. (2004). Kin support among blacks and whites: Race and family organization. *American Sociological Review, 69,* 812–837.

Schneider, D. (2011). Wealth and the marital divide. *American Journal of Sociology, 117,* 627–667.

Shoemaker, N. (1991). Native American families. In J. H. Hawes & E. Nybakkin (Eds.), *American families: A research guide and historical handbook* (pp. 291–317). New York: Greenwood Press.

Smith, T. W., Davern, M., Freese, J., & Hout, M. (2017). General social surveys, 1972–2016. Machine readable data file. Chicago: National Opinion Research Center.

Snipp, C. M. (2002). American Indian and Alaska native children in the 2000 census: A kids count/prb report. Retrieved January 29, 2009, from http://www.prb.org/pdf/indian_alaska_children.pdf

Stack, C. B. (1974). *All our kin: Strategies for survival in a black community.* New York: Harper and Row.

Suarez, Z. E. (1993). Cuban exiles: From golden exiles to social undesirables. In H. McAdoo (Ed.), *Family ethnicity: Strength in diversity* (pp. 164–176). Newbury Park, CA: Sage Publications.

Swidler, A. (2001). *Talk of love: How culture matters.* Chicago: University of Chicago Press.

Taylor, P. (2014). *The next America: Boomers, millennials, and the looming generational showdown.* New York: PublicAffairs.

Teachman, J. (2007). Race, military service, and marital timing: Evidence from the NLSY-79. *Demography, 44,* 389–404.

The New York Times. (2007, July 24). Transcript: Fourth democratic debate.

Twine, F., & Gallagher, C. (2007). The future of whiteness: A map of the "third wave". *Ethnic and Racial Studies, 31,* 4–24.

U.S. Bureau of the Census. (2011a). Overview of race and Hispanic origin: 2010. Retrieved August 26, 2019, from https://www.census.gov/prod/cen2010/briefs/c2010br-02.pdf

U.S. Bureau of the Census. (2011b). Table 1. Detailed living arrangements of children by race, Hispanic origin, and age: 2009. Retrieved August 5, 2018, from https://www.census.gov/hhes/socdemo/children/data/sipp/living2009/tab01.pdf

U.S. Bureau of the Census. (2017). Table FINC-01. Selected characteristics of families by total money income in 2016. *Current Population Survey, Annual Social and Economic Supplement.* Retrieved August 7, 2018, from https://www.census.gov/data/tables/time-series/demo/income-poverty/cps-finc/finc-01.html

U.S. Bureau of the Census. (2018a). Table FM-2. All parent/child situations by type, race, and Hispanic origin of householder or reference person: 1970 to present. *Families and Living Arrangements.* Retrieved January 17, 2019, from https://www.census.gov/data/tables/time-series/demo/families/families.html

U.S. Bureau of the Census. (2018b). Using two separate questions for race and ethnicity in 2018 end-to-end Census test and 2020 Census. *2020 Census Program Memorandum Series.* Retrieved August 5, 2020, from https://www.census.gov/programs-surveys/decennial-census/2020-census/planning-management/memo-series/2020-memo-2018_02.html

U.S. House of Representatives Committee on Post Office and Civil Service. (1994). Hearings: Review of federal measurements of race and ethnicity *Serial no. 103–7* (pp. 105–106). Washington, DC: U.S. Government Printing Office.

U.S. National Center for Health Statistics. (1995). Births to unmarried mothers: United States, 1980–92. *Vital and Health Statistics, Series 21, no. 53.* Retrieved February 2, 2009, from http://www.cdc.gov/nchs/data/series/sr_21/sr21_053.pdf

U.S. National Center for Health Statistics. (2017). Births: Final data for 2015. *National Vital Statistics Report, Vol. 66, no. 1.* Retrieved August 9, 2017, from https://www.cdc.gov/nchs/data/nvsr/nvsr66/nvsr66_01.pdf

U.S. National Center for Health Statistics. (2018a). Births: Final data for 2016. *National Vital Statistics Reports.* Retrieved August 5, 2018, from https://www.cdc.gov/nchs/data/nvsr/nvsr67/nvsr67_01.pdf

U.S. National Center for Health Statistics. (2018b). Deaths: Leading causes for 2016. *National Vital Statistics Reports.* Retrieved August 5, 2018, from https://www.cdc.gov/nchs/data/nvsr/nvsr67/nvsr67_06.pdf

U.S. Office of Minority Health. (2018). Profile: American Indian/Alaska native. Retrieved August 1, 2018, from https://minorityhealth.hhs.gov/omh/browse.aspx?lvl=3&lvlid=62

Western, B., & Wildeman, C. (2009). The black family and mass incarceration. *The Annals of the American Academy of Political and Social Science, 621,* 221–242.

Wilson, K. L., & Portes, A. (1980). Immigrant enclaves: An analysis of the labor market experiences of Cubans in Miami. *American Journal of Sociology, 86,* 295–319.

Wilson, W. J. (1987). *The truly disadvantaged: The inner city, the underclass, and public policy.* Chicago: University of Chicago Press.

Wilson, W. J. (1996). *When work disappears.* New York: Knopf.

Wright, L. (1994). One drop of blood. *The New Yorker,* pp. 46–55.

Zhou, M., & Bankston III, C. L. (1998). *Growing up American: How Vietnamese children adapt to life in the United States.* New York: Russell Sage Foundation.

Part Three

Sexuality, Partnership, and Marriage

In the next three chapters, we move from a focus on the effects of gender, race-ethnicity, and class to a consideration of how intimate relationships are built from the ground up, how they are structured as partnerships and marriages, and how family members care for each other. These chapters examine the challenges that people experience as they come to form partnerships and marriages. Chapter 6 discusses the great changes in sexual attitudes and practices over the past half-century. It looks at the family lives of LGBTQ individuals. It also covers childbearing outside of marriage, which is a consequence of changing sexual practices. Attention then shifts in Chapter 7 to marriage and cohabitation. We will first study courtship patterns in the past, the rise and fall of dating, the increase in independent living, and living apart relationships. We will then review how marriage changed to a companionship in the early 1900s and how it recently has changed again to a more individualized kind of partnership. We will also examine the complex phenomenon of cohabitation, or "living together." Chapter 8 will examine the complex connections between work and families. We will first study the growth in dual-earner couples as married women have entered the paid labor force. We will also examine the important, largely unpaid, caring work that family members, most of them women, do for their partners, children, parents, and kin. We will also consider changes in who does the housework and the child care in dual-earner families. Finally, we'll look at how the workplace can become more family friendly.

Chapter Six

Sexualities

Looking Forward

1. What determines people's sexual identities?
2. Is "sexual identity" still a useful way to think about people's sexuality?
3. What are the family lives of LGBTQ individuals like?
4. What are the patterns of sexual activity in committed relationships and outside of relationships?
5. What is the nature of the teenage pregnancy "problem"?

Sexual Identities

Kinsey Report a 1948 book by Alfred Kinsey detailing the results of thousands of interviews with men about their sexual behavior

No one did more to demonstrate that the boundaries between heterosexuality and homosexuality are unclear in American society than Alfred Kinsey, a zoology professor at the University of Indiana. In 1948 he published the results of thousands of interviews with men about their sexual behavior. Kinsey's dry, statistical book with 173 figures and 162 tables, often referred to as the **Kinsey Report,** became an immediate best seller. His findings on homosexuality shocked the country: Half of all men in his sample, he reported, acknowledged having had erotic feelings toward other men; one-third had at least one sexual experience with another man; one out of eight had sexual experiences predominantly with other men for at least three years; and 4 percent had had sexual experiences exclusively with other men (Kinsey, Pomeroy, & Martin, 1948). Kinsey concluded from his study that sexual orientation was a continuum running from exclusively heterosexual behavior to a mixture of heterosexual and homosexual behavior to exclusively homosexual behavior. Thus the book contained two far-reaching conclusions. First, the proportion of men whose experiences were predominantly homosexual was higher than most had imagined. Although Kinsey gave a range of figures, the one that came to dominate public discussion was that 10 percent of males were "more or less exclusively homosexual" for at least three years between the ages of 16 and 55 (Kinsey et al., 1948). Second, an even larger number of men had some homosexual experience or feelings.

Although Kinsey's general conclusions still stand, his figures are not representative of the U.S. population now and probably were not then either. His study was based entirely on interviews with volunteers, the vast majority of them white, well educated, young, and from the Midwest and Northeast. Since then, new data have been collected that provide more representative percentages. And scholars have put forth theoretical perspectives that help to interpret these numbers.

THE DETERMINANTS OF SEXUAL IDENTITIES

Some sociologists and like-minded scholars take the position that sexual identities are completely determined by society. Others take the position that biological influences may also play a significant role in determining people's sexual identities. Here is the case for each of these viewpoints.

social constructionist perspective (on sexuality) the belief that human sexual identities are entirely socially constructed

The Social Constructionist Perspective What we might call the **social constructionist perspective** on human sexual identities is that sexual identities are *entirely* socially created (Seidman, 2003). Advocates of this perspective point to many kinds of evidence. They note the unclear boundaries of the two-gender, heterosexually dominant model. For instance, they might cite the between-man-and-woman genders such as the two-spirits. They might remind us of the deep friendships of women in the nineteenth century (Smith-Rosenberg, 1975). They would note that in much of ancient Greece and Rome, men were allowed, even expected, to desire sex with other men or boys as well as with women (Ariès, 1985b). The Greek biographer and historian Plutarch wrote:

> *The noble lover of beauty engages in love wherever he sees excellence and splendid natural endowment without regard for any difference in physiological detail. The lover of human beauty [will] be fairly and equably disposed toward both sexes, instead of supposing that males and females are as different in the matter of love as they are in their clothes.*[1]

Yet although the Greeks had words for specific sexual tastes, they had no general term comparable to "homosexuality" (Weinrich & Williams, 1991).

The social constructionists would also argue that even today sexual identities vary from culture to culture. For example, in Brazil and some other Latin American countries, a man who always takes the active, penetrating role in sex with other men would not necessarily be thought of as a "homosexual," whereas a man who always takes the passive role would (Rebhun, 1999). In other words, a man's sexuality depends on whether he plays the "masculine" role in sex, in which case he may be considered heterosexual even if he sometimes has sex with other men. Cultural and historical variations such as these lead sociologists to argue that the sexual categories we use are defined by the society we live in.

The social constructionists would also point to the findings from national surveys about sexual life. Between 2011 and 2013, a U.S. government agency asked detailed questions about sexual life in a random-sample survey of Americans ages 18 to 44, the National Survey of Family Growth. (Although the researchers strongly defend their methods, some observers have expressed skepticism about the possibility of doing a survey on sexual behavior. See *How Do Sociologists Know What They Know?:* Asking about Sensitive Behavior.)

The NSFG measured sexual orientation in several ways, three of which are shown in Figure 6.1 (on page 156). Each person was asked whether he or she had had any same-sex sexual contact in their lifetime; the set of two bars on the left shows that 17.4 percent of women and 6.2 percent of men said yes. The second set of bars reports responses to a question, "People are different in their sexual attraction to other people. Which best describes your feelings?" Then a range of responses was presented, from "only attracted" to the opposite sex to "mostly" to "equally attracted to males and females" to "mostly" and "only" attracted to the same sex. The bars show that 19.0 percent of women reported at least some attraction to the same sex (in other words, they did *not* choose "only attracted to males"), compared to 7.9 percent of men. The last set of bars shows responses to a question on sexual identity: "Do you think of yourself as . . . Heterosexual, Homosexual, Bisexual, or Something else?" Among women 6.8 percent chose homosexual or bisexual, and among men 3.9 percent did. An additional 1 percent of women and men refused to answer the question or said that they did not know. Women were more likely to choose bisexual (5.5 percent) than homosexual, while men were equally likely to choose homosexual or bisexual.

[1] Quoted in Boswell (1982).

How Do Sociologists Know What They Know?

Asking about Sensitive Behavior

How do sociologists collect information on people's behaviors and attitudes? For the most part, they ask them. The most common way of doing so is through the random sample survey. Typically, a survey research organization will be hired to randomly select households and to ask the occupants a list of questions. In 1992, the National Opinion Research Center, one of the leading academic survey research organizations, asked a random sample of 3,432 adults detailed questions about their sexual activities and preferences. Researchers from the University of Chicago, who had written the questions, tabulated the results and published *The Social Organization of Sexuality* (Laumann et al., 1994). In the 2000s and 2010s, the U.S. National Center for Health Statistics used similar questions in national surveys. Some of the results are presented in Figures 6.1 and 6.2 (on pages 156 and 166). Several other surveys have included questions on sexuality (Add Health, 2014; VanHaitsma, Paik, & Laumann, 2004).

But can those findings be trusted? After all, the interviewers were inquiring about some of the most private and sensitive aspects of behavior. Biologist Richard Lewontin, writing in the *New York Review of Books* (Lewontin, 1995a), ridiculed the Chicago sociologists for believing the responses of their subjects. His scathing critique, and the subsequent exchange of letters between social scientists and him, addressed the limits of survey-based sociological research.

Lewontin's main objection is that sociologists can't be sure that people tell the truth when asked about their behavior, especially when the topic is as sensitive as sexuality. Some people may lie, while others may not even admit the truth to themselves. Lewontin also pointed to a discrepancy in the data: Men reported 75 percent more sexual partners in the previous five years than did women. A few complexities aside, the average number of sexual partners of men and women should be almost the same. The authors examine this discrepancy and conclude that the most likely cause is that men exaggerate or women understate the number of partners when asked. Writes Lewontin: "If one takes the authors at their word, it would seem futile to take seriously the other results of the study" (1995a, p. 29).

The authors responded that although they "readily admit that we were not always successful in securing full disclosure," they "spent a great deal of time worrying about how we could check the reliability and honesty of our respondents' answers" (Laumann et al., 1995, p. 43). They used techniques such as asking similar questions at different points in the interview to see if a person's responses were consistent. For some sensitive questions, the respondents were given a form to fill out that they could return in a sealed envelope.

Lewontin was not appeased. For him, the sex survey is an example of sociology reaching for knowledge that is beyond its grasp. When they accept self-reports of sensitive behaviors and statistically analyze them, he argues, sociologists are trying too hard to imitate the natural sciences. Without adequate ways to measure information such as sexual behavior, and above all without the possibility of performing experiments, he maintains, sociology is limited:

FIGURE 6.1
Prevalence of three measures of same-sex sexual activity, women and men, aged 18 to 44, in the United States, 2011–2013. (*Source:* U. S. National Center for Health Statistics, 2016.)

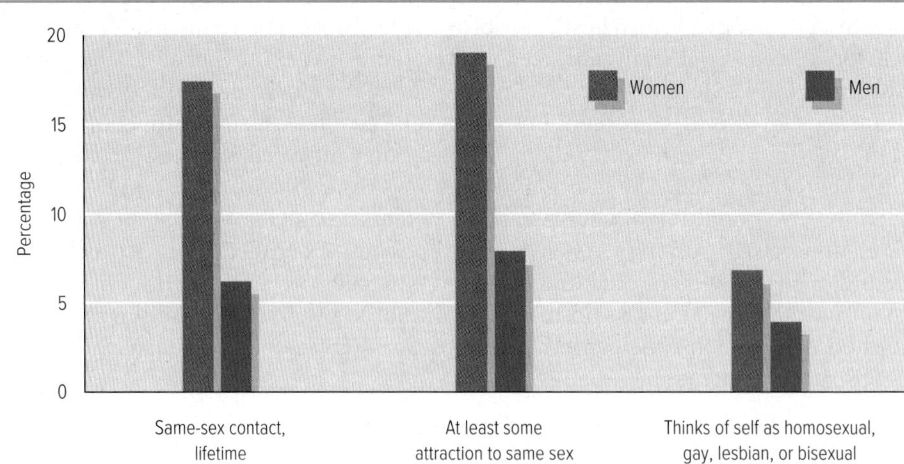

[Sociologists] are asking about the most complex and difficult phenomena in the most complex and recalcitrant organisms, without that liberty to manipulate their objects of study which is enjoyed by natural scientists. In comparison, the task of the molecular biologist is trivial. . . . Like it or not, there are a lot of questions that cannot be answered, and even more that cannot be answered exactly. There is nothing shameful in that admission. (Lewontin, 1995b, p. 44)

Lewontin's argument must be taken seriously by sociologists. There are indeed limits on how much sociologists can learn about human behavior, and random sample surveys and statistical analyses can't surmount these limits. For some problems, sociologists might be better off abandoning surveys and turning to the kind of intensive, long-term field observations that anthropologists and some sociologists do—even though the findings from field studies aren't necessarily representative of the population under study.

Does it follow that we should reject all findings from the study of sexual behavior because it is likely that men exaggerated, or women understated, their number of partners? This is a matter of judgment. My answer would be no. For one thing, comparisons among different groups represented in both older and newer samples are likely to be valid even if the individual responses aren't entirely accurate.

In addition, survey researchers have developed a better technique for asking about sensitive topics—the audio computer-assisted self-interview. Interviewees are given a laptop and provided with earphones. They see and hear questions that no one else in the room can see or hear. They respond merely by pressing number keys on the laptop, as instructed by the program. Studies have shown that this technique raises substantially the reported rates of injection drug usage, violent behavior, risky sex, and abortion (Turner, Forsyth, et al., 1998; Turner, Ku et al., 1998). This technique is now standard procedure for in-person interviews. Researchers also pay careful attention to issues of sampling, questionnaire design, and building trust with respondents (Michaels, 2013; Paik, 2015).

Yet, we should be wary of pushing survey research techniques beyond the limit of their usefulness. The sex surveys press on that limit. The more sensitive the material and the more subjective the questions, the more skeptical readers should be. Nevertheless, we needn't dismiss the contributions of survey research to understanding sensitive issues. We should seek to supplement surveys with other, more intensive forms of data gathering. And we should recognize that there may be some questions about society that are beyond the capability of sociology to answer.

Ask Yourself

1. If you were asked to participate in a study of college students' sexual behavior, would you answer all the questions truthfully? Would you participate in the study?
2. Why is knowing about people's sexual behavior and attitudes important? Give a specific example.

The NSFG survey, therefore, shows that the percentage of Americans who think of themselves as homosexual or bisexual is lower than the percentages who have ever had a same-sex sexual experience or who find same-sex activity at least somewhat appealing. Its findings confirm Kinsey's claim that sexual orientation is multidimensional and that no single number can adequately represent its prevalence. This conclusion suggests that there is no clear dividing line between heterosexuality and homosexuality and that the distinction is at least in part socially created.

In addition, the NSFG suggests that women's sexual identities may be more fluid than men's: More women find same-sex experiences at least somewhat attractive and more describe themselves as bisexual than homosexual. Men's heterosexuality seems more precarious—more easily questioned and lost—than women's: In a survey experiment, researchers found that when subjects were told that a man who had previously only dated women had one same-sex sexual encounter, they tended to question his heterosexuality; but when similar subjects were told that a woman who had previously only dated men had one same-sex encounter, they were not as likely to question her heterosexuality (Mize & Manago, 2018). It is as if a heterosexual identity is a fragile accomplishment for a man that must be maintained by strict boundaries.

integrative perspective (on sexuality) the belief that human sexual identities are determined by both social and biological factors

The Integrative Perspective Does biology also play a role in people's sexual identities? Almost no sociologists take the position that human sexuality is entirely driven by genes and hormones. However, some sociologists (I am one of them) take what Schwartz and Rutter (1998) call the **integrative perspective** on human sexuality: They argue that it is influenced by both social and biological factors. They would claim that while the social construction of sexual identities is very important, people may also be born with a sexual nature–a tendency to be attracted to partners of the opposite or the same gender. These sociologists reject the argument that genes and hormones have no influence on sexuality just because some societies have in-between genders and because the boundaries between the orientations are unclear. They point to two kinds of evidence: twin studies and genome-wide-association studies.

The twin studies take advantage of the varying genetic resemblance of different kinds of pairs of siblings. Identical twins share 100 percent of their genetic material, while fraternal twins and nontwin sibling pairs share, on average, 50 percent of their genetic material. Consequently, if same-sex attraction were partly genetic in origin, one might expect the greatest similarity of sexual orientation among identical-twin pairs such as two sisters who look exactly alike and were raised in the same household. One might expect less similarity among twin sisters who don't look alike or among two sisters who aren't twins. In one study, researchers recruited a national sample of pairs of siblings, some of them identical twins, some of them fraternal twins, and some of them not twins. They studied this question: If one of the twins described himself or herself as having a homosexual or bisexual orientation, what percentage of the time did the other twin also have a homosexual or bisexual orientation? The answer is 32 percent of the time among identical twins, against 15 percent of the time among fraternal twin and nontwin pairs. The higher percentage among identical twins supports the possibility that sexual orientation is partially genetically linked (Kendler, Thornton, Gilman, & Kessler, 2000).

As geneticists have mastered the technology of sequencing the genome–mapping out the genetic code of individuals based on samples of their DNA–the twin studies are being replaced by studies in which genetic resemblance is measured by comparing the entire genomes of individuals. One study of predominantly white men compared variations between the genomes of those who identified as homosexual and the genomes of those who identified as heterosexual. The researchers identified several locations on the genomes where the heterosexual and homosexual groups of men tended to differ (Sanders et al., 2017). The researchers cautioned that studies with larger samples (theirs was about 2,300) are needed before we can be confident that these differences hold. Moreover, they noted that biological influences on sexual orientation are likely to be found at multiple genetic locations–in other words, there is no such thing as a single, "gay" gene.

In addition, both the twin studies and the genomic studies, also suggest that sexual orientation is *not* completely genetically determined. After all, 68 percent of the identical twin pairs–who shared the same genetic material–had different sexual orientations in the twin study cited above. It is possible that something in the twins' environments may have influenced them differently. As is the case with gender differences, any biological effects probably operate not by determining a person's sexual orientation but rather by creating predispositions toward one orientation or the other. Social and cultural factors then further influence sexual orientation. But unlike gender differences—where substantial evidence exists of the different treatment boys and girls receive from parents, peers, schools, and the like—there is little evidence that parents or peers treat children who will grow up to identify as LGBTQ adults differently than they do other children. Moreover, the general failure of psychiatrists and psychologists to change the sexual orientation of gay and lesbian clients who wish to do so has undermined the credibility of the psychoanalytic explanation for same-sex attraction, which emphasizes unresolved issues of identification with one's parents. Nor is there any evidence that children and adolescents learn same-sex attraction from adults. So, although social and cultural factors quite likely play a role in sexual orientation, no satisfactory theories have been advanced to explain their role.

The biological studies have been controversial, in large part because of their political implications. Some observers argue that if attraction to people of the same gender is not a lifestyle choice but rather an inherent, immutable part of an individual's personality, there is little justification for restricting the legal rights of LGBTQ individuals. Other advocates argue that the studies are less consequential because civil rights should not depend on whether a person's style of life is cultural or biological in origin. To be sure, research into the biological origins of sexual orientation need not have political significance. Rather, its purpose could be the same as that of most of the research discussed in this book—to increase our understanding of why people behave as they do in their family and personal lives. The great variation from society to society in the ways that sexual orientation is structured—the two-spirit tradition, the acceptance of same-sex relations among the ancient Greeks and Romans, the mental illness model of the United States in the first half of the twentieth century, the emergence of an open lesbian and gay subculture in the 1960 and 1970s, to the national legalization of same-sex marriage in 2015—shows that social forces are an important part of the explanation for the behaviors and attitudes that emerge. But it seems likely that biological forces are also part of the story.

Points of Agreement and Disagreement In sum, almost all sociologists agree that the type of society a person lives in influences such characteristics as whether individuals become exclusively heterosexual or identify as LGBTQs, what social groups they draw their partners from, and what range of sexual acts they undertake. The main disagreement, then, between partisans of the social constructionist and integrative perspectives is whether society *completely* determines sexual identities. The former group would say that the influence of biology is minimal, whereas the latter group would say that both society and biology matter.

Quick Review

- Some sociologists believe that sexual identity is entirely socially created; they cite variations over time and from society to society.
- Surveys suggest that a substantial number of people have some homoerotic feelings but a smaller percentage are exclusively gay or lesbian.
- Other sociologists believe that both biological and social factors determine sexual identities; they point to genetic studies and twin studies.

QUESTIONING SEXUAL IDENTITIES

Over the past few decades, a newer perspective has emerged which questions the whole idea of fixed, stable sexual identities. Whereas the older literature focused on questions such as the extent to which a person's gay or lesbian identity is socially constructed, the newer literature focuses on whether it is meaningful to speak of a gay, lesbian, or heterosexual identity at all. In reality, the newer perspective says, such identities are always shifting, unstable, and arbitrary. There are many kinds of "gay identities," the writers argue, including the resident in a "gay" neighborhood who openly lives with a partner; the business executive who restricts his social life to weekends; and the married suburbanite who occasionally and furtively has sex with men (Brekhus, 2003). Because of this diversity, it is argued, you cannot simply label someone as gay (or straight). To use these labels is to buy into a system of heteronormativity in which heterosexuals regulate everyone's sexual behavior along rigid and constraining lines. Instead, sociologists are urged to examine the entire system by which we classify people's sexual lives in a way that privileges the people we call heterosexual and puts the rest at a disadvantage.

As noted in Chapter 1, the name that the advocates of this point of view, who span cultural studies, comparative literature, history, sociology, and other disciplines, have chosen for their perspective is queer theory. The essence of queer theory is the view that sexual life is artificially organized into categories that reflect the power of heterosexual norms. These norms restrict the possibilities for a more fluid, changing sexual identity in order to protect the dominance of heterosexuality as it is currently organized. Queer theorists reject a sharp split of sexual activity into either a straight or gay way of life. They also reject the subdiscipline of gay and lesbian studies, arguing that to accept these categories as the starting point is to accept what must be questioned: the restrictive organization of sexuality (Gamson & Moon, 2004). Instead they urge that we study how this organization came about and how it is maintained.

One does not have to agree with all the claims of queer theory to appreciate the point that the labels we attach to people—she's a lesbian, he's straight—are complex social constructions that give social advantages to the heterosexual people and create disadvantages for LGBTQ people. Queer theorists and many others believe these inequalities to be oppressive. But what this perspective reminds us is that these inequalities, whether understandable or not, were consciously created rather than being "natural." One must also agree that the boundaries of sexual identities are more fluid than people ordinarily think. Queer theory contributes the insight that a rigid split between heterosexual and homosexual is not "natural" but rather reflects prevailing heterosexual norms in our society.

Quick Review

- Queer theorists claim that sexual identities are always unstable and arbitrary.
- They argue that we should reject the concept of sexual identities as meaningful, fixed categories.
- They urge instead that we study the ways in which conventional sexual identities are organized according to norms that privilege heterosexuals.

LGBTQ Family Life

How do people's sexual identities affect their family lives? In particular, how do sexual minorities–individuals who identify as lesbian, gay, bisexual, or queer–form and live family lives? And how do gender nonconforming individuals–transgender or genderqueer–do so? The answers to these questions are of interest not only because they can enlighten us about LGBTQ families but also because, by comparison, they can deepen our understanding of the often taken-for-granted nature of heterosexual family life. Let us examine three aspects: How LGBTQ people define their families, how they come to be parents, and how they divide the division of labor at home.

DEFINING FAMILY

A generation ago, when attitudes toward sexual minorities were less positive and same-sex marriage was unthinkable, gay and lesbian individuals often faced hostility and rejection from their families of origin (their parents and siblings). Consequently, they often had to construct their own families–to build the kind of ties that heterosexuals took for granted. They did so by forming strong bonds with close friends and perhaps other nonbiological relatives such as members of self-help or faith groups. The result was a **chosen family:** a family formed through voluntary ties among individuals who are not biologically or legally related. Relationships with some biological relatives might be good enough for them to be included too. But the emphasis was on building a family: "Gay people really have to work to make family," one person told an observer (Weston, 1991). In some respects, these chosen families are similar to other kinds of voluntary kin such as kin networks found among the poor or complex families formed after divorce and remarriage.

chosen family a family formed through voluntary ties among individuals who are not biologically or legally related

Chosen families were more common among middle-class gay and lesbian individuals than among the less affluent, it appears (Carrington, 1999). The reason is that maintaining large friendship-based families takes time and money. People with better paying, more flexible jobs could more easily arrange social events and spend more on travel and dining. In addition, nonwhite individuals sometimes had less extensive friendship networks and were more likely to rely on biological kin (Carrington, 1999). It is likely that substantial class and racial–ethnic differences existed–and may continue to exist–in the ways that sexual minorities organize their personal lives (Moore & Stambolis-Ruhstorfer, 2013).

Are chosen families still common in the aftermath of the greater acceptance of sexual minorities and the legalization of same-sex marriage? More recent studies of sexual minorities suggest that they are indeed still common but usually exist in combination with biologically related families (Hull & Ortyl, 2018). When asked whom they consider to be in their families, most individuals mentioned *both* chosen family members (close friends) *and* biologically or legally related family members (parents, stepparents). Very few did not list anyone who could be considered a chosen family member, but on the other hand, very few listed only chosen family members. The greater level of acceptance by their biological kin today may allow sexual minorities to include ties to parents and siblings. Transgender and genderqueer people were more likely to mention chosen families, which may reflect less acceptance by biological kin. In sum, sexual minorities appear to define their families in ways that combine voluntary kin and biological kin (Soler, Caldwell, Córdova, Harper, & Bauermeister, 2018).

BECOMING PARENTS

There are four ways that an LBGT individual can become a parent (Moore & Stambolis-Ruhstorfer, 2013). The first way is for a person to have a child in a heterosexual relationship, end that relationship, come out as LGBTQ, and retain custody of the child. Because women retain custody more often than men after a breakup, most of these families include a LGBTQ mother, her children, and her partner if she has one. This type of family is probably declining in numbers as the more open climate leads fewer LGBTQ individuals to enter into heterosexual marriages. The second type of LGBTQ parenthood is through the use of assisted reproductive technology. As an example, a child may be conceived through donor insemination–the insertion of donated semen into the uterus of an ovulating woman. Or a gay man may have a child by hiring a gestational surrogate–commonly known as a surrogate mother–who agrees to be inseminated with his sperm and then to transfer the child to him at birth. Surrogacy is still controversial; entering into a contract to pay a surrogate is legal in many states but illegal in others. Some states allow only married couples to use the services of a surrogate. Several European countries have banned paid surrogacy (Finkelstein, MacDougall, Kintominas, & Olsen, 2016.) Critics argue that surrogacy exploits the woman who carries the child and dehumanizes the child by turning it into a commodity, whereas others counter that some surrogates find it personally and financially rewarding to carry children (Jacobson, 2016). The third way is through adoption. Same-sex couples are more likely to adopt children who have been in foster care than are different-sex couples (Gates, 2013), probably because foster care children are harder to place and therefore more available to same-sex couples. And the fourth way is simply to form a lasting partnership with another LGBTQ person who has already acquired a child through one of these means.

In 2013, about 200,000 children were being raised by same-sex couples and an additional 1.1 to 2.0 million children under age 18 had a lesbian, gay, or bisexual parent who was not living with a partner, according to the best estimate (Gates, 2014). During the years prior to the Supreme Court decision that legalized same-sex marriage (*Obergefell v. Hodges,* 2015), there was much interest in comparing the well-being of children living with lesbian or gay parents with children living with heterosexual parents. It's not easy to make the comparison. Lesbian and gay parents may differ from heterosexual parents in ways that have little to do with their sexuality. For instance, lesbian and gay parents are more likely to be black or Hispanic, less likely to have a college degree, more likely to report low incomes, and more likely to be foreign born than heterosexual parents (Brewster, Tillman, & Jokinen-Gordon, 2014; Gates, 2013). In other words, they are more disadvantaged, on average, than heterosexual parents, which could affect their children's development. Moreover, some scholars question why children living with heterosexual parents should be the standard to which all other children are compared (Stacey & Biblarz, 2001).

Those difficulties notwithstanding, the results of several national studies show little difference between children raised in lesbian families, on the one hand, and children raised in heterosexual families. (There is little data on children raised by gay male fathers.) The American Sociological Associate submitted a friend-of-the-court brief on the topic to the Supreme Court in 2013; and an updated version was published as a journal article a year later (Manning, Fettro, & Lamidi, 2014). The authors concluded, "To date the consensus in the recent social science literature is clear: children living with two same-sex parents fare just as well as children residing with two different-sex parents" (p. 499). Some of the studies reviewed in the article did show more difficulties among children with same-sex parents, but once the investigators adjusted for the more disadvantaged social and economic status of the same-sex parents, the differences were greatly reduced. Another study that was considered in some of the court cases did suggest that adults whose parents had same-sex relationships were not doing as well (Regnerus, 2012a, 2012b), but it has received sharp criticism (Rosenfeld, 2015). Yet even the authors of the sociological association brief state that more research is needed on the topic.

DIVIDING THE HOUSEHOLD LABOR

Traditionally, women in different-sex marriages have performed most of the child care and housework and men have been the main wage earners. That has begun to change, as we will see in Chapter 8, but it's still the case that different-sex married couples tend to have a division of labor, with women doing more at home and men doing more in the labor market. Mid-twentieth-century economists and sociologists (Parsons & Bales, 1955; Becker, 1973) claimed that a sharp division of labor was efficient, in the sense that it was the best way to get all of the tasks of family life accomplished. Beneath this talk about efficiency was an unspoken sense that women were better at home work than men–that it came more naturally to them than it did to men and that they preferred it to paid work. More recently, sociologists have argued that the traditional division of labor reflects strong social norms about the kinds of work that women and men are supposed to do rather than any gains in efficiency or differences in natural abilities. In other words, it is the socially constructed gender differences in marital roles that drives the differences in women's and men's work. Same-sex couples allow us explore this issue because we can observe what the partners do in a relationship in which there are no gender differences because both partners have the same gender. If we still see a sharp division of labor between the partners, then perhaps there are some gains in efficiency, unrelated to gender, if one partner specializes in homework and the other in market work. But if we see substantial sharing of both home work and market work among same-sex couples, we might conclude that the division of labor in different-sex partnerships is heavily influenced by social norms that prescribe the different tasks that women and men are supposed to do.

A number of small-scale studies of same-sex couples are beginning to provide answers to these questions. Nearly all were conducted prior to the national legalization of same-sex marriage, so we cannot determine the role of marriage itself. Still, nearly all the studies suggest that same-sex couples divide housework and child care more equitably than do different-sex couples (Goldberg, 2013). Two women, or two men, it seems, tend to share cleaning the house and caring for the children more than do a woman and a man. These findings provide evidence, albeit tentative, that the specialized division of labor found among different-sex couples is influenced by social norms about proper gender roles.

Nevertheless, a more equitable division of labor doesn't mean that the division is *completely* equal. The same studies also show that some degree of specialization exists among most of the same-sex couples that have been studied. That is to say, one person usually does more than 50 percent of the work at home and the other usually does more than 50 percent of the wage and salary work. The partners justify this specialization by citing one or more of several factors: Time availability (one partner works more outside of the home and therefore has less time to do chores at home); earning power (one partner commands a higher salary than the other partner can command); or different preferences (one partner prefers to do child care more than the other one does) (Carrington, 1999; Kelly & Hauck, 2015; Panozzo, 2015). So there may be some gains in efficiency to specialization—just not to the degree that mid-twentieth-century social scientists thought. And there may be differing individual preferences for home versus market work that result in a less than 50/50 split of all of the family's work.

A caveat: These conclusions all treat gender as a fixed category, as social theorists in the past have done. Yet as queer theorists would suggest, the fluidity of gender and sexual identities in contemporary partnerships can create specialized roles in new and unexpected ways. Consider relationships in which a cisgender woman is partnered with a transgendered person who is making a transition from woman to man. What is the likely division of labor in such as partnership? Studies suggest that the cisgender women in these partnerships tend to undertake a more feminine set of tasks in order to support the emerging masculinity of the transgender men with whom they are living (Pfeffer, 2010). We are just beginning to learn about the roles and responsibilities of partnerships that involve transgendered individuals.

Quick Review

- LGBTQ individuals commonly construct family ties from biological kin such as parents and siblings and from nonbiologically related close friends whom they choose to consider family members.
- There are several routes to parenthood for LGBTQ individuals, including donor insemination, surrogacy, and adoption.
- Children raised by same-sex parents from birth appear to be similar to children raised by heterosexual parents.
- Individuals in same-sex partnerships tend to share responsibilities more equitably than do individuals in different-sex partnerships.
- Still, some specialization in home or work tasks remains in most same-sex partnerships.

Sexuality In and Out of Relationships

People's sexual lives today have been influenced by the increasing acceptability of sexual activity outside of marriage. To understand that story, we need to step back a bit. There have been three eras in the attitudes toward sexuality and love in the United States. Before about 1890, sexual attraction and romantic love were thought to be inappropriate bases for choosing a spouse. Rather, one chose a spouse for practical reasons such as the ability to manage a farm or run a household. Moreover, even within marriage, sexual expression was thought to be an activity best done in moderation. From about 1890 to about 1960, in contrast, sexual attraction and romantic love were increasingly viewed as not only appropriate but, in fact, crucial criteria. Within marriage, people increasingly valued the emotional fulfillment they could obtain through sex and romantic love. The idea of a sexual identity, based on one's attitudes and practices, passed into common usage. Still, sexual expression outside marriage continued to be seen as illicit.

Since the 1960s, the positive value given to sexual expression and gratification has continued and even increased. Young people were shaking off the restrictions of their parents' generation. By 1974, a majority of young adults under age 30 in a national survey said that sex before marriage was "not wrong at all" (Smith, Davern, Freese, & Hout, 2017). In addition, sexual activity has become defined even more as a private matter. In 1965, for example, the Supreme Court ruled that a state law prohibiting the use of contraceptives violated marital privacy by allowing police to search the "sacred precincts of marital bedrooms" (*Griswold* v. *Connecticut,* 1965). In 1972, the Court, using similar reasoning, overturned laws prohibiting the sale of contraceptives to unmarried persons (*Eisenstadt* v. *Baird,* 1972). The rationale for these laws had been that sexual activity was carried out in order to have children and that the state had an interest in seeing that married couples did, in fact, have children and that unmarried persons did not. In this way, the state could promote and control the reproduction of the population. By the time of these court decisions, however, sex had become primarily a means of individual fulfillment. Therefore, the rationale for state intervention had weakened.

This changing view of sexual activity is part of the broader growth of individualism during the twentieth century. In the post-1960 era, cultural changes were spurred, in part, by the increasing economic independence of women, which made it possible for young adult women to postpone marriage without postponing intimate sexual relationships. In turn, young men were able to initiate sexual relationships with women without making a commitment to support them. (Women's economic independence will be discussed in more detail in Chapter 8.) The changes in sexual behavior were also guided greatly by the availability of more effective means of contraception, notably the birth control pill. Among 25-year-old women in the 1950s and early 1960s, about half had had sex without being married. In contrast, among 25-year-old women in the 2000s, about 90 percent had had sex without being married (Wu, Martin, & England 2017).

We know less about trends in same-sex sexual activity, but it does appear that greater change has occurred among women than among men. In a national survey, women who entered adulthood around 2010 reported higher levels of same-sex sexual activity, and higher percentages identifying as lesbian or bisexual, than did women who entered adulthood around 1990 (England, Mishel, & Caudillo, 2016). There was no upward trend for men, however, in behavior or identification. The authors speculate that this gender difference may be another example of the asymmetry of gender change, in which women have changed more than men (see Chapter 3).

The changes over time in different-sex activity have also been less dramatic for men, for whom the sexual double standard always allowed more nonmarital sexual activity than it allowed women. Still, the double standard has now disappeared. Figure 6.2 shows the number of different-sex sexual partners in the past 12 months reported by never-married, noncohabiting women and men in the 2002 and 2006–2008 NSFG surveys. Under the old double standard, we would expect that far more women than men would report having had no sex partners; but the percentage reporting no partners is only slightly higher for women than for men (although men were more likely to report having had two or more partners).

SEXUALITY IN COMMITTED RELATIONSHIPS

Given the increases in sexual activity outside marriage, you might expect that married persons would be increasingly likely to have **extramarital sex.** Indeed, some authors have suggested that marital relationships could coexist with, and perhaps even be enriched by, extramarital affairs (Kipnis, 2003). Yet monogamy—having just one sex partner—is still the rule rather than the exception among married

extramarital sex sexual activity by a married person with someone other than his or her spouse

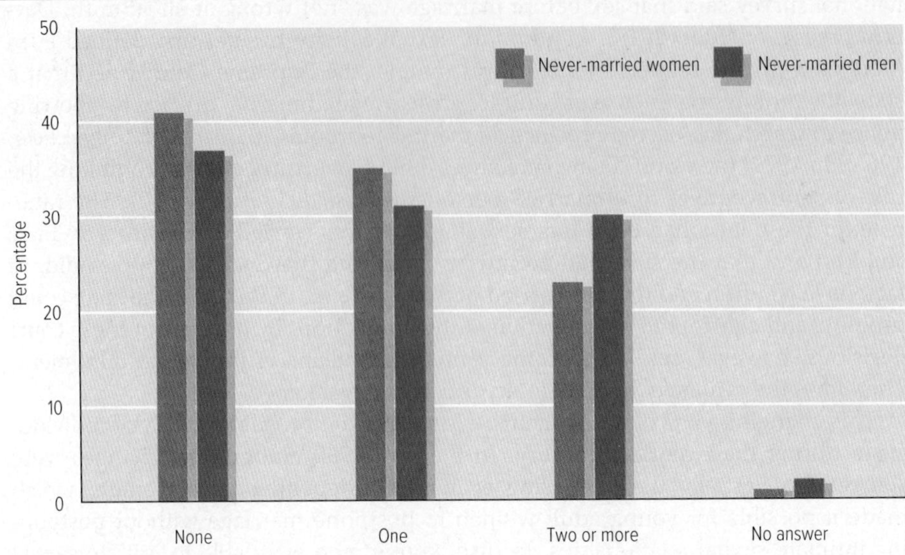

FIGURE 6.2 Number of different-sex sexual partners in the past 12 months, for never-married, noncohabiting women and men, ages 15 to 44, in the United States, 2002 and 2006–2008. (*Source:* U.S. National Center for Health Statistics, 2011)

persons. Consider trends in public opinion. There is no doubt that the American public has become more tolerant of sexual activity among persons who have not yet (and may never be) married. Almost every year since 1972, the General Social Survey, or GSS, an annual or biennial national survey of American adults, has asked people their opinions about both premarital and extramarital sex. Between 1972 and 2016, the proportion who agreed that *premarital* sex was "always wrong" declined from 72 percent to 41 percent. During the same period, however, the proportion agreeing that *extramarital* sex was "always wrong" increased from 70 to 75 percent.[2]

Even people in cohabiting relationships seem to be monogamous. Consider the responses of women to a question in the 2006–2010 NSFG on the number of sexual partners they had had in the previous 12 months. As other studies would lead us to expect, 99 percent of the women who were married reported having only one partner. But 91 percent of women who were cohabiting also reported having one partner. It would appear that the norm of monogamy extends to the behavior of most cohabiting couples. So individuals who have a series of committed relationships—cohabiting or marital—usually follow a pattern we can call **serial monogamy:** a succession of monogamous sexual relationships. Only among women who were not living with a partner did substantial numbers report having multiple partners: 67 percent said one sexual partner, 20 percent said two, and 13 percent reported three or more. But note that even among the unpartnered, a clear majority reported no more than one partner.[3]

serial monogamy a succession of monogamous sexual relationships

The quality and quantity of sexual relations matters for the health and well-being of the partners in both different-sex and same-sex committed partnerships

[2] Author's calculations. The question on extramarital sex was first asked in 1973; for both questions I have excluded "Don't know" and "No answer" responses (Smith, Davern, Freese, & Hout, 2017).

[3] The question was asked of women who had had sex in the previous 12 months. The results apply to different-sex partners; there were too few women in committed relationships with same-sex partners to calculate reliable percentages. Source: author's calculations from the National Survey of Family Growth, 2006–2010 survey round (U.S. National Survey of Family Growth, 2015).

(Schwartz, Serafini, & Cantor, 2013) although it's difficult to know what's the cause and what's the effect: Do sexually satisfied couples have better relationships, or do better relationships lead to more satisfying sex lives? The cause-and-effect arrow probably points both ways. In addition, having children also affects a couple's sex life: Sexual frequency declines during pregnancy and remains lower than prior to the pregnancy while the children are young. Sexual frequency also tends to decline with the increasing duration of the relationship, although the partners' satisfaction with their sex lives does not necessarily decline as sharply as the frequency does (Liu, 2003; Schwartz, Serafini, & Cantor, 2013).

SEXUAL ACTIVITY OUTSIDE OF RELATIONSHIPS

Sexual activity outside of relationships of any kind is increasingly prevalent. When young adults pair off, it is sometimes in the form of a "hookup," a phenomenon that seems to have begun in the 1980s and become common in the 2000s (Bogle, 2008; England, Shafer, & Fogarty, 2008). **Hooking up** is a sexual encounter with no expectation of further involvement. Unlike dating, it is not necessary, or even desirable, that either of the individuals have a romantic attraction to the other. The hookup scene is heteronormative; we know much less about the extent of same-sex hookup activity (Rupp, Taylor, Regev-Messalem, Fogarty, & England 2014). Hookups commonly occur at parties or other group settings and often involve alcohol, which serves to loosen inhibitions and provide a rationale for acting in a sexually forward manner (Bogle, 2008). In a survey of Stanford undergraduates, men said they had consumed an average of five drinks, and women said three drinks, before hooking up (England & Thomas, 2007). In a large online survey of students at 21 four-year colleges and universities, 69 percent of women reported at least one hookup by senior year (England, Shafer, & Fogarty 2008). A hookup does not necessarily imply sexual intercourse. About one-third of students in the online survey reported only kissing and nongenital touching; about one-third reported genital touching or oral sex; and a little more than one-third reported intercourse. The increased popularity of the hookup, however, does not mean that college students never have relationships. In the online survey, 73 percent of women reported being in a relationship of six months or more while in college (England, Shafer, & Fogarty, 2008).

hooking up a sexual encounter with no expectation of further involvement

The hookup culture can be seen in a positive or negative light. On the positive side, hooking up may be a rational response to the increasingly long stage of life between sexual maturity and the older ages at marriage we see today. It may be especially attractive to students who wish to postpone marrying and having children until after they have obtained a college degree and established their careers. During this long transition to adulthood, they may seek sexual pleasure but not serious relationships that could distract them from their goals (Armstong, Hamilton, & England, 2010). In the online survey, 69 percent of women and 71 percent of men agreed that "One disadvantage of being in an exclusive relationship in college is that it might interfere with moving to another city for a job or graduate school when I graduate" (England & Bearak, 2014). Hooking up seems to be more common among white students from economically privileged backgrounds–the kinds of students who are most likely to adopt a strategy of postponing marriage and childbearing–than among nonwhite students or students from moderate- to low-income backgrounds (Hamilton & Armstrong, 2009; Owen, Rhoades, Stanley, & Fincham, 2010). Less privileged college students, who are more likely to make a quicker transition to family formation, may be more uncomfortable with sex outside of relationships.

On the negative side, the hookup culture, seems to retain the sexual double standard that often favors men over women. The ambiguity of the hookup—neither partner knows whether the other has any romantic interest—places a person who would like to have a romantic relationship at a disadvantage. Young women, according to studies of hooking up, tend to be more troubled by this lack of commitment than young men (Bogle, 2008). College women report more satisfaction with sex that occurred within the context of a relationship than in a hookup (Armstrong, England, & Fogarty, 2012). Even the nature of the sexual activity seems to favor men; in the online survey, men were far more likely to report having an orgasm during a hookup than were women (Armstrong, England, & Fogarty, 2012). Moreover, women who engaged in multiple hookups were more likely to be stigmatized as sexually loose than were similar men. In the online sample, 69 percent of men agreed that "If women hook up or have sex with lots of people, I respect them less"; but only 37 percent of men agreed that "If men hook up or have sex with lots of people, I respect them less" (England & Bearak, 2014). Both the positive and negative views of hookups, of course, could be valid.

Adolescent Sexuality and Pregnancy

One consequence of the cultural changes in sexuality is the rise in childbearing outside of marriage. Starting in the mid-1960s, young adults' sexual lives changed in two ways. First, having sexual intercourse prior to marriage, often many years before, became common. Figure 6.3 displays the findings of a series of national surveys of unmarried adolescent girls, aged 15 to 19, since 1971 and of boys the same ages since 1988. The percentage who had ever had sexual intercourse rose sharply during the 1970s and then peaked in the late 1980s. Second, between the mid-1950s and 2017, the age at which half of all first marriages occurred rose by seven years for men and nearly eight years for women (U.S. Bureau of the Census, 2018b). Consequently, far more young women and men remain single throughout late adolescence and early adulthood. The combination of earlier sexual activity and later marriage has lengthened the stage of life when young adults can have a child outside of marriage.

CHANGES IN SEXUAL BEHAVIOR

Adolescent sexual activity, however, has declined since the 1980s, particularly for boys, as shown in Figure 6.3. In 1988, never-married adolescent boys were more likely to have had sexual intercourse (60 percent) than were comparable girls (51 percent), reflecting a long-standing pattern. But by the 2011–2015 period, the difference had narrowed between boys (44 percent) and girls (42 percent). Sociologists don't fully understand why the decline has occurred. One factor is the virtual disappearance of teenage marriage: In 2018, less than 1 percent of 15- to 19-year olds were married (U.S. Bureau of the Census 2018a). Another factor may have been education in school about the risk of contracting HIV through sexual intercourse. Class and racial differences in premarital sexual activity were also smaller at the end of the century because the rise in adolescent sexual activity had been greater among the middle class than among the poor, more noticeably among whites than among blacks (Forrest & Singh, 1990; U.S. National Center for Health Statistics, 2017).

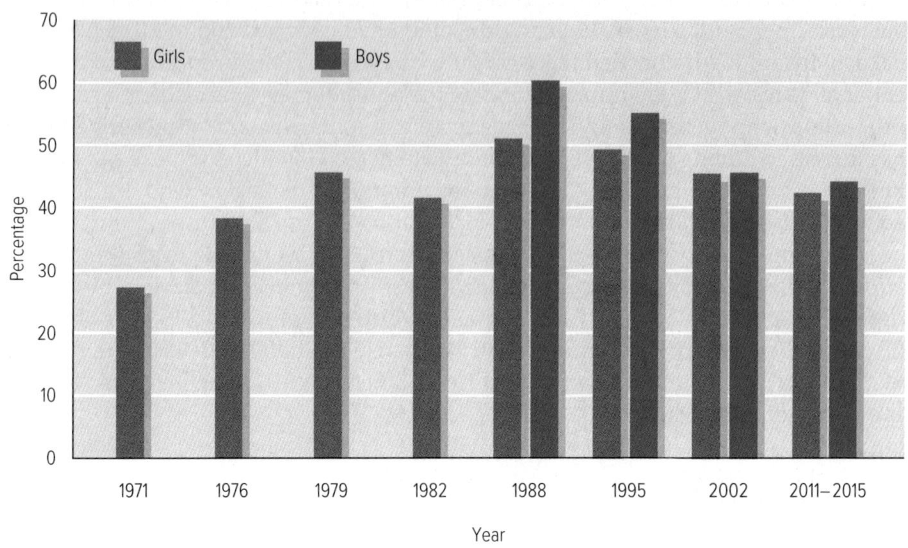

FIGURE 6.3
Number of 15- to 19-year-olds who have ever had sexual intercourse, 1971–2013 for girls, 1988–2013 for boys, in the United States. (*Sources:* U.S. National Research Council, 1987; and U.S. National Center for Health Statistics, 2017. For 1971–1982, percentages are for girls residing in metropolitan areas only. However, the 1982 percentage, which is available for both the U.S. and metropolitan areas, is nearly identical.)

Summing up these trends:

- Adolescent sexual activity is more common today than it was in the middle of the twentieth century, although it has declined since the 1980s.
- The historical difference in the sexual activity of adolescent boys and girls has lessened.
- The increases in adolescent sexual activity have been greater for the middle class and whites than for other groups, although sexual activity is still more common among the poor and African Americans.

Yet even with the declines that have occurred since the 1990s, adolescent sexual activity still was much more widespread than it had been at midcentury, especially for girls. Coupled with a rising age at marriage, this increase in sexual activity among adolescents led to a greater proportion of teenage pregnancies and births outside marriage.

THE TEENAGE PREGNANCY "PROBLEM"

Most people have read or heard something about the teenage pregnancy "problem," but few people have a good understanding of exactly what the problem is. About 450,000 15- to 19-year-old women in the United States become pregnant each year. About 39 percent of these pregnancies are ended by an abortion or a miscarriage, leaving about 275,000 births (Alan Guttmacher Institute, 2017). Despite widespread talk about an "epidemic" of teenage childbearing, this is a lower number of births than was the case 10 or 20 years ago. In fact, the birthrate for teenage girls is at an all-time low (U.S. National Center for Health Statistics, 2019). That is to say, the probability that a teenage girl will have a baby in a given year is lower than at any time since the federal government began to keep statistics in the 1940s.

Then what is the problem? Marriage, or rather the lack of it. Marriage among teenagers has decreased faster than birthrates have. A pregnant 18- or 19-year-old who got married in 1960 would have had plenty of company–31 percent of all

18- to 19-year-old women were married. But to marry at those ages today is to stand out: Just 2 percent of 18- to 19-year-old women had ever married in 2014.[4] As sexual activity among unmarried teenagers increased and as the proportion of teenagers of all races who were unmarried rose, the consequence was a sharp rise in the proportion who were risking a pregnancy outside marriage. Contraceptive usage has increased among teenagers, but over the long run, the increased use has merely kept pace with the increasing numbers of unmarried teenagers who are sexually active. Consequently, the **nonmarital birth ratio**—the proportion of all births that occur to unmarried women—has increased sharply for teenagers, even though the *birthrate*—the probability that a teenager (married or not) will have a birth—has declined. For example, in 1970 the nonmarital birth ratio for 15- to 19-year-olds was 22 percent (U.S. National Center for Health Statistics, 2000); by 2017 it had risen to 89 percent (U.S. National Center for Health Statistics, 2018). The increased ratio is the source of public concern.

nonmarital birth ratio the proportion of all births that occur to unmarried women

THE CONSEQUENCES FOR TEENAGE MOTHERS

Despite support from their parents and other kin, adolescents who bear children appear worse off later in life, on average, than adolescents who wait until their twenties to begin having children. Teenage mothers complete fewer years of schooling, have jobs that pay less, are more likely to be dependent on public assistance payments, and are less likely to have stable marriages. The more difficult issue to resolve is whether these differences are due to having a child as a teenager per se or to the kinds of impoverished backgrounds common among teenage mothers. This is an example of a **selection effect,** the principle that whenever individuals sort, or "select," themselves into groups nonrandomly, some of the differences among the groups reflect preexisting differences among the individuals. Selection effects frequently complicate the interpretation of data that sociologists collect.

selection effect the principle that whenever individuals sort, or "select," themselves into groups nonrandomly, some of the differences among the groups reflect preexisting differences among the individuals

For example, suppose we want to know whether teenage mothers grow up to be poor at a higher rate because of the effects of (1) having a child as a teenager or (2) coming from low-income families. To truly settle this issue, a truth-seeking but cold-blooded social scientist would want to conduct the following experiment: Obtain a list of all families with teenage girls in the United States and then assign at random some of the girls to have children and others to remain childless until their twenties. Because of the random assignment, teenage childbearing would be about as likely to occur in middle-class families as in poor families. In this way, the social scientist could eliminate family background as a cause of any differences that emerge between teenage mothers and nonmothers.

In the real world, of course, teenage pregnancies don't occur randomly; rather, they are more likely to occur in families that were poor before the teenager gave birth. The teenage childbearers are self-selected, in a sense, from less-fortunate families. It is very difficult to separate out the selection effect of family background from the true causal effect of having the baby per se. Studies suggest that some of the apparent effect of teenage childbearing is indeed a selection effect—in other words, teenage mothers probably would grow up to have somewhat lower incomes even if they had waited until after age 19 to have children (Geronimus, 1991;

[4] Author's calculation from American Community Survey data.

Geronimus & Korenman, 1992; Hotz, McElroy, & Sanders, 1996). But some studies still suggest that the economic circumstances of teenage mothers remain modestly worse after the selection effect is accounted for (Ashcraft, Fernández-Val, & Lang, 2013). For example, these young women may be somewhat less likely to graduate from high school and somewhat more likely to have reduced annual incomes as young adults. Moreover, the effects are greater for middle-class young women who become pregnant than for poor women who become pregnant (Diaz & Fiel, 2016). It may be that having a baby as a teenager poses few penalties for young women who are already poor, because they are likely to remain poor regardless of whether they bear children or not. (See *Families and Public Policy:* The Rise and Fall of the Teenage Pregnancy Problem.)

Moreover, the life course of teenage mothers varies substantially. Some of those who drop out of school later return to school and obtain a high school diploma or its equivalent. In 1995 and 1996, Frank Furstenberg located and reinterviewed about 200 women who had been in a study of teenage mothers he had conducted 30 years earlier (Furstenberg, 1976). Only 51 percent of these women had graduated from high school by the time they were age 21, and few of the dropouts were in school. But by the 30-year reinterview, 80 percent had obtained a high school degree or its equivalent by taking classes as adults. Two-thirds were working full-time, and a majority were earning enough to be classified as working-class or middle-class (Furstenberg, 2007). They were not a prosperous group, but they were far better off than one would have predicted when they were teenage mothers. Furstenberg suggests that they might not be much better off today even if they had not given birth as teenagers.

To sum up what we know about teenage mothers:

- They are disadvantaged in education, income, and employment.
- Some, although probably not all, of their disadvantages are due to other factors in their lives, such as growing up in low-income families.
- There is much variation in the way their lives turn out.

Quick Review

- Sexual activity among teenagers is much more common than it was prior to the 1970s.
- Both the birthrate and the marriage rate have been declining among teenagers.
- The proportion of teenage births that are to unmarried girls and women has increased.
- Some of the problems shown by teenage mothers reflect disadvantages they had prior to becoming pregnant.

Sexuality and Family Life

As recently as the 1950s, heterosexual marriage was the only morally approved venue for sexual activity; and the only approved purpose of marital sex was to have children. Recall that prior to a 1965 Supreme Court ruling, a state could ban the sale of contraceptives entirely; and prior to a 1972 ruling, sales could

Families and Public Policy

The Rise and Fall of the Teenage Pregnancy Problem

During the 2008 Presidential campaign, the public learned that Bristol Palin, the unmarried 17-year-old daughter of Republican vice-presidential nominee Sarah Palin, was pregnant. After Bristol's baby Tripp was born in late December, the family released a statement welcoming the grandson but cautioning teenagers to avoid pregnancy. "Teenagers need to prevent pregnancy to begin with—this isn't ideal," the statement quoted Bristol as saying, "but I'm fortunate to have a supportive family which is dealing with this together."

In fact, family planning experts have been issuing warnings about teenage pregnancy for decades. In the late 1960s, alarmed by the initial signs of a sharp rise in births to unmarried teenagers, government demographer Arthur Campbell famously warned:

> *The girl who has an illegitimate child at the age of 16 suddenly has 90 percent of her life's script written for her. She will probably drop out of school . . . she will probably not be able to find a steady job that pays enough to provide for her and her child. . . . Her life choices are few, and most of them are bad. (quoted in Ericksen & Steffen, 1999, p. 88)*

What has happened to the teenage pregnancy problem, however, must have surprised Campbell. At first, as birthrates rose, and as surveys during the 1970s showed a worrisome rise in teenage sexual activity, the public became alarmed. Teenage pregnancy became a major social issue. Advocacy groups urged better contraception or less sexual activity, or both. But then came research suggesting that some of the problems faced by teenage mothers were really problems of poverty, not early motherhood, and might have occurred even if they had postponed childbearing until the teenage years were over. This is the so-called selectivity argument for why teenage mothers have difficulties, which I have discussed elsewhere in this section. A study that followed a group of teenage mothers for 30 years found some of them doing better than expected (Furstenberg, 2007). Perhaps not all of them had 90 percent of their life's scripts written.

As the controversy raged over whether teenage pregnancy was the root cause of young mothers' difficulties, another trend, unnoticed at first, got underway: The birthrates of teenage mothers began to decrease. Since the 1980s, levels of sexual activity among teens declined

be limited to married couples. Many individuals who would today come out as gay or lesbian entered into heterosexual marriages and had children in the mid-twentieth century because that was the only respectable way to have a family life. Living with a sexual partner without marrying was seen as shameful. Contraception was unreliable—the birth control pill was not available until the 1960s. The Kinsey Report shocked Americans in 1948 because it suggested the unthinkable—that the expression of sexuality was more varied than the focus on heterosexual marriage suggested.

Since the mid-twentieth century, the domain of sexuality—sexual activity, attraction, and orientation—has expanded far beyond heterosexual marriage. Sexual expression is much broader than in the past, and the variety of acceptable family living arrangements has greatly increased. Today, much that was shocking in the 1950s is commonplace: premarital sex, different-sex and same-sex cohabiting relationships, same-sex marriage, unmarried teenagers having children, single parenthood, gay and lesbian public identities, and so forth. As we will see in the next chapter, more than half of young adults live with a partner prior to marrying. And a majority of adults now believe that sexual relations

and the use of contraceptives increased. By the late-2010s, teenage birthrates had dropped to levels not seen in two decades (U.S. National Center for Health Statistics, 2019). In contrast, births to unmarried women in their twenties rose sharply because women were postponing marriage but not postponing having children as much. Whereas in 1970 teenagers accounted for 50 percent of all nonmarital births, by 2017 they accounted for only 11 percent (U.S. National Center for Health Statistics, 2018).

By the late-2000s, the birthrates for unmarried women in their twenties had far exceeded the birthrates for unmarried teens. Organizations took note, and some began to reorient their activities. For instance, the National Campaign to Prevent Teen Pregnancy, which was founded in 1996 to work exclusively on decreasing teenage pregnancy, expanded its mission a decade later to include unwanted pregnancies among women in their twenties. Its leaders argued that teenage pregnancy was still a cause for concern, but that teenagers had made more progress in reducing unwanted pregnancies than had older women. They changed the name of the organization to the National Campaign to Prevent Teen and Unplanned Pregnancy.

In noting the decline in teenage births and the large share of nonmarital births to women in their twenties today, I do not mean to suggest that teenage pregnancy is benign or that we should ignore it. As Bristol Palin said, it is not ideal. Teenage birthrates are still higher in the United States than in nearly all other Western countries (Singh & Darroch, 2000). And teenage motherhood may somewhat lower the chances of graduating from high school and college and reduce economic well-being later in life, especially for middle-class young women (Diaz & Fiel, 2016). Teenagers would be better off if the rate fell further. Nevertheless, we can now see that teenage pregnancy is part of a larger problem of nonmarital, and sometimes unwanted, pregnancies among women and their partners. It is this larger problem that more and more advocacy groups and researchers are now focusing on.

Ask Yourself

1. Do you know anyone who has given birth as a teenager? If so, how has her life turned out?
2. Does it make sense to broaden the focus of pregnancy prevention programs to include women in their twenties?

between two adults of the same sex is "not wrong at all" (Smith, Davern, Freese, & Hout, 2017). This transformation is a mark of how diverse both sexual expression and family life have become. In fact, sexual activity outside of any family context (e.g., sex between two non partnered individuals) is now routine. The tight social control of sexual activity that existed in the past has weakened. Instead individuals are freer to choose whether to have sex based on their personal satisfaction.

As we come to terms with the great changes in sexuality and family life, social theorists are pushing us to consider new frontiers. For instance, queer theorists challenge us to forgo the heterosexual, gay, or lesbian identities that have defined our sense of ourselves as sexual beings and our roles in families. These new ideas may seem strange to some of us; but then again, the idea that marriage could be just one of several outlets for sexual expression would have seemed strange to most Americans in the mid-twentieth century. Informed by a broader understanding of sexuality and family life, we will now turn to a consideration of the great changes that have occurred in marriage and cohabitation.

Looking Back

1. **What determines people's sexual identities?** Social constructionists believe that sexual identities, such as "heterosexual" and "gay," are entirely created by the way society is organized—the dominant norms and values, the legal privileges and restrictions, and so forth. They note the different ways in which sexual identities have been expressed in other societies cross-culturally and historically. They cite surveys which suggest a continuum, rather than a sharp line, between heterosexuality and homosexuality. Other social scientists think that there is a biological component to sexual identities. They cite evidence from behavioral genetic and twin studies.

2. **Is "sexual identity" still a useful way to think about people's sexuality?** Queer theorists question whether stable, fixed sexual identities really exist and whether they are useful concepts for understanding social change. They point to the multiple forms that each "identity" takes. They charge that current social norms restrict sexual behavior and force people into arbitrary categories. Those who disagree say that the categories we commonly use have important consequences for the lives of Americans and should be used to study topics such as parenthood, marriage, and other contested issues.

3. **What are the family lives of LGBTQ individuals like?** LGBTQ individuals who faced hostility and rejection from their families of origin had to construct their own by forming strong bonds with close friends and other nonbiological relatives. Today, they often combine these chosen families with biological kin. LGBTQ individuals can become parents in several ways: Using reproductive technology such as donor insemination or surrogacy, having a child in a prior heterosexual partnership, or adopting a child. The results of several national studies show little difference between children raised in lesbian families, on the one hand, and children raised in heterosexual families. Same-sex couples divide housework and child care more equitably than do different-sex couples, although some specialization of roles often exists.

4. **What are the patterns of sexual activity in committed relationships and outside of relationships?** During the twentieth century, the positive value placed on sexual expression in marriage increased. Despite increases in premarital sexual activity, most people still believe that one should be sexually monogamous during marriage; and cohabiting couples are largely monogamous, too. Many people therefore go through a series of committed relationships in which they have only one sexual partner, a pattern called serial monogamy. Sexual activity completely outside the context of a relationship, as in hooking up, has become common. The hookup culture can be seen as a way to manage the long stage between sexual maturity and marriage. But it seems to retain the sexual double standard that favors men over women.

5. **What is the nature of the teenage pregnancy "problem"?** Over the past half-century, the proportion of teenage births that occur outside of marriage has risen sharply because of a decline in marriage among teenagers. Bearing a child as a teenager somewhat reduces a woman's chances of leading an economically successful adult life. Yet some of the disadvantages observed in these cases occur because teenage mothers tend to come from disadvantaged families, not solely because they had a child at a young age.

Study Questions

1. What cultural features of American society influence people's senses of their sexual identity?
2. Does it make a difference whether there is a biological component to sexual identities? If so, why?
3. What is the case for discarding the concept of a sexual identity?
4. Is the rise of the hookup culture a positive development for college students?
5. Compare trends in attitudes toward premarital sex with trends in attitudes toward extramarital sex.
6. Why has concern about teenage pregnancy grown if the likelihood that a teenager will give birth has been declining?
7. Explain what a "selection effect" is.
8. What was the social significance of the Kinsey Report?

Key Terms

chosen family 161
extramarital sex 165
hooking up 167
integrative perspective (on sexuality) 158
Kinsey Report 154
nonmarital birth ratio 170
selection effect 170
serial monogamy 166
social constructionist perspective (on sexuality) 154

Thinking about Families

The Public Family	The Private Family
Has the contemporary American culture gone too far in accepting sex without romantic love?	**Should the government be involved in discouraging teenage pregnancy?**

References

Eisenstadt v. Baird, 438 405 (U.S. 1972).

Griswold v. Connecticut, 381 479 (U.S. 1965).

Obergefell v. Hodges, 576 (U.S. 2015).

Alan Guttmacher Institute. (2017). Adolescent sexual and reproductive health in the United States. *Fact Sheet.* https://www.guttmacher.org/fact-sheet/american-teens-sexual-and-reproductive-health#

Ariès, P. (1985). Thoughts on the history of homosexuality. In P. Aries & Benjin (Eds.), *Western sexuality* (pp. 62–75).

Armstrong, E. A., England, P., & Fogarty, A. C. K. (2012). Accounting for women's orgasm and sexual enjoyment in college hookups and relationships. *American Sociological Review, 77*(3), 435–462.

Armstrong, E. A., Hamilton, L., & England, P. (2010). Is hooking up bad for young women? *Contexts, 9*(3), 22–27.

Ashcraft, A., Fernández-Val, I., & Lang, K. (2013). The consequences of teenage childbearing: Consistent estimates when abortion makes miscarriage non-random. *The Economic Journal, 123*(571), 875–905.

Becker, G. S. (1973). A theory of marriage: Part i. *The Journal of Political Economy,* 813–846.

Bogle, K. (2008). *Hooking up: Sex, dating, and relationships on campus.* New York: New York University Press.

Carrington, C. (1999). *No place like home: Relationships and family life among lesbians and gay men.* Chicago: University of Chicago Press.

Diaz, C. J., & Fiel, J. E. (2016). The effect(s) of teen pregnancy: Reconciling theory, methods, and findings. *Demography, 53,* 85–116.

England, P., & Bearak, J. (2014). The sexual double standard and gender differences in attitudes toward casual sex among U.S. University students. *Demographic Research, 30*(46), 1327–1338.

England, P., Mishel, E., & Caudillo, M. L. (2016). Increases in sex with same-sex partners and bisexual identity across cohorts of women (but not men). *Sociological Science, 3,* 951–970.

England, P., Shafer, E. F., & Fogarty, A. C. K. (2008). Hooking up and forming romantic relationships on today's college campuses. In M. Kimmel & A. Aronson (Eds.), *The gendered society reader* (pp. 531–547). New York: Oxford University Press.

England, P., & Thomas, R. J. (2007). The decline of the date and the rise of the college hook up. In A. S. Skolnick & H. H. Skolnick (Eds.), *Family in transition, 14th edition* (pp. 151–162). Boston: Allyn and Bacon.

Ericksen, J. A., & Steffen, S. A. (1999). *Kiss and tell: Surveying sex in the twentieth century.* Cambridge MA: Harvard University Press.

Finkelstein, A., MacDougall, S., Kintominas, A., & Olsen, A. (2016). Surrogacy law and policy in the U.S.: A national conversation informed by global lawmaking. *Columbia Law School Sexuality & Gender Law Clinic.* Retrieved April 27, 2019, from https://web.law.columbia.edu/sites/default/files/microsites/gendersexuality/files/columbia_sexuality_and_gender_law_clinic-surrogacy_law_and_policy_report-june 2016.pdf

Forrest, J. D., & Singh, S. (1990). The sexual and reproductive behavior of American women. *Family Planning Perspectives, 22,* 206–214.

Furstenberg, F. F. (1976). *Unplanned parenthood: The social consequences of teenage childbearing.* New York: Free Press.

Furstenberg, F. F. (2007). *Destinies of the disadvantaged: The politics of teen childbearing.* New York: Russell Sage Foundation.

Gamson, J., & Moon, D. (2004). The sociology of sexualities: Queer and beyond. *Annual Review of Sociology, 30,* 47–64.

Gates, G. J. (2013). LGBT parenting in the United States. *Williams Institute.* Retrieved January 5, 2016, from http://williamsinstitute.law.ucla.edu/wp-content/uploads/LGBT-Parenting.pdf

Gates, G. J. (2014). LGB families and relationships: Analyses of the 2013 national health interview survey. *Williams Institute.* Retrieved January 5, 2016, from http://williamsinstitute.law.ucla.edu/wp-content/uploads/lgbfamilies-nhis-sep-2014.pdf

Geronimus, A. T. (1991). Teenage childbearing and social and reproductive disadvantage: The evolution of complex questions and the demise of simple answers. *Family Relations, 40,* 463–471.

Geronimus, A. T., & Korenman, S. (1992). The socioeconomic consequences of teen childbearing reconsidered. *Quarterly Journal of Economics, 107,* 1187–1214.

Goldberg, A. E. (2013). "Doing" and "undoing" gender: The meaning and division of housework in same-sex couples. *Journal of Family Theory & Review, 5*(2), 85–104.

Hamilton, L., & Armstrong, E. A. (2009). Gendered sexuality in young adulthood. *Gender & Society, 23,* 589–616.

Hotz, V. J., McElroy, S. W., & Sanders, S. G. (1996). The costs and consequences of teenage childbearing for the mothers and the government. *Chicago Policy Review, 1,* 55–94.

Hull, K. E., & Ortyl, T. A. (2018). Conventional and cutting-edge: Definitions of family in LGBT communities. *Sexuality Research and Social Policy,* published online ahead of print.

Jacobson, H. (2016). *Labor of love: Gestational surrogacy and the work of making babies.* New Brunswick, NJ: Rutgers University Press.

Kelly, M., & Hauck, E. (2015). Doing housework, redoing gender: Queer couples negotiate the household division of labor. *Journal of GLBT Family Studies, 11*(5), 438–464.

Kendler, K. S., Thornton, L. M., Gilman, S. E., & Kessler, R. C. (2000). Sexual orientation in a U.S. national sample of twin and nontwin sibling pairs. *American Journal of Psychiatry,* 157(11), 1843–1846.

Kinsey, A. C., Pomeroy, W. B., & Martin, C. E. (1948). *Sexual behavior in the human male.* Philadelphia: Saunders, W.B.

Kipnis, L. (2003). *Against love: A polemic.* New York: Pantheon.

Laumann, E. O., Gagnon, J. H., Michael, R. T., & Michaels, S. (1995, May 25). Sex, lies, and science: An exchange. *New York Review of Books.*

Lewontin, R. (1995a, April 20). Sex lies and social science. *The New York Review of Books,* 24–29.

Lewontin, R. (1995b, May 25). Sex, lies, and social science: An exchange. *New York Review of Books,* 43–44.

Liu, C. (2003). Does quality of marital sex decline with duration? *Archives of Sexual Behavior, 32*(1), 55–60.

Manning, W. D., Fettro, M. N., & Lamidi, E. (2014). Child well-being in same-sex parent families: Review of research prepared for American sociological Association amicus brief. *Population Research and Policy Review, 33*(4), 485–502.

Michaels, S. (2013). Sexual behavior and practices: Data and measurement. In A. K. Baumle (Ed.), *International handbook on the demography of sexuality* (pp. 11–20). Dordrecht: Springer.

Moore, M. R., & Stambolis-Ruhstorfer, M. (2013). LGBT sexuality and families at the start of the twenty-first century. *Annual Review of Sociology, 39,* 491–507.

Owen, J. J., Rhoades, G. K., Stanley, S. M., & Fincham, F. D. (2010). "Hooking up" among college students: Demographic and psychosocial correlates. *Archives of Sexual Behavior, 39:653–663.*

Paik, A. (2015). Surveying sexualities: Minimizing survey error in study of sexuality. In J. DeLamater & R. F. Plante (Eds.), *Handbook of the sociology of sexualities* (pp. 93–107). Dordrecht: Springer.

Panozzo, D. (2015). Child care responsibility in gay male-parented families: Predictive and correlative factors. *Journal of GLBT Family Studies, 11*(3), 248–277.

Parsons, T., & Bales, R. F. (1955). *Family, socialization, and the interaction process.* New York: The Free Press.

Pfeffer, C. A. (2010). "Women's work"? Women partners of transgender men doing housework and emotion work. *Journal of Marriage and Family, 72*(1), 165–183.

Rebhun, L. A. (1999). *The heart is unknown country: Love in the changing economy of Northeast Brazil.* Stanford, CA: Stanford University Press.

Regnerus, M. (2012a). How different are the adult children of parents who have same-sex relationships? Findings from the new family structures study. *Social Science Research, 41*(4), 752–770.

Regnerus, M. (2012b). Parental same-sex relationships, family instability, and subsequent life outcomes for adult children: Answering critics of the new family structures study with additional analyses. *Social Science Research, 41*(6), 1367–1377.

Rosenfeld, M. J. (2015). Revisiting the data from the new family structure study: Taking family instability into account. *Sociological Science, 2,* 478–501.

Rupp, L. J., Taylor, V., Regev-Messalem, S., Fogarty, A. C., & England, P. (2014). Queer women in the hookup scene: Beyond the closet? *Gender & Society, 28*(2), 212–235.

Sanders, A. R., Beecham, G. W., Guo, S., Dawood, K., Rieger, G., Badner, J. A., et al. (2017). Genome-wide association study of male sexual orientation. *Scientific reports, 7*(1), 16950.

Schwartz, P., & Rutter, V. (1998). *The gender of sexuality.* Thousand Oaks, CA: Pine Forge Press.

Schwartz, P., Serafini, B. J., & Cantor, R. (2013). Sex in committed relationships *International handbook on the demography of sexuality* (pp. 131–165): Springer.

Seidman, S. (2003). *The social construction of sexuality.* New York: W. W. Norton.

Singh, S., & Darroch, J. E. (2000). Adolescent pregnancy and childbearing: Levels and trends in developed countries. *Family Planning Perspectives, 32,* 14–23.

Smith, T. W., Davern, M., Freese, J., & Hout, M. (2017). General social surveys, 1972–2016. Machine readable data file. Chicago: National Opinion Research Center.

Smith-Rosenberg, C. (1975). The female world of love and ritual: Relations between women in nineteenth-century America. *Signs, 1*(1), 1–29.

Soler, J. H., Caldwell, C. H., Córdova, D., Harper, G., & Bauermeister, J. A. (2018). Who counts as family? Family typologies, family support, and family undermining among young adult gay and bisexual men. *Sexuality Research and Social Policy, 15*(2), 123–138.

Stacey, J., & Biblarz, T. J. (2001). (how) does the sexual orientation of parents matter. *American Sociological Review,* 66(2), 159–183.

Turner, C. F., Forsyth, B. H., O'Reilly, J. M., Cooley, P. C., Smith, T. K., Rogers, S. M., & Miller, H. G. (1998). Automated self-interviewing and the survey measurement of sensitive behaviors. In M. P. Couper, R. P. Baker, J. Bethlehem, C. Z. F. Clark, J. Martin, W. L. Nicholls II, & J. M. O'Reilly (Eds.), *Computer assisted survey information collection.* New York: Wiley.

Turner, C. F., Ku, L. C., Rogers, S. M., Lindberg, L. D., Pleck, J. H., & Sonenstein, F. L. (1998). Adolescent sexual behavior, drug use, and violence: Increased reporting with computer survey technology. *Science, 280(May* 8), 867–873.

U.S. Bureau of the Census. (2018a). Table A1. Marital status of people 15 years and over, by age, sex, and personal earnings: 2018. *America's Families and Living Arrangements.* Retrieved February 16, 2019, from https://www2.census.gov/programs-surveys/demo/tables/families/2018/cps-2018/taba1-all.xls

U.S. Bureau of the Census. (2018b). Table MS-2. Estimated median age at first marriage, by sex: 1890 to the present. *Historical Marital Status Tables.* Retrieved November 16, 2018, from https://www2.census.gov/programs-surveys/demo/tables/families/time-series/marital/ms2.xls

U.S. National Center for Health Statistics. (2000). Nonmarital childbearing in the United States, 1940–1999. *National Vital Statistics Reports, Vol. 48, no. 16.* Retrieved February 4, 2009, from http://www.cdc.gov/nchs/data/nvsr/nvsr48/nvs48_16.pdf

U.S. National Center for Health Statistics. (2011). Sexual behavior, sexual attraction, and sexual identity in the United States: Data from the 2006–2008 national survey of family growth. *National Health Statistics Reports, no. 36.* Retrieved January 4, 2012, from http://www.cdc.gov/nchs/data/nhsr/nhsr036.pdf

U.S. National Center for Health Statistics. (2016). Sexual behavior, sexual attraction, and sexual orientation among adults aged 18–44 in the United States: Data from the 2011–2013 national survey of family growth. *National Health Statistics Reports, number 88.* Retrieved January 7, 2016, from http://www.cdc.gov/nchs/data/nhsr/nhsr088.pdf

U.S. National Center for Health Statistics. (2017). Sexual activity and contraceptive use among teenagers in the United States, 2011-2015. *National Health Statistics Reports.* Retrieved August 25, 2018, from https://www.cdc.gov/nchs/data/nhsr/nhsr104.pdf

U.S. National Center for Health Statistics. (2018).

U.S. National Center for Health Statistics. (2018). Births: Final data for 2017. *National Vital Statistics Reports.* Retrieved March 19, 2019, from https://www.cdc.gov/nchs/data/nvsr/nvsr67/nvsr67_08-508.pdf

U.S. National Center for Health Statistics. (2019). Births in the United States, 2018. *NCHS Data Brief, no. 346.* Retrieved September 11, 2019, from https://www.cdc.gov/nchs/data/databriefs/db346-h.pdf

U.S. National Survey of Family Growth. (2015). Questionnaires, datasets, and related documentation. Retrieved May 15, 2016, from http://www.cdc.gov/nchs/nsfg/nsfg_questionnaires.htm

Weinrich, J. D., & Williams, W. L. (1991). Strange customs, familiar lives: Homosexualities in other cultures. In J. C. Gonsioreck & J. D. Weinrich (Eds.), *Homosexuality: Research implications for public policy* (pp. 44–59). Newbury ParK, CA: Sage Publications.

Weston, K. (1991). *Families we choose: Lesbians, gays, kinship.* New York: Columbia University Press.

Wu, L. L., Martin, S. P., & England, P. (2017). The decoupling of sex and marriage in the United States: Cohort trends in who did and did not delay sex until marriage. *Sociological Science, 4,* 151–175.

Chapter Seven

Cohabitation and Marriage

Looking Forward

1. How has the process by which young adults find intimate partners changed?
2. What is the role of cohabitation in the American family system?
3. How has marriage changed over the past century?
4. What is marriage like today?
5. How does the marriage market work?
6. Is a stable, gender-egalitarian style of marriage emerging?

Between 1882 and 1884, Isabella Maud Rittenhouse was courted by several suitors. Maud's diary, discussed by Steven Seidman, reveals that two stood out (Seidman, 1991). The first was Robert Witherspoon, a handsome, charming, educated, and cultivated man, to whom Maud was powerfully attracted. The other was Elmer Comings, a rather plain-looking and socially awkward man who was, nevertheless, hardworking, reliable, and responsible. Today, the choice between them would be easy: 9 out of 10 Mauds would pick Robert, the object of romantic love, over unexciting Elmer. The real Maud, however, chose Elmer. Her reasoning shows how different the relationship among sex, love, and marriage was in the Victorian era than it is now.

To Maud and to most other nineteenth-century women and men, marrying someone because of strong romantic feelings was considered risky. Passionate, romantic love was thought to be a base emotion that faded away quickly, leaving little support for the couple. Far longer lasting was a spiritual love in which the partners joined together in a moral, uplifting marriage. The spiritual relationship rested upon a deep knowledge of each other and a sense of mutual obligation. Spiritual love was "true love," a union not only of the heart but also of the soul and the mind. Strong sexual attraction was equated with "romantic love," a dangerous emotional state that was hard to control. True love was much to be preferred.

There were practical reasons rooted in the structure of nineteenth-century society why people thought this way. The general standard of living was far lower than it is today, and most married women did not work outside the home. In order to have a comfortable life, it was crucial for a woman to marry an economically reliable, hardworking man. Correspondingly, a man needed to marry a woman who would raise children, manage a home, and perhaps earn money by taking in boarders or assembling small goods such as hats at home. Feelings of romantic love could tempt a person to choose passion over partnership. Indulging in passion was a luxury most nineteenth-century people could not afford.

Maud decided that her romantic love for Robert was immature and that she could not overlook some lapses of character. She wrote that he had "beauty of feature and charm of tongue with little regard for truth and high moral worth"; whereas Elmer, "though not graceful . . . and handsome . . . [had an] inward nobility in him." Maud was well aware that she was rejecting romance when she rejected Robert: "If I do marry [Elmer] it will be with a respectful affection and not with a passionate *lover* love."[1] Moreover, Maud knew that, unlike Robert, Elmer did not

[1] All quotations are from Seidman (1991).

share her knowledge of and interest in the arts and literature: "All the time I am planning to bring him up to a standard where I *can* love him." Thus, she girded for the task of marrying Elmer. Fortunately for her—although not for Elmer—she broke off the courtship when Elmer entered into some suspicious business dealings that cast doubt on his character. But even in ending the courtship, Maud relied on practical and ethical considerations rather than on her feelings.

This separation between romantic love and sex, on the one hand, and marriage, on the other hand, was typical of the cultural tradition of the Western nation-states prior to the twentieth century. One historian studied the detailed writings on marital sexual activity by 25 medieval theologians and found that only 2 of them ever addressed the subject of love (Flandrin, 1985). Sexual relations that were too passionate were thought to be immoral and to compete with a person's worship of God. Sensual pleasures were for the love affairs a person had outside of his or her marriage—never sanctioned by theologians but tolerated, in practice, for men only. St. Jerome, quoting the Roman philosopher Seneca, wrote:

> *A prudent man should love his wife with discretion, and so control his desire and not be led into copulation. Nothing is more impure than to love one's wife as if she were a mistress . . . Men should appear before their wives not as lovers but as husbands. (Ariès, 1985a)*

This separation between erotic love and marriage evaporated during the twentieth century. Both Seneca and Maud would be surprised by an article in a social science journal which reported that men and women who were married, or who expected their current relationships to last a lifetime, reported greater pleasure from their sex lives than men and women with short-term partners (Waite & Joyner, 2001). More surprising still would be the increase in sexual activity outside the context of any kind of long-term relationship, the increase in childbearing outside of marriage, and the public nature of LGBTQ partnerships. All these changes, to which we have become accustomed, were nearly unthinkable until the twentieth century and, in the case of same-sex marriages, not accepted until the twenty-first century.

Since Maud's time, then, expectations about marriage have changed dramatically. Most people view romantic love, compatibility, and companionship as essential to a good marriage. In this chapter, we will examine the expectations people have today about their marriage partners and, more generally, about the meaning of their unions. I define a **union** as a stable, intimate relationship between two people who live in the same household, but may or may not be married. Increasingly, people's expectations are played out first in a cohabiting union and then in marriage. Consequently, we need to study the growth of cohabitation over the past few decades. Then we will turn to the changing nature of marriage.

union a stable, intimate relationship between two people who live in the same household but may or may not be married

Forming a Union

Maud's deliberate decision-making process shows that the choice of a husband was largely hers to make. Parental influence was more direct in most societies historically, and it is still more direct in some developing nations today. For instance, in rural villages throughout the developing world, parents who have land or wealth to pass on to their children are especially likely to have a voice. In many Asian nations, it is still common for parents, even prosperous city dwellers, to play a role in the choice of their children's spouses.

AMERICAN COURTSHIP

But by the 1800s most young adults in the United States at least shared with their parents the responsibility for choosing a spouse. Indeed, young adults from the lower economic classes probably had substantial autonomy because there was little property for parents to worry about. (Among the upper classes, parents undoubtedly retained a stronger role.) Young people went about finding a spouse through courtship, a process that had been developed in Europe. **Courtship** is a publicly visible process with rules and restrictions through which young men and women find a partner to marry. The words *publicly visible* emphasize the important role of the community–and, in particular, parents–in watching over, and participating in, the courting a young adult does. For instance, in early modern Britain, the first stages of courtship occurred mainly outdoors, in plain view of peers and kin (Gillis, 1985). By and large, it was acceptable for casually acquainted young men and young women to be seen together only at public events such as festivals, games, or dances, and even then only in groups. At dances young people changed partners so frequently that no couple spent too much time together.

courtship a publicly visible process with rules and restrictions through which young men and women find a partner to marry

This centuries-old system of courtship met its demise after 1900. Its decline in the United States was linked to great social and economic changes: migration from rural areas (and from overseas) to cities, the rise of industrial capitalism, higher standards of living, and the lengthening of adolescence. As more and more people moved to cities and worked in factories and offices, the number of potential partners and the places where they could meet grew. Consequently, it became harder for parents to monitor and oversee the process. And as standards of living rose, it became possible for young adults to keep some of their earnings or to receive allowances from their parents. Thus, young people began to accumulate a key resource: spending money. The city provided plenty of places to spend it, most notably the movie theater and the dance hall. Rising standards of living also allowed many families to buy an automobile. This marvel of technology let young couples wander far from home; it also gave them a private place for necking (kissing) and petting (touching below the neck). As a result, courtship, in the words of historian Beth Bailey, went from "front porch to back seat" (Bailey, 1988).

In addition, a new view of the teenage years arose: They were seen as a time during which teens needed to develop their personalities and capabilities free of the pressures of the adult world (Kett, 2003). In an influential 1904 book, psychologist G. Stanley Hall popularized the term "adolescence" for this newly recognized stage of life (Hall, 1904). Attention to adolescence emerged as child labor laws restricted how much younger teenagers could work and as more prosperous middle-class families no longer needed their children to work. Moreover, it arose as changes in the economy made it clear to parents that children needed at least a high school education in order to obtain better-paying jobs. Consequently, adolescence was embodied most clearly in the high school, which removed teenagers from the world of adults. Not until the early decades of the twentieth century did a majority of teenagers enroll in high school (Mintz, 2004). College enrollments also increased early in the century and then skyrocketed after World War II. The high school and college years gave adolescents a protected time in which they could create and participate in their own subculture, relatively free of parental involvement.

THE RISE AND FALL OF DATING

After the turn of the twentieth century, a new system of courtship based on dating evolved. Although some might think that dating has been around for a long time, it was rare until 1900 or so, and the term was not even used until then. Under the old way of courting, a young man had called at the house of a young woman and had spent the evening chatting, often with her parents within earshot. The spirit of the change was captured in a 1924 short story in *Harper's* magazine. A man comes calling at the home of a young woman, expecting to spend the evening in her parlor. But when she opens the door, she has her hat on—a clear sign that she expects to go out.[2] As the story suggests, suddenly a young man was expected to take a young woman somewhere on a date—which meant he had to spend money. A firm rule of the dating system was that the young man paid the expenses. In return, he enjoyed the company of the young woman. Dating placed courtship on an economic basis. Young men provided goods such as movie tickets or restaurant meals in exchange for companionship and, often, necking and petting. Through these rules, argues Bailey, dating shifted the balance of power in courtship from women to men (Bailey, 1988). Under the old system, women received men in their own homes, at times they chose, and usually with their parents nearby. (During a girl's first season of receiving callers, her mother might initially invite the young men.) Now the evening was initiated and controlled by males, and it depended on cash earnings, which favored men over women.

Dating also shifted power from parents to teenagers and young adults. The movement of activity away from public gatherings and the home made it much harder for parents to influence the process. Rather, adolescents became oriented toward the dating system of their peer group—the other adolescents in the local school or neighborhood. With the triumph of dating, courtship moved from a parent- and other-adult-run system to a peer-run system where the participants made the rules and punished the offenders.

The dating system probably had its heyday in the 20-year period—1945 to 1965—after World War II. Throughout the period, college enrollments rose sharply and most young adults at least completed high school. Postwar parents had grown up in the dating system, and so there was less parent–child disagreement about it than had been the case in the 1920s and 1930s. At the same time, young people in the 1950s may have started to date earlier than their parents.[3] In a national survey of high school students conducted in 1960, about two-thirds of all boys and three-fourths of all girls stated that they had begun to date by grade 9; virtually all had dated by grade 12 (Modell, 1989).[4]

But as age at marriage began to rise in the 1960s and 1970s, the dating system became less closely connected to marriage. Steady dating in high school seemed more and more remote from serious attempts to find a spouse. What's more, cohabitation, perhaps a new stage of courtship, became a common event in young adults' lives prior to marriage. Also, the sharp rise in premarital intercourse for

[2] This story is cited in both Rothman (1984) and Bailey (1988). It is cited by Bailey as Black (1924).

[3] Both Bailey and Rothman suggest that adolescents began to date at younger ages in the 1950s. But when a random sample of Detroit-area women in 1984 was asked to recall when they had begun to date, there was little difference in the responses of those who had married before the war versus after the war; see Whyte (1990).

[4] The data came from the Project Talent survey of 4,000 high school students nationwide.

teenage boys and girls demonstrated that the dating system was increasingly ineffective in holding sexual activity to petting. Adolescents began to socialize more often in larger, mixed-sex groups (Modell, 1989).

ONLINE MATCHMAKING AND COMMITMENT

Over the past two decades, the Internet has emerged as an important way in which individuals find partners to live with or marry; and its use has grown dramatically. A national survey conducted in 2017 found that among heterosexual couples, meeting online has become the most popular way to meet, surpassing meeting through friends for the first time around 2013 (Rosenfeld, Thomas, & Hausen, 2019). That was a higher proportion than those who had found their spouses in any of three traditional ways: family, friends, or work. Observers of this trend do not agree on what to make of it. Some of them view it as undermining our ability to make commitments because there is always a potentially better partner in cyberspace, accessible with one click (Turkle, 2011). Yet the evidence so far shows that people who met their cohabiting partners or spouses online do not end their relationships sooner than people who met offline (Cacioppo, Gonzaga, Ogburn, & VanderWeele, 2013; Rosenfeld, 2017). One reason may be that the online sites that specialize in serious searches, such as eHarmony and Match.com, require participants to post a great deal of information about themselves, which may make them efficient mechanisms for finding a compatible partner (Rosenfeld, 2017). In addition, the Internet is particularly important for people who are looking for partners with characteristics that are relatively uncommon because it is harder to find these partners through traditional means. More than 60 percent of partnered gay men and lesbians, for example, reported in one national study that they had met their partners through online sites, making it by far the most widespread way of finding partners (Rosenfeld & Thomas 2012).

INDEPENDENT LIVING

Once out of college, many young adults live on their own, rather than with their parents. Many non-college-graduates live on their own, too. This is a recent phenomenon. Figure 7.1 shows the percentage of unmarried women and men in their twenties who headed their own households from 1880 to 2010, according to historical census data. You can see how uncommon heading one's household was in the late-nineteenth and early-twentieth centuries. Standards of living were lower, more people lived in rural areas, there was less housing, and women's lives were more constrained. Most unmarried young adults helped support their families by turning over their wages to their parents. But in the second half of the century, the percentage living on their own rose sharply. Standards of living increased, and it became common—even expected—for young adults to keep their wages. Women became more independent as they obtained college degrees and worked outside of the home. In addition, the rise in independent living was consistent with the broader growth of expressive individualism, which uncoupled sexual activity from marriage (with help from the introduction of the birth control pill in the 1960s). Even with declines since 2000 (which may be due to the Great Recession of the late 2000s), far more unmarried young adults head their own households than in the past.

As the typical age at marriage rose in the late twentieth century, it became common for emerging adults to set up an independent household years before

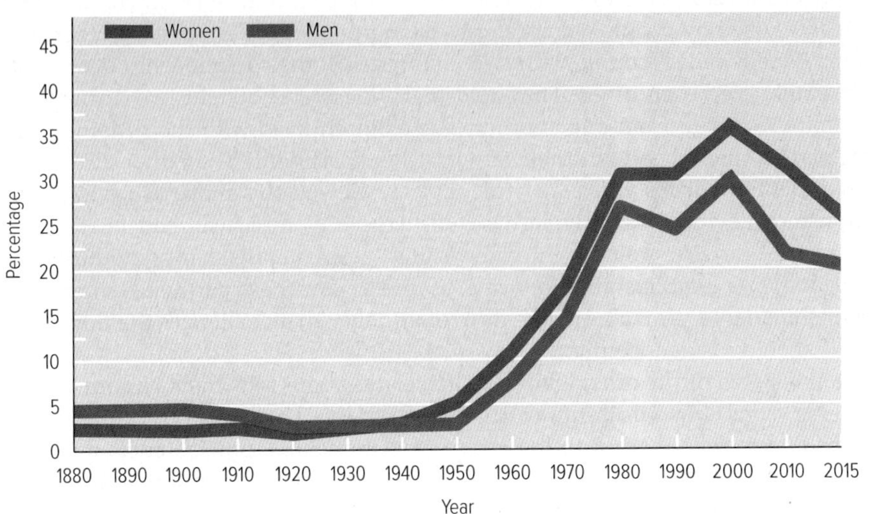

FIGURE 7.1 Percentage of unmarried men and women aged 20–29 who headed their own household, 1880 to 2015. (*Source:* Rosenfeld, 2007, and author's calculations)

they married. Observers have been concerned that the rise in emerging adults living alone has increased the degree of isolation and loneliness in American society. But adults who are living alone are more socially active than are married couples (and probably cohabiting couples, too): They are more likely to visit friends, stay in contact electronically or by telephone, or join a social group. "Living alone and being alone," writes Eric Klinenberg (2012, p. 19), "are hardly the same." Nevertheless, the percentage of unmarried emerging adults who headed their own households dropped sharply between 2000 and 2010, as Figure 7.1 shows, largely due to the Great Recession, which reduced their employment opportunities. More of them chose to remain in, or to move back to, their parental homes.

LIVING APART RELATIONSHIPS

An adult who lives independently may nevertheless have an intimate partnership with someone living elsewhere. The phenomenon of what we might call **living apart relationships,** in which two people define themselves as couples but live in separate households, was first noted in Europe (Haskey, 2005; Castro-Martin, Domínguez-Folgueras, & Martín-García, 2008; Levin, 2004).[5] In the United States, the best estimate, based on a 2013 survey, is that 3.5 percent of people ages 18 to 65 are in a living apart relationship. It is defined as one in which the survey respondent said that she or he had a partner but was not living with that person and also agreed that that she or he was in a "committed long-term relationship and choose to live apart."[6]

living apart relationship a relationship in which two people define themselves as a couple but do not live together

[5] These arrangements are often referred to as *living apart together* relationships or LAT relationships; but the term *living apart relationships* is simpler and preferable (Stoilova et al., 2014).

[6] The estimate was provided by Susan Brown, National Center for Family and Marriage Research, Bowling Green State University.

There are several types of living apart relationships (Stoilova et al., 2014). Some are freely chosen by people who prefer to be more independent of each other. For instance, one Swedish couple with two children saw their relationship deteriorating but still loved each other. They sold their house and bought two apartments a few minutes' walk from one another. The children lived with their mother, but spent part of their time with their father at his apartment. The father also spent some of his time at his wife's apartment. They viewed this move as saving their relationship (Levin, 2004). Similarly, a Portuguese woman who had been living apart for several years told an interviewer that permanently sharing a household is not good for a relationship (Stoilova et al., 2014). For these partners, living apart relationships serve as an alternative form of intimacy that challenges the norm that couples should reside together.

Yet the partners in other living apart relationships see their circumstances as arising from constraints rather than free choice. These couples believe that circumstances force them into living apart relationships. For instance, a couple may prefer to live together, but each partner may have a good job which he or she does not wish to give up, even though the jobs are in different cities. The presence of children from previous relationships may also serve as a constraint; researchers have uncovered many living apart relationships in which one or both partners is raising children from a previous relationship and prefers not to alter the household. A divorced mother who cares for her children during the week may prefer to live apart from her partner and then spend time with him when her ex-husband has the children on the weekends. In a Canadian survey, 23 percent of the women in living apart relationships were living with children (Milan & Peters, 2003).

For partners who freely chose to live apart or who face constraints such as jobs in different cities, living apart relationships can have a long duration. Other kinds of living apart relationships are likely to have shorter durations, such as transitional relationship in which the partners view themselves as cohabiting or marrying soon, or an undecided relationship in which one or both partners is unsure whether they want to commit to living together (Stoilova et al., 2014). The transitional or undecided living apart relationships may be more common during the stage of life we called emerging adulthood in Chapter 2. As people age out of that stage, the chances may increase that they will live with their partners. In the Canadian survey, living apart relationships were more common among people in their twenties than among older people; and about half of those in living apart relationships expected to live with their partners at a future time (Milan & Peters, 2003).

In fact, the line between living apart and living together may be so fuzzy that the partners themselves may not be sure whether they are living together. In a study of moderate-income early adults in the Toledo, Ohio, area who had cohabited, two sociologists found that it was not always easy to determine when a cohabiting relationship began (Manning & Smock, 2005). For half the individuals, living together was not a deliberate decision but more of a "slide" into cohabitation: "Respondents say, 'it wasn't planned,' 'it just snuck up on me,' or 'it just happened'" (p. 996). Emerging adults with separate residences may gradually spend more and more time together, and they may keep their residences for a while even after they are cohabiting full time. Living apart relationships show that the boundaries around the category "family" are becoming fluid and blurred, much as the boundaries between sexual identities are becoming blurred.

Quick Review

- In the 1800s, young adults found spouses through the publicly visible process of courtship.
- The rise of dating in the twentieth century shifted much of the control over meeting partners from adults to their children and their children's peer group.
- Dating declined late in the twentieth century.
- More Americans now find a spouse online than by traditional means such as family, friends, or work.
- Single young adults are much more likely to live separately from parents than was the case a century ago.
- Some partners view themselves as couples and yet live apart in what are called living apart relationships.

Cohabitation

cohabitation the sharing of a household by unmarried persons who have a sexual relationship

By **cohabitation,** commonly called "living together," I mean a living arrangement in which two adults who are not married to each other but who have a sexual relationship share the same house or apartment. Before the 1960s, cohabitation in the United States was common mainly among the poor and near poor. With little in the way of resources to share and little prospect of leaving money or possessions to their children, the poor had less reason to marry. For many, cohabitation had served as an acceptable substitute for legal marriage. But beginning around 1970, the proportion of all young adults who lived with someone prior to marrying increased sharply. By the early 2010s, 64 percent of women aged 19 to 44 had cohabited; and 70 percent of recently married women had cohabited prior to marrying (Hemez & Manning, 2017a, 2017b). As cohabitation has become more common, its role in the family system has increased. States and localities have been implementing legal changes that give cohabiting couples rights that once were reserved for married couples. (See *Families and Public Policy:* The Legal Rights of Cohabiting Couples.)

Although the common image is one of a childless couple, many cohabiting couples have children in their households: In 2017, 37 percent of different-sex unmarried couples had the children of one or both partners present, including 66 percent of Hispanics, 46 percent of African Americans, and 29 percent of non-Hispanic whites (U.S. Bureau of the Census, 2017). In fact, more than half of the births listed in official statistics as occurring outside of marriage are in reality births to cohabiting couples rather than to single mothers living without partners (Wu, 2017). (Cohabiting mothers are counted simply as "unmarried" because birth certificates, on which these statistics are based, ask whether the mother is married but not whether she is living with a partner.) Over the past decade or two, most of the rise in childbearing outside of marriage has been the result of births to cohabiting couples, not births to women living alone.

Cohabitation has been increasing among individuals of all social classes. Figure 7.2 shows the percentage of women aged 19 to 44 who had ever cohabited, separated according to how much education they had attained, for five time periods from 1987 to 2011–2013. The percentage rose over time for all educational groups. Cohabiting relationships in the United States are shorter, on average, than in most other Western countries (Andersson, Thomson, & Duntava, 2017). Within three years, two-thirds of all cohabiting relationships have ended either by marriage or by dissolutions (Copen, Daniels, & Mosher, 2013).

Families and Public Policy

The Legal Rights of Cohabiting Couples

Getting married is not only a way for couples to express their love and commitment to each other but also a way for them to obtain important practical and financial advantages not available to couples who cohabit or live apart. In most nations the law has long recognized marriage as a privileged relationship in which the spouses have special rights and responsibilities. Here is a partial list of rights and responsibilities that married couples have but cohabiting couples, in most jurisdictions in the United States, do not have:

- They can include each other as beneficiaries on pension and annuity plans offered by their employers, and they can purchase health insurance for each other through their employers.
- They can file a joint income tax return, which may reduce their tax liability.
- They can receive Social Security survivors' benefits if their spouse dies, and they can inherit from each other even when there is no will.
- They are jointly responsible for their children, and each can give legal permission to schools, doctors, and the like, for trips, operations, and so forth.
- They can adopt children together.
- In the event of a divorce, they are both normally entitled to either custody or visitation rights.

This list reflects the view, virtually unchallenged until a few decades ago, that marriage constitutes the only legitimate context for the raising of children. It also reflects the ideal, prominent in the first half of the twentieth century, that families should have one wage earner (the husband), who should be able to provide health insurance, survivors' benefits, and so on, to his wife.

Yet social changes have made the granting of rights solely to married couples debatable. For instance, 25 percent of births in the 2009–2013 period occurred to women who were cohabiting with the fathers of their children (Manning, Brown, & Stykes, 2015). Cohabitation itself is so common that some observers question the rationale for denying cohabiting couples similar rights to those married couples have. They argue that there is little difference between a cohabiting couple raising children and a married couple raising children—and that the former ought to have the same rights and receive the same benefits as the latter. Others favor retaining the privileged place of marriage for any of several reasons: because of a moral or religious belief that marriage is the only proper setting for having and raising children; because of a pragmatic belief that marriage provides a more stable two-parent setting than cohabitation; or because of a wish to avoid further spending by government or business that would be triggered by treating cohabitors like spouses.

In the United States, states and municipalities are moving toward granting cohabiting couples some of the rights and responsibilities that married couples have. Canada has gone further: Under the Modernization of Benefits and Obligations Act of 2000, legal distinctions between married and unmarried same-sex and opposite-sex couples were eliminated for couples who have lived together for at least a year.

In France, where almost 9 out of 10 unions begin outside of marriage, opposite-sex and same-sex cohabiting couples may enter into Civil Solidarity Pacts, which give them most but not all of the rights and responsibilities of married couples after the pact has existed for three years (Martin & Théry, 2001). Some Scandinavian countries also have registered partnerships for opposite-sex couples (Lyall, 2004). Others, such as the United Kingdom, have domestic partnerships exclusively for same-sex couples.

The debate over the legal rights of cohabiting couples reflects the weakening role of marriage in the institution of the family. Although still dominant, marriage is no longer the only acceptable way for couples to live together. Rather, cohabitation is broadly tolerated. This toleration is so recent, however, that there is little consensus on the rights and responsibilities partners should have toward each other and toward the children in their households. Family law in the United States still assumes that most couples with children are married, and it serves them fairly well. But it has not caught up to the reality that many parents are cohabiting, and it does not provide them with the rights and protections that they need (Carbone & Cahn, 2014).

Ask Yourself

1. Are any of the couples you know cohabiting? If so, have their relationships reached the point at which legal considerations would be meaningful to them?
2. Should couples who are cohabiting have the same legal rights as married couples? Why or why not?

COHABITATION AND CLASS

Yet although cohabitation has increased across the board, it differs by social class (Sassler & Miller, 2017). Figure 7.2 shows that the more education a woman had, the less likely she was to have ever cohabited at all time periods. So although college-educated young adults are sometimes thought of as a cultural vanguard, they have been the least likely to live with a partner before marrying. The meaning of cohabitation—what individuals who are living together think that their relationship signifies—also varies by social class, although there is substantial variation and overlap. Let us examine these meanings.

College-Educated Cohabitants College-educated young adults, as Chapter 4 demonstrated, are much more likely to wait until after marriage to have their first child than are less-educated young adults. As a result, they do not have children while cohabiting as often as people with less education. Fifteen percent of college-educated cohabiting women had a child (of either partner) in their households in 2017, compared to 35 percent of cohabiting women who graduated from high school but did not have a four-year college degree (U.S. Bureau of the Census, 2017).

Among the highly educated, cohabitation is often a testing ground for marriage. Childless college-educated couples may live together as a way of determining whether they are compatible enough to get married. They may cohabit after college while pursuing graduate school or starting careers. Some of them may already be formally engaged and have wedding dates set. Few will have children prior to making the decision to marry, and few will cohabit for more than two or three years without marrying or breaking up. By and large, college-educated adults use cohabitation as a step in a family-building process. Most eventually marry, and they wait until after they marry to start having children.

Moderately Educated Cohabitants Cohabitation among moderately educated young adults—those who have graduated from high school but do not have a four-year college degree—is less closely tied to marriage. These individuals may

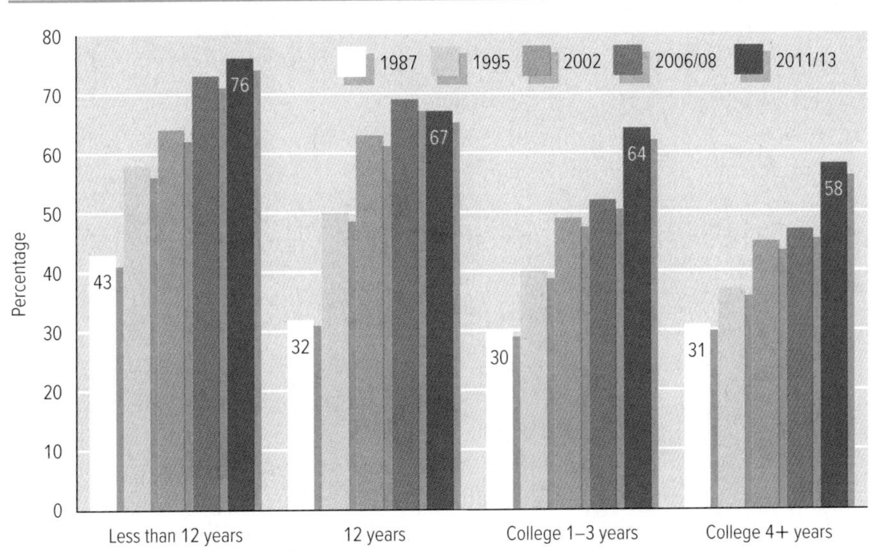

FIGURE 7.2
Percentage of women aged 19 to 44 who had ever cohabited, by educational attainment: 1987 to 2011–2013. (*Source:* Manning & Stykes, 2015)

wish to eventually marry, but they do not think it is possible, or even desirable, at the moment. Marriage may not be foremost in their mind when they begin to live together. In a study of young adults in the Toledo, Ohio, area, who typically had graduated from high school and perhaps had some college courses, the authors reported that many childless cohabiting adults seemed to drift into living together without much thought as to what the relationship might become in the long run and sometimes even without a deliberate decision to cohabit. In fact, none of the 115 cohabiting young adults in this study said that he or she was deciding between marriage and cohabitation at the start of the union (Manning & Smock, 2005). The process of moving in may occur rather quickly for moderately educated couples, often within the first six months of their relationships. The rapid movement into cohabitation may lead to conflicts and communication differences that make marriage to one's partner seem unattractive (Sassler & Miller, 2017).

For moderately educated cohabiting adults who already have children together, the experience may have unfolded differently. Rather than first living together and then having a child, it is common for unmarried couples to begin living together *after* the woman becomes pregnant, whether or not the pregnancy was planned (Reed, 2006). In one study, nearly 40 percent of all couples who were cohabiting at the time of the birth of their first child had begun to live together after the woman became pregnant (Rackin & Gibson-Davis, 2012). Rather than drifting into cohabitation, they decide to live together as a response to the impending birth. They do often think about marriage as a long-term goal. But few think that just because they have a child, they should marry.

Whether or not children are present, most moderately educated cohabitants eventually think about the issue of marriage. Few will remain together for long without marrying (Sassler & Miller, 2017). But their standards for marriage are high. In the Toledo study, many did not want to marry until they had a financial package in place that often included homeownership, being out of debt, and having a stable, adequate income. A 25-year-old woman told the authors that she and her partner were interested in getting married, but they had a lot to accomplish beforehand:

> *Um, we have certain things that we want to do before we get married. We both want very good jobs, and we both want a house, we both want reliable transportation. I'm about to start taking cake decorating classes, and so I can have me some good income, and he–he's trying his best you know? He's been looking out for jobs everywhere, and we–we're trying. We just want to have–we gotta have everything we need before we say, "Let's get married." (Smock, Manning, & Porter, 2005)*

If they fail to acquire everything they need, couples such as this one are likely to dissolve their unions within a few years.

The Least-Educated Cohabitants Cohabitants who did not graduate from high school, most of whom have low-incomes, can be even further removed from considering marriage. Some low-income women see no prospect of finding a man who is suitable for marriage. They may live instead in **serial cohabitation** (Lichter & Qian, 2008) with two or more live-in partners with little or no thought of marriage, interspersed with romantic relationships that do not involve living together.

serial cohabitation living with two or more partners without marrying them

They may enter into cohabiting relationships because of pregnancy, as is the case with the moderately educated; and these relationships are rarely stable. In a study of the parents of nearly 5,000 babies born in urban hospitals, about half of the fathers who were living with the mothers at the birth of their child were no longer romantically involved with the mother five years later (Bendheim-Thoman Center for Child Wellbeing, 2007). Low-income mothers may also enter into cohabiting relationships because of dire financial need. In these instances, the mothers expect that their partners will provide financial support while they are co-residing. In a small number of cases, women may even allow destitute former partners to live with them without restarting sexual relationships (Cross-Barnet, Cherlin, & Burton, 2011). In all, marriage is uncommon among low-income cohabitants: Only about one-fourth of poor cohabiting couples marry their partners within five years, compared to about two-thirds of nonpoor cohabiting couples (Lichter, Turner, & Sassler, 2010). For these individuals, a mixture of cohabiting and non-cohabiting romantic relationships is often a long-term substitute to marriage.

Summing Up While there is much variation in the complex and growing phenomenon of cohabitation, an overall pattern is apparent: The more education that cohabitants have, the more likely they are to marry (Kuo & Raley, 2016). This is true in Canada as well as in the United States (Wright, 2018). Among college graduates, cohabiting relationships are often a stage in the marriage process. As well-educated young adults postpone marriage and invest in careers, they choose to live with partners whom they may wish to marry and someday—after marrying—have children with. Among the moderately educated, cohabitation is more often a short term alternative to marriage. It is a living arrangement that provides intimacy, financial savings, and sometimes co-parenting for couples who do not have the resources that they think are necessary for marriage. Most moderately educated individuals will eventually marry, although not necessarily with the person they first lived with. And among the least educated, cohabitation is an alternative to marriage that may be long-term. But rather than having one long-term cohabiting relationship, it is common for the least-educated to have a series of relationships, some involving cohabiting and some not.

Quick Review

- Cohabitation is a rapidly growing and diverse living arrangement.
- For most couples, it is a short-term partnership that ends in either a marriage or a dissolution within a few years.
- It is more common among the less-educated.
- The more education that cohabitants have, the more closely their relationships are linked to marriage.

Marriage

Marriage is no longer the nearly universal experience it was in the mid-twentieth century. In fact, at current rates only about three-fourths of American young adults would ever marry (Martin, Astone, & Peters, 2014), which would be the lowest percentage on record—and the records go back to the mid-1800s (Cherlin, 1992). The decline is mostly concentrated among young adults without college degrees. In contrast, the decline among college graduates has been less: 84 percent of women college graduates and 81 percent of men are projected to eventually marry (although even those percentages are low by historical standards).

The decline has been especially sharp among African Americans, among whom about half of all women and men are projected to eventually marry. Marriage, in other words, is becoming a less central part of family life for Americans, particularly for the less-educated and for nonwhites. Studies suggest that low- and moderate-income couples are hesitant to marry until they have achieved stable, satisfactory incomes—in other words, they may be willing to cohabit, but they see a marriage bar they must reach before they will marry (Gibson-Davis, 2007; Ishizuka, 2018). As for the meaning that marriage has for husbands and wives, the literature suggests two great changes that occurred during the twentieth and early twenty-first centuries.

FROM INSTITUTION TO COMPANIONSHIP

Family life in preindustrial Western nations was guided more by law and custom than by affection and emotional stimulation. The local government in Plymouth Colony, you will recall, kept a close watch over the conduct of family members. Parents played a greater role in selecting a spouse for their children than was the case in later centuries. In general, husbands and fathers had greater authority than they do today: Religion and law certified the father as head of the family, with broad powers over his wife (whose property he could sell) and his children (who remained with him in the event of a divorce). In addition, the marginal existence of poor farm families and the modest standard of living of most urban families made the family's subsistence a higher priority than the personal development of the parents and children.

institutional marriage a marriage in which the emphasis is on male authority, duty, and conformity to social norms

The Institutional Marriage We might call this pre-twentieth-century form of marriage the **institutional marriage.** A social institution, you will remember, consists of a set of rules and roles that define a social unit of importance to society. Marriage prior to the twentieth century fit this description. It was held together by clear rules and roles: The husband was expected to be the head of the household, the wife was to be dutiful and submissive, and the children obedient. Although the husband and wife may have been fond of each other, romantic love wasn't necessary or even desirable—which is why Maud Rittenhouse chose Elmer over Robert. Rather, spouses were expected to work together under the husband's authority to manage the farm, raise children, and keep food on the table. The local community, the church, and the law all supported the rules and roles of the institutional marriage.

But in the early twentieth century, progressive writers argued that an active sex life was central to a happy marriage. In the 1920s, Robert and Helen Lynd conducted a famous study of life in Muncie, Indiana, which they selected as a typical American town and called "Middletown" (Lynd & Lynd, 1929). The Lynds reported that, compared with the 1890s, young adults were more likely to view romantic love as the only valid basis for marriage. In this new romantic climate, they wrote, women were more concerned with "youthful beauty." Throughout the country, mass production and rising incomes made fashionable clothing affordable. Advice columnist Dorothy Dix told her readers that "good looks are a girl's trump card." And she counseled, "Dress well and thereby appear fifty percent better looking than you are. . . . Make yourself charming" (May, 1980).

The Companionate Marriage In a 1945 textbook, Ernest Burgess, the leading family sociologist of the first half of the twentieth century, famously described this transition in the meaning of marriage:

> *The central thesis of this volume is that the family in historical times has been, and at present is, in transition from an institution to a companionship. In the past the important factors unifying the family have been external, formal, and authoritarian, as the law, the mores, public opinion, tradition, the authority of the family head, rigid discipline, and elaborate ritual. At present, in the new emerging form of the companionship family, its unity inheres less and less in community pressures and more and more in such interpersonal relations as the mutual affection, the sympathetic understanding, and the comradeship of its members. (Burgess & Locke, 1945)*

Burgess meant the family-as-institution and the family-as-companionship to be seen as ideal types. Thus, he cautioned that purely institutional or purely companionship families exist "nowhere in time or space." In the spirit of the ideal type, we can call the kind of marriage that was emerging in the 1940s the **companionate marriage.** It emphasized affection, friendship, and sexual gratification. Keep in mind, however, that the style of marriage Burgess saw emerging was the single-earner, breadwinner–homemaker marriage that flourished in the 1950s—not the dual-earner family that emerged only in the second half of the twentieth century. The husband and wife in the companionate marriage ideally adhered to a sharp division of labor (he worked outside the home, she worked inside the home). Nevertheless, they were supposed to be each other's companions—friends, lovers—to an extent not imagined by the spouses in the institutional marriages a generation or two earlier. Husbands' authority, although still substantial, was less than in the institutional marriage. Young women were increasingly seen as needing higher education, not so they could establish careers but rather so they could be stimulating conversationalists and efficient homemakers. By midcentury, large state universities enrolled hundreds of thousands of bright young women who majored in home economics or consumer science and joked that what they really hoped to get at college was an "MRS." degree.

companionate marriage a marriage in which the emphasis is on affection, friendship, and sexual gratification

FROM COMPANIONSHIP TO INDIVIDUALIZATION

The companionate marriage reached its peak at midcentury. The spouses who married at young ages and in record numbers in the late 1940s and the 1950s were its exemplars. Most wives, except among the poor, did not work outside the home. Instead, they focused on creating an emotionally satisfying home life centered on affectionate relations between spouses and on child rearing—these were, after all, the parents who produced the baby boom. They found meaning in the successful performance of their social roles: the homemaker who raised children well and was a pleasant companion and friend to her husband; the man who supported his family through steady employment, enjoyed the company of his wife, and was a loving, if sometimes distant, father.

By the mid-1960s, however, the breadwinner–homemaker companionate marriage was losing ground as both a cultural ideal and a demographic reality. It was gradually overtaken by family forms that Burgess had not foreseen, particularly marriages in which both the husband and the wife worked outside the home. Although women continued to do most of the housework and child care, the roles of wives and husbands became more flexible and open to negotiation. Moreover, an even more individualistic perspective on the rewards of marriage took root. When people evaluated how satisfied they were with their marriages, they thought more in terms of individual satisfaction with how their own lives were developing than in terms of satisfaction gained through building a family.

Toward the Individualistic Marriage In other words, it mattered less how well they were performing the roles society expected of them, such as earning money, raising children, or working hard on the job. It mattered more how much they enjoyed their jobs, how much emotional gratification they were getting from their marriages, how gratifying their sex lives were, and how pleased they were with the ways their lives were changing and developing. Being a good citizen or a responsible parent was less important; being emotionally satisfied was more important. Feeling that you were meeting your obligations to others was less central; feeling that you had opportunities to grow as a person was more central. Starting in the 1960s popular magazine articles offering marital advice emphasized three themes that characterized beliefs about the post-1960-style marriage. The first was "self-development," the belief that each person should develop a fulfilling, independent self instead of merely sacrificing oneself to one's partner. Second, roles within marriage should be flexible and negotiable; and third, communication and openness in confronting problems are essential (Cancian, 1987).

This shift produced the second great change in the meaning of marriage during the twentieth century. Given its emphasis on self-development, flexible roles, and open communication, we might call the form that emerged after 1960 the **individualistic marriage.** It, too, is something of an ideal type: Even people who evaluate their satisfaction in very individualistic terms may also take pride in being a good parent. But its general form represents an important break with the meaning of marriage in the past. The change in meaning that accompanied the transition to the individualized marriage has been called a shift "from role to self" (Cancian, 1987).

individualistic marriage a marriage in which the emphasis is on self-development, flexible roles, and open communication

The Influence of Economic Change In addition, both transitions—from the institutional marriage to the companionate marriage, and from the companionate marriage to the individualistic marriage—had economic roots. First, both are related to changes in the nature of work. The transition from institution to companionship occurred as the United States was becoming increasingly industrialized and urbanized. Husbands (although not wives at first) took jobs that paid wages. Farm families needed to function as production units—as small-scale firms if you will—in order to be successful. In most agricultural societies, older men retained substantial authority to run these production units. Wage work, in contrast, provided young adults with some independence from their parents: They could move away to jobs in the city. Their parents had less control over whom they married. Moreover, men's authority was reduced in urban marriages because of the demise of the family as production unit. Later, the transition from companionship to individualistic marriage occurred as married women took paid jobs in large numbers. In doing so, they gained greater independence from men and were exposed to new ideas beyond the home. Women as well as men could now think in terms of their own individual development through adulthood. These circumstances supported the emergence of a more individualistic perspective on the rewards of marriage.

Second, both transitions are related to increases in families' standards of living. When most people's living standards were so low that they had difficulty earning enough money for food and shelter, few had time for personal fulfillment. People needed to pool earnings and housework with spouses and children in order to subsist, and marriage was therefore more of an economic partnership. The rising standard of living during the twentieth century gave more people the luxury of focusing on their own feelings of satisfaction. They did so first in the context of the companionate marriage in which a higher standard of living allowed many wives to stay home rather than work for pay. But increasingly high standards of living meant that people could live alone if their marriages were not personally fulfilling, and this development accelerated the transition from companionate marriage to individualistic marriage.

Quick Review

- In the institutional marriage, wives' and husbands' behavior is governed by strong social norms, tradition, and law. Men have substantial authority.
- In the companionate marriage, the spouses expect affection, friendship, and sexual gratification and find satisfaction in being good parents and spouses.
- In the individualistic marriage, each spouse expects self-fulfillment, intimacy, and continuing personal growth.
- Industrialization and urbanization hastened the transition to the companionate marriage.
- The increase in married women working for wages, as well as rising standards of living, underlay the transition to the individualistic marriage.

The Current Context of Marriage

Overall, research and writing on the changing meaning of marriage suggest that it is now situated in a very different context than in the past. This is true in at least two senses. First, individuals now have a great deal of choice in how they live their personal lives. It used to be that young adults got married, and only then moved in together, and only then had children. Today, more forms of marriage and more alternatives to marriage are socially acceptable. You may fit marriage into your life in many ways: You may first live with a partner, or sequentially with several partners, without thinking about whether the arrangement will lead to marriage. You may have children with your eventual spouse or with someone else before marrying. You may marry someone of the same gender and build a shared marital world. Moreover, you can have partnerships and children without ever marrying at all. Elsewhere I have called this the **deinstitutionalization of marriage:** the idea that alternatives to marriage are more acceptable and more prevalent than in the past, with the result that marriage is much less dominant as a context for intimate partnerships, childbearing, and family life (Cherlin, 2004). Within marriages and cohabiting unions, roles are more flexible and negotiable, although women still do more than their share of the household work and child rearing (as we will see in the next chapter).

deinstitutionalization of marriage the idea that alternatives to marriage are more acceptable and more prevalent than in the past

The second difference is in the nature of the rewards that people seek through marriage and other close relationships. People want the individualistic rewards of what's often called personal growth or self-development—a sense that your inner life is changing and developing in a way that gives you great satisfaction—and deeper intimacy. People try to attain these rewards through more open communication and mutually shared disclosures about feelings with their partners. To attain personal growth, they may feel justified in insisting on changes in a relationship that no longer allows them to grow in the directions they wish. In contrast, they are less likely than in the past to focus on the rewards to be found in fulfilling socially valued roles such as the good parent or the loyal and supportive spouse. The result of these changing contexts is that social norms about family and personal life count for less than they did during the heyday of the companionate marriage, and far less than during the period of the institutional marriage. Instead, personal choice and self-development loom large in people's construction of their marital careers.

WHY DO PEOPLE STILL MARRY?

There is, however, a puzzle within the story of the changes in marriage that needs solving: Why do most people still want to marry? After all, with the many choices adults have, it's not necessary, strictly speaking, to marry anymore. To be sure, fewer Americans are marrying than during the peak years of marriage in the mid-twentieth century, but a majority still do. Among people born around 1990, 79 percent of women and 75 percent of men are projected to have married by 2020 (Martin, Astone, & Peters, 2014). A survey of high school seniors conducted annually since 1976 shows no decline in the importance they attach to marriage. The percentage who respond that "having a good marriage and family life" is extremely important has remained constant, at about 80 percent for young women and 70 percent for young men (Bachman, Johnston, & O'Malley, 2014). Clearly, marriage remains important to many people in the United States. Consequently, I think the interesting question is not why so few people are marrying, but rather, why so many people are marrying, or planning to marry, or hoping to marry, when cohabitation and single parenthood are widely acceptable options.

MARRIAGE AS THE CAPSTONE EXPERIENCE

What has happened, I would argue, is that although the practical importance of being married has declined, its symbolic importance has increased. Marriage is less dominant than it was–you don't have to marry anymore. But it is also more distinctive than it was–precisely because it is optional, it causes married couples to stand out from others. It has evolved from a marker of conformity (doing what every adult was virtually required to do) to a marker of prestige (attaining a special status). Today, marriage is a status young couples build up to, often by living with a partner beforehand, by gaining steady employment or starting a career, by putting away some savings, and even by having children. A half-century ago, marriage's place in the life course used to come before those investments were made, but now it often comes afterward. It used to be the foundation of adult personal life; now it is sometimes the capstone–the last brick put in place when the structure is finally complete.

This new meaning of marriage is not limited to the college-educated. We saw it earlier in the chapter in the attitudes of cohabitants without college degrees, who will not marry until all the bricks are in place. Edin and Kefalas (2005), who studied childbearing and intimate relationships among mothers in low- and moderate-income Philadelphia neighborhoods, wrote,

> *In some sense, marriage is a form of social bragging about the quality of the couple's relationship, a powerfully symbolic way of elevating one's relationship above others in the community, particularly in a community where marriage is rare.*

Two generations ago, young adults got married *before* they had everything they needed. But cohabiting was not an option back then, so they faced the choice of marrying or not living together. Today, with cohabitation as an acceptable option, many young adults are postponing marriage until they pass the milestones that used to occur early in marriage.

THE WEDDING AS A STATUS SYMBOL

Even the wedding has become an individual achievement. In the distant past, a wedding was an event at which two kinship groups formed an alliance. More recently, it has been an event organized and paid for by parents, at which they display their approval and support for their child's marriage. In both cases, it has been the ritual that provides legal and social approval for having children. But in keeping with the individualistic marriage, it is now becoming an event centered on and often controlled by the couple themselves, having less to do with family approval or having children than in the past.

You might think, then, that weddings would become smaller and that many couples would forgo a public wedding altogether. But that does not appear to have happened for most couples. The wedding, it seems, has become an important symbol of the partners' personal achievements and a stage to display their self-development. Studies suggest that the percentage of weddings held in a religious institution, the percentage with receptions, and the percentage followed by a honeymoon have increased (Whyte, 1990). In recent decades, then, when partners decide that their relationship has finally reached the stage where they can marry, they generally want a ritual-filled wedding to celebrate it (Boden, 2003; Bulcroft, Bulcroft, Bradley, & Simpson, 2000; Bulcroft, Bulcroft, Smeins, & Cranage, 1997; Ingraham, 1999; Mead, 2007).

Even low- and moderate-income couples who have limited funds and who may already have children and may be living together seem to view a substantial wedding as a requirement for marriage. Some of the young adults in the Toledo study said that merely going "downtown" for a civil ceremony at a courthouse or a justice of the peace's office did not constitute an acceptable wedding. A home health care aide said she was waiting for her boyfriend to change his mind about a church wedding because, "until he does, we just won't get married. I'm not going downtown. . . . I say, you don't want a big wedding, we're not going to get married" (Smock, Manning, & Porter, 2005). The authors of the Philadelphia study write, "Having the wherewithal to throw a 'big' wedding is a vivid display that the couple has achieved enough financial security to do more than live from paycheck to paycheck" (Edin & Kefalas, 2005). The couples in these studies wanted to make a statement through their weddings, a statement both to themselves and to their friends and family that they had passed a milestone in their personal development. Through wedding ceremonies, the purchase of a home, and the acquisition of other accoutrements of married life, individuals hoped to display their attainment of a prestigious, comfortable, stable style of life. People marry now not only for the social benefits that marriage provides but also for the personal achievement–the capstone experience–it represents.

MARRIAGE AS INVESTMENT

But the practical gains of marriage have not completely disappeared. True, families now buy products and services that wives used to make at home (think of restaurant meals). Labor-saving devices allow household partners to produce goods with less time and effort (think of wrinkle-resistant clothes that don't need ironing). Yet some advantages still remain, especially for marriages in which both spouses bring home decent incomes. Suppose you want to buy a home with your partner. Most couples take out a mortgage that entails making monthly payments for 20 or 30 years. Before you sign the mortgage papers, you need to be confident that your partnership will be around for that long. You would probably be more confident if you were married than if you were cohabiting because a marriage is harder to end: Divorce laws stipulate that assets must be divided and arrangements for children be agreed upon. Family and friends who helped celebrate your wedding will want to know what went wrong. Therefore, marriage, more so than cohabitation, lowers the risk that your partner will renege on agreements that have been made by moving out. In this sense, marriage is a commitment device–a way to increase the likelihood that your partner will stay committed to you in the long term. It conveys what we might call **enforceable trust**–the ability to call on the law and on family and friends to help enforce the agreements you have made with a partner (Cherlin, 2000; Portes & Sensenbrenner, 1993). As a result, you can invest in the partnership with less fear of abandonment.

enforceable trust the ability to enforce the agreements one has made with a partner

The largest investment that couples typically make is in raising children. Over the past few decades, the amount of money that parents spend on their children has increased, and as noted in Chapter 4, the increase has been greatest among parents with high incomes (Kornrich & Furstenberg, 2013). The latter are more likely to follow the expensive child-rearing strategy that Lareau (2011) called "concerted cultivation": music lessons, summer camp, SAT prep courses, travel, and high-tuition colleges (see Chapter 4). For these parents, the stronger commitment that marriage provides is more valuable than it is for lower-income parents who don't spend as much on their children (Lundberg, Pollak, & Stearns, 2016). Consequently, the greater trust that marriage provides for sharing the costs of expensive consumption and investment may be one reason why the percentage ever marrying is higher, and the divorce rate is lower, among college graduates: Marriage is of greater financial value to them. Low- and moderate-income couples are less likely to buy a large house or send their child to an elite college, and therefore getting married, relative to cohabiting, provides them with few financial benefits.

Quick Review

- People have more choices today about how to live their personal lives.
- The rewards that people seek in marriages and other close relationships center on personal growth and deeper intimacy.
- Marriage is still important as a symbol of status and prestige.
- Increasingly, young adults are delaying marriage until they have accomplished other goals such as obtaining steady employment or buying a home.
- Marriage still provides partners with greater trust that long-term investments can be made in buying a home or in child rearing.

MARRIAGE AND RELIGION

Organized religion in the United States has always supported marriage, and it has continued to do so throughout the transitions to the companionate and independent marriages. The United States is probably the most religious nation in the Western world. A comparable set of surveys conducted in more than 60 nations between 1999 and 2001 shows that Americans go to church more often than do people in every other Western nation except Ireland and that they think of themselves as "religious persons" more than in any Western nation except Italy. Moreover, they tend to believe that what they learn from religion is relevant to their family lives. When asked, "Generally speaking, do you think that the churches in your country are giving adequate answers to . . . the problems of family life?" more Americans (61 percent) said yes than did people in any other Western country (Inglehart et al., 2004).

Conservative (or evangelical) Protestant and Mormon young adults, particularly those who attend church regularly and say that religion is important, tend to marry at earlier ages than other young adults (Lehrer, 2004; Xu, Hudspeth, & Bartkowski, 2005; Eggebeen & Dew, 2009). Among married persons, those who are active religiously describe themselves as somewhat happier with their marriages (Fincham & Beach, 2010); and they also tend to report better mental health (Waite & Lehrer, 2003). Couples who attend religious services frequently have a lower risk of divorce than do those who attend less often (Bramlett & Mosher, 2002). (I will have more to say about divorce risks in Chapter 12.) It is not clear, however, whether religious activity causes these differences or whether other, unmeasured factors cause both greater well-being and more religious activity.

In recent years, churches have been an expanding base for counseling, educational programs, and other attempts at "marriage strengthening." For example, churches have participated in the development of programs to teach communication skills to engaged or recently married couples so that they will be better equipped to discuss and resolve problems that may arise (Markman et al., 2004). The main exception to the emphasis on marriage among religious groups is among African American churches. Although these churches are strong supporters of African American families, they emphasize marriage relatively less and extended family ties relatively more than do predominantly white churches (Gilkes, 1995).

SAME-SEX MARRIAGE

The most sweeping change in marriage in memory is its extension to same-sex couples. After more than a decade of fierce debate, controversial court rulings, and shifting public opinion, the change was completed in 2015 when the Supreme Court, in *Obergefell* v. *Hodges* (2015), ruled that restricting marriage to different-sex couples was unconstitutional. Justice Anthony Kennedy, who wrote the opinion for the five-justice majority, argued for a fundamental right to marriage. He wrote of same-sex partners with children:

> *Without the recognition, stability and predictability marriage offers, their children suffer the stigma of knowing their families are somehow lesser. They also suffer the significant material costs of being raised by unmarried parents, relegated through no fault of their own to a more difficult and uncertain family life. The marriage laws at issue here thus harm and humiliate the children of same-sex couples.*

Marriage, according to the majority of the justices, is an important status that benefits parents and children and that cannot be denied on the basis of the gender of the partners. Their sexual orientation is irrelevant to their right of access to this legal institution.

The four justices who dissented argued that the ruling was a grave mistake. Chief Justice John Roberts wrote:

> *As a result, the Court invalidates the marriage laws of more than half the states and orders the transformation of a social institution that has formed the basis of human society for millennia, for the Kalahari Bushmen and the Han Chinese, the Carthaginians and the Aztecs. Just who do we think we are?*

To the minority of the Court, the heterosexual nature of marriage from ancient days to the present is so basic that it cannot be transcended without altering the institution beyond recognition.

Suddenly same-sex marriage was legal in all 50 states. The next question was how many same-sex couples would avail themselves of the opportunity to marry? The answer is quite a few. By 2017, a majority of all same-sex couples who were living together–61 percent, by one estimate (Gallup Organization, 2017)–had taken advantage of changes in state laws, and then in the nation after *Obergefell,* by marrying. This high take-up rate suggests that marriage is a meaningful marker of a successful personal life for many Americans, whatever their sexual orientation. Nevertheless, the high take-up rate may also reflect a backlog of couples who were in long-term relationships and were therefore inclined to affirm their commitment through marriage. It isn't clear whether younger, recently formed couples will be as eager to wed. Nevertheless, same-sex marriage is now firmly a part of the American family system. It is so new that sociologists don't yet know much about it; but we can expect to learn more in the coming years from studies that are just getting underway.

IS MARRIAGE GOOD FOR YOU?

Do individuals benefit from being married? A substantial body of literature shows that married men appear advantaged compared with unmarried men in many ways and that, to a lesser extent, married women seem advantaged as well. (We do not yet know the effect of marriage on same-sex partners.) But it is difficult to know whether marriage *causes* these differences. For example, married men and women live longer, on average, than do unmarried men and women. One study estimated that unmarried men have a 33 percent higher risk of dying than do married men; and unmarried women have a 14 percent higher risk of dying than do married women (Rendall, Weden, Favreault, & Waldron, 2011). A number of studies have found evidence that married men and women have substantially better health than unmarried men and women, in terms of life expectancy, self-rated health, and psychological distress (Carr & Springer, 2010).

There are two possible reasons for these findings:

1. *Being married actually causes people to feel better and live longer.* Marriage might be good for one's physical and mental health in two ways. First, it may deter people from undertaking risky behavior. For instance, married men and women are less likely to abuse alcohol or drugs (Duncan, Wilkerson, & England, 2006). Marriage may provide people with a sense of responsibility to children and spouses that leads them to take fewer risks. In addition, marriage may provide a partner who monitors a person's health closely and urges a healthier lifestyle. Second, married people have higher incomes and more wealth, in part because of economies of scale (two people can share a home or a car). A higher standard of living eases stress and makes people less likely to abuse alcohol or drugs.

2. *Mentally and physically healthier people are more likely to get married and to stay married.* As women and men choose partners, we would expect them to favor the healthy and the happy over the troubled and the ill. So there should be *positive selection into* marriage: People with positive qualities are more likely to enter into it. Recall the discussion of the selection effect on teenage childbearing: Young women who have children as adolescents are not a random sample of all adolescents. Similarly, people who marry are not a random sample of all adults; rather, they represent the most attractive 70 to 80 percent of the population in the marriage market. Moreover, people with poorer mental health have marriages that are more troubled and are therefore more likely to divorce. So as couples age, there is *negative selection out of* marriage: People with negative characteristics are more likely to leave it. Because of selection into and out of marriage, we would expect currently married individuals to be physically and mentally healthier even if what goes on in a marriage has nothing to do with it.

Because sociologists cannot randomly assign some people to marry and others to stay single and then study them, we cannot say definitively whether being married actually causes people's health and mood to improve or whether we are merely witnessing a selection effect. Most likely, both a true causal effect and a selection effect occur (Carr & Springer, 2010). The findings for men, in particular, are so strong and consistent across a number of studies of different domains of life as to suggest that some of the advantages shown by married men are caused by the marriage relationship itself. And it is likely that there are benefits for women as well. If the effects of marriage were purely due to selection, we would expect that as people get older, the difference between the married and unmarried would increase—because the unmarried group would be composed more and more of unhealthy individuals who never married or who divorced. But data on death rates and treatment for mental illness do not show a gap between the married and the unmarried that increases with age (Rendall et al., 2011). Marriage might benefit men more than women because unmarried men have fewer social resources to draw on. As Chapter 10 will show, women are enmeshed in support networks with other women—mothers, sisters, grandmothers—much more than men are. In contrast, men tend to rely heavily on their wives for social support; and they therefore have more to gain from marrying.

Quick Review

- People who are actively religious marry earlier and have somewhat happier marriages.
- The advantages married people show may be partly due to selection and partly to marriage itself.

THE MARRIAGE MARKET

Despite the rise of cohabitation, the great majority of Americans eventually marry. When sociologists and economists study who marries whom, they often make an analogy to the labor market, in which people seeking employment look for employers who will hire them at an acceptable wage. In the **marriage market,** unmarried individuals (or their parents) search for others who will marry them (or their children). Instead of an acceptable wage, the searchers require that a partner have an acceptable set of desired characteristics, such as a college education, good looks, a pleasant disposition, and so forth.

marriage market an analogy to the labor market in which single individuals (or their parents) search for others who will marry them (or their children)

There are three components to this market model of marriage. The first component is simply a group of people who are actively looking for a spouse at the same place at the same time. They constitute the *supply* of men and women who are in the marriage market. The second component is *preferences.* Each person has an idea of his or her own preferred characteristics in a spouse. Some people may care more about good looks, others more about personality or earning potential. A person will try to find a mate who ranks as high as possible on the characteristics she or he prefers. And that same person will probably have a minimum set of characteristics that she or he will accept. The third component is *resources.* These are the characteristics a person possesses that are attractive to others. In a sense resources are the flip side of preferences: Resources are what I have that a partner might want; preferences are what I want a partner to have.

So people who are looking for spouses, who have preferences about the qualities they want, and who have resources to offer create a marriage market. To be sure, it is difficult in real life to decide just who is looking for a spouse and who isn't. The growth of cohabitation makes this problem even more difficult. Moreover, this depiction of searchers as rational, calculating individuals who tote up the pluses and minuses of prospects is at odds with the popular image of people falling in love with each other. Clearly, the market metaphor can't explain everything about who marries whom. Nevertheless, in the aggregate, the behavior of unmarried persons resembles that of job searchers enough that the metaphor is useful.[7]

Sometimes preferences and resources are so incompatible that the market can't provide acceptable spouses for all who are looking. One explanation for the drop in the African American marriage rate is that decent-paying industrial jobs–making steel or cars or television sets–have moved to firms in developing countries or have been automated, so that men without college educations (and African American men are less likely to have attended college) have a harder time finding a job that can support a family. Therefore African American women, so this argument goes, can't find enough employed African American men to marry (Wilson, 1987). Recent studies have indeed found that women's marriage rates are lower in areas where more men were unemployed, although the effect has not been large enough to fully explain racial differences in marriage patterns. High levels of homicide, imprisonment, and drug use also remove some black men from the marriage market.

The Specialization Model In the predominant marriage bargain of the mid-twentieth century, men placed a greater emphasis on the homemaking skills of their wives; conversely, women placed a greater emphasis on the earning potential of their spouses. This is the bargain hailed in the writings of functionalist sociologist Talcott Parsons and his associates in the 1950s (Parsons & Bales, 1955). It is also the bargain implied by the theory of the division of labor advanced by economist Gary Becker, whose theoretical work since the 1960s pioneered the economic approach to studying the family (1991).

Becker drew his model from the theory of international trade, under which each country is said to have a "comparative advantage" in producing particular goods relative to other countries. For example, a poor, underdeveloped country with land and farmers but few factories might be able to produce grain more "efficiently" than tractors. In contrast, a developed country such as the United States, with its assembly line factories and skilled workers, may be able to produce tractors (and other manufactured goods) more efficiently than grain. If so, according to the theory, each

[7] The job search analogy has been carried furthest by Oppenheimer (1988).

country will benefit if the underdeveloped country specializes in producing grain, some of which it can trade for tractors, and the developed country specializes in producing tractors, some of which it can trade for grain. Becker's application of this model to the family is straightforward: If women are more "efficient" at housework and child care relative to earning money—either because they are better at caring for children or because they tend to be paid less than men—and men are more efficient at earning money rather than at housework and child care, both will benefit if the wife specializes in housework and child care and the husband specializes in paid work outside the home. Consequently, the model predicts that in the marriage market women will search for good providers and men will search for good homemakers. We might call this the **specialization model** of the marriage market.

specialization model model of the marriage market in which women specialize in housework and child care and men specialize in paid work outside the home

The Income-Pooling Model In general, the specialization model of the marriage market predicted that women with less education and lower earnings would be *more* likely to marry than better-educated, higher-earning women. The former group, it was said, has more to gain by marrying a man who will earn money while they specialize in housework and child care. But a new bargain has emerged, in which both spouses work for pay and pool their incomes. We can call this the **income-pooling model** of marriage. Under this model, a woman with greater earning potential should be more likely to marry because she is more attractive to men seeking to pool incomes. This now seems to be the case: Women with four-year college degrees are more likely to marry than are women without them, and the gap has been widening (Martin, Astone, & Peters, 2014). Studies also show that men with higher earning potential are more likely to marry women with higher earning potential than they were a generation or two ago—suggesting a shift from a specialization model to an income-pooling model (Torr, 2011). Comparisons across countries also support this shift in the marriage market. Ono (2003) found that in Japan, where few women work and the specialization model would seem to apply, women with more income are less likely to marry, whereas in Sweden and the United States, where many women work and the income-pooling model is gaining strength, women with more income are more likely to marry.

income-pooling model a model of the marriage market in which both spouses work for pay and pool their incomes

It appears, then, that the marriage bargain now includes the preference, for most couples, that both spouses will contribute to the family's income. Why has this change occurred? In part, it reflects the greater acceptance of married women's work outside the home. In addition, it reflects the prolonged stagnation of men's wages since the early 1970s. Valerie Oppenheimer (2003) found that young men with a recent history of unstable employment are less likely to marry than are men with stable employment; but they are *more* likely to cohabit—as if cohabiting is a fallback position for young men whose employment situations are not adequate for marrying. Her article implies that the declining employment prospects of less-educated young men may be a factor in the increase in cohabitation and the later age at first marriage.

Quick Review

- A specialization model of the marriage market, in which men traded earning potential for women's housework and childbearing efforts, predominated in the mid-twentieth century.
- An income-pooling model, in which women and men both offer earning potential, arose over the past few decades.
- The greater acceptance of married women's work outside the home and the declining earning power of men without college educations underlie this transition.

Social Change and Intimate Unions

Prior to about 1960, marriage was the only acceptable way for adults to have intimate partnerships and to raise children. So dominant was marriage that people who never married were viewed as having incomplete lives and as being perhaps defective in some way. Never-married older women were derided as "spinsters" or "old maids." A historian labeled the period from 1850 to 1960 in Britain, which had similar trends, "the age of mandatory marriage" (Gillis, 1985). During this age a strict division of labor arose, in which husbands were to work outside the home and wives were to manage the home and care for children. But great changes have occurred since the mid-twentieth century.

CHANGES IN UNION FORMATION

union formation the process of beginning to live with a partner through cohabitation or marriage

Table 7.1 summarizes the changes since the 1950s in **union formation,** the process of beginning to live with a partner through cohabitation or marriage. In the 1950s, most young women and many young men did not have sex until they were engaged or married. If a premarital pregnancy occurred, the mother and father usually married quickly to avoid the stigma of an "illegitimate" birth. Cohabitation was scandalous and virtually unknown among the middle class; and even among the poor it was less common than today. Nearly everyone married, and they did so at younger ages than before or since. The birthrate rose to a twentieth-century high. Women

Table 7.1 Changes in Union Formation Since the Mid-Twentieth Century

	1950s	2010s
When do sexual relations begin?	For a majority of women and many men, sexual relations began only after engagement or marriage.	Sexual relations typically begin many years before a union is formed.
What happens when premarital pregnancies occur?	Usually led to a hasty marriage because childbearing outside of marriage was highly stigmatized.	Much less likely to lead to marriage because childbearing outside of marriage is more acceptable.
Who cohabits?	Cohabitation is common only among the poor; it is not considered respectable among the nonpoor.	Most young adults will cohabit before they marry. It has become an important part of the process of finding a marital partner.
Who marries and when?	About 95 percent of whites and almost 90 percent of blacks married; average age at marriage was younger than in any other decade.	About 80 percent of whites will marry, and about half of blacks will marry. Typical ages at marriage are about seven years older than in the 1950s.
What is the economic bargain?	Men typically exchanged their earning power for women's housework and child-rearing effort. Middle-class and working-class married women rarely worked outside the home.	Men and women typically pool their earnings and achieve economies of scale (i.e., only one mortgage to pay for). Women with higher earning potential are more likely to marry.
What is the cultural expectation?	Companionship and satisfaction through playing the roles of spouse and parent.	Ongoing self-development, intimacy, and communication.

expected to stay at home after marrying, and men expected to be the family's sole earner—the so-called good provider (Bernard, 1981). Husbands and wives expected to be loving companions and friends and to derive great pleasure from being successful spouses and parents.

In the early twenty-first century, nearly all these conditions have changed. Most young adults begin to have sex many years before they marry, and better birth control technology and legalized abortion make it easier for them to do so. The typical age at marriage is much higher than at midcentury, and the proportion of people who never marry has grown. Unmarried women can give birth to children outside of marriage with little stigma. More than half of all young adults cohabit prior to marrying. For some, cohabitation is an alternative to marriage, whereas for others, it is a way to see whether they and their partners are compatible enough to marry.

The marital bargain has also changed. It is based more on a pooling of joint earnings than on an exchange of men's earnings for women's housework and child care. Men are still required to be good, steady earners in order to be acceptable as husbands; but increasingly women are expected to be good earners as well. Although women still provide more of the housework and child care, the marital bargain typically calls for men to do more work at home than was the case at midcentury. On an emotional level, wives and husbands are increasingly concerned with self-development, intimacy, and communicating their feelings and desires. In addition, LGBTQ couples can now marry or live openly in cohabiting relationships.

Many of the changes since the mid-twentieth century have weakened the role of marriage in personal life. In fact, given the greater acceptability of alternative living arrangements, one might ask why so many people still marry. One reason is that marriage still allows a partner to have greater trust in the commitment the other partner has to the relationship. Marriage requires a commitment to a long-term, possibly lifelong, relationship, although that advantage is weaker than it used to be. The greater commitment is especially useful for high-income couples who make large, long-term investments in homes and child rearing.

In addition, marriage is still a marker of prestige and distinction. In fact, as fewer people marry and young adults take longer to do it, the prestige that marriage confers may be growing. Marriage is now, in part, a step people take to distinguish themselves from others. Some cohabiting couples are postponing marriage until after they have achieved job stability, have amassed enough savings to buy a home, and in some cases have had children together. Marriage used to be the foundation of adult personal life; now it is sometimes the crowning achievement. Church ceremonies and wedding parties seem to be popular, even among people who aren't particularly religious, in part because they demonstrate commitment, but also because they show family and friends that one's personal life is a success. Nevertheless, despite these advantages, it is clear that marriage does not hold as privileged a position in our family system as it did in the mid-twentieth century. The gains to marriage, relative to alternatives, are perceived to be lower on average today than they were a half-century ago.

TOWARD THE EGALITARIAN MARRIAGE?

As we have seen, divorce has decreased sharply among college-educated young adults since about 1980 (Schwartz & Han, 2014). Moreover, college graduates are more likely to marry than are people with less education (Martin, Astone, & Peters, 2014), and they are much more likely to wait to have children until after they marry

(Manning & Stykes, 2015). Consequently, some observers are claiming that these well-educated young adults are the vanguard of an emerging phase of family life based on stable, egalitarian partnerships and high investment in children–a happy ending of sorts to a half-century of turbulent family change. In Europe, where these developments do not seem limited to college graduates, the claim is that stable, gender-egalitarian partnerships are increasingly common among nearly all social classes (Esping-Andersen & Billari, 2015). In a **gender-egalitarian marriage,** both spouses share the housework and child care much more equitably than in the past. To be sure, more than one kind of egalitarianism may exist. Some couples in Europe, while endorsing the right of women to work outside the home and the desirability of having men to do more work in the home, believe that it's perfectly acceptable for women to choose to stay home and care for children (Knight & Brinton, 2017).

gender-egalitarian marriage a marriage in which both spouses share the housework and child care much more equitably than in the past

What we may be witnessing, so these authors state, is the completion of the "gender revolution" (Goldscheider, Bernhardt, & Lappegård, 2015): In the first half of the gender revolution, which took place in the later decades of the twentieth century, the movement of women into the workforce destabilized the breadwinner–homemaker marriages that were prevalent in the post–World War II era. These trends created a double burden on women, who were still expected to do most of the domestic work in the home even though they were employed. As a result, divorce rates rose, cohabitation increased, and birthrates fell. In the second half of the gender revolution, which we are experiencing now, men are increasingly sharing domestic tasks, which relieves the double burden on women. Therefore, marital relations are more harmonious and divorce rates are declining. Birthrates, although still low by historical standards, have risen in many Western countries. The advocates for this point of view concede that some national populations are proceeding through the second half of the gender revolution faster than others, but they argue that the path is clear throughout the West.

The announcement of a new egalitarian era may seem premature to Americans. To be sure, over the past several decades the proportion of domestic work that men in partnerships do has increased substantially in the United States (Kan, Sullivan, & Gershuny, 2011), as we will see in the next chapter. Yet much of the increase occurred prior to the 2000s, and men still perform only about one-third of the work. Women still do substantially more than their fair share by egalitarian standards. As a result, some American scholars are expressing concern over the possibility that the gender revolution has stalled (England, 2010), as noted in Chapter 3. In response, the gender-egalitarian theorists acknowledge as much but argue that the process is well underway (Goldscheider, Bernhardt, & Lappegård, 2015). Same-sex marriages may reinforce this trend because LGBTQ couples tend to share domestic work more equitably and flexibly than different-sex couples.

Are we likely to see the spread of stable egalitarian marriages throughout American society? That may depend on the future employment opportunities in the kinds of jobs that men tend to take. It is still the case that men are viewed as good marriage material only if they can provide steady earnings from work. A 2014 national survey found that 78 percent of never-married American women said that whether a man had a steady job would be a very important criterion for them in choosing a spouse or partner, whereas just 46 percent of never-married men said it would be important that their spouse or partner have a steady job (Pew Research Center, 2014). A man's willingness to share the housework makes him an attractive partner only if he also has the potential to be a good earner. Highly educated women with good earnings prospects themselves are able to attract men who have egalitarian attitudes and good earning potential because most of these men want to pool two incomes in order to achieve middle-class status. Yet as described in Chapter 4, the changes in the American economy due to the globalization and automation of production have made it increasingly hard for young men without college degrees to meet the expectation of being a steady earner. Consequently, a woman with less education may be less likely to find a man with adequate earning power. Even if she can find a man with egalitarian attitudes, she may decide that a life-time partnership with him is risky compared to alternatives such as a low-commitment cohabiting union or lone parenting.

As a result, the emergence of a gender-egalitarian equilibrium of committed, domestic–work-sharing couples in long-term relationships is likely to be more common among privileged, college-educated Americans than among Americans with less education. The same decision-making logic that produces egalitarian partnerships among college-educated young adults may also produce weaker partnerships or lone parenthood among the less-educated. Perhaps gender-egalitarian partnerships will be widespread in European countries that have more generous social welfare programs. But in the United States, the new egalitarian equilibrium is likely to be confined to the more privileged classes (Cherlin, 2016).

Looking Back

1. **How has the process by which young adults find intimate partners changed?** In the United States and other Western nations, for centuries young adults went about finding a spouse through the publicly visible process of courtship. The practice declined in the United States after 1900 due to migration to large cities, growing affluence, and the emergence of adolescence as a protected time between childhood and adulthood. The rise of dating after 1900 placed courtship on an economic basis and transferred power from young women (and their parents) to young men. The heyday of dating was probably 1945 to 1965; toward the end of the century, it declined. In recent decades, young adults have increasingly lived independently. Some enter into living apart relationships that can be short-term or long-term.

2. **How has marriage changed over the past century?** The institutional marriage was held together by community pressure and the authority of the family head. But by the mid-twentieth century, it had been eclipsed by the companionship marriage, which was held together more by mutual affection and intimacy. The ideal type of companionate marriage was the single-earner breadwinner–homemaker family that flourished in the 1950s. Beginning in the late 1960s, this model was overtaken by the individualistic marriage, in which both spouses were increasingly concerned with personal growth and self-fulfillment. In the individualistic marriage, the relationship between spouses tends to be seen as an ongoing project that is open to negotiation and change.

3. **What is marriage like today?** Although Americans now have more choices about their personal lives, most still marry. More Americans now find a spouse online than by traditional means such as family, friends, or work. Marriage still provides some benefits that cohabitation does not, such as greater trust in one's partner's commitment. However, people also see marriage as a symbol of achieving a successful adult life. They build up to marriage, postponing it until they have all of the prerequisites in place. They use religious wedding ceremonies (rather than courthouse weddings) to display their personal achievements to friends and relatives. In 2015, the Supreme Court extended the right to marry to same-sex couples.

4. **What is the role of cohabitation in the American family system?** Prior to 1970, cohabitation was found largely among the poor. Since then the practice has expanded greatly at all income levels. In the United States today,

a majority of marriages are now preceded by a period of cohabitation. These unions tend to lead within a few years to either marriage or breakup. Cohabitation is a diverse phenomenon that includes not only childless young adults, but also couples with children. A majority of the children who are officially born outside of marriage are actually born to two cohabiting parents. The nature of cohabitation varies by social class. For college-educated young adults, cohabitation is often a stage in the marriage process. For the non-college-education, cohabitation is not as closely linked to marriage.

5. **How does the marriage market work?** The marriage market—a model that is widely used by social scientists—consists of individuals who are searching for a spouse in a particular geographic area, who have a set of preferences concerning the type of person they wish to find and a set of resources to offer in return. The predominant marriage bargain at mid-twentieth century, based on the specialization model of marriage, involved a husband who traded his earnings in return for child care and housework by his wife. This model of marriage no longer fits the present-day marriage market. In particular, evidence suggests that both men and women now prefer partners with good earnings potential.

6. **Is a stable, gender-egalitarian style of marriage emerging?** A more stable, gender-egalitarian marriage may be emerging among college-educated young adults. In this model of marriage, the spouses share domestic work more equitably than in the past. Because the double burden of housework and paid work is eased for wives, marriages are more harmonious and the risk of divorce falls. But egalitarian marriages only succeed if the man has steady earnings. Consequently, they may not emerge among less-educated young adults, whose employment opportunities are restricted by globalization and automation.

Study Questions

1. What are the differences between nineteenth-century courtship and twentieth-century dating?
2. How do the cohabiting relationships of college-educated young adults differ from the cohabiting relationships of less-educated, lower-income young adults?
3. What did Burgess mean when he wrote that marriage was "in transition from an institution to a companionship"?
4. What distinguishes the individualistic marriage from the companionate marriage?
5. What does it mean to say that marriage has become a "capstone" experience?
6. Why is it difficult to tell whether marriage improves the well-being of women and men?
7. How has the typical marriage bargain changed between the mid-twentieth century and today?
8. Is marriage so weakened as an institution that it is likely to become just one of many possible adult lifestyles?

Key Terms

Thinking about Families

The Private Family	The Public Family
Do people expect too much emotional satisfaction from a cohabiting partner or spouse?	**Should the public be concerned about the rise of cohabitation and childbearing outside marriage?**

References

Andersson, G., Thomson, E., & Duntava, A. (2017). Life-table representations of family dynamics in the 21st century. *Demographic Research, 37*(Article 35), 1081–1230.

Ariès, P. (1985a). Love in married life. In P. Aries & Benjin (Eds.), *Western sexuality* (pp. 130–139). Oxford: Basil Blackwell.

Bachman, J. G., Johnston, L. D., & O'Malley, P. M. (2014). Monitoring the future: Questionnaire responses from the nation's high school seniors. Retrieved November 27, 2015, from http://www.monitoringthefuture.org/datavolumes/2012/2012dv.pdf

Bailey, B. L. (1988). *From front porch to back seat: Courtship in twentieth-century America.* Baltimore: Johns Hopkins University Press.

Becker, G. S. (1991). *A treatise on the family (enlarged edition).* Cambridge, MA: Harvard University Press.

Bendheim-Thoman Center for Child Wellbeing. (2007). Parents' relationship status five years after a nonmarital birth. *Fragile Families Research Brief, no. 39.* Retrieved November 18, 2013, from http://fragilefamilies.princeton.edu/sites/fragilefamilies/files/researchbrief39.pdf

Bernard, J. (1981). The good provider role: Its rise and fall. *American Psychologist, 36.*

Black, A. (1924). Is the young person coming back? *Harper's* (August), 340.

Boden, S. (2003). *Consumerism, romance, and the wedding experience.* Hampshire: Palgrave Macmillan.

Bramlett, M. D., & Mosher, W. D. (2002). Cohabitation, marriage, divorce and remarriage in the United States. Series 22, no 2. Retrieved June 2003 from www.cdc.gov/nchs/data/series/sr_23/sr23_022.pdf

Bulcroft, R. A., Bulcroft, K., Bradley, K., & Simpson, C. (2000). The management and production of risk in romantic relationships: A postmodern paradox. *Journal of Family History, 25,* 63–92.

Burgess, E. W., & Locke, H. J. (1945). *The family: From institution to companionship.* New York: American Book Company.

Cacioppo, J. T., Cacioppo, S., Gonzaga, G. C., Ogburn, E. L., & VanderWeele, T. J. (2013). Marital satisfaction and break-ups differ across on-line and off-line meeting venues. *Proceedings of the National Academy of Sciences, 110*(25), 10135–10140.

Cancian, F. M. (1987). *Love in America: Gender and self-development.* Cambridge, England: Cambridge University Press.

Carbone, J., & Cahn, N. (2014). *Marriage markets: How inequality is remaking the American family.* New York: Oxford University Press.

Carr, D., & Springer, K. W. (2010). Advances in families and health research in the 21st century. *Journal of Marriage and Family, 72*(3), 743–761.

Cherlin, A. J. (1992). *Marriage, divorce, remarriage: Revised and enlarged edition.* Cambridge, MA: Harvard University Press.

Cherlin, A. J. (2000). Toward a new home socioeconomics of union formation. In L. J. Waite, C. Bachrach, M. Hindin, E. Thomson, & A. Thornton (Eds.), *Ties that bind: Perspectives on marriage and cohabitation* (pp. 126–144). Hawthorne: Aldine de Gruyter.

Cherlin, A. J. (2004). The deinstitutionalization of American marriage. *Journal of Marriage and Family, 66*(4), 848–861.

Cherlin, A. J. (2016). A happy ending to a half-century of family change? *Population and Development Review, 42*(1), 121–129.

Copen, C. E., Daniels, K., & Mosher, W. D. (2013). *First premarital cohabitation in the United States: 2006–2010 national survey of family growth:* U.S. National Center for Health Statistics.

Cross-Barnet, C., Cherlin, A. J., & Burton, L. M. (2011). Bound by children: Intermittent cohabitation and living together apart. *Family Relations, 60,* 633–647.

Duncan, G. J., Wilkerson, B., & England, P. (2006). Cleaning up their act: The effects of marriage and cohabitation on licit and illicit drug use. *Demography, 43*(4), 691–710.

Edin, K., & Kefalas, M. J. (2005). *Promises I can keep: Why poor women put motherhood before marriage.* Berkeley: University of California Press.

Eggebean, D., & Dew, J. (2009). The role of religion in adolescence for family formation in young adulthood. *Journal of Marriage and Family, 71,* 108–121.

Esping-Andersen, G., & Billari, F. C. (2015). Re-theorizing family demographics. *Population and Development Review, 41*(1), 1–31.

Flandrin, J.-L. (1985). Sex in married life in the early middle ages: The church's teaching and behavioral reality.

In P. Aries & A. Bejin (Eds.), *Western sexuality: Practice and precept in past and present times* (pp. 114–129). Oxford: Basil Blackwell.

Fincham, F. D., & Beach, S. R. H. (2010). Marriage in the new millennium: A decade in review. *Journal of Marriage and Family, 72*(3), 630–649.

Finkel, E. J., Hui, C. M., Carswell, K. L., & Larson, G. M. (2014). The suffocation of marriage: Climbing mount Maslow without enough oxygen. *Psychological Inquiry, 25*(1), 1–41.

Gallup Organization. (2017). In U.S., 10.2% of LGBT adults now married to same-sex spouse. *Social & Policy Issues.* Retrieved April 27, 2019, from https://news.gallup.com/poll/212702/lgbt-adults-married-sex-spouse.aspx

Gibson-Davis, C. M. (2007). Expectations and the economic bar to marriage among low income couples. In K. Edin & P. England (Eds.), *Unmarried couples with children* (pp. 84–103). New York: Russell Sage Foundation.

Gilkes, C. T. (1995). The storm and the light: Church, family, work, and social crisis in the African-American experience. In N. Ammerman & W. C. Roof (Eds.), *Work, family, and religion in contemporary society* (pp. 177–198). New York: Routledge.

Gillis, J. R. (1985). *For better or worse: British marriages, 1600 to the present.* Oxford: Oxford University Press.

Goldscheider, F., Bernhardt, E., & Lappegård, T. (2015). The gender revolution: A framework for understanding changing family and demographic behavior. *Population and Development Review, 41*(2), 207–239.

Hall, G. S. (1904). *Adolescence: Its psychology and its relations to anthropology, sociology, sex, crime, religion and education.* New York: Appleton.

Hemez, P., & Manning, W. D. (2017a). Over twenty-five years of change in cohabitation experience in the U.S., 19872013. *National Center for Family and Marriage Research, Family Profile FP-17-02.* Retrieved August 28, 2018, from https://www.bgsu.edu/ncfmr/resources/data/family-profiles/hemez-manning-25-years-changecohabitation-fp-17-02.html

Hemez, P., & Manning, W. D. (2017b). Thirty years of change in women's premarital cohabitation experience. *National Center for Family and Marriage Research, Family Profile 17-05.* Retrieved August 28, 2018, from http://www.bgsu.edu/ncfmr/resources/data/family-profiles/hemez-manning-30-yrs-change-womenpremarital-cohab-fp-17-05.html

Inglehart, R., Basáñez, M., Díez-Medrano, J., Halman, L., & Luijkx, R. (2004). *Human beliefs and values: A cross-cultural sourcebook based on the 1999–2002 values surveys.* Mexico City: Siglo Veintiuno Editores.

Ingraham, C. (1999). *White weddings: Romancing heterosexuality in popular culture.* New York: Routledge.

Ishizuka, P. (2018). The economic foundations of cohabiting couples' union transitions. *Demography, 55*(2), 535–557.

Kan, M. Y., Sullivan, O., & Gershuny, J. (2011). Gender convergence in domestic work: Discerning the effects of interactional and institutional barriers from largescale data. *Sociology, 45*(2), 234–251.

Kett, J. F. (2003). Reflections on the history of adolescence in America. *History of the Family, 8,* 345–179.

Klinenberg, E. (2012). *Going solo: The extraordinary rise and surprising appeal of living alone.* New York: Penguin Press.

Kornrich, S., & Furstenberg, F. (2013). Investing in children: Changes in parental spending on children, 1972–2007. *Demography, 50*(1), 1–23.

Kuo, J. C.-L., & Raley, R. K. (2016). Diverging patterns of union transition among cohabitors by race/ethnicity and education: Trends and marital intentions in the United States. *Demography, 53*(4), 921–935.

Lareau, A. (2011). *Unequal childhoods: Class, race, and family life, second edition.* Berkeley: University of California Press.

Lehrer, E. L. (2004). Religion as a determinant of economic and demographic behavior in the United States. *Population and Development Review, 30,* 707–726.

Levin, I. (2004). Living apart together: A new family form. *Current Sociology, 52,* 223–240.

Lichter, D. T., & Qian, Z. (2008). Serial cohabitation and the marital life course. *Journal of Marriage and Family, 70*(4), 861–878.

Lichter, D. T., Turner, R. N., & Sassler, S. (2010). National estimates of the rise in serial cohabitation. *Social Science Research, 39,* 754–765.

Lundberg, S. J., Pollak, R. A., & Stearns, J. (2016). Family inequality: Diverging patterns in marriage, cohabitation, and childbearing. *Journal of Economic Perspectives, 30*(2), 79–101.

Lyall, S. (2004, February 15). In Europe, lovers now propose: Marry me a little. *The New York Times,* p. A3.

Lynd, R. S., & Lynd, H. M. (1929). *Middletown: A study in modern American culture.* New York: Harcourt, Brace, and World.

Manning, W. D., Brown, S. L., & Stykes, B. (2015). Trends in births to single and cohabiting mothers, 1980–2013. *National Center for Family and Marriage Research, Family Profile FP-15-03.* Retrieved November 26, 2015, from https://www.bgsu.edu/content/dam/BGSU/college-of-arts-and-sciences/NCFMR/documents/FP/FP-15-03-birth-trends-single-cohabiting-moms.pdf.

Manning, W. D., & Smock, P. J. (2005). Measuring and modeling cohabitation: New perspectives from qualitative data. *Journal of Marriage and Family, 67*(4), 989–1002.

Manning, W. D., & Stykes, B. (2015). Twenty-five years of change in cohabitation in the U.S., 1987–2013. *National Center for Family and Marriage Research, Family Profile FP-15-01.* Retrieved January 12, 2015, from http://www.bgsu.edu/content/dam/BGSU/college-of-arts-and-sciences/NCFMR/documents/FP/FP-15-01-twenty-five-yrs-cohab-us.pdf

Markman, H. J., Whitton, S. W., Kline, G. H., Stanley, S. M., Thompson, H., & St. Peters, M. (2004). Use of an empirically based marriage education program by religious organizations: Results of a dissemination trial. *Family Relations, 53,* 504–512.

Martin, S. P., Astone, N. M., & Peters, H. E. (2014). Fewer marriages, more divergence: Marriage projections for millennials to age 40. Retrieved January 12, 2015, from http://www.urban.org/UploadedPDF/413110-Fewer-Marriages-More-Divergence.pdf?RSSFeed=Urban.xml

Martin, C., & Théry, I. (2001). The PACS and marriage and cohabitation in France. *International Journal of Law, Policy and the Family, 15,* 135–158.

May, E. T. (1980). *Great expectations: Marriage and divorce in post-Victorian America.* Chicago: University of Chicago Press.

Mead, R. (2007). *One perfect day: The selling of the American wedding.* New York: Penguin.

Milan, A., & Peters, A. (2003, summer). Couples living apart. *Canadian Social Trends,* 2–6.

Mintz, S. (2004). *Huck's raft: A history of American childhood.* Cambridge, MA: The Belknap Press of Harvard University Press.

Modell, J. J. (1989). *Into one's own: From youth to adulthood in the United States.* Berkeley: University of California Press. Obergefell v. Hodges, 576 (U.S. 2015).

Ono, H. (2003). Women's economic standing, marriage timing, and cross-national contexts of gender. *Journal of Marriage and Family, 65,* 275–286.

Oppenheimer, V. K. (2003). Cohabiting and marriage during young men's career-development process. *Demography, 40,* 127–149.

Parsons, T., & Bales, R. F. (1955). *Family, socialization, and the interaction process.* New York: The Free Press.

Pew Research Center. (2014). Record share of Americans have never married. Retrieved October 9, 2014, from http://www.pewsocialtrends.org/2014/09/24/record-share-of-Americans-have-never-married/#what-never-married-adults-are-looking-for-in-a-potential-spouse

Portes, A., & Sensenbrenner, J. (1993). Embeddedness and immigration: Notes on the social determinants of economic action. *American Journal of Sociology, 98,* 1320–1350.

Rackin, H., & Gibson-Davis, C. M. (2012). The role of pre- and postconception relationships for first-time parents. *Journal of Marriage and Family, 74*(3), 526–539.

Reed, J. M. (2006). Not crossing the "extra line": How cohabitors with children view their unions. *Journal of Marriage and Family, 68,* 1117–1131.

Rendall, M. S., Weden, M. M., Favreault, M. M., & Waldron, H. (2011). The protective effect of marriage for survival: A review and update. *Demography* (48), 481–506.

Rosenfeld, M. J. (2007). *The age of independence: Interracial unions, same-sex unions, and the changing American family.* Cambridge, MA: Harvard University Press.

Rosenfeld, M. J. (2017). Marriage, choice, and couplehood in the age of the internet. *Sociological Science, 4,* 490–510.

Rosenfeld, M. J., & Thomas, R. J. (2012). Searching for a mate: The rise of the internet as a social intermediary. *American Sociological Review, 77*(4), 523–547.

Rosenfeld, M. J., Thomas, R. J., & Hausen, S. (2019). Disintermediating your friends: How online dating in the United States displaces other ways of meeting. *Proceedings of the National Academy of Sciences, 116*(36), 17753–17758.

Rothman, E. K. (1984). *Hands and hearts: A history of courtship in America.* Cambridge, Mass: Harvard University Press.

Sassler, S., & Miller, A. J. (2017). *Cohabitation nation: Gender, class, and the remaking of relationships.* Berkeley: University of California Press.

Schwartz, C. R., & Han, H. (2014). The reversal of the gender gap in education and trends in marital dissolution. *American Sociological Review, 79*(4), 605–629.

Seidman, S. (1991). *Romantic longings: Love in America.* New York: Routledge.

Smock, P. J., Manning, W. D., & Porter, M. (2005). "Everything's there except money": How money shapes decisions to marry among cohabitors *Journal of Marriage and Family, 67*(3), 680–696.

Stoilova, M., Roseneil, S., Crowhurst, I., Hellesund, T., & Santos, A. C. (2014). Living apart relationships in contemporary Europe: Accounts of togetherness and apartness. *Sociology, 48*(6), 1075–1091.

Torr, B. M. (2011). The changing relationship between education and marriage in the United States, 1940–2000. *Journal of Family History, 36*(4), 483–503.

Turkle, S. (2011). *Alone together: Why we expect more from our technology, and less from each other.* New York: Basic Books.

U.S. Bureau of the Census. (2017).

U.S. Bureau of the Census. (2017). Table UC3. Opposite sex unmarried couples by presence of biological children under 18, and age, earnings, education, and race and Hhispanic origin of both partners: 2017. Retrieved May 21, 2016, from https://www2.census.gov/programs-surveys/demo/tables/families/2017/cps-2017/tabuc3-all.xls

Waite, L. J., & Joyner, K. (2001). Emotional satisfaction and physical pleasure in sexual unions: Time horizon, sexual behavior, and sexual exclusivity. *Journal of Marriage and Family, 63,* 247–264.

Waite, L. J., & Lehrer, E. L. (2003). The benefits from marriage and religion in the United States: A comparative analysis. *Population and Development Review, 29,* 255–275.

Whyte, M. K. (1990). *Dating, mating and marriage.* New York: Aldine de Gruyter.

Wilson, W. J. (1987). *The truly disadvantaged: The inner city, the underclass, and public policy.* Chicago: University of Chicago Press.

Wright, L. (2018). Union transitions and fertility within first premarital cohabitations in Canada: Diverging patterns by education. *Demography, 55* (in press).

Wu, H. (2017). Trends in births to single and cohabiting mothers, 1980–2014. *Family Profiles, FP-17-04, National Center for Family and Marriage Research.* Retrieved July 23, 2018, from https://www.bgsu.edu/ncfmr/resources/data/family-profiles/wu-trends-births-single-cohabiting-mothers-fp-17-04.html

Xu, X., Hudspeth, C. D., & Bartkowski, J. P. (2005). The timing of first marriage: Are there religious variations? *Journal of Family Issues, 26,* 584–618.

Chapter Eight

Work and Families

Looking Forward

1. How has married women's work changed over the past half-century?
2. How does our society treat the labor of caring for others?
3. How has the division of labor in marriages changed?
4. What are some of the strains working parents can experience?
5. How is the workplace responding to the needs of working parents?

It's true that most husbands in different-sex marriages do less child care than their wives. But there's a lot of variation—sometimes in unexpected ways. Think about married men who have two very different occupations: physicians and emergency medical technicians (EMTs). Doctors are highly educated, cosmopolitan professionals who see patients at their offices and in hospitals. EMTs are high-school educated and have a certificate from a training institute or a community college. They race from disaster to disaster, reaching into smashed cars or rushing into burning buildings to rescue the injured and resuscitate the nearly dead. Who do you think does more child care?

Answer: The EMTs. That's according to a study by Dan Clawson and Naomi Gerstel (2014). How and why do they do more than the physicians? Nearly half of the EMTs in the study work different shifts than their employed wives so that they can split the child care during the work week. This tag-team arrangement can strain a marriage, but it ensures that one parent is always home with the children when they aren't in school. "It gets a little hectic," one EMT told the authors. "It gives me what I want: time with my family, good pay—well, reasonable pay" (p. 185). In fact, most of the EMTs prioritized spending time with their families rather than pursuing overtime assignments that would have boosted their incomes. They talked about picking their kids up from school and feeding them dinner. And they said that if they were needed at home in a pinch, they would be there. One EMT said

> *If there was a family emergency, the good thing about where we work, I'd leave . . . So I would get up and leave, because it's family and friends first. I have no problem, and you can dock me a day's pay (p. 182).*

Physicians, on the other hand, spoke of the need to work long hours. They felt obligated to respond quickly when a patient was ill. They also talked about how they and their wives had become accustomed to an expensive lifestyle that required long working hours to earn enough to maintain it. One of them said, "We have got used to a particular way of living. I have to work the hours I do to get what we now think we need" (p. 188). Forty percent of them had stay-at-home wives, but even when their wives were employed, it was the wives who changed their schedules when a child was sick or a nanny didn't show up. Whereas the EMTs showed up to feed and bathe the kids, the male physicians tended to show up for visible events, such as their children's athletic contests or dance recitals. The authors called them "public fathers," who could be seen at the school concert, as opposed to the "private fathers," who did most of their parenting at home.

The contrast between the physicians and the EMTs shows that it is possible for men to organize their time in ways that make them nearly equal child care partners with their wives. But it also shows the pressures on men to provide an ample income, even if their wives are working too. And it shows how employment constrains the parenting of both men and women, whether it means being docked a day's pay in order to stay home with a sick child or working evenings and weekends to manage a caseload of patients.

Some of the difficulty stems from the ways that businesses and schools are organized: both still operate as if every employee with children had a stay-at-home spouse and that every school child had a stay-at-home parent. Although this has never been true of all families, it was much more common in the mid-twentieth century than it is today. Let's examine the great changes since then and their implications for combining work and family roles today.

From Single-Earner to Dual-Earner Marriages

Figure 8.1 shows the low levels of married women's work outside the home at the middle of the twentieth century and the spectacular rise since then. The two lines show the percentage of married women with children who were in the labor force for every year between 1948 and 2016. Government statistical agencies consider the **labor force** to be all people who are either working outside the home or looking for such work. In 1948, only about one-fourth of married women whose youngest children were at least six years old (and therefore in school) were in the labor force, as were only about one-tenth of married women with children under age six.

labor force all people who are either working outside the home or looking for work

The rates rose sharply through the 1990s, leveled off around 2000, and have declined slightly since then. For the moment, at least, the historic rise in married women's labor force participation rates seems to have peaked. In 2016, 73 percent of all married women with school-aged children, and 63 percent of those with preschool-aged children, were in the labor force (U.S. Bureau of Labor Statistics, 2017). Some may prefer to remain at home full time while others cite the difficulty of combining paid work and family responsibilities (Stone, 2007).

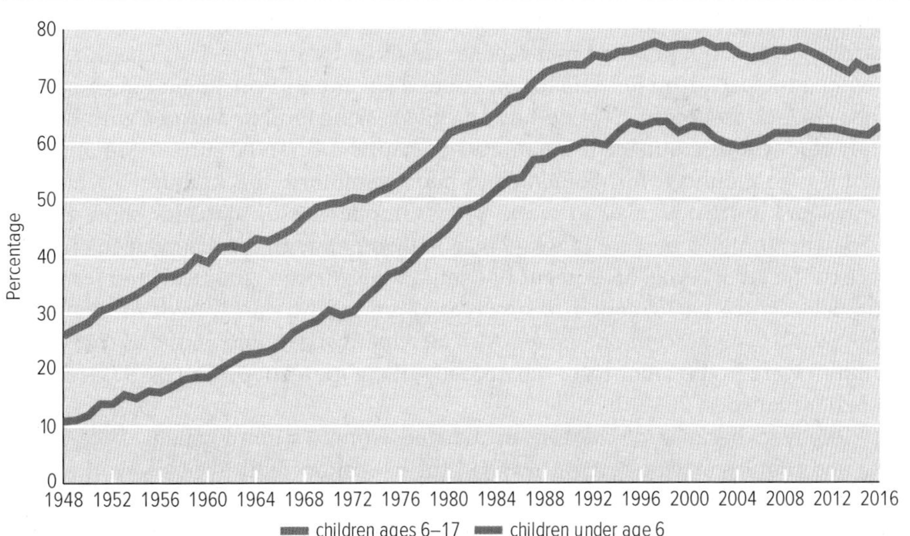

FIGURE 8.1 Labor force participation rates of married women with children under age 18, by age of youngest child, 1948–2016. (*Sources:* U.S. Bureau of Labor Statistics, 2017; and earlier reports.)

BEHIND THE RISE

service sector workers who provide personal services such as education, health care, communication, restaurant meals, legal representation, entertainment, and so forth

Several factors contributed to the increase in married women's labor force participation. During the twentieth century, the service sector of the economy expanded greatly. The **service sector** consists of the workers who provide personal services such as education, health care, communication, restaurant meals, legal representation, entertainment, and so forth. Many of the jobs in the service sector had come to be stereotyped as women's work; these jobs usually required some education but paid less than men's work. Examples include secretary, nurse, and elementary school teacher. As the demand for these kinds of jobs increased, wages increased (although they remained lower than men's wages) and more married women were drawn into the labor force (Oppenheimer, 1970).

In addition, as the population shifted from farms to cities, each generation (except for the parents of the baby boomers) had fewer children. There was no longer a need for lots of child labor to help on the farm; moreover, the rising wages of women in the labor force meant that women who stayed home were passing up more and more income. As a result, parents' preferred strategy was to have fewer children and to invest more resources in each–to pay for college education or job training courses, for example. This strategy reduced the number of years in which young children would be present in the home and therefore freed married women sooner from child care, the major responsibility that had kept them out of the labor force. Moreover, the decline in the wages of men without college educations since the early 1970s has motivated many wives to take paying jobs. Finally, the high divorce rate of the past several decades made it increasingly risky for married women to leave the labor force and let their job skills deteriorate. Given the low amount of child support payments that most divorced women receive (see Chapter 12), they need to be able to rely on their earning power.

A PROFOUND CHANGE

This great movement of married women into the labor force is one of the most important changes in American family life in the past century. It has profoundly altered women's and men's lives. It has affected the balance of power between women and men. It has been instrumental in the shift from the companionship marriage to the independent marriage, as described in the previous chapter. It has provided the backdrop for debates on issues such as abortion, about which women whose identity is bound up in home and child rearing tend to disagree with women who value working outside the home (see Chapter 14). To be sure, the change has been less pronounced for women from poor or minority backgrounds, who have always had a greater need to work. For example, census statistics show that in 1975, when only 35 percent of white married women with preschool-aged children were in the labor force, 55 percent of comparable African American women were. Still, labor force participation has increased among African American women as well: By 2016, 69 percent of married African American women with preschool-aged children were in the labor force (compared with 63 percent of whites) (U.S. Bureau of Labor Statistics, 2017).

Moreover, because of the rise in married women's employment, dual-earner married couples are the rule rather than the exception: Both spouses worked outside the home in 59 percent of all marriages with children present in 2015. And wives' earnings are becoming a more important component of the family's income.

In 2015, the median employed wife contributed 37 percent of her family's income (meaning that half provided more than that, and half less than that), up from 27 percent in 1970 (U.S. Bureau of Labor Statistics, 2017). It is even becoming common for wives to out-earn their husbands. Twenty-nine percent of employed wives in dual-earner marriages earned more than their husbands in 2016 (U.S. Bureau of Labor Statistics, 2017). Still, husbands are the main earners in a majority of married-couple households. And wives who could potentially earn more than their husbands tend to be employed less often than one would expect, as if they feel the need to avoid breaking the norm that husbands should be the breadwinners (Bertrand, Kamenica, & Pan, 2015).

Quick Review

- The percentage of married women who work outside the home increased greatly during the second half of the twentieth century.
- The expansion of the service sector of the economy and the drop in the number of children per family contributed to the increase.
- In the 2000s and 2010s, married women's rates of labor force participation remained high, although with a slight decline.
- Both spouses are employed in a majority of married couples, and it is becoming more common for wives to out-earn their husbands.

The Division of Labor in Marriages

We have seen that the role of women in the paid labor market has changed dramatically over the past half-century. Great changes have also occurred in the roles of women and men in the home. In addition, how sociologists think about housework and child care has evolved, as a new perspective—care work studies—has arisen in response to the trends.

RETHINKING CARE WORK

It's clear that society can no longer rely on the unpaid labor of stay-at-home wives and mothers to provide the care that family members need. In this sense, the movement of women into the labor force has created a "crisis in care" (Glenn, 2000). The crisis has also spawned a growing body of social research, theory, and advocacy on the topic of caring. In this new literature, "care work" has emerged as the central concept—one might even speak of a care work movement (Stone, 2000). Some authors conceive of care work very broadly, but I will propose a narrower definition consistent with this book's focus on families. Let us define **care work** as activity in which one person meets the needs of spouses, partners, children, parents, or others who cannot fully care for themselves. The person who does the care work is the caregiver, and the person who gets the care is the care receiver. Within families, children, the frail elderly, and the ill or disabled are the obvious care receivers. But wives and husbands also perform care work by providing emotional support and household goods and services to each other.

care work activity in which one person meets the needs of spouses, partners, children, parents, or others who cannot fully care for themselves

Breaking the Work/Family Boundary The writers in the care work movement argue that the separation between what goes on in families and what goes on in the world of work is artificial and should be abolished. As the suffix "work" in care work suggests, these authors maintain that what caregivers do should be thought of as work. This seems obvious when one thinks about workers in child care centers. The care work movement suggests that we view caring labor not just through the lens of the private family but also through the lens of the public family. To be sure, care work provides private, emotional satisfaction for family members, but it also provides a publicly useful service.

Valuing Caring Labor The writers also maintain that caring labor is often underpaid, undervalued, and even demeaned relative to other kinds of work (Tronto, 1993). Care is often considered "women's work," a phrase that often implies unpaid or low-paid work of marginal importance. Women constitute the vast majority of paid caregivers: 94 percent of child care workers and 89 percent of health aides, for example, in 2017 (U.S. Bureau of Labor Statistics, 2018b). Moreover, they are disproportionately drawn from the less advantaged racial-ethnic groups—such as immigrant Hispanic and Asian women.

People who perform paid care work earn less than people who do comparable work that does not involve care. Three researchers estimated the "wage penalty" that women who are employed at child care centers or as nannies pay for doing care work: Even taking into account the skills required for the job, the education needed, and the prior work experience they tend to have, women who are employed as child care workers earn 26 percent less than women who work at comparable non–care-giving work jobs (England, Budig, & Folbre, 2002). Other statistics tell the same story of low pay for child care work: A government earnings survey in 2017 reported that child care workers had average hourly earnings of $11.42, which was 28 cents less than the average hourly earnings of parking lot attendants (U.S. Bureau of Labor Statistics, 2018c).

Paula England (2005) presents three possible reasons why care work does not pay as much as non–care work:

1. As noted above, people tend to devalue and even demean labor that is thought of as "women's work," which care work historically has been. Employers either underestimate the value of the work women do or are culturally biased against paying women as much as they pay men for comparable work. For example, they may still believe it's more important to pay men well because they should be the breadwinners for their families—a common position a half-century ago.
2. Labor that creates public goods, such as children who will grow up to be responsible members of society, tends to be underpaid. The reason is that it is difficult to stop people from "free-riding," obtaining the benefits of the public goods without having to pay for them. I don't have to pay child care workers to benefit from the next generation of responsible workers because I will receive a Social Security check based on the taxes they will pay whether or not I have children.
3. Many people find satisfaction in caring for others. In other words, they may find caring work intrinsically fulfilling and be willing to accept lower pay for a caring job than for a non–care work job. Child care workers may enjoy caring

for children and accept low pay to enter the field, or they may get attached to the children they are caring for and not leave the job for a higher paying one. Employers of child care workers may, in a sense, take advantage of people's desire to help others by offering low wages.

The care work movement urges that caregivers such as child care workers and nursing home aides receive higher pay and greater respect.

Quick Review

- The movement of wives into the paid workforce limits their ability to provide unpaid caring work in the home.
- The resulting "crisis in care" has focused attention on care work, the face-to-face caregiving that used to be done in families by wives who weren't working for wages.
- From the care work perspective, the caring that goes on in families should be considered as "work" whether or not the caregivers are paid.
- Caring labor is often undervalued; it is also done disproportionately by women and members of minority racial-ethnic groups.

WHO'S DOING THE CARE WORK?

Do young adults want to share the care work as well as the paid work? Most of the New York area young adults in one study said that they hoped to create marriages or committed partnerships that would be egalitarian in sharing both kinds of work (Gerson, 2010). Young men were looking for a partner to share not only the child care but also the responsibility of earning enough to support a family. Young women were looking for a partner who would not just earn a good living but also participate fully in life at home. The term "egalitarian" didn't necessarily mean a strict 50/50 division of paid work and home work; it connoted a major investment by each partner in both employment and family life. It meant being flexible in the tasks each partner performed and mutually supportive of the other's roles. The wish for egalitarian partnerships was so widespread that it was even expressed by most of the young adults who had grown up in homes where mothers and fathers played traditional roles. In fact, some observers argue that a gender-egalitarian model of partnership is emerging throughout the Western nations (Esping-Andersen & Billari, 2015; Goldscheider, Bernhardt, & Lappegård, 2015).

Is such a trend occurring in the United States? We have already seen how much more involved American women are in the world of paid work. How much change has there been in the home? Let's examine almost 50 years of information from American **time-diary studies,** in which a random sample of people were asked to keep a record of what they were doing every minute during a time period–usually a single day (Sayer, 2016). The results of comparable time-diary studies conducted from 1965 to 2012 are shown in Figure 8.2. It displays the number of minutes per day that women and men aged 25 to 59 spent in housework and child care. (Note that the chart is for all women and men in that age range rather than just for married women and men.) We can draw three conclusions from the chart:

time-diary studies surveys in which people are asked to keep a record of what they were doing every minute during a time period

1. The gap between women and men has narrowed. In 1965, women spent six times as much time doing housework and child care as men. In 2012, women spent about twice as much time on these tasks as did men.

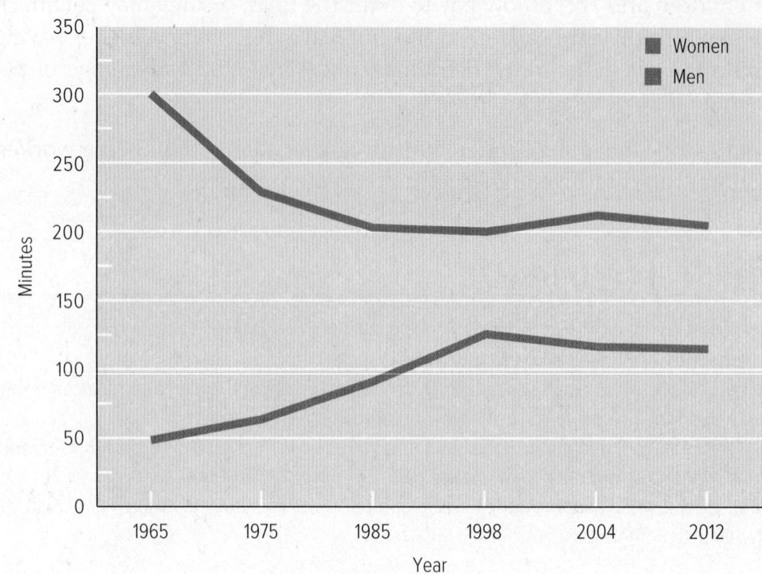

FIGURE 8.2
Minutes per day spent in housework and child care, Americans aged 25 to 59, by gender. (*Source:* Sayer, 2016)

2. The gap narrowed primarily because women reduced the amount of time they spent on housework and child care. Women spent about 100 minutes less on these tasks in 2012 than in 1965. Men spent about 65 minutes more on these tasks in 2012 than in 1965. In other words, the majority of the narrowing occurred because women cut back their time rather than because men expanded theirs.
3. There gap narrowed substantially between the 1965 and 1998 time-diary studies, but there has been no further narrowing since then. In fact, the gap had widened slightly by 2012.

Overall, there has been a substantial convergence in the time that women and men devote to housework and child care. But women have changed more than men, and despite the reduction in women's time, they still do more than men. Moreover, there has been little change since the turn of the twenty-first century.

CULTURAL IDEALS AND DOMESTIC WORK

How does the amount of work that wives and husbands do outside the home relate to the amount of work they do inside the home? This is an important everyday issue for tens of millions of dual-earner couples. Social exchange theory predicts that if wives' earnings increase relative to their husbands' earnings, they should become less dependent and their household power should increase. They should be able to use that power to get their husbands to do more child care and housework. If, however, the idea that women should care for children is still a culturally ingrained mode of thinking, then wives' employment may not make much difference (Pavalko & Wolfe, 2016).

Time-diary studies show that, contrary to social exchange theory, husbands do not increase the total amount of time they spend with their children when their wives are employed. So cultural ideals may still lead to an imbalance in who does the care, even when wives have paid work. Husbands do, however, change what they are doing during the time spent with their children. In particular, they take more responsibility for routine care such as feeding them or dressing them. In nationally representative time-diary surveys conducted in 2003 through 2007, fathers whose wives were employed reported being alone with their children for three to six hours more than men with non-employed wives (Raley, Bianchi, & Wang, 2012). During this alone time, they can't rely on their wife's presence to help them out. These shifts suggest that employed wives are able to negotiate for their husbands to be more involved in physical caregiving, consistent with the exchange perspective.

In addition, as the mother's income rises, the couple is likely to purchase more outside care for children, such as use of a day care center. The same goes for housework: Another look at Figure 8.2 shows that the total time that men and women spent in domestic work declined between 1965 and 2003 because the time women spent decreased more than the time men spent rose. Married couples today are more likely to purchase services to replace some of the housework that wives used to perform, such as cooking and cleaning. Daily lives depend not only on the couples' labor but also on cleaning services and fast food restaurants. Married couples may also have become accustomed to slightly less clean homes and more wrinkled clothing than in the past.

UNMARRIED MOTHERS AND DOMESTIC WORK

What about single and cohabiting mothers? How much work do they undertake at home, compared to married mothers, and how much leisure time do they have? You might think that single mothers would do more housework than married mothers and have less leisure time because they don't have a partner to share the work with. Cohabiting mothers might also do more housework than married mothers because their partners might not be as committed as are married partners. But studies of different-sex partnerships show surprisingly that single and cohabiting mothers tend to do less housework, have more leisure time, and sleep more than married mothers (Passias, Sayer, & Pepin, 2017; Pepin, Sayer, & Casper, 2018). In other words, it is married mothers who seem to do the most work at home, have the least leisure, and sleep the least. Researchers speculate that women who are married may feel pressure to "do gender" by having cleaner homes or doing more cooking in order to fulfill the expected feminine role of the wife. It also may be the case that husbands, by virtue of doing less around the house, create more housework for their wives than they do. Single mothers, without these pressures, have more leisure time, although they tend to spend it alone in passive activities, notably watching television. When married mothers have leisure time, they are more likely to spend it in social activities.

THE CURRENT STATE OF SHARING

What, then, should we conclude about the current division of labor between husbands and wives in dual-earner families? Husbands still tend to work longer hours for pay and do less childcare and housework than their employed wives. On average, husbands in dual-earner marriages with preschool-aged children present do about 40 percent of the child care and housework, according to time-use surveys from 2003 to 2005 (Milkie, Raley, & Bianchi, 2009). This 40/60 split of the child care and housework is more equitable than would have been the case a few decades ago; moreover, we have seen that fathers are taking on more responsibility in caring for their children while their wives work. Nevertheless, 40/60 isn't 50/50, and wives still tend to do more unpaid work.

Employed wives also have less leisure than husbands; elsewhere in the same surveys wives report spending less time with just adults and less time watching TV than do fathers–a total of seven fewer hours of leisure per week. That's about two weeks less leisure time over the course of a year of 24 hour days. In her classic 1980s study of the "second shift" that employed mothers worked when they came home, Arlie Hochschild estimated that they had about four weeks less leisure time per year. "So twenty-five years didn't rid women of an extra shift," she wrote in the afterword to a recent, revised edition. "But it did cut the length of it in half" (Hochschild, 2012).

When wives work part-time, according to the same surveys, they do more child care and housework than do wives who work full time, not surprisingly. But fathers with wives employed part-time are hardly any different from fathers whose wives work full-time. Fathers don't seem to adjust their time allocation to the amount of time their wives work. It's wives, not husbands, who seem to make most of the adjustments. The more money the wife makes, the more the family spends on substitutes for housework (restaurant meals) or child care (day care centers). But families do not seem to spend the husband's income on substitutes (Gupta, 2007), just as they don't seem to adjust the father's time in housework and child care when wives increase time spent in paid work. It is as if husbands are still culturally entitled to work outside the home regardless of what their wives are doing, and their income goes for housing, utilities, and other day-to-day expenses. The tacit agreement is that the wife will do more of the housework in return. If a job reduces her ability to do household work, then the family may set aside some of her earnings–but not the husband's earnings–to pay others to do what she cannot. It is a reminder that couples still do not see women's and men's earnings as fully equivalent, despite the great increases in wives' earnings over the past several decades, and that wives are still expected to be the major caregivers at home.

Overall, we see a mixture of persistence and change in the division of labor between employed wives and husbands. Fathers do more in the home than they used to. Yet although it's more acceptable for husbands to do half the housework and the childcare, only a minority does. Fathers take more responsibility when their wives work for pay, but wives feel more pressure. If young adults consider a 40/60 split to be equitable, then many of the women and men in the New York City study mentioned earlier should be able to establish marriages that meet their hopes. If young adults consider only a 50/50 split to be equitable, then fewer will find the kinds of marriages they are looking for unless changes in husbands' and wives' roles continue.

All of these conclusions apply to different-sex marriages. We do not yet have enough information on same-sex marriages to state with confidence what the state of sharing is among them. There are, however, many studies of same-sex cohabiting couples, most of them consisting of partners who identify as lesbian rather than of partners who identify as gay men. These studies show that same-sex couples tend to divide housework and child care more equally than do different-sex couples (Goldberg, Smith, & Perry-Jenkins, 2012). Nevertheless, many same-sex couples do show more of a division of labor when they have children present, with one partner doing more paid work and the other doing more child care (Antecol and Steinberger, 2013; Schneebaum, 2013). Perhaps there are gains in efficiency to specializing in market work versus domestic work, as economists have theorized (Becker,

1991), that are independent of the genders of the partners. But the division of labor observed in same-sex couples is not as sharp as in breadwinner-homemaker heterosexual marriages, and the same-sex partners, unaffected by gender ideology, may view the division as voluntary and fair (Goldberg, 2013; Brewster, 2017).

Quick Review

- Over the past few decades, the share of housework and child care done by husbands in different-sex marriages has increased, although they still do less, on average, than their wives.
- The total time spent doing housework has declined, and couples are purchasing more services.
- Husbands in dual-earner marriages take more responsibility of caring for children by themselves.
- Wives feel more pressure and do more multitasking.
- Cohabiting and single mothers do less domestic work than do married women.
- Sharing in same-sex couples is more equal, but there is some dividing of market and home work when children are present.

Work-Family Balance

Ultimately, the division of labor at home and at work contributes to the larger issue of whether today's families can successfully combine paid work with unpaid family work; whether stress from work corrodes the daily interactions of spouses, parents, and children; whether, in the opposite direction, stress from family life reduces performance at work; and whether the joint demands of work and family are so consuming as to leave no time for relaxation and recreation. These larger questions are ways of asking whether the activities in one's life are in balance. Of course, whether life is balanced is a subjective judgment–the combination of work and family activities that I find most satisfying may not satisfy you. But for all of us, the way that paid employment is organized–who does it, when they do it, where they do it, what the job conditions are like, and so forth–greatly affects our ability to achieve the balance we seek.

Some observers have suggested that balancing work and family has become more difficult for Americans because they are working longer hours. Yet a closer look reveals that while some Americans are overworked, others are underworked. Jacobs and Gerson (2004) compared census data from 1970 and 2000 and found two very different trends. People with professional and managerial jobs were indeed working more hours in 2000 than in 1970, but people in lower-level occupations were working fewer hours.

PROFESSIONAL AND TECHNICAL WORKERS: LONG HOURS

Most college-educated, higher-level workers receive weekly salaries that remain the same no matter how many hours they work. Consequently, employers have an incentive to pressure them to work longer hours, especially given the downsizing of the workforce in many firms. Moreover, new technology such as smartphones and tablets have blurred the distinction between work and leisure as organizations expect employees to respond to messages at any time (Wajcman, 2016). The percentage of Americans who work very long weeks (50 hours or more) is higher than in Canada and most European countries, including the United Kingdom, France, and Germany (Jacobs & Gerson, 2004). And dual-earner couples in the United States work a higher number of total hours than do couples in these countries, in large part because American women work more hours than do women in most of the other countries. Yet despite the number of parents who are working long hours, fewer preschool children are in publicly financed child care in the United States than in most of these countries. So although more parents work long hours in the United States, public support for child care is relatively low.

LESS-EDUCATED WORKERS: FEWER, AND LESS PREDICTABLE, HOURS

Less-educated workers tend to receive hourly wages, which means that their employers have to pay them more for every extra hour worked. Instead of encouraging these employees to work longer hours, employers have tended to hire more part-time workers. Or they hire workers for a limited time, sometimes through subcontractors. Often part-time or limited-time workers are not eligible for fringe benefits such as health insurance, which provides further savings to employers. In this way, the labor market seems to be moving in opposite directions at the top and bottom, toward longer hours among the college educated and shorter hours among the less well-educated (Kalleberg, 2011).

Yet the problems for workers in the lower levels of the labor market include not only getting enough hours of work but also controlling the times that they get. Many wage workers don't know what hours their employers will want them to work until soon before they are supposed to start. One national study showed that 41 percent of early-career workers who get paid by the hour did not know when they were expected to work until a week or less before the actual date. For workers who were mothers and fathers the percentages were even higher (Lambert, Fugiel, and Henly, 2014). This unpredictability is so common that two scholars call it, with some irony, **normal unpredictability**, by which they mean the pervasiveness–the widespread nature–of unpredictability in job hours and schedules which makes it difficult for workers to control time (Gerstel & Clawson, 2018). It is a major challenge for working parents in lower–white-collar, blue-collar, and service occupations. A change with little warning in one parent's schedule may cause the other one to scramble to change her or his schedule to accommodate children's needs; and it may cause a grandmother who provides child care to change her schedule. Add in the unpredictability of families' daily routines–a child is too sick to attend school, a day care provider is on vacation–and the unpredictability of both work and family life can create intense stress.

normal unpredictability the pervasiveness of unpredictability in job hours and schedules which makes it difficult for workers to control time

WHEN DEMANDS OF WORK AND FAMILY LIFE CONFLICT

A pair of surveys conducted 25 years apart show how feelings of conflict between work and family have increased. In 1977, 34 percent of workers said they felt "some" or "a lot" of interference between their jobs and their family lives, while 45 percent gave that response in 2002 (Families and Work Institute, 2002; see also Nomaguchi, 2009). In the General Social Surveys of 2010 through 2014, employed adults were asked "How often do the demands of your job interfere with your family life?" Forty-eight percent of people who were married with children at home said "often" or "sometimes" (Smith, Davern, Freese, & Hout, 2017). Nor was work interference limited to married couples. Forty-two percent of single parents and even 21 percent of single adults not living with children said that their jobs interfered with their family lives often or sometimes.

Task Size There are two senses in which work could interfere with family life. The first is what we might call task size: the sheer size and scope of the demands of the job. Task size is mainly a problem for professional and managerial employees who work long hours. Their jobs often place unlimited demands on their time and energy and become all-consuming, almost like religious callings. And yet family life also demands an unlimited commitment, so that work and family become "competing devotions" (Blair-Loy, 2003) that are very difficult to reconcile. Individuals are caught between trying to fulfill the cultural ideals of what it means to be a good worker and a good parent. The tools of modern communication—the smart phone, the tablet, the laptop—allow professionals and managers to do some of their work at home, which can help ease the strain but which also can make it worse by making the workplace always accessible.

Task Stress The second sense in which work could interfere is to increase emotional stress. Task stress is not necessarily correlated with task size. Many professionals who work long hours find their jobs rewarding and not unduly stressful. Rather, task stress is more likely to be found among less-educated Americans, who perform physically difficult or dangerous work, or who have little job security and could be laid off at any time, or who work under close supervision without the ability to check on their children by calling home. They may bring that stress home with them in what researchers call **spillover,** the transfer of mood or behavior between work and home.

spillover the transfer of mood or behavior between work and home

Two psychologists studied the effects of work-to-home spillover on the marriages of 19 male police officers who, at the end of each workday for a month, completed questionnaires about their level of job stress (Roberts & Levenson, 2001). Once per week the officers and their wives came to a university laboratory, where they were wired to machines that monitored their physiological responses. They were then told to discuss the day's activities. On days when the police officers reported more job stress, they showed heightened arousal in their autonomic nervous system—the "fight or flight" response that people may feel if surprised by something unpleasant. They also displayed less positive emotion and more negative emotion in their conversations with their wives. These reactions—the arousal, the greater negative emotion in conversations—have been shown to be correlated with marital distress and divorce in other studies conducted by the authors and their collaborators.

Task stress can also affect parents whose work hours are unpredictable or who do not work a standard daytime, Monday through Friday, schedule. The lack of predictability makes it difficult to arrange care for children. Eighteen percent of all workers had evening, night, or rotating (sometimes day, sometime evenings, sometimes night) schedules, according to a 2004 government survey; and 17 percent said that they usually worked either Saturday or Sunday or both (McMenamin, 2007). Nonstandard work has increased as the service sector of the economy has grown. Evenings and weekends are when people eat at restaurants and do their shopping. The growing health care industry must care for patients around the clock. But child care providers mostly work a standard schedule; few day care centers, for instance, are open evenings, nights, or weekends. So parents working these nonstandard shifts must find other means of obtaining child care.

One way in which dual-earner couples manage nonstandard work hours is to work different shifts, like the families of the EMTs described at the beginning of this chapter. Perhaps one-third of all dual-earner couples with preschool-aged children have at least one spouse working an evening, night, or rotating shift (Presser, 1999); and many of these couples are sharing the child care. It is an arrangement that can provide good care, but couples working different shifts may have little time for each other and their relationships may suffer. For instance, when wives work a fixed night schedule, their risk of divorce increases (Presser, 2000; Kalil, Ziol-Guest, & Epstein, 2010). Single parents working nonstandard hours face an even more difficult situation because they don't have a spouse they can rely on for assistance. Overall, the children of parents who work nonstandard hours may be at risk of poorer academic or emotional development (Han & Waldfogel, 2007; Joshi & Bogen, 2007; Han & Fox, 2011).

Family emergencies can also bring about work-related stress. Let's suppose that your daughter breaks her arm on the playground and that you need to deal with it. Can you take time off from work? If you are fortunate enough to be among the top 10 percent of wage earners in the nation, you probably can: 61 percent of them were allowed to take paid personal leave days. But the less you earn, the less likely you are to have that work benefit; only 10 percent of people in the bottom 10 percent of wage earners could take paid personal leave (U.S. Bureau of Labor Statistics, 2015). Some low-wage workers could even be fired for taking a day off to get their children to the doctor's office. A pediatrician at a Johns Hopkins clinic in a low-income neighborhood told me the rule of thumb her experience has taught her: When a child breaks a leg, a parent often loses a job. Low- and moderate-income workers typically do not have the kind of flexible work environment that professionals and managers take for granted.

TOWARD A FAMILY-RESPONSIVE WORKPLACE?

The concerns of workers, and increasingly of the managers who employ them, about easing the conflicting demands of work and family have led to a movement toward what is called the **family-responsive workplace**—meaning a work setting in which job conditions are designed to allow employees to meet their family responsibilities more easily. Advocates argue that it will be beneficial not only to employees but also to employers (Levin-Epstein, 2007). Fewer workers, it is said, will quit work because of family responsibilities, which will save employers the costs of recruiting and training replacements. Workers will be less stressed, it is claimed, which will increase productivity. Employers have, in fact, become more responsive to employees' family concerns, if only out of self-interest: American firms have improved in areas such as child care leave flexibility (Bloom, Sadun, Scur, & Van Reenen, 2015). Employers who wish to recruit and retain good workers realize that they must make their jobs attractive to people who are caring for children—and to the growing number who are caring for elderly parents.

family-responsive workplace a work setting in which job conditions are designed to allow employees to meet their family responsibilities more easily

Although some small employers and many mid-size employers offer family-friendly policies, large firms tend to offer the most extensive policies, such as child care assistance, paid sick leave, and some form of paid maternity leave. Large firms invest more money in training new workers, so they have more to lose if an employee quits due to family constraints. Because of higher sales revenues, large firms can more easily pass along the costs of policies. Since large firms tend to have better-paying, steadier jobs and better-educated workforces, a two-tiered class system is developing in which well-educated managers and professionals and better-paid blue-collar factory workers tend to be offered more assistance than are less-advantaged workers.

The most common, and most widely used, employee benefit is **flextime,** a policy that allows employees to choose, within limits, when they will begin and end their working hours. For example, a company might allow its employees to begin work anytime between 7:00 and 9:00 A.M. and to leave anytime from 3:00 to 5:00 P.M., as long as they work eight hours. In 2004, 30 percent of wage and salary workers could vary the start and end of their work days to some degree, a sharp rise from 14 percent in 1987 (McMenamin, 2007). Again, college-educated employees benefit more than high school educated employees: The more prestigious the occupational category, the more likely workers are to have flextime. Employed parents use flextime to match their work schedules to the school or day care schedules of their children. Flextime doesn't necessarily increase the amount of time parents can spend with their children, but it does allow them to avoid stressful conflicts between childcare and job responsibilities.

flextime a policy that allows employees to choose, within limits, when they will begin and end their working hours

To be able to spend more time with their children, especially when they are infants or when they are sick, employed parents need other options. One of these is **parental leave,** time off from work to care for a child, with a guarantee that the employee can have her or his job back when she or he returns. All other wealthy nations require employers to grant parental leave with at least partial pay (Pew Research Center, 2016). In this regard, as in many family policies, the United States lags behind. Canada, for instance, provides one year of leave at 53 percent of the worker's wage (OECD, 2017). In the United States in 1993, Congress passed the Family and Medical Leave Act, which requires companies with 50 or more employees to provide 12 weeks of *unpaid* leave for birth, adoption, foster care, or personal or family illness. Employers must allow employees to return to their jobs at the end of the leave. Although support for paid parental leave is growing in the United States, it remains a contentious issue. (See *Families and Public Policy:* Paid Parental Leave.)

parental leave time off from work to care for a child

The spread of computers, smart phones, and fax machines allows employees to work at home, or indeed anywhere. Experts in work and family policies touted the growth in **telecommuting**–doing work from home using electronic communication–as a new way to allow workers to combine work and caregiving. In 2017, 38 percent of workers with a bachelor's degree worked at home on a typical day, as did 12 percent of workers with a high school degree (U.S. Bureau of Labor Statistics, 2018a). But the trend toward doing more work at home has been a mixed blessing. While it does allow workers to be home with a child, parents report difficulty in actually caring for a child while attempting to focus on work. Having electronic access helps employees manage their work but it also makes it difficult for them to leave work behind, so the anxieties of the workplace are more likely to invade the home. In fact, people who work long hours report *more* work-to-family interference when they control their own schedules than when they don't–quite possibly because it's more difficult for them to separate their work from their home life (Schieman, Milkie, & Glavin, 2009).

telecommuting doing work from home using electronic communication

Although the spread of family-friendly policies such as flexible schedules and caregiving leaves is necessary to create a family-responsive workplace, they will be insufficient unless workers use them. That depends on the culture of the workplace which, Joan Williams (2010) argues, is still shaped by the masculine norms of the mid-twentieth century, when men were expected to focus completely on work and to rely on their wives to take care of home and family. Men still don't like to admit to their supervisors that they need to go home for family emergencies, Williams writes, because it would show insufficient commitment to their jobs. In some firms, employees fear that they will be shunted aside and denied promotions if they take advantage of

Families and Public Policy: Paid Parental Leave

A half-century ago, women workers who became pregnant were expected to give up their jobs and stay home to raise the child. In fact, teachers in some school systems were required to leave their jobs if they gave birth. Today those norms are long gone. Mothers tend to return to the workforce quickly, their incomes needed to pay the mortgage or their career ladder in jeopardy. Fifty-eight percent of all married mothers with children under one were working for pay in 2017 (U.S. Bureau of Labor Statistics, 2018d). Some of these mothers (and some of their husbands) would prefer to stay home with a new baby for several months or perhaps a year, but few employers allow it and few parents can afford it. In response, the federal government passed the Family and Medical Leave Act in 1993, which requires firms with 50 or more employees to allow new parents up to 12 weeks of unpaid leave. Yet because the leave is unpaid, many parents cannot afford to take it.

Some workers can cobble together a sort-of paid leave by combining sick leave, pregnancy disability leave, and vacation days. And some employers—typically large ones that can better afford it—offer some paid leave. Even when it is offered, however, the culture of some firms discourages employees from taking it out of fear that they will not be perceived as fully committed employees worthy of good assignments and promotions (Blair-Loy, 2003).

All other wealthy countries provide parental leave with pay. Many of the nations in the European unions offer leaves of a half a year or more with partial pay (OECD, 2017). The United States lags behind for two reasons. First, the American government provides fewer protections against loss of earnings in general than do other nations. American workers are at the mercy of the labor market more than workers in most other nations. Second, European nations have been concerned for decades, and in some cases for centuries, with encouraging births. These modest-sized nations, surrounded by others, have long been anxious about keeping the size of their populations up to a level where they could field an army capable of defending the country. Americans have not worried about birthrates. We have an ocean separating us from potential adversaries, and we have a tradition of expanding the size of the nation through immigration. So the American government has not felt the need to subsidize births by providing paid leave.

Now, however, with so many dual-earner couples and employed single mothers, support is growing for paid parental leave in the United States. Four states—California, New Jersey, New York, and Rhode Island—currently provide for paid family leave. The State of Washington and Washington D.C. enacted programs that will take effect in the near future. The U.S. Congress has considered various paid parental leave bills, but as of 2019 none had passed. Opponents have criticized the cost of the measures, while supporters have argued that they would increase the retention of employees who give birth and assist firms in the recruitment of prospective employees.

California's paid leave law appears to have increased mothers' work effort, as supporters had argued. After the law went into effect, the work hours of mothers of one- to three-year-old children increased (Rossin-Slater, Ruhm, & Waldfogel, 2013). In other words, mothers seem to have used paid leave as a temporary break from work, rather than quitting work altogether after they gave birth. Paid leave remains an important issue on the family policy agenda.

Ask Yourself

1. Do you know any couples who are trying to raise a family while both of them work full-time? If so, what is their major problem? Could a change in public policy help to solve it?
2. Should American workers receive paid parental leaves, like workers in some European countries?

flexible schedules or caregiving leaves. Looking at what has happened to work-family balance over the past few decades, one gets the sense that the conditions of family life have changed more than the conditions of work. Egalitarian norms that encourage sharing the housework and child care are stronger than in the past, and husbands contribute more than they used to. But at least in the United States, the norm of the fully-committed worker with no family responsibilities is still present. Thus, individuals are caught between trying to fulfill the cultural ideals of what it means to be a good worker and a good parent. To solve this dilemma requires a "culture of flexibility" (Families and Work Institute, 2011), an atmosphere in which supervisors who are knowledgeable about family-friendly benefits encourage employees to use the benefits and do not penalize them for doing so. More broadly, it requires a culture in which being a good worker and a good parent are not defined as mutually exclusive.

Quick Review

- A greater percentage of American workers, and American dual-earner couples, put in very long work weeks than do workers in most other developed nations.
- Less-educated workers face the problem of unpredictable work hours.
- Work can interfere with family life because long hours conflict with family time or because workers bring home the stress they experience.
- Family life can interfere with work if parents' jobs do not allow the flexibility they need to deal with family emergencies.
- Parents who earn more or work in large firms receive more benefits to help them balance their family and paid work lives.

Looking Back

1. **How has married women's work changed over the past half-century?** In the second half of the twentieth century, married women entered the labor force in large numbers. A majority of married women with young children are now employed outside the home. The rise of the service sector and the long-term decline in fertility are two important reasons for women's increase in labor force participation. In the 2000s, married women's labor force participation declined slightly but remains at a high level.

2. **How does our society treat the labor of caring for others?** Much of the caring labor in families was provided by wives in the home. It was not considered "work" because it was unpaid and consisted of caring for people. As women have moved into the paid labor force, the value of the caring they provided has become evident and has proven difficult to replace. Some authors suggest that we must place a higher value on caring labor—paid and unpaid.

3. **How has the division of labor in marriages changed?** Wives in different-sex marriages have greatly reduced the amount of housework they do, while husbands have increased theirs. As a result, the relative amount of housework done by husbands and wives has become less unequal. Husbands take more responsibility for the routine care of their children when their wives work. Wives, however, feel more pressure and do more multitasking. Overall, the total amount of housework being done has declined; couples are buying more services, such as restaurant meals, than they used to. Same-sex couples divide the tasks more equally but still show some specialization.

4. **What are some of the strains working parents can experience?** Work can interfere with family life through the amount of work to be done, which may intrude into family time, from the unpredictability of work hours, or from the stress of the workplace. One increasingly common way for dual-earner couples to manage child care is to work split shifts, a practice that provides children with parental care but can strain a marriage to the point of divorce.

5. **How is the workplace responding to the needs of working parents?** Workers are concerned about meshing their jobs with their family responsibilities, and corporations and government are responding. Large corporations are increasingly providing assistance such as caregiving leave and flexible hours. So far, these and other reforms have benefited college-educated workers and employees of large corporations more than high school educated workers and employees of small corporations. To be effective, family-friendly reforms will require a more flexible culture in the workplace.

Study Questions

1. How has the life of the typical married woman changed since the middle of the twentieth century?
2. How has the life of the typical married man changed?
3. How have the changes in work outside and inside the home changed the quality of marriages?
4. Why do jobs that involve caring for others typically pay low wages?
5. Why do some Americans feel overworked while others feel underworked?
6. Does work interfere with family life the same way for a professional as it does for a factory worker or service provider?
7. Why do well-paid workers typically receive more family-related benefits than workers who earn less?
8. How do the cultural expectations of being a good worker and a good parent clash?

Key Terms

care work 217
family-responsive workplace 226
flextime 227
labor force 215
normal unpredictability 224
parental leave 227
service sector 216
spillover 225
telecommuting 227
time-diary studies 219

Thinking about Families

The Public Family	The Private Family
Are benefits such as family leave or tax credits for child care unfair to workers without children?	**Might couples' feelings toward each other be different if they shared the housework and child care equally?**

References

Antecol, H., & Steinberger, M. D. (2013). Labor supply differences between married heterosexual women and partnered lesbians: A semi-parametric decomposition approach. *Economic Inquiry, 51*(1), 783–805.

Bertrand, M., Kamenica, E., & Pan, J. (2015). Gender identity and relative income within households. *Quarterly Journal of Economics, 130*(2), 571–614.

Blair-Loy, M. (2003). *Competing devotions: Career and family among women executives.* Cambridge, MA: Harvard University Press.

Bloom, N., Sadun, R., Scur, D., & Van Reenen, J. (2015). Helping firms by helping employees? Work-life balance in America. *Center for American Progress.* Retrieved January 3, 2016, from https://cdnAmerican-progress.org/wp- OECD. (2017). Table pf2.1. A summary of paid leave entitlements available to mothers. *Family Database.* Retrieved October 17, 2018, from https://www.oecd.org/els/soc/PF2_1_Parental_leave_systems.pdfcontent/uploads/2015/12/18071628/Bloom-report-update.pdf

Brewster, M. E. (2017). Lesbian women and household labor division: A systematic review of scholarly research from 2000 to 2015. *Journal of lesbian studies, 21*(1), 47–69.

Clawson, D., & Gerstel, N. (2014). *Unequal time: Gender, class, and family in employment schedule.* New York: Russell Sage Foundation.

England, P. (2005). Emerging theories of care work. *Annual Review of Sociology, 31,* 381–399.

England, P., Budig, M., & Folbre, N. (2002). Wages of virtue: The relative pay of care work. *Social Problems, 49,* 455–173.

Esping-Andersen, G., & Billari, F. C. (2015). Re-theorizing family demographics. *Population and Development Review, 41*(1), 1-31.

Families and Work Institute. (2002). Highlights of the national study of the changing workforce. Retrieved

February 24, 2009, from http://familiesandwork.org/site/research/summary/nscw2002summ.pdf

Families and Work Institute. (2011). Workplace flexibility in the United States: A status report. Retrieved January 22, 2012, from http://familiesandwork.org/site/research/reports/www_us_workflex.pdf

Gerstel, N., & Clawson, D. (2018). Control over time: Employers, workers, and families shaping work schedules. *Annual Review of Sociology, 44,* 77–97.

Gerson, K. (2010). *The unfinished revolution: How a new generation is reshaping family, work, and gender in America.* New York Oxford University Press.

Glenn, E. N. (2000). Creating a caring society. *Contemporary Sociology, 29,* 84–94.

Goldberg, A. E. (2013). "Doing" and "undoing" gender: The meaning and division of housework in same-sex couples. *Journal of Family Theory & Review, 5*(2), 85–104.

Goldberg, A. E., Smith, J. Z., & Perry-Jenkins, M. (2012). The division of labor in lesbian, gay, and heterosexual new adoptive parents. *Journal of Marriage and Family,* 74(4), 812–828.

Goldscheider, F., Bernhardt, E., & Lappegård, T. (2015). The gender revolution: A framework for understanding changing family and demographic behavior. *Population and Development Review, 41*(2), 207–239.

Gupta, S. (2007). Autonomy, dependence, or display? The relationship between married women's earnings and housework. *Journal of Marriage and Family, 69,* 399–417.

Han, W.-j., & Fox, L. E. (2011). Parental work schedules and children's cognitive trajectories. *Journal of Marriage and Family, 73,* 962–980.

Han, W.-j., & Waldfogel, J. (2007). Parental work schedules, family process, and early adolescents' risky behavior. *Children and Youth Services Review, 29,* 1249–1266.

Hochschild, A. (2012). *The second shift: Working families and the revolution at home. Revised and with a new afterword.* New York: Penguin.

Jacobs, J. A., & Gerson, K. (2004). *The time divide: Work, family, and social policy in the 21st century.* Cambridge, MA: Harvard University Press.

Joshi, P., & Bogen, K. (2007). Nonstandard schedules and young children's behavioral outcomes among working low-income families. *Journal of Marriage and Family, 69,* 139–156.

Kalil, A., Ziol-Guest, K. M., & Epstein, J. L. (2010). Nonstandard work and marital instability: Evidence from the National Longitudinal survey of youth. *Journal of Marriage and Family, 72,* 1289–1300.

Kalleberg, A. L. (2011). *Good jobs, bad jobs: The rise of polarized and precarious employment systems in the United States, 1970s to 2000s.* New York: Russell Sage Foundation.

Lambert, S. J., Fugiel, P. J., & Henly, J. R. (2014). Schedule unpredictability among early career workers in the US labor market: A national snapshot. *EINet (Employment Instability, Family Well-being, and Social Policy Network), University of Chicago.* Retrieved October 16, 2018, from https://www.ssa.uchicago.edu/sites/default/files/uploads/lambert.fugiel.henly_.executive_summary.b_0.pdf

Levin-Epstein, J. (2007, February). Responsive workplaces: The business case for employment that values fairness and families. *The American Prospect.* Retrieved February 25, 2016, from http://www.prospect.org/cs/articles?article=responsive_workplaces

McMenamin, T. M. (2007). A time to work: Recent trends in shift work and flexible schedules. *Monthly Labor Review* (December), 3–15.

Milkie, M. A., Raley, S. B., & Bianchi, S. M. (2009). Taking on the second shift: Time allocations and time pressures of U.S. Parents with preschoolers. *Social Forces, 88,* 487–518.

Nomaguchi, K. M. (2009). Change in work-family conflict among employed parents between 1977 and 1997. *Journal of Marriage and Family,* 71(15–32).

OECD. (2017). Table pf2.1. A summary of paid leave entitlements available to mothers. *Family Database.* Retrieved October 17, 2018, from https://www.oecd.org/els/soc/PF2_1_Parental_leave_systems.pdf

Oppenheimer, V. K. (1970). *The female labor force in the United States, population monograph series, 5.* Berkeley: Institute of International Studies, University of California.

Passias, E. J., Sayer, L., & Pepin, J. R. (2017). Who experiences leisure deficits? Mothers' marital status and leisure time. *Journal of Marriage and Family, 79*(August), 1001–1022.

Pepin, J. R., Sayer, L. C., & Casper, L. M. (2018). Marital status and mothers' time use: Childcare, housework, leisure, and sleep. *Demography, 55,* 107–133.

Presser, H. B. (2000). Non-standard work schedules and marital instability. *Journal of Marriage and the Family, 62,* 93–110.

Raley, S., Bianchi, S. M., & Wang, W. (2012). When do fathers care? Mothers' economic contribution and fathers' involvement in child care. *American Journal of Sociology, 117*(5), 1422–1459.

Roberts, N. A., & Levenson, R. W. (2001). The remains of the workday: Impact of job stress and exhaustion on marital interaction in police couples. *Journal of Marriage and Family, 63,* 1052–1067.

Rossin-Slater, M., Ruhm, C. J., & Waldfogel, J. (2013). The effects of California's paid family leave program on mothers' leave-taking and subsequent labor market outcomes. *Journal of Policy Analysis and Management,* 32(2), 224–245.

Sayer, L. C. (2016). Trends in women's and men's time use, 1965-2012: Back to the future? In S. M. McHale, V. King, J. Van Hook, & A. Booth (Eds.), *Gender and couple relationships* (pp. 43-78). Dordrecht: Springer.

Schieman, S., Milkie, M. A., & Glavin, P. (2009). When work interferes with life: Work-nonwork interference and the influence of work-related demands and resources. *American Sociological Review, 74*, 966–988.

Schneebaum, A. (2013). *The economics of same-sex couple households: Essays on work, wages, and poverty.* (PhD dissertation), University of Massachusetts, Amherst.

Smith, T. W., Davern, M., Freese, J., & Hout, M. (2017). General social surveys, 1972–2016. Machine readable data file. Chicago: National Opinion Research Center.

Stone, D. (2000, March 13). Why we need a care movement. *The Nation*, 13–15.

Stone, P. (2007). *Opting out? Why women really quit careers and head home.* Berkeley: University of California Press.

Tronto, J. C. (1993). *Moral boundaries: A political argument for an ethic of care.* New York: Routledge.

U.S. Bureau of labor Statistics. (2015). Employee benefits survey, paid time-off benefits, March 2015, table 32. Retrieved October 17, 2018, from http://www.bls.gov/ncs/ebs/benefits/2015/ownership/civilian/table32a.pdf

U.S. Bureau of Labor Statistics. (2017). Women in the labor force: A databook. *Report 1071.* Retrieved October 13, 2018, from https://www.bls.gov/opub/reports/womens-databook/2017/home.htm

U.S. Bureau of Labor Statistics. (2018a). American time use survey - 2017 results. *News Release USDL-18-1058.* Retrieved October 17, 2018, from https://www.bls.gov/news.release/pdf/atus.pdf

U.S. Bureau of Labor Statistics. (2018b). Labor force statistics from the current population survey: 11. Employed persons by detailed occupation, sex, race, and hispanic or latino ethnicity. *Household Data Annual Averages* Retrieved October 13, 2018, from https://www.bls.gov/cps/cpsaat11.htm

U.S. Bureau of Labor Statistics. (2018c). May 2017 national occupational employment and wage estimates: United States. *Occupational Employment Statistics.* Retrieved October 13, 2018, from https://www.bls.gov/oes/current/oes_nat.htm#00-0000

U.S. Bureau of Labor Statistics. (2018d). Table 6. Employment status of mothers with own children under 3 years old by single year of age of youngest child and marital status, 2016–2017 annual averages. *Economic News Release.* Retrieved September 12, 2019, from https://www.bls.gov/news.release/famee.t06.htm

Wajcman, J. (2016). *Pressed for time: The acceleration of life in digital capitalism.* Chicago: University of Chicago Press.

Williams, J. C. (2010). *Reshaping the work-family debate: Why men and class matter.* Cambridge, MA: Harvard University Press.

Part Four

Links across the Generations

In this part, we shift from same-generational relations of spouses and partners to intergenerational relations between parents and children. How adequately parents are meeting their overall responsibilities for raising children is a topic of much discussion and concern. In addition, working-age adults bear most of the responsibility for supporting and taking care of the older population. The increasing number of older persons raises the question of whether family care will continue to be adequate. In the terms of this book, the issue is whether the public family is meeting its caretaking responsibilities for children and the older population. Chapter 9 examines the care of children by their parents. No public issue involving the family has received more attention in recent years than the well-being of children. The chapter begins by asking two questions: What are parents supposed to do for children? And what might prevent parents from doing what they are supposed to do? It then evaluates the complex question of whether children's well-being has declined. In Chapter 10 the focus shifts from the young to the old. The chapter first reviews the substantial changes that occurred in the lives of the older population during the twentieth century. It subsequently examines the assistance provided to, and provided by, the older people, as well as levels of contact and affection between older people and their adult children and grandchildren.

Chapter Nine

Children and Parents

Looking Forward

1. What are the main goals in socializing children, and how do parents differ in the way they fulfill their role?
2. How does the socialization of children vary by ethnicity, class, gender, and the sexual orientation of parents?
3. What barriers must parents overcome in socializing their children?
4. How much time do parents and children spend together?
5. How has the well-being of American children changed over time?

In 2018 the proportion of American family households that had children under 18 was 41 percent, a modern-day low (U.S. Bureau of the Census, 2018a). The high point was reached in the early 1960s, at the end of the baby boom, when the proportion was 57 percent. It fell below 50 percent in 1985 and has continued to drop ever since. The main and most obvious reason for the decline is that people are having fewer children than they were during the baby boom. Even among families that have children under 18, the most common number of children is one, and only 21 percent have more than two. Children, as I argued in Chapter 1, are a public good. With their numbers relatively low, the United States will need all of them to lead productive adult lives in the coming decades. So it is important that we raise them well. In part, that is a collective responsibility: Our schools and our health system must not fail them. But for the most part, the responsibility for raising today's children falls on their parents. We need them to succeed in raising them well. This raises two questions that will be the subject of this chapter: What are parents supposed to do for children? And what might prevent them from doing what they are supposed to do?

What Are Parents Supposed to Do for Children?

For the first several years of life, at least, families provide the main setting in which children's fundamental needs are met. In the United States, parents are given broad powers to shape their children's lives. What are the lessons children need to learn from their families, and how are those lessons shaped by social forces such as ethnicity, class, and gender? What behaviors by parents provide the best foundation for children's development?

First and foremost, parents, and sometimes other adult relatives, supply most of the love, nurturing, and care that children need in order to develop a basic sense of trust in other human beings. They also train young children in the skills they need to become more autonomous, such as dressing and feeding themselves. Later they provide the guidance, support, and discipline children need in order to become competent members of their society. In other words, family members socialize their children. Indeed, families are the major source of primary socialization–the settings for the first lessons children learn about their society.

SOCIALIZATION AS SUPPORT AND CONTROL

As parents socialize their children, they act in two broad ways. First, they provide emotional support–love, affection, warmth, nurturing, or acceptance. Emotional support shows children that parents care about their actions. It makes children feel more positively about themselves. Because children want to continue receiving such support, they try to act in ways they think will please their parents. Second, parents exercise control–they seek to limit or change children's behavior. Sometimes parental control is coercive, consisting of the use or threat of punishment or force. But control also may be inductive–that is, based on setting consistent limits, explaining the reasons for these limits to the child, requesting that the child comply, and praising her or his compliance. Parents may also exercise control by threatening to withdraw their love if the child does not behave well.

Numerous studies have examined the ways in which parents combine various aspects of support and control. In what is probably the most influential analysis, psychologist Diana Baumrind distinguished among three styles of parental behavior (Baumrind, 1971). In the **authoritative style,** parents combine high levels of emotional support with consistent, moderate control. Children are provided with warmth and affection and with firm, consistent discipline. But the discipline is moderate and is based on requests and explanations rather than on the use of force or punishment. Baumrind and others claim that authoritative parenting produces children who are more socially competent–meaning that they have higher self-esteem, cooperate better with others, develop a better moral sense, and are more independent. The two other styles of behavior, it is claimed, produce children who are less competent and who may show more behavior problems, anxiety, or depression. In the **permissive style,** parents provide support but exercise little control over their children by any means. And in the **authoritarian style,** parents combine low support with coercive attempts at control. The implication of this research tradition is that children are socialized best when parents set clear standards, enforce them consistently but without harsh punishment, and provide substantial emotional support. One can spare the rod without spoiling the child, it seems, but setting no limits on children's behavior is virtually as bad as relying solely on the stick.

authoritative style (of parenting) a parenting style in which parents combine high levels of emotional support with consistent, moderate control of their children

permissive style (of parenting) a parenting style in which parents provide emotional support but exercise little control over their children

authoritarian style (of parenting) a parenting style in which parents combine low levels of emotional support with coercive attempts at control of their children

SOCIALIZATION AND ETHNICITY

The three-category classification of parenting styles is still widely cited, and the authoritative style is generally seen as more effective than the authoritarian style. Some scholars have questioned whether the model can be applied to racial and ethnic minority families. African American parents, for instance, are somewhat more likely than white parents to use physical punishment; and Asian American parents are more likely than white parents to insist on discipline and obedience (McLoyd, Cauce, Takeuchi, & Wilson, 2000). Within African American or Asian American culture, according to critics, these actions may not have the negative meaning that whites, especially middle-class whites, attach to them (Chao, 1994; McLoyd, Kaplan, Hardaway, & Wood, 2007). In fact, one study found that parents' physical discipline–mostly spanking or slapping–in the first five years of a child's life and during early adolescence was associated with more behavior problems among eleventh-grade European American children but fewer behavior problems among eleventh-grade African American children (Lansford, Deater-Deckard, Dodge, Bates, & Pettit, 2004). Another study found that white early adolescents (with an average age of 12) perceived their mothers as less warm if their mothers used harsh parenting methods such as spanking them with their hands when they had done something wrong, but African American early adolescents did not see mothers who spanked them as less warm. White early adolescents also perceived their mothers as less warm if their mothers did not explain to them why they were being punished, but African American early adolescents did not. The authors suggest that when physical discipline is more commonly accepted, children may interpret this style of parenting as expressing warmth and love, especially in low-income African American families, for whom their findings were strongest (Jackson-Newsom, Buchanan, & McDonald, 2008). These studies suggest that researchers must be cautious in applying Baumrind's classification scheme to racial and ethnic minority parents.

One of the primary tasks in socialization, in fact, is to familiarize children with the culture in which they are growing up. Consider the acquisition of language. Learning to talk not only allows children to communicate with others, but also carries important lessons about their society. A French child learns two words for *you:* Siblings and friends are called *tu,* and parents and other adults are called *vous.* Thus, the child learns which relationships are characterized by equality and intimacy and which are characterized by respect and social distance. A Japanese girl learns to show deference to men by addressing them differently than she does women. At a conference I attended in Tokyo, a female Japanese professor was criticized by a male colleague—in Japanese. She replied to him in English. When asked later why she responded in English, she said that, had she chosen Japanese, she would have had to use the "respect language" a polite woman must employ when addressing a man. In English, she could respond as a linguistic equal.

norm a widely accepted rule about how people should behave

value a goal or principle that is held in high esteem by a society

Socialization also involves teaching children norms and values. **Norms** are widely accepted rules about how people should behave. **Values** are goals and principles that are held in high esteem by a society. The norms and values may be those of the dominant culture in the society, of a subculture, or of both. Families begin this process; schools, churches, peer groups, and even the media carry it on. For example, Japanese children learn to place a higher value on loyalty to the group in situations where an American child would learn to value independent action. When asked about desirable characteristics for children, Japanese mothers are more likely than American mothers to mention interdependence: fitting in with the group, getting along with others (Rothbaum, Kakinuma, Nagaoka, & Azuma, 2007).

SOCIALIZATION AND SOCIAL CLASS

In Chapter 4, we reviewed studies showing that middle-class parents tend to socialize their children somewhat differently than working-class and low-income parents. These differences can be overstated; there are many commonalities, such as a consumer culture that drives lower-income and higher-income parents alike to purchase expensive sneakers and personal electronic devices for their children (Pugh, 2009). Still, the class differences seem important. To review, middle-class parents tend to emphasize autonomy and self-direction. They seek actively to enhance their children's talents and opinions, in a style that Lareau (2011) called "concerted cultivation." Working-class and lower-income parents, on the other hand, are more likely to emphasize obedience and conformity. They seek to provide a safe, loving environment in which children can grow on their own—in Lareau's terms, they aim for "the accomplishment of natural growth." Kohn (1969; Kohn & Schooler,

1978) claimed that the differing parenting styles derive from the occupational conditions of the parents. Middle-class parents whose jobs provide autonomy and self-direction are more likely to emphasize those values with their children. Thus, middle-class parents socialize their children, in effect, to grow up and take middle-class jobs. (Although an overemphasis on autonomy can leave children unprepared to accept the rules and routines of large organizations.) (Streib, 2018) Working-class parents, with their emphasis on obedience and conformity, socialize their children for the kinds of blue- and pink-collar jobs the parents have held.

SOCIALIZATION AND GENDER

Chapter 3 presented evidence that parents socialize their daughters differently than their sons; here that discussion will be briefly summarized. Researchers now think of socialization as a two-way process in which children and parents influence each other. Because of their predispositions or because of other factors that may make them behave differently, children can influence how parents treat them. Parents then make decisions that reinforce these differences, such as buying stereotypically female toys for girls and stereotypically male toys for boys. The distinctions parents make may reflect, in part, biologically based differences between girls and boys (Painter-Brick, 1998); yet parents' actions also tend to magnify and exaggerate gender differences. The emphasis in sociological studies of this process has been on the conscious social learning children do as they are rewarded for some behaviors and punished for others—and as they watch and imitate adults of the same gender. Schools, peer groups, and the media further exaggerate gender differences, so that adult gender roles are far more distinctive than any inherent differences might warrant.

RELIGION AND SOCIALIZATION

Do religious denominations differ in what they say parents are supposed to do for their children? Are some religious beliefs more consistent with authoritarian than authoritative parenting? Some social scientists have suggested that conservative Protestantism leads fathers to be more authoritarian with their children. The argument is that conservative Protestantism—the denominations and independent churches sometimes called evangelical or fundamentalist, such as the Southern Baptist Convention, the United Pentecostal Church, and the Assemblies of God—teaches that men are the head of the family and therefore encourages a strict, discipline-oriented, distant style of fathering (Gottman, 1998). But national surveys that ask parents about their religious activities and their relationships with their children suggest that the story is not that simple (Wilcox, 2004). Yes, conservative Protestant men are more likely to believe in traditional gender roles: It's better if the husband is the earner and the wife stays home to raise the family, the wife should do more of the housework, and so forth. But they are also more likely to combine discipline with what sociologists call "emotion work" (Hochschild, 1979), the act of influencing and managing the emotions of others—in this case their wives and children.

W. Bradford Wilcox (1998, 2004) reports that conservative Protestant fathers who frequently attend church spank their children more often, which fits the authoritarian style, but in other ways they are quite authoritative: They hug and praise their children more than other fathers, yell at them less, and spend more time in leisure activities like playing together or having private talks. Wilcox argues that conservative Protestant churches teach that being the household head means, in part, being an involved father. The churches urge fathers not just to be disciplinarians but also to be emotionally expressive toward their children and to spend time with them. As a result, Wilcox argues, fathers become "soft patriarchs" who combine strict discipline with warmth and involvement in a style that blends the authoritarian with the authoritative. Religious fathers from "mainline" Protestant groups, such as the Episcopal, Lutheran, Presbyterian, and Methodist churches, are less authoritarian–they spank their children less–but they aren't as involved in activities with them and are less likely to set rules for television viewing or to know where their children are when they're not at home. So while conservative Protestant fathers may be disciplinarians, they also are involved in their children's lives.

WHAT'S IMPORTANT?

Social class and gender differences do exist, then, in how children are socialized. Nevertheless, it is possible to make some general statements about what parents are supposed to do. First, they should provide support to their children. This includes material support such as food, clothes, and shelter, as well as emotional support such as love and nurturing. The need for the former is obvious: Without material support, the child is in physical danger. Yet without emotional support, she or he is likely to grow up without a sense of security or a capability for trusting and loving other people. Second, parents should provide control. They must supervise and monitor their children's behavior not only to help them avoid physical harm but also to teach children the limits of acceptable behavior.

One could supplement this basic list according to one's values. Some might stress the importance of religious and ethical training–an upbringing that teaches children about the spiritual and moral side of life. Those who believe that people of both genders should undertake a wide range of behaviors that are now stereotyped as masculine or feminine–who believe, for example, that men should provide more care for children and women should have better opportunities for careers–might add that parents should encourage more **androgynous behavior** (i.e., behavior that has the characteristics of both genders) in their children. From this perspective, boys should be encouraged to be more nurturing and girls more aggressive. Similarly, those who believe that the values passed along to working-class children limit their occupational achievements might add that parents of all classes ought to encourage autonomous behavior in their children.

androgynous behavior behavior that has the characteristics of both genders

Does the sheer amount of time that mothers spend with children matter? Some people believe that children do best when parents, and especially mothers, spend lots of time and energy caring for them–a style sometimes called *intensive mothering* (Hays, 1996). The evidence, however, suggests that children's development may not be closely tied to how much time their mothers spend with them. According to a national study in which parents recorded on an almost minute-by-minute basis what they were doing with their time during one day, and that also measured the well-being of their children, how much time mothers spent with children ages 3 to 11 was not associated with behavior problems, such as whether the child was cruel or mean to others, or emotional problems, such as whether the child was too fearful or anxious (Milkie, Nomagushi, & Denny, 2015). Nevertheless, we shouldn't conclude that it makes no difference how much time mothers devote to children. Rather, it could be that mothers who recognize that their children have problems respond by increasing the amount of time they spend with them, which would create the false appearance that more time "causes" more problems (Waldfogel, 2016). Still, the lesson is that simply counting the number of hours a mother spends with her children is not a good way to predict how well her children are faring.

Quick Review

- Parents socialize their children by providing emotional support and control and by teaching them about norms and values.
- Authoritative parenting—combining warmth with consistent, moderate discipline—is thought to be most beneficial, but this conclusion may not apply to racial-ethnic minority groups.
- Middle-class parents tend to emphasize autonomy and self-direction, while working-class and lower-income parents tend to emphasize obedience and conformity.
- Parents tend to socialize their daughters differently than their sons, creating or magnifying gender differences.
- Conservative Protestant men tend to combine strict discipline with an involved style of fatherhood.

WHAT DIFFERENCE DO FATHERS MAKE?

Most of the literature on parenting focuses on mothers rather than fathers—an understandable emphasis, since mothers do more child rearing than fathers in nearly all societies. But over the past few decades, scholars have conducted a great deal of research on the role of fathers in child rearing. Most studies were conducted in the context of families with two different-sex parents and in which the mother is the primary caregiver. These studies suggest that fathers do make a difference in their children's lives (Marsiglio, Amato, Day, & Lamb, 2000; Pleck, 2007). For example, adolescents in two-parent families who reported a more positive relationship with their fathers (for instance, by agreeing with the statement "I really enjoy spending time with him" or reporting that he often helped the adolescent do important things) were subsequently less likely to engage in delinquent acts (such as damaging or destroying property or stealing something) than were adolescents with a less positive relationship, even after taking into account how positive the relationship between the adolescent and the mother was (Bronte-Tinkew, Moore, & Carrano, 2006).

Fathers have both direct and indirect effects on their children's development. They influence children directly by interacting with them: talking to them, playing with them, asserting authority, and so forth. For instance, toddlers whose fathers provide more supportive behavior to them (for instance, by encouraging and assisting them during play sessions) show greater vocabulary and cognitive gains, whether or not their mothers are supportive (Tamis-LeMonda, Shannon, Cabrera, & Lamb, 2004). Fathers can influence children indirectly in two ways. First, they can provide financially for the family, which is the traditional role of the father. Having a steady, adequate income benefits everyone in the family by ensuring that basic needs will be met. Second, they can be supportive of the mother—cooperating with her in child rearing, responding positively to the parenting she does. Children whose fathers support them in these indirect ways are better adjusted at home and at school (Cabrera, Tamis-LeMonda, Bradley, Hofferth, & Lamb, 2000).

A large proportion of children either experience their parents' divorce or are born to single mothers (see Chapter 12). Most of these children live with their mothers.

One might think that the more time these children spend with their fathers, the better their development would be, but a majority of studies on this topic do not show a strong link between the frequency by itself of a father's visits and child development (Marsiglio et al., 2000; Sobolewski & King, 2005). (Although a father who rarely sees his children has little influence on them.) What studies do show is that children whose nonresident fathers have an authoritative parenting style (e.g., who encourage their children and discuss their problems) tend to develop better than children whose visits with their fathers are purely recreational (Amato & Gilbreth, 1999). Within limits, then, the way nonresidential fathers behave as parents seems to make more of a difference than how often they see their children. Even among fathers who live with their children, the simple amount of time they spend together is less important than how actively engaged they are and how much responsibility they take for the children's care (Palkovitz, 2002).

ADOPTION

Adoptive families are usually successful, and most adopted children exhibit normal emotional development. A minority of adopted children, however, do show elevated levels of emotional or behavioral difficulties (Brodzinsky, Schechter, & Marantz, 1992; Zill & Wilcox, 2018). These difficulties may stem from events prior to the adoption, such as maternal substance abuse during pregnancy, time spent in multiple foster homes, or neglect in an overseas orphanage. But despite the successes of the majority, adoption may still be, in the words of one observer, "a devalued status" (Fisher, 2003). Most people may admire it in the abstract, but many seemingly good candidates for adoptive parenthood, such as middle-class couples who are unsuccessful in efforts to conceive a child, avoid it in practice, either out of a strong preference for biological children or a fear that an adoption will not work out.

About 2 percent of all children under age 18 in the United States are adopted (Child Trends, 2012). The nature of adoption has been changing over the past few decades. A half-century ago, the typical adoption used to involve an unmarried, white mother placing an infant for adoption with an unrelated married couple. But after the introduction of the birth control pill in the 1960s and the legalization of abortion in the 1970s, the number of unplanned births declined sharply. Moreover, the stigma of raising children outside of marriage decreased. As a result, the proportion of white, unmarried mothers who gave up their newborns for adoption declined from almost 20 percent in the early 1970s to 2 percent in the first half of the 1990s (U.S. National Center for Health Statistics, 1999). (The proportion of African American mothers who give up their newborns for adoption has always been lower and is estimated at about 2 percent.) But other forms of adoption have become more common.

Domestic Adoption Of all children who are adopted from within the United States, about half are adopted through private agencies and about half are adopted through the foster care system (Vandivere, Malm, & Radel, 2009). Children adopted through the foster care system tend to be more disadvantaged. About two-thirds of them are from racial-ethnic minority groups (National Center for Family and Marriage Research, 2011). More than half have special health needs such as learning disabilities (Vandivere, Malm, & Radel, 2009). Most parents adopting from foster care said they did so because they wanted to provide a permanent home for a child (Vandivere,

Malm, & Radel, 2009). Children who have been placed in foster care and whose parents' rights to them have been terminated due to neglect or abuse are sometimes adopted by their foster parents or by kin such as aunts or grandparents. (See Chapter 11, *Families and Public Policy:* The Swinging Pendulum of Foster Care Policy.)

Transnational Adoption Adoptions of children from other countries peaked at about 23,000 in the mid-2000s and have since declined. At that time, about one-fourth of all adopted children had been born in other countries (Vandivere, Malm, & Radel, 2009). There were 5,370 transnational adoptions in 2016 (Pew Research Center, 2017). The rise of transnational adoptions prior to the mid-2000s mainly reflected the declining number of American children who are placed for adoption at birth. Both the rise and fall also reflect geopolitics, population policies, and the globalization of the adoption market.

For instance, the Chinese government, concerned that birthrates were too high, instituted a policy whereby most families were limited to having a single child. Given the traditional preference of Chinese parents for sons, the one-child policy led to a flood of abandoned girl babies in Chinese orphanages. While discouraging Chinese families from adopting these girls, the government created an agency to work with international organizations that found willing adoptive parents in the West. But nations are also sensitive to the perception that they cannot care for their own children and tend to eventually reduce foreign options. China has since instituted tighter restrictions on the characteristics of parents who may adopt Chinese babies (most would-be parents must be married, for instance, and must have good physical and mental health records) and has encouraged adoption by Chinese parents. Nevertheless, China remained the top sending country in the late-2010s (U.S. Department of Homeland Security, 2018). Russia banned U.S. adoptions and encouraged Russians to adopt children after several incidents of alleged abuse, including an American parent who sent an adopted child back to Russia alone on an airplane because of what she said were severe psychological problems (Levy, 2010). Before the ban Russia sent the second largest number of babies; currently, Ethiopia is the second largest sender.

Transnational adoption could not occur without modern means of communication and transportation. Adopting a child internationally is a long and complex process for the prospective parents. Typically, two government agencies, one in the sending and one in the receiving country, are involved, along with a nonprofit social service agency with representatives in both countries. Paperwork, interviews, and permits are required. As a last step, the adopting parents must travel to the sending country to obtain final approvals and to return with a child. It is an option that barely existed a half-century ago. Now it is an integral part of the globalization of family life.

LGBTQ PARENTHOOD

As noted in Chapter 6, there are several ways in which LGBTQ individuals can become parents. Until a few decades ago, living openly as a lesbian or gay couple that was raising children was so far outside of accepted family behavior as to be nearly impossible. As recently as 1990, when survey researchers asked a national sample of Americans whether sexual relations between two adults of the same sex was always wrong, almost always wrong, wrong only sometimes, or not wrong at all, 73 percent responded "always wrong" (Yang, 1997). Given this high level of disapproval of same-sex behavior and relationships, many individuals who might today live openly as gay or lesbian parents entered into different-sex marriages and had children. But as attitudes began to change, some of these individuals ended their marriages and raised their children alone or with same-sex partners. Consequently, the earliest openly-LGBTQ parents tended to be women who identified as lesbian (men rarely retained custody after divorce) and whose children had been born into different-sex marriages. Studies of the relative well-being of the children in these families, compared to children raised by different-sex parents, are hard to interpret because one cannot easily distinguish between the effects of parental divorce and of living with lesbian parents. Nevertheless, early studies of the well-being of children raised by two lesbian parents compared to children raised by two different-sex parents showed little difference between the two groups (Patterson, 2000).

However, as attitudes changed (when the same question was asked of a national sample in 2018, 31 percent responded "always wrong" (Smith, Davern, Freese, & Morgan, 2019)), it became more common for same-sex couples to plan for children who would be born after the couples began their relationships. Women who identified as lesbians conceived children through donor insemination – the insertion of donated semen into the uteruses of ovulating women. Some gay men hired surrogate mothers who carried fetuses inseminated with their (or their partners') sperm. Other LGBTQ individuals adopted children, often from the foster care system. These children, intentionally acquired by openly-LGBTQ individuals, are becoming increasingly common. Overall, as noted in Chapter 6, about 200,000 children under 18 were being raised by same-sex couples in 2013, and between 1.1 and 2.0 million children under 18 had an LGBTQ parent who was not married or cohabiting (Gates,2014). LGBTQ parents tend to be more disadvantaged than parents who identify as heterosexual: They are less likely to have a college degree, more likely to report low incomes, and more likely to be black or Hispanic (Brewster, Tillman, & Jokinen-Gordon, 2014; Gates, 2013).

There was continued interest in the well-being of children who are being raised by LGBTQ parents, especially during the period just before the Supreme Court ruling that legalized same-sex marriage (*Obergefell v. Hodges*, 2015). The American Sociological Association filed a friend-of-the-court brief that later appeared in the form of an academic journal article; its authors concluded, "To date, the consensus in the recent social-science literature is clear: children living with two same-sex parents fare just as well as children residing with different sex parents" (Manning, Fettro, & Lamidi, 2014, p. 499). And yet, more studies would be welcome – including studies that move beyond the same-sex-parents v. different-sex-parents comparisons. We need to know more about what daily life in LGBTQ families with children is like: what challenges parents face, how parenthood and childhood are experienced, and how these families interact with school and community. As these families become increasingly numerous, we are likely to learn more about them.

Quick Review

- Fathers influence their children's development directly through interacting with them.
- Fathers influence their children's development indirectly by providing financial support and by supporting the parenting behaviors of mothers.
- Children adopted from foster care tend to be more disadvantaged and have more health problems than children adopted through private agencies.
- Children adopted transnationally move largely from poorer countries to wealthier countries.
- Children with same-sex parents are increasingly acquired through donor insemination, surrogacy, or adoption.

What Might Prevent Parents from Doing What They Are Supposed to Do?

Yet even parents with the best intentions sometimes cannot care for their children and socialize them as well as they would like to. The larger society sometimes interferes, as when a parent loses a job or a family cannot climb out of poverty. The transformation of the U.S. economy over the past few decades has hurt many parents and made child rearing more difficult. Social change also may interfere: Some observers have argued that recent changes in the organization of families make successful parenting more difficult. Among the changes causing these alleged difficulties are the great increase in the proportion of children who are cared for by someone other than a parent because their parents work for pay, the increase in the divorce rate since the 1960s, and the increasing proportion of children born outside marriage. In this section, the effects of these developments on the quality of parenting will be examined.

UNEMPLOYMENT AND POVERTY

On the most basic level, low income means fewer clothes and less food. It can mean being evicted from your apartment. It can mean that your children's bedroom has peeling, lead-filled paint. The effects of poverty on children can start before they are born. Pregnant, poor women are more likely to receive inadequate prenatal care and to engage in behaviors harmful to the fetus—such as smoking and using drugs, which reduce birth weight (Aber, Jones, & Cohen, 2000).

In addition, the consequences of unemployment and poverty can be more subtle. They can change the ways parents act toward each other, and they can also change the way parents and children interact. Consider the declining fortunes of rural communities, a topic of great interest since rural Americans voted in large numbers for President Donald Trump in the 2016 presidential election. The problems of rural America have existed for several decades: In 1987, sociologist Glen Elder, psychologist Rand Conger, and several collaborators studied 76 families in a rural Iowa county (Elder, Conger, Foster, & Ardelt, 1992). All were white, a majority were middle class, and each consisted of a married couple and at least two children, one of whom was in seventh grade. After obtaining background information from the family members, the research team set up a video camera. While the tape rolled, they asked the parents to spend 30 minutes reviewing the history and present status of their marriage. Then they taped a 15-minute discussion in which the parents attempted to solve a problem in their marriage. They then taped one of the parents and the seventh-grader in two discussions: talking about a family activity and talking about a family problem such as doing chores or getting along with a younger sibling. Finally, they taped the other parent and the seventh-grader in the same two discussions. Over the next several months, trained raters viewed and reviewed the videotapes, coding the kinds of behaviors each person displayed, such as warmth, affection, or anger.

Unemployment Nineteen of the fathers had lost their jobs, had had their hours cut back, or had been demoted in the preceding year. Other families had experienced a drop-in income or very little growth. The researchers combined these events into a measure of how much "economic pressure" each family was facing. (Even though most of the mothers were employed outside the home, the researchers focused on fathers, who were still the main earners in nearly all the families.) Studies of families during the Great Depression had shown that men who had lost their jobs were tense and irritable in their relations with wives and explosive and punishing in their relations with their children (Liker & Elder, 1983). The tapes showed similar behavior: Fathers in families under economic pressure were more irritable and hostile toward their wives and children. Their wives often replied in kind. One daughter said that at dinnertime "we are kinda cautious, like walking on hot ground or something" (Elder et al., 1992). The interviews revealed that fathers under economic pressure tended to be depressed, lacking energy and interest—more so than their wives. One father said, "There would be some good days, but there would be more bad ones than good ones. Kind of lethargic. Oh, I know it's gotta be done, but I'll do it tomorrow. We kind of floated." Moreover, during the taped discussions, children whose fathers were more hostile and irritable were themselves more sullen, angry, and abrasive. In their interviews, these children admitted to more symptoms of depression (e.g., feeling lonely, hopeless, no interest) and aggressiveness (e.g., I am tempted to break a rule if I don't like it; I do the opposite of what a bossy person says; I yell back if I'm yelled at).

The study suggests a chain of events running from economic difficulties to children's behavior problems. The loss of a job or a drop-in income causes psychological distress for the husband, who is still expected to be the family's main earner. The distress in turn leads to depression and to angry, explosive exchanges with his wife and children. And the children then become more depressed, hostile, and aggressive. It is possible, however, that causation could run the opposite way: Men who are depressed and hostile may be more likely to lose their jobs and to have children with similar characteristics. Still, the sequence proposed by the Iowa researchers is plausible and is supported by other studies (Price, Choi, & Vinokur, 2002).

Poverty Studies of poor urban families show similar dynamics (Edin & Kissane, 2010). A parent in poverty may be depressed about job prospects, anxious about paying the bills, or angry about crime and drugs in the neighborhood. Such a parent has few psychological resources left to devote to her or his children. In a term borrowed from electronic data transmission, she may have less "bandwidth" left to deal with children's problems (Mullainathan & Shafir, 2013). Instead of reasoning with the child or explaining why a certain behavior is good or bad, a depressed and anxious parent may respond to perceived misbehavior simply by threatening harsh punishment—but may then give in if the child refuses to obey. Thus, the child obtains little emotional support and receives discipline that is inconsistent, harsh, and punitive. As noted earlier, this style of parenting has been associated with diminished social competence among children, although some scholars question its application to racial-ethnic minority groups. There are many other potential pathways in which poverty could affect children's well-being. For instance, children in poverty tend to have parents who have less education and who may provide less cognitive stimulation, such as reading less to the child. They tend to live in neighborhoods where schools are of lower quality. The continual stress produced by their environment could lead to higher overall levels of stress hormones in their bodies, which in turn could affect brain development and lead to behavior problems (Evans, Chen, Miller, & Seeman, 2012). One set of studies suggests that low income has more of an effect on children's school achievement than it does on their behavior; moreover, low income seems to be more detrimental to younger children than to adolescents (Duncan & Brooks-Gunn, 1997).

FAMILY INSTABILITY

Given the increases in divorce, cohabiting relationships, and single parenthood, another factor that might prevent parents from doing what they are supposed to do is the growing instability of family life. Children today experience more changes in the composition of the households they live in. Moreover, American children experience more changes than do children in any other Western country. Figure 9.1 compares the percentage of children living with their mothers, who experience three or more of their mothers' partnerships by age 15, in 12 countries. For example, consider a child whose mother is married when the child is born; the mother later separates from her husband and lives for a time as a single parent, then cohabits with a man and then ends that relationship, and then lives with another man, all before the child turns 16. That child will have experienced three maternal partnerships—three men living in his or her house. Figure 9.1 shows that in some countries such as Belgium and Italy, 0.1 percent, or one in a thousand, children experience this much turnover. In Sweden, 2.6 percent of children experience this much turnover, the highest rate in Western Europe. But in the United States, 8.2 percent of children experience this much turnover, triple the rate in Sweden. Instability is much higher in the United States because Americans have high rates of marrying, divorcing, and remarrying, and they start and end cohabiting relationships more quickly (Andersson, Thomson, & Duntava, 2017; Cherlin, 2009).

Different Kinds of Households There are two ways in which this high level of instability could affect children negatively. First, it exposes them to several kinds of households, each of which could be problematic:

- A divorcing household. Chapter 12 will examine the effects of divorce and remarriage in detail. To summarize, experiencing one's parents' divorce raises the risk of experiencing outcomes such as dropping out of school, having a child as a teenager, or receiving public assistance. Still, most children do not experience these undesirable outcomes despite the increased risk.
- A single-parent household. Stable single-parent families can be good environments for children, and any difficulties they have may stem more from having low incomes than from not having a second parent present. Even so, living with one parent can sometimes be a handicap for children, even after low income is taken into account. Other potential difficulties include higher rates of depression (Carlson & Corcoran, 2001) and less effective monitoring and supervision (Astone & McLanahan, 1991). As with parenting styles, racial and ethnic differences may be important: The association between having a single parent and child outcomes such as delinquency

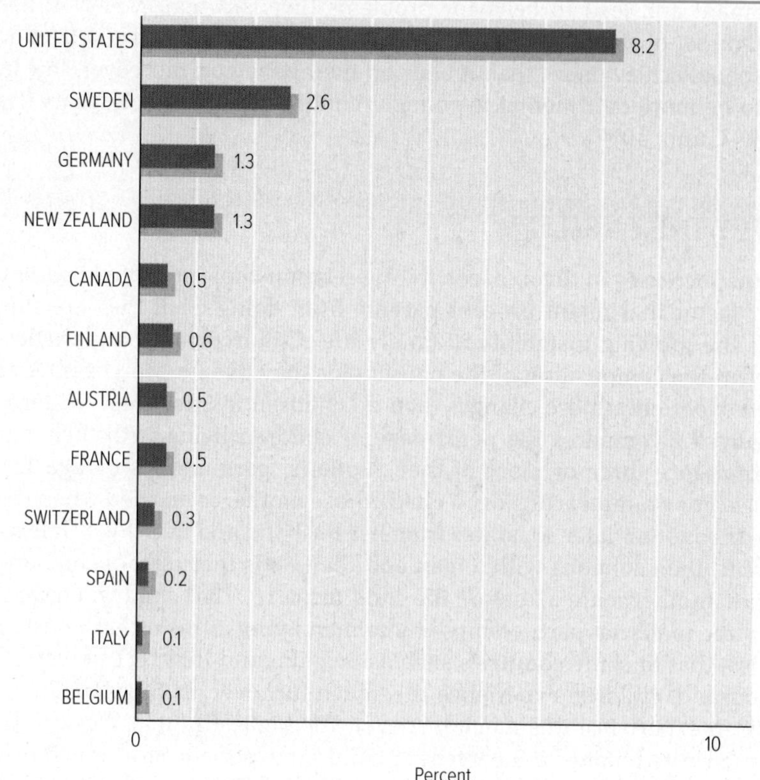

FIGURE 9.1 Percentage of children, living with their mothers, who experience three or more maternal partnerships by age 15. (*Source:* Jeffrey Timberlake, unpublished tabulations subsequent to Heuveline, P., J. M. Timberlake, and F. F. Furstenberg, Jr. (2003). "Shifting Childrearing to Single Mothers: Results from 17 Western Countries." *Population and Development Review* 29(1), 47–71.)

may be weaker among African Americans than among whites (Dunifon & Kowaleski-Jones, 2002).

- A household with a parent and her or his cohabiting partner. A biological parent might be willing to live with a partner she or he would not be willing to marry; and these partners may devote less time and energy to child rearing than would a married parent. In any case, in one national study, children living with a biological parent who was cohabiting (e.g., a mother and her boyfriend) were less engaged with school (skipped school more often, had trouble getting homework done) than children in most other kinds of families (Brown, 2006). In another study, children living with a biological parent who was cohabiting were less likely to graduate from high school than were children in a two-biological-parent family, or children living with a remarried parent, or children living with a divorced parent who had never re-partnered (Raley, Frisco, & Wildsmith, 2005). Families in which a biological parent is cohabiting with a partner may be particularly unfavorable environments for children.

Multiple Transitions The second way in which a high level of instability could affect children negatively is through the sheer number of transitions to which the child has to adjust, regardless of the type of family that is formed. Repeated movements of parents' partners in and out of the home could produce disruptions in the child's family system that could undermine her or his sense of security and trust. Researchers report that the number of transitions that children experience is associated with undesirable outcomes such as behavior problems at home and in school (Cavanagh & Huston, 2006; Fomby & Cherlin, 2007; Osborne & McLanahan, 2007; Cavanagh & Huston, 2008). Moreover, the association is not limited to family transitions: The sum total of instability across a number of domains, including residential moves, changes in child care arrangements, and changes in mothers' employment have also been shown to correlate with children's behavior problems (Fomby & Mollborn, 2017). It is not clear, however, whether this is a cause-and-effect association (a greater number of transitions cause more problems) or whether it reflects underlying, unmeasured factors that cause both the parents to have more partners and their children to have more problems. And if it is causal, the precise mechanisms are not well understood. The researchers typically suggest that frequent transitions cause greater family stress, which affects children.

FAMILY COMPLEXITY

Because of the increasing number of partners that adults have during their lifetimes, it's becoming more common to have children with more than one partner—what demographers are calling **multipartner fertility** (hereafter MPF). This phenomenon is leading to complex family households in which different children have different sets of parents, and in which half-siblings (who share one parent) and step-siblings (who are from parents' previous relationships) are common. Some MPF has long existed: A man or woman whose spouse dies might remarry and have more children, or a divorced woman or man might remarry and have more children. But cohabiting relationships have accelerated the process because they are much less stable than marriages. After cohabiting relationships end, parents may go on to have children with other partners. A second, important source of the rise of MPF is the considerable amount of childbearing outside of any kind of partnership. In 1950, only 4 percent of all children were born to unpartnered parents; but in 2010–2014, 15 percent were (Wu, 2017). Parents who give birth to a child without a partner are much more likely to subsequently have children with another partner.

multipartner fertility having children with more than one partner during one's lifetime

About 13 percent of men and 19 percent of women in their forties have had children with more than one partner. But that includes people who have fewer than two children. If we consider just people who have had two or more children, 23 percent of men and 28 percent of women in their forties have had children with more than one partner (Guzzo, 2014). MPF is more common among mothers who had their first children at an early age, who were African American, have lower levels of education, or who attended religious services less often (Carlson & Furstenberg, 2006; Guzzo & Furstenberg, 2007a, 2007b). Having a child by more than one partner is not necessarily a problem, but it complicates child rearing. Women who had children with multiple partners were less likely, according to one study, to say that they had family or friends they could count on for social support, such as a small loan or a place to stay—although whether the lack of support is a cause or an effect of MPF is unclear (Harknett & Knab, 2007). Both instability (the number of parental transitions) and complexity (MPF) appear to be associated with children's behavior problems (Fomby & Osborne, 2017).

IMMIGRATION STATUS

Immigrant parents and their children may face difficulties if they do not have legal residence in the United States. In 2010, an estimated 5.5 million children were living with at least one unauthorized immigrant parent; and the vast majority of these children were born in the United States and therefore were United States citizens (Yoshikawa & Kholoptseva, 2013). The children of unauthorized parents may be vulnerable to having their parents detained or deported. Just the fear of losing a parent could lead to children's anxiety, which could interfere with their progress at school. One mother recalls how her children would call her when she was at the supermarket and say, "Are the police going to get you because you don't have papers? Please don't go out or someone will take you" (Berger Cardoso, Scott, Faulkner, & Barros Lane, 2018, p. 309). Although unauthorized parents are ineligible for most public benefits, their United-States-born children, as citizens, are eligible for some benefits such as the Children's Health Insurance Program. Their unauthorized parents, however, may be reluctant to enroll them in programs for which they qualify out of fear that they, the parents, could be identified and deported as a result. In addition, their parents may not be informed about benefits because of their limited English proficiency. Overall, unauthorized parents face a difficult task in raising their United-States-born children. In one study, unauthorized parents from Mexico reported more parenting strain (feeling worn out or tired from raising a family, etc.) than did United-States-born Mexican parents (Noah & Landale, 2018).

MASS INCARCERATION

mass incarceration extremely high rates of imprisonment, particularly of African American males

Another development over the past quarter-century, sadly, also prevents parents from doing what they are supposed to do: **mass incarceration,** the term sociologists use for the extremely high rates of imprisonment today, particularly of African American males. The percentage of Americans imprisoned or jailed has grown enormously since about 1980. A major factor in its growth has been an increase in arrests for nonviolent drug-related crimes and increases in the sentences that the violators receive—including laws that limit a judge's discretion by requiring mandatory minimum sentences. Nationally, over half of all prisoners have children under age 18 (U.S. Bureau of Justice Statistics, 2008). As a result, American children are at an increased risk of having a parent in prison. The problem is worse for children with parents who have not graduated from high school. By one estimate, 15 percent of white children in this group and 62 percent of black children will, at current rates, have a parent in prison before they reach age 18. But the numbers are considerable for the children of parents with high school educations, too: 4 percent of white children and 16 of black children will experience a parent's incarceration before they reach age 18 (Pettit, 2012).

The imprisonment of fathers leaves mothers to cope with raising children on their own. It leaves children with fathers who are not in their daily lives but not completely gone, either—fathers who can be visited, who make collect telephone calls home, and who write letters, but who cannot be counted on for support. The anxiety-producing state of having a parent who is not present but not totally absent is an example of what is called "ambiguous loss" (Voss, 1999). Children may grieve the loss of their fathers, but that loss cannot be fully resolved because the fathers remain a shadow presence in their lives. Young boys whose fathers are incarcerated tend to show more physically aggressive behavior (Wildeman, 2010). Mass incarceration also affects children because when their fathers are released from prison, they often have a difficult time finding employment.

In the first year after their release, fathers who have stable housing (e.g., living with their own mothers), who retain a good relationship with their children's mothers, and who do not lapse into crime and drugs have better relationships with their children (Western & Smith, 2018). But crushing child support debt can interfere: In many states, court-ordered child support payments continue to be assessed while men are in prison, so that upon their release they face a bill for thousands, and sometimes tens of thousands, of dollars (Haney, 2018). Their inability to pay off these debts hampers their efforts to reconnect with their children.

Quick Review

- Unemployment and poverty can change the way parents act toward each other and the way they interact with their children.
- American children experience more instability in parents' spouses and partners entering and exiting their households than do children in other Western countries.
- Family instability could affect children by exposing them to kinds of households that may increase the risk of negative outcomes such as behavior problems.
- Family instability could also affect children because of the difficulties of adjusting to the frequent movements of parents and parents' partners into and out of the household.
- Mass incarceration is leaving many children with imprisoned parents who, upon release, face challenges in maintaining relationships with their children.

TIME APART

Because of the great increase in the proportion of mothers who work outside the home, more children face daily periods of separation from their parents. Neither parent may be available to care for a preschool child or to be home when an older child returns from school. The issue is usually framed in terms of "working mothers" even though fathers are working outside the home and could provide care when they are home. This development raises two questions: How much less time do children spend with their parents? and What are the consequences of spending more time apart?

How Parents Compensate for Time Apart You would think children must be spending much less time with their parents now than in the past. But studies suggest that the increase in time apart has been smaller than one would expect (Bianchi, Robinson, & Milkie, 2006). Employed parents seem to compensate during nonemployed hours for some of the time they spend away from their children. Booth, Clarke-Stewart, Vandell, McCartney, and Owen (2002) compared the time spent with parents by two groups of infants in a national study: those who were in child care 30 hours or more per week and those who were not in child care at all. ("Child care" is the term commonly used for nonparental care provided to children while their parents work.) Although the mothers of the first group could potentially have spent 30 fewer hours with their infants, they actually spent only 12 fewer hours with them, on average. Thus, they had compensated for more than half the hours their children were in child care settings.

How are they doing it? First, they are cutting back on housework. Second, they have less leisure time. Married women, for instance, spend less time reading, visiting people, and participating in clubs or other organizations. All parents are spending less time eating, suggesting quicker meals. Third, they are combining activities much more–working or trying to relax while taking care of their children at the same time, for example (Bianchi et al., 2006). Fourth, in the time that they have with their children, parents are making a priority of intensive activities such as playing or reading to them, rather than just monitoring them (Bittman, Craig, & Folbre, 2004). Overall, family life would seem to be a bit more hectic for parents, with less time for leisure and household tasks. But as a result, children's time apart from parents has not increased as much as labor force trends would lead one to expect.

The Consequences of Nonparental Care More than 60 percent of all preschool-aged children today spend some time each week in child care (U.S. Bureau of the Census, 2013). Some observers worry that nonparental child care is inferior to the care parents can provide. Several older studies suggested that if mothers returned to paid work while their children were still in the first year or two of life, their children's development could suffer (e.g., Brooks-Gunn, Han, & Waldfogel, 2002). But newer studies are showing that mothers' employment while their children are young is not harmful (Lombardi & Coley, 2014, 2017). Perhaps changes such as more readily available child care options and greater involvement of fathers in caring for young children have reduced the negative effects found in the older studies. The long-term effects of mothers' early employment on their children also seems modest (Vandell et al. 2010). The best conclusion is that children do not experience substantially more cognitive or emotional problems later in childhood if their mothers return to work quickly after their births.

Quick Review

- Working parents spend nearly as much time with their children as do nonemployed parents.
- Working parents cut back on other uses of time such as housework and leisure.
- The effects on children's development of mothers returning to work in the early years of their lives appear to be modest.

The Well-Being of American Children

Now that we have studied what parents should do for their children and how social changes may have aided or hindered parents' tasks, we are ready to confront what is probably the most critical question to be asked about the public family: Has the well-being of children declined? This is a question that, in recent years, has often been posed and answered affirmatively by national commissions, politicians, and editorial writers. Yet the American public believes that children's well-being is worse than it actually is. Half or more of participants in national surveys in 2002 and 2003 estimated that at least 30 percent of children live in poverty (almost twice the true figure at the time), that about 20 percent have no health insurance (the true figure was about 12 percent), and that the number of children on welfare has increased or stayed the same since the welfare laws were changed in 1996 (the true number has dropped sharply) (Guzman, Lippman, Moore, & O'Hare, 2003). (We should also examine how children's well-being is studied by sociologists and other participants in this debate: See *How Do Sociologists Know What They Know?*: Measuring the Well-Being of Children.) The answer to the question of how children are doing depends on which children you are talking about.

How Do Sociologists Know What They Know?

Measuring the Well-Being of Children

Concern about the well-being of American children has created a demand by policy-makers, journalists, and other observers for better information about the well-being of children. Until the 1980s, the federal government collected relatively little information about children. Family sociologists were focused on the conjugal family of husband, wife, and children—but paid little attention to the children themselves. The rise in divorce and in childbearing outside of marriage in the 1960s and 1970s increased the demand for better knowledge about the consequences for children, and academic researchers and government agencies began to respond.

The first questions they had to consider were the following: How do you measure children's well-being in the large-scale surveys that the federal government tends to fund and that sociologists study? And what aspects of children's lives are important for well-being? The most obvious areas are basic needs such as a child's standard of living and health. The Bureau of the Census gathers information annually about income levels and poverty of households with children. In 1981, the government fielded the first child health supplement to the National Health Interview Survey, a large, ongoing survey of Americans' health. The data from these and other government surveys are made available (with names and addresses deleted to ensure confidentiality) to sociologists who wish to analyze them.

But these indicators tell only part of the story. Sociologists and psychologists are interested in two other important domains: *cognitive* indicators of what children are learning and *socioemotional* indicators of how they are feeling and behaving. Cognitive indicators are relatively straightforward; sociologists studying random samples of children and their families can ask permission to talk to children's teachers and to obtain test scores from their schools. For pre-school-aged children, of course, there are no test scores to obtain. As a result, survey researchers interested in young children sometimes administer short tests directly to them. For example, a child might be shown a progressively more difficult series of pictures and asked to identify each one.

More difficult to measure are the socioemotional aspects of well-being. For younger children, the best strategy for survey researchers is to ask parents questions about their children's behavior. Older children can be asked directly about problematic behavior.

For instance, since 1975 a federally funded national study, Monitoring the Future, has annually asked nationwide samples of 8th-, 10th-, and 12th-graders about drug use. To be sure, we cannot determine whether students are being fully truthful in their responses. (See *How Do Sociologists Know What They Know?* Asking about Sensitive Behavior, page 156) But even so, changes in their responses from year to year are likely to represent real increases or decreases. For example, the surveys showed that the percentage of twelfth graders who had used marijuana in the past year declined to a low point of 21.9 percent in 1992 but has risen since then to 37.1 percent in 2017 (Miech, Johnston, O'Malley, Bachman, Schulenberg, & Patrick, 2018).

Demographer Kenneth Land and his colleagues have developed an "index of child well-being," a number they have calculated for each year from 1975 to 2013. They combine 28 statistical indicators in domains such as health, economic well-being, safety/behavioral concerns, and emotional/spiritual well-being. They state that their index declined through 1993 but increased slightly since then and was 3 percent higher in 2013 than in 1975, suggesting very modest progress (Land, 2014). But not everyone agrees that it's possible to derive a single number that adequately reflects a condition as complex as children's well-being.

Overall, far more information on children's well-being is available from survey research today, compared with two decades ago. In recent years, interest in indicators of children's well-being has been so high that federal government agencies have coordinated their data gathering. Their annual compendium, "America's Children: Key National Indicators of Well-Being," (Federal Interagency Forum on Child and Family Statistics, 2018) provides very useful information for sociologists and for students writing papers on the well-being of children and is available on the Internet. I have used their compendium to construct Figure 9.2 in this chapter.

Ask Yourself

1. Have you ever responded to a survey of children's well-being? If so, were you truthful in your responses?
2. Which measures of children's well-being—income and health, cognitive achievement, or socioemotional status—do you think are most critical? Explain your viewpoint.

WHICH CHILDREN?

Over the past few decades, the fortunes of children have diverged, with some doing better while some are doing worse. Figure 9.2 shows what this trend has meant for children over the period from 1980 to 2016. It divides all children into five groups, depending on how their family's income compares to the federal poverty line (which was $20,160 for a family of three in 2016):

Extreme poverty: Less than 50 percent of the poverty line.

Below poverty, but above extreme poverty: Between 50 and 99 percent of the poverty line.

Low income: Between 100 and 199 percent of the poverty line.

Medium income: Between 200 and 399 percent of the poverty line.

High income: 400 percent or more of the poverty line.

The chart stacks these five groups of families one on top of the other like a five-layer cake so that the height equals 100 percent of all families in every year. What changes from year to year is the thickness of each layer of the cake, which represents the proportion of children in each group.

You can see that the proportion of children in the high-income group grew markedly. In 1980, 17 percent of children lived in high-income families. The thickness of the top layer increased over time, so that by 2016, 31.8 percent lived in high-income families. What this means is that an increasing share of all children were living in families that were prospering economically, which is good news. But a further look at the chart shows that the medium-income group of children contracted sharply: whereas it included 41 percent of all children in 1980, it included 29 percent in 2016. In contrast, the size of the below poverty or extreme poverty groups remained about the same, which is bad news. In sum, during this 33-year period, the proportion of well-off children increased while children in low-to-middle-income families were squeezed, and the proportion of children in poverty or extreme poverty remained steady.

DIVERGING DESTINIES

Like the diverging demographics of families in different status groups that were described in Chapter 4, the trends in well-being we have reviewed suggest what one observer called "diverging destinies" for America's children (McLanahan &

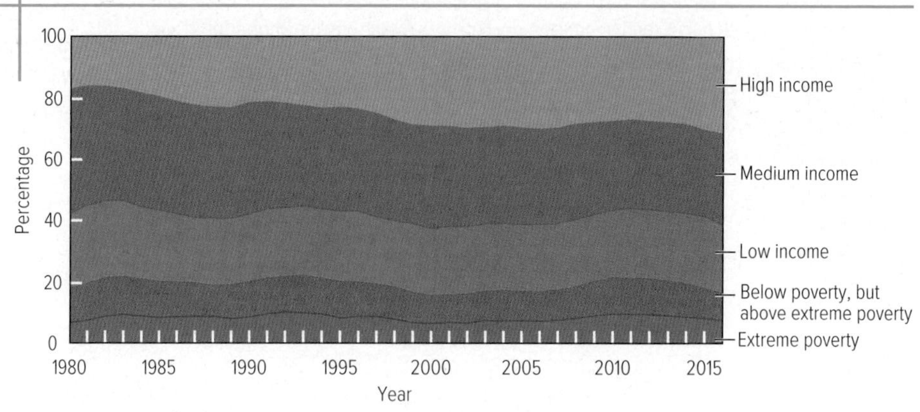

FIGURE 9.2
Percentage of U.S. children who were living in "extreme poverty," "below poverty but above extreme poverty," "low income," "medium income," and "high income" families, 1980–2016. (*Source:* Federal Interagency Forum on Child and Family Statistics, 2018)

Jacobson, 2015). In the first half of the twentieth century, most children, rich or poor, white or black, lived in two-parent families (Tolnay, 2004). But since then, as divorce and childbearing outside of marriage increased, the living arrangements of children have diverged by income. Most of the decline in two-parent families took place among people with less education and lower incomes. In 1960 about one-fourth of all poor families were headed by single mothers; but by the 2000s about half were headed by single mothers. In addition, by the end of the century, more than half of the wealthier families had two earners, reflecting the movement of married women into the workforce (Levy, 1998).

Poor and Wealthy Children As a result of these trends, you can tell more about a child's standard of living by the type of family he or she is living in than was the case a half-century ago. Children whose families are prosperous–those who are in the top layer of Figure 9.2–usually live with two parents, both of whom work outside the home. The incomes of two-parent, two-earner families have grown much more than the incomes of other kinds of families (U.S. Bureau of the Census, 2018b). Children who are poor–those in the bottom two layers–are more likely to live with one parent. To the extent that living in a single-parent family makes it more difficult to escape from poverty, poor children may be experiencing hardships for a longer period of their lives. Moreover, there are strong racial and ethnic differences in whether children are well-off or not. Hispanic and African American children are underrepresented in the top, "high income" layer of Figure 9.2; and as one moves downs the layers, the percentages of Hispanics and African Americans generally rise.

Children in the Middle It is among children from families in the narrowing middle of Figure 9.2, neither poor nor affluent, many of which have been hard-pressed to maintain their standard of living, that a judgment about trends in well-being is most difficult. My own sense is that, on average, the children in the middle have experienced a moderate downward drift in well-being. They are less likely to live with two parents than in the past, and their families have become less stable and more complex. They have grown up during a period of economic belt tightening by the working and middle classes. Even a moderate deterioration in well-being among children in the middle is cause for concern to those who believe in the idea of progress–the idea that our society ought to be improving the lives of its citizens rather than backsliding. It also raises the question of whether children have a basic right to an upbringing that meets high standards. (See *Families and Public Policy:* Do Children Have Rights?) I think that changes in the family contributed to this deterioration, but I'm not convinced the family was the major actor. The family itself was acted upon by larger forces such as the globalization of the economy and a cultural shift toward ever-greater individualism. Yet parents are not merely passively acted on by social forces; they must be assigned some responsibility for the consequences of their actions, such as getting divorced and having children in short-term cohabiting unions.

And although I am skeptical of those who claim that there is a pervasive crisis in the well-being of American children, I do think that a real crisis is occurring among children at the bottom of the income distribution. Their share of the population has not decreased significantly in decades. They are the most likely group to have unstable and complex families and to have parents who did not graduate from high school. They also have a higher concentration of Hispanics and African Americans. The families of children such as these are continually struggling to keep their heads above water without much success.

Families and Public Policy

Do Children Have Rights?

In 1989, the United Nations established the Convention on the Rights of the Child, an international treaty designed to protect children and ensure their basic needs (Office of the United Nations High Commissioner for Human Rights, 2016). The treaty requires states to take steps to protect the economic, social, and cultural rights of children. Only two countries in the world have not ratified the treaty: Somalia and the United States.

According to the Constitution, international treaties must be approved by a two-thirds majority of the United States Senate, and opposition in the Senate has been strong enough to prevent the Convention from being approved. Some Americans believe that the treaty undermines the authority of parents over their children, which they see as a basic, nonnegotiable principle. The Convention does say that all nations "shall respect the responsibilities, rights and duties of parents . . . to provide, in a manner consistent with the evolving capacities of the child, appropriate direction and guidance." But it's that clause, "in a manner consistent with the evolving capacities of the child," that makes opponents uneasy. It seems to suggest that there are limits on parental authority, especially among pre-teens and adolescents.

In a report critical of the Convention, Marshall and Smith (2006) cited Article 13 as an example of how it infringes on parental rights and authority:

> *The child shall have the right to freedom of expression; this right shall include freedom to seek, receive and impart information and ideas of all kinds, regardless of frontiers, either orally, in writing or in print, in the form of art, or through any other media of the child's choice.*

Critics would argue that parents should have the authority to monitor and restrict the information that their children, even their teenagers, receive. For instance, parents may block certain television channels from being viewed in their homes. Supporters of the treaty would argue that it does not prevent parents from making restrictions that are in the broad interests of their children, such as blocking sexually explicit cable channels or pornographic Web sites. Yet the wording of the Article suggests to some that children may surf the Internet as they please.

The fact is that nations and groups differ on what restrictions should be placed on children. For example, some poor nations would disagree with the American law that children have the right to go to school to age 16. Even within a particular society there are disagreements. In the United States, for instance, many schools distribute contraceptives to students without their parents' consent, much to the dismay of some parents. More controversially, a pregnant teenager may obtain an abortion without her parents' permission in most of the nation. Many parents approve of these measures, but a minority do not.

Some advocates for children's rights argue that children should have the right not only to have their interests protected (adequate food, shelter, education, etc.) but also to voice opinions over how they are treated. Article 12 says:

> *States Parties shall assure to the child who is capable of forming his or her own views the right to express those views freely in all matters affecting the child, the views of the child being given due weight in accordance with the age and maturity of the child.*

Some international agencies have added children's empowerment and participation to their goals for assisting families. These goals are generally not considered by American organizations. Nevertheless, older children in the United States are often allowed to testify in contested divorce cases as to which parent they wish to reside with. Exactly how old the children have to be in order that their opinions count is a matter of debate.

The United Nations subsequently added two optional protocols to the Convention, covering matters that are almost universally condemned: conscripting children into the military and trafficking in child prostitution and child pornography. The United States did sign on to these addenda. But opposition to the main body of the treaty remains strong.

Ask Yourself

1. What restrictions did you have on your rights growing up?
2. At what age should children be granted a say in matters such as which parent they would prefer to reside with after a divorce?

Quick Review

- Over the past few decades, the proportion of children in economically prosperous families has increased.
- Over the same period, the proportion in poverty or extreme poverty has remained about the same.
- Children at the top are probably doing better than in the recent past; children at the bottom are doing worse.
- Trends in the well-being of children in the narrowing middle are harder to assess; they may have experienced a moderate decline in well-being.

Looking Back

1. **What are the main goals in socializing children and how do parents differ in the way they fulfill their role?** By socializing their children, parents equip them to function well in society. Among other things, parents teach children norms (widely accepted rules about how to behave) and values (goals and principles that are held in high esteem in a society). Parents provide both material and emotional support to their children and exercise control over them. A combination of high levels of emotional support and consistent, moderate discipline, called an authoritative parenting style, seems to produce children who are most socially competent, although it may be less applicable to minority-group families.

2. **How does the socialization of children vary by ethnicity, class, gender, and the sexual orientation of parents?** In racial and ethnic groups such as African Americans and Asian Americans, parents rely more on strong discipline than white parents. Working-class parents stress obedience and conformity more than middle-class parents; conversely, middle-class parents stress autonomy and self-direction more than working-class parents. Members of each social class emphasize values that are consistent with the kinds of jobs they perform. Parents also socialize boys and girls differently, so that any preexisting differences are exaggerated in childhood and adult behavior. Evidence on children who grow up with LGBTQ parents from birth suggests that they do not differ much from children with heterosexual parents.

3. **What barriers must parents overcome in socializing their children?** Unemployment and poverty can affect the way parents act toward each other and toward their children. Job loss or low earnings can cause a parent to become depressed and angry; fathers in these situations are likely to have angry, explosive exchanges with their wives and children. Family instability and complexity could affect children because of exposure to types of household that may increase negative outcomes such as behavior problems or by exposure to the difficulties of adjusting to the frequent movements of parents and parents' partners into and out of the home. Immigrant parents may have special difficulties if they are not authorized to be in the United States. Mass incarceration is affecting parenting among African Americans. There is evidence of small long-term effects of nonparental child care.

4. **How much time do parents and children spend together?** While it seems as though parents should be spending less time with their children because so many mothers have entered the paid workforce over the past half-century, parents are spending nearly as much time with children as they did several decades ago. They accomplish this feat in several ways including doing less housework and cutting back on leisure time. The effects of mothers returning to work while their children are young are modest.

5. **How has the well-being of American children changed over time?** Comparisons between the "average" child today and the "average" child a few decades ago can be

misleading. Economic inequality has increased since the early 1970s: The percentage of children at the top of the income ladder has risen, whereas the middle group has decreased in size, and the bottom group has stayed the same size. The growing proportion of children who live in relatively wealthy settings tends to be doing well. Children in the poorest families tend not to be doing well. Children in the shrinking middle group may have suffered a moderate reduction in well-being over the past few decades.

Study Questions

1. Why might authoritative parenting be more effective in some social settings than in others?
2. Why might adoption be a "devalued status"?
3. In what ways might we expect children in LGBTQ families to be similar to children in heterosexual families? In what ways might we expect them to be different?
4. How does a father's unemployment change the relationships among parents and children in a household?
5. How might experiencing several parents and parents' partners enter and exit the home affect children?
6. How does having a father in prison affect family life?
7. Why is it too simplistic to conclude, as some observers have, that children's well-being has declined among all social classes and races/ethnicities in recent decades?

Key Terms

androgynous behavior 240
authoritarian style (of parenting) 237
authoritative style (of parenting) 237
mass incarceration 250
multipartner fertility 249
norm 238
permissive style (of parenting) 237
value 238

Thinking about Families

The Public Family	The Private Family
What are the crucial duties society expects of parents in raising their children?	**What kind of satisfaction do parents get from raising children?**

References

Aber, J. L., Jones, S., & Cohen, J. (2000). The impact of poverty on the mental health and development of very young children. In C. H. Zeanah (Ed.), *Handbook of infant mental health, second edition.* (pp. 113–128). New York: Guilford Press.

Amato, P. R., & Gilbreth, J. G. (1999). Non-resistant fathers and children's wellbeing. *Journal of Marriage and the Family, 61*, 557–573.

Andersson, G., Thomson, E., & Duntava, A. (2017). Life-table representations of family dynamics in the 21st century. *Demographic Research, 37*(Article 35), 1081–1230.

Astone, N. M., & McLanahan, S. S. (1991). Family structure, parental practices, and high school completion. *American Sociological Review, 56,* 309–320.

Baumrind, D. (1971). Current patterns of parental authority. *Developmental Psychology Monographs, vol. 4, no. 1, pt. 2.*

Berger Cardoso, J., Scott, J. L., Faulkner, M., & Barros Lane, L. (2018). Parenting in the context of deportation risk. *Journal of Marriage and Family, 80*(2), 301–316.

Bianchi, S. M., Robinson, J. P., & Milkie, M. A. (2006). *Changing rhythms of American family life.* New York: Russell Sage Foundation.

Bittman, M., Craig, L., & Folbre, N. (2004). Packaging care: What happens when children receive nonparental care? In N. Folbre & M. Bittman (Eds.), *Family time: The social organization of care* (pp. 134–151). London: Routledge.

Booth, C. L., Clarke-Stewart, A., Vandell, D. L., McCartney, K., & Owen, M. T. (2002). Child-care usage and mother-infant quality time. *Journal of Marriage and Family, 64,* 16–26.

Brewster, K. L., Tillman, K. H., & Jokinen-Gordon, H. (2014). Demographic characteristics of lesbian parents in the United States. *Population Research and Policy Review, 33*(4), 503–526.

Brodzinsky, D. M., Schechter, M. D., & Marantz, R. (1992). *Being adopted: The lifelong search for self.* New York: Doubleday.

Bronte-Tinkew, J., Moore, K., & Carrano, J. (2006). The father-child relationship, parenting styles, and adolescent risk behaviors in intact families. *Journal of Family Issues, 27,* 850–881.

Brooks–Gunn, J., Han, W. J., & Waldfogel, J. (2002). Maternal employment and child cognitive outcomes in the first three years of life: The NICHD study of early child care. *Child Development, 73*(4), 1052–1072.

Brown, S. L. (2006). Family structure transitions and adolescent well-being. *Demography, 43,* 447–461. Cabrera, N. J., Tamis-LeMonda, C. S., Bradley, R. H., Hofferth, S., & Lamb, M. E. (2000). Fatherhood in the twenty-first century. *Child Development, 71,* 127–136.

Carlson, M. J., & Corcoran, M. E. (2001). Family structure and children's behavioral and cognitive outcomes. *Journal of Marriage and the Family, 63,* 779–792.

Carlson, M. J., & Furstenberg, F. F., Jr. (2006). The prevalence and correlates of multipartnered fertility among urban U.S. Parents. *Journal of Marriage and Family, 68,* 718–732.

Cavanagh, S. E., & Huston, A. C. (2006). Family instability and children's early problem behavior. *Social Forces, 85*(1), 551–581.

Cavanagh, S. E., & Huston, A. C. (2008). The timing of family instability and children's well-being. *Journal of Marriage and Family, 70,* 1258–1270.

Chao, R. (1994). Beyond parental control and authorization parenting style: Understanding Chinese parenting through the cultural norm of training. *Child Development, 65,* 1111–1119.

Cherlin, A. J. (2009). *The marriage-go-round: The state of marriage and the family in America today.* New York: Alfred A. Knopf.

Child Trends. (2012). Adopted children. Retrieved November 19, 2018, from https://www.childtrends.org/wpcontent/uploads/2012/08/113_Adopted_Children-1.pdf

Duncan, G. J., & Brooks-Gunn, J. (1997). Income effects across the life span: Integration and interpretation. In G. J. Duncan & J. Brooks-Dunn (Eds.), *The consequences of growing up poor* (pp. 596–610). New York: Russell Sage Foundation.

Dunifon, R., & Kowaleski-Jones, L. (2002). Who's in the house? Race differences in cohabitation, single parenthood, and child development. *Child Development, 73,* 1249–1264.

Dunifon, R., & Kowaleski-Jones, L. (2002). Who's in the house? Race differences in cohabitation, single parenthood, and child development. *Child Development, 73,* 1249–1264.

Edin, K., & Kissane, R. J. (2010). Poverty and the American family: A decade in review. *Journal of Marriage and Family, 72,* 460–479.

Elder, G. H. J., Conger, R. D., Foster, M. E., & Ardelt, M. (1992). Families under economic pressure. *Journal of Family Issues, 13,* 5–37.

Evans, G. W., Chen, E., Miller, G., & Seeman, T. (2012). How poverty gets under the skin: A life course perspective. In V. Malholms & R. King (Eds.), *The Oxford handbook of poverty and child development* (pp. In press). New York: Oxford University Press. Fisher, A. P. (2003). Still "not quite as good as having your own"? Toward a sociology of adoption. *Annual Review of Sociology, 29,* 335–361.

Federal Interagency Forum and Child and Family Statistics. (2018). America's children: Key national indicators of well-being, 2018. Retrieved November 18, 2018, from https://www.childstats.gov/americaschildren/poverty.asp

Fomby, P., & Cherlin, A. J. (2007). Family instability and child well-being. *American Sociological Review, 72*(2), 181–204.

Fomby, P., & Mollborn, S. (2017). Ecological instability and children's classroom behavior in kindergarten. *Demography, 54,* 1627–1651.

Fomby, P., & Osborne, C. (2017). Family instability, multipartner fertility, and behavior in middle childhood. *Journal of Marriage and Family, 79*(February), 75–93.

Gates, G. J. (2013). LGBT parenting in the United States. *Williams Institute.* Retrieved January 5, 2016, from http://williamsinstitute.law.ucla.edu/wp-content/uploads/LGBT-Parenting.pdf

Gates, G. J. (2014). LGB families and relationships: Analyses of the 2013 national health interview survey *Williams Institute* Retrieved January 5, 2016, from http://williamsinstitute.law.ucla.edu/wp-content/uploads/lgb-families-nhis-sep-2014.pdf

Gottman, J. M. (1998). Toward a process model of men in marriages and families. In A. Booth & A. C. Crouter (Eds.), *Men in families: When do they get involved? What difference does it make?* (pp. 149–192). Mahwah, NJ: Lawrence Erlbaum Associates.

Guzman, L., Lippman, L., Moore, K. A., & O'Hare, W. (2003). How are children doing: The mismatch between public perception and statistical reality. Washington, DC: Child Trends.

Guzzo, K. B. (2014). New partners, more kids: Multiplepartner fertility in the United States. *Annals of the American Academy of Political and Social Science, 654*(1), 66–86.

Guzzo, K. B., & Furstenberg, F. F. (2007a). Multipartnered fertility among American men. *Demography, 44,* 583–601.

Guzzo, K. B., & Furstenberg, F. F. J. (2007b). Multipartnered fertility among young women with a nonmarital first birth: Prevalence and risk factors. *Perspectives on Sexual and Reproductive Health, 39,* 29–38.

Haney, L. (2018). Incarcerated fatherhood: The entanglements of child support debt and mass imprisonment. *American Journal of Sociology, 124*(1), 1–48.

Harknett, K., & Knab, J. (2007). More kin, less support: Multipartnered fertility and perceived support among mothers. *Journal of Marriage and Family, 69,* 237–253.

Hays, S. (1996). *The cultural contradictions of motherhood.* New Haven: Yale University Press.

Heuveline, P., Timberlake, J. M., & Furstenberg, F. F., Jr. (2003). Shifting childrearing to single mothers: Results from 17 Western countries. *Population and Development Review, 29*(1), 47–71.

Jackson-Newsom, J., Buchanan, C. M., & McDonald, R. M. (2008). Parenting and perceived maternal warmth in European American and African American adolescents. *Journal of Marriage and Family, 70,* 62–75.

Kohn, M. L. (1969). *Class and conformity: A study in values.* Homewood, IL: Dorsey Press.

Kohn, M. L., & Schooler, C. (1978). The reciprocal effects of the substantive complexity of work and intellectual flexibility: A longitudinal assessment. *American Journal of Sociology, 84,* 24–52.

Lansford, J. E., Deater-Deckard, K., Dodge, K. A., Bates, J. E., & Pettit, G. S. (2004). Ethnic differences in the link between physical discipline and later adolescent externalizing behaviors. *Journal of Child Psychology and Psychiatry, 45,* 801–812.

Lareau, A. (2011). *Unequal childhoods: Class, race, and family life, second edition.* Berkeley: University of California Press.

Levy, F. (1998). *The new dollars and dreams: American incomes and economic change.* New York: Russell Sage Foundation.

Liker, J. K., & Elder, G. H. Jr. (1983). Economic hardship and marital relations in the 1930's. *American Sociological Review, 48,* 343–359.

Lombardi, C. M., & Coley, R. L. (2014). Early maternal employment and children's school readiness in contemporary families. *Developmental Psychology, 50*(8), 2071.

Lombardi, C. M., & Coley, R. L. (2017). Early maternal employment and children's academic and behavioral skills in Australia and the United Kingdom. *Child Development, 88*(1), 263–281.

Manning, W. D., Fettro, M. N., & Lamidi, E. (2014). Child well-being in same-sex parent families: Review of research prepared for American Sociological Association amicus brief. *Population Research and Policy Review, 33*(4), 485–502.

Marshall, J., & Smith, G. V. (2006). Human rights and social issues at the U.N.: A guide for U.S. Policymakers. Retrieved January 5, 2016, from http://www.heritage.org/Research/WorldwideFreedom/bg1965.cfm

Marsiglio, W., Amato, P. R., Day, R. D., & Lamb, M. E. (2000). Scholarship on fatherhood in the 1990s and beyond. *Journal of Marriage and the Family, 62,* 1173–1191.

McLanahan, S., & Jacobsen, W. (2015). Diverging destinies revisited. In P. R. Amato, A. Booth, S. M. McHale, & J. Van Hook (Eds.), *Families in an era of increasing inequality* (pp. 3–23). Dordrecht: Springer.

McLoyd, V. C., Cauce, A. M., Takeuchi, D., & Wilson, L. (2000). Marital processes and parental socialization in families of color: A decade review of research. *Journal of Marriage and the Family, 62,* 1070–1093.

McLoyd, V. C., Kaplan, R., Hardaway, C. R., & Wood, D. (2007). Does endorsement of physical discipline matter? Assessing moderating influences on the maternal and child psychological correlates of physical discipline in African American families. *Journal of Family Psychology, 21,* 162–175.

Miech, R. A., Johnston, L. D., O'Malley, P. M., Bachman, J. G., Schulenberg, J. E., & Patrick, M. E. (2018). Monitoring the future national survey results on drug use, 1975–2017: Volume i, secondary school students. Retrieved November 19, 2018, from http://monitoringthefuture.org//pubs/monographs/mtf-vol1_2017.pdf

Milkie, M. A., Nomaguchi, K. M., & Denny, K. (2015). Does the amount of time mothers spend with children or adolescents matter? *Journal of Marriage and Family, 77*(April), 355–372.

Mullainathan, S., & Shafir, E. (2013). *Scarcity: Why having too little means so much.* New York: Macmillan.

Noah, A. J., & Landale, N. S. (2018). Parenting strain among Mexican-origin mothers: Differences by parental legal status and neighborhood. *Journal of Marriage and Family, 80*(April), 317–333.

Obergefell v. Hodges, 576 (U.S. 2015).

Office of the United Nations High Commissioner for Human Rights. (2016). Convention on the rights of the child. Retrieved January 5, 2016, from http://www.ohchr.org/en/professionalinterest/pages/crc.aspx

Osborne, C., & McLanahan, S. (2007). Partnership instability and child well-being. *Journal of Marriage and Family, 69,* 1065–1083.

Painter-Brick, C. (Ed.). (1998). *Biosocial perspectives on children.* Cambridge: Cambridge University Press.

Patterson, C. J. (2000). Family relationships of lesbians and gay men. *Journal of Marriage and Family, 62,* 1052–1069.

Pettit, B. (2012). *Invisible men: Mass incarceration and the myth of black progress.* New York: Russell Sage Foundation.

Pew Research Center. (2017). Amid decline in international adoptions to U.S., boys outnumber girls for the first time. Retrieved November 17, 2018, from http://www.pewresearch.org/fact-tank/2017/10/17/amid-decline-in-international-adoptions-to-u-s-boys-outnumber-girls-for-the-first-time/

Pleck, J. H. (2007). Why could father involvement benefit children? Theoretical perspectives. *Applied Developmental Science 11,* 196–202.

Price, R. H., Choi, J. N., & Vinokur, A. D. (2002). Links in the chain of adversity following job loss: How financial strain and loss of personal control lead to depression, impaired functioning, and poor health. *Journal of Occupational Health Psychology, 7,* 302–312.

Pugh, A. J. (2009). *Longing and belonging: Parents, children, and the consumer culture.* Berkeley: University of California Press.

Raley, R. K., Frisco, M. L., & Wildsmith, E. (2005). Maternal cohabitation and educational success. *Sociology of Education* (78), 144–164.

Rothbaum, F., Kakinuma, M., Nagaoka, R., & Azuma, H. (2007). Attachment and AMAE: Parent—child closeness in the United States and Japan. *Journal of Cross-Cultural Psychology, 38,* 465–486.

Smith, T. W., Davern, M., Freese, J., & Morgan, S. L. (2019). General social surveys, 1972-2018. [machine readable data file.]. Chicago: National Opinion Research Center.

Sobolewski, J. M., & King, V. (2005). The importance of the coparental relationship for nonresident fathers' ties to children. *Journal of Marriage and Family, 67,* 1196–1212.

Streib, J. (2018). Class, culture, and downward mobility. *Poetics, 69,* in press.

Tamis-LeMonda, C. S., Shannon, J. D., Cabrera, N. J., & Lamb, M. E. (2004). Fathers and mothers at play with their 2- and 3- year-olds: Contributions to language and cognitive development. *Child Development, 75,* 1806–1820.

Tolnay, S. E. (2004). The living arrangements of African American and immigrant children, 1880–2000. *Journal of Family History, 29,* 421–445.

U.S. Bureau of the Census. (2013). Who's minding the kids? Child care arrangements: Spring 2011. *Household Economics Studies P70-135.* Retrieved January 7, 2016, from http://www.census.gov/prod/2013pubs/p70–135.pdf

U.S. Bureau of the Census. (2018a). Table F2. Family households, by type, age of own children, and educational attainment of householder: 2018. Retrieved November 17, 2018, from https://www2.census.gov/programs-surveys/demo/tables/families/2018/cps-2018/tabf2-all.xls

U.S. Bureau of the Census. (2018b). Table F-13. Work experience of husband and wife–all married-couple families by median and mean income: 1976 to 2014. Retrieved November 18, 2018, from https://www2.census.gov/programs-surveys/cps/tables/time-series/historical-income-families/f13ar.xls

U.S. Bureau of Justice Statistics. (2008). Parents in prison and their minor children. *NCJ 222984.* Retrieved February 7, 2014, from http://www.bjs.gov/content/pub/pdf/pptmc.pdf

U.S. Department of Homeland Security. (2018). Yearbook of immigration statistics 2017. Retrieved November 17, 2018, from https://www.dhs.gov/immigration-statistics/yearbook/2017

U.S. National Center for Health Statistics. (1999). Adoption, adoption seeking, and relinquishment for adoption in the United States. Advance Data, Number 306. Retrieved October 16, 2003, from http://www.cdc.gov/nchs/data/ad/ad306.pdf

Vandell, D. L., Belsky, J., Burchinal, M., Stenberg, L., Vandergrift, N., & NICHD Early Child Care Research Network. (2010). Do effects of early child care extend to age 15 years? Results from the NICHD study of early child care and youth development. *Child Development, 81,* 737–756.

Vandivere, S., Malm, K., & Radel, L. (2009). *Adoption USA: A chartbook based on the 2007 national survey of adoptive parents.* Washington DC: U.S. Department of Health and Human Services, Office of the Assistant Secretary for Planning and Evaluation.

Waldfogel, J. (2016). How important is parental time? It depends: Comment on Milkie, Nomaguchi, and Denny (2015). Waldfogel, J. (2016). How important is parental time? It depends: Comment on Milkie, Nomaguchi, and Denny (2015). *Journal of Marriage and Family, 78*(February), 266–269.

Western, B., & Smith, N. (2018). Formerly incarcerated parents and their children. *Demography, 55*(3), 823–847.

Wilcox, W. B. (1998). Conservative Protestant childrearing: Authoritarian or authoritative? *American Sociological Review, 63,* 796–809.

Wilcox, W. B. (2004). *Soft patriarchs, new men: How Christianity shapes fathers and husbands.* Chicago: University of Chicago Press.

Wildeman, C. (2010). Paternal incarceration and children's physically aggressive behaviors: Evidence from the fragile families and child wellbeing study. *Social Forces, 89,* 285–310.

Wu, H. (2017). Trends in births to single and cohabiting mothers, 1980–2014. *Family Profiles, FP-17-04, National Center for Family and Marriage Research.* Retrieved July 23, 2018, from https://www.bgsu.edu/ncfmr/resources/data/family-profiles/wu-trends-births-single-cohabiting-mothers-fp-17-04.html

Yang, A. S. (1997). Trends: Attitudes toward homosexuality. *Public Opinion Quarterly, 61*(3), 477–507.

Yoshikawa, H., & Kholoptseva, J. (2013). Unauthorized immigrant parents and their children's development. Retrieved November 17, 2018, from http://observatoriocolef.org/_admin/documentos/childrenspdf.pdf

Zill, N., & Wilcox, W. B. (2018). The adoptive difference: New evidence in how adopted children perform in school. Retrieved November 17, 2018, from https://ifstudies.org/blog/the-adoptive-difference-new-evidence-onhow-adopted-children-perform-in-school

Chapter Ten

Older People and Their Families

Looking Forward

1. How has grandparenthood changed over the past century?
2. How much support do older adults provide to, and receive from, their kin?
3. Who cares for the frail aged?
4. Are older adults isolated from their kin?
5. What sources of tension exist in intergenerational relations?

In early 2005, a reporter for *The New York Times* called me to say that she was working on a story about grandparents and grandchildren in an age of high divorce and remarriage rates. Some grandchildren, she said, had more than four grandparents because one or more grandparents had divorced and remarried, bringing a stepgrandparent into the family. Did I know anything about this? Yes, I replied, not only because I study families, but also because I was one of eight grandparents of two young children. All four of their biological grandparents had divorced and remarried before they were born. Their maternal grandmother had married me. I was technically one of their stepgrandparents, but that sociological distinction was lost on them. They eagerly accepted the attention and affection of all eight: Grandma Peach, Grandma Linda, Oma (German for granny) Gerda, Nanny, Papa Andy (me), Papa Jay, Papa David, and Papa Dude. "The upside of all this is that children can have more grandparents who love them," the reporter quoted me as saying. "What message it will give them about marriage, I'm not quite sure" (Harmon, 2005).

In fact, the more-than-four grandparents phenomenon is so new that no one is sure what influence it may have on family life. For one thing, the divorce rate reached its current peak in 1980, so that the adults who drove its rise are only now aging into later life. (We will discuss divorce and remarriage in Chapter 12.) For another, people are living longer than they used to, making it possible for so many grandchildren to have so many grandparents. Until the last few generations, it was far less common for children to have four (let alone eight) living grandparents (Uhlenberg, 2004). Now grandparents are a dime a dozen, it seems, and many are active and independent.

This is not to say that all older adults are healthy and active. As the older population has expanded, so has the number of frail persons in need of care. The cost of the technology-driven health care provided to the increasing numbers of frail older adults has risen dramatically in recent years and has become a major problem for the nation. In addition, a disproportionately large part of the older population sits precariously just above the poverty line—not poor, but not by much. The incidence of poverty is greater for older women than for men, as we shall see.

This chapter will focus on the family lives of older adults—their interactions with spouses, children, grandchildren, and other relatives. As birthrates and death rates both decline, there are relatively more older people and relatively fewer younger people in the population. Whether society will be able to adequately meet the needs of the older population is an issue of great importance from the perspective of the public family. Spouses and relatives, as will be demonstrated, provide most of the assistance to older adults. Providing adequate assistance is likely to be more difficult now that the huge baby boom generation is retiring. Other changes in family life, such as the increase in women's work outside the home and the rise in divorce, may also affect the task of caring for the older population.

But it would be a mistake to think of older adults only as *recipients* of assistance because they are also important *providers* of assistance to children and grand children. Much of that assistance is provided on an as-needed basis: help with a down payment for a house, help when employed parents need child care, help when a daughter separates from her husband. In fact, over the past few decades, the percentage of grandchildren who are living in their grandparents' homes—sometimes without either parent present—has been increasing. We will examine more closely the assistance that older adults give to their families.

Although recent trends in the well-being of children are mixed, as noted in the previous chapter, recent trends in the well-being of the older population deserve at least two cheers. Programs for older people have been the one indisputable success of U.S. social welfare policy since the Great Depression. In fact, so successful have the programs been, and so far have both death rates and birthrates fallen, that most people fail to realize how new is the kind of life most older Americans are leading today—a longer, healthier life in which they provide substantial assistance to their family members. In order to understand what has happened, we need to begin by looking back in history.

The Modernization of Old Age

We tend to associate grandparents with old-fashioned families—the large, rural, three-generation kind. We have a nostalgic image of Grandma, Grandpa, Aunt Bess, Mom, Dad, and the kids sitting around the hearth, baking bread and telling stories. Correspondingly, many observers think that the role of older people in families has become less important since the farm gave way to the factory. According to this view, industrialization meant that older people could no longer teach their children and grandchildren the skills needed to make a living. Moreover, older people no longer controlled the resources—such as farmland—that gave them influence over the lives of the young. There is some truth to this perspective. But the historical facts suggest that grandparenthood—as a distinct and nearly universal stage of life—is a post–World War II phenomenon. To be sure, there have always been grandparents around, but never this many and never with so few of their own children left to raise.

MORTALITY DECLINE

The Statistics First of all, a century ago—even 50 years ago—far fewer people lived long enough to become grandparents. Much of the decline in adult **mortality** (the demographers' term for deaths in a population) from preindustrial levels occurred in the twentieth century. Only about 37 percent of all women born in 1870 survived to age 65; in contrast, about 77 percent of women born in 1930 reached age 65 (Uhlenberg, 1979, 1980). The number of years that the average 40-year-old woman could expect to live increased by 12 between 1900 and 2000, and for men it increased by 9. The trends for whites and nonwhites are similar, but in every decade the life expectancy of nonwhites has been lower than that of whites. In 2016, white

mortality the number of deaths in a population

babies had a life expectancy of 79 years, compared with 75 years for black babies (U.S. National Center for Health Statistics, 2018).

health span the number of years a person can expect to live while in good health.

A more difficult question is whether the gains in life expectancy that have been occurring recently have added healthy years or infirm years at the end of life. **Health span** is the term for the number of years that a person can expect to live while in good health. Although there has been some decline of mild disabilities among the older population in recent decades, the prevalence of serious disabilities (severe arthritis, physical limitations due to a stroke) has not declined as much. So while we continue to keep people alive for a longer and longer period of time–a major accomplishment in itself–we are not keeping them alive and fully healthy for much longer than was the case a few decades ago (Crimmins, 2015).

older population the group of people aged 65 years and over

The Social Consequences The decline in mortality during the twentieth and early twenty-first centuries has had two consequences. First, both women and men can expect to live much longer lives than was the case several decades ago. Second, women tend to outlive men. In 2016, the average female baby could expect to live 81 years, the average male baby 76 years (U.S. National Center for Health Statistics, 2018). A century ago the sex difference was much smaller because many more women died in childbirth. So it is the case today that (1) there are many more older people in the population than there used to be and (2) 56 percent of older people are women. Figure 10.1 shows the projected growth of the U.S. population aged 65 and over from 2020 to 2060. Under the usual convention, which I will follow, the **older population** is defined as all persons aged 65 and over. This is an arbitrary cut-off point that is used because until recently 65 was the age at which a person could retire and receive full Social Security benefits. Most 65-year-old persons are healthy and active, however, and the government has raised the retirement age to 67 for people born after 1960. Figure 10.1 shows that the older population is projected to increase by two-thirds by 2060 to about 95 million, compared to about 57 million in 2020. By 2045, when today's college students will be middle-aged, one in five Americans will be age 65 or over.

FIGURE 10.1
Projected population 65 years old and over in the United States: 2020 to 2060.
Source: U.S. Bureau of the Census, 2018a.

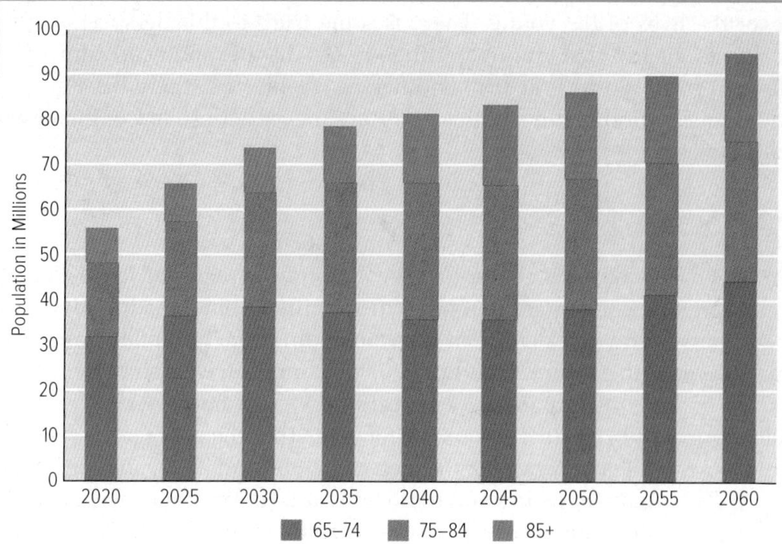

Moreover, the greatest growth will occur among the age 75 to 84 population (the middle section of each bar) and the 85 and over population (the top section). In other words, not only will the older population increase but it will itself become older and older, increasingly top-heavy with those in their seventies, eighties, and nineties. As the older population has expanded, **gerontologists** (social and biological scientists who specialize in the study of aging) invented the following terms to differentiate among the aged: **young-old** for those 65 to 74, **old-old** for those 75 to 84, and **oldest-old** for those 85 and over. Now they are talking about **centenarians**—people who are at least 100 years old. In 2010, there were about 50,000 centenarians, more than 80 percent of them women.

gerontologist a social/-biological scientist who specializes in the study of aging

young-old the group of older people 65 to 74 years of age

old-old the group of older people 75 to 84 years of age

oldest-old the group of older people 85 years of age and over

centenarian a person who is 100 years old or older

The sharp decline in mortality has caused a profound change in the relationship between older persons and their children and grandchildren. For the first time in history, as I noted at the beginning of this chapter, most adults live long enough to get to know most of their grandchildren, and most children have the opportunity to know most of their grandparents. The chances were only 50–50 that a child born at the beginning of the twentieth century would still have two living grandparents when he or she reached the age of 15. In contrast, the comparable chances rose to 9 in 10 for a 15-year-old in the 1970s (Uhlenberg, 1980). Currently, then, nearly all children have the opportunity to get to know at least two of their grandparents—and many get to know three or four (or even eight). But children born at the beginning of the century were not nearly as fortunate.

FERTILITY DECLINE

The decline in **fertility** (the demographer's term for births in a population) is the second reason why grandparenthood on a large scale is a recent phenomenon. As recently as the late 1800s, American women gave birth to more than four children, on average (Ryder, 1980). Many parents still were raising their younger children after their older children left home and married. Under these conditions, being a grandparent took a backseat to the day-to-day tasks of raising the children who were still at home. Today, in contrast, the birthrate is much lower, and parents are much more likely to be finished raising their children before any of their grandchildren are born. When a person becomes a grandparent now, there are fewer family roles competing for her or his time and attention. Grandparenthood is more of a separate stage of family life, unfettered by child care obligations—one that carries its own distinct identity. It was not always so.

fertility the number of births in a population

The combination of falling mortality and fertility rates has also altered the bonds of kinship that people have. Because birthrates have fallen, younger people tend to have fewer brothers and sisters than their parents and grandparents. So the horizontal bonds of kinship—those to relatives in the same generation as you—have tended to shrink. In contrast, lower mortality means that you have a much greater chance of having living parents well into your middle years than your parents or grandparents had. Vertical kinship ties—those to relatives in preceding or following generations—have tended to grow. The result is a kinship structure with growing links up and down the generations and withering links across them sometimes referred to as the "beanpole family" (Bengtson, 2001). A number of gerontologists have argued that lowered mortality rates are making the four- and five-generation family (e.g., my grandparents, my parents, me, my children, and my grandchildren) common. Yet although there are more of these linkages than there used to be, they are still the exception rather than the rule. A survey in the Boston area showed that at no stage of the adult life course up through age 70 did more than 20 percent of the respondents belong to more than a three-generation linkage of kin. And the number in five-generation linkages never topped 2 percent. At all ages, the most common generational depth was three. In young adulthood, the three generations were typically my grandparents, my parents, and me; in middle age the three were my parents, me, and my children; and at older ages they were me, my children, and my grandchildren.

The authors of the Boston study, Alice and Peter Rossi, conclude:

> *The truly remarkable demographic change over the twentieth century is the impact of increased longevity on the number of years when the majority of the population may still have at least one living parent. (Rossi & Rossi, 1990)*

The watershed age, they argue, is 50. Prior to age 50, there is little drop-off in the percentage of adults who have at least one living parent; at about age 50 the percentage declines sharply. And at about the same age, the percentage who have grandchildren increases sharply: The median age at becoming a grandparent in the United States is 49 for women and 52 for men (Leopold & Skopek, 2015). Thus, the lives of most parents and children now overlap by about 50 years. As the parent generation begin to lose their aging parents, they often begin to acquire grandchildren.

RISING STANDARD OF LIVING

Older people also have more money, on average, than they did a few decades ago. As recently as 1960, older Americans were an economically deprived group: 35 percent had incomes below the poverty line, compared with 22 percent of the total population. Now they have caught up: Their poverty rate of 9.2 percent for 2017 was lower than the rate for younger adults (U.S. Bureau of the Census, 2018b). The main reason they are no longer disadvantaged is Social Security, the federal government program that provides retirement benefits to persons aged 62 and over. Beginning in the 1950s and 1960s, Congress expanded Social Security coverage, so that nearly all workers, except some who are employed by government, are now covered. And since the 1960s, Congress has increased Social Security benefits far faster than the increase in the cost of living. As a result, the average monthly benefit has doubled in purchasing power since 1960, even after taking inflation into account. Today's older adults benefited from the society-wide rise in economic welfare in the 1950s and 1960s, when they were working; then, as they reached retirement, they benefited from the increase in Social Security benefits.

Variations by Age, Race, and Gender Still, there are sharp variations by age, race, and gender in the proportion of the older population who are poor. Overall, the old-old are more likely to be poor than those who are younger, older women are more likely to be poor than men, and African Americans and Hispanics are more likely to be poor than whites. For example, in 2017, 8.2 percent of persons aged 65 to 74 were poor, compared with 10.6 percent of those aged 75 and over. Only 7.5 percent of older men were poor, compared with 10.5 percent of women. And 7.0 percent of the non-Hispanic white aged were poor, compared with 19.3 percent of blacks and 17.0 percent of Hispanics (U.S. Bureau of the Census, 2018c).

Moreover, as I said earlier, a larger percentage of the older population have incomes that place them just above the poverty level. In 2017, 10.5 percent had incomes between 100 and 150 percent of the poverty level, compared with 7.2 percent of all adults under the age of 65 (U.S. Bureau of the Census, 2018c). This nearly poor group is in some ways more vulnerable to economic and health crises than the poor older population because they fall between the poor, who can qualify for additional public assistance, and the middle class, who can supplement their Social Security checks with savings and pensions. Although nearly all older persons are covered by **Medicare,** the government program of health insurance for the older population, Medicare pays for less than half of their health expenditures. Moreover, it pays nothing for nursing home care. Persons with incomes below the poverty line are also eligible for **Medicaid,** the government health insurance program for the poor of all ages, which does pay for nursing home costs. Middle-class older persons can afford to purchase private health insurance to pay the bills Medicare doesn't cover. But those with incomes that are just above the poverty line typically have too much income to qualify for Medicaid and too little to buy private insurance.

Medicare the government program of health insurance for all older people

Medicaid the government program of health insurance for people with incomes below the poverty line

It is also uncertain whether the Social Security and Medicare systems will provide the older population of the future with the same level of benefits that they would receive today. Low birthrates today mean that there will be fewer workers in a decade or two to pay Social Security taxes for the growing number of older people. In 2016, there were nearly four people of working age (20 to 64) for every older person; by 2035, according to current estimates, there will be less than three people of working age for every older person (U.S. Bureau of the Census, 2018a). In addition, the increases in the number of old-old and oldest-old may strain the already costly Medicare system. (See *Families and Public Policy:* Financing Social Security and Medicare.)

Social Consequences Nevertheless, because of the general rise in their standard of living, older parents and their adult children are less dependent on one another economically. Family life in the early decades of the twentieth century was precarious; lower wages, the absence of social welfare programs, and crises of unemployment, illness, and death forced people to rely on their kin for support to a much greater extent than is true today. There were no such things as unemployment compensation, welfare checks, food stamps, Medicare, Social Security benefits, or government loans to students. Often there was only your family. Some older people provided assistance to their kin, such as finding a job for a relative, caring for the sick, or minding the grandchildren while the parents worked. Sometimes grandparents, their children, and their grandchildren pooled their resources into a common family fund so that all could subsist. When older parents became frail, their children cared for them at home. Historical accounts suggest that intensive intergenerational cooperation was more common than it is today because it was needed more.[1]

SEPARATE LIVING ARRANGEMENTS

Since the mid-twentieth century, the percentage of older women who live alone has increased greatly. To a lesser extent, so has the percentage of older men. Figure 10.2 displays trends in living arrangements between 1940 and 1980 for persons aged 60 and over, and it also displays living arrangements in 2000 and 2010 for persons aged

[1] See, for example, Anderson (1971); Hareven (1982).

Families and Public Policy: Financing Social Security and Medicare

Until the recent debates about how to finance Social Security, many people believed in a myth: The government saved the Social Security taxes they paid—as if the money were put in a drawer with their name on it—and paid it back to them when they retired. In fact, Social Security is a pay-as-you-go system in which the taxes workers pay today are mostly given to today's older recipients. But as the proportion of the population that is older rises, the tax burden on the younger, working-age population becomes greater. The problem could become severe in the near future as the large baby boom generation retires.

Even today, the expenditures are huge: Social Security benefits accounted for 24 percent of the federal budget in 2016—$311 billion more than all expenditures on national defense. Benefits under Medicare, the government health insurance program for the aged, constituted another 16 percent (Center on Budget and Policy Priorities, 2017). In other words, 40 percent of the federal budget was spent on benefits for the older population.

In 2005, President George W. Bush proposed to partially replace Social Security with a new system based on investing some of people's Social Security taxes in the stock and bond markets (Kosterlitz, 2005). Under this plan, part of the taxes workers pay would indeed be saved under their names, just as the myth suggested, only instead of keeping the money in a drawer the government would invest it. Partial privatization, as the plan is called, would eventually save federal money, since the government would reduce the benefits it pays to retired workers and substitute the proceeds of their personal accounts. Supporters of the plan touted it as a way to reduce the growth of Social Security spending while relying on private investments. Critics of the plan, however, opposed investing people's tax dollars in the markets because the returns are not guaranteed. Although in the past the returns from stocks and bonds have been substantial, no one can be certain what future returns will be, as the Great Recession of 2007 to 2009 showed. President Bush was unable to get the plan through Congress.

Although the public pays more attention to the cost of Social Security than to the cost of Medicare, Social Security is actually in better shape. In 1983, Congress passed legislation that greatly strengthened the long-term financial status of the system. Among other things, the legislation increased the payroll taxes that workers and their employers pay into the government's Social Security trust fund. The legislation also raised the age at which people can retire and receive full benefits from 65 to 67 in 2027.

65 and over.[2] Living arrangements are grouped into four categories: (1) living alone; (2) living with their spouse; (3) living without a spouse but with other relatives; or (4) living with nonrelatives only. The upper panel is for women, the lower for men. Among women, there was a sharp increase in the percentage who were living alone—as you can see from the increasing size of the uppermost section of each bar, moving from left to right. Conversely, there was a sharp fall in the percentage who were living without a spouse but with other relatives (such as a daughter or son). By 2010, it was nearly as common for an older woman to live alone as to live with a husband.

This shift toward older women's living alone has occurred for three reasons. First, women have been outliving men by a greater and greater margin each decade, so that the number of older widows has grown much larger, and fewer widows remarry because of the imbalance between the sexes. In 2010, there were four times as many unmarried widowed older women than there were unmarried widowed older men (U.S. Bureau of the Census, 2014). Second, it is less common now for a child to remain at home with his or her parents after reaching adulthood than in the past (although there has been some reversal of this pattern in recent years, as we will see). It used to be common for a child to remain with a farm

[2] Figure 10.2 excludes older people who were living in nursing homes.

(Although a two-year increase may seem modest, it will save money because 3 to 4 percent of 65-year-olds die within two years, and others will keep working and paying taxes.) Due to the increased payroll taxes, the Social Security trust fund is collecting surpluses that theoretically should be saved to pay for future costs. Unfortunately, politicians are finding it difficult to resist the temptation to use the surpluses to reduce the federal budget deficit today rather than to save them for the future. Consequently, the surpluses may not provide as much help as they should.

Little has been done, however, to control the spiraling growth of Medicare payments. Three factors are contributing to the growth: the increase in the older population, the growing share of the older population that is in the old-old and oldest-old categories (and therefore at greatest risk of serious illness and disability), and the increasing cost of health care. The Affordable Care Act, the major health care reform law enacted in 2010, included provisions that were designed to reduce spending on Medicare. For instance, it reduced the growth in payment rates to doctors who treat Medicare patients. It increased the premiums that higher-income beneficiaries must pay for supplementary coverage. It succeeded in reducing the rate of growth of Medicare expenditures. But it did not solve the problem (Kaiser Family Foundation, 2015).

Further steps may be needed. The government could raise the payroll tax that pays for Medicare, as has been done with the Social Security payroll tax. Workers see one combined deduction on their paychecks for Social Security and Medicare; given the recent increases in this deduction, there could be opposition to further hikes. The government could also raise the age of eligibility for Medicare. In addition, older people who are better off economically could be charged larger deductibles (the amount an individual must pay for a service before Medicare pays anything) or larger copayments (the percentage of the cost of a service that the individual, not Medicare, must pay after the deductible is met). But it is very difficult to make major changes in popular programs for the older population.

Ask Yourself

1. Do you have older relatives who receive Medicare benefits? If so, how important is government health insurance to them? If the government did not offer Medicare benefits, would your relatives, or their children, be able to afford their medical care?
2. Should Medicare beneficiaries be charged according to their ability to pay? Explain your reasoning.

family and to take over the farm when the older generation retired, but far fewer farm families exist today. With the decline of farming and the rise of wage labor, children have better economic opportunities outside of their parents' home than in the past. Third, older Americans tend to prefer to live near their children but not with them—a cultural preference that has been labeled "intimacy at a distance" (Rosenmayr & Kockeis, 1965). They want to see their children and grandchildren but maintain their independent residences. As the incomes of the older population have increased, they have been able to fulfill this preference by renting or owning their own housing units.

Nevertheless, Figure 10.2 shows a very different pattern for older men than for older women. To be sure, the percentage living alone has increased for men, as indicated by the top section of the bars, but the increase has been modest. At all times since 1940, the vast majority of older men have been married and sharing a household with their wives. Moreover, the proportion who were married *increased* between 1940 and 1980—as you can see by the next-to-the-top section of each bar. This marriage bonanza for older men was the flip side of the spouse drought for older women. Men had a higher risk of dying than women, but if they managed to live longer than their wives, their remarriage prospects were better than were older women's. The current generation of older men has been cared for by women throughout

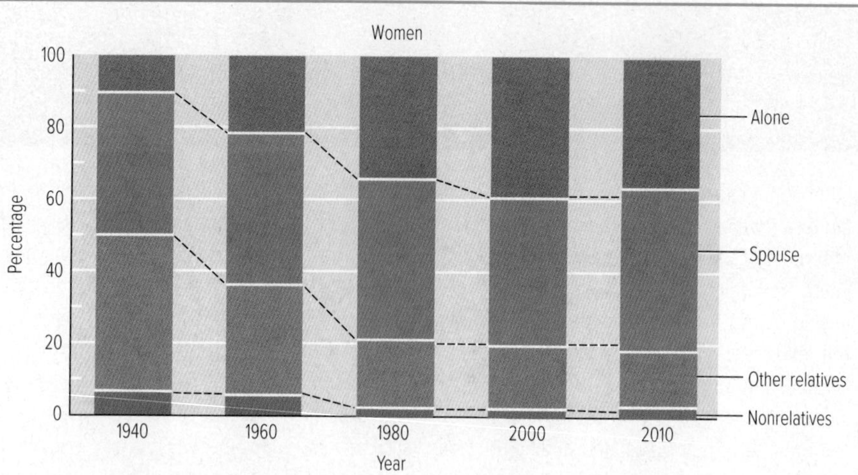

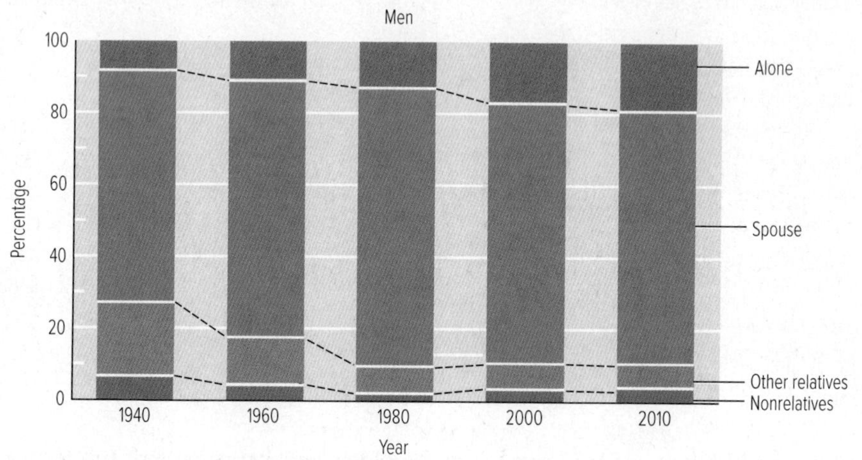

FIGURE 10.2 Living arrangements of women and men 60 years old and over in the United States, 1940 to 1980, and for women and men 65 years old and over, 2000 and 2010. *Sources:* Sweet & Bumpass, 1987; U.S. Bureau of the Census, 2001, 2014.

their lives—by their mothers when they were growing up and by their wives (many of whom did not work outside the home after marriage) in middle age. They continue to be cared for by women in old age. Most older widows, on the other hand, must continue to care for themselves or to rely on relatives living mostly in other households. And so the older years have taken on an increasingly different character for women than for men—women more likely to be living apart from kin, men more likely to be living with their wives. (The rise in divorce in early and mid-adulthood has also separated the worlds of men and women; more on that in a few pages.)

CONTACT

Given the rise in independent living among the older population, you might think that grandparents must be isolated from their children and grandchildren. But that is not the case. About 75 to 80 percent of older people live within an hour's drive of at least one of their children (Agree & Glaser, 2009). Moreover, grandparents typically see at least some of their grandchildren regularly. In a national survey, 39 percent of grandparents reported that at least one set of grandchildren lived less than

10 miles from them; and a majority reported that they saw at least one grandchild every week (Uhlenberg & Hammill, 1998). Studies of children also show high levels of contact. Among children in a national study who did not live with their grandparents, half of preschoolers and one-third of elementary-schoolers spent time with a grandparent in a typical week (Dunifon, Near, & Ziol-Guest, 2018).

Many studies have shown that one of the strongest predictors of how often grandparents see their grandchildren is how far apart they live (Cherlin & Furstenberg, 1992; Dunifon & Bajracharya, 2012). The dominance of distance illustrates both the strength and the vulnerability of the grandparent–parent–grandchild relationship. As for its strength: When grandchildren live close by, grandparents see them regularly, except under unusual circumstances. The pull grandparents exert when they live nearby shows how strong is the sense of obligation among adult children to keep in touch with their parents and their in-laws as well as how useful grandparents can be in helping care for young grandchildren. The uniformly high frequency of contact among nearby kin suggests that the bond among grandparents, their adult children, and their grandchildren is still strong.

On the other hand, when adult children move away, grandparents' access to their grandchildren drops dramatically. To be sure, adult children who have weaker ties to their parents may be the ones who tend to move from their hometowns. Job possibilities, marriage, and many other events also enter into the decision to move. Still, from the grandparents' point of view, whether or not adult children live close by involves a large element of luck. When a son takes a job in another state or a daughter-in-law moves away after a divorce, the grandparent is rarely able to overcome this impediment to regular contact.

In addition to living close by, grandparents see their grandchildren more frequently if they have a close relationship with the mother of the grandchild—their daughter or daughter-in-law. Middle-aged women do the work of "kin keeping" more often than middle-aged men, and studies show that their ties with older and younger generations are stronger and more consistent, on average, than men's (Rossi & Rossi, 1990). In general, grandmothers see their grandchildren more than grandfathers do, and grandmothers on the mother's side see even more of them than grandmothers on the father's side (Uhlenberg & Hammill, 1998). And if there is a divorce in the parents' generation, grandparents on the father's side often see less of their grandchildren because the grandchildren usually reside with the mother (Jappens & Van Bavel, 2016).

Quick Review

- Because of dramatic declines in mortality, grandparents' and grandchildren's lives overlap much more than in the past. Also, women tend to live longer than men.
- Because of declines in fertility, most grandparents are no longer raising children, which makes grandparenthood a more distinct stage of life.
- A rising standard of living, due in large part to Social Security, has made the older people less dependent on their children.
- Older women are much more likely to be living alone than in the past, and older men are more likely to be married than in the past.
- Although most grandparents live apart from their grandchildren, they tend to see at least some of them often.

Intergenerational Support

In middle and old age, as in childhood, most people in need of assistance turn to their kin. The majority of help that the older population and their adult children receive comes from one another. And because of lengthening life expectancy, this stage of mutual assistance lasts longer than ever before. But although adult children will provide assistance during the years when they have aging parents, most of them will *receive* substantial help from their aging parents as well. Until their last years, most aging parents are relatively healthy and economically independent.

In fact, the role of older parents as providers of support to their children has increased over the past generation. The employment struggles of young adults have led more of them to live in their parents' homes well into their twenties or early thirties. The struggles of low-income parents to support their children has led to a growth in the percentage of grandchildren who live with their grandparents, sometimes without the parent generation present. Overall, the extended family has been making something of a comeback lately, with older parents in the role of householders and providers assisting their children and grandchildren rather than in the historical role of dependents who are being cared for by their children and grandchildren.

MUTUAL ASSISTANCE

Why do older persons and their adult children provide so much assistance to each other? While it may seem natural that they do, there are patterns to this behavior that need explanation, such as these: Until they are very old or very ill, older persons typically give more assistance to their adult children than the children give to them (Agree & Glaser, 2009). They tend to give more assistance to adult children with greater needs and to adult children who have provided them with more assistance (Suitor, Sechrist, & Pillemer, 2007). Adult children who earn higher wages spend less time caring for their parents (Bianchi, Hotz, McGarry, & Seltzer, 2008). People give more assistance to biological parents and children than to stepparents and stepchildren (Cox, 2008). Two perspectives, altruism and exchange, have been proposed to explain these patterns, and both probably influence intergenerational assistance.

Altruism The first is altruism–caring about others, wanting to make their lives easier and better. People behave more altruistically toward close relatives than toward others. They tend to feel most obligated to help their children, second most to help their grandchildren, and then their parents and grandparents (Nock, Kingston, & Holian, 2008). Sociologists would say that these altruistic sentiments reflect strong social norms about how to live one's family life. We are taught that a good person cares for her or his children and gives time and effort generously to them. American law reinforces that norm: It is a crime to grossly mistreat one's children or to abandon them. And although it is not a crime to abandon one's older parents when they are in need, most people would be ashamed to do so. These norms about family life, however, have limits. For instance, they say little about whether a person has an obligation to help a step-relative, perhaps accounting for the lower level of assistance that studies show.

Evolutionary theorists would add that stepparents may provide less assistance to stepchildren (and vice versa) because they are not genetically related. More generally, evolutionary theorists would argue that much of our altruistic family behavior reflects our biologically based drive to reproduce our genes, so when assisting a family member aids that goal, we are more likely to do it (Cox, 2008). That is why, so the theory goes, more assistance flows down the generations from parents to children than flows upward from children to parents until the parents are old and frail: Older parents have a continuing, genetic interest in ensuring the survival and well-being of their children and grandchildren. In practice it's very difficult to sort out the influence of social norms from the influence of evolutionary pressures. The altruistic behavior we witness probably reflects a mixture of the two. In fact, one reason social norms about family life are so strong may be that they often reinforce our evolutionary interests.

Exchange The second perspective on intergenerational assistance is exchange theory, which we have seen before in this book. It suggests that in deciding whether to assist family members, individuals consider the benefits that they would receive and the costs that they would incur; and if the benefits exceed the costs, they act. No one suggests that most people make decisions about intergenerational caregiving in a cold, hard-hearted way. Nevertheless, people do seem to weigh the pluses and minuses. For instance, a high-earning adult child with an ailing mother may make the following calculation: My time is worth a lot of money, so I will gain more and lose less if, instead of taking time from work to care for my mother, I hire someone to care for her. A low-earning child, faced with the same trade-off, might decide to provide care herself.

Sometimes these calculations of the benefits and costs of providing assistance take a subtler form called **generalized exchange.** In this situation I help an individual in my family with the expectation that at a later time I will be able to request assistance from anyone in the family—not necessarily the individual I helped (Takahashi, 2000). It's the same principle that might lead you to stop your car to help someone who is changing a flat tire, not because you expect that person to ever help you but rather because you expect that if you have a flat tire, *someone* will help you. As long as enough people behave as you do, you will be right. Similarly, I may choose to help one of my children with the down payment on a house today, and two years later I may help the other child with school fees for a grandchild, with the expectation that if I need assistance later in life, someone in my little family system will reciprocate. In this way, my assistance creates a generalized obligation, an indirect IOU of sorts, that I can carry in my pocket and, in time of need, present to either child. As long as our family has built up relations of trust and reciprocity, I will be likely to collect.

generalized exchange the provision of assistance to one member of a family with the expectation that someone in the family will reciprocate at a later time

In practice, the mutual assistance between older parents and their adult children represents a mixture of altruism and exchange. Adult children and older parents provide assistance up and down the generations of their families both because they have strong emotional bonds and because they think that they will receive help in return when they need it. Altruism (and its cousins, emotional closeness and love) helps to explain why older parents provide more assistance to children who need it more. Exchange helps to explain why they provide more assistance to children who have given more assistance to them. When asked who is most likely to provide them with assistance, older parents tend to choose daughters rather than sons because they may feel emotionally closer to daughters and because they are likely to have a history of receiving more assistance from their daughters (Fingerman, Pillemer, Silverstein, & Suitor, 2012).

MOVING IN WITH GRANDPARENTS

Grandparents often help care for their grandchildren. Indeed, in 2011, grandparents were the primary source of child care for 21 percent of preschool-aged children whose mothers worked outside the home (U.S. Bureau of the Census, 2013). In addition, over the past few decades a modest but growing percentage of grandchildren have been living with grandparents. In all, 7.6 million children lived with their grandparents in 2011 (U.S. Bureau of the Census, 2013). Observers have particularly noted the growing percentage who are living in their grandparents' homes (as opposed to living in their parents' homes with grandparents present). Children who are living in their grandparents' homes are likely to be receiving support and care from them. Between 1970 and 2011, the percentage of children who lived in their grandparents' homes more than doubled. The growth occurred primarily in homes where one parent was present or where neither parent was present rather than in families where both parents were present.

Multigenerational Households Households in which grandparents, grandchildren, and one parent are present are usually formed in circumstances such as when a mother of a young child takes a job, or an unmarried parent gives birth, or a parent moves in after a divorce. In these **multigenerational households,** as we will call households in which at least three generations of family members reside, grandparents can provide important child-rearing assistance. The number of multigenerational households increased from about three million in 1990 to about four million in 2000 and about five million in 2010. The continuing immigration from Latin America and Asia may have played a role because in these cultures multigenerational living is more common. Only 2.7 percent of non-Hispanic white households were multigenerational in 2010, compared to 7.4 percent of African American households, 8.1 percent of Asian households, and 9.8 percent of Hispanic households (U.S. Bureau of the Census, 2012).

multigenerational households households in which at least three generations of family members reside

Grandfamilies About 1.6 million children, comprising about 2 percent of all children in the United States, are living with grandparents without the parent generation being present (Dunifon, 2018). These families are now common enough to have a name: **grandfamilies.** In most cases, parents have voluntarily decided to let their children be raised in the grandparent's home–often, the father is not in the picture and the mother, perhaps due to being substance abuser, or to being unable to handle her child, or to being a young teenager at the time of the birth, feels unable to raise the child and places the child with her own mother: the grandmother. Sometimes a Court mandates that a child be removed from a parent and sent to live with grandparents. Grandfamilies tend to have low incomes, and they are more common among African Americans than among Hispanics or non-Hispanic whites (Dunifon, 2018). For the grandparents and grandchildren involved, grandfamilies are sites of love, affection, and gratitude, on the one hand, but also sources of ambivalence and tension. Grandchildren appreciate what their grandparents are doing for them. But at the same time, they may have ambivalent feelings about their living arrangements. "At least you're being raised," one girl said to Rachel Dunifon (2018, pp. 107–108), "and not just, like, somewhere where you don't know nobody and you're getting sent from foster home to foster home . . . At least you're not walking around feeling like nobody cares about you." Her use of "at least" suggests that she may think that living with one's parents is better but

grandfamilies families in which grandparents are raising grandchildren without the parents being present

that she's grateful to her grandmother. She and others may have lingering anger at the parents who are not in their lives. Grandparent caregivers may feel ambivalent, too: They value having a close relationship with their grandchildren, but they also are older and are often facing health difficulties and financial limitations that make it difficult for them to take on a parent-like role.

Rewards and Costs Overall, the movement of more grandchildren into their grandparents' homes seems to represent a response to family crises rather than a greater preference for intergenerational living. Although some middle-class mothers have moved in with their parents after a separation or divorce, most of the families involved in this trend tend to be poor or near-poor. So while the typical middle-class grandparent attains "intimacy at a distance," a growing share of poor and near-poor grandparents are directly involved in raising their grandchildren. This is particularly true among African American grandparents, 30 percent of whom, in one national survey, reported having the primary responsibility for raising a grandchild for at least six months at some point in their lives (Fuller-Thomson & Minkler, 2000). I will return shortly to the intergenerational ambivalence that family situations such as these can produce.

THE RETURN OF THE EXTENDED FAMILY?

So far we have discussed three kinds of households in which older parents are living with their adult children, their grandchildren, or both. There are households in which adult children in their twenties and early thirties are living at home, perhaps unable to find employment in a tough economy. There are multigenerational households in which grandparents, adult children, and grandchildren co-reside, sometimes as a way of coping with low incomes. And there are grandfamilies in which grandparents care for their grandchildren with the middle generation present. I will refer to these three family forms for simplicity as extended-family households. All three have grown recently, and as they grow, they challenge the idea that the simple household consisting only of parents and their non-adult children has become the dominant living arrangement. Are we seeing a large-scale return of the extended family household? How do recent changes compare with long-term trends in intergenerational co-residence? Figure 10.3 provides some answers to those questions. In compiling it, the authors (Pew Research Center, 2010; Fry & Passel, 2014) combined the three kinds of households we are focusing on: (1) older parents who are co-residing with adult children age 25 and older; (2) multigenerational households in which three or more generations of family members live together; and (3) grandfamilies. The figure shows the percentage of all households that met one of these criteria from 1900 to 2012.

The figure demonstrates, first, that the increase in recent decades has been substantial but that the percentage of extended-family households today is still far below the levels of the first half of the twentieth century. As you can see, the percentage of extended-family households was much higher in the period from 1900 to 1940 than in subsequent years. During this period, as noted earlier, family life was more precarious, and young adults married at later ages and often remained at home until marriage. Second, the figure shows a sharp decline from 1940 to 1980. This was a period of growing prosperity, increasing government support for the older population, and the lowest marriage ages of the century. Third, the figure demonstrates that the more recent increase in extended-family households began

FIGURE 10.3 Percentage of the Population Living in Two-Adult Generation, Multigenerational, or Grandfamily Households, 1900 to 2012. *Source:* Pew Research Center 2010; Fry & Passel, 2014.

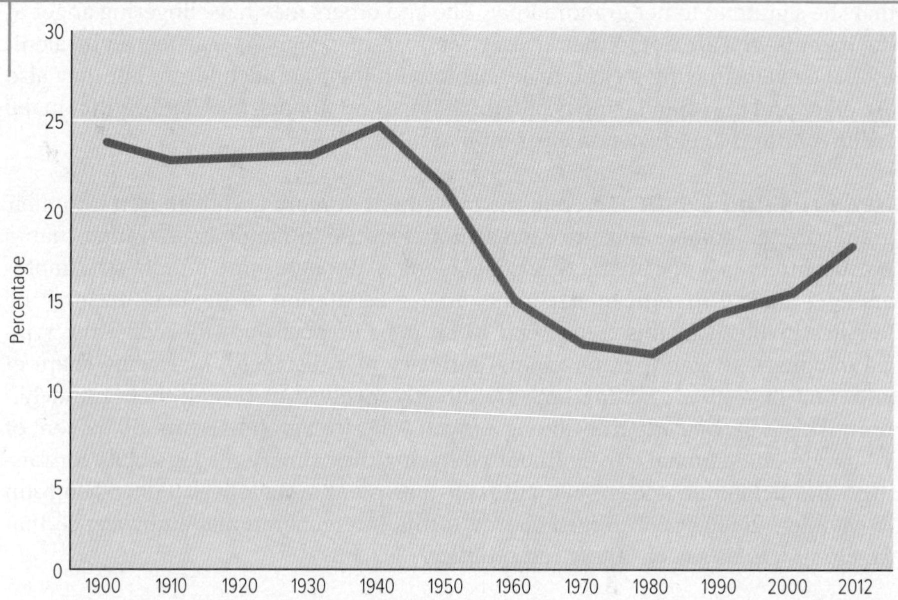

in the 1980s. It reflects older ages at marriage and later exits of young adults from home; increases in divorce and childbearing outside of marriage that led many single parents to live with their older parents at least temporarily; the growth of immigrant populations with stronger cultural traditions of multigenerational living; and the rise of grandfamilies in which grandparents are raising grandchildren.

Extended-family households are clearly playing a greater role in American family than was the case 20 or 30 years ago. Will the share of extended-family households ever reach early twentieth-century levels? It is always difficult to predict the demographic future. As late as the 1970s, for instance, no sociologist predicted that the percentage of extended-family households would soon begin to increase. Nevertheless, I think there are several factors which make reaching early twentieth-century levels unlikely. Standards of living are higher than a century ago, which encourages independent living. Government support for the older population encourages them to live in separate households, and better health allows them to be independent longer into old age. It is commonplace for young adults to cohabit with partners prior to marrying, so that the effect of later marriage on household composition is reduced. As immigrants adapt to American culture, it is likely that fewer of them will live in extended-family households. In any case, at current rates of increase, it would take decades more for extended-family households to reach early twentieth-century levels.

Quick Review

- Until they are very old or ill, older people provide more assistance to their children and grandchildren than they receive.
- Both altruism and social exchange underlie this assistance.
- A growing number of young adults are remaining in their parents' homes.
- More grandparents are caring for their grandchildren, sometimes in grandfamilies in which no parent is present.
- The increase in extended-family households since 1980 has been substantial, but levels remain lower than in the early twentieth century.

CARE OF OLDER PERSONS WITH DISABILITIES

You might think that most seriously impaired older persons are cared for in nursing homes, but that is not so. More are living in the community (that is, in private homes or apartments, not institutions) than in nursing homes and the percentage living in the community is increasing. In order to measure physical impairment, gerontologists have developed standard questions about the activities a person needs help with. The most common set, **activities of daily living**, or ADLs, refers to personal care, including bathing, dressing, eating, getting into and out of bed, walking indoors, and using the toilet. Among all older persons with limitations in one or more ADLs in 1994, two-thirds were living in the community. Even among those with limitations in two or more ADLs, the percentage living in the community rose from 57.5 percent in 1984 to 69.5 percent in 2004 (Redfoot & Houser, 2010).

activities of daily living (ADLs) personal care activities, including bathing, dressing, getting into or out of bed, walking indoors, and using the toilet

At least 90 percent of the care of disabled older people who live in the community is received from family members (Houser, Gibson, & Redfoot, 2010). According to a 1999 national survey of dependent older persons, 80 percent of their primary caregivers were spouses and children and an additional 10 percent or so were other family members (Wolff & Kasper, 2006). Moreover, women do more of the care of the older population than do men. Two-thirds of the caregivers identified in the survey of the dependent older persons were women (Wolff & Kasper, 2006). And there is a rough hierarchy of caregivers. If the older person's spouse is alive and reasonably healthy, she or he will normally become the primary caregiver; if the spouse is not alive, an adult daughter is usually next in line; and if there is no daughter who can manage the care, another relative, such as a son or a sister, may be called upon (Gatz, Bengtson, & Blum, 1990). Since a majority of older women survive their husbands, this hierarchy means, in practice, that older women are likely to be cared for eventually by their daughters, although sons do contribute.

These mostly female caregivers not only assist their relatives but also perform a critical public service. Without the care that they provide, our already expensive government health care programs would be much more costly. Since Medicare does not pay for nursing home care, individuals must pay nursing home costs by spending their own money first. Only when individuals have spent most of their savings–and therefore meet the government requirements for being poor–are they eligible for Medicaid, which will then step in and pay the bills. Typically, persons of modest means who enter nursing homes–the costs of which average more than $50,000 per year–"spend down" their assets in several months and then turn to Medicaid. Medicaid and Medicare spending for nursing home care totaled about $72 billion in 2011 (Eiken et al., 2014). Individuals in care spent another $40 billion out of their own pockets.

About 2.5 percent of the older people in the United States resided in nursing homes in 2016 (U.S. Administration on Aging, 2017). As was noted in the discussion of Figure 10.1, the oldest-old, those aged 85 and over, are the fastest-growing segment. Some of them will reside in a nursing home at some point during their last years. From the public standpoint, it is crucial to hold down the number of persons who will need institutionalized care.

THE REWARDS AND COSTS OF CAREGIVING

The informal care system has depended on the availability and goodwill of middle-aged women. A few decades ago, most married women were not employed outside the home; presumably, they had more time to devote to caring for an aging parent. But a majority of married women now work outside the home. As family caregivers increasingly combine working outside the home with caregiving for an older spouse or parent, one might imagine that their levels of stress would increase. Yet having other roles to play (employee, wife) may lower the stress that caregivers of the older people feel. Having a job you like, for instance, may take your mind off your caregiving responsibilities, making it easier to provide care. From this perspective, the stress caregivers feel largely derives from the care they give, not from an overload of responsibilities. Success or social support in one role may compensate for the stress provoked by another.

Moreover, adult children with disabled parents may find the situation stressful even if they are not the main caregivers. According to one national survey of adults in their fifties, those who had a parent who needed extensive care were, in some circumstances, more depressed if they were *not* the main caregiver than if they were (Amirkhanyan & Wolf, 2003). The authors suggest that caregivers feel the stress of having a disabled parent but also reap the rewards of providing care, whereas their husbands, wives, or siblings feel the stress but get none of the rewards. And the rewards can be substantial: becoming closer to a parent, making a difference in his or her daily life, gaining a greater sense of the meaning of life. Caregiving to an older parent is not simply a burden, as difficult as it may be. It can also give people a sense of connectedness and satisfaction.

Quick Review

- Family members provide more of the care of frail older persons than do nursing homes.
- Caring for older people can be both rewarding and stressful.

The Quality of Intergenerational Ties

Beyond giving and receiving care when needed, what can be said about the quality of the relationships between older people and their kin today? What social forces strengthen intergenerational kinship bonds and sustain close emotional relationships? What social forces act to undermine these bonds and undercut emotional closeness? In addressing these questions, sociologists have used the concepts of intergenerational solidarity and intergenerational conflict to help us to understand what brings the generations together or pushes them apart. A newer concept, intergenerational ambivalence, allows us to examine the role of mixed feelings across the generations.

INTERGENERATIONAL SOLIDARITY

The concept of solidarity is a broad one, and, fittingly, *solidarity* is a word with many connotations. When asked, a word processing program pops up the following synonyms: cooperation, fellowship, harmony, unity, stability, and reliability. An unabridged dictionary defines solidarity as "an entire union of interests and responsibilities in a group," and it quotes a phrase from Joseph Conrad: "Solidarity that knits together innumerable hearts" (*Webster's Third New International Dictionary*, electronic version). We might say, after Conrad, that **intergenerational solidarity** refers to the characteristics of family relationships that knit the generations together.

intergenerational solidarity the characteristics of family relationships that knit the generations together

With respect to the older parents and their adult children, three broad characteristics of intergenerational solidarity have received the most attention from social scientists (Silverstein & Bengtson, 1997):

- *Contact:* How frequently parents and children see each other and are in touch electronically through telephone calls or e-mail messages.
- *Assistance:* The amount of assistance, in time, goods, or money, that parents and children provide to each other.
- *Affinity:* How emotionally close parents and children feel and how much they agree on values, attitudes, and beliefs.

We have already discussed contact and assistance. Let us focus on affinity. It is relevant for judging whether the older population obtains the closeness and emotional support they wish—and whether they provide closeness and emotional support to their children and grandchildren. It is the kind of question included under the umbrella of the private family.

Hand in hand with the demographic and economic changes in the lives of the older population have come great changes in the emotional content of their relationships with their children and grandchildren. During the twentieth century, there appears to have been an increasing emphasis on bonds of sentiment: love, affection, and companionship. There is no evidence that the emotional ties between parents and children have grown weaker. As part of the research for a book we wrote about grandparents (Cherlin & Furstenberg, 1992) Frank Furstenberg and I talked with many grandparents at senior citizens' centers. When we asked grandparents whether grandparenthood had changed since they were grandchildren, we heard stories of their childhood that differed from our idyllic image of the past. Their grandparents, we were told, were respected, admired figures who often assisted other family members. But again and again, we heard them talk about the emotional distance between themselves and their grandparents:

> *The only grandmother I remember is my father's mother, and she lived with us.*
>
> *INTERVIEWER: What was it like, having your grandmother live with you?*
>
> *Terrible [laughter]! She was old, she was strict. . . . We weren't allowed to sass her, I guess that was the whole trouble. No matter what she did to you, you had to take it. . . . She was good, though. . . . She used to do all the patching of the pants, and she was helpful. But, oh, she was strict. You weren't allowed to do anything, she'd tell on you right away.*
>
> *INTERVIEWER: So what difference do you think there is between being a grandparent when you were a grandchild and being a grandparent now?*
>
> *It's different. My grandma never gave us any love.*
>
> *INTERVIEWER: No?*
>
> *Nooo. My goodness, no, no. No, never took us anyplace, just sat there and yelled at you all the time.*
>
> *INTERVIEWER: Did you have a lot of respect for your grandmother?*
>
> *Oh, we had to whether we wanted to or not, we had to.*

Grandma may have helped out, and she certainly was respected, even loved, but she was often an emotionally distant figure. This is not to say that affection was absent from the relations between young and old. But there has been a shift in the balance between respect and affection. Grandparents today are closer emotionally to their grandchildren than in the past.

Granted, it is hard to judge the accuracy of these recollections of two generations ago. But the story that the grandparents consistently told us fits with the demographic and economic developments that have been discussed. It is easier for today's grandparents to have a pleasurable, emotion-laden relationship with their grandchildren because they are more likely to live long enough to develop the relationship, because they are not still busy raising their own children, because they can travel long distances more easily and communicate by Skype, or smartphone, or e-mail, and because they have fewer grandchildren and more economic resources to devote to them. Earlier in the nation's history, the generations were often bound up in economic cooperation that took precedence over affection and companionship. In fact, there may be a trade-off between bonds of obligation and authority, on the one hand, and bonds of sentiment. Historian David Hackett Fischer, in his book on the history of aging in America, noted the following differences between the nation's early and later years:

> *Even as most (though not all) elderly people were apt to hold more power than they would possess in a later period, they were also apt to receive less affection, less love, less sympathy from those younger than themselves. The elderly were kept at an emotional distance by the young. (Fischer, 1978)*

Conversely, in modern America:

> *As elders lost their authority within the society, they gained something in return. Within the sphere of an individual family, ties of affection may have grown stronger as ties of family obligation grew weak. (Fischer, 1978)*

This increasing emphasis on affection appears to be continuing among older people and their children and grandchildren today. Warm, emotionally close relations are the most common style in the United States and other wealthy nations (Silverstein, Gans, Lowenstein, Giarrusso, & Bengtson, 2010).

Quick Review

- Intergenerational solidarity depends on frequent contact, emotional closeness, and mutual support.
- Sentiment and affection have become increasingly central to intergenerational relations, whereas the authority of older people may have declined.

INTERGENERATIONAL CONFLICT AND AMBIVALENCE

intergenerational conflict discord among family members that pulls the generations apart

Yet intergenerational relations aren't always warm, and older parents and adult children don't always get along. Tensions, criticisms, and arguments occur, not just among family members who are alienated from each other but also among family members who generally get along well. **Intergenerational conflict** refers to discord among family members that pulls the generations apart. In its mild forms, it can intrude from time to time into the relationships of emotionally close kin. In its more virulent forms, it can underlie a hostile relationship. Intergenerational conflict commonly occurs over communication and interaction styles (such as being overly critical, dominating, or treating family members in ways that are perceived as unfair) and habits and lifestyles (such as using alcohol or drugs, adopting a particular style of dress, or engaging in types of recreation that some find objectionable).

Together, the concepts of solidarity and conflict define a wide range of intergenerational behaviors and attitudes.

Scholars have suggested, however, that another middle-ground concept is necessary to fully understand intergenerational relations today: intergenerational ambivalence (Connidis & McMullin, 2002; Lüscher & Pillemer, 1998; Pillemer & Lüscher, 2003). It refers to the contradictory emotions or mixed feelings that family members may hold toward each other.

For instance, adult children may have conflicting feelings about caring for ailing parents. On the one hand, they may find caring for parents deeply fulfilling and meaningful. On the other hand, they may feel resentful of the demands that caring makes on their time and energy. Even in the mind of a dedicated, loving caregiver, these contradictory feelings may coexist. In one national study, women who began to care for an older parent reported both an increase in depression and a greater sense of purpose in life (Marks, Lambert, & Choi, 2002). The older parent may also feel ambivalent toward the adult child—at once understanding that children have independent lives to lead and yet desiring care from them.

Ambivalence is a broad concept, applicable to many situations in which a person can have conflicting feelings. Sociologists focus on situations in which ambivalence is socially structured, meaning that it reflects contradictions of authority, power, or social norms (Connidis, 2015). Let us define **intergenerational ambivalence** as socially structured contradictory emotions in an intergenerational relationship. The conditions of contemporary life probably make ambivalence more common now than in the past (Connidis & McMullin, 2002). As noted earlier, more grandparents are being called upon to care for their grandchildren in circumstances that can lead to ambivalent feelings. Or consider gender differences in social norms about caregiving. Women are still expected to do more of the care of older parents; and they, in fact, do provide the bulk of care (Agree & Glaser, 2009). More middle-aged children have living parents today than in the past because of increases in life expectancy. Yet women also have greater opportunities to work outside the home than in the past. Adult daughters' greater responsibilities for providing care, combined with greater opportunities for self-advancement in the workplace, can create ambivalence. Middle-aged sons may also feel ambivalence about caregiving, but because they aren't expected to be the primary caregivers, they may more easily resolve their feelings by hiring a caregiver. Middle-aged daughters, in contrast, may be more likely to provide the care themselves because that's what they are expected to do—and leave their ambivalent feelings intact.

intergenerational ambivalence socially structured contradictory emotions in an intergenerational relationship

Several studies confirm the prediction that women feel more ambivalence than men in their relations with older parents: Older women seem to report more ambivalent feelings toward their daughters than toward their sons, as indicated by their greater agreement with statements such as mother and daughter "get on each other's nerves but nevertheless we feel very close" (Pillemer & Suiter, 2002; Pillemer et al., 2012). Another study of rural Iowa families found that women who were caring for parents reported more ambivalence than men who were caring for parents: The women were more likely to agree with both positive statements (e.g., feeling appreciated and loved) and negative statements (feelings of conflict, tension, or disagreement) about their relationship to their parent (Willson, Shuey, & Elder, 2003). These ambivalent feelings do not necessarily prevent caregiving, but they suggest that caregiving often creates simultaneous positive and negative feelings for the provider and the recipient of care.

Ambivalence may be a property not just of the relationship between two family members but also of relationships within the larger family group. For instance, an older adult with more than one child may be grateful for the care provided by some of her children but disappointed by the lack of care from others. If we just look at her feelings about each child separately, we may not see any ambivalence: She either feels positively or negatively toward each child. But when we consider her feelings toward her children as a group, we see ambivalent feelings. This group level process consisting of mixed feelings across multiple children has been called **collective ambivalence** (Connidis, 2015; Silverstein & Giarrusso, 2010). For instance in a national survey, the happiness of older parents was associated with not only their positive relationships with the adult children they felt closer to but also their less positive relations with the adult children they felt least close to (Ward, 2008). Their happiness, in other words, corresponded to their feelings about their children collectively.

collective ambivalence mixed feelings across multiple children

The Family National Guard

In all, how important a part of the American family system are intergenerational relations? Gerontologist Vern L. Bengtson is the leading advocate of the view that intergenerational relations are very important. In fact, Bengtson (2001; see also Bengtson, Biblarz, & Roberts, 2002) suggests that with the decline of the two-parent nuclear family, intergenerational relations are becoming more important than nuclear family ties to many Americans—and will continue to be important in the twenty-first century. Bengtson argues that the increasing longevity and better health of the older population mean that adult children are fortunate enough to have parents available to them well into midlife. He would note how commonly older parents take in daughters and grandchildren after a divorce or care for grandchildren when parents are unable to do so. He contrasts the durability and longevity of parent–child–grandchild bonds with the increasing fragility of marriage bonds.

There is much to be said for this argument, but it does have limitations. Among the nonpoor, grandparents tend to leave the child rearing to parents, live independently, and seek "intimacy at a distance." Relations between many divorced older men and their adult children are strained, and it's not clear how much mutual support stepparents and stepchildren will provide to each other over the life course. Some skeptics believe that there has been a loss of family feeling since the time when most older people were living with their children. They charge that modern grandparents, in their rush to retire in the Sun Belt, have abandoned their bonds to their grandchildren.

Perhaps the best way to balance these views is to think of grandparents as the family national guard (Hagestad, 1985). In the middle classes, at least, the guard is usually on inactive reserve—keeping in contact with children and grandchildren, having pleasant relations, but providing (and receiving) little assistance. When a crisis occurs in an adult child's or a grandchild's life—a divorce, a birth outside of marriage, a sudden illness—the family national guard is called up. The key questions are how often the guard shows up for duty when called and how long they stay active. Because older Americans lead longer, healthier lives than in the past, more of them are available. Because most feel emotionally close to their children and grandchildren, they are motivated to help. So in most circumstances, grandparents willingly provide substantial assistance. But active duty has its costs, and, like the national guard, most grandparents prefer to return to inactive duty—to resume their independent lives.

When Furstenberg and I were writing our book, we visited a senior citizens' center in a Jewish neighborhood in Baltimore. There we talked with a group of grandparents who told us that the new development in the neighborhood was the immigration of many families from Russia. With some envy, they described to us the relationships the Russian grandparents had with their grandchildren: "The grandparents live with their children and grandchildren." "They go on vacation together." "They go out to eat together." "They are very involved in the care of their grandchildren." After listening to these remarks, one of us asked whether anyone in the group would trade places with the immigrant grandparents in order to have their type of relationship. The question was met with immediate cries of "No way!" "No" and "I'm satisfied." The questioner pursued the point further: "Why wouldn't you trade places? There are all these strong family ties?" A woman replied, "I don't think I could live with my children," and a chorus of "No" and "No way" followed.

One grandmother said, simply, "It's too late." What she meant was that, given the opportunity for independence, most American grandparents had already seized it and couldn't give it up. To live with their children, they would have to adjust their daily schedules to fit their children's busy lives. It's easy to look at current living arrangements and criticize the older population for emphasizing autonomy and personal satisfaction in their daily lives. But they are merely engulfed in the same flood of self-fulfillment that has washed over their children and grandchildren. To ask grandparents to lead a retreat to a family system that emphasizes cooperation over companionship, obligations over independence, duty over love, is perhaps unfair. This is the first generation in which most older Americans have had a choice in these matters; should they be criticized for making the same choices as everyone else?

Quick Review

- The older population and their children may have ambivalent feelings toward each other that are socially structured.
- Social changes such as more women working outside the home may have increased intergenerational ambivalence.
- Some observers argue that social change is making intergenerational relations a more important part of family life.

Looking Back

1. **How has grandparenthood changed over the past century?** Today most adults live long enough to get to know their grandchildren because adult life expectancy has lengthened substantially, particularly for women. And because birthrates are lower, and most adults have finished raising their children by the time they become grandparents, grandparenthood is now a more distinct stage of life. Declining births mean that the average person has fewer links to kin in the same generation; but because of declining mortality the average person has more links to kin in preceding or succeeding generations. Moreover, over the past half-century the incomes of older people have risen dramatically, thanks to the expansion of the Social Security

rolls, increases in Social Security benefits, and the growth of private pension programs.

2. **How much support do the older people provide to, and receive from, their kin?** Most of the help that the older people and their adult children receive is mutual. The principles of altruism and exchange underlie this assistance. Except when they are ill, the olders provide more help than they receive. Among those who need care, most older men get it from their wives, while most older women must rely on daughters and other relatives. A modest but increasing percentage of grandparents are caring for the grandchildren in their own homes. These grandparents tend to have lower incomes and poorer health, and their caregiving is usually in response to a crisis in their adult children's lives.

3. **Who cares for the frail aged?** The majority of seriously disabled older persons are cared for in their homes by family members, rather than in a hospital or nursing home. The most common family caregiver other than a spouse is an adult daughter. In the future, fewer adult daughters will be available as caregivers, both because more of them will be employed and because the older generation will have fewer adult children. Caring for an aging family member can be both rewarding and stressful. Higher rates of divorce and remarriage among older Americans may reduce the number of caregivers available to them.

4. **Are older adults isolated from their kin?** Older adults value both their independence and contact with their kin. Most have frequent contact with at least one child, especially with those who live nearby. There is a greater emphasis on affection and companionship, and a lesser emphasis on economic cooperation, in intergenerational relations now. Some observers suggest that the quality of intergenerational relations has declined, but others counter that older people and their children have chosen a style of relating to one another—that is, separate residences and fairly frequent contact—that suits them both.

5. **What sources of tension exist in intergenerational relations?** Despite the generally positive feelings the older people and their children have for each other, ambivalent feelings do exist. Those who are giving or receiving substantial care may find it both rewarding and tension-producing. Women experience ambivalence more than men because they are expected to provide care. In addition, older men who have separated from the mothers of their children may be unable, later in life, to rely on their adult children for support.

Study Questions

1. How have the great declines in adult mortality and fertility altered old age?
2. Should the trend toward the older generation living apart from their children be viewed as a positive or negative development for family relations?
3. How do the lives of older women differ from the lives of older men?
4. How do the lives of older non-Hispanic whites differ from the lives of older African Americans and Hispanics?
5. In what ways are women the family caregivers and kin-keepers?
6. Under what kinds of circumstances would intergenerational ambivalence be high in a family?
7. What is the evidence that intergenerational relations, as some suggest, are becoming a more important part of American family life?

Key Terms

activities of daily living (ADLs) 279
centenarian 267
collective ambivalence 284
fertility 267
generalized exchange 275
gerontologist 267
grandfamilies 276
health span 266
intergenerational ambivalence 283
intergenerational conflict 282
intergenerational solidarity 280
Medicaid 269
Medicare 269
mortality 265
multigenerational households 276
old-old 267
older population 266
oldest-old 267
young-old 267

Thinking about Families

The Private Family	The Public Family
Should we be surprised that American grandparents want to live near their grandchildren but not with them?	**Together, the federal and state governments spend twice as much money on Social Security and Medicare as the federal government spends on the entire defense budget. Is government spending too much money on the older generation?**

References

Agree, E. M., & Glaser, K. (2009). Demography of informal caregiving. In P. Uhlenberg (Ed.), *International handbook of population aging* (pp. 647–668): Springer.

Amirkhanyan, A. A., & Wolf, D. A. (2003). Caregiver stress and noncaregiver stress: Exploring the pathways of psychiatric morbidity. *The Gerontologist, 43,* 817–827.

Bengtson, V. L. (2001). Beyond the nuclear family: The increasing importance of multigenerational bonds. *Journal of Marriage and Family, 63,* 1–16.

Bengtson, V. L., Biblarz, T. J., & Roberts, R. E. L. (2002). *How families still matter: A longitudinal study of youths in two generations.* Cambridge: Cambridge University Press.

Bianchi, S. M., Hotz, V. J., McGarry, K., & Seltzer, J. (2008). Intergenerational ties: Theories, trends, and challenges. In A. Booth, A. C. Crouter, S. Bianchi, & J. Seltzer (Eds.), *Intergenerational caregiving* (pp. 3–43). Washington, DC: Urban Institute Press.

Center on Budget and Policy Priorities. (2017). Chart book: SNAP helps struggling families put food on the table. Retrieved May 26, 2017.

Cherlin, A. J., & Furstenberg, F. F., Jr. (1992). *The new American grandparent: A place in the family, a life apart.* Cambridge, MA: Harvard University Press.

Connidis, I. A. (2015). Exploring ambivalence in family ties: Progress and prospects. *Journal of Marriage and Family,* 77(February), 77–95.

Connidis, I. A., & McMullin, J. A. (2002). Sociological ambivalence and family ties: A critical perspective. *Journal of Marriage and Family, 64,* 558–567.

Cox, D. (2008). Intergenerational caregiving and exchange: Economic and evolutionary approaches. In A. Booth, A. C. Crouter, S. Bianchi, & J. Seltzer (Eds.), *Intergenerational caregiving* (pp. 81–125). Washington, DC: The Urban Institute Press.

Crimmins, E. M. (2015). Lifespan and healthspan: Past, present, and promise. *Gerontologist,* 55(6), 901–911.

Dunifon, R. E. (2018). *You've always been there for me: Understanding the lives of grandchildren raised by grandparents* New Brunswick NJ: Rutgers University Press.

Dunifon, R., & Bajracharya, A. (2012). The role of grandparents in the lives of youth. *Journal of Family Issues,* 33(9), 1168–1194.

Dunifon, R. E., Near, C. E., & Ziol-Guest, K. M. (2018). Backup parents, playmates, friends: Grandparents' time with grandchildren. *Journal of Marriage and Family,* 80(3), 752–767.

Eiken, S., Sredl, K., Gold, L., Kasten, J., Burwell, B., & Saucier, P. (2014). Medicaid expenditures for longterm services and supports in FY 2012: Truven Health Analytics.

Fingerman, K. L., Pillemer, K., Silverstein, M., & Suitor, J. J. (2012). The baby boomers' intergenerational relationships. *The Gerontologist, 52,* 199–209.

Fischer, D. H. (1978). *Growing old in America.* New York: Oxford University Press.

Fry, R., & Passel, J. S. (2014). In post-recession era, young adults drive continuing rise in multi-generational living. *Pew Research Center, Social and Demographic Trends.* Retrieved May 28, 2016, from http://www.pewsocialtrends.org/2014/07/17/in-post-recession-era-young-adults-drive-continuing-rise-inmulti-generational-living/

Fuller-Thomson, E., & Minkler, M. (2000). African American grandparents raising grandchildren: A national profile of demographic and health characteristics. *Health & Social Work, 25,* 109–118.

Gatz, M., Bengston, V. L., & Blum, M. J. (1990). *Care giving families* (3rd ed.). Orlando, FL: Academic Press.

Hagestad, G. (1985). Continuity and connectedness. In V. L. Bengtsen & J. F. Robinson (Eds.), *Grandparenthood* (pp. 31–48). Beverly Hills, Ca: Sage.

Harmon, A. (2005, March 20). Ask them (all 8 of them) about their grandson. *The New York Times,* pp. 1, 18.

Houser, A., Gibson, M. J., & Redfoot, D. L. (2010). Trends in family caregiving and paid home care for older people with disabilities in the community: Data from the national long-term care survey: AARP Public Policy Institute.

Jappens, M., & Van Bavel, J. (2016). Parental divorce, residence arrangements, and contact between grandchildren and grandparents. *Journal of Marriage and Family, Online ahead of publication.*

Kaiser Family Foundation. (2015). The facts on Medicare spending and financing. Retrieved January 14, 2016, from http://files.kff.org/attachment/fact-sheet-the-facts-on-medicare-spending-and-financing

Kosterlitz, J. (2005). Inside the new social security accounts. *National Journal, 37, issue 1/2,* 21–23.

Leopold, T., & Skopek, J. (2015). The demography of grandparenthood: An international profile. *Social Forces,* 94(2), 801–832.

Lüscher, K., & Pillemer, K. (1998). Intergenerational ambivalence: A new approach to the study of parentchild relations in later life. *Journal of Marriage and Family, 60,* 413–425.

Marks, N. G., Lambert, J. D., & Choi, H. (2002). Transitions to caregiving, gender, and psychological well-being. *Journal of Marriage and Family, 64,* 657–667.

Nock, S. L., Kingston, P. W., & Holian, L. M. (2008). Intergenerational caregiving. In A. Booth, A. C. Crouter, S. Bianchi, & J. Seltzer (Eds.), *Intergenerational caregiving* (pp. 279–316). Washington, DC: The Urban Institute Press.

Pew Research Center. (2010). The return of the multigenerational family household. Retrieved November 20, 2018, from http://www.pewsocialtrends.org/2010/03/18/the-return-of-the-multi-generational-family-household/

Pillemer, K., & Lüscher, K. (Eds.). (2003) *Intergenerational ambivalences: New perspectives on parent-child relations in later life.* Stamford, CT: Elsevier/ JAI Press. Redfoot, D. L., & Houser, A. (2010). More older people with disabilities living in the community: Trends from the national long-term care survey, 1984–2004: AARP Public Policy Institute. Elsevier/ JAI Press.

Pillemer, K., Munsch, C. L., Fuller-Rowell, T., Riffin, C., & Suitor, J. J. (2012). Ambivalence toward adult children: Differences between mothers and fathers. *Journal of Marriage and Family,* 74(5), 1101–1113.

Pillemer, K., & Suiter, J. J. (2002). Explaining mothers' ambivalence toward their adult children. *Journal of Marriage and Family, 64,* 602–613

Rosenmayr, L., & Kockeis, E. (1965). *Umwelt und familie alter menschen.* Berlin: Luchterland-Verlag.

Rossi, A. S., & Rossi, P. H. (1990). *Of human bonding: Parent-child relations across the life course.* New York: Aldine de Gruyter.

Ryder, N. B. (1980). Components of temporal variations in American fertility. In R. W. Hiorns (Ed.), *Demographic patterns in developed societies* (pp. 15–54). London: Taylor and Francis.

Silverstein, M., & Bengston, V. L. (1997). Intergenerational solidarity and the structure of adult child-parent relationships in American families. *American Journal of Sociology, 103,* 429–460.

Silverstein, M., & Giarrusso, R. (2010). Aging and family life: A decade review. *Journal of Marriage and Family, 72,* 1039–1058.

Silverstein, M., Gans, D., Lowenstein, A., Giarrusso, R., & Bengtson, V. L. (2010). Older parent-child relationships in six developed nations: Comparisons at the intersection of affection and conflict. *Journal of Marriage and Family,* 72(4), 1006–1021.

Suitor, J. J., Sechrist, J., & Pillemer, K. (2007). Differences in mothers' support for adult children in black and white families. *Research on Aging, 29,* 410–435.

Sweet, J. A., & Bumpass, L. L. (1987). *American families and households.* New York: Russell Sage Foundation.

Takahashi, N. (2000). The emergence of generalized exchange. *American Journal of Sociology,* 105(1105–1134).

U.S. Administration on Aging. (2017). A profile of older Americans: 2017. Retrieved November 20, 2018, from https://acl.gov/sites/default/files/Aging%20and%20Disability%20in%20America/2017OlderAmericansProfile.pdf

U.S. Bureau of the Census. (2001). The 65 years and over population: 2000. Retrieved March 6, 2009, from http://www.census.gov/prod/2001pubs/c2kbr01-10.pdf.

U.S. Bureau of the Census. (2012). Table PCT14: Presence of multigenerational households. *2010 Census Summary File 1.* Retrieved January 27, 2012, from http://factfinder2.census.gov

U.S. Bureau of the Census. (2013). Who's minding the kids? Child care arrangements: Spring 2011. *Household Economics Studies P70-135.* Retrieved January 7, 2016, from http://www.census.gov/prod/2013pubs/p70-135.pdf

U.S. Bureau of the Census. (2014). 65+ in the United States: 2010. *Current Population Reports, P23-212.* Retrieved January 6, 2016, from https://www.census.gov/content/dam/Census/library/publications/2014/demo/p23-212.pdf

U.S. Bureau of the Census. (2018a). Detailed age and sex composition of the population. *2017 National Population Projections Tables.* Retrieved November 20, 2018, from https://www2.census.gov/programs-surveys/popproj/tables/2017/2017-summary-tables/np2017-t3.xlsx

U.S. Bureau of the Census. (2018b). Income and poverty in the United States: 2017. Retrieved December 18, 2018, from https://www.census.gov/content/dam/Census/library/publications/2018/demo/p60-263.pdf

U.S. Bureau of the Census. (2018c). POV01. Age and sex of all people, family members and unrelated individuals iterated by income-to-poverty ratio and race. *Annual Social and Economic (ASEC) Supplement.* Retrieved November 20, 2018, from https://www.census.gov/data/tables/time-series/demo/income-poverty/cps-pov/pov-01.2017.html

U.S. National Center for Health Statistics. (2018). Deaths: Final data for 2016. *National Vital Statistics Reports.* Retrieved November 20, 2018, from https://www.cdc.gov/nchs/data/nvsr/nvsr67/nvsr67_05.pdf

Uhlenberg, P. (1979). Demographic change and the problems of the aged. In M. W. Riley (Ed.), *Aging from birth to death* (pp. 153–166). Boulder, CO: Westview Press.

Uhlenberg, P. (1980). Death and the family. *Journal of Family History, 5,* 313–320.

Uhlenberg, P. (2004). Historical forces shaping grandparent-grandchild relationships: Demography and beyond. *Annual Review of Gerontology and Geriatrics, 24,* 77–97.

Uhlenberg, P., & Hammill, B. G. (1998). Frequency of grandparent contact with grandchild sets: Six factors that make a difference. *The Gerontologist, 38,* 276–285.

Ward, R. A. (2008). Multiple parent-adult child relations and well-being in middle and later life. *Journal of Gerontology: Social Sciences, 63B,* S239–S247.

Willson, A. E., Shuey, K. M., & Elder, G. H., Jr. (2003). Ambivalence in the relationship of adult children to aging parents and in-laws. *Journal of Marriage and Family, 65,* 1055–1072.

Wolff, J. L., & Kasper, J. D. (2006). Caregivers of frail elders: Updating a national profile. *The Gerontologist, 46,* 344–356.

Part Five

Conflict, Disruption, and Reconstitution

Conflict between intimate partners has a public significance beyond the immediate family context. It spans both the private family, where it affects the quality of emotional support, intimacy, and cooperation, and the public family, where its social consequences are played out on a larger scale. Conflict between adults can also lead to the dissolution of cohabiting and marital unions. Chapter 11 considers violence and abuse between spouses and partners and by parents against children. After a brief review of the history of domestic violence, the chapter summarizes current knowledge. The most important theories of domestic violence are presented, followed by an examination of sexual aggression and violence in dating relationships and a discussion of public policies. Marital conflict, these days, often leads to divorce. Perhaps 40 percent of all marriages in the United States at current rates would end in divorce. Chapter 12 probes the causes and consequences of this high level of dissolution and repartnering in cohabiting relationships and marriage. It examines the process that disrupting couples experience and the consequences for both children and adults. It describes the new kinds of family relationships and kinship networks that form after remarriages or after parents cohabit with a new partner.

Chapter Eleven

Domestic Violence

Looking Forward

1. When did domestic violence become a social issue?
2. What do we know about violence between intimate partners?
3. What is the extent of child abuse?
4. What do we know about sexual aggression and violence in emerging adulthood?
5. Why does domestic violence occur?
6. What are the public policy issues concerning domestic violence?

On September 26, 2016, a mother brought the body of her six-year-old child, Zymere Perkins, to the emergency room of St. Luke's Hospital in New York City. The hospital staff estimated that he had been dead for about 17 hours. The mother didn't offer any explanation for why the child was dead. The boy had blood in one eye, bruises on his torso, abdomen, neck, and arms, a scratch on his neck, and a laceration on the side of his head. The medical examiner later ruled that the death of Zymere was a homicide resulting from chronic-abuse trauma injuries. His death became a public issue when it was revealed that the New York City agency responsible for child welfare had investigated the family five times and had found evidence that the mother's romantic partner had beaten and abused Zymere, yet the agency had never removed the child from his mother's care (Nahmias, 2016). Cases such as this one often lead to demands that child welfare service workers be more aggressive in removing children from potentially abusive parents. Yet removing children from their homes has its own risks, as when children separated from their families drift through the foster care system.

domestic violence violent acts between family members or between partners in intimate or dating relationships

The problem is that the public hears about child abuse or intimate partner violence mainly through sensational cases such as Zymere's death or football star O.J. Simpson's 1995 trial for the murder of his former wife. A few decades ago, even social scientists ignored **domestic violence,** which will be defined in this chapter as violent acts between family members or between partners in intimate or dating relationships. Not a single article on the topic appeared in *Journal of Marriage and the Family,* the major scholarly journal in the field, between its founding in 1939 and 1969 (O'Brien, 1971). Now, however, hardly an issue appears without one. In fact, the increase in research has been so sudden and so massive that it requires an explanation. It wasn't spurred by an increase in domestic violence, because there isn't convincing evidence of an increase, as will be noted later. Rather, its rise initially reflected the increased political power of the feminist movement, which viewed domestic violence as an important barrier to women's equality, and the increasing cultural emphasis on the rights of the individual, including children, the older population, and more recently, individuals in same-sex relationships. To appreciate what has occurred, it is necessary first to examine the history of domestic violence as a social problem.

Domestic Violence in Historical Perspective

The recent attention to highly publicized cases of child abuse and wife battering is not the first outpouring of public concern about domestic violence. Rather, the history of domestic violence in the United States shows short periods of public attention separated by longer periods of neglect. The periods of attention have had less to do with the prevalence of violence than with the power of various political and social groups (Pleck, 1987).

EARLY HISTORY

Domestic violence is not new. Historians have documented numerous cases in early modern Europe (the period roughly between 1500 and 1800) that were caused by sexual jealousy, disagreements over money, or excessive alcohol consumption (Muravyeva, 2013). In the New England colonies, the Puritans believed that it was the responsibility of the government to enforce moral behavior, even if that meant intervening in the affairs of the family. And moral behavior excluded violent acts by husbands against their wives. The well-known minister Cotton Mather told his congregants that for "a man to Beat his Wife was as bad as any Sacriledge" and that "any such a Rascal were better buried alive, than show his Head among his Neighbours any more" (Pleck, 1987). Friends, neighbors, and fellow churchgoers watched over a family's conduct in ways we would view today as nosy, if not meddlesome. In 1641, the Massachusetts Bay Colony enacted the first law against wife beating in the Western world, according to historian Elizabeth Pleck; it also prohibited parents from exercising "any unnatural severitie" with their children (Pleck, 1987).

How strictly this law was enforced, however, is unclear because the number of persons actually charged with wife beating was small. The Puritans must have felt the tension between respecting the integrity of the family and intervening to protect women and children from abuse. After the Puritans, government officials in most eras were even more reluctant to intervene. Indeed, the history of the issue of domestic violence is, in large part, a story of conflict between the goals of preserving the family unit and of protecting women and children. When intervention was seen as shoring up the family (as among the Puritans), it received broader support; when it was perceived as undermining men's authority and contributing to divorce, it received less.[1]

A peak of concern occurred in the late 1800s, when the child protection movement arose. In 1874, the first society for the prevention of cruelty to children was founded; 40 years later there were 494 of them. Pleck argues that the growth of these societies, usually started by leaders of the local social elite, reflected a desire to control the behavior of the unruly, growing immigrant and working-class populations. In addition, I think, the growth came at a time when attitudes toward children were evolving from seeing them as economic assets to seeing them as emotionally rewarding beings to be nurtured (Zelizer, 1985). Still, leaders of the movement were careful to reassure parents that their authority to discipline their children, even by occasional physical punishment, was not in question. The founder of the New York Society for the Prevention of Cruelty to Children assured nervous supporters that he favored "a good wholesome flogging for disobedient children," although he wished to protect children from "undue parental severity"

[1] This paragraph, and the next several, draw heavily from Pleck (1987).

(Pleck, 1987). And the few organizations that sought to help battered wives had to fight suspicion that they were encouraging the breakup of the family.

THE TWENTIETH CENTURY

The Political Model of Domestic Violence During the twentieth century, two ways of thinking about domestic violence emerged. The first is what might be called the *political model* of domestic violence–political not in the sense of Democrats and Republicans but rather in the sense of the relations of power and authority between men and women. Historian Linda Gordon has argued that domestic violence has been a politically constructed problem in two senses:

> *First, the very definition of what constitutes unacceptable domestic violence, and appropriate responses to it, developed and then varied according to political moods and the force of certain political movements. Second, violence among family members . . . usually arises out of power struggles in which individuals are contesting real resources and benefits. These contests arise not only from personal aspirations but also from changing social norms and conditions. (Gordon, 1988)*

The struggles are usually about men's power to control the behavior of women. Resorting to force is a way for a husband to compel his wife to behave as the husband wishes. Traditionally, social structure has supported men's control over women through law and social custom. Laws that allowed husbands to use some degree of physical force against their wives are an example. The political model implies that domestic violence is deeply rooted in laws and customs that reinforce male dominance and is unlikely to be ended without political action by women's groups and their allies.

The Medical Model of Domestic Violence The second way of thinking is the *medical model,* under which domestic violence is seen as an illness and a source of injuries. In contrast to the political model, the main concern is not with relations of power but rather with illness and well-being. Health and social welfare professionals who have campaigned against child abuse, for example, have focused attention on the physical and mental harm that children suffer from physical and sexual violence. Some have argued that both the victims and the perpetrators of violence suffer from various "syndromes," illness-like complexes of symptoms, injuries, and attitudes, that need to be treated. The professionals point to links between being violent and such personal problems as a history of abuse as a child, alcoholism, or mental illness. The medical model therefore conceives of the problem as though it can be solved by the intervention of health and social welfare professionals, much as they might attack schizophrenia or tuberculosis.

The first two decades of the twentieth century were a time when domestic relations courts, which treated family disputes more as social welfare cases than as criminal cases, were established throughout the states. But the issue of domestic violence was relatively quiescent until 1962, when pediatrician C. Henry Kempe and his colleagues, troubled by X-ray pictures of broken bones in children and reports of maltreatment, published an article titled "The Battered Child Syndrome" (Kempe, Silverman, Steele, Droegemuller, & Silver, 1962). Kempe and his colleagues brought the medical model of domestic violence to the public's attention. In their view, child abuse was centered on a "syndrome" of repeated violence and inadequate parenting. This perspective created sympathetic concern not only for the blameless victims but also for the abusers, who seemed to be fighting a mental illness that needed treatment. In these ways the "syndrome" attracted broad public interest; within five years, every state had enacted laws that required medical personnel to report suspected cases of child abuse.

Still, there was little attention paid to wife beating until the mid-1970s, when feminist groups succeeded in making violence against women into a political problem. A decade earlier, the feminist movement had undergone a major revival, boosted by the parallel growth of the civil rights movement. Some feminist groups focused on combating rape. Part of their strategy was the formation of services for rape victims, such as hot lines, crisis centers, and legal support. The issue of rape led organizers to the issue of sexual and physical violence directed toward married women. The movement's fundamental goal was not to treat the injuries of the victims or ease the personal problems of the perpetrators—valuable as those steps might be—but rather to remove the social supports for male violence, such as a reluctance to prosecute alleged offenders. Consequently, activists worked for changes in the law, funds for crisis centers and shelters for battered women, and the rejection of social norms that tolerated violence directed at women. With feminist influence at a high point in the 1970s, political pressure for action grew. By the end of the 1970s, nearly every state had enacted laws to protect women from violence through a mixture of support services, requirements that physicians report suspected cases, and tougher criminal procedures. The inclusion of LGBTQ individuals in these networks did not occur until much later. In 2013, Congress reauthorized the Violence Against Women Act, which for the first time extended support services to victims of violence in same-sex partnerships (LeTrent, 2013).

Quick Review

- The New England colonies passed the first laws against wife beating in the Western world.
- The issue of domestic violence historically has reflected a conflict between the goals of preserving the family unit and protecting women and children.
- A political model of domestic violence, reflecting relations of power and authority, arose in the twentieth century.
- A medical model of domestic violence, which views it as an illness and a source of injury, also developed in the twentieth century.

Intimate Partner Violence

The beatings that many people in shelters have endured from spouses and live-in partners would fit anyone's definition of family violence. But how far in the other direction should the concept of domestic violence go? Is a slap in the face domestic violence, or should the term be reserved for more serious acts of aggression? There is disagreement among the public and academic researchers about exactly what constitutes domestic violence. It's not even clear how to define the term "domestic." Most early studies of adult domestic violence focused on married and cohabiting couples, but most recent studies have focused on the broader concept of "intimate partners," or boyfriends and girlfriends.

TWO KINDS OF VIOLENCE?

When sociologists began to study the extent of violent acts among intimate partners in random-sample surveys of the general population, they asked people whether, and how often, in the previous year they had engaged in behaviors against their spouses or cohabiting partners that ranged from the less serious (e.g., grabbing, pushing, or slapping) to the more serious (e.g., hitting with a fist) to the very serious (e.g., threatening or using a knife or gun) (Straus, 1979; Straus et al., 1996). Surprisingly, men and women in these surveys were about equally likely to report engaging in these acts in the previous year, although most acts were of the less serious kind. This pattern has been confirmed in other surveys (Fergusson, Horwood, & Ridder, 2005). In other words, surveys suggest that both women and men at times initiate violence against their intimate partners. In contrast to the picture of battered women and violent men that the shelter and social services studies show, surveys paint pictures of violent couples in which both partners engage in aggression.

situational couple violence violence that arises from a specific situation in which one or both partners act aggressively in anger

To reconcile this seeming contradiction, some researchers argue that there are two distinct types of intimate partner violence. Michael Johnson calls the first kind **situational couple violence** (Johnson, 2017). It is the more common kind of conflict; and it usually involves the less serious kinds of aggression. It typically occurs when a specific dispute leads one partner to get angry and to lash out at the other, and it rarely escalates into serious violence or injury. That is, it arises from a particular situation rather than from a larger, long-term pattern of violence. Moreover, men and women are about equally likely to initiate it. Most of the violent acts reported in surveys are of this type.

coercive controlling violence a pattern in which a man seeks to control the behavior of his partner through repeated, serious, violent acts

Johnson and his colleagues claim that a second, more serious kind of violence exists: **coercive controlling violence** (Hardesty et al., 2015; Johnson, 2017). This is the type of violence, they argue, that researchers who study shelters or the legal system see. While it affects a much smaller share of the national population than does situational couple violence, its consequences are more dire. It involves a pattern of violence such as repeatedly beating one's partner; it is therefore more likely to cause injuries; and unlike situational violence, it is mostly perpetrated by men. Johnson argues that the heart of the distinction between these two types is that the men who engage in coercive controlling violence are trying to control their partner's behavior: whom they see, whom they talk to, when they leave the house, where they go, and so forth. These men may also seek to dominate their wives, girlfriends, or boyfriends by keeping them economically dependent and by instilling fear of the consequences of disobeying them. The key difference is motivation: control rather than mere anger. Table 11.1 compares these two hypothetical kinds of domestic violence.

Table 11.1 Characteristics of Situational Couple Violence and Coercive Controlling Violence

	SITUATIONAL COUPLE VIOLENCE	COERCIVE CONTROLLING VIOLENCE
Prevalence	Common	Less common
Type of aggression	Less serious (e.g., slapping)	More serious (e.g., beating up)
Gender of perpetrators	Both men and women	Mostly men
Motivation	Anger	Control

Without doubt, far more seriously injured and abused women than men show up at shelters or hospital emergency rooms or testify at the trials of abusive partners who have been arrested. Even among studies of the general population, women are more likely to be reported engaging in the less serious acts such as slapping or kicking, whereas men are more likely to be reported engaging in serious acts such as beating up or choking; and women are more likely to report being injured than are men. So while a majority of violent incidents involving couples may involve minor acts of aggression by both spouses, it seems clear that a minority of incidents do involve serious aggressions by men which cause injuries in women.

The research and debate about distinguishing types of intimate partner aggression can be seen as an extension into the twenty-first century of the tensions between the political and medical models of domestic violence. The idea of situational couple violence fits the medical model; however, in this case the doctor is not a pediatrician like C. Henry Kempe but rather a clinical psychologist or a psychiatrist. The problem is framed as a dysfunctional couple who cannot resolve conflicts peacefully. This framing suggests remedies such as family psychotherapy or marital counseling. In contrast, the idea of coercive controlling violence fits the political model. Here the problem is framed as a controlling male who dominates his wife, girlfriend, or boyfriend in part by inflicting serious and even life-threatening violence. The remedy is to remove the violent man from the household and prevent him from having contact with his partner. This remedy suggests not psychotherapy but rather legal action: an arrest, a restraining order, or incarceration. Researchers and advocates for battered women were incensed by the findings from sociological surveys that women seemed to engage in partner violence as often as men because they saw no battered men at their shelters, only women who had been the victims of severe violence at the hands of controlling men. Johnson (1995) first proposed his distinction in order to show that both models of intimate partner violence had their place. In a sense, he and his colleagues are arguing that the medical model may be more appropriate for the majority of incidents, but that the political model may still be valid for the minority of incidents that cause serious injury and trauma.

Nevertheless, it's still debatable whether two distinct, easily identifiable kinds of intimate partner violence exist (Anderson, 2010). Alternatively, we could think of them as the two end points of a continuum on which we could place individuals according to factors such as severity and frequency of violence and levels of psychopathology. Some couples progress from mild to extreme violence while others do not, for reasons that are not well understood (Holtzworth-Monroe, 2005). We do not know how many of the serious incidents involve men who are engaging in a pattern of controlling partners through violence and how many are merely expressing anger and hostility. Clinicians have found that some couples exhibit symptoms of both kinds in intimate partner violence (Capaldi & Kim, 2007). Consequently, it is best to see Johnson's two kinds of violence as ideal types—conceptual models that help us to understand sociologically the motivations and forces behind the intimate partner violence we see, rather than as guidelines for clinical diagnosis of a violent individual undergoing treatment.

TRENDS AND PREVALENCE IN INTIMATE PARTNER VIOLENCE

In this mixture of concern and debate, one important question often gets lost: How much intimate partner violence is there? We know little about how much violence

How Do Sociologists Know What They Know? Advocates and Estimates: How Large (or Small) Are Social Problems?

The government announced in 2006 that between 1979 and 2004 the number of rapes per 1,000 people in the United States dropped by 85 percent, according to the National Crime Victimization Survey. (The figure is for all rapes, not just the rapes by intimate partners that are discussed in this chapter.) This was good news, except to some advocates for victims of rape and sexual abuse. "When the conversation gets bogged down around, 'How prevalent is this problem?' you can't even get to the next steps, of 'Now, what are we going to do about it?'" Jennifer Pollitt Hill, executive director of the Maryland Coalition Against Sexual Assault, told the *Washington Post* (Fahrenthold, 2006). In other words, Hill was suggesting that stories reporting a decline in rape are unhelpful because they make it more difficult for advocacy groups to win support for services and laws that could help rape victims. It would be better not to talk about it. Dean Kilpatrick, director of the National Crime Victims Research and Treatment Center in Charleston, South Carolina, told the *Post*, "If there's been a change, it's been a very small change." He said that high-profile rape cases may have persuaded more rape victims to stay silent so that their personal lives would not be publicly scrutinized. But it is hard to see how that factor could explain a drastic 15-year drop.

Hill and Kilpatrick were responding no differently than many advocates for (and against) social causes when they describe the scope of the problem they care about. When it would benefit their perspective for the problem to be defined broadly, they tend to describe it as large (e.g., the rate of rape has not really declined; let's stop talking about how it has declined). Consider homelessness. In the 1980s, advocates for the homeless repeated an estimate by activist Mitch Snyder that two to three million people were homeless. Although observers who argued that Synder's estimate was too large were criticized by some advocates, Synder later admitted that his estimate was based on little more than guesswork. No one really knew how many homeless persons there were.

When it is beneficial to advocates' perspectives to define a problem as modest, they tend to describe it as small. Robert Rector of the conservative Heritage Foundation believes that the problem of poverty in the United States has been exaggerated and that government programs to assist the poor are ineffective and too costly. He therefore has argued that many of the families whose incomes

there was in the distant past. The official records of court proceedings can tell us only about the rare instances when abuse came to the attention of the legal system. Consequently, it's impossible to know whether domestic violence has increased, decreased, fluctuated, or stayed the same over the past 100 years. Most likely, what has changed the most over the past century is not the prevalence of intimate partner violence but the amount of attention we have paid to it. (See *How Do Sociologists Know What They Know?:* Advocates and Estimates: How Large [or Small] Are Social Problems?)

Trends Nevertheless, we do have good evidence from Bureau of Justice statistics on the trend in rates of intimate partner violence since 1994, and the results are heartening. Serious but nonfatal intimate partner violence against women (rape or sexual assault, robbery, or aggravated assault) declined by 72 percent between 1994 and 2011. Simple assault by an intimate partner (causing or intending to cause bodily harm) declined by 70 percent over the same period. The rate of serious but nonfatal intimate partner violence against men declined by 64 percent, and the rate of simple assault declined by 44 percent. Homicides by intimates declined by 23 percent for women and 55 percent for men (U.S. Bureau of Justice Statistics, 2013). Some observers believe that the decline partially reflects the passage in 1994 of the Violence against Women Act, which provided sensitivity training in interpersonal violence for police and funded legal services for victims.

fall below the official poverty line are not really poor. The living standards of the officially poor, he notes, are higher today than in the past: nearly three-fourths own a car; 97 percent have a television, 89 percent have microwave ovens, a third have a dishwasher. "Most of America's 'poor' live in material conditions that would be judged as comfortable or well-off just a few generations ago," he wrote in a background paper (Rector, 2007). But liberal poverty analysts counter that although the standard of living of the poor has increased, the standard of living of the non-poor has increased much more. As a result, the gap between the poor and the non-poor is wider than in the past. "In the early 1960s," wrote Rebecca M. Blank and Mark H. Greenberg, "the poverty line was just under 50 percent of median income for a family of four. By 2007, it was at 28 percent of the median" (Blank & Greenberg, 2008).

This is not to say that any of the advocates described here are distorting the data or lying. There is more than one way of defining most social problems. It is probably true, for example, that rape and sexual assaults are still underreported in government surveys, as advocates would claim. So the problem is larger than official statistics show. It is difficult to find all of the homeless, who hide in the abandoned buildings and alleyways of low-income neighborhoods. And it is true that the absolute level of living has probably risen for most of the poor compared to the mid-twentieth century.

My point is only that, as a consumer of social statistics, you should always ask yourself what the biases are of the people who are presenting you with the numbers. If they have a strong stake in convincing you that the problem is large in scope, they will probably choose an expansive definition of it. If they want to convince you the problem is not serious, they'll usually choose a much narrower definition. Evaluate not only their numbers but also their social and political arguments with this tendency in mind.

Ask Yourself

1. In doing student research or observing local politics, have you noticed dramatic differences in the statistics people quote to support their positions? If so, give an example. Did you understand the reason for the discrepancy?
2. What other reasons besides bias might help to explain conflicting statistics on social problems?

Another factor in the decline is a changed social climate on intimate partner violence which has discouraged would-be perpetrators. For example, attention to rape by intimates—especially by husbands—is fairly recent. Until a few decades ago, laws against rape specifically excluded sexual relations between husband and wife. The long-accepted legal principle was that by marrying, wives give their consent to sexual intercourse, so their husbands may demand it, by force if necessary. Some advocates of family privacy and the traditional authority of the husband still agree with that position. But as attitudes toward physical violence in marriage changed, forced sexual acts among married couples increasingly came into question. By the mid-1990s, almost every state had fully or partially repealed the exemption of spouses from rape statutes (Bennice & Resick, 2003).

It is possible but unlikely that the reductions in violence since 1994 merely represent changes in what people are likely to report to survey interviewers or to law enforcement professionals. In two comparable national surveys in 1980 and 2000, the number of serious quarrels among couples did not decline—suggesting that they argued in 2000 as much as ever. But the number of violent incidents did decline (Amato, Booth, Johnson, & Rogers, 2007). If anything, the changing climate concerning intimate partner violence should have made people *more* likely to report violence in recent surveys, but instead they reported less. It seems reasonable to conclude that the level of intimate partner violence has dropped substantially in recent years.

Prevalence Still, the current risks of intimate partner violence remain disturbing. Based on a national survey, the Centers for Disease Control and Prevention estimated that as of 2010 the lifetime chance of a woman being raped, physically assaulted or stalked by an intimate was 36 percent (U.S. Centers for Disease Control and Prevention, 2010). Intimate partnerships remain a major risk site for homicide for women: The percentage of women who were killed by someone they know rose from 30 to 39 percent from 1993 to 2010. For men, the comparable figure is just 3 percent (U.S. Bureau of Justice Statistics, 2013). Women were also more likely to be seriously injured by intimate partners than were men (13 percent to 5 percent).

Social surveys have provided estimates of intimate partner violence among LGBTQ individuals. The 2010 Centers for Disease Control and Prevention survey found that rates are as high or higher among people who identify as gay or lesbian as among people who identify as heterosexual (U.S. Centers for Disease Control and Prevention, 2013). For reasons that researchers do not yet understand, women who identify as bisexual report sharply higher rates of intimate partner violence than do lesbian, gay, or heterosexual individuals. For instance, in the 2010 survey, the lifetime prevalence of severe intimate partner violence was 29 percent for lesbians, 24 percent for heterosexual women, and 49 percent for bisexual women. The comparable figures were 16 percent for gay men and 19 percent for heterosexual men. (There were too few bisexual men in the survey to provide reliable numbers.) Nearly all of the victimization of bisexual women was perpetrated by men, and in the case of rape, their victimization started in adolescence more so than among lesbians who were raped. We will need to await further studies on bisexual women to help determine the reasons for their higher rates of victimization by intimates.

WHICH PARTNERSHIPS ARE AT RISK?

Some intimate partnerships are more likely to lead to violence than others. Whether the couple is married seems to matter, as does their social class.

Marital Status In crime victimization surveys, women in intact, different-sex marriages report the lowest levels of intimate partner violence and women who are separated but not divorced in different-sex marriages report the highest levels (U.S. Bureau of Justice Statistics, 2012). Other studies of different-sex partnerships suggest that married women have a substantially lower rate of intimate partner violence than do cohabiting women (U.S. National Institute of Justice, 2000). It is too soon to know whether married same-sex partners have lower rates than separated or cohabiting same-sex partners. There are several possible explanations for these findings. Women who have separated but not divorced are more likely to have recently ended their relationships because they were violent; consequently, violent incidents may have caused the separations. The lower risk for married women than for cohabiting women could be a selection effect: Women may refuse to marry cohabiting partners who seem violent (Kenney & McLanahan, 2006; Repetti, 2001). And it could be that marriage transforms the relationships of the partners in ways that reduce the likelihood of violence through, for instance, greater commitment or a greater propensity to forgive partners for transgressions (Fincham, Stanley, & Beach, 2007).

Social Class Although domestic violence affects all social classes, several studies report higher rates of domestic violence among low-income than among middle-income couples (U.S. Bureau of Justice Statistics, 1995; Sorenson, Upchurch,

& Shen, 1996) and among unemployed men than among employed men (Capaldi, Knoble, Shortt, & Kim, 2012). Part of this difference may reflect a greater reluctance of middle-income individuals to admit to violence or a greater vigilance toward poor families by social welfare agencies. Still it appears that there is at least a modest association between lower social class and violence against spouses and partners. Johnson (2008) found that having less education is strongly associated with being a coercive controlling partner. But these findings do not necessarily mean that less-educated or low-income couples are inherently more violent; rather, they may be responding to factors such as frustration over lack of resources or social isolation. A study of the 1987–1988 National Survey of Families and Households found that employment instability and financial strain increased the likelihood of intimate violence against women, as did living in a neighborhood of concentrated poverty and disadvantage (Benson, Fox, DeMaris, & Van Wyk, 2003). So both a couple's own economic difficulties and the difficulties of their neighborhood can influence the level of intimate violence.

In fact, there are theoretical reasons to expect these associations: Nearly a half-century ago, William Goode suggested that men with more income and education have additional resources besides force that they can use to control the behavior of their wives (Goode, 1971). This relationship between social class and violence against wives also holds in developing countries: A Bangkok, Thailand, survey found that men with more income, education, and prestigious occupations were less likely to have hit, slapped, or kicked their wives (Hoffman, Demo, & Edwards, 1994). Married women in an Egyptian national survey who had a higher household standard of living were less likely to report that their husbands had acted violently toward them (Yount & Li, 2010). In general, when wives and husbands have more resources available to them, husbands tend to be less violent.

Quick Review

- Most incidents of intimate partner violence involve minor acts of aggression that usually do not lead to injuries and that are initiated by both men and women.
- A minority of incidents involve serious acts of aggression that more often lead to injuries and are initiated by men in order to control their partners.
- Rates of intimate partner violence have declined
- Married couples have lower rates of violence than other couples.
- Violence against spouses and romantic partners occurs in all social classes but is more common in less-educated, lower income families.

CHILD ABUSE

Hitting children is the most tolerated form of family violence. Among parents of 19- to 35-month-old children who were interviewed in a 2000 national survey, 65 percent said that they had spanked their children at some point (Regalado, Sareen, Inkelas, Wissow, & Halfon, 2004). Although it is difficult to make historical comparisons, the use of physical force against children may have been more prevalent in colonial times than ever since. The Puritans believed children were born tainted with sin and expressed their diabolical nature through stubbornness, willfulness, and disobedience. Consequently, good parents had a moral duty to defeat such expressions of sin. When two- and three-year olds first began to act contrary, the task of the father was to "break the child's will" and instill obedience through stern discipline. Even a century ago, physical force was probably more common than it is now. No one today could imagine the head of a children's welfare organization announcing his or her support for flogging.

child abuse an act by a parent or caretaker that results in death, serious physical or emotional harm, sexual abuse, or exploitation

Even if we grant parents the right to spank or slap, at some point physical force shades into abuse. As with violence between spouses and partners, there is no single definition of exactly what constitutes **child abuse.** The U.S. Congress uses a definition that includes an act by a parent or caretaker which results in death, serious physical or emotional harm, sexual abuse or exploitation (U.S. Administration for Children and Families, 2018). Information on the incidence of child abuse comes from the National Incidence Study of Child Abuse and Neglect (NIS), a series of national surveys of child welfare professionals, conducted in 1980, 1986, 1993, and 2005–2006. The NIS obtained information from a broad range of professionals who serve children; they were asked to report on any children they had seen who appeared to be abused or neglected (Sedlak et al., 2010). Although this survey missed children who did not come to the attention of community professionals, it still provides some of the best information. Figure 11.1 shows the rate of abuse and neglect per 1,000 children in the 1993 and the 2005–2006 surveys.[2] The first two bars are for all forms of maltreatment combined. They show that the overall rate of child maltreatment cases declined from about 23 out of every 1,000 children in 1993 to about 17 out of every 1,000 children in 2005–2006. The other pairs of bars show the trends between 1993 and 2005–2006 for specific kinds of maltreatment. All of them show declines. Thus, child abuse and neglect appear to have declined during this period. Other, more recent surveys suggest that the decline has continued (Child Trends, 2018).

Note that the rates were higher (and therefore the bars in Figure 11.1 are higher) for neglect than for the abuse categories. In fact, 60 percent of the cases were reported for neglect rather than for abuse. More than half of the neglect cases

FIGURE 11.1
Rates of maltreatment per 1,000 children, 1993 and 2005 to 2006.
Source: Sedlak et al., 2010.

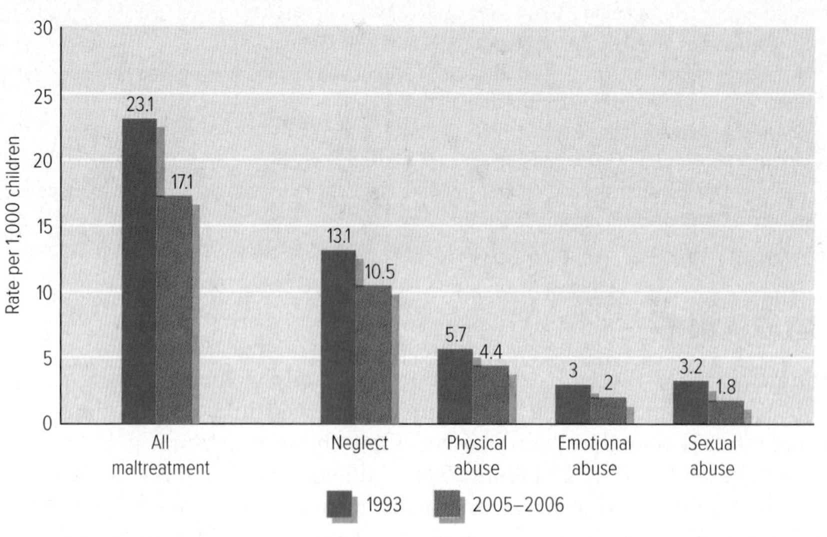

[2] The figure displays rates according to the "harm standard," which requires a judgment that actual harm had occurred to the child, rather than the more lenient "endangerment standard," which only requires a judgment that the child is at risk of harm (Sedlak et al., 2010).

referred to educational neglect, which typically means that the children weren't attending school regularly and that their parents were not making much effort to have them attend. The remainder of the cases of neglect referred to physical neglect, which usually means that children were left unattended or poorly supervised by their parents, and emotional neglect, which includes situations such as inadequate nurturance or exposure to bad behaviors and environments. Only about one-third of all the reported cases of maltreatment were for physical abuse or sexual abuse, the kinds of child-related domestic violence that are of greatest public concern.

The NIS also suggests that child maltreatment was not equally likely in all families. Children whose parents had incomes of below $15,000 per year or who had not graduated from high school or who participated in a poverty program had rates of maltreatment that were five times higher than children whose parents had none of these characteristics. Children whose parents were unemployed had twice the rate of maltreatment as children whose parents were employed (Sedlak et al., 2010). As was true for intimate partner violence, there is good theoretical reason to think that the hardships of poverty and unemployment might lead distressed parents to have less patience with their children or at least to be more neglectful. In fact, family disadvantage is more closely associated with neglect than it is with abuse in the NIS. It is poor families that are more often forced to leave a child unattended while adults work, or that have little faith in the present system of education and therefore don't make sure their children attend school.

Sexual Abuse and Its Consequences The NIS indicates a relatively low incidence of child sexual abuse–1.8 cases per 1,000 children. But social surveys suggest that the problem is more common. In a 1992 survey of sexual activity, the adult subjects were asked, "Before you [reached puberty] did anyone touch you sexually?" (Laumann et al., 1994). Seventeen percent of the women and 12 percent of the men said yes. Among the women, nearly all the touching had been done by men (63 percent) or adolescent boys (28 percent) rather than by women. Men, however, were most likely to report touching by adolescent girls (45 percent), followed by men (23 percent) and adolescent boys (15 percent). Nearly all the incidents for both sexes had involved touching genitals, with a minority reporting vaginal, oral, or anal sex.

The interviewers also asked who did the touching (Laumann et al., 1994). Among women, the most common responses were an older relative (29 percent) or a family friend (29 percent); even more men named a family friend (40 percent). As for cases of sexual abuse that would fit the usual legal definition of **incest**–sexual relations between a child and her or his parent, brother, or sister–16 percent of women who had been touched named a father or brother. Thus, our best estimate is that, overall, about 3 percent of adult American women (that is, 16 percent of the 17 percent who reported touching by anyone) had experienced incest as children. The percentage of women whose experiences fit the definition of incest may be even lower today, given the apparent decline in the rate of child sexual abuse. As for abuse at preschools or schools, only 3 percent of the women who were touched and 4 percent of the men reported that a teacher had done the touching.

incest sexual relations with one's child, brother, or sister

A large research literature suggests that having been sexually abused as a child can have profound long-term consequences for an adult's sexual behavior and intimate relationships (Loeb et al., 2002). The seriousness of the consequences is associated with factors such as the number of incidents, the severity and duration of the incidents, and the age of the child during the incidents. Traumatic sexual experiences can produce inappropriate sexual behavior and feelings of betrayal, lack of trust, and powerlessness (Kendall-Tackett, Williams, & Finkelhor, 1993). They can produce later-life consequences such as poor self-image, depression, and lack of a clear sense of boundaries between oneself and others (Briere & Elliott, 1994). In adolescence and adulthood, these conditions can lead to early onset of sexual activity, riskier sexual activity, and multiple partners (Fergusson, Horwood, & Lynskey, 1997; Thompson, Potter, Sanderson, & Maibach, 1997). As adults, women who were sexually abused as children may have more frequent sexual encounters and relationships from which they derive less pleasure than other women. The 1992 national survey of sexual activity found that women who said they had been touched sexually as children by older persons were, as adults, more likely to experience forced sex, to have multiple sex partners, to engage in riskier sexual behavior, and to experience difficulties such as greater anxiety about sex and less pleasurable sex (Laumann et al., 1994). One-fourth of about 2,000 low-income women in Boston, Chicago, and San Antonio reported that they had been sexually abused as children; and these women were more likely to have had a series of short-term intimate relationships, many of them violent, in adulthood (Cherlin, Burton, Hurt, & Purvin, 2004).

Physical Abuse and Its Consequences Physical abuse can lead to some of the same consequences as sexual abuse, such as lower self-esteem, lack of trust, and depression. In addition, physical abuse can lead to brain injuries and growth retardation (English, 1998). Young children are at the greatest risk of dying from physical abuse: Of the estimated 1,580 child maltreatment deaths in 2014, approximately three-fourths were under age three. The majority of deaths involve neglect, either alone or in combination with another type of maltreatment, such as leaving a child unsupervised in the bathtub (Commission to Eliminate Child Abuse and Neglect Fatalities, 2016). Physical abuse is also associated with behavior problems such as aggression and increased risk of arrest for violence (English, 1998; English, Widom, & Brandford, 2001). Some children, however, do not show lasting consequences of physical abuse; these children tend to have been abused fewer times and to have had a supportive adult available to them.

Poly-victimization Three-fourths of the low-income women in the study of Boston, Chicago, and San Antonio who reported experiencing sexual abuse also reported experiencing physical abuse (Cherlin et al., 2004). This overlap raises the question of what it means to experience more than one type of abuse. Researchers have studied this question by obtaining information on all of the types of maltreatment children have experienced, including not only sexual and physical abuse but also being victimized by theft or other violent crimes, by witnessing violent crime or abuse, and by bullying. They define **poly-victimization** as experiencing multiple types of child maltreatment (Anderson, 2010). It is not uncommon: 22 percent of the children in a national sample had experienced four or more types of victimization during the previous year; and these children were reported to be more anxious, depressed, and aggressive (Finkelhor, Ormrod, & Turner, 2007). The claim is that experiencing several types of maltreatment has a cumulative effect, even after considering the effects of each type of maltreatment separately, as if poly-victimization were to overload the brain's capacity to cope with traumatic events. That claim may be true, but it is also possible that the seeming effects of poly-victimization may

poly-victimization experiencing multiple types of child maltreatment

reflect other causes of distress such as preexisting psychological problems or living in a disadvantaged neighborhood.

Poverty or Abuse? More generally, some of the problems that physically or sexually abused children display, such as depression or aggressive behavior, may be related to growing up in low-income families and disadvantaged neighborhoods, rather than resulting from the abuse itself. Consequently, some of the problems that abused children show would probably have occurred even if they hadn't been abused. In fact, some critics argue that child protective workers sometimes overreact to families in which the real problem is poverty, not maltreatment. When they remove a child from his or her parents in cases of neglect without physical or sexual abuse, according to the critics, workers often make his or her problems worse. Such children are usually sent into the foster-care system, which has its own problems and is not a clear improvement over living at home. (See *Families and Public Policy:* The Swinging Pendulum of Foster Care Policy, on p. 314.) An alternative strategy is to focus social services on assisting the parents of these children (Besharov & Laumann, 1997).

ELDER ABUSE

Another kind of domestic violence that has drawn public attention is **elder abuse,** which we might define as abuse or neglect of an elderly person by a caregiver.

elder abuse abuse or neglect of an elderly person by a caregiver

A modest proportion of the older population reports ever being physically abused (1.8 percent) or sexually abused (0.3%) since turning age 60. But 13.5 percent report ever being mistreated emotionally, such as by verbal abuse, humiliation, harassment, or being ignored. Others report that family members have spent their money (3.4 percent in the past year) (Acierno, Hernandez, Amstadter, Resnick, Steve, Muzzy, and Kilpatrick, 2010). Abuse is more common among what was called in Chapter 10 the young-old population, those age 65 to 74, than among the old-old or the oldest-old. Researchers think that the problem is worse among the young-old because they are more likely to be living with spouses and adult children than are older adults of advanced age—and spouses and children are the most common abusers of the older population (Lachs & Pillemer, 2015). So elder abuse has a family dimension to it; in this case, unfortunately, living with family members increases the likelihood that an older adult will be abused, compared to older people who are living alone or are in assisted living or skilled nursing facilities.

Quick Review

- Definitions of child abuse range from a narrow focus on serious physical harm to an inclusion of sexual abuse without injury and various forms of neglect.
- More than half of official reports of child abuse are for neglect.
- Like adult domestic violence, child abuse occurs in all social classes but is more common in lower-income families.
- Childhood sexual abuse can have long-term negative consequences for sexual behavior and intimate relationships in adulthood.
- Some older persons are emotionally, physically, or sexually abused by their caregivers.

Families and Public Policy

The Swinging Pendulum of Foster Care Policy

Foster care—the removal of children from their parental home and their placement in another home—is a program with few admirers and many critics. It involves a difficult choice between two worthy goals: protecting the integrity of the family unit and protecting children from physical and mental harm. In most circumstances, the children are removed without their parents' permission after a child protective worker investigates a report of abuse or neglect. Consequently, foster care embodies the most severe form of state interference between parents and children—seizing the children against the parents' will. Because child protective workers tend to be middle class and the affected children tend to be poor, it is sometimes criticized as a class-based intrusion into family life. Because it substitutes state-directed care for parental care, it is sometimes criticized as antifamily. Because it fails to return many children to their families in a timely manner, it is criticized for warehousing children from problem families, rather than helping the parents provide better care. Yet few would disagree that children should be protected from some parents—the drug-addicted, the physically or sexually abusive, for instance—who are not fit to raise them.

In the late 1970s, when about 500,000 children were living in foster care, a policy consensus formed: Alarmed by the numbers of children in care, both conservatives and liberals agreed that child protective workers should place a higher priority on helping troubled parents keep their children and care better for them. If a foster care placement was needed, greater efforts should be made to return the children to a permanent home—either by sending them back to their parents or, if absolutely necessary, by putting them up for adoption. Congress codified this consensus in the Adoption Assistance and Child Welfare Act of 1980.[1]

The new consensus worked as intended for several years. As the pendulum swung toward keeping children with their parents, the number of children in foster care declined to about 275,000 in 1983 through 1985. Then it rose again during the 1990s, due in part to the rapid spread of crack cocaine usage. The surge in abandoned and drug-impaired infants led some experts to call for seizing more at-risk children from parents.

In the early 2000s, as crack cocaine usage declined, the foster care caseload began to drop again. Then came the most recent crisis: Rising addiction and death rates due to the abuse of prescription pain relievers, heroin, and fentanyl—the latter, a synthetic opioid far more potent than heroin. Foster care caseloads rose, especially in regions where the opioid crisis was more severe. In fact, a government study found that, between 2011 and 2016, a 10 percent increase in the overdose death rate in a county corresponded to a 4.4 percent increase in children placed in foster care (U.S. Office of the Assistant Secretary for Planning and Evaluation, 2018). The proportion of children entering the foster care system due to parental substance abuse increased from

Sexual Aggression and Violence in Emerging Adulthood

During the new life stage of emerging adulthood that was discussed in Chapter 2—the period between the late teens and about age 30—individuals may have numerous sexual relationships, ranging from hook-ups to dating to cohabiting to marriage. Each is potentially vulnerable to physical and sexual aggression. In fact, rates of violence and abuse peak during emerging adulthood: Between one-fourth and one-half of emerging adults report violence in a relationship within the past year (Halpern-Meekin, Manning, Giordano, & Longmore, 2013). Among women, those who are cohabiting report more violence than those who are married, and both groups report more violence than women who are dating (Brown & Bulanda, 2008). Violence seems to be particularly high in relationships that are characterized by repeated breakups and reconciliations: Seventeen-to-twenty-four-year olds who had experienced a breakup followed by a reunion reported more physical conflict

10 percent in 2000 to over 30 percent in 2016. And the total number of children in foster care rose to 443,000 in 2017 (U.S. Administration for Children and Families, 2018). The pendulum was swinging back.

Yet neither option—vigilance and early removal of children perceived to be in danger, or increased efforts to help troubled parents so that they can keep their children—has worked well. The foster care system was designed on the basis of assumptions about families that no longer hold. It assumed that the family problems leading to foster care were temporary—as when a mother became ill with a disease such as tuberculosis and needed six months or a year to recuperate. It assumed that large numbers of mothers who did not work outside the home could be found to care temporarily for children whose parents couldn't care for them. It didn't foresee families sleeping in homeless shelters and drug-addicted newborns abandoned in nurseries. In addition, it probably ignored levels of child abuse that today would be unacceptable.

The heart of the problem is that there still are no good alternatives to parental care for children. Long-term foster care, with children frequently shuttled from family to family, is problematic. Yet abusive or neglectful parents also harm children. One innovation is to place children in the homes of relatives and pay them. In 2017, 32 percent of foster children were placed in relatives' foster homes (U.S. Administration for Children and Families, 2018). This so-called kinship care option preserves some of the child's family bonds and seems preferable to care by nonrelatives, but it is not without problems. Relatives may have more difficulty than strangers in restricting visits by abusive parents. Moreover, they tend to keep children for a longer period of time than other foster parents; yet they are sometimes reluctant to adopt the children for fear of angering the parents. Thus, kinship care can conflict with the goal of finding a permanent home for foster children. In addition, foster parents typically receive substantially more money per child than parents do under Temporary Assistance for Needy Families (the cash welfare program), creating a possible incentive for families receiving TANF to place the children in kinship foster care.

The only real, long-term hope of stopping the swings of the foster care pendulum is to prevent more children from being abused and neglected in the first place. That would require an assault on poverty, unemployment, substance abuse, and family breakups. Meanwhile, the quandary of what to do about abusive and neglectful parents and their children continues.

Ask Yourself

1. Do you know anyone with experience as a foster parent? If so, what was that person's opinion of the foster care system?
2. Which do you think is more important, protecting a family's integrity or protecting children from abuse?

[1]Public Law 96–272.

than those who were in stably together or stably broken-up relationships (Halpern-Meekin et al., 2013). The issue that provokes the most acrimony and violence is sexual infidelity—"cheating" in the vernacular—especially when it is reinforced with language that a partner thinks is disrespectful or rude (Giordano, Copp, Longmore, & Manning, 2015).

Emerging adulthood includes attendance at college for many young people. Unfortunately, sexual aggression and violence are common among college students. A 2005 study of undergraduate students at two large public universities, one in the South and one in the Midwest, found that 19 percent of the women reported experiencing completed or attempted sexual assault since entering college (Krebs, Lindquist, Warner, Fisher, & Martin, 2009). A majority of those who experienced completed sexual assault did so while under the influence of alcohol or drugs. More than 3 percent of the women reported experiencing physically forced rape. Another survey found that in about 80 percent of the cases, college student women knew the offender in sexual assaults and rapes; and about half occurred while the student was pursuing leisure activities while away from home

(U.S. Bureau of Justice Statistics, 2014). Women who frequently drink enough to get drunk, who are unmarried, and who have been a victim of sexual assault before the current school year are more likely to be victimized (U.S. National Institute of Justice, 2000.) Students who report having any same-sex sexual experiences tend to report higher levels of sexual violence than do students who report exclusively different-sex experiences (Edwards et al., 2015).

Young men who commit sexual aggression against acquaintances are more likely to show hostility toward women and to believe that men are supposed to be more dominant and women more subordinate (Abbey & McAuslan, 2004). The men also show greater physiological arousal when presented with rape scenarios in psychology experiments, are more likely to consider violence against women acceptable, and are more sexually active than men who don't commit sexual aggression. Much of the research on sexual aggression and physical violence among young adults stems from a time when dating was the predominant setting in which college students were sexually intimate. But with the demise of dating and the rise of the hook-up culture, it is not clear how relevant these past studies are to sexual activity among college students. The potential for abuse and aggression is substantial in hookups because the partners may not know each other well. On the other hand, the ephemeral nature of the hookup—the lack of any future contact—may make it less subject to violence than are relationships. Issues of jealousy and commitment may not arise in a hookup, so the most powerful emotions that drive intimate violence among emerging adults may be absent (Armstrong, Hamilton, & England, 2010). To date, however, studies suggest that college women who participate in hookups are more likely to experience sexual violence than are those who do not (Ford, 2017). Hooking up appears to be a risk factor for sexual assault.

Quick Review

- Rates of violence peak during the life stage of emerging adulthood.
- Violence seems to be highest in relationships with repeated break-ups and reconciliations. Sexual aggression and violence are common among college students.
- Most sexual assaults on college campuses are committed by someone the victim knows.
- Alcohol abuse and hookups are risk factors for sexual violence.

Explanations

Why do people abuse their spouses, partners, or children? According to the political model of domestic violence, assaults against spouses and partners arise, in part, from power struggles between men and women. Men have an advantage in struggles against women because of their greater physical strength, on average, and because of a social system that often reinforces male dominance. During the many thousands of years humans spent as hunter-gatherers, male strength was central to the life of bands. Men defended the band's territory against intrusions by other bands, and men armed with spears hunted animals. It is likely that men used their strength to compete for women and to dominate them. Later, in larger social groups, men were often able to shape laws and norms—such as the belief that the husband should be the head of the household—to their advantage so that they didn't need to use force to achieve their ends. The system of male dominance that still appears to some extent in virtually every society today is based in part upon the use of, or the threat of the use of, force against women.

But most heterosexual men, despite their advantage in strength and despite cultural beliefs, don't hit their wives. And most gay men don't hit their spouses and partners. In addition, both men and women sometimes abuse their children. Consequently, the general notion of male dominance isn't useful in explaining why some men are violent and others are not or why parents abuse their children. Many other explanations have been proposed, most of which have some plausibility. These explanations are often referred to as "theories" of domestic violence, although most of them are just collections of related propositions. Some of these perspectives emphasize psychological factors, whereas others emphasize social structural factors. At the present time, we don't know enough to tie them together into a single, coherent explanation. Let's focus on the ones I think are the most important.

SOCIAL LEARNING PERSPECTIVE

The explanation that is probably cited the most draws upon the **social learning perspective** developed by social psychologists. According to this perspective, individuals learn behavior they will later exhibit by observing what others do and seeing the consequences of these actions. Thus, children from violent homes are said to learn by observation and personal experience that aggressive or violent behavior is an acceptable and often successful way of controlling others and getting what you want (Bandura, 1973). In fact, a number of studies do show that children who grow up in homes characterized by domestic violence are more likely, as adults, to act violently toward their spouses and children. (All children may, to some extent, learn that violent behavior is acceptable through watching the pervasive violence in television programs, video games, and films.)

social learning perspective the theory that individuals learn behavior they will later exhibit by observing what others do and seeing the consequences of these actions

For example, in 1999 researchers mailed a questionnaire to several hundred people in upstate New York who, 25 years earlier, had been randomly selected for a psychological study. In the questionnaire, the subjects were asked whether they had seen or heard as a child physical fights between their parents or between a parent and the parent's partner; 26 percent responded that they had, and 14 percent said they had seen two or more incidents. They were also asked a series of questions about whether their current relationships were violent: were they ever physically threatened by their partner and did *they* threaten their partner; were they ever kicked, bitten, or hit with a fist by their partner, or did *they* ever kick, bite, or hit their partner with a fist; and so forth. Even after taking into account the extensive information they had on file about these individuals since childhood, they found that individuals who had seen two or more violent incidents as children were more than twice as likely to have acted violently toward their own current partners or to have been on the receiving end of violent acts by their current partners (Ehrensaft et al., 2003).

This pattern of findings can be interpreted in two ways. The glass-half-empty interpretation is that people are far more likely to assault their partners if they have witnessed hitting or been hit by their parents. This interpretation shows why the social learning perspective does help us to understand why some people are violent. The glass-half-full interpretation is that the vast majority of people who have witnessed hitting or been hit by their parents do *not* beat their spouses. In fact, a review of over 100 studies found that the correlation between being raised in a physically violent home and being an adult perpetrator or victim of physical intimate partner violence was modest in size (Smith-Marek et al., 2015). This second interpretation shows the limitations of the social learning perspective as an explanation for violent behavior: It doesn't explain why most people who have been exposed to violence are not themselves violent.

FRUSTRATION–AGGRESSION PERSPECTIVE

frustration–aggression perspective the theory that aggressive behavior occurs when a person is blocked from achieving a goal

An alternative explanation is derived from the **frustration–aggression perspective.** Here the central idea is that aggressive behavior occurs when a person is blocked from achieving a goal, such as when economic inequalities cause men and women to work for low wages, high unemployment rates make it hard to find a job, or racial discrimination limits the opportunities of people from racial-ethnic groups. When these conditions occur, it is said, the person may displace his or her frustration and anger onto a safer target—such as his or her spouse or children. These targets are safer than employers or strangers because there is less chance of being arrested, being hit hard in return, or losing one's job. Consider, for instance, the sharp economic downturn that occurred in the late 2000s, commonly known as the Great Recession. In areas of the country where the unemployment rate was increasing rapidly, men acted in a more coercive controlling way toward their romantic partners, even after taking into account whether the men were themselves unemployed (Schneider, Harknett, & McLanahan, 2016). In places where unemployment was increasing fast, women in a national survey were more likely to agree with one or more statements about their male partners such as: "He tries to keep you from seeing or talking with your friends or family," "He tries to prevent you from going to work or school," and "He slaps or kicks you." It is as if the uncertainty and anxiety of a rapid economic downturn increased some men's controlling behavior toward intimate partners.

In contrast to the social learning approach, violent behavior is not viewed as directed toward a specific end, such as dominating a partner. Rather, violence is seen as an emotional outburst of displaced anger, usually by a man. So this perspective suggests that, regardless of what people have learned about violence as children, they will be more likely to act violently if they are frustrated by forces they feel are blocking their ability to get a job, move out of a dangerous neighborhood, or attain other important goals. Consequently, the frustration–aggression approach helps us to understand why domestic violence is somewhat more common among the lower social classes, whose members are more likely to be blocked from attaining their goals (but who may also be more likely to have grown up in violent homes).

The frustration–aggression approach raises the question of where a person's basic tendency to act violently (when blocked or frustrated) comes from, other than social learning. Biological processes such as inherited genes could play a role: Pairs of identical twins in the Add Health national survey showed greater similarity than pairs of fraternal twins in whether they had ever insisted or made a partner have sexual relations when the partner did not want to (Barnes, TenEyck, Boutwell, & Beaver, 2013). Since identical twins share 100 percent of their genes while fraternal twins share on average 50 percent, the greater similarity in the behavior of the identical twins could reflect genetic influences. I raise this possibility not to excuse the behavior of violent men. Most people can (and do) control their urges and predispositions. Still, men with a greater biological predisposition toward aggression might be more likely than others to assault their partners and children if they are frustrated and angry about events occurring outside the home.

SOCIAL EXCHANGE PERSPECTIVE

A third explanation draws upon the **social exchange perspective.** This explanation proposes that people calculate whether to engage in a particular behavior by considering the rewards and costs of that behavior and the rewards of alternatives to it. The model here is that of the rational actor. It suggests that a man may decide whether to beat his partner by considering the rewards (he can control her; he can let out his anger and frustration at the rest of the world) against the costs of violence (she might seek a divorce) and the rewards of not being violent (she will continue to do much of the child care and contribute the paycheck from her job). This approach helps to explain why wives are more likely to be the victims of violence if they don't work for wages; in that case, the costs of violence to the husband (she might seek a divorce) are lower and the rewards of not being violent (she will contribute earnings) are lower because the wife is not employed. The social exchange perspective also helps to explain the greater violence against women among the lower social classes. Men with more income can influence their wives' actions by exchanging money for the desired behavior. With money they can get the same rewards poorer men must use force to obtain, but without incurring the high costs of force—such as the possibility that the wife will seek a divorce.

social exchange perspective the theory that people calculate whether to engage in a particular behavior by considering the rewards and costs of that behavior and the rewards of alternatives to it

Quick Review

- The social learning perspective emphasizes that people learn through observation and experience that violent behavior against intimates is acceptable.
- The frustration–aggression perspective emphasizes that violent behavior results when a person is blocked from achieving a goal.
- The social exchange perspective suggests that people engage in violent behavior against intimates when the rewards exceed the costs.

Domestic Violence and Public Policy

In the epilogue to her book on U.S. social policy against domestic violence since the Puritans, Pleck wrote:

> *The history of social policy against domestic violence has been one of persistent, even inherent conflict between protecting the victim and preserving the family, and the gradual development of alternatives within and outside the family for victims of abuse. (Pleck, 1987)*

In the mid-1970s, this often dormant conflict surfaced again, as the feminist movement raised the issue. There is a subtext to the protect-the-victim versus preserve-the-family discourse. Public policies that protect the victim restrict men's use of their superior physical force and therefore decrease the power of men over women. That is why feminist groups worked so hard to bring the problems of battered women to the public's attention, to create crisis centers, shelters, and support services, and to modify the law in nearly all states. Wrote Gordon (1988), "Defining wife-beating as a social problem . . . was one of the great achievements of feminism."

POLICY CHOICES

Today, several decades after domestic violence reemerged as an issue, the political landscape has been transformed. To a large extent, the liberal-feminist view has carried the day. Consequently, the differences between conservatives and liberals on domestic violence are much smaller than when feminists first raised the issue. A half-century ago, one could still find principled conservative defenders of the idea that a husband could, within limits, hit his wife as a corrective action. Today one would be hard pressed to find more than a handful of defenders of physical violence against wives, husbands, or intimate partners in any circumstances. While conservatives may still favor the two-married-parent family with the husband as the head, they tend to endorse the role of the husband as a "soft patriarch" (Wilcox, 2004) who is affectionate and appreciative toward his wife and who spend lots of time in joint activities with his children. The soft patriarch may still spank his kids, but he would not approve of any greater physical discipline than that and would not strike his wife. In fact, Evangelical Protestant husbands who attend church regularly have lower rates of domestic violence than do most other kinds of fathers (Wilcox, 2004). So while conservatives may still object to expansive definitions of domestic violence that would, for instance, ban all forms of corporal punishment against children, they oppose physical and sexual violence among intimate partners.

SOCIAL PROGRAMS

Moreover, advocates have found it challenging to translate protect-the-victim policy into effective programs. Consider the spread since the early 1980s of mandatory arrest policies in domestic violence complaints. This approach was influenced by an experiment conducted by the Minneapolis police force in 1981 and 1982. When responding to domestic violence complaints, the police randomly assigned the offender to one of three treatments: arresting him, ordering him to leave the home for eight hours, or trying to mediate the dispute. The results, based on subsequent arrest records and interviews with the victims, showed that arresting the suspect resulted in the lowest level of repeat violence (Sherman & Berk, 1984).

Intrigued officials at the Department of Justice decided to support replications of the experiment in other cities. But many state governments—eager to take action against the problem—legislated mandatory arrest policies without waiting for the results of the replications. The results of the experiments in other localities suggest, in the words of one review article, a "modest preventative effect" of mandatory arrest policies (Maxwell, Garner, & Fagan, 2002). The authors suggested that while these policies may be helpful in reducing intimate partner violence, they are far from a cure-all. In order to make greater progress in reducing intimate partner violence, organizations will need to identify men at higher risk of repeat offenses—due to factors such as alcohol abuse, prior arrest records, and unemployment—and treat them or restrict their actions. But our knowledge of how to go about this larger task is incomplete (Leisenring, 2008).

These issues illustrate the difficulty of designing programs to address intimate partner violence. Still, in an era of greater gender equality and acceptance of same-sex relationships, the image of a bruised and battered partner has led most Americans to approve of government efforts to protect her or him. The Violence against Women Act, which was reauthorized by Congress in 2013, enjoys wide support, and its extension to LGBTQ people is an advance. It is hard to imagine returning to a time when men could hit their wives with impunity, the violent acts of same-sex partners were outside of the law, and parents could boast of giving their children a good wholesome flogging.

Quick Review

- Public policy discussions about domestic violence often have a preserve-the-family versus protect-the-victim theme.
- Starting in the 1970s, feminists succeeded in moving social norms and policies toward protecting the victims.
- Policy disagreements between conservatives and liberals are smaller than in the past.
- Measures to protect the victims of intimate partner violence, regardless of gender or sexual orientation, have broad support.

Looking Back

1. **When did domestic violence become a social issue?** Domestic violence has been a social issue at various points throughout U.S. history. The Puritans, who took a strong stand against wife beating, passed the first laws against it. A period of renewed interest occurred in the late 1800s, and another in the 1960s. Two theoretical models, a medical model and a political model, have been applied to this social problem. The current interest and activity are largely a result of political and social action by feminist groups and by health and social welfare professionals.

2. **What do we know about violence between intimate partners?** The more common kind is situational incidents in which spouses become angry and engage in minor violent acts. Women seem as likely to initiate these incidents as men. The less common but more serious kind is a pattern of serious violent acts usually carried out by a man against a woman. In many of these cases, the man is seeking to control his partner's behavior. Women are more likely to be the victims of aggressive acts over their lifetimes than are men. Domestic violence is more common among cohabiting couples than among married couples, and more common among low-income families than higher-income families. Over the past two decades or so, intimate partner violence appears to have declined substantially.

3. **What is the extent of child abuse?** Though the physical abuse of children has probably decreased over the long term, surveys continue to show disturbing levels of child abuse by parents. More than half the reported cases refer to educational or physical neglect; less than one-third, to physical or sexual abuse. Child neglect and, to a lesser extent, physical abuse are somewhat more common among low-income families than others. Some cases of neglect may reflect the constraints of poverty more than abuse by parents. Childhood sexual and physical abuse can have long-term undesirable consequences. Severely neglected or abused children are sometimes placed in foster care. In the late 1980s and 1990s, the number of children in foster care rose and there is a continuing debate about whether government social programs should emphasize the preservation of families or the protection of children.

4. **What do we know about sexual aggression and violence in emerging adulthood?** Rates of violence and abuse peak during emerging adulthood. Among women, those who are cohabiting report more violence than those who are married. Most sexual assaults on college campuses are committed by someone the victim knows. Alcohol abuse and hookups are risk factors for sexual assault. Students who report any same-sex sexual experiences report higher levels of sexual violence. Young men who commit sexual aggression against women acquaintances are more likely to show hostility to women and to believe that men should be dominant.

5. **Why does domestic violence occur?** Assaults against spouses and partners arise in part from power struggles between men and women. Men have an advantage in these struggles because of their greater physical strength, and because of a social system that often reinforces male dominance. But most men, gay or heterosexual, do not hit their partners, so other explanations are needed for domestic violence. According to the social learning approach, children from violent homes will learn that violent behavior is an acceptable and often successful means of controlling others; consequently, they will be more likely as adults to use violence against spouse and children. The frustration–aggression approach emphasizes that individuals who are blocked from attaining a goal may displace their frustration and anger onto their spouses and children. The social exchange approach suggests that people calculate the rewards and costs of violent behavior and the alternatives to it. According to this approach, partners who have some economic resources are less likely than others to be victimized, as cross-cultural studies show.

6. **What are the public policy issues concerning domestic violence?** The long-term fundamental tension has been between preserving the family and protecting the victim. Feminists raised the issue of domestic violence in the 1970s and have largely succeeded in moving social norms and public policy toward protecting the victims. Conservatives may still favor the husband-headed family, but they advocate no physical violence other than perhaps spanking children. Legal protection has been extended to LGBTQ people. Crafting successful policies to protect victim of domestic violence has been challenging.

Study Questions

1. How would the political and medical models of domestic violence differ in the way that the perpetrators of violence are viewed?
2. How narrowly or broadly should domestic violence be defined?
3. What are some likely explanations for why domestic violence appears to be more common among lower-income families?
4. Much of the data on the number of new cases of child abuse come from reports by state child welfare agencies. What are the likely biases of this way of collecting information?
5. What are some of the long-term consequences of childhood sexual and physical abuse?
6. How does the trade-off between family reunification and child protection affect the foster care system?
7. Why are so many cases of rape and sexual assault carried out by acquaintances of the victims?
8. What patterns of domestic violence does the social learning perspective explain well? What patterns doesn't it explain well?

Key Terms

child abuse 304
coercive controlling violence 298
domestic violence 294
elder abuse 307
frustration–aggression perspective 312
incest 305
poly-victimization 306
situational couple violence 298
social exchange perspective 313
social learning perspective 311

Thinking about Families

The Public Family	The Private Family
Should child protective workers leave children with parents who have not been violent, but who seem likely to be violent in the future, or should they take children away from potentially violent parents?	**Is rape a concept that should be applied to married couples?**

References

Abbey, A., & McAuslan, P. (2004). A longitudinal examination of male college students' perpetration of sexual assault. *Journal of Consulting and Clinical Psychology, 72,* 747–756.

Acierno, R., Hernandez, M. A., Amstadter, A. B., Resnick, H. S., Steve, K., Muzzy, W., & Kilpatrick, D. G. (2010). Prevalence and correlates of emotional, physical, sexual, and financial abuse and potential neglect in the United States: The national elder mistreatment study. *American Journal of Public Health, 100*(2), 292–297.

Amato, P. R., Booth, A., Johnson, D. R., & Rogers, S. J. (2007). *Alone together: How marriage in America is changing.* Cambridge, MA: Harvard University Press.

Anderson, K. L. (2010). Conflict, power, and violence in families. *Journal of Marriage and Family, 72,* 726–742.

Armstrong, E. A., Hamilton, L., & England, P. (2010). Is hooking up bad for young women? *Contexts, 9*(3), 22–27.

Bandura, A. (1973). *Aggression: A social learning analysis.* Englewood Cliffs, NJ: Prentice-Hall.

Barnes, J. C., TenEyck, M., Boutwell, B. B., & Beaver, K. C. (2013). Indicators of domestic/intimate partner violence are structured by genetic and nonshared environment influences. *Journal of Psychiatric Research, 47,* 371–376.

Bennice, J. A., & Resick, P. A. (2003). Marital rape: History, research, and practice. *Trauma, Violence, & Abuse, 4,* 228–246.

Benson, M. L., Fox, G. L., DeMaris, A., & Van Wyk, J. (2003). Neighborhood disadvantage, individual economic distress and violence against women in intimate relationships. *Journal of Quantitative Criminology, 19,* 207–235.

Besharov, D. J., & Laumann, L. A. (1997). Don't call it child abuse if it's really poverty. *Journal of Children and Poverty, 3,* 5–34.

Blank, R. M., & Greenberg, M. H. (2008). Improving the measurement of poverty. *Hamilton Project Discussion Paper.*

Retrieved March 25, 2009, from http://www.brookings.edu/papers/2008/12_poverty_measurement_blank.aspx

Briere, J., & Elliot, D. M. (1994). Immediate and longterm impacts of child sexual abuse. *The Future of Children, 4,* 54–59.

Brown, S. L., & Bulanda, J. R. (2008). Relationship violence in young adulthood: A comparison of daters, cohabitors, and marrieds. *Social Science Research,* 37(1), 73–87.

Capaldi, D. M., & Kim, H. K. (2007). Typological approaches to violence in couples: A critique and alternative conceptual approach. *Clinical Psychology Review, 27,* 253–265.

Capaldi, D. M., Knoble, N. B., Shortt, J. W., & Kim, H. K. (2012). A systematic review of risk factors for intimate partner violence. *Partner Abuse, 3*(2), 231–280.

Cherlin, A. J., Burton, L. M., Hurt, T. R., & Purvin, D. M. (2004). The influence of physical and sexual abuse on marriage and cohabitation. *American Sociological Review, 69,* 768–789.

Child Trends. (2018). Child maltreatment. Retrieved December 8, 2018, from https://www.childtrends.org/indicators/child-maltreatment

Edwards, K. M., Sylaska, K. M., Barry, J. E., Moynihan, M. M., Banyard, V. L., Cohn, E. S., Walsh, Wendy A.,& Ward, S. K. (2015). Physical dating violence, sexual violence, and unwanted pursuit victimization a comparison of incidence rates among sexual-minority and heterosexual college students. *Journal of interpersonal violence,* 30(4), 580–600 Chapter 11

Ehrensaft, M. K., Cohen, P., Brown, J., Smailes, E., Chen, H., & Johnson, J. G. (2003). Intergenerational transmission of partner violence: A 20-year prospective study. *Journal of Consulting and Clinical Psychology, 71* , 741–752.

English, D. J. (1998). The extent and consequences of child maltreatment. *The Future of Children, 8*(1), 39–53.

English, D. J., Widom, C. S., & Brandford, C. (2001). Childhood victimization and delinquency, adult criminality, and violent criminal behavior: A replication and extension, final report (NCJ 192291). Washington, DC: National Institute of Justice.

Fahrenthold, D. A. (2006, June 19). Statistics show drop in U.S. Rape cases. *The Washington Post.*

Fergusson, D. M., Horwood, L. J., & Lynskey, M. T. (1997). Childhood sexual abuse, adolescent sexual behaviors, and sexual revictimization. *Child Abuse and Neglect, 21,* 789–803.

Fergusson, D. M., Horwood, L. J., & Ridder, E. M. (2005). Partner violence and mental health outcomes in a New Zealand birth cohort. *Journal of Marriage and Family, 67,* 1103–1119.

Fincham, F. D., Stanley, S. M., & Beach, S. R. H. (2007). Transformative processes in marriage: An analysis of emerging trends. *Journal of Marriage and Family, 69,* 275–292.

Finkelhor, D., Ormrod, R. K., & Turner, H. A. (2007). Poly-victimization: A neglected component in child victimization. *Child abuse & neglect, 31*(1), 7–26.

Ford, J. V. (2017). Sexual assault on college hookups: The role of alcohol and acquaintances. *Sociological Forum, 32*(2), 381–405.

Giordano, P. C., Copp, J. E., Longmore, M. A., & Manning, W. D. (2015). Contested domains, verbal "amplifiers," and intimate partner violence in young adulthood. *Social Forces, 94*(2), 923–951.

Goode, W. J. (1971). Force and violence in the family. *Journal of Marriage and the Family, 33,* 624–636.

Gordon, L. (1988). *Heroes of their own lives: The politics and history of family violence.* New York: Viking.

Halpern-Meekin, S., Manning, W. D., Giordano, P. C., & Longmore, M. A. (2013). Relationship churning, physical violence, and verbal abuse in young adult relationships. *Journal of Marriage and Family, 75*(1), 2–12.

Hardesty, J. L., Crossman, K. A., Haselschwerdt, M. L., Raffaelli, M., Ogolsky, B. G., & Johnson, M. P. (2015). Toward a standard approach to operationalizing coercive control and classifying violence types. *Journal of Marriage and Family, //*(August), 833–843.

Hoffman, K. L., Demo, D. H., & Edwards, J. N. (1994). Physical wife abuse in a non-Western society: An integrated theoretical approach. *Journal of Marriage and the Family, 56,* 131–146.

Holtzworth-Monroe, A. (2005). Male versus female intimate partner violence: Putting controversial findings into context. *Journal of Marriage and Family, 67,* 1120–1125.

Johnson, M. P. (1995). Patriarchal terrorism and common couple violence: Two forms of violence against women. *Journal of Marriage and Family, 57,* 283–294.

Johnson, M. P. (2017). A personal social history of a typology of intimate partner violence. *Journal of Family Theory & Review,* 9(June), 150–164.

Kempe, H. C., Silverman, F. N., Steele, B. F., Droegemuller, W., & Silver, H. K. (1962). The battered child syndrome. *Journal of the American Medical Association, 181,* 17–24.

Kendall-Tackett, K. A., Williams, L. M., & Finkelhor, D. (1993). Impact of sexual abuse on children: A review and synthesis of recent empirical studies. *Psychological bulletin, 113,* 164–180.

Kenney, C. T., & McLanahan, S. S. (2006). Why are cohabiting relationships more violent than marriages? *Demography, 43,* 127–140.

Krebs, C. P., Lindquist, C. H., Warner, T. D., Fisher, B. S., & Martin, S. L. (2009). College women's experiences with physically forced, alcohol-or other drug-enabled, and drug-facilitated sexual assault before and since entering college. *Journal of American College Health,* 57(6), 639–649.

Lachs, M. S., & Pillemer, K. (2004). Elder abuse. *The Lancet, 364,* 1363–1272.

Laumann, E. O., Gagnon, J. H., Michael, R. T., & Michaels, S. (1994). *The social organization of sexuality: Sexual practices in the United States.* Chicago: University of Chicago Press.

Leisenring, A. (2008). Controversies surrounding mandatory arrest policies and the police response to intimate partner violence. *Sociology Compass, 2,* 451–466.

LeTrent, S. (2013). Violence against women act shines a light on same-sex abuse. *CNN.* Retrieved January 10, 2016, from http://www.cnn.com/2013/03/14/living/same-sex-domestic-violence-and-vawa/

Loeb, T. B., Williams, J. K., Vargas Carmona, J., Rivkin, I., Wyatt, G. E., Chin, D., & Asuan-O'Brien, A. (2002). Child sexual abuse: Associations with the sexual functioning of adolescents and adults. *Annual Review of Sex Research, 13,* 307–345.

Maxwell, C. D., Garner, J. H., & Fagan, J. A. (2002). The preventive effects of arrest on intimate partner violence: Research, policy and theory. *Criminology & Public Policy, 2,* 51–80.

Nahmias, L. (2016). City and state release separate reports on the death of Zymere Perkins. Retrieved December 11, 2018, from https://www.politico.com/states/new-york/albany/story/2016/12/city-and-state-release-separatereports-on-child-abuse-death-of-six-year-old-harlem-boy-zymere-perkins-108061

O'Brien, J. E. (1971). Violence in divorce prone families. *Journal of Marriage and the Family, 33,* 692-698.

Pleck, E. (1987). *Domestic tyranny: The making of American social policy against family violence from colonial times to the present* U.S. Office of the Assistant Secretary for Planning and Evaluation. (2018). The relationship between substance use indicators and child welfare caseloads. *ASPE Research Brief.* Retrieved 2018, December 10, from https://aspe.hhs.gov/system/files/pdf/258831/SubstanceUseCWCaseloads.pdf

Repetti, R. L. (2001). Searching for the roots of marital conflict in uxoricides and uxorious husbands. In A. Booth, A. C. Crouter, & M. Clements (Eds.), *Couples in conflict* (pp. 47–55). Mahwah, NJ: Lawrence Erlbaum.

Schneider, D., Harknett, K., & McLanahan, S. S. (2016). Intimate partner violence in the great recession. *Demography, 53*(2), 471–505.

Sedlak, A. J., Mettenburg, J., Basena, M., Petta, I., McPherson, K., Greene, A., & Li, S. (2010). Fourth national incidence study of child abuse and neglect (nis–4): Report to Congress. *U.S. Administration for Children and Families.* Retrieved February 8, 2012, from http://www.acf.hhs.gov/programs/opre/abuse_neglect/natl_incid/reports/natl_incid/nis4_report_congress_full_pdf_jan2010.pdf.

Sherman, L., W., & Berk, R. A. (1984). *The Minneapolis domestic violence experiment.* Washington, DC: The Police Foundation.

Smith-Marek, E. N., Cafferky, B., Dharnidharka, P., Mallory, A. B., Dominguez, M., High, J., et al. (2015). Effects of childhood experiences of family violence on adult partner violence: A meta-analytic review. *Journal of Family Theory & Review, 7*(4), 498–519.

Sorenson, S. B., Upchurch, D. M., & Shen, H. (1996). Violence and injury in marital arguments: Risk patterns and gender differences. *American Journal of Public Health, 86,* 35–40.

Straus, M. A. (1979). Measuring intrafamily conflict and violence. *Journal of Marriage and the Family, 41,* 75–88.

Straus, M. A., Hamby, S. L., Boney-McCoy, S., & Sugarman, D. B. (1996). The revised conflict tactics scales (cts2): Development and preliminary psychometric data. *Journal of Family Issues, 17,* 283–316.

Thompson, N. J., Potter, J. S., Sanderson, C. A., & Maibach, E. A. (1997). The relationship of sexual abuse and HIV risk behaviors among heterosexual adult female STD patients. *Child Abuse and Neglect, 21,* 149–156.

U.S. Administration for Children and Families. (2018). The AFCARS report no. 25. Retrieved December 10, 2018, from https://www.acf.hhs.gov/sites/default/files/cb/afcarsreport25.pdf

U.S. Bureau of Justice Statistics. (1995). Violence against women: Estimates from the redesigned survey. Washington, DC: U.S. Government Printing Office.

U.S. Bureau of Justice Statistics. (2012). Intimate partner violence in the United States. Retrieved February 10, 2012, from http://bjs.ojp.usdoj.gov/content/intimate/ipv.cfm

U.S. Bureau of Justice Statistics. (2013). Intimate partner violence: Attributes of victimization, 1993–2011. *Intimate Partner Violence.* Retrieved January 10, 2016, from http://www.bjs.gov/index.cfm?ty=pbdetail&iid=4801

U.S. Bureau of Justice Statistics. (2014). Rape and sexual assault victimization among college-age females, 1995–2013. Retrieved December 15, 2018, from https://www.bjs.gov/content/pub/pdf/rsavcaf9513.pdf

U.S. Centers for Disease Control and Prevention. (2010). Intimate partner violence in the United States–2010. *National Center for Injury Prevention and Control.* Retrieved January 10, 2016, from http://www.cdc.gov/violenceprevention/pdf/cdc_nisvs_ipv_report_2013_v17_single_a.pdf

U.S. Centers for Disease Control and Prevention. (2013). The national intimate partner and sexual violence survey (NISVS): 2010 findings on victimization by sexual orientation. *National Center for Injury Prevention and Control.* Retrieved January 11, 2016, from http://www.cdc.gov/violenceprevention/pdf/nisvs_sofindings.pdfU.S. National Institute of Justice. (2000). Extent, nature and consequences of intimate partner violence. Retrieved February 25, 2016, from https://www.ncjrs.gov/pdffiles1/nij/181867.pdf

U.S. National Institute of Justice. (2000). Extent, nature and consequences of intimate partner violence. Retrieved February 25, 2016, from https://www.ncjrs.gov/pdffiles1/nij/181867.pdf

U.S. Office of the Assistant Secretary for Planning and Evaluation. (2018). The relationship between substance use indicators and child welfare caseloads. *ASPE Research Brief.* Retrieved 2018, December 10, from https://aspe.hhs.gov/system/files/pdf/258831/SubstanceUseCWCaseloads.pdf

Wilcox, W. B. (2004). *Soft patriarchs, new men: How Christianity shapes fathers and husbands.* Chicago: University of Chicago Press.

Yount, K. M., & Li, L. (2010). Domestic violence against married women in Egypt. *Sex Roles, 63,* 332–347.

Zelizer, V. (1985). *Pricing the priceless child: The changing social value of children.* New York: Basic Books.

Chapter Twelve

Union Dissolution and Repartnering

Looking Forward

1. What are the ways in which American children experience the end of their parents' unions?
2. What factors have influenced the level of union dissolution?
3. What happens to children in the aftermath of the dissolution of their parents' marriage or cohabiting union?
4. What are the forms of stepfamily life?
5. How does the well-being of children in stepfamilies compare to the well-being of children in other kinds of families?
6. How have the trends in union dissolution and repartnering altered family life?

There are three ways that children can experience the end of their parents' union. Until about 100 years ago, the way most did so was through the deaths of their fathers or mothers (Ellwood & Jencks, 2004). Death rates for adults in mid-life were far higher than today, and children could not take it for granted that both of their parents would live long enough to see them through their teenage years. But starting in the early 1900s, adult death rates began a century-long decline (U.S. National Center for Health Statistics, 2018), and today it is rare for a child to have a parent die. During the decades-long decline, however, the second way that children can experience the end of their parents' union became much more common: divorce. The divorce rate, as noted in Chapter 2, doubled in the 1960s and 1970s and reached a high plateau in 1980. At that time, nearly two-thirds of children living in single-parent families were residing with a divorced or separated parent, rather than a widowed parent.

Demographers disagree on the overall trend in divorce since 1980, but there's no doubt that the sharp increases that characterized the 1960s and 1970s have ended (Kennedy & Ruggles, 2014). Moreover, the risk of divorce has declined substantially among college graduates (Martin, 2006). My reading of the data is that there has been a modest decline among non-college-graduates as well. (See *How Do Sociologists Know What They Know?* Measuring the Divorce Rate.) But as divorce rates have plateaued or dropped, a third way for children to experience the disruption of their parents' union has become more common: witnessing the breakup of their unmarried cohabiting parents' union. One in four children is now born to cohabiting parents (Wu, 2017). If their unions end, these parents cannot go to court to get a divorce decree because they were never married. The beginning and end of their relationships never show up in the nation's marriage and divorce statistics. By 2013, less than half of children living in single-parent families were residing with a divorced or separated parent; most of the rest were living with an unmarried parent who either had ended a cohabiting union or had never lived with the other parent.[1]

From a child's perspective, there is great variation in the experience of parental cohabitation. The breakup of a cohabiting union can be as consequential for children as is the divorce of married parents. The cohabiting partner who leaves the household could be the biological father or mother of the child, or that partner

[1] The figures on children in single-parent families in 1980 and 2013 are calculations by the author. In 2013, among all children living with one parent, 46 percent were living with divorced and separated parents; and 45 percent were living with never married parents (U.S. Bureau of the Census, 1985, 2013). A small number were living with widowed parents.

How Do Sociologists Know What They Know?

Measuring the Divorce Rate

A reporter calls a sociologist who does research on divorce and asks, "What's the most recent statistic for the divorce rate in the United States?" "In 2016," the sociologist replies, "17 out of every 1,000 married women divorced." "Seventeen out of a thousand," she responds, "No way! That's tiny. The divorce rate has got to be much higher than that."

"Well," says the sociologist, "another way of saying it is that about 40 percent of all marriages would end in divorce at current rates." "Great," the reporter replies, "and what year is that for?" "It's not for a year," the sociologist tries to explain, "it's a projection based on rates among older women . . ." But he can tell that the reporter is losing patience fast. She wants a figure and a year, not a lecture in demography, and she's writing a story on a deadline.

In fact, it's hard to answer the question, "what's the current divorce rate?" in a way that is both precise and meaningful. The difficulty is that the most meaningful statistic describes the proportion of all current marriages that will end in divorce, but it's impossible to know that proportion until everyone who is now married has grown old and died. So sociologists try to estimate this lifetime figure, but their estimates are just educated guesses. The precise statistic is based on the number of divorces in the most recent year for which data are available, but it doesn't tell us much about people's experience with divorce.

The 17-out-of-1,000 rate is the precise statistic; it represents the number of divorces in the United States in 2016 divided by the number of married women (and then multiplied by 1,000) (Hemez, 2017). It includes women who have been married for many years as well as those who married only recently. It gives the probability that a married woman would have become divorced in 2016: 17 ÷ 1,000, or a little less than 2 percent. So 2016, about 2 percent of married women obtained divorces.

This does indeed sound like a very low figure, given all of the public concern about divorce. No wonder reporters are unhappy with it. It is a *cross-sectional rate,* meaning a rate at one point in time. It provides a snapshot of the experiences of married American women during a single year. In the following year, 2017, the 983 of every 1,000 women who did *not* divorce in 2016 were still at risk of divorcing, and another 17 or so probably did. In 2018, yet another 17 or so would obtain divorces, and so on, year after year, into the future. Consequently, although the average woman married in 2016 had a 2 percent chance of becoming divorced *in 2016,* she had a far higher chance of becoming divorced *over the rest of her married life.*

Just how high her lifetime chances are, we cannot know with certainty. But let us conduct the following thought experiment: Suppose the risks of divorce were to stay the same for the next 30 years: 17 out of 1000 per year. Now think of a hypothetical woman whose wedding is today. We could fast-forward her through time and calculate her risk of divorce over the first 30 years of her marriage—because we are assuming that her risks will remain the same as those observed today.

If we were to do this calculation, we would find that the 30-year probability of divorce for a young woman marrying today about 40 percent. But it's important to recognize that this figure is just a projection of current risks into the future. In fact, it's unlikely that divorce risks will stay the same.

The utility of the long-term estimate, then, is not that it will prove accurate 30 years from now—it may not—but rather that it indicates the underlying force of divorce that is implied by the behavior of married people today. The long-term estimate, in other words, answers an important *what if* question: What if the risks of divorce at each duration of marriage stayed the same as they are now; what long-term level of divorce would these current risks imply? This is the question most readers want an answer to, even if the answer is necessarily uncertain.

Ask Yourself

1. How many couples in your family have divorced in the past year? In the past 10 years? The past 20? Is your family's divorce rate similar to the divorce rate for the country as a whole?
2. In general, do news reporters do a good enough job of explaining the significance of social statistics such as the divorce rate? What are the dangers of misreporting such statistics?

FIGURE 12.1
Percentage of all Children Born to Cohabiting or Married parents who Experience the Dissolution of Their Parent's Union by Age 15.

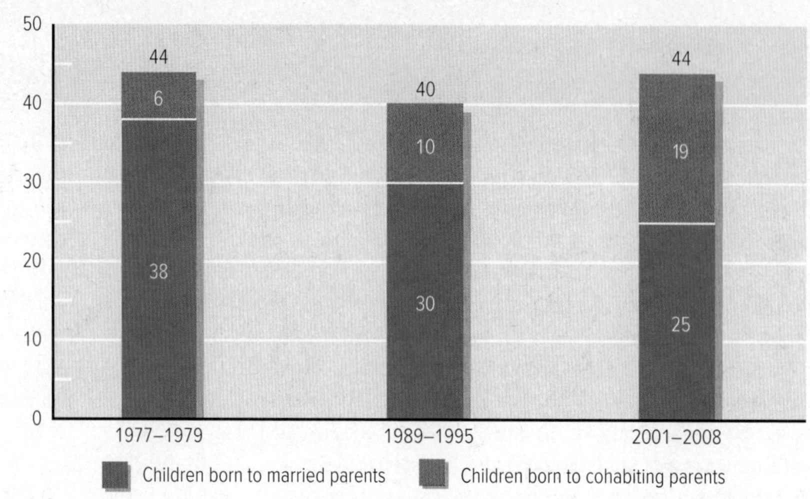

might be someone who has assumed a stepparent-like role in the child's life. The breakup may worsen the financial situation of the parent with whom the children remain. On the other hand, that partner may be a short-term live-in boyfriend who contributed little money to the family pot; who had little to do with the children; and whose departure won't alter their lives much. While continuing to study the consequences of divorce, we need to broaden our focus to also include the breakup of cohabiting unions. In order to do so, I will write about **union dissolution,** meaning both the legal ending of a marital union and the informal ending of a cohabiting union, and **union repartnering,** meaning the formation of new unions either by remarriage or a new cohabiting union.

union dissolution the legal ending of a marital union or the informal ending of a cohabiting union

union repartnering the formation of new unions either by remarriage or a new cohabiting union

What proportion of children experience the dissolution of their parents' union? Figure 12.1 presents estimates that I have calculated for three points in time for which comparable data are available: 1977 to 1999; 1989 to 1995; and 2001 to 2008.[2] You can see that in the earliest and latest of the three periods, an identical 44 percent of children are estimated to experience a dissolution. The middle period is a bit lower, at 40 percent. Overall, then, the percentage of children experiencing a dissolution of their parents' unions has changed very little since the late 1970s. But note that the *type* of dissolution has changed. For each period, the figure divides the total percentage of children experiencing dissolution into two parts: children who were born to married parents and children who were born to cohabiting parents. In the earliest period, the experience of children born to married parents dominated. They experienced the breakdown of their parents' *marriages.* As we move toward the present, however, more and more of the dissolution occurred to children born to *cohabiting* parents. Some of those parents never married and therefore never legally separated or divorced, but rather simply ended their partnerships. If this trend continues, we may soon see a time when a majority of children who experience dissolution will be born to cohabiting parents.

[2] I used the following sources: For dissolutions in 1977–1979, Bumpass (1984). For dissolutions in 1989–1995, Andersson & Philipov (2002). For dissolutions in 2001–2008, Andersson, Thomson, & Duntava (2017). For the proportion of children born to married parents and to cohabiting parents, Wu (2017). The comparisons over time are not exact (e.g., Bumpass (1984) gives the percentage experiencing a disruption by age 16, and the others report it by age 15). I would estimate that the numbers are accurate to plus or minus two percentage points.

It makes a difference for children whether the dissolutions they experience result from being born to married parents or to cohabiting parents. The dissolutions of cohabiting parents occur much sooner after the children's birth than do the dissolutions of parents who were married when the children were born (Andersson, Thomson, & Duntava, 2017). About half of cohabiting couples who have a child together will have ended their unions by the time their child is five years old, even if they had married in the interim years (Bendheim-Thoman Center for Child Well-being, 2007). In fact, the risk of disruption for children born into cohabiting unions is about twice as high as the risk of divorce for children born to married parents (Andersson, Thomson, & Duntava, 2017). The rise in cohabitation as a setting for childbirth has increased children's chances of living in unstable families over the past few decades (Rackin & Gibson-Davis, 2018). Then why does Figure 12.1 show no increase in the *total* percentage of children experiencing dissolution? Because divorce rates have been declining since a peak around 1980, so that children born to married parents are less likely to see their parents part.

When two childless adults, whether married or cohabiting, end their union, the breakup, although emotionally painful, is straightforward. If they were cohabiting, they basically walk away. If they were married, they conclude their legal business and often do not see each other again. When children are involved, however, a clean break is not possible. Even though the ties between the parents are severed, the breakup does not sever the ties between each parent and the children. In many cases, the mother keeps custody of the children, forming a single-parent family that may endure for years. The father's relationship–often reduced to regular visits, or less–is problematic. Indeed, some fathers fade from their children's lives. Nevertheless, a growing number of fathers are obtaining shared custody of their children.

The story of parental repartnering, until recently, has been a story of remarriage. In the past, the vast majority of new unions were formalized by marriage. Today that is not the whole story. After a breakup, most parents will form another partnership, but it won't necessarily involve marriage. In 2018, there were 2.4 million children who were living with a biological parent and that parent's unmarried partner who was not the biological parent of the child (U.S. Bureau of the Census, 2018b). In some cases, this second partnership will fail and a parent may move on to a third one. Repartnering further complicates adults' and children's lives. It introduces a stepparent into the child's family but doesn't subtract a biological parent–unlike remarriage after a parental death. It can bring a bewildering network of quasi-relatives that extends over several households. In short, repartnering necessitates another major adjustment for adults and children who may have struggled to adjust to single-parent life.

These developments have greatly altered American family life. They have also been a source of concern. What do we know about the causes and consequences of union dissolution? About the effects of repartnering and remarriage on stepparents and stepchildren? How are union dissolution and repartnering altering the nature of the family? These are the questions to be pursued in this chapter.

Societal Influences on Union Dissolution

Broad cultural and economic trends in American society have influenced levels of union dissolution. We have examined these trends in previous chapters. A brief discussion of them follows here. A summary is provided in Table 12.1.

Table 12.1 Social Influences on Union Dissolution

Cultural change	A greater emphasis on personal fulfillment made dissolution a more acceptable option for people who felt unfulfilled by their unions.
Cohabitation	The increase in cohabiting unions, which have a higher probability of ending in a dissolution than do marriages, has been the main driver of rising union dissolution among young adults.
Men's employment opportunities	As young men's economic opportunities decreased since the early 1970s, their reduced earning potential may have caused stress in marriages and a turn toward cohabiting rather than marrying.
Women's employment opportunities	Women's growing employment opportunities led to a rise in the number of wives working outside the home. Under the specialization model of marriage, employment raised the risk of divorce, but under the income-pooling model, employment seems to lower it.
Age at entry into union	People who begin their unions at older ages have a lower rate of dissolution. The rising age at marriage is an important reason for the decline in divorce over the past few decades.
Race and ethnicity	African Americans have higher rates of union dissolution than most other groups. Low income and unemployment, a lesser emphasis on marriage in African American kinship, and discrimination in job and housing markets may contribute.

CULTURAL CHANGE

The most important cultural change has been the growing place of individualism and personal fulfillment in intimate unions. Cultural critics claim that this emphasis erodes bonds of obligation and trust. As a framework for thinking about relationships, it is alleged, the emphasis on personal fulfillment results in a vocabulary that is rich in ways of thinking about individual well-being but impoverished in ways of thinking about commitment (Bellah, Madsen, Sullivan, Swidler, & Tipton, 1985). For instance, numerous books, articles, lecture series, courses, and support groups exist on self-actualization or self-development or human potential, but much less intellectual activity is centered on maintaining personal responsibilities and obligations to others. Put another way, a focus on personal fulfillment represents a shift toward the concerns of the private family as against the concerns of the public family. Married couples today place more emphasis on individual satisfaction than in the middle of the twentieth century. At that time, a spouse who wanted a divorce needed to prove to a judge that her or his partner was guilty of something very wrong such as desertion or violent behavior. Then in the 1970s, most states enacted unilateral divorce laws, commonly known as "no-fault" divorce, under which one spouse could obtain a divorce even if the other spouse objected. From the unilateral divorce perspective, divorce is an acceptable option for people who feel personally unfulfilled; indeed *not* divorcing in the face of personal dissatisfaction comes to need justification. The growing emphasis on personal fulfillment almost certainly contributed to the sharp rise in divorce in the 1960s and 1970s. The recent decline in divorce rates, centered on college graduates, may imply something of a cultural reversal. But individualism remains a stronger factor than in the nation's past.

COHABITATION

Cohabitation is almost by definition a more individualistic type of union than is marriage. But unlike marriage, it is largely unregulated by law: When it starts and when it ends are solely up to the partners, and either of them can end the relationship at any time without taking any legal action. Their commitment to each other is understood to be limited. In nearly all Western countries, cohabiting unions have a higher probability of ending in a dissolution than do marriages (Andersson, Thomson, & Duntava, 2017). In the United States, the proportion of young adults who have ever cohabited has increased while the proportion who have ever married has decreased (Lamidi & Manning, 2016). Cohabitation has therefore become the main driver of rising union dissolution among young adults. In other words, the amount of union dissolution among young adults has increased in the United States not because they are getting married and divorced more often (they are not) but rather because they are increasingly likely to enter into short-term cohabiting unions. (Eickmeyer, 2018). Figure 12.1 showed that children born to cohabiting parents have become a growing proportion of all children who see their parents' union end.

MEN'S EMPLOYMENT

Men are still culturally expected to work steadily in order to be seen as good husbands. In the older, specialization model of the marriage market, men traded their wages for women's housework and child care services. In the newer, income-pooling model of the marriage market, men and women combine their incomes. But even in the income-pooling model, the expectation is that men will contribute financially. While it may now be *desirable* for a wife to work steadily outside of the home, it remains *mandatory* that the husband work steadily. If he does not provide a steady income, the chances that his marriage will end in divorce increase, many studies show (Burstein, 2007; Killewald, 2016). Since the 1970s, the employment opportunities for men without college educations have been declining because of the globalization and computerization of production. These less-educated young men and their partners have turned toward cohabiting unions. The greatest growth in cohabiting relationships has been among those with a high school degree but not a bachelor's degree (Manning & Stykes, 2015). Unless their financial position improves, these cohabiting couples are less likely to marry and more likely to dissolve their relationships (Seltzer, 2004). When an unemployed man in the Toledo study of cohabiting young adults was asked why he hadn't married his girlfriend, he replied, "I don't really know 'cause the love is there uh ... trust is there. Everything's there except money" (Smock, Manning, & Porter, 2005, p. 687). Moreover, some of the participants in the study said that the man's job was more important than the woman's job—that he should "provide for" or "support" a family. "What would make me ready?" one man said. "Knowing that I could provide" (p. 691). The turn toward cohabitation has likely increased the rates of union dissolution experienced by young adults without bachelor's degrees. Conversely, the transformed economy has increased opportunities for college-educated professionals and managers. The strong job market they enjoy may explain why divorce has declined among college-educated couples.

WOMEN'S EMPLOYMENT

While the effect of men's employment on union dissolution is straightforward, the effect of women's employment is complex. Women's employment theoretically could have contrasting effects:

- *Independence effect.* Employment could raise the likelihood of a breakup by providing an opportunity for the woman to support herself independently of her partner. This opportunity would make dissolution a more attractive option for women who were unhappy with their marriages or cohabiting unions.

- *Income effect.* On the other hand, employment could lower the likelihood of dissolution because the increase in the family's income could relieve financial pressures and thereby reduce tensions in the relationship.

Which effect predominates seems to depend on which cultural model of gender roles is dominant. In the specialization model of marriage that was dominant in the mid-twentieth century, wives were not supposed to work outside the home. They were highly dependent on their husbands' earnings. When they did work, their employment undermined the breadwinner–homemaker bargain that was the heart of the specialization model. Studies from this period suggest that wives' employment, on balance, increased the risk of divorce (Becker, Landes, & Michael, 1977). In other words, the independence effect of women's earnings predominated several decades ago. With the rise of the income-pooling model of marriage, however, both spouses are supposed to work for pay. Wives' earnings are an acceptable way for a family to increase its income. Wives' earnings also can bring them more bargaining leverage on issues such as how much housework and child care each spouse does. Newer studies suggest that wives' incomes may now *lower* the risk of divorce for most couples—especially when they are married to men who also have substantial earnings (Sayer & Bianchi, 2000; Burstein, 2007; Goldscheider, Bernhardt, & Lappegård, 2015).

The change from wives' income being destabilizing to stabilizing seems to have begun at some point in the last quarter of the twentieth century and is still in progress (Sweeney, 2002; Sweeney & Cancian, 2004). It is consistent with the greater emphasis on individualism and personal fulfillment because it allows both women and men to participate in the labor market. Along with the trend toward a more egalitarian division of housework and child care, the spread of the income-pooling model appears to reflect the emergence of a new cultural climate in which greater equality in men's and women's roles inside and outside the home, rather than a sharp division of labor, leads to greater stability in marriage. This change helps to explain why the divorce rate has been declining recently among college-educated married couples, in which both the husband and the wife typically have stable, substantial earnings.

AGE AT ENTRY INTO UNION

As young adults age out of their teenage years and into their twenties, they gain maturity. They have a better sense of what kinds of persons they will be as adults and what their needs in a partner will be. Moreover, they will be choosing among older partners who have had more time to finish their education and start their work lives, thereby revealing more of what their adult life course may be like. In other words, after their teenage years they should be in a better position to make a match that will last. Moreover, early cohabiting unions or marriages are often precipitated by an unplanned pregnancy, and it is known that a pre-union birth raises the likelihood dissolution (Amato, 2010). It does so partly because it brings together a couple who might not otherwise have chosen to live together. It also may be more difficult, on a practical level, for a couple to make a partnership work if a young child is present from day one. Consequently, the older a person is at entry into a marriage or a cohabiting union, the lower is the chance that it will end in dissolution, at least through one's early thirties (Lehrer, 2008). The rising age at marriage is an important reason for the declines in divorce over the past few decades (Rotz, 2016; Cohen, 2019).

RACE AND ETHNICITY

African Americans have substantially higher rates of marital separation and divorce than most other racial-ethnic groups (Payne, 2018); about one-half of the marriages of black women end within 15 years compared to about one-third of white women's marriages (Raley & Bumpass, 2003). Similarly, African America women who are cohabiting are less likely to marry their partners and more likely to break up with them (Bramlett & Mosher, 2002). Although lower income, unemployment, and lower educational level are important sources of this racial difference, these factors alone cannot account for it. It is possible that the lesser emphasis in African American culture on marriage, relative to extended kinship ties, also plays a role. African Americans, who can rely more heavily on mothers, grandmothers, and other kin, have less need to stay married; they also have an alternative source of support if a marriage ends (Orbuch, Veroff, & Hunter, 1999).

In addition, black women who separate from their husbands are considerably less likely to obtain a legal divorce, and again the differences are not due solely to economics or education. Within three years of separating, 57 percent of black women had obtained a divorce, according to a survey, compared with 66 percent of Hispanic women and 91 percent of non-Hispanic white women (Bramlett & Mosher, 2002). What these statistics imply is that black women have a higher likelihood of separating from husbands, but they turn these separations into divorces at a much slower pace.

Nevertheless, discrimination and unequal access to jobs and income may still play a role in the marriage differential between African Americans and whites. As noted in a discussion of racially based differences in marriage in Chapter 5, the military provides something of a natural experiment with regard to family life: it is an institution with less discrimination than in civilian life and in which blacks receive similar salaries and benefits (such as health insurance) as do whites. This is particularly true in the Army, which has the highest proportion of blacks of all branches of the armed services and has substantial numbers of blacks in supervisory positions. Teachman and Tedrow (2008) compared the risk of divorce for married black soldiers on active duty to married blacks who were in the reserves. Both active-duty and reserve-duty soldiers must meet the same entrance requirements to join the service (for instance, being a high school graduate), but reservists experience the potential discrimination of the civilian labor and housing markets, whereas soldiers on active duty do not. They found that black soldiers while on active duty had a much lower risk of divorce than did black reservists; in fact, their risk of divorce was comparable to that of white civilians. The implication is that the discrimination and unequal treatment of civilian life may be a reason for the higher divorce rates of African Americans.

How Union Dissolution Affects Children

At least one partner chooses to leave in every case of union dissolution. Presumably, then, at least one partner's well-being is enhanced by the breakup. But children do not choose that their parents end their union. While the end of a violent, dysfunctional union might benefit the children involved, it isn't true in general that children's well-being is enhanced by their parents' breakup. In fact, there are good reasons to think that their well-being should be, in many cases, diminished. They lose the benefits of having both of their parents living in the same household with them. They must go through an emotionally difficult process of adjusting to the breakup. Sometimes they must cope with continuing, bitter conflict between their parents. Nevertheless, most of them manage to cope with the dissolution without major long-term problems. A discussion of the important aspects of their experiences follows.

CHILD CUSTODY

legal custody (of children after a dissolution) the right to make important decisions about the children and the obligation to have legal responsibility for them

physical custody (of children after a dissolution) the right of a divorced spouse to have one's children live with one

joint legal custody (of children after a dissolution) the retaining by both parents of an equal right to make important decisions concerning their children

joint physical custody (of children after a dissolution) an arrangement whereby the children of divorced parents spend substantial time in the household of each parent

There is first the matter of custody: Who will have responsibility for the children, and where will they live? **Legal custody** refers to having the right to make important decisions about the children and to having legal responsibility for them. **Physical custody** refers to where they actually live. In the United States in the past, the two kinds of custody were usually merged; the father typically had custody in both senses prior to the mid-nineteenth century, the mother, after that. Family law throughout much of the twentieth century was based on a presumption that maternal custody was better for young children; indeed, custody was awarded to the mother in about 85 percent of the cases (Weitzman, 1985). In most states, however, that presumption has been replaced with the rule that the court should decide according to the "best interests of the child"—a standard that formally favors neither parent.

Moreover, many states are moving toward a presumption in favor of **joint legal custody,** which means that both parents retain an equal right to make important decisions concerning the children (as opposed to sole legal custody, in which one spouse can make the decisions without consulting the other) (Bartlett, 1999). A decree of joint legal custody is essentially a decree that the parents' responsibilities toward their children have not changed; despite the breakup, they both remain responsible. Most recently, in a growing number of cases, divorcing parents are agreeing to **joint physical custody,** under which the children spend substantial time in each household. For instance, the proportion of divorces in Wisconsin in which children are mandated to spend at least 25 percent of their time with their mothers and at least 25 percent with their fathers increased from 8 percent to 50 percent between 1988 to 2010 (Meyer, Cancian, & Cook, 2017). Conversely, the proportion in which the children spend nearly all of their time with their mothers declined from 76 percent to 42 percent. Joint physical custody is now the most common arrangement in Wisconsin; and in about two-thirds of these arrangements, the children are spending an equal amount of time with each parent. The old presumption that children should remain solely in the custody of their mothers after a divorce has weakened. We know less, however, about children's relationships with both parents after the dissolution of a cohabiting union because in most cases there is no legal agreement.

CONTACT

Fathers who don't live with their children, whom I will call nonresident fathers, have increased the amount of involvement they have with their children, whether or not they had been married to the mother at the time of the child's birth. Figure 12.2 shows the change in involvement for nonresident fathers. The authors of the study on which the graph is based (Amato, Meyers, & Emery, 2009) divided nonresident fathers into three groups: *uninvolved fathers,* who had neither seen their child nor paid any child support in the past year; *involved fathers,* who had seen their child weekly or more often in the past year and had also paid some child support; and a

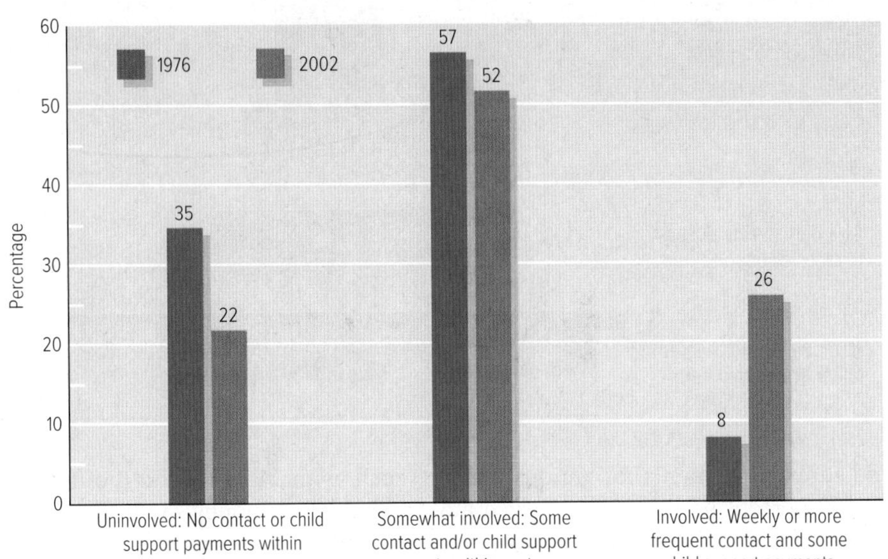

FIGURE 12.2
Involvement of nonresident fathers with their children, 1976 and 2002. (*Source:* Amato, Meyers, & Emery, 2009)

middle group I will call *somewhat involved fathers,* who had seen their child in the past year but less frequently than weekly, and/or had paid some child support in the past year. These are crude categories, to be sure, but national surveys in 1976 and 2002 can be used to see how the proportions have changed over time. The results show that the percentage of "involved" fathers increased sharply from 8 to 26 percent, whereas the percentage of "uninvolved" fathers decreased from 35 to 22 percent. The uninvolved fathers represent a mixture of fathers whose involvement with their children started at a high level but declined over time and fathers who had little contact with their children starting at the first year after the separation. The former group was more likely to have had their children while married to the mother, whereas the latter group was more likely to have had their children at a younger age and outside of marriage (Cheadle, Amato, & King, 2010). The authors of the study suggest that the increase in "involved" fathers may reflect a growing cultural norm that nonresident fathers should remain in their children's lives. The spread of this norm would be beneficial to children: research shows that children's adjustment to dissolution is better when they have regular contact with their fathers, except in the small number of cases in which fathers have serious problems such as substance abuse or violent behavior (Kelly, 2007).

ECONOMIC SUPPORT

Many fathers seem to fade from their children's lives in part because they will not or cannot contribute to their children's support. Figure 12.3 displays the child support pyramid. The figures are from a Bureau of the Census study of the 11.1 million separated, divorced, or remarried mothers who in 2015 had children under the age of 21 who were living with them and whose fathers were absent from the household. The base of the pyramid represents all these women. Moving up the pyramid, we can see that only 45 percent had been awarded child support payments and were supposed to receive them in 2015. (Most of the rest had not been awarded

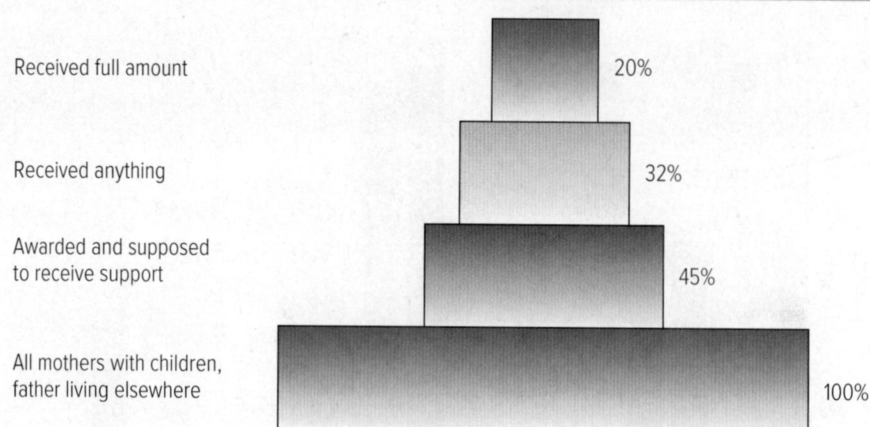

FIGURE 12.3
The child support pyramid: award and receipt of child support payments to women with children under the age of 21 living in their households who have fathers living elsewhere, 2015. (*Source:* U.S. Bureau of the Census, 2018a)

child support payments for various reasons, such as inability to find the father.) Only 32 percent had actually received any child support money in 2015; and 20 percent had received the full amount of child support that was due them (U.S. Bureau of the Census, 2018a).

Custodial mothers are often hit hard economically when they end a relationship with the fathers of their children. Most do not receive child support, as Figure 12.3 shows. When a union that involves children ends, whether marital or cohabiting, women's incomes tend to drop sharply at first (Avellar & Smock, 2005). Over the past few decades, divorced custodial mothers have been able to compensate for this drop better than (previously) cohabiting custodial mothers, largely because the earnings of divorced mothers have increased more. The rising number of cohabiting custodial mothers, and their financial troubles, is contributing to income inequality in American society (Ananat & Michaels, 2008; Tach & Eads, 2015).

Although most single-parent families are headed by mothers, the number of single-father families has been growing. Between 1980 and 2018, the number of single fathers living with their own children under 18 increased from 690,000 to 2.1 million. These families now constitute 18 percent of all single-parent families with children (U.S. Bureau of the Census, 2018d). In addition, there are hundreds of thousands of custodial fathers who have remarried and therefore are not counted in the single-father total. Single fathers tend to have higher incomes than single mothers because men's wages are typically higher than women's. However, single fathers tend to have lower incomes and less education than married fathers. Nineteen percent had incomes below the government poverty line in 2016 (U.S. Bureau of the Census, 2018c). Yet few single fathers are granted child support awards, since most have higher incomes than their ex-wives.

Quick Review

- Joint legal custody is now common after union dissolution, and joint physical custody is growing.
- Most children live with their mothers after a divorce. Nonresident fathers are more likely to be involved in their children's lives than in the past, but minorities do not see their children or support them.
- Mothers and the children in their custody tend to experience a decline in their standard of living; less than half of custodial mothers receive child support payments from the fathers.
- The number of single fathers raising children has increased.

Families and Public Policy

Child Support Obligations

Children in single-parent families would benefit if every absent parent paid child support to the custodial parent. This was the goal of several laws that were enacted in the 1980s and 1990s. Since 1994, for example, all parents who have been ordered by the courts to pay child support have had their payments deducted automatically from their paychecks. Moreover, states are now required to adopt guidelines for the amount of child support a parent should pay, according to income and number of children; judges must follow these guidelines or state in writing why they didn't.

In fact, toughening child support enforcement has been one of the most popular family policies among both conservatives and liberals. Conservatives favor tougher enforcement because making fathers pay is consistent with their belief that parents should take responsibility for the well-being of their children. (Although the law applies equally to absent mothers who owe child support payments, in practice the vast majority of payments are collected from fathers and distributed to mothers.) The new measures send a message to fathers that they can leave their unions, but they can't leave their children. Conservatives hope that the measures will deter men from fathering children they can't, or don't intend to, support. Liberals favor tougher measures because increased collection of child support payments will provide more economic support to children in low-income single-parent families.

These measures produced a rise in child support orders and payments until the mid-2000s. Since then, however, the proportion of custodial parents who have a child support order in place has declined (Meyer, Cancian, & Chen, 2015). One reason for the decline is the increasing percentage of custodial parents who have never married the other parent. Legal support orders are much less common among never-married parents. So the growth in the percentage of children born to cohabiting parents who do not marry has resulted in a lower likelihood that children in single-parent families are receiving support from their other parent. In addition, orders have decreased because of the great growth in the number of parents who are awarded joint custody. In these instances, both parents may be providing substantial support to their children, and they (or a judge considering their case) may think a child support order is less necessary.

Moreover, child support enforcement measures tend to help middle-class single parents and their children more than poor single parents and their children. Most middle-class noncustodial fathers are employed and can make some child support payments. Many poor fathers, however are not working steadily and may not be able to make the child support payments a court has ordered. As they fall behind, they build up an "arrearage" of back payments they owe the mothers of their children. In many states, the arrearage continues to accumulate even if they are in prison. It may get so high that it discourages fathers from working because so much of their income would go toward paying down the arrearage. Consequently, some experts warn that child support programs that rely solely on enforcement of child support orders will not work for poor families. Rather, these experts advocate programs to increase the earnings capacity of single fathers, so that they can afford to pay the child support they owe (Mincy, Jethwani, & Klempin, 2014).

Ask Yourself

1. Do you know anyone who has had difficulty collecting court-ordered child support payments? If so, was the problem caused by the absent parent's inability to pay or simply an unwillingness to pay?
2. Besides the measures described here, what other steps could government take to improve the economic well-being of children in single-parent families?

PSYCHOSOCIAL EFFECTS

The experience of a parental union dissolution could potentially affect the well-being of children: their emotional and behavioral development, their school achievement, their long-term mental health, or the work and family lives they seek out when they reach adulthood. Unfortunately, nearly all of the research is about the consequences of marital separation and divorce rather than about the consequences of the dissolution of a cohabiting union. Here is what we know.

crisis period a period during the first year or two after parents separate when both the custodial parent and the children experience difficulties in dealing with the situation

The Crisis Period The first year or two after married parents separate is a time of dramatic change during which both the custodial parents and the children—most whom are intensely upset when they learn of the separation—often experience difficulties (Kim, 2011). Developmental psychologists have called this time the **crisis period** (Chase-Lansdale & Hetherington, 1990; Hetherington & Kelly, 2002). After the breakup, the custodial parent (typically the mother) is often angry, upset, and depressed. One consequence, according to observers, is the "diminished parenting" that often occurs during the crisis period (Wallerstein & Kelly, 1980; Wallerstein, Lewis, & Blakeslee, 2000). Distracted, distressed parents may have difficulties providing the daily mixture of emotional support and moderate, consistent discipline that psychologists called "authoritative parenting." Instead, parents seem to be emotionally distant and preoccupied, prone to ignore misbehavior or to lash out with harsh discipline. For example, a child misbehaves, prompting the harried, depressed parent to respond angrily. Her response can set off more negative behavior: A toy is thrown on the floor or a bowl of cereal is knocked off the table. The parent responds even more angrily, further provoking the child.

Most divorcing parents are able to greatly reduce their conflict with each other by two or three years after they break up (Kelly, 2007), but for a minority the disputes and difficulties continue. A continuing high level of conflict is probably the most widely cited factor in harming children's adjustment after a divorce. When parents fight, children tend to become fearful and distressed—whether the parents are married or divorced. After the breakup, children have fewer problems if their parents can cooperate (Buchanan, Maccoby, & Dornbusch, 1996; Hetherington & Kelly, 2002). Some of the conflict that harms children, however, can begin before the breakup. And some of the problems that children exhibit after a divorce might have occurred to some extent even if their conflicted parents had remained together.

Multiple Transitions Apart from exposure to the parents' distress and conflict, the breakup forces children to adjust to jarring transitions. The first, of course, is the departure of a parent from the home. This is not necessarily the last transition, however. The financial settlement between middle-class, divorcing parents sometimes requires that the family's house be sold. As a result, children must often move to a new neighborhood, begin classes at a new school, and make new friends. Some divorced mothers move in with their parents temporarily while they make the transition to single parenting. Other adults will probably move in and out of the child's household as parents repartner. Children from cohabiting-parent families that break up are particularly likely to experience multiple transitions. The cumulative stress of these multiple transitions may cause difficulties, as was discussed in Chapter 9. The idea is that the number of transitions in family living arrangements that a child makes—how many times parents or parent-figures move in and out of the household—may cause as many adjustment problems as living in any particular kind of family (Amato, 2010). Transitions out of two-parent families are more problematic for children than transitions into them (Lee & McLanahan, 2015).

Long-term Adjustment After the crisis period, the majority of children resume normal development (Emery, 1999). Still, one study found that, six years after the disruption, 20 to 25 percent of young adolescents were displaying serious behavior problems, as opposed to 10 percent of young adolescents who were still living with both parents (Hetherington & Clingempeel, 1992; Hetherington & Kelly, 2002). The researchers found that the problems of some boys in the crisis period had persisted; in addition, girls were now displaying as many problems as boys. Early adolescence is a time when tension between parents and children can increase as the children try to become more independent. It is possible that this task is more difficult for children whose parents have divorced. According to the Hetherington and Clingempeel study, single mothers monitored their children's behavior less closely and engaged in more arguments with them than did married mothers. Moreover, the researchers speculated that children who are just coming to terms with their own burgeoning sexuality may have a more difficult adjustment when they must confront intimate relationships between a parent and that parent's new boy- or girlfriend or spouse.

How do children of divorced parents fare over the long term? The psychologist Judith Wallerstein followed a group of such children for 25 years. Her books about their well-being after 10 years (Wallerstein & Blakeslee, 1989) and 25 years (Wallerstein, Lewis, & Blakeslee, 2000) report widespread, lasting difficulties in personal relationships. At the 25-year mark, a minority had managed to establish successful personal lives, but only with great effort. The legacy of divorce, Wallerstein claims, doesn't fade away:

> *Contrary to what we have long thought, the major impact of divorce does not occur during childhood or adolescence. Rather, it rises in adulthood as serious romantic relationships move center stage. When it comes time to choose a life mate and build a family, the effects of divorce crescendo.*

Because these young adults didn't have the chance to observe successful marriages, Wallerstein maintains, they didn't learn how to create one. Faced with the choice of a partner or a spouse, their anxiety rises; they fear repeating their parents' mistakes. Lacking a good model to follow, they are more likely to make bad choices. Overall, Wallerstein states, only about half the women and one-third of the men in the group were able to establish successful personal lives by the 25-year mark.

But the negative long-term effects of divorce probably are not as widespread as Wallerstein claims. Some portion of what she labels as the effects of divorce on children probably weren't connected to the divorce. And the typical family that experiences divorce won't have as tough a time as Wallerstein's families did: Many of the parents in her modest sample of 60 families had extensive psychiatric histories. Parents with better mental health than those in her sample can more easily avoid the worst of the anger, anxiety, and depression that comes with divorce. They are better able to maintain the children's daily routines at home or in school. And their children can more easily avoid the extremes of anxiety and self-doubt that plagued the children in Wallerstein's study.

Rather than solely reflecting Wallerstein's pessimistic picture, the long-term view seems to encompass both a glass-half-full and a glass-half-empty perspective. When parents divorce, or when single parents raise children outside marriage, their children run a higher risk of experiencing undesirable events (such as dropping out of school) in young adulthood and beyond. Nevertheless, most children from single-parent families will not, as a consequence, experience such problems. Hetherington reported that in her 20-year study, 80 percent of the children were eventually able to adapt and become "reasonably well adjusted" (Hetherington & Kelly, 2002). This is not to say that parental divorce has no lasting effect whatsoever on most children. Even young adults who are happy and successful—college graduates with good jobs and good marriages—may nevertheless feel a sense of loss over or painful memories of childhoods spent coping with parents' divorces (Marquardt, 2005).

In the terms of two psychologists, they may show "distress" but not "disorder" (Laumann-Billings & Emery, 2000).

It is possible that some of these long-term difficulties are due to the poor quality of the parents' marriages, rather than to the divorces themselves. A study by Paul R. Amato and Alan Booth (1997) attempted to disentangle these two possibilities. The study began as telephone interviews with a nationally representative sample of married couples in 1980. The interviewers asked their respondents multiple questions on marital quality, including marital happiness, marital interaction (e.g., "How often do you eat your main meals together?"), marital conflict ("How many serious quarrels have you had in the past two months?"), and divorce proneness (e.g., "Has the thought of getting a divorce or separation crossed your mind in the last three years?"). The researchers divided all of the families into two groups, low conflict and high conflict, using all of the information. Then in 1992 all of the children who had lived with their parents in 1980 and who were now age 19 or older were interviewed.

The investigators report that offspring who experienced high marital conflict in 1980 were doing *better* in 1992 if their parents had divorced than if they had stayed together; on the other hand, offspring from low-conflict families were doing worse if their parents had divorced. This finding confirms the oft-stated but rarely substantiated belief that if family conflict is severe, children may benefit from a divorce. But the researchers caution that only a minority of the divorces that occurred were in high-conflict marriages (such as marriages with physical abuse or frequent serious quarrels). For that minority, the consequences of experiencing continuing conflict between their parents probably would have been worse than the consequences of the divorce. But the majority of offspring who experienced parental divorce probably would have been better off if their parents had stayed together.

Genetically Informed Studies It is possible that divorce itself is just a marker for other, less observable factors that are the real causes of the seeming effects of divorce on children. One alternative explanation is that parents and children in divorced families share genetic tendencies that make it more likely that the parents will divorce *and* that the children will show behavior problems. If so, then the naïve social scientist, seeing a correlation between parental divorce and children's problems, may mistakenly assume that divorce causes the problems when, in fact, both the divorce and the children's problems are the result of a genetic tendency toward, say, antisocial behavior or depression. If that's the case, we ought to see differences in the responses to divorce between people who share inherited genes and those who do not.

Researchers in the field of behavioral genetics study people of varying degrees of genetic relatedness to see whether evidence exists of possible genetic causes of behavior. One study, for example, compared the academic achievement and behavior problems of children after a divorce in two types of families (O'Connor, Caspi, DeFries, & Plomin, 2000). In the first type, the children were adopted and therefore they shared no genes with their parents. In the second type, the children were the biological offspring of the parents. If the apparent "effects" of divorce are really the effects of common genetically based tendencies, the researchers reasoned, then the adopted children should show fewer difficulties after the divorce because they have not inherited any problematic tendencies from their adoptive parents, whereas the biological children may have. But that is not what they found. Rather, the adopted children showed as many problems as the biological children. This finding, the researchers argued, suggests that divorce may truly have effects on children's behavior since the difficulties the adopted children showed cannot be due to genetic inheritance (see also D'Onofrio et al., 2005).

Still, some children may have genetic tendencies that make them more sensitive to the effects of living with two biological parents or not. Recent studies are taking advantage of technologies that can analyze a person's genes from a DNA sample. In one study, for instance, the researchers classified adolescents by whether or not they had variant forms of genes that had been associated with antisocial behavior. They then found that adolescents with the variant form of one gene were more likely to engage in serious delinquent behavior (for instance, selling drugs or using a weapon to get something from someone) than were other adolescents if they were living with a single parent or with stepparents. But they were *not* more likely to engage in serious delinquent behavior than were other adolescents if they were living with their two biological parents (Guo, Roettger, & Cai, 2008). This study suggests that it is the interaction of genetic tendencies (whether a child has a predisposition toward greater antisocial behavior) and the family environment (whether a child is living with two biological parents or not) that determines whether children and adolescents exhibit behavior problems such as serious delinquent behavior.

A similar study compared the responses to family instability among children who varied in their genetic sensitivity to changes in their environment (Mitchell et al., 2015). Some children—particularly boys—seem to be genetically predisposed to have greater reactions to changes in their environments than do other children. The study found that when the more genetically reactive children experienced a change such as the departure from the household of a biological parent, they showed increased behavior problems such as being disobedient at school or home. In contrast, children who did not have the genetic predisposition were more likely to adapt to the departure of a biological parent without showing behavior problems.

The emerging picture from these genetically informed studies is that the effects of union dissolution and family instability on children are due to a **gene–environment interaction:** A situation in which a change in the environment (such as the departure of a biological parent from the home) has an effect that is most pronounced on children with a genetic sensitivity to that environmental change. Those who have a genetic tendency to be more sensitive or reactive to new environments show the greatest behavioral change. Union dissolution, it seems, has a true causal effect, but it doesn't affect all children the same way. Their genes play a role in how they react.

gene–environment interaction a situation in which a change in the environment has a greater effect on people with a genetic sensitivity to that change

In Sum Overall, the research literature on the effects of union dissolution on children suggests the following conclusions:

- Almost all children experience an initial period of intense emotional upset after their parents separate.
- Most resume normal development without serious problems within about two years after the separation.
- A minority of children experience some long-term problems as a result of the breakup that may persist into adulthood.

From the glass-half-empty perspective, we can conclude that union dissolution may cause a substantial percentage increase in the number of individuals who may need the help of a mental health professional or who may not obtain as much education as they should or who may be unemployed more often than they should.

As a society, we should be troubled by this development. From the glass-half-full perspective, however, it seems that most individuals do not suffer serious long-term harm as a result of their parents' separation. We need to keep both perspectives in mind when considering the effects of union dissolution.

Quick Review

- Nearly all children and parents are upset and distressed during the first year or two after the separation, sometimes called the "crisis period."
- The loss of a parent from the home, continuing parental conflict, and multiple transitions are factors that often cause difficulties for children during the crisis period.
- After the crisis period, a majority of children resume normal development, but minorities do experience continuing difficulties.
- For some children, the effects of divorce may last into or even peak in adulthood.
- The difficulties children show after parents separate reflect an interaction between genetic tendencies and family experiences.

Repartnering

The breakup of a union is not the end of the changes faced by parents and children. A majority of parents will either live with another partner or marry one, or do both. If divorced parents marry their new partners, they will form what is conventionally thought of as a stepfamily: (A) a marriage that is a second (or higher order) marriage for at least one of the spouses; and (B) in which one or both spouses have children from their previous marriages. Note that if condition (A) is satisfied but not condition (B), we are looking at a remarriage but not a stepfamily because no children from a previous relationship are involved. We might define a conventional stepfamily as formed by a legal marriage in which at least one parent is legally divorced and has children from a previous marriage. It is conventional because it harks back to the mid-twentieth-century time when most single-parent families were formed as a result of a divorce (rather than the dissolution of a cohabiting union or childbearing by a single parent) and the vast majority of single parents who found a new live-in partner married that person.

Yet because of the great changes in family life since the mid-twentieth century, the twenty-first-century American stepfamily is more diverse (Stewart, 2007). To be sure, there still are many families that have the conventional form. But we now need to expand the concept to other forms: families in which the partners are cohabiting rather than married; families in which the children come not from a previous marriage but from nonmarital relationships; and indeed families in which neither parent has ever legally married, divorced, or remarried.

Consider how cohabitation complicates the picture. It's even more common for couples to live together prior to a remarriage than it is prior to a first marriage. Three-fourths of marital stepfamilies begin as cohabiting unions (Guzzo, 2015). Moreover, many additional cohabiting unions fit the stepfamily form but never result in marriage, either because the couple breaks up (most commonly) or because they remain together for a long period of time without ever formalizing their relationship through a marriage (less common in the United States than in some European countries). Some of the new partners in these cohabiting families invest enough time and effort into being a presence in the daily lives of their partner's biological children to be considered stepparents by any standard except remarriage. Others, however, remain in the home briefly and never play a role in the children's lives.

Or consider the families that form when a woman who has had a child in a previous relationship but never married the father subsequently marries another man. She and her husband may be in their first marriages, rather than in remarriages, and yet her new family takes on the structure of a stepfamily. In some cases, her previous partner, the father of her child, may continue to be part of the child's life, and the stepfamily will function much the way a remarriage following a divorce often does. In other cases, however, the mother may have had only a casual relationship with the father and he may never have been a part of the child's life. In this case, the family may function more like a conventional first-marriage family. In yet other cases, the mother and the father may have had children with several other partners in a pattern I described in Chapter 9 as multipartner fertility, creating multiple links with previous partners and biological children living elsewhere.

So let me define a **stepfamily** in a broader way than we conventionally have thought of one. It is a family in which

stepfamily a family in which two adults are married or cohabiting and at least one has a child from a previous marriage or relationship

1. Two adults are married or cohabiting, and
2. At least one adult has a child from a previous marriage or relationship.

This definition does not require that the adults be married; nor does it require that all the children live in the same household. Under this broad definition, at least one-fourth of stepfamilies involve cohabiting couples rather than married couples, according to national figures, and nearly two-thirds of children first enter stepfamily life through cohabitation rather than marriage (Guzzo, 2015). I will use the term **cohabiting stepfamily** to mean only the kind of stepfamily in which the partners are cohabiting; I will use the parallel term **married stepfamily** to mean only those in which the partners are married. Our definition also does not require that the biological parent in the stepfamily was previously married to, and then divorced, the biological father of her children. Rather, it allows for previous relationships to have been outside of marriage.

cohabiting stepfamily a stepfamily in which the partners are cohabiting without marrying

married stepfamily a stepfamily in which the partners are married

This way of conceptualizing stepfamilies is becoming more common in the research literature (Stewart, 2007). But most of the research on stepfamilies has been conducted within the framework of divorce and remarriage because cohabitation did not play a major role until the last few decades. This restricted definition, focused on divorce and remarriage, has made it easy for researchers to determine whether a stepfamily actually exists: In addition to the presence of stepchildren, the partners must be married. Under our broader definition of stepfamilies, it may be unclear whether a stepfamily exists. Recall the discussion in Chapter 1 of boundary ambiguity, the state in which family members are uncertain about who is in or out of the family. Only one-half of teenagers who were in cohabiting stepfamilies according to their mothers' reports, you may remember, considered the cohabiting partners to be part of their families, as if their mothers were single parents in the other half. Some of the men in these households may have been more tenuously attached to the family than the mother reported, perhaps not sleeping there some nights; and some of the teenagers may have had distant relationships with men who were present and did not think of them as parent-like figures.

In any case, stepfamilies are quite common, no matter how you measure them. Forty-two percent of American adults said in a national survey that they had at least one steprelative: a stepsibling (meaning a nonbiologically related person they considered to be like a brother or sister), a half-sibling (meaning a person with whom they shared one biological parent), a stepparent, or a stepchild. Having a steprelative is more common among young adults than among older adults, a difference that reflects the rising number of cohabiting stepfamilies in recent years. And it is more common among adults without a college degree, which reflects their higher rates of union dissolution (Pew Research Center, 2011). From a child's perspective, living in a stepfamily household is also becoming common. In 2009, 16 percent of all children lived in a household in which a stepparent, stepsibling, or half-sibling was present (U.S. Bureau of the Census 2011). This statistic only includes children whose stepsiblings live in their household. Other children, whose numbers are hard to estimate, have contact with stepsiblings or half-siblings living in other households, as is the case when one's biological father has children who live with his ex-wife but sometimes visit the new household.

Quick Review

- Stepfamilies are increasingly diverse.
- Stepfamilies can be formed by families in which the partners marry and families in which the partners cohabit.
- The proportion of cohabiting stepfamilies has grown in recent decades.
- Having a steprelative has become common in the United States.

Care and Assistance in Stepfamilies

You might think that the addition of a stepparent would improve the overall well-being of children whose parents had ended a previous partnership. For one thing, when a single mother finds a new partner, her household income usually rises dramatically because men's wages are higher, on average, than women's wages. Consequently, if a decline in the standard of living hurts the well-being of children in single-parent families, an increase after the mother starts a new partnership should improve it. In addition, the stepparent adds a second adult to the home. He or she can provide assistance to the custodial parent and back up the custodial parent's monitoring and control of the children's behavior. A stepparent can also provide an adult role model for a child of the same gender.

Despite these advantages, children in stepfamilies show lower levels of well-being than children in two-biological-parent families (Sweeney, 2010). In fact, some studies find no difference between children in stepfamilies and children in single-parent families (Ganong & Coleman, 2004) or that just children from advantaged backgrounds benefit from their mother's remarriage (Wagmiller, Gershoff, Veliz, & Clements, 2010). The presence of half-siblings or stepsiblings is associated with small but consistently negative declines in children's well-being (Sanner, Russell, Coleman, & Ganong, 2018). To be sure, most children in stepfamilies do not demonstrate serious problems (Hetherington & Jodl, 1994). But the risk of having problems is higher in stepfamilies.

COHABITING V. MARRIED STEPFAMILIES

Moreover, the risk is particularly high in cohabiting stepfamilies (Sweeney, 2010). For instance, adolescents in cohabiting stepfamilies are more likely to drink or smoke (Brown & Rinelli, 2010). A study showed that they were more likely to engage in antisocial behavior such as stealing, getting suspended from school, or running away from home (Apel & Kaukinen, 2008). Not all studies show differences, but enough evidence exists to question whether children benefit from the addition of a cohabiting stepparent to their households.

There are plausible reasons why cohabiting stepparents may be problematic for children. First, a wide variation exists in the level of commitment and involvement among cohabiting stepparents. They have no clearly defined obligations–their role is even less institutionalized than is the role of the married stepparent. There is no wedding ceremony, no public acknowledgment of a cohabiting stepparent's entry into the household. Some cohabiting stepparents may be very engaged with the children whereas others have little to do with them. Second, many cohabiting partnerships are short-term; cohabiting stepparents may have recently arrived and may soon be gone. They may not see themselves as stepparents, and the stepchildren may not see them as such–as was the case in the survey of mothers and their adolescent children who differed in their reports on whether a stepfather was present in the household. This boundary ambiguity probably reflects men who have an intimate relationship with the mother, spend most nights in the household, but do not engage the children. It is these kinds of cohabiting stepparents who are of little benefit to the children. Other stepparents, in contrast, may involve themselves in children's lives and become valued members of the family. In addition, parents with certain unknown personal characteristics that impair family cohesion could be self-selecting into the population of cohabiting stepfamilies.

INTERGENERATIONAL SUPPORT

We also need to think about the consequences of stepfamily life for support up and down the generations in families. Parents often provide assistance to their adult children, who may still live with them or who may receive help caring for the grandchildren. And middle-aged adults often provide care to their older parents. But what if the adult children are stepchildren and the older parents are stepparents? Will families exchange as much care and money as they would for biological adult children and older parents? This is an important question because without help from their families, many older parents would be left without adequate care–we might, for instance, need many more nursing homes–and many adult children would be left without a place to live. In theory, having steprelatives could lead to more intergenerational assistance because steprelatives expand the total number of relatives that a person has, and the more people you can call on for aid, the more likely you should be to receive it. But studies show that family members tend to provide less assistance to steprelatives than to biological relatives (Pezzin, Pollak, & Schone, 2008; Seltzer & Bianchi, 2013). Overall, according to data from a well-known national study, the Panel Study of Income Dynamics, families that have adult stepchildren or older stepparents provide less assistance up and down the generations than do comparable families with only biological relatives (Wiemers, Seltzer, Schoeni, Hotz, & Bianchi, 2019). The decrease in assistance from adult stepchildren to older stepparents is especially noticeable if the adult stepchild's biological parent is no longer married to, or living with, the stepparent. After a stepfamily has dissolved, the amount of contact between the adult stepchildren and the older stepparent declines (Noël-Miller, 2013). If the number of families with steprelatives continues to increase in the future, as seems likely, we could see declining levels of assistance across the generations—a problem for a society such as ours that still relies heavily on family care.

Quick Review

- The well-being of children in stepfamilies is lower than that of children in two-biological-parent families and roughly equivalent to that of children in single-parent families.
- The number of transitions children have experienced may impair their adjustment to stepfamilies.
- Children in stepfamilies leave home at an earlier age than children in two-biological-parent or single-parent households.
- Children in cohabiting stepfamilies seem to fare worse than children in married stepfamilies.
- Families with steprelatives provide less assistance up and down the generations than do families with only biological relatives.

Union Dissolution and Repartnering: Taking Stock

What can be learned from studying union dissolution and repartnering? The evidence we have reviewed suggests three themes.

THE ROLE OF COHABITING UNIONS

The study of union dissolution and repartnering used to center on marriage: the ending of marriages through legal separation and divorce and the beginning of remarriages. Moreover, the United States used to have by far the highest divorce rate of any developed nation. But as the American divorce rate has declined, other nations are catching up (OECD, 2018). To be sure, there are still plenty of divorces and remarriages in the United States. Yet over the last two or three decades, the main driver of instability in intimate partnerships has been the rise of cohabitation. Cohabiting unions have become much more common than in the past, and they remain more fragile than marriages. They are affecting a growing number of children. The proportion of all children who are born to cohabiting parents has risen steadily to about one out of four. Those children are exposed to a high risk of experiencing parental dissolution and repartnering. By age 15, 73 percent of American children born to cohabiting parents are likely to see their parents' union dissolve—a higher rate than in nearly all North American and European countries (only Russia comes close). And American children who experience a parental separation are more likely to see their residential parent form a new union than are children in Europe (Andersson, Thomson, & Duntava, 2017). In this way, cohabiting unions are driving the sheer amount of turnover, of churning, in the family lives of American children at a rate not seen in any other developed country (Cherlin, 2009).

NEW KINSHIP TIES

The official Bureau of the Census definition of a family is two or more people living in the same household and related by blood, marriage, or adoption. It is not clear how long this definition will survive because divorce, nonmarital childbearing, cohabitation, and remarriage are breaking the correspondence between family and household. Until recently, the unchallenged family unit in Western nations was the conjugal family of husband, wife, and children residing in the same household. At some points in the life cycle of the family they might have welcomed elderly parents, or young servants and apprentices, into their household. They also had many relatives living in other households. There was, however, a clear demarcation between the members of one's own household, who were the core of the family system, and those beyond the household's boundaries, who were the periphery. The correspondence between family and household is so deeply ingrained that we take it for granted. For example, our entire government apparatus for collecting statistics on "families" actually surveys households. Statistically, we may have to give up the idea that we can count families simply by knocking on doors. We may have to accept that a family can be defined only in reference to a person, not a household.

In addition, the rise in divorce, nonmarital childbearing, cohabitation, and remarriage is increasing the importance of what I called in Chapter 1 voluntary kinship, the ties that people have to actively construct, as opposed to assigned kinship, the ties that people automatically acquire at birth or through first marriage. In this regard, kinship after relationship dissolution and repartnering is similar to the extended kin networks among low-income and racial-ethnic populations. In these situations, individuals find it in their interest to build their own family ties. Being a father or a mother was once a status assigned to a person automatically at the birth of his or her child. To be sure, people have children through their own efforts; nevertheless, one does not have to do anything else to be a biological parent, nor can one easily resign from the post. Being a grandparent was ascribed similarly. All that is still the case when children are born to, and raised by, two married parents.

The creation of stepfamilies, though, adds a number of other potential kinship positions. Whether these positions are filled depends on the actions of the individuals involved. The most obvious positions are stepfather and stepmother. There is wide variation in the roles stepparents play. Some are parent-like figures who are intensely involved with their stepchildren. Many others are more like friends or uncles and aunts. Others, particularly stepparents who don't live with their stepchildren every day, are more distant. In all cases, how much like a family member a stepparent becomes depends in large part on the effort he or she puts into developing a close relationship with stepchildren and also on the stepchild's actions. Intergenerational ties to stepgrandparents are even more dependent on individual action; they range from no contact to a kinlike role, depending in large part on the investment the stepgrandparents make.

Yet the challenge of voluntary kinship is as follows: Kinship ties that can be created by people's actions can also be ended by lack of action. In contrast, it is much harder to end assigned kinship ties. Therefore, voluntary kinship ties are more likely to change over the course of one's life than assigned kinship ties. Voluntary ties may even change from year to year, as a stepparent moves into or out of the household or as contact diminishes with a stepgranddaughter who moves out of state. Just as containment within one household made families easy to spot, so, too, assignment at birth and first marriage made kinship easy to track. Now, family and kinship require new mental maps that can change from year to year. We are just beginning to draw them.

THE IMPACT ON CHILDREN

There is, finally, the important question of how children are coping with all of this dissolution and repartnering. I would argue that the effects are neither minor nor massive. On the one hand, the evidence suggests that most children who experience these events do not have serious, long-lasting problems because of them. On the other hand, it is clear that a minority of children do experience lasting problems that appear to be caused by dissolution or repartnering. Some of these problems might have occurred even if the children's families had remained intact. Other problems, though, seem clearly linked to the disruption and its aftermath.

Let us suppose, for the sake of argument, that 10 percent of children from two-biological-parent families will grow up to have serious mental health problems as adults. Further, let us suppose that the prevalence of serious mental health problems is twice as high–20 percent–among children in single-parent families and stepfamilies. A little algebra will show that if 4 in 10 children experience single-parent or stepfamily life, the overall rate of serious mental health problems in the population would rise to 14 percent when this generation reaches adulthood.[3] An overall rise from an expected 10 percent (if there were no breakups in the population) to 14 percent may not seem like much. But it would require a 40 percent expansion of mental health facilities around the country and the training of 40 percent more mental health professionals. At current population levels, it would alter the lives of an additional three million people in each generation. It would mean that about 1 in 7, rather than 1 in 10, adults might need clinical help. In sum, it would mean a significant decline in mental health.

Consequently, even if only a minority of children will experience long-term problems, we should be troubled by this possibility. Some people might wish to work toward reducing union dissolution, and indeed the divorce rate has declined, especially among the college-educated. But we might also wish to assist parents and children in unions that are dissolving. We might promote conflict-resolution strategies for them, urge that children be kept out of conflict, and provide guidelines on how to minimize the impact of a dissolution. We might wish to encourage support groups and services in schools. In sum, we might take whatever steps we can to reduce the negative effects of union dissolution and repartnering on children.

Quick Review

- The growing emphasis on personal fulfillment has made marriage more fragile.
- Newer living arrangements are increasing the frequency with which people are creating their own kinship ties.
- The changes in single-parent families have altered children's lives.

[3] $(0.40 \times 0.20) + (0.60 \times 0.10) = 0.14$, or 14 percent.

Looking Back

1. **What are the ways in which American children experience the end of their parents' unions?** The predominant way that children experienced union dissolution used to be because of the death of one of their parents. As the divorce rate rose, more children experienced a dissolution because of divorce than because of parental death. Today it is also common for children to experience the dissolution of their parents' cohabiting unions. The percentage of children living with parents who are cohabiting has increased; and these cohabiting unions have higher rates of dissolution than do marriages. If the dissolutions of both marriages and cohabiting unions are considered together, it is likely that about 44 percent of all children born to two parents who live in the household will experience the breakup of their parents' unions by age 15. Some parents will remarry, while some others will cohabit with new partners without remarrying.

2. **What factors have influenced the level of union dissolution?** On a societal level, the increased emphasis on personal fulfillment as a criterion for judging marriages and cohabiting unions has contributed to higher dissolution rates. The rise in cohabitation has been an important factor in union dissolution. The diverging trends in union dissolution since about 1980 may reflect the labor market advantages of college graduates and the disadvantage of those without college degrees. Middle-class women's earning potential now seems to support marriage rather than to encourage alternatives. A union is more likely to dissolve if the partners are young when they marry, or if they are African Americans.

3. **What happens to children in the aftermath of the dissolution of their parents' marriage or cohabiting union?** In an increasing number of cases, divorcing parents are agreeing to joint physical custody, under which the children spend substantial time in each household. Nonresident fathers are more likely to be involved in their children's lives than a few decades ago. Only a minority of custodial parents receive child support payments from the noncustodial parent. Overall, the incomes of mothers tend to fall after a union dissolution. In the short term, custodial parents may have trouble maintaining the children's daily routines and providing appropriate emotional support. Children whose parents end cohabiting unions are at risk of multiple transitions of parents, parents' partners, and stepparents into and out of the home.

4. **What are the forms of stepfamily life?** Stepfamilies take many forms. Some display the remarriage-after-divorce-based form that was dominant in the twentieth century: two married parents, at least one of them in a second marriage, and at least one stepchild. But a majority of stepfamilies today begin with a cohabiting couple and stepchildren. Some stepfamilies are formed after a mother has a child outside of marriage as a single parent and then begins a relationship with a new partner. A broad definition of stepfamilies is needed to encompass these and other forms.

5. **How does the well-being of children in stepfamilies compare to the well-being of children in other kinds of families?** Many studies show that the well-being of children in stepfamilies is no better, on average, than the well-being of children in single-parent households after a divorce or union dissolution. Both groups show lower levels of well-being than children in biological two-parent families. Children in cohabiting stepfamilies appear to fare worse than children in married stepfamilies.

6. **How have the trends in union dissolution and repartnering altered family life?** These trends have altered family life in important ways. The main driver of instability in intimate partnerships is the rise of cohabitation. The nature of kinship has been altered, and the correspondence of family in household has been broken. People are constructing new kinship ties to fit the new types of families they are forming. While these new family forms may cause short-term distress for many children and increase the risk of long-term harm to them, the majority of children who experience these changes will grow up without serious long-term problems.

Study Questions

1. Why might wives' paid employment outside the home have two, potentially offsetting, effects on the likelihood of divorce?
2. What is the evidence that the effects of union dissolution on children are not simply due to genetic influences?
3. How are the custodial and visiting arrangements for children after a dissolution likely to be different from how they were in the past?
4. Why might the "glass-half-empty/ half-full" metaphor fit the effects of union dissolution on children?
5. What are the different forms that make up stepfamilies?
6. Why isn't the well-being of children in stepfamilies better than that of children in single-parent families?
7. How concerned should we as a society be about the effects of union dissolution and repartnering on children?

Key Terms

cohabiting stepfamily 339
crisis period 334
gene–environment interaction 337
joint legal custody (of children after a dissolution) 330
joint physical custody (of children after a dissolution) 330
legal custody (of children after a dissolution) 330
married stepfamily 339
physical custody (of children after a dissolution) 330
stepfamily 339
union dissolution 324
union repartnering 324

Thinking about Families

The Public Family	The Private Family
By and large, do stepfamilies do a good enough job of raising the next generation?	**What are the sources of the tension that sometimes exists between stepparents and stepchildren?**

References

Amato, P. R. (2010). Research on divorce: Continuing trends and new developments. *Journal of Marriage and Family, 72*, 650–666.

Amato, P. R., & Booth, A. (1997). *A generation at risk: Growing up in an era of family upheaval.* Cambridge, MA: Harvard University Press.

Amato, P. R., Meyers, C. E., & Emery, R. E. (2009). Changes in nonresident father-child contact from 1976 to 2002. *Family Relations, 58*, 41–53.

Ananat, E. O., & Michaels, G. (2008). The effect of marital breakup on the income distribution of women with children. *Journal of Human Resources, 43*(3), 611–629.

Andersson, G., & Philipov, D. (2002). Life-table representations of family dynamics in Sweden, hungary, and 14 others ffs countries: A project of descriptions of demographic behavior. *Demographic Research, 7*, 67–145.

Andersson, G., Thomson, E., & Duntava, A. (2017). Life-table representations of family dynamics in the

21st century. *Demographic Research, 37*(Article 35), 1081–1230.

Apel, R., & Kaukinen, C. (2008). On the relationship between family structure and antisocial behavior: Parental cohabitation and blended households. *Criminology, 46,* 35–69.

Avellar, S., & Smock, P. J. (2005). The economic consequences of the dissolution of cohabiting unions. *Journal of Marriage and Family, 67,* 315–327.

Bartlett, K. T. (1999). Improving the law relating to post-divorce arrangements for children. In E. M. Hetherington (Ed.), *Coping with divorce, single parenting, and remarriage* (pp. 71–102). Mahwah, NJ: Lawrence Erlbaum Associates.

Becker, G. S., Landes, E. M., & Michael, R. T. (1977). An economic analysis of marital instability. *Journal of Political Economy, 85,* 1141–1187.

Bellah, R., Madsen, R., Sullivan, W. M., Swidler, A., & Tipton, S. M. (1985). *Habits of the heart: Individualism and commitment in America.* Berkeley: University of California Press.

Bendheim-Thoman Center for Child Wellbeing. (2007). Parents' relationship status five years after a nonmarital birth. *Fragile Families Research Brief, no. 39.* Retrieved November 18, 2013, from http://www.fragilefamilies.princeton.edu/briefs/ResearchBrief39.pdf

Bramlett, M. D., & Mosher, W. D. (2002). Cohabitation, marriage, divorce and remarriage in the United States. Series 22, no 2. Retrieved June 2003 from www.cdc.gov/nchs/data/series/sr_23/sr23_022.pdf

Brown, S. L., & Rinelli, L. N. (2010). Family structure, family processes, and adolescent smoking and drinking. *Journal of Research on Adolescence, 20,* 259–273.

Buchanan, C. M., Maccoby, E. E., & Dornbusch, S. F. (1996). *Adolescents after divorce.* Cambridge, MA: Harvard University Press.

Bumpass, L. L. (1984). Children and marital disruption: A replication and update. *Demography, 21,* 71–82.

Burstein, N. R. (2007). Economic influences on divorce *Journal of Policy Analysis and Management, 26,* 387–429.

Chase-Lansdale, L., & Hetherington, M. E. (1990). The impact of divorce on life-span development: Short and long term effects. In P. B. Baltes (Ed.), *Life-span development, and behavior* (Vol. 10, pp. 105–150). Hillsdale, NJ.: Lawrence Erlbaum Associates.

Cheadle, J. E., Amato, P. R., & King, V. (2010). Patterns of nonresident father contact. *Demography, 47,* 205–225.

Cherlin, A. J. (2009). *The marriage-go-round: The state of marriage and the family in America today.* New York: Alfred A. Knopf.

Cohen, P. N. (2019). *The coming divorce decline.* Paper presented at the Annual Meeting of the Population Association of America, Austin TX.

D'Onofrio, B. M., Turkheimer, E., Emery, R. E., Slutske, W. S., Heath, A. C., Madden, P. A., & Martin, N. G. (2005). A genetically informed study of marital instability and its association with offspring psychopathology. *Journal of Abnormal Psychology, 114,* 570–586.

Eickmeyer, K. J. (2018). Cohort trends in union dissolution during young adulthood. *Journal of Marriage and Family, 81,* (June), 760–770.

Ellwood, D. T., & Jencks, C. (2004). The spread of single parent families in the United States since 1960. In D. P. Moynihan, T. Smeeding, & L. Rainwater (Eds.), *The future of the family* (pp. 26–65). New York: Russell Sage Foundation.

Emery, R. E. (1999). *Marriage, divorce, and children's adjustment* (Second ed.). Beverly Hills: Sage.

Ganong, L. H., & Coleman, M. (2004). *Stepfamily relationships: Development, dynamics, and interventions.* New York: Kluwer Academic/Plenum Publishers.

Goldscheider, F., Bernhardt, E., & Lappegård, T. (2015). The gender revolution: A framework for understanding changing family and demographic behavior. *Population and Development Review, 41*(2), 207–239.

Guo, G., Roettger, M. E., & Cai, T. (2008). The integration of genetic propensities into social-control models of delinquency and violence among male youths. *American Sociological Review, 73,* 543–568.

Guo, G., Roettger, M. E., & Cai, T. (2008). The integration of genetic propensities into social-control models of delinquency and violence among male youths. *American Sociological Review, 73,* 543–568.

Guzzo, K. B. (2015). Twenty-five years of change in repartnering and stepfamily formation. *Center for Family and Demographic Research, Working Paper 2015–17.* Retrieved January 28, 2016, from https://www.bgsu.edu/arts-and-sciences/center-for-family-demographic-research/research-at-cfdr/working-papers-table.html

Hemez, P. (2017). Divorce rate in the U.S. *National Center for Family and Marriage Research, Family Profile FP-17–24.* Retrieved January 16, 2019, from https://www.bgsu.edu/ncfmr/resources/data/family-profiles/hemezdivorce-rate-2016-fp-17-24.html

Hetherington, E. M., & Clingempeel, G. (1992). Coping with marital transitions. *Monographs of the Society for Research in Child Development, 57.*

Hetherington, E. M., & Jodl, K. M. (1994). Stepfamilies as settings for child development. In A. Booth & J. Dunn (Eds.*),Stepfamilies: Who benefits? Who does not?* (pp. 55–79). Hillsdale, NJ: Lawrence Erlbaum.

Hetherington, E. M., & Kelly, J. (2002). *For better or for worse: Divorce reconsidered.* New York: W. W. Norton.

Kelly, J. B. (2007). Children's living arrangements following separation and divorce: Insights from empirical and clinical research. *Family Process, 46,* 35–42.

Kennedy, S., & Ruggles, S. (2014). Breaking up is hard to count: The rise of divorce in the United States, 1980–2010. *Demography, 51*(2), 587–598.

Killewald, A. (2016). Money, work, and marital stability: Assessing change in the gendered determinants of divorce. *American Sociological Review, 81*(4), 696–719.

Kim, H. S. (2011). Consequences of parental divorce for child development. *American Sociological Review, 76*(3), 487–511.

Lamidi, E., & Manning, W. D. (2016). Marriage and cohabitation experiences among young adults. *Family Profiles, FP-16–17, National Center for Family and Marriage Research.* Retrieved January 17, 2019, from https://www.bgsu.edu/ncfmr/resources/data/family-profiles/lamidi-manning-marriage-cohabitation-youngadults-fp-16-17.html

Laumann-Billings, L., & Emery, R. E. (2000). Distress among young adults from divorced families. *Journal of Family Psychology, 14,* 671–687.

Lee, D., & McLanahan, S. (2015). Family structure transitions and child development instability, selection, and population heterogeneity. *American Sociological Review, 80*(4), 738–763.

Lehrer, E. L. (2008). Age at marriage and marital instability: Revisiting the Becker-Landes-Michael hypothesis. *Demography, 21*(2), 463—484.

Manning, W. D., & Stykes, B. (2015). Twenty-five years of change in cohabitation in the U.S., 1987–2013. *National Center for Family and Marriage Research, Family Profile FP-15–01.* Retrieved January 12, 2015, from http:// www.bgsu.edu/content/dam/BGSU/college-of-arts-and-sciences/NCFMR/documents/FP/FP-15-01-twenty-five-yrs-cohab-us.pdf

Martin, S. P. (2006). Trends in marital dissolution by women's education in the United States. *Demographic Research, 15,* 537–560.

Meyer, D. R., Cancian, M., & Chen, Y. (2015). Why are child support orders becoming less likely after divorce? *Social Service Review, 89*(2), 301–334.

Meyer, D. R., Cancian, M., & Cook, S. T. (2017). The growth in shared custody in the United States: Patterns and Implications. *Family Court Review, 55*(4), 500–512.

Mincy, R. B., Jethwani, M., & Klempin, S. (2014). *Failing our fathers: Confronting the crisis of economically vulnerable nonresident fathers.* New York: Oxford University Press.

Mitchell, C., McLanahan, S., Notterman, D., Hobcraft, J., Brooks-Gunn, J., & Garfinkel, I. (2015). Family structure instability, genetic sensitivity, and child well-being. *American Journal of Sociology, 120*(4), 1195–1225.

Noël-Miller, C. M. (2013). Former stepparents' contact with their stepchildren after midlife. *Journals of Gerontology Series B: Psychological Sciences and Social Sciences, 68*(3), 409–419l.

O'Connor, T. G., Caspi, A., DeFries, J. C., & Plomin, R. (2000). Are associations between parental divorce and children's adjustment genetically mediated? An adoption study. *Developmental Psychology, 36,* 429–437.

O'Connor, T. G., Caspi, A., DeFries, J. C., & Plomin, R. (2000). Are associations between parental divorce and children's adjustment genetically mediated? An adoption study. *Developmental Psychology, 36,* 429–437.

OECD. (2018). Sf3.1: Marriage and divorce rates. *Family Database.* Retrieved January 18, 2019, from http://www.oecd.org/els/family/database.htm

Orbuch, T. L., Veroff, J., & Hunter, A. G. (1999). Black couples, white couples: The early years of marriage. In E. M. Hetherington (Ed.), *Coping with divorce, single parenting, and remarriage* (pp. 23–43). Mahwah, NJ: Lawrence Erlbaum Associates.

Pew Research Center. (2011). A portrait of stepfamilies. Retrieved January 28, 2016, from http://www.pewsocialtrends.org/2011/01/13/a-portrait-of-stepfamilies/

Pezzin, L. E., Pollak, R. A., & Schone, B. S. (2008). Parental marital disruption, family type, and transfers to disabled elderly parents. *Journal of Gerontology: Social Sciences, 63B,* S349–S358.

Rackin, H., & Gibson-Davis, C. (2018). Social class divergence in family transitions: The importance of cohabitation. *Journal of Marriage and Family, 80*(October), 1271–1286.

Raley, R. K., & Bumpass, L. L. (2003). The topography of the divorce plateau: Levels and trends in union stability in the United States after 1980. *Demographic Research, 8,* 245–259.

Rotz, D. (2016). Why have divorce rates fallen? The role of women's age at marriage. *Journal of Human Resources, 51*(4), 961–1002.

Sanner, C., Russell, L. T., Coleman, M., & Ganong, L. (2018). Half-sibling and stepsibling relationships: A systematic integrative review. *Journal of Family Theory & Review, 10*(4), 765–684.

Sayer, L. C., & Bianchi, S. M. (2000). Women's economic independence and the probability of divorce: A review and reexamination. *Journal of Family Issues, 21,* 906–943.

Seltzer, J. A. (2004). Cohabitation in the United States and Britain: Demography, kinship, and the future. *Journal of Marriage and Family, 66*(4), 921–928.

Seltzer, J. A., & Bianchi, S. M. (2013). Demographic change and parent-child relationships in adulthood. *Annual Review of Sociology, 39,* 275–290.

Smock, P. J., Manning, W. D., & Porter, M. (2005). "Everything's there except money": How money shapes decisions to marry among cohabitors *Journal of Marriage and Family, 67*(3), 680–696.

Stewart, S. D. (2007). *Brave new stepfamilies: Diverse paths toward stepfamily living.* Thousand Oaks, CA: Sage.

Sweeney, M. M. (2002). Two decades of family change: The shift in economic foundations of marriage. *American Sociological Review, 67*(1), 132–147.

Sweeney, M. M., & Cancian, M. (2004). The changing importance of white women's economic prospects for assortative mating. *Journal of Marriage and Family, 66*, 1015–1028.

Sweeney, M. M. (2010). Remarriage and stepfamilies: Strategic sites for family scholarship in the 21st century. *Journal of Marriage and Family, 72*, 667–684.

Tach, L., & Eads, A. (2015). Trends in the economic consequences of marital and cohabiting dissolution in the United States. *Demography, 52*(2), 431–452.

Teachman, J. D., & Tedrow, L. (2008). Divorce, race, and military service: More than equal pay and equal opportunity. *Journal of Marriage and Family, 70*, 1030–1044.

U.S. Bureau of the Census. (2011). Table 1. Detailed living arrangements of children by race, hispanic origin, and age: 2009. Retrieved August 5, 2018, from https://www.census.gov/hhes/socdemo/children/data/sipp/living2009/tab01.pdf

U.S. Bureau of the Census. (2013). Table C3. Living arrangement of children under 18 years and marital status of parents, by age, sex, race, and Hispanic origin and selected characteristics of the child for all children: 2013. *America's Families and Living Arrangements: 2013: Children (C table series)*. Retrieved June 20, 2014, from https://www.census.gov/hhes/families/files/cps2013/tabC3-all.xls

U.S. Bureau of the Census. (2018a). Custodial mothers and fathers and their child support: 2015. *P60-262*. Retrieved January 17, 2019, from https://www.census.gov/content/dam/Census/library/publications/2018/demo/P60-262.pdf

U.S. Bureau of the Census. (2018b). Table C3. Living arrangements of children under 18 years and marital status of parents, by age, sex, race, and hispanic origin and selected characteristics of the child for all children: 2018. *America's Families and Living Arrangements*. Retrieved December 18, 2018, from https://www.census.gov/data/tables/2018/demo/families/cps-2018.html

U.S. Bureau of the Census. (2018c). Table FG-5. One-parent unmarried family groups with own children under 18, by labor force status of the reference person: 2016. *America's Families and Living Arrangements, Table FG-5*. Retrieved January 17, 2019

U.S. Bureau of the Census. (2018d). Table FM-2. All parent/child situations by type, race, and hispanic origin of the householder or reference person: 1970 to present. Retrieved May 26, 2019, from https://www2.census.gov/programs-surveys/demo/tables/families/time-series/families/fm2.xls

U.S. National Center for Health Statistics. (2018). United States life tables, 2015. *National Vital Statistics Reports, vol. 67, no. 7*. Retrieved December 18, 2018, from https://www.cdc.gov/nchs/data/nvsr/nvsr67/nvsr67_07-508.pdf

Wagmiller, R. L., Gershoff, E., Veliz, P., & Clements, M. (2010). Does children's academic achievement improve when single mothers marry? *Sociology of Education, 83*(3), 201–226.

Wallerstein, J. S., & Blakeslee, S. (1989). *Second chances: Men, women and children a decade after divorce*. New York: Ticknor and Fields.

Wallerstein, J. S., & Kelly, J. B. (1980). *Surviving the breakup: How children and parents cope with divorce*. New York: Basic Books.

Wallerstein, J. S., Lewis, J. M., & Blakeslee, S. (2000). *The unexpected legacy of divorce*. New York: Hyperion.

Weitzman, L. J. (1985). *The divorce revolution: The unexpected social and economic consequences for women and their children in America*. New York: The Free Press.

Wiemers, E. E., Seltzer, J. A., Schoeni, R. F., Hotz, V. J., & Bianchi, S. M. (2019). Stepfamily structure and transfers between generations in U.S. Families. *Demography, 56*(1), 229–260.

Wu, H. (2017). Trends in births to single and cohabiting mothers, 1980–2014. *Family Profiles, FP-17–04, National Center for Family and Marriage Research*. Retrieved July 23, 2018, from https://www.bgsu.edu/ncfmr/resources/data/family-profiles/wu-trends-births-single-cohabiting-mothers-fp-17-04.html

Part Six

Family, Society, and World

Where do all the great social changes of the twentieth and early twenty-first centuries leave the institution of the family? Chapter 13 examines the changes in family life around the world in the past half-century. We will see a mixed picture of sharp changes in some regions of the world and lesser changes elsewhere. We will also learn how globalization is tying together the families of the world. Chapter 14 examines government policy toward families. We begin by studying the relationship in the past and present between the family and the state. An understanding of conservative and liberal interpretations of this relationship helps us better comprehend current political debates. We then turn to some important issues affecting families, important changes in policies and programs that have affected low-income families. Finally, we examine a series of current debates over family policy, such as how much to help employed parents manage the demands of their work and family lives, whether the government should enact programs to encourage young adults to marry, and how to encourage responsible fatherhood.

Chapter Thirteen

International Family Change

Looking Forward

1. What is the convergence thesis and has it proven to be true?
2. How has parental control of children's marriage choices changed in the global south?
3. What is the companionate ideal and how has it spread?
4. How has globalization altered family patterns in the Western world and the global south?
5. What is the "return to historical complexity" interpretation of recent family change in the West?

In 1990, I attended an international conference in Tokyo on the Japanese family. A college professor told me this story to illustrate how much marriage had changed in Japan. His father met the woman he would marry for the first time on their wedding day. The marriage had been arranged solely by the parents of the bride and groom. When my friend was a young man, he considered his parents to be enlightened because they permitted him to meet the woman they had selected as his wife a few times before they married. Recently, he said with a smile, his daughter had come home and asked him if he would like to meet the man she had decided to marry. Today, a generation later, even more family change has come to Japan. Its divorce rate is now equal to the high rates of some wealthy Western nations (although still lower than in the United States). Living together before marrying, which was shameful in 1990, has become relatively common. The scope of the changes from the generation of my friend's father to the generation of young adults who are partnering today is breathtaking. Family life looks much more like the United States or Western Europe than was the case a half-century ago. The main question that my anxious hosts at the conference had for me was whether the Japanese family was turning into the American family. I assured them that because of Japan's distinctive cultural traditions, it was not. I am no longer certain that was the right answer.

Yet there are aspects of Japanese family patterns that remain strikingly different from the West. (Recall from Chapter 1 that the Western nations comprise the countries of Western Europe and the United States, Canada, Australia, and New Zealand.) For instance, only about 2 percent of children are born outside of marriage (compared to about 40 percent in the United States), and only about 20 percent of the Japanese believe it's acceptable for a woman to have children without marrying (Choe, Bumpass, Tsuya, & Rindfuss, 2014). Moreover, Japanese adults remain responsible for the care of their older parents much more so than Americans. It's still considered improper to send one's parents to a nursing home; instead, children are supposed to care for their parents when needed. The Japanese regard the tendency of Americans to park their ailing parents in nursing homes as callous and uncaring. This mixture of change and persistence in family life can be found in many nations. In some areas of the world, such as East Asia (China, Japan and their neighbors), the changes have been massive. In other areas, such as South Asia (India and its neighbors) change has been more moderate. Many societies have been able to graft new features onto old patterns, creating family patterns that are creative mixtures of the past and the present.

Nearly all of the material in this book so far has been about the United States. An American reader might question whether it is necessary to learn about families in other countries. One justification is to better understand one's own culture by comparing it to cultures elsewhere. Americans might assume that choosing one's own spouse and not marrying until one's twenties or thirties is natural and unremarkable. But an examination of how heavily parents are involved in these decisions in much of the world can lead us to understand the ways in which the Western family system is distinctive. In addition, the world economy is now globalized; national boundaries are more porous; and family trends in one part of the world can influence lives in distant nations. People, money, and jobs move across these boundaries with an ease that was impossible until recently. For instance, immigrants are entering the United States in numbers not seen in a century; and their families are taking on new, transnational forms that include both relatives they leave behind and new ones they acquire. Americans are purchasing goods made by workers in other countries whose family lives are changing as a result of the factory jobs they hold. Globalization has connected the world's population in unprecedented ways. Americans who know little about other societies cannot grasp the great social and economic changes that have occurred. Indeed, Americans who don't understand other cultures may not even realize how their own culture is evolving in a globalized world.

The Convergence Thesis

A half-century ago, a leading sociologist, William J. Goode, wrote a book predicting that as economic development proceeded the world's families would in the future converge toward the Western model of a conjugal family–by which he meant the marriage-based unit of husband, wife, and children (Goode, 1963). He drew upon the prevailing view of national development in the mid-twentieth century: **modernization theory.** It held that the underdeveloped countries of the world would eventually make a transition from traditional to modern in a fashion similar to the transition that had occurred in the West. The first sentence of his book proclaimed, "For the first time in world history a common set of influences–the social forces of industrialization and urbanization–is affecting every known society" (p.1). Modernization theorists believed that the Western model of development was not only inevitable but also beneficial–it was the best path for all countries to take (Thornton, 2005). They believed that as Europe had developed, it had moved from a predominantly extended-family system to a predominantly conjugal family system. Therefore, they associated the conjugal family system with progress and economic development.

modernization theory the idea that poorer countries would eventually make a transition from traditional to modern in the same way as the Western countries did

The basic assumption was that in the olden days families had been larger and more complex, but as they modernized they moved to smaller, simpler–and superior– conjugal form. In the past, it was thought, large extended families were common because farmers needed more child labor and because the generations lived together. We know now, however, that traces of the conjugal family and other supposedly modern family patterns have been found in Europe as far back as the historical records go (Macfarlane, 1978; Mitterauer & Sieder, 1982). The idea that the extended family was the old form in Europe and the conjugal family is the new form is incorrect. Nevertheless, modernization theory's view of the family remains influential.

It certainly influenced Goode. When he published his book, the conjugal family was still dominant in the United States. During the 1950s and early 1960s in the United States, as I noted in Chapter 2, nearly everyone married, they tended to marry young, and they had more children than their parents' generation. The United States dominated the world economically and militarily. Families were prospering. No wonder that Goode thought that the conjugal family was the wave of the future and that someday in the not-too-distant-future the family patterns of nearly all countries would converge to the conjugal family model.

But the first sign of trouble for the convergence occurred almost as soon as the book was printed in 1963. Divorce rates began to rise rapidly in the United States, birth rates declined sharply, cohabitation became common, the typical age at marriage rose, and the proportion of births outside of marriage rose. To be sure, marriage-based families of husband, wife, and children remained an important part of the American family system, but they were not nearly as dominant in 1980 as they were when Goode was writing his book. They are even less dominant today. The model family that the world was supposed to converge upon—the great American conjugal family—was eroding in Goode's backyard.

The supremacy of the conjugal family also weakened in Western Europe. In the nations in the north such as Sweden, Norway, Denmark, and France, the degree of change in some respects exceeded the changes in the United States. For instance, marriage and childbearing became separate parts of adult life to an even greater degree than in America. In 2010 the percentage of children born outside of marriage exceeded 50 percent in Sweden, Norway, and France and was in the mid-forties in the United Kingdom and the Netherlands (Lappegård, 2014). By comparison, 40 percent of American children were born outside of marriage in 2017 (U.S. National Center for Health Statistics, 2018). Most children born outside of marriage in Western Europe were born to cohabiting couples who might remain together for several years before marrying or might never marry at all (Holland, 2013). As in the United States, the kind of Western family that the world was supposed to converge toward declined.

Quick Review

- Modernization theorists such as William J. Goode predicted that family patterns around the world would converge toward the mid-twentieth century Western family.
- World family patterns have changed greatly since William J. Goode first made his prediction that family patterns around the world would converge, but they have not adhered to the Western pattern.
- Change in Western Europe was in some ways greater than in the United States, such as in the separation of childbearing and marriage.

The Global South

global south the less developed nations in Central and South America, Africa, and Asia

Throughout the Western nations, the conjugal family is no longer the dominant force it was when Goode wrote his book. Nor did families in what is called the **global south**—the less-developed nations in Central and South America, Africa, and Asia—move in lockstep toward the Western model as the convergence thesis suggested they should (McDonald, 1992). A few non-Western nations, such as Japan, experienced great economic development and did come to resemble the Western pattern in many ways; but others remained dissimilar—especially those in the most rural and underdeveloped areas of the world, such as sub-Saharan Africa and South Asia. So Goode's central prediction–that family patterns in all nations would move toward the Western conjugal family model–proved wrong (Therborn, 2014). Nevertheless, some of Goode's subsidiary predictions have been borne out, as we will see in this chapter:

- He correctly anticipated a widespread tendency for parents to lose authority over their children's family lives. Parents in many countries used to control who their children wed and when they married; that power has greatly eroded, although it hasn't disappeared.
- He also thought correctly that the idea of a companionate marriage based on romantic love could spread broadly even in societies that have made little progress toward industrialization. The ideal of the love-based marriage has become popular in many countries even when little change in their economies has occurred.

Moreover, there have been other momentous changes that Goode did not even foresee. When he was writing, cohabitation was still uncommon in the West and rare in most of the world. Since then, it has surged in many countries. And we can hardly blame him for failing to anticipate the advent of globalization, which was made possible by computer-based communication that did not exist in the early 1960s–and which has created new forms of personal life such as families that span more than one nation. It's worth examining, then, what has happened–and not happened–to families in the global south in the half-century since Goode's book appeared.[1]

THE DECLINE OF PARENTAL CONTROL

Even though convergence toward the conjugal family did not occur on a world scale, Goode was still accurate in predicting that the power of parents, lineages, and other extended kin over their children would diminish in many nations as industrialization occurred. In particular, parents' ability to influence the decisions that their children make about events of the life course, such as the timing of marriage, choice of spouse, place of residence, and number of children, would diminish. A good indicator of parental control in a society is the typical age at marriage for women. If women's ages at marriage are very low, it usually the case that parents are choosing husbands for their daughters. Few 15-year olds are actively looking for husbands by themselves; yet in some societies, parents may try to negotiate the marriages of their daughters shortly after, or even before, they become able to bear children. In societies such as these, older men traditionally wanted young wives so that they could maximize the number of children they could have. When girls are married at young ages to older men, they have little power in their marriages and lack the authority to make decisions. They are at greater risk of domestic violence. They are often subservient not only to their husbands but also the mothers-in-law with whom they often reside. They typically must drop out of school and consequently receive little education. Their early first births have a higher risk of medical complications. In some societies, largely in sub-Saharan Africa, they are taken as second or third wives in polygynous marriages with men who are much older than they are (International Center for Research on Women, 2010).

[1] This chapter draws upon my article on how the changes in family life that have occurred around the world since Goode's book compare to his predictions (Cherlin, 2012).

Therefore, if we see increases in women's ages at marriage in nations where it has been traditionally very low, we have discovered signals of profound changes in the relations between parents and children and between wives and husbands. To be sure, teenage marriages don't have these negative qualities in all nations at all times. For instance, in the United States in 1960, 24 percent of 14-to-19-year-olds were married (U.S. Bureau of the Census, 1966); yet nearly all chose their own spouse (or chose their own sex partner, got pregnant, and were pressured to marry). But this period represents the exception in the United States. As noted in Chapter 2, marriage ages were unusually low during the baby boom years of the 1950s; and afterward ages at marriage rose to their previous levels. In the global south, in contrast, low ages at marriage have long been common.

Rising Age at Marriage And in fact, over the past several decades, the typical ages at which young adults enter first unions have indeed risen in many regions of the world, which suggests that parental influence on spouse choice has decreased and that wives' authority in their households has increased. According to United Nations data, the mean (average) age at marriage for women in the world as a whole has increased from 21 to 23 since the 1970s (Ortega, 2014).[2] That average increase conceals a great deal of variability, but the overall worldwide trend is clear: There has been a convergence toward older ages at marriage for women (Pesando & GFC Team, 2019). Figure 13.1 shows the decline in teenage marriage in several large nations since about 1970: It presents, based on United Nations data, the percentage of 15- to 19-year-old women who were currently married around 1970 and at a recent date that varies from 2006 to 2011. It is likely that most marriages in this age range were arranged by parents with little consultation with their daughters, except in Brazil and the United States.

You can see that the percentage of adolescent girls who are married has declined sharply in all of the countries. Nevertheless, there is still wide variation. In Bangladesh, where the vast majority of girls married as teenagers in 1970, it is still the

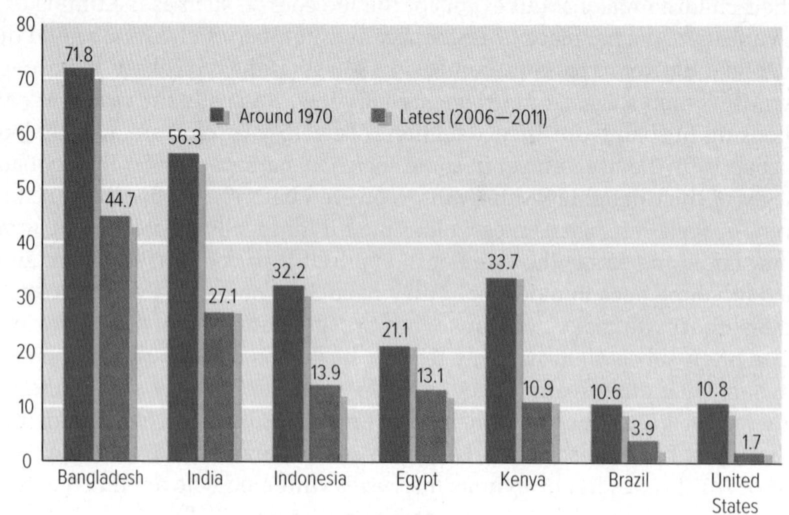

FIGURE 13.1 Percentage of 15- to 19-Year-Old Girls Who Were Married, 1970s to the Present. (*Source:* United Nations, 2013b)

[2] Technically, these are estimates of the "singulate mean age at marriage," the average number of years a person lives before marrying among all people who marry by age 50.

case that more than 40 percent of 15- to 19-year olds are married today—one of the highest levels in the world. The difference between the average ages at marriage for men and women in Bangladesh today is nearly seven years (United Nations, 2013b). In India, more than 20 percent of women in this age range are married; but the average figure for this vast nation combines northern India, where teenage marriage is still common, and southern India, where marriage ages are much higher. In Indonesia, Egypt, and Kenya, the percentage is a bit above 10 percent. In fact, throughout low-income countries in Asia, the Middle East, and North Africa, the percentage is about 10 percent or less. The major world exception today (in addition to Bangladesh and northern India) is a belt of several African nations on the edge of the Sahara Desert, including Mali, Chad, and Niger, where more than 40 percent of 15- to 19-year olds are married and the difference between the average ages at marriages for men and women is six to seven years. The chart also shows that very low proportions of teenagers are married in Brazil and the United States. Early marriage has always been uncommon in the Latin American and North American countries (except during the baby boom), where most young adults have found their own marriage partners.

Hybrid Marriage As the average age at marriage for women has declined, so has **arranged marriage,** in which parents choose their children's spouses with little or no participation by the children themselves. As my friend told me at the Tokyo conference, marriages arranged by parents used to be common in Japan but are rare today. The share of Japanese marriages that were arranged dropped from 63 percent in 1955 to 7 percent in 1998 (East-West Center, 2002). A fall of similar magnitude occurred in China between the 1940s and the 1960s. The Marriage Law of 1950 banned arranged marriages, as befitted a regime headed by Mao Zedong, who ran away from home as a teenager rather than agree to an arranged marriage and who began work as a journalist, publicizing cases in which women had committed suicide rather than go through with arranged marriages (Witke, 1967). So in China government action rather than development produced much of the change in marriages ages. Still, in rural areas of China, parents retained substantial influence over spouse choices through the 1970s (Parish & Whyte, 1978). Eventually, factors such as the freedom to migrate to the city and the lack of family property under the socialist system undercut parental authority in rural areas, giving young adults substantial autonomy (Yan, 2003).

arranged marriage a process in which parents choose their children's spouses with little or no participation by the children themselves

Throughout Asia, traditional arranged marriages in which the children were not consulted about their future spouses have declined greatly (Jones, 2010). Arranged marriage is often contrasted with **love marriage,** the process in which young adults choose their own marriage partners on the basis of love and companionship. Yet the decline of strictly arranged marriages doesn't always mean that young adults are choosing spouses solely on their own, the way Westerners do. It doesn't always imply the triumph of love marriage. Rather, what is emerging in some countries is **hybrid marriage,** in which young adults and their parents work together to find marriage partners (Cherlin, 2012; Allendorf, 2013; Allendorf & Pandian, 2016). Hybrid marriage combines aspects of arranged marriage and love marriage. Young adults have more authority than in the past because parents may give them greater leeway to reject suggested choices. They may allow their children to get to know and like their partners prior to the marriage. Or they may even allow their children to suggest potential mates to them. The children may value their limited autonomy but still see their parents' involvement as making the task of finding a spouse easier.

love marriage a process in which young adults choose their own marriage partners on the basis of love and companionship

hybrid marriage a process in which young adults and their parents work together to find marriage partners

The resulting marriages are neither fully arranged nor fully self-chosen but rather a hybrid of the love marriage and arranged marriage systems. In India, for instance, marriages arranged by parents without the consent of their children have declined; but what has increased the most are not marriages in which spouses are chosen by the children themselves but rather parent-arranged marriages with the children's consent (Banerji & Vanneman, 2009). A young, upper-middle-class Indian man told sociologist Nancy Netting the story of his marriage:

> *My father's friend . . . told me and my father that [they knew] a nice girl, who will also suit your family. . . . Her family sent horoscope and photographs and biodata. She's beautiful. The picture and horoscope were just fine. . . .*
>
> *[My family] met her first . . . and then we [were allowed to meet]. She was just amazing . . . she was exactly meeting my nature . . . We went into a room for a half-hour and I asked her some questions . . . and I told her [about myself]. We agreed to meet a second time; I took her for a ride, she was very bold and said she was fine with me. The third meeting I decided, but I didn't tell her, because I needed to talk to my parents. . . . "Everything's fine," they said. "Go ahead." The three meetings took three weeks (Netting, 2010, pp. 714-15).*

In order for this marriage to happen, both the young man and his parents had to agree. Either generation could have scuttled it.

Particularly in the urban middle classes, parents who are arranging marriages now consider whether their children will be personally happy with the partners they will choose, a criterion that was not traditionally emphasized (Fuller & Narasimhan, 2008). In one variant, couples meet on their own, fall in love, and only then ask their parents' permission to marry—but may well end the relationship if either partner's parents disapprove. One Indian young man first met his girlfriend at an Internet café. He told Netting:

> *She is my first girlfriend and I think maybe she's the last. I never think before . . . for any other girl . . . I told my father everything, and after that he [went to her family and told them] . . . They are [from a higher caste] but her father knows I am very good, and fine for daughter, but her mother doesn't like me. I think not because just caste but I have less education, yet I work hard and have a good business. . . .*
>
> *She's all things my mother and father want. I won't say much about her because I'll be talking always with love . . .*

Two months later, an email message brought this unhappy news:

> *We decided to stop our relation because of her mother . . . & no girls of India is going against her mother.*

Despite her strong emotional bond to the young man, the young woman would not marry against her mother's wishes. However, two months later, another email reported:

> *I want to give u best news that finally her parents agreed for her marriage with me . . . Her father & brother support me lots & finally they change her mother's mind . . . [Next month] is date selected for my marriage (Netting, 2010, p. 721).*

Without the young woman's mother's change of heart, the wedding would not have gone forward.

In hybrid forms of spouse choice such as these, parents and children collaborate to find a partner who will provide love and companionship to the child in addition to working on the family's behalf. Instead of simply rejecting arranged marriage, well-educated Indians seem to be adapting it to a wage- and salary-based economy and to urban life.

The story of two Turkish young adults also shows the hybrid nature of marriage choice. Ali met Fadime on a minibus that traveled between their villages. According to anthropologist Kimberly Hart (2007), they created a secret, romantic relationship supported by love letters and glances exchanged on the minibus. Up to that point, their relationship looked like a love marriage. But they felt that they needed to obtain the permission of their parents to marry. The mother of Fadime, the would-be bride, was favorably disposed but explained a problem: Fadime's older brother was unmarried, and tradition dictated that siblings marry in the order of their birth. So Fadime could not marry before her brother did. Upon hearing of this problem, the mother of Ali, the would-be groom, set about finding an unmarried girl in her village who she might match with Fadime's brother, thus solving the marriage-order problem. She found a suitable girl, and the two families matched her with Fadime's brother. The brother and his potential bride were allowed time to develop an affectionate relationship through telephone conversations, gifts, and family ceremonies. Meanwhile, Ali and Fadime waited patiently for their turn to marry. Finally, the older brother married the girl from Ali's village, and many villagers remarked that the couple had fallen in love. Their marriage cleared the way for Ali and Fadime to also marry. By the end of the story, neither marriage seemed to be totally a love marriage or totally an arranged marriage. It is in the space between love marriage and arranged marriage that many marriages are formed, with young adults gaining authority but parents still playing an important role.

THE SPREAD OF THE COMPANIONATE IDEAL

Parental control over their children's marriage behavior has also been reduced by the spread of the idea that marriage should be based on love and companionship. Rather than serving the needs of parents and other kin, marriage, from this viewpoint, should center on the emotional satisfaction of the husband and wife. In Chapter 7 I called this style the companionate marriage, in which the emphasis is on affection, friendship, and sexual gratification. The mid-twentieth-century modernization theorists thought that this new style of marriage would spread as nations industrialized; but it now appears that companionate marriage has spread even in nations that aren't very industrialized. For instance, older women in a Mexican village say that what was most important when they married was that a husband "respected you." They described how the ideal of marriage has changed over a generation from *respeto* (respect) to *confianza* (trust, intimacy). Among the older generation, if a husband showed respect to his wife, his sexual infidelity was not seen as a failing serious enough to warrant a separation or a divorce. But among the younger generation, a woman expects her husband to be an intimate companion and would view his infidelity as a serious threat to her marriage (Hirsch, 2003). Reports from a large number of non-Western settings show that young adults are increasingly oriented toward romantic love, shared interests, and companionship in a spouse.

How Social Norms Change The social norm of companionship can spread through media such as television and movies even without much economic development. And the spread of companionships often goes hand in hand with declines in arranged marriage, increases in age at marriage, and other changes in family life. In the Chitwan Valley in Nepal, a region where traditionally most marriages had been arranged by parents, the first movie theater was built in 1969. The first all-weather road linking the largest town to cities outside the area was completed in 1979; and better transportation subsequently led to more opportunity for wage labor. Television first appeared in the late 1980s. By taking retrospective life histories from a sample of residents, researchers were able to determine that people who had listened to radio, seen a movie, and watched television were more likely to have played a role in the process of choosing their spouse, even controlling for whether they had ever worked outside of their family group. From the mass media, the residents saw and heard mostly Western messages, which provided the news that the wealthiest and most advanced people in the world chose their own spouses and married for love and companionship (Ghimire, Axxin, Yabiku, & Thornton, 2006). Over the last half of the century, the proportion of people who had participated at all in the selection of their spouses rose from less than 10 percent to about half; and the mean age at marriage rose from 15 to 21 (Axxin, Ghimire, & Barber, 2008).

Similar findings about mass media have been reported in other countries. Using data on five states in India from 2003 to 2008, researchers found that the entry of cable TV led to increases in people's positive views of women's autonomy, to enrollment gains in schools, and to declines in pregnancy rates (Jensen & Oster, 2009). In Brazil, the spread from region to region since 1965 of the television network that airs most of the popular *novellas,* or soap operas, was associated with a reduction in the probability that women in the region would give birth in a given year. Most of the female characters in the *novellas,* the authors note, are beautiful, healthy, middle-class–and either childless or have one child (La Ferrara, Chong, & Duryea, 2008). An anthropologist told of people in an impoverished neighborhood in Northeast Brazil watching *novellas* in which characters meaningfully said to each other, in Portuguese-accented, borrowed English, *Ai lóvi iú,* and in the process learned a lesson on the importance of romantic love (Rebhun, 1999). Residents in a village in Iraq that is near the Syrian and Turkish borders blamed the introduction of satellite TV for a surge in suicides by girls who faced arranged marriages. They cited a Turkish soap opera, "Forbidden Love," about the romantic lives of the upper class. A 16-year-old girl who had unsuccessfully tried to kill herself rather than submit to an arranged marriage told a reporter that she had watched the program. "I wish I had that life," she said (Arango, 2012).

The media are not the only channel through which Western ideas of companionate marriage can spread. In Papua New Guinea, Christian missionaries took up residence in societies where, traditionally, married men and married women had lived in separate housing and encouraged them to build "family houses" where they could live together in companionate marriages (Wardlow, 2006). In Africa and in Latin America, Pentecostal Christianity is growing rapidly and encouraging parishioners to focus on the conjugal family. Moreover, the spread of mass education to the low-income nations has undermined parental control over decisions about marriage and childbearing (Caldwell, 2006). Education–even elementary education–changes attitudes and values by showing children that a source of authority outside of the family exists, by removing them from control of their parents for a large part of their daily lives, and by teaching them useful new skills that their parents lack. In these ways, education encourages children and adolescents to be more autonomous in their decision-making and reduces parental authority. Teenage marriages tend to drop. A man in Northern India explained to sociologist Keera Allendorf the influences of education and the media on family life this way:

In the past, people were mostly uneducated. They had a traditional concept, but now everything has become modern. Every kind of facility is there now. Television was not there in the past. They did not have knowledge. They used to focus only on their old culture. They were busy in farming. But now people have learned many things. They watch television. They read newspapers. People went abroad after being educated and everything has been advanced (Allendorf, 2013, p. 465).

This broader knowledge of the world has eroded parental control over who marries whom. The infusion of Western values, through reading materials in schools and through messages in the mass media, has increased the salience of romantic love.

To be sure, economic circumstances affect whether new social norms are accepted. Had there been no changes in the availability of wage labor or in land use, the messages of the mass media about love and companionship might not have stuck. In general, the higher the level of economic development in a country, the later people tend to marry (Jones & Yeung, 2014). The TV watchers in Northeast Brazil had migrated to cities where low-wage jobs existed. They were no longer tied to their parents' farms; they could make decisions independently. But the spread of new ideas can be seen even in settings where there have been modest changes in the economy. Thornton (2005) argues that although Western ideas about the family are often opposed or resisted at first, many of these ideas are nevertheless adopted, often in modified forms, because the Western-style family is so closely associated with national development–and national development is seen as the path to prosperity. He calls these ideas **developmental idealism,** the belief that Western-style families and economic development are beneficial for all countries. The spread of developmental idealism carries the messages that both the economic system and the social organization of the Western developed countries are superior and should be aspired to. Individuals see the Western family and other facets of Western social organization as part of the process of development and, therefore, as ideals to be emulated. So it follows that people *should* change their family lives to be closer to the Western model. This view of the superiority of the Western way of life, while abandoned by many intellectuals in the West, is apparently still alive on the streets of the non-Western world.

developmental idealism the belief that Western-style families and economic development are beneficial for all countries

The Spread of Postmodern Ideals But you have to wonder which version of the Western family is being emulated these days. Certainly the version shown in contemporary Western movies and television programs and in Latin American soap operas differs sharply from the stable, marriage-based conjugal family of the Western family that dominated family life in the age I called in Chapter 1 the modern era: the long period from the beginning of industrialization to the mid-to-late twentieth century. During that time most children were born within marriages, cohabitation was uncommon, and divorce rates were relatively low. That was the modern family. Yet as I noted, that era has been superseded by the late-modern era, sometimes called the postmodern era. If young adults in the global south are seeking today to form families that are like the West, they may be emulating the postmodern family rather than the modern family. Said otherwise, they may be learning about family patterns which encompass not only modern characteristics such as self-choice of spouse but also postmodern characteristics such as cohabitation, high rates of divorce, very low birth rates, and a general orientation toward individual growth and development. If so, their societies may move quickly from traditional family patterns to postmodern patterns without spending much time in between—as though families could fly from the 1800s directly to the 2000s while avoiding most of the twentieth century. When the first wave of industrialization in non-Western nations was occurring in the 1950s and 1960s, much was written about "latecomers." In particular, the Japanese were seen as benefiting from coming late to the process of industrialization because they could quickly import and utilize the knowledge and technology that had slowly built up during the much longer industrializing process in the West (Levy, 1972). Similarly, it may be that some of the latecomers to family change are catching up to the West by skipping the companionate form that dominated the modern era and moving directly from the institutional marriage to individualistic marriage (see Chapter 7).

The Cohabitation Boom So we see, for instance, a great increase in cohabitation in Latin America and in East Asia. The Latin American cohabitation boom has been largest in Brazil, the most populous country in the region. Among all 25- to 29-year-old Brazilians who were in a union (marital or cohabiting), 7 percent were cohabiting in 1970; but by 2010, 57 percent were cohabiting (Esteve, Lesthaeghe, López-Gay, & García-Román, 2016). Many Latin American nations have long had stable informal unions, sometime called consensual unions. These informal unions were more common among the poor and served as an alternative to marriage. Young women entered into them as teenagers and quickly had children. Researchers call these kinds of unions "traditional cohabitation" (Covre-Sussai, Meuleman, Botterman, & Matthijs, 2014). In recent decades a new form of "modern cohabitation" has emerged: Its key characteristics are that, first, unlike traditional cohabitation, it is more common among better-educated young adults and, second, these young adults start their cohabiting unions later—nearly all wait until after their teenage years. The reasons behind the growth of modern cohabitation in Latin America are similar to the reasons for the increase in cohabitation in Western nations such as the United States, including increased autonomy of women, increasing educational opportunities, and a more individualistic view of intimate partnerships.

In East Asia, we see Japan once again undergoing a rapid, latecomer transition. The percentage of women who ever cohabited doubled from 10 percent to 21 percent in Japan from the generation that was in its twenties in the 1970s to the generation that was in its twenties in the 1990s (Raymo, Iwasawa, & Bumpass, 2009). Unmarried Japanese women in their twenties are more negative about marriage than are their American counterparts; for example, 69 percent say that their degree of personal freedom would become worse if they married, compared to 29 percent of Americans—a reflection, perhaps, of the greater inequalities between husbands and wives in Japan (Tsuya, Mason, & Bumpass, 2004). Younger Japanese women and men are more supportive of the idea that they can have a full and satisfying life without getting married then are older Japanese men and women (Bumpass & Choe, 2004).

The increase of cohabitation in China, the most populous country in the world, has also been dramatic. Among Chinese who married before 1980, premarital cohabitation was almost nonexistent. But among those who married in the decade of the 2000s, about 30 percent had cohabited first (Xu, Li, & Yu, 2014; Yu & Xie, 2015;). The 1980s marked the start of the transformation of China from a planned economy to a form of market economy. Millions of young adults left rural areas and moved to cities to find employment in factories or offices; their parents, left behind in rural China, had less control over who their children married than in the past—and whether their children cohabited prior to marrying. Urban young adults had greater exposure to Western ideals of family life, which included cohabitation, than did their rural counterparts–another example of developmental idealism. Young women's employment provided them with greater independence and gave them the freedom to choose cohabitation. And the high cost of housing in urban areas made cohabiting with a partner an appealing way to split the costs. As in Latin America, then, both economic development and exposure to Western ideals supported a great increase in cohabitation among better-educated young adults. Cohabitation patterns have become more similar around the world (Pesando, 2019).

The Decline of Fertility When Goode wrote his book, the United States was just emerging from the baby boom, and the average young adult woman was on track to have three children. He thought that was about right for an advanced country–not too large, not too small. He could have called it the Goldilocks fertility rate; and he expected little change. But birth rates plummeted in the United States, and in other Western countries; and more surprisingly, they began to drop in much of the global south. The total fertility rate (TFR), which I defined in Chapter 5 as the average number of births that a woman would have over her lifetime if current birthrates were to remain the same, was 4.7 for the entire world in 1970; it fell to 3.2 in 1990 and to 2.4 in 2011 (United Nations, 2013a). A TFR of about 2.1 is necessary to reproduce the population from generation to generation; and the world is approaching that level. Currently, a belt of countries through the middle of Africa still have high fertility rates, but the TFR has come down almost everywhere else: 2.6 in India; 2.3 in Mexico; and below-replacement levels of 1.8 in Brazil and 1.6 in China.

The decline in China was achieved in part by a government policy that limited most couples to having one child. The program achieved its goal of swiftly reducing the population growth rate. But it collided with the Chinese preference for having sons rather than daughters due to the tradition that sons remain with their parents after marrying, bring in daughters-in-law, and care for their parents in older age. Chinese couples used methods such as ultrasound scans and sex-selective abortions to avoid having daughters as first children. As a result an oversupply of boys now exists relative to girls; and 10 to 15 percent of the boys will not be able to find wives when they reach adulthood (Jiang, Feldman, & Li, 2014). This may not seem high to an American or a European who is accustomed to relatively high numbers of people who will never marry; but it is unprecedented in China, where marriage has been nearly universal. Moreover, China does not have a well-developed social security system. Older adults must rely on their children for care; those without children to help will struggle to find alternative means of support. The situation is an example of how traditional cultural patterns can influence the course of family change in unforeseen ways.

Quick Review

- Substantial changes in family life have occurred in many of the nations of the global south.
- Age at marriage has increased and arranged marriages have become less common, reflecting a decline in parental control of their children's family lives.
- The ideal of the companionate marriage has spread broadly, even in settings where national development has been modest. Cohabitation has increased in many regions of the world.
- Fertility rates have dropped sharply in world; in China the government-induced decline has clashed with a traditional preference for sons.

Globalization and Family Change

In the half-century since Goode's book appeared, the world revolution of which he wrote—the spread of industrialization—has not played out the way that modernization theorists anticipated. Africa has been largely left behind; South Asia and the Middle East have struggled; progress in Southeast Asia (Indonesia and its neighbors) and Latin America has been uneven; and only in East Asia has consistent economic growth occurred. Moreover, viewing the process of development of one nation, or even of one region, at a time is no longer an adequate way to assess economic and social change. Rather we must now consider the consequences of globalization, which I defined in Chapter 1 as the increasing flow of goods, services, money, migrants, and information across the nations of the world.

THE GLOBALIZATION OF PRODUCTION

globalization of production the movement to the global south of the production of goods and services that Westerners consume

Advances in technology, such as computer-based electronic communication, along with a lowering of barriers to trade and investment, have facilitated the **globalization of production,** by which I mean the movement to the global south of the production of goods (such as electronics) and services (such as call centers) that Westerners consume. All of the mid-century theorists expected the economies of the industrialized nations to grow indefinitely; none would have predicted the decline in industrial jobs that has occurred in the West as factory production has moved overseas or has been computerized. None foresaw the kind of industrialization in which factories in the global south specialize in the labor-intensive production of goods that used to be manufactured in the West, while most of the control over design, marketing, and sales—and most of the profits—remain in the West. None expected the rise of global coordination on a supra-national level, exemplified by the multinational corporations that manage production networks across many countries. It is as if another dimension of space has been added to the world since Goode and his contemporaries sought to predict the future of family life, and those whose vision was limited to the lesser dimensions of the nation state-level could not see it.

What, then, has the globalization of production done to family life? In the global south the increasing employment of women is changing family patterns. Employers in many low-income countries seem to think that women will work for lower wages than men and that they are easier to control than are men (for instance, less likely to complain or to go on strike) (Benería, 2003; Trask, 2010). Women dominate the workforce in occupations such as assembling electronic goods or making clothes. Some of these jobs are done in factories. Others are done at home, as when employers drop off parts for electronic devices or toys and later pick up the assembled products. Employers often subcontract tasks to middlemen who in turn hire a predominantly female, home-based workforce.

The increase in women working for pay has brought both benefits and costs to family life in the global south. As for the benefits: Women's wages, although very low by developed country standards, have allowed them to raise their family's standard of living, such as by improving their children's diet or purchasing a refrigerator. Studies show that when wives have control over money they tend to spend more of it on their children than when husbands have control of it (Lundberg, Pollak, & Wales, 1997). Women who are earning wages have been able to gain more independence and bargaining power in their households (as have employed women in Western countries—see Chapter 8). Their increased earnings have made their husbands less likely to physically abuse them, and in more extreme circumstances they have been able to use their earnings to escape abusive marriages. Moreover, working at home has allowed them to combine earning money with the childcare and household work that they are still expected to do.

Yet the costs have been substantial, too. Wages are so low, and employment so unstable, that a family may need multiple sources of income to subsist from day to day, entailing long hours of work by both parents. Women may have little control over when they work and how long they work. The lack of institutionalized child care centers or subsidies sometimes means that younger children are left in the care of older ones. A daughter may be forced to drop out of school in order to care for her siblings, thus ending her chance to get a good education (Trask, 2010). Many husbands have not increased their share of the domestic work, creating a crushing double burden for wives whose jobs may require long working hours and six- or seven-day work weeks (Heymann, 2006).

Consequently, families in the global south cannot easily be sorted into winners and losers in the globalization of production. Although one could undoubtedly find some families for whom the effects have been completely positive and others for whom the effects have been completely negative, there are many more for whom the effects have been both positive and negative. The ability to earn money through factory work or home production, even if wages are low, is an opportunity that women in low-income countries cannot easily pass up. It can increase their independence and boost their children's standard of living. But it can also make their lives increasingly harried by the long hours of paid and unpaid work that make up their day. It can leave their children without adult care and can cut short the education of caregiving daughters. It can leave women exploited by employers who are not bound by contracts and labor laws. The globalization of production is a decidedly mixed blessing for the families in the poorer nations of the world.

TRANSNATIONAL FAMILIES

The improvements in global communication and transportation have also influenced family life through immigration, which became a major political issue in the United States. Millions of families in the global south send members to work in wealthy nations in order to earn higher wages and send most of their earnings back. The cash payments sent to family members in the country of origin are called **remittances.** Mexican immigrants in the United States sent $33.5 billion in remittances in 2018 (Bank of Mexico, 2019). Until recently, however, nearly all of the people who migrated to wealthy countries to send money back home were men. Many of them were fathers who had left their children, and often their wives, in the home country. This arrangement is still very common in Mexico. A study found that 1 out of 11 Mexican children can expect to see their fathers immigrate to the United States by age 15 (Nobles, 2011). Since the gendered expectation is that a father's main task is to provide economically for his children, researchers paid little attention to the consequences of this migration stream for family life. But the number of women migrating to the wealthy countries in order to send money home has increased sharply, although figures are hard to come by. Some of these women have left their children behind. Since the gendered expectation—and the reality—is that mothers are the main caregivers for children, observers have expressed concern about the consequences of this immigration stream for children and for the immigrant mothers themselves.

remittances cash payments that immigrants send back to families in their countries of origin

The growing migration of women is a result of at least three factors. The first is the growth in wealthy countries of the kind of low-wage service jobs that women have traditionally done. For instance, because more middle-class mothers in the United States now work outside the home, the demand has risen for nannies to care for their children while they work. It is common for dual-earner American families to hire caregivers from countries such as Mexico and the Philippines, many of whom have left their own children in the care of others in their home countries, and who are willing to work for low wages (Ehrenreich & Hochschild, 2003). Elsewhere, the demand for caregivers for the frail older population has grown. In Italy, where it is expected that adult children will care for their parents at home, families are hiring immigrant women from less-prosperous Eastern European nations, many of them in the country without documentation, to live with their parents and care for them. Since the workers are not authorized to be in the country, families can pay low wages, avoid paying employer taxes, and demand long hours (Colombo, 2007; Da Roit, 2007; Palese, Oliverio, Girardo, Fabbro, & Saiani, 2004).

The second factor is the development of inexpensive means of computer-based communication across long distances: cell phone calls, text messages, video services, long-distance calling cards, email, and so forth. Better means of communication allow immigrant mothers to stay in touch with their children. The third factor is inexpensive air travel, which allows immigrants from overseas to return home periodically. In the past, immigrants had little contact with their families. A European immigrant to the United States in 1900 could only send letters that might take a month or two to be delivered. Today, a caregiver in the United States can remain a part of her children's lives: she can call them weekly, keep track of how they are doing in school, and return home for a major family event. As a result, the families of today's immigrants transcend national boundaries. Many families have begun to think of themselves as living in two (or more) countries at once. They are **transnational families:** families that maintain continual contact between members in the sending and receiving countries (Baldassar, Kilkey, Merla, & Wilding, 2014).

transnational families families that maintain continual contact between members in the sending and receiving countries

Mothers (and fathers) who migrate do not make the decision lightly. They do it to provide their children with financial support for what they think will be a better life. A restaurant worker in the United States can make as much as a well-educated professional in many of the poorer countries of the world. Still, mothers may feel guilty about leaving their children and may have difficulty maintaining an emotional connection (Dreby, 2010). Mothers who migrate tend to reunite sooner with their children—either by returning home or bringing them to the United States—than do fathers who migrate (Suárez-Orozco, Todorova, & Louie, 2002). Typically, mothers leave their children in the care of a maternal grandmother or other relatives; and they do it in societies in which kin such as grandparents traditionally play a larger role in family life than is the case in the United States. The money that parents send home can pay for a better diet, clothes for school, or medical treatment—basic expenditures that an American family would take for granted. The money that a mother sends home also can help the grandmother, too—perhaps paying for a better roof or an additional room for her house. In these ways, the children left behind and their caregivers can benefit from the sacrifices that the mothers make. A group of Guatemalan children who were interviewed seemed to understand the benefits of remittances from migrant parents. One youth told a researcher, "That money helps us to pay for our studies, so that we can have a better life" (Lykes & Sibley, 2013).

Yet the question still remains of the effect of mothers' migration on the well-being of the children left behind. Several studies have found higher rates of anxiety and loneliness among the children of transnational migrants (Lykes & Sibley, 2013). A survey of families in Mexico found that households in which a former caregiver had migrated to the United States were more likely to have children with academic and behavioral problems (Lahaie, Hayes, Piper, & Heymann, 2009). Over time, parents and children may drift further apart. Children may resent their mother's absence, or may simply be lonely; and they may withdraw emotionally from their mothers in phone calls and messages. The transnational family can become complex if, for instance, a divorced mother finds a new partner in the United States and has a child with him (Dreby, 2010). As they reach the teenage years, children in the home country may be more difficult for grandmothers to control. The separation can be trying for all three generations involved.

Nevertheless, family bonds remain. In one Mexican town, when children were asked to draw a picture of their family, 70 percent those with migrant parents included them in the picture. Just 38 percent of those with divorced parents, in contrast, included them in the picture (Dreby, 2010). In nations in which the migration of mothers is very common, the family and community may adapt. For instance, in the Philippines, where women outnumber men among international migrant workers, children with a parent overseas showed a level of psychological well-being no different from children whose parents had not migrated (Graham & Jordan, 2011).

It is difficult, consequently, to make an overall judgment of the effects of transnational family life on the lives of children in the sending countries (Mazzuato & Schans, 2011). Any attempt to do so is fraught with questions that depend upon one's values more than on hard data. These questions include the importance of economic advancement versus the emotional loss of separation; the extent to which the increasing ease of electronic communication can compensate for distance; the proper role of parents versus other kin such as grandmothers in raising children; and whether Western ideals of the independent conjugal family should apply. The issue is complex, and no simple answer is satisfactory.

Quick Review

- The globalization of production has had a worldwide effect on family life.
- In the global south women are working for pay in both the formal and informal sectors of the economy.
- The great increase in women working for pay has brought both benefits (more independence and bargaining power) and costs (child care problems) in the global south.
- An increase in mothers who immigrate to wealthy countries without their children has led to a growth in transnational families.
- Transnational families can strain the ties between mothers and children, but the funds sent home also provide benefits to the children and their caretakers.

Family Change in the Western Nations

Family patterns have also changed greatly throughout the Western world in the past half-century. Social theorists writing in the mid-twentieth century, such as Goode (1963), expected that the conjugal family of husband, wife, and children would continue to dominate family life in the Western countries. Functionalist theorists such as Talcott Parsons (1942, 1943) thought that the conjugal family fit best with an industrialized society. They argued, first, that wage and salary workers in industrialized societies need to be able to move geographically to where the best employment opportunities are located. Second, since only the husband had a job in the typical conjugal family, the entire family could easily move from place to place as the husband followed the opportunities in the labor market. Therefore, the conjugal family fit the needs of industrial society and was the most "functional" family form, to use the key term of Parsons and his followers. Given the dominance of breadwinner-homemaker marriages at the time in the United States, it was easy for observers to imagine that that the uniformity of family life–nearly everyone married, they did so at early ages, they had children within marriage, most wives stayed home when the children were young, and divorce rates were modest–would continue. But it did not: family patterns in the United States and other Western countries became much more diverse over the ensuing half-century. In place of uniformity came the co-existence of many different patterns of family and personal life. Today we commonly see not just married-couple families but also cohabiting couples with and without children, single parents, stepfamilies, and childless single adults.

GLOBALIZATION AND FAMILY DIVERSITY IN THE WEST

Globalization has played a role in the growing diversity of family life in the Western nations. For instance, as factory production shifted to nations in the global south, a gap in family life opened between the college-educated and the less-educated in the United States, the United Kingdom, and to a lesser extent, other Western European countries (Kiernan, 2011). High school educated American and British young adults face a much weaker job market because the kinds of mid-level jobs that their parents used to take have moved to countries such as China where workers earn far less. Young adults still think that a man must have a steady, adequately paying job in order to support a marriage. With good job opportunities scarce–and with nonmarital childbearing much more acceptable than it used to be–young, high school educated adults hesitate to marry and increasingly have children before marrying. Furthermore, the cohabiting unions they form have a high risk of breaking up; and if they marry, their risk of divorce is higher than among the college educated.

College-educated individuals, on the other hand, still have access to the managerial and professional jobs that have remained in the developed nations even as factory and clerical work has left. As a result, this group is doing relatively well economically. In the United States, at least, the college-educated are increasingly living family lives that we might call **neo-traditional.** Marriage rates are high; and most children are born to married couples; and divorce rates have dropped. This marriage-centered style of life harks back to the mid-twentieth century, although with some important differences: unlike the 1950s family, couples may cohabit before they marry, most wives work outside the home, and relations between husbands and wives are more egalitarian. Far from being a cultural vanguard, college-educated young adults are leading more conventional family lives than are the less-educated. In sum, college-educated adults and their families are emerging as the group that has benefited the most from the globalization of production. In contrast, this great transformation of employment has constrained the family lives of less-educated adults and their families, leaving them disadvantaged by globalization.

neo-traditional a style of family life centered on marriage but which may be preceded by cohabitation and in which wives work outside the home

THE RETURN TO COMPLEXITY

Since the collective memories of people alive today only reach back to the mid-twentieth century, we might be tempted to think that the uniformity of family patterns in the 1950s represented the way family life always was. But that's not so; in many ways, the mid-twentieth-century family was the historical outlier. The Swedish sociologist Göran Therborn (2004, 2014) argued that family patterns in the Western nations in the mid-twentieth century were more uniform than they had been in the past and more uniform than they are today. Therefore, it was the uniformity of the mid-twentieth century that was most distinctive and unusual period in historical perspective. In the centuries leading up to the 1900s, informal marriage and nonmarital births had, in some Western European countries at some time points, exceeded the levels of the 1950s and 1960s. And because of high death rates, widowhood was much more common in the distant past than in the mid-twentieth century. The increases in cohabitation, nonmarital births, and divorce during the last half of the twentieth century have returned the West to a more diverse set of family patterns. What has occurred to the family in recent decades, Therborn argues, is "a return to its historical complexity" (2004, p. 314). That is to say, we have seen a return to family diversity, in contrast to the uniformity of family patterns in the mid-twentieth century.

Figure 13.2 illustrates this historical pattern with respect to marital dissolution in the United States. When the rate of marital dissolution due to death or divorce is higher, families are more diverse because there are more single parents and stepfamilies; when it is lower, families are more uniform. The figure shows, based on census data, the percentage of women aged 30 to 59 who were currently widowed

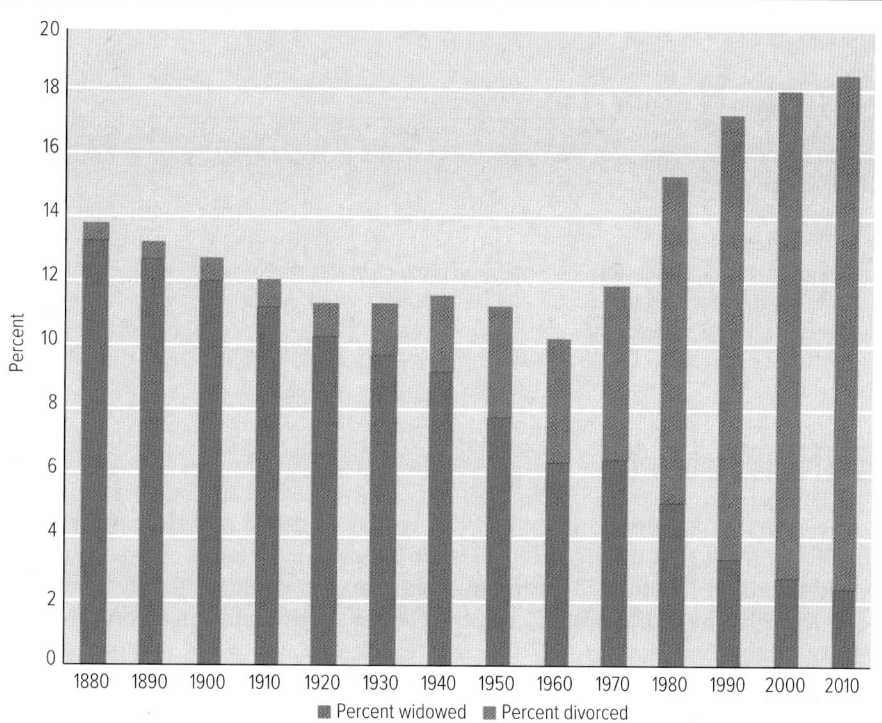

FIGURE 13.2
Percentage of 30- to 59- Year-Old Women Who Were Currently Widowed or Divorced: 1880 to 2010. (*Source:* Ruggles et al., 2010)

or divorced in every decade between 1880 and 2010. The blue portion of each bar shows those who were widowed, and the red portion shows those who were divorced. Note that the heights of the bars sink to a minimum in 1960, at which time fewer women were widowed than in the past and fewer were divorced than would be the case in the future. This was the time of the lowest levels of marital dissolution: people who got married (and that encompassed almost everyone in the 1950s and 1960s) stayed married. Notice that from the viewpoint of 1960, the heights of the bars ascend to their highest levels in 1880 when looking into the past and to 1990 to 2010 when looking into the future. (If we could look back further than 1880, we would probably see even higher bars.) Family patterns were more diverse at the end points, with substantial percentages of the population experiencing marital dissolution.

But note that the blue and red portions of the bars are of very different lengths in 1880 compared to 2010. In 1880 widowhood was common but divorce was rare, whereas in 2010 divorce was common but widowhood was rare. Therefore, the components of marital dissolution are different than in the past; and they have different implications for family life. While divorce leaves children with ties to parents living elsewhere, death removes those parents. Moreover, divorce may have a more negative effect on children than losing a parent by death (McLanahan & Sandefur, 1994), either because of the social support we provide to widows and widowers or because of the conflict and tensions that underlie most divorces. Therefore, the diversity of the late nineteenth century (lots of single-parent families and stepfamilies due to widowhood) had different consequences for parents and children than does the current diversity (lots of single-parent families and stepfamilies due to divorce). The idea of a return to historical complexity should not be taken to mean that Western family life is now the same as it was prior to the uniformity of the mid-twentieth century. We have experienced a return to diverse patterns, but not a return to old ways, of family life.

Quick Review

- Family patterns in the Western nations became more diverse over the past half-century as the dominance of marriage diminished.
- College-educated Westerners have gained the most from globalization and still live marriage-centered family lives.
- The mid-twentieth century was the more unusual period in historical perspective.
- The diversity of family patterns in the past had different consequences for family life than the diversity of family patterns today.

The Past and the Future

A half-century after Goode's book in 1963, we know that the world convergence in family patterns that he predicted did not happen—if for no other reason than the mid-twentieth century, breadwinner-homemaker conjugal family to which Goode thought the world would converge began a sharp decline soon after his book was published. Rather, the Western family became more diverse in new ways he did not anticipate. Moreover, only limited family change occurred in India and neighboring countries; and economic crises and AIDS tore the fabric of the Sub-Saharan African family. Yet the amount of change across East Asia was astonishing and, for the most part, consistent with Goode's hypothesis of the decline of family control and the increase in the autonomy of the couple. Moreover, the idea of romantic love and companionship seemed to spread almost everywhere across the globe, as he suggested it would. Hybrid forms of the process of marriage emerged that combined old traditions of family involvement with a new emphasis on love and companionship. In Latin America, which Goode did not study, signs of the postmodern family can be seen even before the transition to the modern conjugal family is complete. Patterns of cohabitation became more similar around the world, as did the timing of women's marriages and first births (Pesando, 2019).

No other scholar, it must be said, did much better at predicting the future. Not a single demographer in the United States in the 1940s predicted the 1950s baby boom. No social scientist predicted the decline in divorce that we have seen among the college-educated since about 1980. As recently as 1990, clueless sociologists such as me were assuring the Japanese that they would never look like the Western family. When social scientists are asked to make predictions, they almost always say that all current trends will continue—as if they were extending a straight-line-graph infinitely into the future. Most of the time they are correct, but only because what's happening today usually will continue to happen tomorrow. Yet that's not a good basis for predictions. Consequently, one lesson we can learn from these failures is how difficult it is for social scientists to predict the future of the family. The next time you hear such a prediction, greet it with skepticism.

In addition, the incorrect predictions of the mid-twentieth century demonstrate the error of thinking that current family patterns represent the endpoint of social change. In the late 1940s and the 1950s, the United States had emerged from World War II as the unchallenged economic power in the world. As workers' wages rose, they married early and moved to the burgeoning suburbs. American sociologists, surveying this prosperous landscape, assumed that the American family had reached the highest stage of its social development. Sociologists pronounced the conjugal family with a breadwinner husband and a homemaker wife to be ideally suited to advanced societies. It seemed like the end of family history. But in fact the Western family would soon undergo a half-century of massive change and families in the global south would fail to converge to the Western conjugal model. We should not repeat this error by concluding that, having weathered the disruptions of the past half-century, we are now entering a period of stability. In fact, there is no more reason to think that we have reached the endpoint of family change than there was in 1963. The prediction that's most likely to be correct is that a half-century from now, family patterns around the world will be different than they are today.

Quick Review

- Family patterns around the world did not converge to the Western conjugal family model.
- The pace of family change around the world was uneven, with the greatest changes occurring in East Asia (China, Japan, and their neighbors).
- The record of social scientists in predicting the future of the family is weak.
- Family change is likely to continue around the world in the next half-century.

Looking Back

1. **What is the convergence thesis and has it proven to be true?** The convergence thesis asserted that family patterns around the world would converge toward the Western conjugal family model as industrialization proceeded. When formulated by William J. Goode in the 1960s, it was based on modernization theory: the idea that all the nations of the world would industrialize as the Western nations already had. It has not proven accurate. Family patterns around the world remain diverse and even the Western family has moved away from the conjugal model. Nevertheless, some aspects of family life have become more similar around the world.

2. **How has parental control of children's marriage choices changed in the global south?** In nearly all countries in which parents had completely controlled marriage choices, young adults now have a say in the process. The typical ages at which women marry have risen, which suggests that parental influence has lessened and the wives have more authority in their marriages. Strictly arranged marriages have declined; but in some societies it has been replaced not with complete self-choice by the young adults based on love but rather with a hybrid process in which both parents and children are involved. Parents may allow their children to accept or reject a potential spouse they recommend; or in some cases the young adults may meet on their own but ask their parents' permission to wed.

3. **What is the companionate ideal and how has it spread?** The companionate ideal is the belief that the relations between spouses should be based primarily on love and companionship rather than male authority or traditional roles. It spread in the West in the twentieth century. Goode predicted that it would spread widely in the global south even without substantial economic development, and his predictions proved true. The ideas of romantic love and companionship spread through means such as movies and television. Fertility rates fell. Religious groups can also spread the message of Western-style love; and education can open people's minds to new ideas. In some countries, however, a transition directly to postmodern family forms such as cohabitation seems to be occurring.

4. **How has globalization altered family patterns in the Western world and the global south?** The flow of goods, money, and migrants across borders has altered family lives in the wealthy Western countries and in the countries in the global south. In the latter countries, increased factory production has drawn women with young children into the workforce in areas where no good child care options exist. Their children's well-being may be threatened. On the other hand, mothers' increased earnings can lift their family's standard of living. In the wealthy nations, middle-class families with young children may hire female migrants as home child care workers; and many of these migrants leave their children in the care of others in their country of origin. They therefore create transnational families.

5. **What is the "return to historical complexity" interpretation of recent family change in the West?** Family patterns in the mid-twentieth century had a degree of uniformity that was historically unusual. For instance, marriage in the United States was nearly universal and people married at a young age. Some observers take that period as typical and view the greater diversity of family patterns as a new development. But diversity has been the rule rather than the exception in family history; therefore, what we are seeing is a *return* to having diverse family forms. Nevertheless, the kinds of family patterns that are common in today's diversity (such as parental divorce) are different from the patterns that were common in pre-twentieth century diversity (such as parental death).

Study Questions

1. Why should an American college student study family life in the poorer nations of the world?
2. What theoretical perspective on development underlay Goode's prediction of convergence?
3. What is the social position of wives who are married at young ages to substantially older men?
4. What has been the attraction the companionate ideal to young adults in the global south?
5. Why did the government of China's one-child policy have unintended consequences?
6. What are the plusses and minuses for mothers from the global south who migrate to wealthy countries to care for children, often leaving their own children behind?
7. In what sense were family patterns more uniform in the mid-twentieth century than before or afterward?
8. What lessons might someone who wishes to predict what family life will look like 50 years from now draw from the mixed record of Goode's predictions?

Key Terms

arranged marriage 359
developmental idealism 363
global south 356
globalization of production 366
hybrid marriage 359
love marriage 359
modernization theory 355
neo-traditional 370
remittances 367
transnational families 368

Thinking about Families

The Public Family	The Private Family
Should national governments try to influence the number of children that young adults have when birth rates are very high—or when, as in many countries today, they are very low?	**Should American parents feel guilty about hiring nannies who leave their own children behind in their countries of origin?**

References

Allendorf, K. (2013). Schemas of marital change: From arranged marriages to eloping for love. *Journal of Marriage and Family, 75*(2), 453–469.

Arango, T. (2012, 6 June). Where arranged marriages are customary, suicide grows more common. *The New York Times.*

Axxin, W., Ghimire, D. J., & Barber, J. S. (2008). The influence of ideational dimensions of social change on family formation in Nepal. In R. Jayakody, A. Thornton, & W. Axxin (Eds.), *International family change: Ideational perspectives* (pp. 251–280). New York: Lawrence Erlbaum Associates.

Baldassar, L., Kilkey, M., Merla, L., & Wilding, R. (2014). Transnational families. In J. Treas, J. Scott, & M. Richards (Eds.), *The Wiley Blackwell companion to the sociology of families* (pp. 155–174). Chichester, UK: Wiley Blackwell.

Bandura, A. (1973). *Aggression: A social learning analysis.* Englewood Cliffs, NJ: Prentice -Hall.

Banerji, M., & Vanneman, R. (2009). *Does love make a difference? Marriage type and post marriage decision-making power.* Paper presented at the Annual Meeting of the Population Association of America, Detroit.

Bank of Mexico. (2019). Revenues by workers' remittances, period: Jan 1995–Dec 2018. *Balance of Payments.* Retrieved February 22, 2019, from http://www.banxico.org.mx/SieInternet/consultarDirectorioInternetAction.do?accion=consultarCuadro&idCuadro=CE81§or=1&locale=en

Benería, L. (2003). *Gender, development, and globalization: Economics as if all people mattered.* New York: Routledge.

Bumpass, L. L., & Choe, M. K. (2004). Attitudes relating to marriage and family life. In N. O. Tsuya & L. L. Bumpass (Eds.), *Marriage, work, and family life in comparative perspective: Japan, South Korea, and the United States* (pp. 19–38). Honolulu: University of Hawaii Press.

Caldwell, J. C. (2006). *Demographic transition theory.* Dordrecht, The Netherlands: Springer.

Cherlin, A. J. (2012). Goode's *World revolution and family patterns:* A reconsideration at fifty years. *Population and Development Review, 38,* 577–607.

Choe, M. K., Bumpass, L. L., Tsuya, N. O., & Rindfuss, R. R. (2014). Nontraditional family-related attitudes in Japan: Macro and micro determinants. *Population and Development Review, 40*(2), 241–271.

Colombo, A. D. (2007). 'They call me a housekeeper, but I do everything.' Who are domestic workers today in Italy and what do they do? *Journal of Modern Italian Studies, 12,* 207–237.

Covre-Sussai, M., Meuleman, B., Botterman, S., & Matthijs, K. (2014). Traditional and modern cohabitation in Latin America: A comparative typology. *Demographic Research, 32*(32), 873–914.

Da Roit, B. (2007). Changing intergenerational solidarities within families in a Mediterranean welfare state. *Current Sociology, 55,* 251–269.

Dreby, J. (2010). *Divided by borders: Mexican migrants and their children.* Berkeley: University of California Press. East-West Center. (2002). The future of population in Asia. Honolulu, HI: East-West Center.

Ehrenreich, B., & Hochschild, A. (2003). *Global woman: Nannies, maids, and sex workers in the new economy:* Metropolitan Books.

Esteve, A., Lesthaeghe, R. J., López-Gay, A., & García-Román. (2016). The rise of cohabitation in Latin America and the Caribbean, 1970–2011. In A. Esteve & R. J. Lesthaeghe (Eds.), *Cohabitation and marriage in the Americas: Geo-historical legacies and new trends* (pp. 25–57). Switzerland: Springer International Publishing.

Fuller, C. J., & Narasimhan, H. (2008). Companionate marriage in India: The changing marriage system in a middle-class Brahman subcaste. *Journal of the Royal Anthropological Institute, 14,* 736–754.

Ghimire, D. J., Axxin, W. G., Yabiku, S. T., & Thornton, A. (2006). Social change, premarital nonfamily experience, and spouse choice in an arranged marriage society. *American Journal of Sociology, 111,* 1181–1218.

Goode, W. J. (1963). *World revolution and family patterns.* New York: The Free Press.

Graham, E., & Jordan, L. P. (2011). Migrant parents and the psychological well-being of left-behind children in Southeast Asia. *Journal of Marriage and Family, 73,* 763–787.

Hart, K. (2007). Love by arrangement: The ambiguity of "spousal choice" in a Turkish village. *Journal of the Royal Anthropological Institute, 13*(2), 345–362.

Heymann, J. (2006). *Forgotten families: Ending the growing crisis confronting children and working parents in the global economy.* Oxford: Oxford University Press.

Hirsch, J. S. (2003). *A courtship after marriage: Sexuality and love in Mexican transnational families.* Berkeley: University of California Press.

International Center for Research on Women. (2010). Child marriage facts and figures. Retrieved April 9, 2014, from http://www.icrw.org/child-marriage-facts-and-figures

Jensen, R., & Oster, E. (2009). The power of TV: Cable television and women's status in India. *Quarterly Journal of Economics, 124*(1057–1094).

Jiang, Q., Feldman, M. W., & Li, S. (2014). Marriage squeeze, never-married proportion, and mean age at first marriage in china. *Population Research and Policy Review, 33,* 189–204.

Jones, G. W., & Yeung, W.-J. J. (2014). Marriage in Asia. *Journal of Family Issues, 35*(12), 1567–1583.

Kiernan, K. (2011). *Fragile families beyond divorce.* Paper presented at the Conference on Divorce, Milan, October 27–29.

La Ferrara, E., Chong, A., & Duryea, S. (2008). Soap operas and fertility: Evidence from Brazil: Bureau for Research and Economic Analysis of Development, Working Paper no. 172.

Lahaie, C., Hayes, J. A., Piper, T. M., & Heymann, J. (2009). Work and family divided across borders: The impact of parental migration on Mexican children in transnational families. *Community, Work & Family, 12*(3), 299–312.

Lappegård, T. (2014). Changing European families. In J. Treas, J. Scott, & M. Richards (Eds.), *The Wiley-Blackwell companion to the sociology of families* (pp. 20–42). Chichester, UK: Wiley.

Levy, M. J. (1972). *Modernization: Latecomers and survivors.* New York: Basic Books.Macfarlane, A.

(1978). *The origins of English individualism.* Oxford: Basil Blackwell.

Lundberg, S. J., Pollak, R. A., & Wales, T. J. (1997). Do husbands and wives pool their resources? Evidence from the United Kingdom child benefit. *Journal of Human Resources, 32,* 463–480.

Lykes, M. B., & Sibley, E. (2013). Exploring meaning-making with adolescents 'left behind' by migration. *Education Action Research, 21*(4), 565–581.

Mazzuato, V., & Schans, D. (2011). Transnational families and the well-being of children: Conceptual and methodological challenges. *Journal of Marriage and Family, 73,* 704–712.

McDonald, P. (1992). Convergence or compromise in historical family change? In E. Berquó & P. Xenos (Eds.), *Family systems and cultural change* (pp. 15–30) Oxford: Clarendon Press.

McLanahan, S. S., & Sandefur, G. (1994). *Growing up with a single parent: What hurts, what helps.* Cambridge, MA: Harvard University Press.

Mitterauer, M., & Sieder, R. (1982). *The European family.* Chicago: University of Chicago.

Netting, N. S. (2010). Marital ideoscapes in 21st-century India: Creative combinations of love and responsibility. *Journal of Family Issues, 31*(6), 707–726.

Nobles, J. (2011). Parenting from abroad: Migration, nonresident father involvement, and children's education in Mexico. *Journal of Marriage and Family, 73*(August), 729–746.

Ortega, J. A. (2014). A characterization of world union patterns at the national and regional level. *Population Research and Policy Review, 33,* 161–188.

Palese, A., Oliverio, F., Girardo, M. F., Fabbro, E., & Saiani, L. (2004). Difficulties and workload of foreign caregivers: A descriptive analysis. *Diversity in Health and Social Care, 1,* 31–18.

Parish, W. L., & Whyte, M. K. (1978). *Village and family in contemporary China.* Chicago: University of Chicago Press.

Parsons, T. (1942). Age and sex in the social structure of the United States. *American Sociological Review, 7*(5), 604–616.

Parsons, T. (1943). The kinship system of the contemporary United States. *American Anthropologist, 45*(1SW), 22–38.

Pesando, L. M. (2019). Global family change: Persistent diversity with development. *Population and Development Review, 45*(1), 133–168.

Raymo, J. M., Iwasawa, M., & Bumpass, L. (2009). Cohabitation and family formation in Japan. *Demography, 46,* 785–803.

Rebhun, L. A. (1999). *The heart is unknown country: Love in the changing economy of northeast brazil.* Stanford, CA: Stanford University Press.

Suárez-Orozco, C., Todorova, I., & Louie, J. (2002). Making up for lost time: The experience of separation and reunification among immigrant families. *Family Process, 41,* 625–643.

Therborn, G. (2004). *Between sex and power: Family in the world, 1900-2000.* London: Routledge.

Therborn, G. (2014). Family systems of the world: Are they converging? In J. Treas, J. Scott, & M. Richards (Eds.), *The Wiley Blackwell companion to the sociology of families* (pp. 3–19). Chichester, UK: Wiley Blackwell.

Thornton, A. (2005). *Reading history sideways: The fallacy and enduring impact of the developmental paradigm on family life.* Chicago: University of Chicago Press.

Trask, B. S. (2010). *Globalization and families: Accelerated systemic social change.* New York: Springer. Tribe, L. (1990). *Abortion: The clash of absolutes.* New York: W.W. Norton.

Tsuya, N. O., Mason, K. O., & Bumpass, L. L. (2004). Views of marriage among never-married young adults. In N. O.

Tsuya & L. L. Bumpass (Eds.), *Marriage, work, and family life in comparative perspective: Japan, south Korea, and the United States* (pp. 39–53). Honolulu: University of Hawaii Press.

United Nations. (2013a). UNdata: Total fertility rate. Retrieved April 19, 2014, from http://data.un.org/Default.aspx

United Nations. (2013b). World marriage data 2012. Retrieved April 9, 2014, from http://www.un.org/esa/population/publications/WMD2012/MainFrame.html

U.S. Bureau of the Census. (1966). Marital status *U.S. Census of Population, 1960: Final Report PC(2)-4E.* Washington, DC: U.S. Government Printing Office.

U.S. National Center for Health Statistics. (2018). Births: Final data for 2017. *National Vital Statistics Reports.* Retrieved March 19, 2019, from https://www.cdc.gov/nchs/data/nvsr/nvsr67/nvsr67_08-508.pdf

Wardlow, H. (2006). All's fair when love is war: Romantic passion and companionate marriage among the Huli of Papua New Guinea. In J. S. Hirsch & H. Wardlow (Eds.), *Modern loves: The anthropology of romantic courtship and companionate marriage* (pp. 51–77). Ann Arbor: University of Michigan Press.

Witke, R. (1967). Mao Tse-Tung, women, and suicide in the may fourth era. *China Quarterly, 31,* 128–147.

Xu, Q., Li, J., & Yu, X. (2014). Continuity and change in Chinese marriage and the family: Evidence from the CFPS. *Chinese Sociological Review, 47*(1), 30–56.

Yan, Y. (2003). *Private life under socialism: Love, intimacy, and family change in a Chinese village 1949–1999.* Stanford: Stanford University Press.

Yu, J., & Xie, Y. (2015). Cohabitation in China: Tends and determinants. *Population and Development Review, 41*(4), 607–628.

Chapter Fourteen

The Family, the State, and Social Policy

Looking Forward

1. What is the "welfare state"?
2. What are the themes that conservatives and liberals stress in debating family policies?
3. How has American antipoverty policy become more work based?
4. What should be the government's stance toward marriage?
5. How much should the government assist low-income families and middle-class working parents?

Consider two hypothetical families. In family A, a poor single mother struggles to raise two children. She receives cash assistance from the Temporary Assistance for Needy Families program and help with food purchases through the Supplemental Nutritional Assistance Program (formerly Food Stamps) from the government. When she or her children are sick, their care is paid for through Medicaid, the federal program of health insurance for the poor. She lives in a publicly owned housing project that charges less for rent than she would pay if she rented an apartment privately. Her four-year-old goes to government-funded Head Start classes to learn skills that will be useful for school. It is obvious that family A receives a great deal of assistance from the government.

In family B, two employed, college-educated parents are raising two children. They are not receiving cash assistance, and they own their own home. It may seem as though they receive no assistance from the government, but they do. Their elderly parents in Miami Beach and Sun City receive Social Security checks, easing the responsibility of family B to support them. Moreover, the couple deduct some of the interest payments for their home mortgage from their taxable income, which makes it easier for them to own a home. They receive an income tax credit for having children. They take an additional income tax credit for part of the cost of the day care center their four-year-old attends, which makes it easier for both of them to hold jobs outside the home. In addition, when Mr. B was laid off from his job as a computer programmer for three months this past year, he collected federally funded unemployment compensation.

In truth, most American families, including most middle-class families, receive substantial government assistance. It has not always been the case that most families receive assistance. In the colonial era, almost no economic assistance was provided; rather, the family was viewed as an independent entity that ought not to be interfered with—a "little commonwealth" in Demos's phrase (Demos, 1970). In fact, there was relatively little government financial assistance to families throughout the nineteenth century. In the early decades of the twentieth century, however, labor unions gained enough strength to demand higher pay, shorter hours, old-age pensions, and unemployment compensation. Moreover, civic groups led by middle-class women pressed for programs, such as pensions for widows, to assist mothers and children in poverty (Skocpol, 1992).

Then, in 1929 came the economic collapse of the Great Depression. The masses of unemployed workers looked to the government for assistance. Herbert Hoover, a Republican president who opposed most government involvement in the economy, was defeated in the 1932 election by Franklin Delano Roosevelt. Under Roosevelt, the federal government developed a number of programs to assist unemployed workers and their families. Among them was the **Social Security Act of 1935,** which created, among other provisions, Social Security (the system of pensions for the elderly), unemployment compensation (payments to workers who lose their jobs), and aid to mothers with dependent children. The latter program was subsequently renamed Aid to Families with Dependent Children. It was the program of financial assistance to low-income, single-parent families that became commonly known as "welfare." Beginning in the 1960s, government programs to assist families expanded greatly.

Social Security Act of 1935 the federal act that created, among other provisions, Social Security, unemployment compensation, and aid to mothers with dependent children (later renamed Aid to Families with Dependent Children)

Most government involvement is based on a concern about the well-being of children (as in the cash assistance or foster home programs) or of the elderly (as in Social Security). In other words, most government programs that affect families do so out of concern about the proper caretaking and support of dependents—people too young or too old or too ill to care for themselves. Most, therefore, reflect the perspective of the public family. The great attention government pays to these issues of caretaking and dependency shows that the family is still viewed as an important source of care.

Yet many of these measures were conceived at a time when the family was different than it is today—a time when there were far fewer divorces, births outside marriage, married women working outside the home, and unmarried couples living together; a time before birth control pills allowed better control of pregnancy, before medical technology allowed fertilized eggs to be implanted in a woman's uterus, and before large numbers of gay and lesbian couples, some with children, were marrying. For example, the Social Security Act's program of aid to mothers with dependent children (the forerunner of the Temporary Assistance for Needy Families program) was originally designed to help widowed women support their children. Its designers never dreamed that, a few decades later, most of its recipients would be never-married or divorced parents.

In the wake of these changes, public support rose in the 1980s and 1990s for new laws and government policies that would assist families. **Family policy,** which I will define as government policies and programs that directly affect the family, had become a major political issue. Much of the debate centered on two sets of issues: (1) how to respond to childhood poverty and the related increases in nonmarital childbearing and single-parent families, such as by reforming cash assistance, enforcing the child support obligations of absent fathers, or encouraging and supporting marriage; and (2) whether, and how, to assist parents employed outside the home, such as by providing child care subsidies or work leave to care for infants or seriously ill relatives. In all recent presidential campaigns, family issues have been prominent themes.

family policy government policies and programs that directly affect the family

This chapter will probe these policy debates for what they reveal about the underlying themes in public discussions on the family. It will focus on the increasing public concern during the twentieth and early twenty-first centuries about the family's ability to care for dependents—and on the public laws and programs that have been enacted to assist it. It will also address government policy toward marriage in the wake of the legalization of same-sex marriage by the Supreme Court in 2015 (*Obergefell v. Hodges,* 2015). In order to do so, however, it is necessary first to examine more generally the often thorny relationship between the family and the state. The current debates are rooted in long-standing questions about how involved in people's family lives the government should be. More specifically, how actively should the government, through law and social policy, regulate and support the family in its care and nurturing of children, the frail elderly, and the chronically ill? And how is the government to decide what kinds of interventions are best to provide? Issues of gender roles have nearly always been central to these debates; often issues of class and race have also been important. The answers to these questions depend, in part, on ethics and morality—subjects beyond the bounds of sociology. Yet the answers also depend on social structure and social change, subjects to which a sociological inquiry can contribute.

Quick Review

- Both low-income and middle-income families receive substantial assistance from the government.
- Federal government programs of income assistance began with the Social Security Act of 1935.
- Family issues have been part of the political debates during all recent presidential campaigns.

The Development of the Welfare State

state a government that claims the right to rule a given territory and its population and to have a monopoly on force in that territory

nation a people with shared economic and cultural interests

nation–state a term that combines the governmental and cultural connotations of the two words it comprises

I will use the term **state** to mean a government that claims the right to rule a given territory and its population and to have a monopoly of force in that territory. I will use the term **nation** to refer above all to a people with shared economic and cultural interests—people who have a sense of belonging, a common bond. The countries of the world today are most accurately described by the term **nation–state,** which combines the governmental and cultural connotations of the two words it comprises. Yet most people use the simpler term "nation" rather than "nation–state" to refer to countries, and I will sometimes follow this simpler usage. The emergence of nation–states has been the central political development in the world since the late 1400s, when monarchs consolidated territories in England, France, and Spain, breaking the power of medieval lords over their lands. Today, the nation–state system, as embodied in the United Nations, is firmly entrenched throughout most of the world.

THE WELFARE STATE

The economic system in the Western nation–states and in most others is capitalism. It is an economic system in which goods and services are privately produced and sold on a market for profit. Workers offer their labor to the owners of the means of production, such as factories, and accept the highest offer of wages they receive. The owners then try to sell their products at a price high enough to yield a profit after they subtract the wages, rents, and other expenses they have paid. In its purest form, the ideology of capitalism argues that there should be no interference by government in the labor market or in the market for products. Beginning with Adam Smith, capitalist economic theorists have argued that the forces of the market—the interplay of the demand for and supply of goods—produce a socially optimal distribution of wages and prices. The market, in Smith's famous phrase, acts as an "invisible hand" that guides the economy toward an outcome that is the best for all (Smith, 1776).

It is but a short extension to argue that, according to capitalist economic theory, the government should not intervene in family affairs. To intervene is to disturb the workings of the invisible hand and therefore to risk doing more harm than good. For example, some critics of cash assistance to poor families argue that it discourages them from taking jobs, thereby reducing their standard of living in the long run. Yet not to intervene is to do nothing to help people in need or assist groups that might be unjustly disadvantaged in the labor market.

As noted earlier, the view that the government should not intervene in family affairs prevailed in the United States until the hardships of the Depression. Since then, the U.S. Congress has passed substantial legislation to protect workers and their families from the most harmful consequences of the labor market. In the social scientific literature on these laws and programs, authors refer to them as "social welfare" measures, and they write of the **welfare state,** by which they mean a capitalist government that has enacted numerous measures—such as Social Security, unemployment compensation, and a minimum wage—to protect workers and their families from the harshness of the capitalist system and to raise their standard of living above what wages paid in the labor market alone would do. Here the term "welfare" is used not in its common meaning of cash assistance to the poor but rather in the broader sense of the well-being of members of society. These social welfare measures expanded greatly in the 1950s and 1960s, as labor and minority groups pushed for them and as growing affluence allowed the government to raise taxes to support them.

welfare state a capitalist government that has enacted numerous measures to protect workers and their families from the harshness of the capitalist system

THE RISE AND FALL OF THE FAMILY WAGE SYSTEM

The welfare state has treated husbands and fathers differently from wives and mothers. In the terms of feminist theory, the development of the welfare state has been "gendered" (Orloff, 1993; Borchorst, 2000). Beginning around the turn of the twentieth century, reformers campaigned, without much success initially, for laws that would require employers to pay male workers enough so they could support their families without wives (and children) having to work for wages. During the same period, women's organizations and labor unions campaigned, with more success, for protective legislation: laws to limit the number of hours women could work for wages to "protect" them from having to work too long and hard outside the home (Skocpol, 1992). Together, these different objectives for women and men supported the **family wage system,** a division of labor in which the husband earns enough money to support his family and the wife remains home to do housework and child care. This system is now in decline, but an examination of its development is useful for understanding the family policy debates occurring today.

family wage system a division of labor in which the husband earns enough money to support his family and the wife remains home to do housework and child care

The moral vision behind campaigns for the family wage system specified that the family works best when men and women inhabit separate spheres: his, paid work outside the home; hers, unpaid homemaking and child rearing inside the home. This view, as has been discussed, gained in popularity in the nineteenth-century United States as industrialization moved the workplace out of the home. The family wage system was never a reality for many working-class and minority families, whose men could not earn enough to support a family. Nevertheless, it remained the dominant cultural view of the family throughout the first half of the twentieth century.

The Social Security Act of 1935 followed the division of labor implicit in the family wage system. It provided old-age pensions only to persons who "earned" them by working a certain number of years in the paid labor force; originally only industrial and commercial workers were covered. The clear expectation was that these covered workers would overwhelmingly be men. The act therefore ignored the value of the care work done by women at home. In 1939, Congress passed an extension of the act that allowed widows of Social Security recipients to receive continued benefits after their husbands died. Younger women whose husbands died or were absent for other reasons, and who were still raising children, were eligible for the Aid to Dependent Children program–but only if their income was below a certain level. Congress did not anticipate that large numbers of women raising children might need assistance because they were divorced from their husbands or had never had a husband. It did not anticipate that large numbers of women would qualify for Social Security benefits themselves by working outside the home. The system presumed that, until the death of one spouse, families would consist of a husband who would *provide* for the family and a wife who would *care* for the family.

Throughout the 1950s, the prosperous decade in which the breadwinner-homemaker family was much celebrated, the family wage system remained the cultural ideal. Beginning in the 1960s, however, it began to weaken; and by the end of the twentieth century, it had faded away. To be sure, husbands still worked for wages and wives remained at home to do housework and child care in a minority of marriages, but the prestige and popularity of this type of marriage had greatly declined. The factor most responsible for its downfall was the enormous increase in wives working outside the home. Women worked before having children and withdrew only temporarily from the workforce when their children were young. Women who gave up paid work also risked financial hardship if their marriages ended in divorce, as more and more were doing. The rise of cohabitation and childbearing outside of marriage further challenged the dominance of the family wage system. By the 1990s, as the system lay in tatters, the family policies of both conservatives–who had strongly supported it–and of liberals had evolved beyond it. That evolution and the legislation and controversy it has engendered are the story of the rest of this chapter.

Family Policy Debates

In the aftermath of the family wage system, no dominant vision of the family has emerged. Instead, family policy remains a highly contentious topic. Two experts reviewed the field and wrote:

> *Arguably, family policy is still not a term that is widely used by knowledge consumers, such as policymakers, journalists, or the public. It has not yet achieved the status of economic or environmental policy, nor is it even recognized in its own right as a subfield of social policy (Bogenschneider & Corbett, 2010, p. 783).*

The difficulties of enacting family policy stem from disagreement about its goals. Should it support married couples over other kinds of families? Should it provide support for mothers who are employed outside the home? Should it provide low-income parents with economic support or should it encourage them to work? In order to understand what these issues symbolize, it helps to study the kinds of positions that conservative and liberal policymakers have taken in the recent past.

THE CONSERVATIVE VIEWPOINT

Conservatives have sought to encourage and support marriage-based families (Wilson, 2002). In the past, they have championed the breadwinner–homemaker marriage that fits the family wage system; but many conservatives now accept the fact that most married women will work outside the home. From the conservative viewpoint, the declining role of marriage in American family life is largely due to a change in American culture: an erosion of traditional norms and values that supported marriage. These values included strong community disapproval of couples living together, which was seen as shameful prior to the 1960s. They also included the stigma associated with having children outside of marriage, which used to be called "illegitimacy," a word which implies that children born outside marriage are not legitimate members of society. Until recently conservatives tended to minimize the role of the economy in producing family change.

As the earlier discussion of the Social Security Act has shown, the U.S. welfare state was constructed to support the breadwinner–homemaker family. To a large extent, its programs encouraged women to marry and men to be the main providers. For example, programs such as Social Security and unemployment compensation were designed with male recipients in mind. Full-time homemakers can accrue eligibility for Social Security only through marriage, and they cannot receive unemployment benefits. The income tax system also encouraged the formation of breadwinner–homemaker marriages and discouraged the formation of two-earner marriages. Until recently, if a man earned $50,000 and a woman earned nothing, they paid less in taxes if they married than if they stayed single. On the other hand, if a man and a woman each earned $25,000, they paid more in taxes if they married than if they stayed single. So a single-earner couple with an income of $50,000 benefited from marrying, but a dual-earner couple with an income of $50,000 did not.

Conservatives generally favor a modest role for government in supporting families although, as we will see later, conservative support is growing for supporting low- and moderate-income parents who are combining paid work and child rearing. They are concerned that if the benefits of social welfare programs are too generous, the beneficiaries will have less incentive to work and will instead become dependent on government assistance. Yet they are not opposed to all government interventions into family life. Rather, conservatives have defended a particular set of interventions that supported the family wage system. The Depression-era and 1950s roots of these programs lie so far in the past that government's role can seem almost invisible. It's understandable, then, that a politician might mistakenly believe that the government has had no role in shaping the contemporary family.

In fact, conservative groups have long advocated government intervention when court rulings and legislation have undermined their vision of the family. After *Roe v. Wade,* the 1973 Supreme Court decision legalizing abortion, grass-roots conservative organizations joined with religious groups to campaign for restrictive state laws and for a constitutional amendment banning abortion. The antiabortion forces succeeded in passing legislation that prohibited the use of federal funds for performing abortions, thus restricting poor women's ability to obtain them (Tribe, 1990). In 2003, conservatives were able to win passage of a law banning a late-term procedure opponents called a "partial-birth abortion," and the constitutionality of the law was affirmed by the Supreme Court in 2007. Abortion remains one of the most divisive issues pertaining to families (see *Families and Public Policy:* The Abortion Dilemma).

Families and Public Policy: The Abortion Dilemma

Abortion has been one of the most bitterly contested and divisive of issues in our society. It starkly contrasts two visions of women's roles: one that emphasizes childbearing and mothering versus one that emphasizes autonomy and employment.

From the late 1800s to the early 1970s, access to abortion was restricted in the United States, generally available only when physicians certified that it was necessary to save the life of the mother. In the 1960s, feminist groups began to demand access to abortion as a woman's right—thereby making abortion a political issue. With the fertility rate falling to about two births per woman, on average, and with life expectancy lengthening, childbearing no longer lasted most of a woman's adult life. Pro-abortion-rights activists, who prefer to be called "pro-choice," sought to control the timing and numbers of the children they bore. They did so, in part, on behalf of poor women who simply wanted to limit how many children they would have. Yet the pro-choice advocates, as Kristin Luker (1984) has written, also shared a "worldview" in which women and men are equal and deserve equal opportunity to work outside the home. Legal abortions, by helping women to plan when to have children, would help them obtain equal opportunity.

Their cause was aided immensely by a 1973 Supreme Court decision, *Roe v. Wade* (1973). In this case, the Court ruled that women had the constitutional right to terminate a pregnancy by abortion during the first trimester and that in the second trimester the state may regulate access to abortion only for reasons reasonably related to the mother's health. *Roe* made abortions legal, but it also spurred the formation of a strong, national movement against abortion. The "pro-life" forces, as the antiabortion movement came to be known, view human life as beginning at conception and therefore oppose abortion except to save the life of the mother. According to Luker (1984), they share a worldview in which women and men are fundamentally different and women's primary role is to raise children.

Abortion rights also vary by class, because the biggest victory for the pro-life forces was the passage of legislation in 1976 that prohibited the use of government funds to pay for abortions. Since most poor women receive medical care through the government program Medicaid, the law makes it difficult for them to obtain an abortion. Supporters argue that the ban on the use of public funds is morally justified because abortion is repugnant to many taxpayers. Nevertheless, the ban made abortion a class-related issue because middle-class women have an easier time finding the funds to pay for an abortion than do poor women. In a 1989 case, *Webster v. Reproductive Health Services* (1989), a divided Court upheld some restrictions on abortion in a Missouri law. More important, the Court nearly overturned *Roe*, with four members clearly leaning in that direction. The appointment of Justice Brett M. Kavanaugh to the Supreme Court in 2018 created a conservative-leaning majority that may be sympathetic to overturning *Roe*.

Public opinion remains divided. In 2016, 43 years after *Roe*, a national sample of adults was asked, "Please tell me whether or not you think it should be possible for a pregnant woman to obtain a legal abortion if she is married and does not want any more children." Fifty-four percent said no, and 46 percent responded yes (Smith, Davern, Freese, & Hout, 2017). In the early years of the twenty-first century, abortion is still an issue that deeply divides Americans in ways that reflect different views of women's lives.

THE LIBERAL VIEWPOINT

Liberals have accepted, and even defended, the diverse forms of family life we see today, including single-parent families and cohabiting families. Whereas conservatives tend to believe that cultural change has driven the transformation of family life, liberals tend to believe that economic change, such as the globalization and automation of production, has been more important. They argue that government has a responsibility to assist all kinds of families, and they generally support expansions of existing programs and propose new ones. For instance, Katherine S. Newman (2012, p. 202), in a book on the growing number of adult children who are living with their parents rather than moving out and starting their own families, sees the globalized economy and government policies as the keys to whether they can succeed:

> *What becomes of them is as much a matter of what the economy provides in the way of opportunity and what we decide we owe them as citizens, future parents and providers. These are not simply natural outcomes. They are expressions of social solidarity, given shape by the governments we elect and the policies they enact.*

In other words, young adults' prospects of moving out are constrained by the globalized economy, rather than by a lack of industriousness; and government should adopt policies to help them find their way out of the house and into stable jobs.

The kinds of measures advanced by liberals tend to help married couples in which wives are employed outside the home and single parents more than they help breadwinner–homemaker couples. Liberals have consistently advocated more support for employed parents. For example, the child care programs and child tax credits that liberals favor make it less difficult for mothers to participate in the work force. By and large, liberals, a political category in which there is a large overlap with feminists, believe that the breadwinner–homemaker family is at best no better than other family forms or at worst a form that unjustifiably restricts the autonomy of women.

Debates over whether and how government should help families arose in the 1960s, as social change began to undermine the breadwinner–homemaker family that was so prominent in the 1950s. At first, these divisions led to a policy stalemate. For example, in 1971, a Democratic-controlled Congress passed a comprehensive child development bill that would have established a national system of preschools for children ages three to five. But President Richard M. Nixon vetoed the legislation on the grounds that it "would commit the vast moral authority of the national government to the side of communal approaches to child rearing over against the family-centered approach"—in other words, government support for child care would undermine the independent, breadwinner–homemaker family.[1]

WHICH FAMILIES ARE POOR?

But let us suspend this story for a moment to ask how the government determines which families are economically deprived and in need of assistance. Each year the U.S. government calculates an official **poverty line** and publishes statistics on the number of families with incomes below the line.

poverty line a federally defined Income limit defined as the cost of an "economy" diet for a family, multiplied by three

The poverty line is a strange concoction that no one likes but no analyst can do without. It was established in the mid-1960s when federal officials figured out how much it would cost to buy enough food to meet the Agriculture Department's standard for an "economy" diet—and then, on the assumption that families spend one-third of their income on food, simply multiplied by three (Katz, 1989). To account for inflation, this standard (which is adjusted for the number of people in the family) is multiplied every year by the increase in the cost of living. Advocates for the poor claim it is too low and therefore underestimates the low-income population; many conservatives claim it is too high. Its main virtue is that it can be used to examine changes over time in the percentage of families that fall above or below it.

[1] *Congressional Record,* December 10, 1971, pp. 46057–46059. (Text of President Nixon's veto message of the Child Development Act of 1971.)

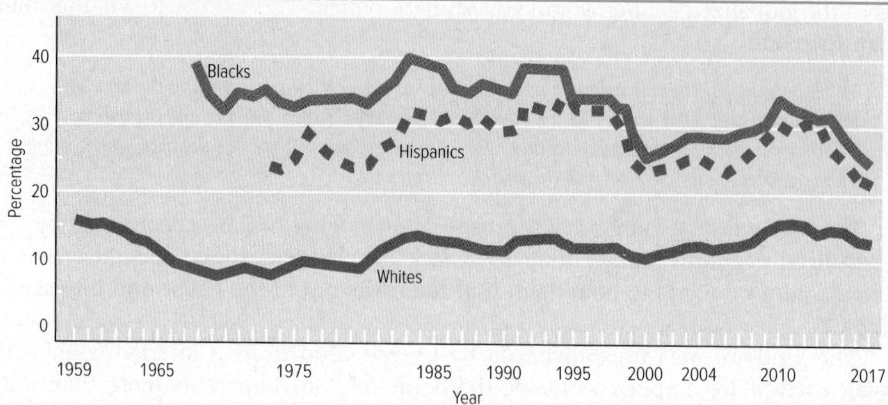

FIGURE 14.1 Percent of families with children under 18 that had incomes below the poverty line, for whites, blacks, and Hispanics, 1959 to 2017. (*Source:* U.S. Bureau of the Census, 2018a)

In 2018, the federal poverty line stood at $25,465 for a family of two adults and two children under 18 and at $20,212 for a family of one adult and two children (U.S. Bureau of the Census, 2018b).

Figure 14.1 shows the percentage of families with children under 18 that fell below the poverty line in each year from 1959 to 2017. Information on African American families is available only from 1967 onward, and for Hispanic families (which may be of any race) from 1972 onward. Poverty rates for families tend to fluctuate with the state of the economy. When the economy was strong in the mid to late 1990s, poverty levels fell. They rose sharply during the late 2000s as the Great Recession took hold and then declined again. In 2017, 12.5 percent of white non-Hispanic families with children under 18 were poor, according to the official definition, as were 21.4 percent of Hispanic families and 21.4 percent of African American families (U.S. Bureau of the Census, 2018a). So African American and Hispanic families remain much more likely to be poor than white families, although African American poverty, as Figure 14.1 shows, is below its historic highs. And even among whites, about one in eight families with children is poor.

Quick Review

- The welfare state emerged in the twentieth century.
- At first, the welfare state supported a family wage system in which fathers were treated differently from mothers.
- Conservatives favor a modest role for government in supporting families and are skeptical of new programs.
- Liberals believe that government has a responsibility to assist all families; they favor expanding government programs.
- The government calculates an official poverty line and determines how many families have incomes that fall below it.

Supporting the Working Poor

Should the government assist poor families? And if so, with what kinds of social welfare programs? These questions have been debated in the Western nations for a long time. Centuries ago, a distinction emerged in both American and British society between the "deserving" and "undeserving" poor (Katz, 1989). There was substantial public sympathy for the deserving poor, those whose poverty is seen as beyond their control. Examples include the disabled, who cannot work because of their physical limitations, and widows, who were seen as victims of their husbands' deaths. Historically, there has been much less sympathy for the undeserving poor, those whose poverty is perceived, whether fairly or not, as somehow their "fault." Able-bodied, non-elderly men are the prime example of the undeserving poor because they are expected to earn a living by working. From this perspective, government should not provide assistance to the undeserving poor because doing so will reduce their incentive to work.

This old distinction between the deserving and undeserving poor still influences government policy toward low-income families today. Conservative policy analysts have been concerned that social welfare benefits paid to families may discourage adults from working. They therefore support programs that provide greater assistance to poor people who are working than to those who are not working. Since about 1980, in fact, American social welfare programs have been increasingly targeted to what we might call the *working poor.* To understand the consequences of this shift for poor families, let us distinguish between two groups of poor families: those that are in **deep poverty,** which we will define as a family income that is less than 50 percent of the federal poverty line, and those that are in **shallow poverty,** defined as an income between 50 percent and 100 percent of the poverty line. In 2018, a single parent with two children would be living in deep poverty if her annual income was less than $10,106. She would be in shallow poverty if her income was greater than that amount but less than $20,212. Families living in deep poverty are less likely to include anyone who is working steadily than are families in shallow poverty.

deep poverty an income of less than 50 percent of the poverty line

shallow poverty an income of between 50 percent and 100 percent of the poverty line

Economist Robert Moffitt has shown that the level of government benefits to families living in deep poverty has declined, while the level of benefits to families living in shallow poverty has increased (Moffitt, 2015). Consider Figure 14.2, which shows the changes in monthly benefits for single-parent families from government programs between 1983 and 2004. Parents who are disabled or elderly are omitted. (The trends are the same for married-parent families.) You can see from the first two bars that the average level of monthly benefits for single-parent families in deep poverty declined substantially during this period. However, the benefit level for single-parent families in shallow poverty increased. So did the benefits for families with incomes of 100 to 200 percent above the poverty line, who are sometimes called the near-poor.

Why did this shift in benefits away from the poorest families occur? The answer is that Congress designed or modified social programs to provide more generous benefits to families that were more likely to have at least one person working steadily and less generous benefits to families in which it was likely that no one was working steadily. Families in deep poverty are more likely to be in the latter group. The intent of this design was to encourage low-income parents to increase their work effort. Let us examine two of those programs, the Earned Income Tax Credit and the Temporary Assistance for Needy Families program.

THE EARNED INCOME TAX CREDIT

Earned Income Tax Credit (EITC) a refundable tax credit to low-income families with children in which at least one parent is employed

The **Earned Income Tax Credit (EITC),** introduced in 1975 but still little known except among low-income families, provided assistance to 25 million workers and their families in 2018 and cost $63 billion (U.S. Internal Revenue Service, 2018).

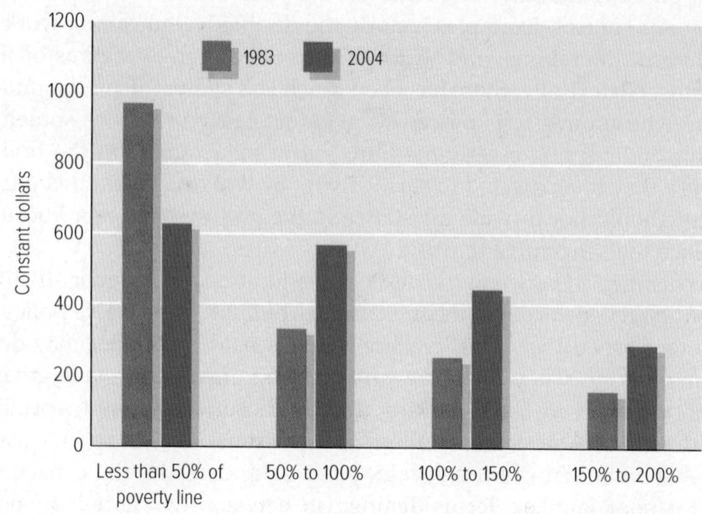

FIGURE 14.2
Monthly benefits received in 1983 and 2004 for single-parent families by private income level. (*Source:* Ruggles et al., 2010)

That amount is twice the cost of the main cash "welfare" program, Temporary Assistance for Needy Families, which we will examine next. The EITC provides a refundable tax credit to low-income families with children in which at least one parent is employed. Even if the family earns so little that its members owe no taxes, they still receive a check for the value of the credit from the government if they file their tax returns. Essentially, the EITC is an income subsidy for parents who work but earn low wages. It has become one of the main antipoverty programs. Conservatives like it for two reasons. First, it goes only to families in which a parent is employed. An unemployed single parent is not eligible. Therefore, the availability of the EITC provides an incentive to work. Second, it applies not only to dual-earner, two-parent families but also to breadwinner–homemaker families because a family qualifies even if only one parent works outside the home. It therefore appears neutral toward wives working outside the home.

Liberals, on their part, like the EITC because it provides income assistance to many low-income families. Liberals also realize that there are relatively few breadwinner–homemaker families among the working poor (who can't afford a stay-at-home parent), so that, in reality, most of the money goes to two-earner families and to employed single parents. Finally, liberal members of Congress in this era realized that a program of tax credits for the working poor went as far as they could convince conservatives to move with regard to income assistance. The EITC has increased several times and provides a maximum benefit of about $6,400 to a family consisting of a single parent with three children and an income of about $14,000 to $21,000. It has become a major source of assistance to poor and near-poor families with at least one earner.

TEMPORARY ASSISTANCE FOR NEEDY FAMILIES

While the history of the EITC is one of expansion, the recent history of the program now known as Temporary Assistance for Needy Families is one of contraction. Changes in the law have reduced the benefits and strengthened the focus on work. As noted earlier, the Aid to Dependent Children program, which was part of the Social Security Act of 1935, was originally designed to support widows and their children. It became commonly known as "welfare." In 1950, Congress increased the benefit level in the hope that poor mothers would be able to stay home and care for their children. Starting about 1970, however, Congress passed a series of laws that encouraged, and later required, mothers receiving benefits to take jobs and leave their children in the care of others. Yet "welfare" remained unpopular with the public. In 1996, after negotiations between President Bill Clinton and the Republican-controlled Congress, the president signed a bill that became known as "welfare reform." It was a stunning rollback of policies toward poor families that had stood since 1935. The bill set a five-year time limit on cash assistance. People still receiving benefits after five years would be cut off. States were free to set an even shorter time limit (and about 20 subsequently did). Recipients also had to accept work within two years of starting to receive benefits or their families would lose their benefits. No longer could poor mothers stay home full-time to care for their children. The emphasis was on temporary assistance and on getting a job. The legislation renamed the time-limited cash assistance program **Temporary Assistance for Needy Families,** or **TANF.** Since 1996, when the new law was passed, the number of TANF recipients has dropped dramatically. By 2015 the number of families receiving benefits had declined by more than two-thirds (U.S. Office of Family Assistance, 2018).

Temporary Assistance for Needy Families (TANF) a federal program of financial assistance to low-income families that began in 1996, following passage of new welfare legislation (see Aid to Families with Dependent Children)

A WORK-FOCUSED WELFARE SYSTEM

Both the EITC and TANF require that a single parents work, or in the case of TANF at least look for work, to receive benefits. What caused such a sweeping reversal of six decades of social policy toward poor families? First, attitudes toward women's roles had changed greatly. By the 1990s, a majority of mothers were working outside the home. It seemed less punitive to require that poor, single mothers attempt to find jobs when the majority of middle-class mothers were employed as well. Encouraging self-reliance and independence among poor mothers seemed consistent with emerging values for nonpoor women. Second, the characteristics of recipients had also changed. No longer are most widowed; rather, the vast majority are separated, divorced, or have never married. Widows, as victims of their husbands' deaths, fall among the deserving poor—their poverty is not their "fault." Yet some observers view unmarried mothers—and perhaps even more so, the fathers of their children—as having chosen, in some sense, an irresponsible path to parenthood and therefore as less deserving of assistance.

Moreover, there is another troubling subtext to the discourse about "deservingness." Not only the marital status but also the racial composition of the TANF population has changed since the early days of the program. African American single-parent families are heavily overrepresented among the persistently poor and, therefore, among TANF recipients. In 2015 African Americans, who constituted 30 percent of TANF recipients, were overrepresented, compared with their percentage of the total U.S. population and even compared with their percentage of the total population with incomes below the poverty line (U.S. Office of Family Assistance, 2018). Scholars who have studied the welfare debate have suggested that racial animosity may underlie some of the public opposition to welfare spending (Grubb & Lazerson, 1988; Quadagno, 1994).

Overall, the new, work-focused social welfare system has provided increased benefits to low- and moderate-income families that are fortunate enough to have at least one steady wage earner. In addition to the EITC, these families may receive a child tax credit to apply against the amount of taxes they owe and may also deduct part of the cost of day care for their children. But families without steady earners (who usually do not have enough income to owe much in federal taxes) do not receive the benefits of any of these work-oriented credits; and, in addition, they are much less likely to be receiving TANF benefits than they would have been before welfare reform. The only major program that still provides benefits without regard to employment is the Supplemental Nutritional Assistance Program, which cost $65 billion in 2018 (U.S. Food and Nutrition Service, 2018). It has expanded substantially, but it does not fully compensate for the increasingly employment-focused social safety net.

Quick Review

- Government social welfare programs have become more focused on supporting work.
- Average benefit levels have declined for the deep poor and increased for the shallow poor and the near poor.
- The Earned Income tax credit, popular with both conservatives and liberals, has expanded in benefit levels and in the number of families claiming it.
- Since the 1996 "welfare reform" bill, TANF benefits have been time-limited and the number of families receiving benefits has decreased greatly.
- The work emphasis comes from the increasing number of working women and the sense that recipients may be less "deserving" (and less white) than in the past.

Current Debates

In recent years, conservatives and liberals have moved toward each other on some issues of family policy, but divisions still exist. In general, liberals are inclined to accept the great changes in family life, such as the increase in single-parent families and in women's work outside the home. They advocate for programs that improve conditions for these families, such as income and employment support for the poor and child care and parental leave assistance for working parents. Conservatives tend to advocate for programs that strengthen traditional family arrangements. They wish to promote marriage, discourage nonmarital births, and ensure that fathers help support their children. Let's examine some of the key family policy issues from these two perspectives—the liberal viewpoint of accepting the changing family and assisting parents and children versus the conservative viewpoint of strengthening family ties by supporting marriage and parental responsibility (Smeeding & Carlson, 2011).

SUPPORTING MARRIAGE

In 2006, Congress passed and President George W. Bush signed a bill extending the welfare reform legislation. This bill included a much debated program, the Healthy Marriage Initiative, that provided the states with up to $100 million per year from 2006 to 2010 to encourage heterosexual marriage and $50 million per year to support "responsible fatherhood" (Center for Law & Social Policy, 2006). Supporters, who were mainly conservative, had argued that the government should encourage low-income women and men to marry in order to ease the hardships of poverty for their children and themselves. Opponents, who were mainly liberal, argued that the government should not be promoting one kind of family over another and that, furthermore, the funds could be better spent on other needs such as providing more child care assistance or discouraging teenage pregnancy.

The debate is not just about research questions—Is it better for children to be raised with two married parents? Can single parents do as good a job if they receive more support?—but also about political and moral issues. These include the autonomy of women, the authority of men, and the wisdom of imposing a particular moral view of family life on those who choose other lifestyles. As we have seen, until the mid-twentieth century, marriage was so central to family life that its dominance was taken for granted. It was an institution in which men held considerable power, in part because of their typically greater earnings and in part because of social norms. Since the 1950s, a number of options have made it possible for women to live full lives outside of marriage. Gains in the labor market provide the opportunity for an independent income. The birth control pill allows for sexual activity without unwanted pregnancies, and the greater acceptability of raising a child outside of marriage allows single women to have the children they want. At the same time, the economic fortunes of men without college educations have diminished, reducing the economic benefits of marriage to women. All told, paths to parenthood and child rearing other than long-term marriage are now more feasible and more attractive.

The supporters of marriage, however, contend that it provides a superior setting for raising children. They acknowledge that many single mothers and fathers are good parents, but they read the evidence as showing that for the most part, one parent can't provide care and supervision as well as two. From this point of view, the key objective of family policy should be to encourage and support marriage in order to reduce the number of children born to unmarried women and their partners.

The centerpieces of the Healthy Marriage Initiative were two large, random-assignment studies of marriage- and relationship-enhancement programs for low-income couples with children (or who were expecting a birth) in multiple sites across the country. The cores of these programs were curricula that teach better communication skills such as how to communicate, resolve conflicts, and build trust. At all sites, couples were randomly allocated to a "treatment" group that was enrolled in the curriculum and a "control" group that was not.

One of the studies, "Building Strong Families," enrolled young, unmarried couples in eight sites around the country who had recently had a child. The results were disappointing: couples who were offered the program were no more likely to have remained together or to have married after three years than were those who weren't offered it (Wood et al., 2012). Across all sites, only 57 percent of couples in the program were still romantically involved after three years. The other study, "Supporting Healthy Marriage," enrolled slightly older couples who had already married and wanted to learn how to strengthen their relationships. After three years, the treatment group had attained small gains in marital happiness, greater warmth and support, positive communication, marital fidelity, and other similar characteristics, compared to the control group. But there was no difference in the proportion that stayed married and no difference in their children's well-being (Lundquist et al., 2014). The results of these two large, random-assignment studies suggest that it is very difficult to design programs that can strengthen relationships and increase marriage among low- and moderate-income couples.

SAME-SEX MARRIAGE

The 2015 Supreme Court decision that legalized same-sex marriage throughout the United States, *Obergefell v. Hodges,* was one of the most consequential changes in marriage law in American history. It ended a political and social debate that just a few years earlier had seemed destined to play out over another decade or two. The decision reflected one of the fastest transformations of public opinion on a social issue that the nation has ever seen. In 2001, Americans opposed the legalization of same-sex marriage by a margin of 57 percent to 35 percent. About half the states amended their constitutions to ban it. But by 2016, Americans favored legalizing same-sex marriage by a margin of 55 percent to 37 percent (Pew Research Center, 2016). And the decision of the Supreme Court overruled all of the state amendments that had banned it.

Advocates for same-sex marriage used two basic arguments: rights and commitment. Marriage provides adults with a number of rights that are unavailable to unmarried couples, such as the ability to file a joint federal tax return, which lowers their taxes. It was unfair, the advocates argued, to deny same-sex couples these rights. But the argument that seemed to carry the day was that same-sex couples wish to express the same emotional commitment to each other that different-sex couples do. For instance, when citizens in Maine voted to legalize same-sex marriage in 2012, they were influenced by television commercials showing typical Maine families that were embracing the commitment their gay children wished to make. "Marriage is a commitment that comes from your heart," one father said. "If my son finds someone that he's in love with and wants to create a bond that's going to last a lifetime, that's marriage in my mind" (Harrison, 2012). This rhetoric found its way into the majority opinion that Justice Anthony Kennedy wrote for the Obergefell case: "The right to marry is fundamental because it supports a two-person union unlike any other in its importance to the committed individuals" (*Obergefell v. Hodges,* 2015, p. 13). In other words, the most powerful argument in support of same-sex marriage came from the domain of the private family –love and commitment to intimate partners–rather than from the domain of the public family, with its concerns over legal rights and responsibilities.

Indeed the legalization of same-sex marriage is a logical consequence of the increasingly individualized meaning of marriage. In the past, most people viewed marriage primarily as an arrangement for having children. Since same-sex partners cannot have biological children together, same-sex marriage was not considered. But by the end of the twentieth century, this view had faded. In 1994 the General Social Survey asked a national sample of adults whether they agreed or disagreed with the statement "The main purpose of marriage these days is to have children." Only 13 percent agreed (Smith, Marsden, & Hout, 2015). Instead, marriage is viewed by most people now as primarily a setting for love and intimacy. Given this changed meaning, the rationale for excluding same-sex partnerships became much weaker. Moreover, many lesbian and gay couples are raising children together, through adoption or donor insemination. When courts examined the issue, they looked at the meaning heterosexuals gave to marriage, and they often found no compelling reason to uphold laws that restricted marriage to opposite-sex partners.

NONMARITAL CHILDBEARING

The objective of reducing nonmarital childbearing is less controversial. Teenage childbearing, in particular, produces a consensus: Most people agree that it ought to be discouraged, although they don't agree on how. Some religious, community, and school groups attempt to discourage adolescent sex by urging abstinence. Other groups accept the current level of sexual activity and urge teenagers to use contraceptives. In fact, as noted in Chapter 6, adolescent sexual activity did decline in the 1990s and 2000s, especially among boys, while contraceptive usage went up–pleasing both the abstinence and contraception camps. Moreover, teenage birthrates declined to all-time lows. Some research suggests that teenage childbearing may be more a reflection of a young woman's disadvantaged background than a cause of future problems. If so, then discouraging teenage childbearing without addressing the underlying disadvantages might not make much difference to a young woman's life chances.

As noted in Chapter 6, nonmarital childbearing is no longer confined to teenagers. In 2017 only 11 percent of all nonmarital births occurred to teenagers. Sixty-two percent occurred to women in their twenties (U.S. National Center for Health Statistics, 2018). It is true that teenagers account for a large share of all *first* nonmarital births; but programs that focus solely on teenagers will miss the much larger number of older unmarried women who give birth. Many of them are in cohabiting relationships with the fathers of their children–relationships with a high risk of breaking up. And a breakup may be followed by having a child with another partner, leading to the problem of multipartner fertility, discussed in Chapter 9. But designing programs that discourage adult women from having children outside of marriage is more difficult. In addition, the case for doing so is more controversial: Many of these births represent childbearing decisions by adults, not adolescents. Some liberals would argue that government should respect their choices, rather than try to discourage them.

Recent studies suggest that long-acting reversible contraceptives, so-call LARCs, could prove very useful for young women who wish to limit their births. These contraceptives include injectable implants and intrauterine devices. LARCs are long lasting and highly effective, and they eliminate the need for a young woman to remember to take a pill every day or to use a contraceptive method when having sex. (Although they do not protect against sexually transmitted infections.) When family planning clinics in Colorado received private funds to allow them to provide LARCs as an option to low-income young women, they found that subsequent birth rates declined by 29 percent among 15- to 19-year olds and by 14 percent among 20- to 24-year olds (Ricketts, Klingler, & Schwalberg, 2014). Some policy analysts believe that increasing the usage of LARCs could substantially reduce unwanted births among young women nationwide (Sawhill, 2014). But a campaign to promote their use among low-income women could be seen by minority-group communities as an attempt to limit their right to have children (McClain, 2015).

RESPONSIBLE FATHERHOOD

As with reducing teenage childbearing, the goal of encouraging fathers to take more responsibility for their children is noncontroversial–but surprisingly complex. Policymakers have focused on fathers who do not live with their children; and in the 1980s and 1990s, they had in mind divorced fathers, many of them middle class, and most of them employed. As part of their divorce decrees, judges often ordered them to pay their former wives a set amount of funds per month in support of their children. To increase the number of fathers who fully met their child support obligations, lawmakers passed a series of bills that enforced this obligation. For example, employers can be required to withhold part of the pay of their workers and to send those funds to the child-support system. These measures did increase compliance with court orders.

But recent attention has shifted to a more difficult problem: how to increase the involvement of low-income fathers who have never married the mothers of their children. And nearly all of the concern has been about child support payments rather than about paternal involvement with their children in a wider sense. State agencies now routinely try to identify the fathers of children whose mothers are receiving public assistance, order them to pay child support, and attempt to collect. But many of these men work in intermittent, low-wage jobs and do not have steady earnings. Moreover, they face a substantial likelihood of spending time in prison, as noted in Chapter 9. All too often, these men pile up "arrears," or unpaid child support amounts, that increase every month, whether they have a job or not and whether they are incarcerated or not. These large arrears can discourage them from working because the law states that a portion of their wages must be withheld to pay the child support they owe. In any case, it is difficult for men with criminal records to find work because many employers won't hire them (Western, 2018).

In addition, given high rates of multi-partner fertility, low-income fathers often have children by more than one mother; consequently, they may live with some of their children but not others. How they should divide their income and their time among these children and their mothers isn't clear (Cancian, Meyer, & Han, 2011). Moreover, although low-income men may value the role of fatherhood and wish to succeed in it, they may have had no good role models when they were children. In any case, problems such as lack of employment, incarceration, and gender distrust between women and men often make it difficult to succeed (Tach & Edin, 2011). Many low-income fathers view themselves as doing the best they can, given their limited resources: supporting themselves, providing financial assistance to the partner and children they are living with, and helping out the mothers of their past children if anything is left over (Nelson & Edin, 2013).

This complex situation suggests to many liberals and some conservatives that government agencies may have gone as far as they can go with policies that only focus on collecting money from fathers. Observers argue that what's needed is to also improve low-income men's position in the labor market so that they can become steady earners. For this reason, it is said, encouraging young adults to stay in school longer, along with providing better job training, would be important (Smeeding & Carlson, 2011). So would discouraging early unplanned pregnancies (Furstenberg, 2011). It's clear that the current policies, designed for a world of middle-class divorced dads, aren't working well among the low-income population; and it will be a challenge to develop better ones (Mincy, Jethwani, & Klempin, 2014).

WORK–FAMILY BALANCE

Chapter 8 presented information about the potential conflicts employed parents feel between their work and family responsibilities: work overload, spillover, and the difficulty some parents face in finding adequate child care. It discussed the movement to create a "family-responsive workplace" that allows workers to fulfill their family responsibilities more easily. Although most conservatives agree that government should provide support to employed parents, liberals want a much broader and more costly set of supports than conservatives. Consider parental leave. In 1993, as noted in Chapter 8, Congress enacted a law requiring large employers to provide their employees with 12 weeks of unpaid leave to care for newborns or deal with other family medical emergencies. Opponents claimed it would place an unfair burden on employers, who would be required to hold open employees' jobs until they returned from parental and medical leaves. Advocates of parental leave, on the other hand, were disappointed that the leave would be unpaid. They argued that low- and moderate-income workers would not be able to afford to take an unpaid leave. The advocates noted that many European countries provide a longer leave with at least partial pay. At least six states, California, Massachusetts, New Jersey, New York, Rhode Island, and Washington, and the District of Columbia either provide paid family leave or have passed legislation that would begin it soon (National Conference of State Legislatures, 2016; National Partnership for Women and Families, 2018). The California program appears to have benefited workers, who were better able to care for their newborns and were more likely to return to the same employer at the end of the leave. And it has not caused major problems for employers, who had feared reductions in productivity and increased turnover (Milkman & Appelbaum, 2013).

More generally, liberal scholars and advocates maintain that the rise of the dual-earner couple has created a harried lifestyle that should be eased for the sake of parents and children. Conservatives counter that the past few decades have seen large increases in government support for working parents, such as the expansion of the EITC, and significant increases in child care funds, much of it targeted to mothers receiving TANF, who must make a transition from welfare to paid employment. Many conservatives would prefer tax credits that would assist all families with at least one worker, including married couples in which the wife is not employed. It is a debate that is likely to remain at the forefront of the family policy agenda in the near future.

Quick Review

- Conservatives favor government programs to support marriage whereas liberals urge support for all family forms.
- The legalization of same-sex marriage marks a historic change in family life.
- Conservatives and liberals both support reducing nonmarital childbearing. Conservatives favor programs that advocate abstinence, whereas liberals prefer sex education and more access to contraception.
- Liberals propose an expanded governmental role in helping parents manage work and family responsibilities, whereas conservatives prefer programs that aid mothers who aren't employed as much as mothers who are employed.

Signs of Convergence?

The arguments between liberals and conservatives about family policy have been entrenched for decades. But lately the two groups have shown some signs of moving toward each other. On the conservative side, some writers are acknowledging that changes in the economy have hurt families—a marked departure from the conservative line that cultural decline is largely to blame (Wehner, 2014). Among liberals, some observers are acknowledging the negative impact of cultural change on trends such as the increase in childbearing outside of marriage, much of it in short-lived cohabiting unions, rather than just pointing to economic causes (Fremstad

& Boteach, 2015). And other liberals support a campaign to get young-adult, low-income women to use long-acting reversible contraceptives (Sawhill, 2014).

In addition, the legalization of same-sex marriage has changed the terms of the debate about public support for marriage. Liberals who opposed marriage-enhancement policies when they were restricted to different-sex couples can now potentially support policies that would assist same-sex as well as different-sex marriages. Some same-sex marriage advocates have already joined forces with long-time proponents of different-sex marriage to promote "inclusive" policies to support all married couples (Blankenhorn, Galston, Rauch, & Whitehead, 2015). Other liberals, however, argue that it is time to eliminate all elements of favoritism toward marriage in government policies (Kahn, 2016).

The issue around which there is the greatest consensus at the national level is paid parental leave which, as noted earlier, several states have enacted. In 2017, a committee of liberal and conservative academics and former government policy-makers issued a joint report in which they unanimously agreed that some type of paid parental leave is needed. Although they disagreed on how to fund it and whether it would be available to middle class parents as well as the low-income parents, the committee agreed on a compromise proposal. It would provide eight weeks of leave from employment for mothers and fathers of newborns at 70 percent wage replacement up to $600 per month (AEI-Brookings Working Group on Paid Family Leave, 2017). In Congress, both Republicans and Democrats have introduced paid family leave legislation, and President Donald Trump mentioned his support for it in his 2019 State of the Union Address (White House, 2019). Many difficulties need to be surmounted, but it is possible that parental leave legislation will be enacted in the near future.

There is also broad support for extending the EITC to childless adults in order to increase the incentives for young men to work. And the tax credit that low and moderate-income families receive if they are raising children was expanded during the 2010s (Center on Budget and Policy Priorities, 2018). To be sure, there are strong, continuing differences between liberals and conservatives. The seeming convergence may disappear as the focus shifts from abstract goals to specific legislation. But even limited signs that the two sides could find common ground is an encouraging development for those who care about the well-being of American families.

Looking Back

1. **What is the "welfare state"?** In the twentieth century, the United States and other Western nation–states enacted numerous social programs to provide support to workers and their families. These "welfare state" measures softened the hardships of the labor market. In the United States, the programs were initially designed under the assumption that husbands would work full-time for wages, and wives would do full-time domestic work in the household. Congress did not anticipate that large numbers of wives would work outside the home or that divorce and childbearing outside of marriage would become more common.

2. **What are the themes that conservatives and liberals stress in debating family policies?** Conservatives believe that heterosexual marriage-based families are the

best family form and provide an optimal environment for raising children. They tend to believe that the upheaval in family life over the past half-century has been a result of cultural change: a deterioration in the values that supported marriage. They also believe in a modest role for government programs in support of family life. Liberals accept and defend the emergence of family diversity. They see family change as rooted in changes in the economy; and they favor more assistance for low-income families and working parents.

3. **How has American antipoverty policy become more work based?** Shifts in government policies have provided more assistance to low-income families with at least one steady earner and less assistance to families without earners. The Earned Income Tax Credit provides substantial assistance to families with children and at least one earner. The welfare reform law placed a lifetime five-year limit on the receipt of cash benefits and required more work effort. Supporters of welfare reform argued that dependence on public benefits was detrimental to low-income families; liberals countered that dependence was a symptom of the deeper problem of poverty.

4. **What should be the government's stance toward marriage?** Conservatives have favored programs to promote marriage. Liberals have opposed marriage promotion programs and the idea that government should favor one kind of family over another. The legalization of same-sex marriage has broadened political support for marriage.

5. **How much should the government assist low-income families and middle-class working parents?** Liberals favor further assistance to low-income families, such as increased child care subsidies. They also favor easing the time crunch on middle-class working parents through measures such as paid parental leave and child care assistance. Conservatives have favored programs to encourage and support marriage among the low-income population. In general, they have not favored assistance to middle-class working parents. But recently there has been some convergence in liberal and conservative views.

Study Questions

1. What kinds of assistance does the government provide to middle-class families?
2. Describe the rise and fall of the family wage system.
3. Why is abortion such a contentious political issue?
4. How does the EITC encourage the poor to work?
5. How does the legalization of same-sex marriage reflect the importance of the private family?
6. What are the arguments for and against greater government support to reduce the strain of working and parenting among the middle-class?
7. What issues underlie the debate about whether the government should support marriage-promotion programs?
8. What are the signs that the conservative and liberal sides may be converging somewhat?

Key Terms

deep poverty 389
Earned Income Tax Credit (EITC) 389
family policy 381
family wage system 383
nation 382
nation–state 382
poverty line 387
shallow poverty 389
Social Security Act of 1935 381
state 382
Temporary Assistance to Needy Families (TANF) 391
welfare state 383

Thinking about Families

The Public Family	The Private Family
Many states now withhold part of a recipient's TANF benefits if she doesn't get her children inoculated against childhood diseases or if her children don't attend school regularly. Do you think this is a good policy?	**Is the government inappropriately invading private life if it tries to encourage people to form one kind of family—say, a married-couple family—rather than another kind?**

References

AEI-Brookings Working Group on Paid Family Leave. (2017). Paid family and medical leave: An issue whose time has come. Retrieved March 20, 2019, from https://www.brookings.edu/wpcontent/uploads/2017/06/es_20170606_paidfamilyleave.pdf

Blankenhorn, D., Galston, W., Rauch, J., & Whitehead, B. D. (2015). Can gay wedlock break political gridlock? *Washington Monthly.* March. Retrieved February 20, 2016, from http://www.washingtonmonthly.com/magazine/marchaprilmay_2015/features/can_gay_wedlock_break_politica054228.php?page=all#

Bogenschneider, K., & Corbett, T. J. (2010). Family policy: Becoming a field of inquiry and subfield of social policy. *Journal of Marriage and the Family, 72*(June), 783–803.

Borchorst, Anette. (2000). Feminist thinking about the welfare state. In M. M. Ferree, J. Lorber, & B. B. Hess (Eds.), *Revisioning gender* (pp. 99–127). Walnut Creek, CA: AltaMira Press.

Cancian, M., Meyer, D. R., & Han, E. (2011). Child support: Responsible fatherhood and the quid pro quo. *Annals of the American Academy of Political and Social Science, 635*(1), 163–191.

Center on Budget and Policy Priorities. (2018). Policy basics: The child tax credit. Retrieved October 29, 2018, from https://www.cbpp.org/research/federal-tax/policy-basics-the-child-tax-credit

Center for Law and Social Policy. (2006). Update on the marriage and fatherhood provisions of the 2006 federal budget and the 2007 budget proposal. Retrieved April 24, 2006, from http://www.clasp.org/publications/marriage_fatherhood_budget2006.pdf

Demos, J. (1970). *A little commonwealth: Family life in Plymouth colony.* Oxford: Oxford University Press.

Fremsted, S., & Boteach, M. (2015). Valuing all our families: Progressive policies that strengthen family commitments and reduce family disparities. *Center for American Progress.* Retrieved February 20, 2016, from https://www.americanprogress.org/issues/poverty/report/2015/01/12/104149/valuing-all-our-families/

Furstenberg, F. F., Jr. (2011). Comment: How do low-income men and fathers matter for children and family life. *Annals of the American Academy of Political and Social Science, 635*(1), 131–137.

Grubb, W. N., & Lazerson, M. (1988). *Broken promises: How Americans fail their children.* Chicago: University of Chicago Press.

Harrison, J. (2012, August 21). New pro-gay marriage ad features Monroe couple. *Bangor Daily News.* Retrieved April 27, 2019, from http://bangordailynews.com/2012/08/21/politics/new-pro-gay-marriage-ad-features-monroe-couple/

Kahn, S. (2016, Winter). Spouses with benefits. *Dissent,* 25–34.

Katz, M. B. (1989). *The undeserving poor: From the war on poverty to the war on welfare.* New York: Pantheon Books.

Luker, K. (1984). *Abortion and the politics of motherhood.* Berkeley, CA: University of California Press.

Lundquist, E., Hsueh, J., Lowenstein, A. E., Faucetta, K., Gubits, D., Michalopoulos, C., & Knox, V. (2014). A family-strengthening program for low-income families: Final impacts from the supporting healthy marriage evaluation *OPRE Report 2014-09A.* Washington DC: Office of Planning, Research and Evaluation, U.S. Administration for Children and Families.

McClain, D. (2015, November 16). The birth-control revolution. *The Nation, 301,* 20–25.

Milkman, R., & Appelbaum, E. (2013). *Unfinished business: Paid family leave in California and the future of U.S. Work-family policy.* Ithaca, NY: Cornell University Press.

Moffitt, R. (2015). The deserving poor, the family, and the U.S. welfare system. *Demography, 52*(3), 729–749.

Mincy, R. B., Jethwani, M., & Klempin, S. (2014). *Failing our fathers: Confronting the crisis of economically vulnerable nonresident fathers.* New York: Oxford University Press.

Nelson, T. J., & Edin, K. (2013). *Doing the best I can: Fathering in the inner city.* Berkeley: University of California Press.

Newman, K. S. (2012). *The accordion family: Boomerang kids, anxious parents, and the private toll of global competition.* Boston: Beacon Press.

Obergefell v. Hodges, 576 (U.S. 2015).

Orloff, A. S. (1993). Gender and the social rights of citizenship: The comparative analysis of gender relations and welfare States. *American Sociological Review, 58,* 303–328.

Pew Research Center. (2016). Changing attitudes on gay marriage. Retrieved May 29, 2016, from http://www.pewforum.org/2016/05/12/changing-attitudes-on-gay-marriage/

Quadagno, J. S. (1994). *The color of welfare: How racism undermined the war on poverty.* New York: Oxford University Press.

Ricketts, S., Klinger, G., & Schwalberg, R. (2014). Game change in Colorado: Widespread use of long-acting reversible contraceptives and rapid decline in births among young, low-income women. *Perspectives on Sexual and Reproductive Health, 46*(3), 125–132.

Roe v. Wade, 410 113 (S. Ct. 1973). Webster v. Reproductive health services, 109 3040 (S. Ct 1989). Obergefell v. Hodges, 576 (U.S. 2015).

Sawhill, I. V. (2014). *Generation unbound: Drifting into sex and parenthood without marriage.* Washington DC: Brookings Institution.

Skocpol, T. (1992). *Protecting mothers and soldiers: The political origins of social policy in the United States.* Cambridge, MA: The Belknap Press of Harvard University Press.

Smeeding, T. M., & Carlson, M. J. (2011). Family change, public response: Social policy in an era of complex families. In M. J. Carlson & P. England (Eds.), *Social class and changing families in an unequal America* (pp. 165–191). Stanford: Stanford University Press.

Smith, A. (1776). *The wealth of nations.*

Smith, T. W., Davern, M., Freese, J., & Hout, M. (2017). General social surveys, 1972–2016. Machine readable data file. Chicago: National Opinion Research Center.

Smith, T. W., Marsden, P. V., & Hout, M. (2015). General social surveys, 1972–2014. Machine readable data file. Chicago: National Opinion Research Center.

Tach, L., & Edin, K. (2011). The relationship contexts of young disadvantaged men. *Annals of the American Academy of Political and Social Science, 635*(1), 76–94.

Tribe, L. (1990). *Abortion: The clash of absolutes.* New York: W.W. Norton.

U.S. Bureau of the Census. (2018a). Historical poverty tables: People and families - 1959 to 2017. Retrieved March 19, 2019, from https://www.census.gov/data/tables/time-series/demo/income-poverty/historical-poverty-people.html

U.S. Bureau of the Census. (2018b). Poverty thresholds for 2018 by size of family and number of children Retrieved March 19, 2019, from https://www.census.gov/data/tables/time-series/demo/income-poverty/historical-poverty-thresholds.html

U.S. Food and Nutrition Service. (2018). Supplemental nutrition assistance program (SNAP). Retrieved March 19, 2019, from http://www.fns.usda.gov/pd/supplemental-nutrition-assistance-program-snap

U.S. Internal Revenue Service. (2018). EITC and other refundable credits. Retrieved March 19, 2019, from https://www.eitc.irs.gov/eitc-central/about-eitc/about-eitc

U.S. National Center for Health Statistics. (2018). Births: Final data for 2017. *National Vital Statistics Reports.* Retrieved March 19, 2019, from https://www.cdc.gov/nchs/data/nvsr/nvsr67/nvsr67_08-508.pdf

U.S. Office of Family Assistance. (2018). Characteristics and financial circumstances of TANF recipients, fiscal year 2015. Retrieved March 19, 2019, from https://www.acf.hhs.gov/ofa/resource/characteristics-and-financial-circumstances-of-tanf-recipients-fiscal-year-2015

Webster v. Reproductive health services, 109 3040 (S. Ct 1989). Wilson, J. Q. (2002). *The marriage problem: How our culture has weakened families.* New York: HarperCollins.

Wehner, P. (2014). The anxieties and worries of middle America. In Y. Network (Ed.), *Room to grow: Conservative reforms for a limited government and a thriving middle class* (pp. 9–14). Washington DC: http://conservativereform.com/wp-content/uploads/2014/05/Room-To-Grow.pdf.

Western, B., & Smith, N. (2018). Formerly incarcerated parents and their children. *Demography, 55*(3), 823–847.

White House. (2019). Remarks by president trump in state of the union address. Retrieved March 20, 2019, from https://www.whitehouse.gov/briefings-statements/remarks-president-trump-state-union-address-2/

Wood, R. G., Moore, Q., Clarkwest, A., Killewald, A., & Monahan, S. (2012). The long-term effects of building strong families: A relationship skills education program for unmarried parents: Executive summary. Retrieved February 25, 2014, from http://www.acf.hhs.gov/sites/default/files/opre/bsf_36_mo_impact_exec_summ.pdf

Glossary

1965 Immigration Act Act passed by the U.S. Congress which ended restrictions that had blocked most Asian immigration and substituted an annual quota.

activities of daily living (ADLs) Personal care activities, including bathing, dressing, getting into and out of bed, walking indoors, and using the toilet.

ADLs See **activities of daily living.**

American Indian The name used for a subset of all Native Americans, namely, those who were living in the territory that later became the 48 contiguous United States.

androgynous behavior Behavior that has the characteristics of both genders.

arranged marriage A process in which parents choose their children's spouses with little or no participation by the children themselves.

Asian American A person living in the United States who comes from or is descended from people who came from an Asian country.

assigned kinship Kinship ties that people more or less automatically acquire when they are born or when they marry.

assimilation The process by which immigrant groups merge their culture and behavior with that of the dominant group in the host country.

assortative marriage The tendency of people to marry others similar to themselves.

asymmetry (of gender change) The greater change in women's lives than in men's lives.

authoritarian style (of parenting) A parenting style in which parents combine low levels of emotional support with coercive attempts at control of their children.

authoritative style (of parenting) A parenting style in which parents combine high levels of emotional support with consistent, moderate control of their children.

baby boom The large number of people born during the late 1940s and 1950s.

barrio A segregated Mexican-American neighborhood in a U.S. city.

bilateral kinship A system in which descent is reckoned through both the mother's and father's lines.

biosocial approach (to gender differences) The theory that both biological and social factors influence gender differences.

birth cohort All people born during a given year or period of years.

boundary ambiguity A situation in which people are uncertain about who is in their family and what roles these people play.

breadwinner–homemaker family A married couple with children in which the father works for pay and the mother does not.

care work Face-to-face activity in which one person meets the needs of another who cannot fully care for her- or himself.

centenarian A person who is 100 years old or older.

child abuse An act by a parent or caretaker that results in death, serious physical or emotional harm, sexual abuse, or exploitation

chosen family A family formed through voluntary ties among individuals who are not biologically or legally related.

cisgender people People who identify with the identity they were assigned at birth.

coercive-controlling violence A pattern in which a man seeks to control the behavior of his partner through repeated, serious, violent acts.

cohabitation The sharing of a household by unmarried persons in a sexual relationship.

cohabiting stepfamily A stepfamily in which the partners are cohabiting without marrying.

collective ambivalence Mixed feelings across multiple children.

compadrazgo In Mexico, a godparent relationship in which a wealthy or influential person outside the kinship group is asked to become the *compadre*, or godparent, of a newborn child, particularly at its baptism.

companionate marriage A marriage in which the emphasis is on affection, friendship, and sexual gratification.

consensual union A cohabiting relationship in which a couple consider themselves to be married but have never had a religious or civil marriage ceremony.

courtship A publicly visible process with rules and restrictions through which young men and women find a partner to marry.

crisis period A period during the first year or two after parents separate when both the custodial parent and the children experience difficulties in dealing with the situation.

cultural lag The tendency for attitudes and values to change more slowly than the material circumstances that underlie them.

deep poverty An income of less than 50 percent of the poverty line.

deinstitutionalization of marriage the idea that alternatives to marriage are more acceptable and more prevalent than in the past.

developmental idealism The belief that Western-style families and economic development are beneficial for all countries.

domestic violence Violent acts between family members or between partners in intimate or dating relationships.

donor insemination A procedure in which semen is inserted into the uterus of an ovulating woman.

Earned Income Tax Credit (EITC) A refundable tax credit to low-income families with a child or children in which at least one parent is employed.

EITC See **Earned Income Tax Credit.**

elder abuse Abuse of an elderly person by a caregiver.

emerging adulthood Period between mid-teens and about 30 when individuals finish their education, enter the labor force, and begin their own families.

enforceable trust The ability to enforce the agreements one has made with a partner.

exchange theory A sociological theory that views people as rational beings who decide whether to exchange goods or services by considering the benefits they will receive, the costs they will incur, and the benefits they might receive if they were to choose an alternative course of action.

expressive individualism A style of life that emphasizes developing one's feelings and emotional satisfaction.

externalities Benefits or costs that accrue to others when an individual or business produces something.

extramarital sex Sexual activity by a married person with someone other than his or her spouse.

family inequality The extent to which some families obtain more income and wealth than do others.

family policy Government policies and programs that directly affect the family.

family-responsive workplace A work setting in which job conditions are designed to allow employees to meet their family responsibilities more easily.

family wage system A division of labor in which the husband earns enough money to support his family and the wife remains home to do housework and child care.

feminist theory A sociological theory that focuses on the domination of women by men.

fertility The number of births in a population.

flextime A policy that allows employees to choose, within limits, when they will begin and end their working hours.

foster care The removal of children from their parental home and their placement in another home.

free-rider problem The tendency for people to obtain public goods by letting others do the work of producing them—metaphorically, the temptation to ride free on the backs of others.

frustration–aggression perspective The theory that aggressive behavior occurs when a person is blocked from achieving a goal.

gender The social and cultural characteristics that distinguish women and men in a society.

gender-egalitarian marriage A marriage in which both spouses share the housework and child care much more equitably than in the past.

gene–environment interaction A situation in which a change in the environment has a greater effect on people with a genetic sensitivity to that change.

generalized exchange The provision of assistance to one member of a family with the expectation that someone in the family will reciprocate at a later time.

gerontologist A social/biological scientist who specializes in the study of aging.

gestation Nine-month development of the fetus inside the mother's uterus.

global south The less developed nations in Central and South America, Africa, and Asia.

globalization The increasing flows of goods and services, money, migrants, and information across the nations of the world.

globalization of production The movement to the global south of the production of goods and services that Westerners consume.

grandfamilies Families in which grandparents are raising grandchildren without the parents being present

health span The number of years a person can expect to live while in good health.

heteronormativity, the idea that heterosexual relationships are the only normal and natural relationships

Hispanic A person living in the United States who traces his or her ancestry to Latin America.

hooking up A sexual encounter with no expectation of further involvement.

hybrid marriage A process in which young adults and their parents work together to find marriage partners.

hypothesis A speculative statement about the relationship between two or more factors.

ideal type A hypothetical model that consists of the most significant characteristics, in extreme form, of a social phenomenon.

immigrant enclave A large, dense, single-ethnic-group, almost self-sufficient community.

incest Sexual relations with one's child, brother, or sister.

income-pooling model A model of the marriage market in which both spouses work for pay and pool their income.

individualism A style of life in which individuals pursue their own interests and place great importance on developing a personally rewarding life.

individualistic marriage A marriage in which the emphasis is on self-development, flexible roles, and open communication.

institutional marriage A marriage in which the emphasis is on male authority, duty, and conformity to social norms.

integrative perspective (on sexuality) The belief that human sexuality is determined by both social and biological factors.

interactionist approach (to gender differences) The theory that gender identification and behavior are based on the day-to-day behavior that reinforces gender distinctions.

intergenerational ambivalence Socially structured contradictory emotions in an intergenerational relationship.

intergenerational conflict Discord among family members that pulls family members apart.

intergenerational solidarity The characteristics of family relationships that knit the generations together.

internal economy The way in which income is allocated to meet the needs of each member of a household, and whose preferences shape how income is spent.

intersectionality The principle that inequalities related to one social identity often overlap with inequalities in other identities.

intersexual A person who is born with ambiguous sexual organs.

joint legal custody (of children after a dissolution) The retaining by both parents of an equal right to make important decisions concerning their children.

joint physical custody (of children after a dissolution) An arrangement whereby the children of divorced parents spend substantial time in the household of each parent.

Kinsey Report A 1948 book by zoology professor Alfred Kinsey detailing the results of thousands of interviews with men about their sexual behavior.

labor force All people who are either working outside the home or looking for work.

late modern or postmodern era The last few decades of the twentieth century and the present day.

legal custody (of children after a dissolution) The right to make important decisions about the children and the obligation to have legal responsibility for them.

life chances The resources and opportunities that people have to provide themselves with material goods and favorable living conditions.

life-course perspective The study of changes in individuals' lives over time, and how those changes are related to historical events.

lineage A form of kinship group in which descent is traced through either the father's or the mother's line.

living apart relationships A relationship in which two people define themselves as a couple but do not live together.

longitudinal survey A survey in which interviews are conducted several times at regular intervals.

love marriage A process in which young adults choose their own marriage partners on the basis of love and companionship.

lower-class families Families whose connection to the economy is so tenuous that they cannot reliably provide for a decent life.

marriage market An analogy to the labor market in which single individuals (or their parents) search for others who will marry them (or their children).

married stepfamily A stepfamily in which the partners are married.

masculinity The set of personal characteristics that society defines as being typical of men.

mass incarceration Extremely high rates of imprisonment, particularly of African American males.

matrilineal Describing a lineage in which descent is traced through the mother's line.

mediating structures Midlevel social institutions and groupings, such as the church, the neighborhood, the civic organization, and the family.

Medicaid The government program of health insurance for people with incomes below the poverty line.

Medicare The government program of health insurance for all older people.

mestizo A person whose ancestors include both Spanish settlers and Native Americans.

middle-class families Families whose connection to the economy provides them with a secure, comfortable income and allows them to live well above a subsistence level.

modernization theory The idea that poorer countries would eventually make a transition from traditional to modern in the same way as the Western countries did.

monogamy The belief that a person should have only one long-term partner at a time, usually through marriage

mortality The number of deaths in a population.

multigenerational households Households in which at least three generations of family members reside.

multipartner fertility Having children with more than one partner during one's lifetime.

nation A people with shared economic and cultural interests.

nation–state A term that combines the governmental and cultural connotations of the two words it comprises.

negative externalities The costs imposed on other individuals or businesses when an individual or business produces something of value to itself.

neo-traditional A style of family life centered on marriage but which may be preceded by cohabitation and in which wives work outside the home.

non-Hispanic whites People who identify their race as white but do not think of themselves as Hispanic.

nonmarital birth ratio The proportion of all births that occur to unmarried women.

norm A widely accepted rule about how people should behave.

objectivity The ability to draw conclusions about a social situation that are unaffected by one's own beliefs.

observational study (also known as **field research)** A study in which the researcher spends time directly observing each participant.

older population The group of people aged 65 years and over.

oldest-old The group of older people 85 years of age and over.

old-old The group of older people 75–84 years of age.

parental leave Time off from work to care for a child.

patrilineal Describing a lineage in which descent is traced through the father's line.

peer group A group of people who have roughly the same age and status as one another.

permissive style (of parenting) A parenting style in which parents provide emotional support but exercise little control over their children.

physical custody (of children after a dissolution) The right to have one's children live with one.

polarization (of the labor market) A growth of job opportunities at the top and bottom of the job market but a lessening of opportunities in the middle.

polyamory The practice of having more than one open romantic relationship at a time

poly-victimization Experiencing multiple types of child maltreatment.

positive externalities Benefits received by others when an individual or business produces something, but for which the producer is not fully compensated.

poverty line A federally defined income limit defined as the cost of an "economy" diet for a family of four, multiplied by three.

primary analysis Analysis of survey data by the people who collected the information.

private family Two or more individuals who maintain a close, emotional relationship and a commitment to each other, and who usually live in the same household and pool their incomes and household labor

public family One or more adults who are jointly caring for dependents, and the dependents themselves.

public goods Things that may be enjoyed by people who do not themselves produce them.

pure relationship An intimate relationship entered into for its own sake and which lasts only as long as both partners are satisfied with it.

queer theory The view that sexuality and gender are artificially organized into categories that reflect the power of heterosexual norms.

racial-ethnic group People who share a common identity and whose members think of themselves as distinct from others by virtue of ancestry, culture, and sometimes physical characteristics.

reference group theory The idea that to understand how people behave, one needs to know to whom, or to what, they are comparing themselves.

reflexivity The process through which individuals take in knowledge, reflect on it, and alter their behavior as a result.

remittances Cash payments sent by immigrants to family members in their country of origin.

role overload The state of having too many roles with conflicting demands.

scientific method A systematic, organized series of steps that ensures maximum objectivity and consistency in researching a problem.

secondary analysis Analysis of survey data by people other than those who collected it.

selection effect The principle that whenever individuals sort, or "select," themselves into groups nonrandomly, some of the differences among the groups reflect preexisting differences among the individuals.

self-identity A person's sense of who he or she is and of where he or she fits in the social structure.

serial cohabitation Living with two or more partners without marrying them.

serial monogamy A succession of monogamous sexual relationships.

service sector Workers who provide personal services such as education, health care, communication, restaurant meals, legal representation, entertainment, and so forth.

sex The biological characteristics through which one can classify a person as male or female.

sexual identity The formation in people's minds of an identity such as heterosexual, gay, lesbian, or bisexual based on romantic and sexual attraction.

shallow poverty An income of between 50 percent and 100 percent of the poverty line.

situational couple violence Violence that arises from a specific situation in which one or both partners act aggressively in anger.

skipped-generation households Households containing grandparents and grandchildren without either parent present.

social capital The resources that a person can access through his or her relationships with other people.

social class An ordering of all persons in a society according to their degrees of economic resources, prestige, and privilege.

social constructionist perspective (on sexuality) The belief that human sexuality is entirely socially constructed.

social exchange perspective The theory that people calculate whether to engage in a particular behavior by considering the rewards and costs of that behavior and the rewards of alternatives to it.

social institution A set of roles and rules that define a social unit of importance to society.

social learning perspective The theory that individuals learn behavior they will later exhibit by observing what others do and seeing the consequences of these actions.

social role A pattern of behaviors associated with a position in society.

Social Security Act of 1935 The federal act that created, among other provisions, Social Security, unemployment compensation, and aid to mothers with dependent children (later renamed Aid to Families with Dependent Children).

social structure The fundamental set of positions that organize society as a whole.

socialization The way in which one learns the ways of a given society or social group so that one can function within it.

socialization approach (to gender differences) The theory that gender identification and behavior are based on children's learning that they will be rewarded for the set of behaviors considered appropriate to their sex but not for those appropriate to the other sex.

specialization model A model of the marriage market in which women specialize in housework and child care and men specialize in paid work outside the home.

spillover The transfer of mood or behavior between work and home.

state A government that claims the right to rule a given territory and its population and to have a monopoly on force in that territory.

status group A group of people who share a common style of life and often identify with each other.

stepfamily A family in which two adults are married or cohabiting and at least one has a child present from a previous marriage or relationship.

survey A study in which individuals from a geographic area are selected, usually at random, and asked a fixed set of questions.

symbolic interaction theory A sociological theory that focuses on people's interpretations of symbolic behavior.

telecommuting Doing work from home using electronic communication.

Temporary Assistance to Needy Families (TANF) A federal program of financial assistance to low-income families that began in 1996, following passage of new welfare legislation. (See **Aid to Families with Dependent Children.**)

time-diary studies Surveys in which people are asked to keep a record of what they are doing every minute during a time period.

total fertility rate (TFR) The average number of children a woman will bear over her lifetime if current birthrates remain the same.

transgender people People who identify with a gender other than the one they were assigned at birth.

transnational families Families that maintain continual contact between members in the sending and receiving countries.

two-spirit people In Native American societies, men or women who dressed like, performed the duties of, and behaved like a member of the opposite sex.

union A stable, intimate relationship between two people who live in the same household but may or may not be married.

union dissolution The legal ending of a marital union or the informal ending of a cohabiting union.

union formation The process of beginning to live with a partner through cohabitation or marriage.

union repartnering The formation of new unions either by remarriage or a new cohabiting union.

upper-class families Families that have amassed wealth and privilege and that often have substantial prestige as well.

utilitarian individualism A style of life that emphasizes self-reliance and personal achievement, especially in one's work life.

value A goal or principle that is held in high esteem by a society.

welfare state A capitalist government that has enacted numerous measures, such as social security, unemployment compensation, and a minimum wage, to protect workers and their families from the harshness of the capitalist system.

Western nations The countries of Western Europe and the non-European English-speaking countries of the United States, Canada, Australia, and New Zealand.

women-centered kinship A kinship structure in which the strongest bonds of support and caregiving occur among a network of women, most of them relatives, who may live in more than one household.

working-class families Families whose income can reliably provide only for the minimum needs of what other people see as a decent life.

young-old The group of older people 65–74 years of age.

Name Index

Page numbers in *italics* indicate illustrations. An *f* indicates figures, *n* indicates footnotes, and *t* indicates tables.

Subject Index

Page numbers in *italics* indicate illustrations. An *f* indicates figures, *n* indicates footnotes, and *t* indicates tables.